W9-DBW-740

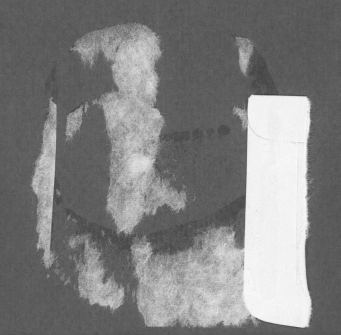

# INTERNATIONAL POLITICS

# INTERNATIONAL

## K. J. Holsti

*University of British Columbia*

**PRENTICE·HALL, INC.**
*Englewood Cliffs, New Jersey*

# Politics

*A Framework for Analysis*

CARL A. RUDISILL LIBRARY
LENOIR RHYNE COLLEGE

327
H74i
76174
Nov. 1971

**International Politics:**
**A Framework for Analysis**
**K. J. Holsti**

© 1967 by PRENTICE-HALL, INC.
Englewood Cliffs, New Jersey

*All rights reserved. No part of this book*
*may be reproduced in any form*
*or by any means without permission*
*in writing from the publisher.*

Current printing (last digit):
10  9  8  7  6

Library of Congress Catalog Card No.: 67–19787

Printed in the United States of America

PRENTICE-HALL INTERNATIONAL, INC., *London*
PRENTICE-HALL OF AUSTRALIA, PTY. LTD., *Sydney*
PRENTICE-HALL OF CANADA, LTD., *Toronto*
PRENTICE-HALL OF INDIA (PRIVATE) LTD., *New Delhi*
PRENTICE-HALL OF JAPAN, INC., *Tokyo*

*to M and P*

# PREFACE

Any reader who reviews the extensive literature on international politics will be struck by the diverse approaches and methods of analysis. These range from works employing intricate descriptions of single events or crises, to broad, theoretical efforts that seek to integrate vast amounts of data into some scheme that will explain the most important aspects of behavior at the international level. All the aproaches have their value, but perhaps ideally one general work should attempt to combine them. The observer of current affairs should relate his tales to generalizations of broader significance, for surely there is some lesson of general applicability to be learned from the Cuban crisis of 1962, the problems of NATO, or the Treaty of Westphalia in 1648. If one is studying an alliance, he should also be able to say something about alliances in general. Similarly, the theorist should ideally formulate his concepts and classifications with reference to historical diplomatic situations.

The recorder of current events has one important advantage over the theorist. His stories, often filled with dramatic events and personalities, are exciting to the reader. A work in theory cannot equally convey drama, but it can more adequately offer broad understanding of political life at the international level. The theorist is in a better position to offer generalizations about the behavior of states regardless of time, place, or personality. This the historian or recorder of current events can do only with difficulty.

My approach to international politics comes closer to that of the theoretician. No single book can cover the field of international politics adequately at all levels of generality, from discussion of the most recent crisis to definition of analytic concepts. In formulating a framework for analysis, I have purposely excluded many aspects of contemporary international affairs on the grounds that they can be—and have been—handled more competently by others. I make little reference to the Secretary-General of the United Nations, the financial problems of that organization, American policy in the Far East, or conflict between Communist China and the Soviet Union. My purpose is, rather, to present a framework which will help the reader to understand what states seek through their governments and political leaders, how they operate in relation to others both in periods of stability and war, what techniques they use to achieve or defend their objectives, how they are restrained by moral, ethical, and legal considerations, and how they resolve their conflicts. To the extent that current affairs and diplomatic history are discussed, I use them as means to an end—as illustrations of general propositions.

The framework, I hope, will also direct the reader to see similarities and differences in the international political processes of different historical eras, and gain some feeling of unity in a field whose data are ordinarily widespread and confusing. I have not, therefore, used the topical approach currently fashionable in general books on the subject. It is useful to know some facts about international trade, international organization, international law, or the conduct of foreign policy in general; but it is more rewarding, I believe, to understand the links between behavior, institutions, and processes. International law, for instance, is not just a body of rules over which legal scholars debate. It should be viewed in its political setting, in the way it is applied in real diplomatic situations. Similarly, instead of discussing the "power" of particular states by comparing their military and industrial capabilities, I believe it is more important to understand how power and influence operate in practice, and to assess the variables that determine whether or not acts of influence will succeed. Stripped of diplomatic verbiage, all governments seek to achieve or defend their objectives through basically similar means, employing threats, rewards, and punishments. When the reader sees the fundamental similarities in the way states conduct their relations, he is less prone to being swayed by the clichés of the cold war or the moral posturing of statesmen. This is not to deny the importance of values and beliefs as bases for judging policies. But the purpose here is to look at international politics in a reasonably systematic fashion, not to suggest solutions to important contemporary problems.

The organization of the book is based on two questions which I believe are crucial to any general study in the field: *why* do states conduct their relations in specified ways, and *how* do they conduct their relations? The first six chapters offer some explanations or hypotheses regarding the sources of state behavior. The main thesis is that no explanation is adequate unless it examines simultaneously the impact of systemic, national, and personality variables on foreign policy objectives and actions. One of the main shortcomings of general analyses of international politics, in my opinion, has been their implicit reliance on only one set of explanatory variables, such as the personalities, values, and aspirations of key policymakers. The second question is seemingly easier to explore because "how" implies description rather than explanation. Yet, in launching the last ten chapters, it soon became apparent that mere description of diplomatic processes would be inadequate. For instance, once the question of how governments bargain with each other has been explored descriptively, a series of problems remain, namely why do certain bargaining strategies fail or succeed. Or, having described generally the impact of ethical or legal limitations on foreign policy actions, a more exacting effort is required to specify under what conditions such limitations are effective. While the second portion of the book thus concerns how states interact, a number of hypotheses explaining why they succeed or fail will also be presented.

Finally, I have tried, where I think the results have been rewarding and the material directly relevant, to apply some of the most recent experimental and theoretical work being conducted by leading scholars in the fields of political science, international relations, social psychology, and other disciplines. This has meant including some material, stripped of its technical language and jargon, from scholarly journals and special monographs which usually evade the public view. Every new idea, approach, or finding in a field that is expanding as rapidly as international relations may be superseded by even newer findings and research methods. I believe it is more important, however, to risk obsolescence than to leave this material in the exclusive domain of academicians.

A work of this scope necessarily relies on the advice, caution, and support of others. I have been particularly fortunate in receiving criticism and encouragement from those closest to me: my wife and my brother. Both read the entire manuscript; both discreetly, but persuasively, kept me on the track when I was tempted to wander off; and both encouraged me when the burden of writing, teaching, and administering approached overbearing proportions. Few writers, I suspect, have been more fortunate. I am also thankful to my brother, Professor Ole R. Holsti of the University of British Columbia, for contributing Chapter XII, an incisive examination of a subject which could fill many books.

The Dean's Committee on Research, Faculty of Graduate Studies, at the University of British Columbia, supplied the funds for research and secretarial assistance over a three-year period. I gratefully acknowledge this assistance. I am also grateful for the permission provided by the publishers of the *Journal of Conflict Resolution* and *Background* to use portions of my articles which previously appeared in those journals. Mr. Richard Riopel of Vancouver encouraged me to undertake the project and helped me to initiate it. I also wish to thank my typists and assistants, Karalee Coleman, Shannon Cornwell, Jane Capleton, Inger Schodt, and Beverly Zack.

K. J. H.

# CONTENTS

**Approaches to
the Study of
International Politics**      1

CHAPTER I

The Development of International Relations as a Field of Study, 4. The Need for Organizing Devices, 13. Levels of Analysis, 15. A Framework for Analysis, 17. International Politics, Foreign Policy, and International Relations, 20. Some Biases in the Study of International Politics, 22. Selected Bibliography, 24.

**International
Systems**      27

CHAPTER II

International Politics in the Chou Dynasty, 1122 B.C.–221 B.C., 29. The External Politics of the Greek City States, 800 B.C.–322 B.C., 42. International Politics in Renaissance Italy, 50. Selected Bibliography, 60.

**The Western
State System**     **61**

CHAPTER III

The International Politics of Eighteenth Century Europe, 62. The International System of the Nineteenth Century, 65. The Contemporary International System, 69. Factors of Stability, Instability, and Change in the Contemporary System, 84. Types of International Systems, 91. Selected Bibliography, 94


**Foreign Policy
Orientations**     **97**

CHAPTER IV

Isolation, 99. Strategies of Non-alignment, 103. Diplomatic Coalitions and Military Alliances, 110. Summary, 120. Selected Bibliography, 121.


**Foreign Policy
Objectives**     **124**

CHAPTER V

Types of Objectives in Historical Systems, 128. "Core" Interests and Values, 132. Middle-Range Objectives, 135. Long-Range Goals, 138. The Interaction of Objectives: Collaboration, Conflict, and Competition, 146. The Interaction of Objectives: Domination and Dependence, 150. Selected Bibliography, 152.


**The Formulation
of Foreign Policy
Objectives**     **155**

CHAPTER VI

Images, Attitudes, Values, Beliefs, and Personal Needs as Components of a Definition of the Situation, 157. The Structure of the International System, Conditions Abroad and Systemic Values as Components of a Definition of the Situation, 169. National Role, 172. Domestic Needs, 173. Objectives and Capabilities, 175. Foreign Policy Objectives as a Function of Public Opinion, 176. Organizational Values, Needs, and Traditions, 181. Relationships Among the Components, 184. Selected Bibliography, 187.

**Power and
the Achievement
of Objectives**     **191**

CHAPTER VII

Capabilities, 197. The Measurement of Capabilities, 198. Variables Affecting the Exercise of Influence, 200. How Influence Is Exercised, 204. Patterns of Influence in the International System, 206. Selected Bibliography, 209.

**The Instruments
of Policy:
Diplomatic Bargaining**     **211**

CHAPTER VIII

The Institutions, Rules, and Personnel of Diplomacy, 212. The Functions of Diplomats, 220. The Purposes of Diplomatic Communication, 226. The Negotiating Process: Bargaining and Capabilities, 228. The Negotiating Process: Inducing Agreement, 230. The Negotiating Process: Diplomatic Styles, 236. Selected Bibliography, 244.

**The Instruments
of Policy:
Propaganda**     **247**

CHAPTER IX

What Is Propaganda? 249. Selecting the Target: Whose Attitudes Can Be Changed? 250. Creating Impact, 256. Techniques of the Propagandist, 257. American Propaganda, 260. Soviet Propaganda, 263. Egypt's Radio Propaganda, 271. The Effectiveness of Propaganda in International Politics, 274. Selected Bibliography, 276.

**Economic Instruments
of Policy**     **279**

CHAPTER X

The Objectives of International Economic Policies, 280.
Techniques of Economic Reward and Punishment, 284.
Economic Rewards and Punishments in Operation, 286.
Economic Penetration and the Establishment of Depend-
encies, 292. Economic Warfare, 295. Foreign Aid as an
Economic Instrument of Policy, 297. Selected Bibliog-
raphy, 307.

**Clandestine Actions
and Military
Intervention**     **310**

CHAPTER XI

Diplomatic Interference in Internal Affairs, 318. Clandestine Political Action, 320. Demonstrations of Force,
322. Subversion, 323. Guerrilla (Unconventional) Warfare, 335. Military Intervention, 338. Conclusion, 340.
Selected Bibliography, 344.

**Weapons, War,
and Political
Influence**     **346**

CHAPTER XII

Weapons as Instruments of Policy, 348. The Spread of
Nuclear Weapons, 350. Deterrence as a Form of Inter-
nation Influence, 352. Deterrence in Crisis Situations,
357. Deterrence Strategies, 364. Summary, 384. Selected Bibliography, 385.

**External Restraints
on Actions**     **387**

CHAPTER XIII

International Law as a Restraint on Policies, 389. The
Use of Legal Norms in Pre-Industrial International Systems, 395. The Growth of European International Law,
399. Contemporary International Law: The Source and

Existence of Legal Norms and Restraints, 402. The Use of Law in the Pursuit of Foreign Policy Objectives, 406. Observing Legal Restraints: The Sanctions of International Law, 411. Foreign Expectations and "World Public Opinion" as External Restraints, 415. Selected Bibliography, 419.

**Internal Restraints
on Actions                                                421**

CHAPTER XIV

Capabilities as Restraints, 422. Domestic Public Opinion as an Internal Restraint, 422. The Role of Ethics and Morality as Internal Restraints, 423. Ethics, Morality, and Values as Psychological and Cultural Restraints, 425. Ethical Restraints in Three Levels of Policy, 430. Ethical Restraints as a Function of the Pattern of Relations Between Nations, 436. The Sanctions for Ethical Foreign Policy Behavior, 438. Summary, 439. Selected Bibliography, 441.

**Resolving International
Conflicts                                                 442**

CHAPTER XV

Behavior Leading to the Resolution of International Conflicts, 445. Procedures for the Pacific Settlement of International Disputes and Conflicts, 455. The Development of Institutions for Pacific Settlement, 459. Behavior and Procedures in International Conflicts: The Record Since 1919, 465. Problems and Prospects of Settlement Through Awards, 469. Selected Bibliography, 474.

**Conflict and
Collaboration in
Security Communities                                      476**

CHAPTER XVI

Background Conditions of Security Communities, 480. Policy-Making and the Handling of Conflicts in Security Communities, 487. Resolving Conflicts in Security Communities: The Record, 492. Selected Bibliography, 495.

**Index                                                   497**

# INTERNATIONAL Politics

# Approaches to
# the study of
# International Politics

After the armies of Imperial Germany invaded Belgium in August, 1914, launching one of the most destructive and futile conflicts in history, the German Foreign Minister, Prince von Bülow, asked his Chancellor why all the diplomatic steps taken to avoid the war had failed. "At last I (Bülow) said to him: 'Well, tell me, at least, how it all happened.' He raised his long, thin arms to heaven and answered in a dull exhausted voice: 'Oh—If I only knew.' "[1] If the German Chancellor did not understand all of the reasons that had led to war, he and his policy-making colleagues knew quite well that many of their decisions were likely to end in catastrophe for both Germany and Europe. He also knew that Germany had only a slight chance of emerging victorious. Since a rational function of war is presumably to achieve a political goal at tolerable costs through the application of force,

[1] Prince Bernhard von Bülow, *Memoirs of Prince von Bülow* (Boston: Little, Brown & Company, 1932), p. 166.

# Chapter I

German policy-makers in the summer of 1914 were not behaving rationally. Was such behavior unique? More than a half century later, Prime Minister Ian D. Smith of the self-governing colony of Rhodesia defied the British government, the United Nations, and most of the states of Africa by unilaterally declaring the independence of the colony. Though Smith and his advisers expected that the British government could not immediately prevent steps toward establishing full Rhodesian independence, they also knew that the declaration of independence would cause grave economic damage to the country, possible war with other African states, or civil war between four million colored Rhodesians and 200,000 white settlers. The British Prime Minister, Harold Wilson, had attempted to forestall the unilateral declaration by threats and promises conveyed through last-minute conferences and telephone calls with Smith. The last call was placed at six o'clock on a Thursday morning in a desperate bid to head off the illegal declaration. Reporting to the House of Commons on that conversation, Wilson recalled that he had "ended the conversation with a heavy heart, feeling that reason had fled the scene and that emotions, unreasoning . . . emotions at that, had taken command [of Prime Minister Smith] regardless of the consequences for Rhodesia, for Africa and for the world."[2]

Taking a longer range perspective, other historical parallels that transcend time, place, and personalities can be noted. In the eighth century B.C. the princes of newly formed states in China successfully challenged the power and authority of the Chinese emperor, thereby putting an end to the Chinese feudal order. Similarly, in 1648 European diplomats and princes congregated in Westphalia to sign a peace treaty ending the Thirty Years' War. They also declared that henceforth the leader of the Holy Roman Empire could no longer extend his dominion into the territories of princes and sovereigns, and that the latter were in no way obliged to respond to the directives of the emperor. This act symbolized the emergence of the modern European nation-state system, replacing the feudal political order which, as in China, had at least theoretically placed an emperor as head, with power radiating down through such lesser political entities as free cities, duchies, and developing dynastic territories.

Every historical occurrence is of course unique: the situations in which statesmen construct alliances, decide to go to war, declare independence, or make peace are all different. Yet, when historical phenomena are analyzed from a certain level of abstraction—not just as facts for their own sake—these situations have many common properties. The events the student of international politics attempts to understand are partly unique

[2] *The New York Times,* November 11, 1965, p. 1.

occurrences, but, as the cases cited above suggest, are also comparable. Smith and the German Chancellor had to make many of the same kinds of calculations before acting, and both acted knowing that their decisions could easily lead to disaster. Both the Chinese princes and the European sovereigns 2,000 years later were determined to put an end to political orders in which emperors could intervene in subordinates' affairs and territories. Regardless of historical and geographical context, policy-makers for different types of political units, whether tribes, city states, empires, or modern nation states, have attempted to achieve objectives or defend their interests by fundamentally similar techniques, of which the use of force or the construction of alliances are only the most obvious examples.

If Thucydides, Frederick the Great, or Louis XIV were to return to life in the latter part of the twentieth century, they would no doubt be astounded by the immense changes in technology, culture, and the lives of average citizens. They would not be familiar with such international institutions as the United Nations or the International Court of Justice, nor would they understand immediately the rationale behind foreign aid programs, or comprehend the destructive capacity of nuclear weapons. But they would recognize the types of threats and rewards modern governments make in attempting to achieve their objectives, the techniques of diplomatic bargaining, and the concern governments have for their international prestige. Certainly they would find little new in the attempts of states to conclude mutually satisfying military alliances or to remain uninvolved in the quarrels of great powers.

The study of international politics, while it must account for the unique, new, and non-recurring phenomenon, is also concerned with processes and patterns of behavior found typically in many historical contexts. All attempts to understand the disparate aspects of political life at the international level implicitly assume some regularities of behavior. The diplomatic historian tends to emphasize the uniqueness of the events he is describing and explaining, but when he employs such concepts as the "balance of power" or "diplomacy" he is referring to classes or types of political behavior that transcend specific historical circumstances. Still, the historian concentrates mainly on single events and occurrences which are related to specific times, places, and personalities.

It is a bias of social scientists to assume the existence of regular patterns of behavior, to explain these in terms of specified variables,[3] and to use

[3] A variable can be defined as any phenomenon or condition, a change in which produces a change in another phenomenon or condition. In the physical realm, for example, variations in temperature cause changes in the properties of water. We know from observation that when the temperature goes below a certain point, water freezes

historical data primarily to elucidate or illustrate the generalizations they are attempting to make. Students of international politics try to understand and explain the causes and nature of war, imperialism, nationalism, or peace without having to describe every war, imperialist, nationalist, or period of stability in diplomatic relations. A valid generalization is one which can be used to describe all events of a given class. Any general statement about these phenomena must be based, of course, on accurate historical observation; but the social scientist is still concerned primarily with classes or types of phenomena rather than with the particular details of each illustration. He is interested in the German Chancellor in 1914 or Prime Minister Smith of Rhodesia as *examples* of the behavior of important policy-makers facing situations of great stress, threat, and consequences; the historian is interested in them as individuals.

## The Development of International Relations as a Field of Study

The line dividing a historian's approach to international relations from that of a social scientist is not as clearcut as the above comments would indicate, for historians frequently attempt to uncover patterns of behavior and elements of recurrence in diplomatic relations, while many political scientists hold that the most valid approach to the subject is careful description of events which are assumed to be unique. In fact, a review of the history of this field of study reveals that most work has used a historical, descriptive, and developmental (e.g., analyzing the conditions which caused or helped bring about certain events or ideas) approach.

---

if all other conditions are held constant. There is an obvious functional relationship between the two variables, temperature and the state of the water. In the social sciences, relationships between variables may be much more difficult to identify and measure because (1) many variables inducing change may be involved simultaneously and (2) it may be impossible to hold all other conditions constant while observation or experimentation is taking place. For example, we may wish to examine the conditions associated with outbreak of war. We could see if there is some type of relationship between the incidence of war and spending on armaments. If through a perusal of historical data we found a high correlation between variations in expenditures on armaments (independent variable) and incidence of war (dependent variable), we could say that the two variables are somehow associated. It would still remain for us to define the exact nature of the relationship and investigate other types of variables, such as perceptions of threat or degree of commitment to objectives, that may be involved in the outbreak of war. We can say with confidence that a lowering of temperature *causes* a change in the state of water, but we could not claim with certainty that rising armaments budgets cause wars, since so many other factors may be involved.

The earliest writings on international relations were largely concerned with proffering practical advice to policy-makers. The Chinese philosopher Mencius in the fourth century B.C., Kautilya, a prime minister under the Indian emperor Chandragupta (326–298 B.C.), and Niccolo Machiavelli wrote works which are studied today for their insight into the kinds of problems that still confront statesmen. But the main purpose of these authors was not so much to provide general analyses of the relations between states as to offer advice on the most effective forms of statecraft. In eighteenth and nineteenth century Europe, diplomatic memoirs, studies on military thought and strategy, and works on international law proliferated. Few authors took the trouble to analyze the behavior of governments in their external relations from a systematic and detached vantage, though a number of observers did suggest that the "balance of power" was a more or less fundamental law of politics at the international level.[4] There were many philosophers, statesmen, lawyers, and military officials who claimed they knew what was wrong with the world, and devised schemes for overcoming these deficiencies. It was not until the twentieth century that attempts at systematic analysis appeared.

Scholars in the United States first began to take serious interest in international problems following America's involvement in Asian and European politics at the turn of the century. Their studies, as well as those of many Europeans before World War I, were oriented largely to analysis of treaties and principles of international law. They were typically legalistic and moral in tone, based on the assumptions that most disputes were raised to be settled, the "shrinking" world was making man more "internationalist," and peace and stability could be constructed through the extension of democracy or construction of international institutions, such as a world court, with power to enforce their decisions. International laws of neutrality and warfare and the problems of arbitration and disarmament were the main subjects considered in courses and texts in international relations.

Academic studies in the 1920's largely continued to expand on the prewar perspectives, though establishment of the League of Nations gave observers something new to write about. Institutes dedicated to the study of international law and organization were formed in Switzerland, Great Britain, and the United States. Articles in scholarly journals contained lengthy descriptions of international conferences and treaties, while popular and academic analysts presented innumerable commentaries on the proceedings of the League of Nations. Aside from these descriptive

---

[4] Cf., Per Mauserth, "Balance of Power Thinking from the Renaissance to the French Revolution," *Journal of Peace Research*, No. 2 (1964), 120–36.

studies—from which one could deduce few generalizations—most work in the field during this decade had a normative orientation: the scholars involved were less concerned with the variables or conditions affecting government behavior in external relations than with judging the policies of states according to their own personal values. The only new development in courses and texts, aside from the analyses of the League of Nations, was an emphasis on description of the "background" conditions of current international affairs.

Hitler's violent assault on the post-war order had important consequences on the ways in which scholars in international relations fields approached their subject. Many observers became impatient with the descriptive, moralistic, and legalistic orientation of the 1920's and realized that, as important as treaties and international organizations were to international relations, objectives such as security and expansion, processes such as trade and diplomacy, and means such as propaganda and subversion had to be studied as well. Hence, while one group of scholars and commentators continued to emphasize the traditional concerns of law, institutions, and current affairs, another branched off to begin more systematic and comparative studies of objectives, processes, and means, as well as those "basic forces" (as they were then called) assumed to affect a state's foreign policy behavior. These studies assessed the phenomenon of nationalism, the influence of geography on a country's foreign policy, and particularly the effect of "power" (or lack of it) on a nation's fate. Not infrequently, these same people were concerned with the strategies the democracies should adopt to ward off the threats posed by Hitler's Germany.

Most important, writers in this school attempted to become more analytical by defining concepts, exploring some ancient myths about international politics, and emphasizing the extent to which all states were equally interested in certain values and interests such as security, power, territory, or peace. While these analysts remained occupied with current problems and described in detail the foreign policies of major powers, behind their teaching and research was the idea that detailed description should be used not only to acquaint the reader or student with facts, but also to illustrate some generalizations or theories about international politics. The emphasis in the classroom and in texts thus turned from efforts to inculcate in students certain attitudes about international politics. ("We must strengthen the League of Nations") to creating understanding about reality, leaving the student to form his own judgments about the best ways to deal with contemporary problems.

Since the end of World War II, the study of international relations has seen important new developments. With the threat to Europe and North

America posed by the Soviet Union after the war, the creation of weapons of mass destruction, and the rise of over 50 new states, policy-makers have had to cope with extremely difficult, dangerous, and, in some cases, unprecedented problems. Most academics, no matter how concerned with creating a scientific field of study could not avoid becoming involved in the great policy and ethical issues of the day. Yet a definite trend away from description, legal analysis, and policy advice has developed in the field. Its objective has not been to assess the main issues in the cold war or describe current international developments, but to create explanatory theories about international phenomena and, in some cases, even to propose the development of a general and predictive "science" of international relations. As could be expected, the different purposes of the study—to understand contemporary problems, offer advice on how to solve them, and create a scientific field of research—have led to distinct schools of thought and different approaches to the subject.

At least four general approaches to the study of international relations exist today, though the distinctions among them are not clearcut or rigid. The first is basically a continuation of the approach popular among scholars in the decade after World War I. Its focus is on the analysis of international institutions and law, the mechanisms which, if properly constructed and employed, could help save our generation from large-scale war. While the originators of this approach concentrated on the texts of treaties and analysis of the legal powers and procedures of international institutions, its contemporary practitioners are more interested in studying the interaction of law, institutions, and politics—the ways, for instance, in which states use treaty arrangements and international organizations for their purposes. They are concerned, as were their predecessors, with suggesting ways to improve present laws and organizations, but are more aware of the political considerations complicating reform programs, and consciously strive to frame their proposals to meet both national aspirations and the prerequisites of international stability.

The second group of scholars is also concerned with the means of avoiding warfare and widespread violence, but rather than emphasizing law and organization, its participants look upon military and defense policies as the best way to secure stability. Instead of focussing on long-range techniques of ordering international relationships, they are concerned with immediate security and strategic problems. Assuming that the best way to prevent war is to prepare for it, they argue that a reasonably stable political order operating under the restraints of international law and institutions can be constructed only if the immediate security needs of the United States, the Soviet Union, and other major powers can be met. Their research and teaching examine the alternative strategies available for coping with the threats posed by cold war. Armed with the research methods and findings of game theory, psychological studies in perceptions, economic models, and historical studies, these scholars and military advisers have scrutinized carefully various military strategies and security programs such as "massive retaliation," the conditions under which a deterrent force is credible to the potential enemy, the problems of "escalating" limited wars, the costs and consequences of civil defense programs, the control over nuclear weapons in NATO, and the economic costs and security consequences of arms control proposals. Some of the issues explored by these scholars and military experts will be summarized in Chapter XII.

A third group of scholars takes the position that while the study of international relations is properly concerned with descriptive, legal, military, and ethical analysis of contemporary problems, its main purpose should be to present general propositions or theories which explain many facets of political behavior at the international level, using historical and contemporary data only as illustrations for these generalizations. It is not enough, they argue, to understand the background conditions of present crises; any trained observer or newspaper pundit can do that. We must also know *why* governments, irrespective of time, place, or historical context, decide to promote revolution abroad, use force, make peace, or withdraw from a position. We must therefore learn about the ways policy-makers behave—how they perceive the external environment, and how psychological characteristics impinge upon policy choices, for example— before we can make any safe generalizations about international politics. But in order to ask the right kinds of questions and get the data needed to test hypotheses and illustrate generalizations, scholars need to construct "theories" to suggest the hypotheses in the first place.

Some members of this group go one step further to argue that the ultimate purpose of scientific analysis is not just explanation, but prediction, and, they maintain, reliable predictions can be made only if the main variables affecting political behavior have been identified, and relationships among the variables specified. These scholars might point out that economists can predict, once the relationship between variables is known, the general consequences of lowering bank interest rates, rise in the supply of money, or increase in public demand for a type of product. What would economists predict about a lowering of bank interest rates? Certainly not that John Smith or Bob Brown would apply for loans. But they could estimate that, in the economy as a whole, there would be an increase of 5 per cent in the volume of borrowing if interest rates were lowered by one quarter per cent. In other words, they can predict *classes* of events, not individual incidents of that class. Similarly, proponents of a predictive science of international politics claim that when enough basic propositions about the behavior of policy-makers have been tested and verified through rigorous research methods, predictive statements about classes of events and trends can be put forward with reasonable confidence. Though we all make casual predictions about specific events in foreign policy or international politics, a number of scholars have already made or tested propositions useful for understanding or predicting behavior in recurring situations. For example, the results of psychological experiments and historical research suggest that in times of crisis and high tension, policy-makers tend to perceive and consider fewer alternative courses of action than when they are not under stress.[5] On a broader scale, we can predict that alliances will tend to disintegrate if the members of the alliance cease to perceive a common potential enemy.

Notice that these statements are not laws; they do not state that in the *next* international crisis Prime Minister X will perceive only one course of action open to him, or that SEATO will be dissolved next year. They are, rather, predictive statements about classes of events, with *probabilistic* or *tendency* characteristics. Exceptions can and will occur, but experimentation or careful historical observation has established that in most instances the dependent variable (perception of fewer alternatives or disintegration of alliances) can be predicted from knowledge of the state of the independent variable (level of tension or stress and degree of perception of a common enemy).

Whether or not prediction is the ultimate purpose of analysis or it is possible to construct a single theory of international politics, members of this third school are convinced that the field can only mature into a science if the methods of physical and social sciences are applied to it. They argue that casual observation, development of historical knowledge, or offering solutions to contemporary problems according to arbitrary value criteria are inadequate substitutes for systematic research employing the most advanced techniques and formal theory. The term "theory" as used by these scholars should not be confused with the formal deductive theories found in the physical sciences or mathematics, where propositions and hypotheses are logically deduced from axioms. The nature of international politics, where literally thousands of variables affect human behavior, makes this type of theoretical activity impossible. But any speculation or research which helps to define terms, formulate concepts, and identify variables affecting behavior, which discovers hidden similarities, establishes classifications (taxonomies) of phenomena, analyzes relationships among variables, or which, in general, helps to create under-

[5] Ole R. Holsti, "Perceptions of Time, Perceptions of Alternatives and Patterns of Communication as Factors in Crisis Decision-Making," *Peace Research Society (International): Papers,* III (Chicago Conference, 1964), 79–120.

standing about the many facts and events of international politics, is a contribution to "theory." Thus, much of the work which goes under the name of "theory" is merely an attempt to come to grips in some *systematic* fashion with a subject whose data are far too widespread for any one individual to comprehend in detail. This concern with theory reflects a desire to arrive at a more basic understanding of international politics and foreign policy than is possible through gathering facts about the most recent international problem. Most of the work of this school could perhaps be better termed "quasi-theory,"[6] as distinct from the formal theory-building of the physical sciences.

In addition to this theorizing activity, in which facts are related to broader concepts and explanatory generalizations, there is also interest in learning about political processes that are often neglected in those studies which concentrate on law, institutions, or current events. This new research delves into such questions as: How are foreign policy decisions arrived at? How do "images," stereotypes, and ideologies affect policy-makers' perceptions of reality and, consequently, their choices among alternative courses of action? Is a strategy of bargaining in which one side threatens to punish more effective than one in which it offers rewards? Or, in what kinds of situations is a threat likely to be credible and therefore effective? How do trust and suspicion affect the propensity of governments to enter into cooperative ventures? How does the political, economic, or social system of a nation affect its foreign policy behavior? What types of social, economic, and political conditions are conducive to successful supranational integration? What types of internal rebellions are most likely to involve outside intervention? Other scholars are involved in research which should tell us much more than we presently know about the effects of public opinion on policy-making, the origins and types of international conflicts, and the types of propaganda most likely to induce desired reactions among the target populations.

In order to conduct research into such questions, old methods of inquiry which relied primarily upon analysis of documents and treaties are no longer adequate. Investigators find it difficult to observe policy-makers in action, and they are too impatient to wait 40 or 50 years until all of the documents are available. Moreover, many aspects of foreign policy-making, diplomatic bargaining, or handling of international conflicts remain undocumented. Thus, scholars working in various areas of the field have recently fashioned a number of research tools which enable them to formulate and test propositions about their subject without having to go through meticulous documentary examination. The com-

---

[6] The term is used by Eugene J. Meehan, *The Theory and Method of Political Analysis* (Homewood, Ill.: The Dorsey Press, 1965), pp. 161–67.

puter, which can analyze the contents and themes of thousands of documents in minutes once a key or dictionary has been formulated, is one important research aid. Surveys and interviews help to obtain information of public attitudes about international problems. One group of scholars has developed a game or simulation of international politics which can be played by laymen. The researchers build into the game many features of reality, so that the pressures faced by lay "policy-makers" (often undergraduate students) become to a certain extent similar to those with which real policy-makers have to cope. By observing the students' behavior (e.g., when they decide to go to war, how they construct alliances, react to a major scientific "breakthrough," handle conflicts, or solve the age-old problem of meeting domestic economic demands while providing arms for security) and by controlling certain aspects of "reality," they are able to test propositions in a manner which would take years of research in government archives. As developed primarily by economists and psychologists, the theory of games can also be helpful in examining the types of conditions and variables, such as trust, suspicion, risk, rewards, or degree of communication, which affect bargaining behavior.

The fourth group of scholars combines the main characteristics of the first with the third: it is deeply concerned with the problems of peace and war, but argues that these can never be understood and ultimately controlled unless a vast amount of reliable knowledge about the subject is first created. The objectives of the research are clearly normative—devising ways to control processes leading to violence—while the techniques are scientific and systematic. This type of scholarship has earned the unfortunate title of "peace research," a term which creates in the minds of many laymen and government officials the notion of fuzzy-headed and naïve intellectuals pontificating from their ivory towers about the ways to secure everlasting peace. Some of the work, however, has made important contributions to our understanding of such problems as the processes leading to war, escalation of violence, the relationship between individual personality characteristics and the phenomena of bigotry, prejudice, and national hostility, the economic effects of disarmament and arms control programs, and the sources of public attitudes towards foreign countries and alien cultures. Whether the findings of these studies will ever be reflected in public policy remains to be seen. Much of the scholarly work on arms control and disarmament in the United States has been made available to the government, and a large amount is being undertaken by government officials themselves or by independent scholars under government contract. Other areas of "peace research" have not yet fared so well, for it is often a difficult political task to translate research findings into policy proposals acceptable to those who run governments.

A unique feature of recent studies of international politics and foreign policy, aside from theoretical activity and attempts to create new research techniques, has been the extent to which they have become interdisciplinary, blending the data, concepts, and insights of all the social sciences. In the past, historians, political scientists, geographers, and legal scholars monopolized the field of international relations; today, anthropologists, economists, sociologists, and psychologists enrich our understanding of international relations by bringing their special skills to problems of common interest or opening previously neglected areas of inquiry. Sociologists and social psychologists help us to understand the nature and origins of public attitudes and opinions which affect foreign policy issues; they have also provided a vast literature dealing with individual behavior in bargaining situations. Economists, aside from their interest in international trade and economic development, provide help in understanding political processes in underdeveloped countries. Anthropologists assist the development of the field by studying war and violence as cultural phenomena, characteristics of mediation and conciliation in primitive societies, and types of problems arising from cross-cultural contacts and economic progress in underdeveloped societies.

As much as the field of study has advanced as a result of new methods and interdisciplinary efforts, these contributions also have their limitations. For example, the literature of social psychology, which at first glance seems so relevant to foreign policy and international politics, is derived largely from experimental work employing small groups of people, usually students, in a laboratory setting. A certain amount of caution is necessary in transferring conclusions obtained in this fashion to diplomatic-political-military situations. No matter how carefully an experiment is constructed, it cannot replicate a real political situation. Results of experiments offered by the social sciences must thus serve primarily as *hypotheses* to be tested against political experience and historical data before they can be verified. If small group experiments suggest that willingness to communicate freely and cooperate vary directly with the amount of trust between people, we should not hastily conclude that the same propositions are necessarily valid in diplomatic relations. It remains the task of those who research in the field of international relations to see if the results of experimental situations can be verified in the diplomatic situation.

Unfortunately, many propositions developed by social scientists are difficult to test in real life. In the example cited above, the social psychologist can easily vary the amount of communication between two students in the laboratory, or inject factors which increase or decrease trust or suspicion to see if they have any effect on the participants'

willingness to collaborate. One cannot manipulate international conferences in the same way, although the social scientists' ingenuity in devising
new methods of research suggests that within the next decade or two such
studies will be possible. When and if that day arrives, many common
sense notions about political processes and behavior at the international
level (including many in this book) will either be substantiated through
precise measurement, modified, or discarded as unfounded "old wives'
tales."

### The Need for Organizing Devices

It was mentioned earlier that some theorizing activity in the field is
undertaken not for the purpose of constructing a predictive theory of
international relations (assuming that it can be done), but for creating
ordering devices or approaches which help the investigator and student
make some sense out of the great diversity of facts and events in international relations. Whatever the name of that device, whether a "quasi-
theory," "model," "conceptual framework," or more simply, a framework
for analysis, its purpose is to help create understanding by ordering facts
and concepts into some meaningful pattern. Gathering of facts or description of events creates understanding of those facts and events, but
otherwise has little broader application. Only when these facts and events
are fitted against some framework of concepts can they be seen essentially
as illustrations of general and recurring processes in international politics.
But an organizing device does more than just relate facts to general
propositions.

Historians use the organizing devices of time, place, and subject matter
(e.g., German foreign policy toward Poland from 1934 to 1939) as a
means of helping them select relevant data, relate the data to each other,
and determine the boundaries of their topic. Without such organizing
devices there would be no place to begin, no limits to help research and
description, and no way to determine what facts, conditions, or events
were relevant to the subject.

Social scientists also use organizing devices, but because they are often
interested in classes of social phenomena rather than specific events
bounded by time, place, and subject, their devices will be more abstract.
For instance, if we want to define the essence of international politics, we
might say "power politics," in which case the boundaries of the subject
would be determined largely by the definition we assign to those two
words. But "power" and "politics" are very abstract concepts, more
difficult to deal with than concepts relating to time and place. Yet, if we

define international politics as "power politics" or "the quest for power," we have, however crude, some framework, approach, or quasi-theory which provides the boundaries of the subject, establishes criteria of relevance, and helps fit some of the many facts of international life together. It designates key variables which help to explain the behavior of states in their external relations. In this case, power—how it is wielded and how much is available—is posited as the key explanatory variable to the understanding of a nation's foreign policies.

There are, of course, certain dangers in employing any approach, theory, model, or framework in social analysis. While these devices help the investigator select data and relate concepts and variables, they may also act as blinders to other significant facets of the subject. Two examples of popular models of international politics will illustrate this point. The Communist view of international politics is one in which classes, not states, are the main political actors. International and class relationships are typified by constant "struggle." Since, the theory argues, the state is the instrument of a society's ruling class, in a capitalist society foreign policies will merely express the monopolists' interests in gaining access to markets, fields of investments, and raw materials. By its very nature a state which represents the interests of the monopolists is an imperialist state, though how imperialist depends upon the stage of capitalist development and class relations within society. Here is a simple theory of international politics that attempts to explain how foreign policy behavior (dependent variable) varies with changes in domestic class relations and the stages of economic development (independent variables). Many "facts" of international relations can be explained by this theory. Certainly Lenin's theory of imperialism provided a reasonably plausible explanation for European and American imperialism around the turn of the century, although long-range predictions based on this theory have been far less impressive.

However, the theory does not account for, and indeed blinds us to, such obvious phenomena as the great quantity of collaborative and cooperative relationships between states with highly developed and essentially private enterprise economies. And, though some modern wars have had economic factors as questions under dispute, the theory does not explain many conflicts in which the economic stakes have been negligible. Because of the blinders created by this model of international politics as an expression of social class struggle, the Communist analyst is at a loss to explain or account for many important aspects of reality. For instance, the theory leads the analyst to see European economic integration as some form of collusion between monopolists to repress the working classes of the Common Market countries, a view ludicrously far from reality.

Another model or approach to international politics which suffers from limitations and lack of explanatory capacity is "power politics." The "power" approach, very popular during the late 1930's and still with considerable repute, assumes that no matter what the long-range objectives of states, their immediate objective is power—the power of one's own state over other states. International politics is conceived as a struggle for power among all states, either for expansion or defense and protection. The study focuses partly on the methods and techniques states use to maximize their power, but primarily on the "elements" of a state's power. Since it is assumed that states are successful to the extent that they have power, the approach demands lengthy consideration and assessment of each nation's "power position," which includes its geography, natural resources, population, technological level, available military resources, and national morale. In other words, because the approach emphasizes just one concept—power—it leads observers to try to discover what constitutes a state's power.

As with the Communist model of international politics, the power approach does explain some aspects of international politics, and it directs researchers to look for certain types of information which are useful to the student. But because of its undue emphasis on power and struggle, it conceals other aspects of international politics which are also important. If some types of relationships can be described as struggle, surely Anglo-American relations are not, for the most part, adequately characterized by this term. As interesting as the "elements" of power may be, they do not determine how effective a state will be in its external relations. A state can be very well endowed with all of the "elements" of power and still not achieve its objectives against even the weakest and smallest states. Thus, while the approach does explain a limited range of phenomena and helps to emphasize the importance of one variable—power—in international politics, it is burdened with its own oversimplicity, lexical definitions, unexamined assumptions, and Hobbesian view of international relationships.

## Levels of Analysis

One final problem about organizing devices needs to be discussed before presenting the framework of analysis employed in this book. What should we use as the major unit of analysis in international politics?[7] Should we focus upon the actions and attitudes of *individual* policy-

[7] J. David Singer, "The Level-of-Analysis Problem in International Relations," in *The International System: Theoretical Essays*, ed. Klaus Knorr and Sidney Verba (Princeton: Princeton University Press, 1961), pp. 77–92; Kenneth W. Waltz, *Man, the State, and War* (New York: Columbia University Press, 1959).

makers? Or can we assume that all policy-makers act essentially the same once confronted with similar situations, and therefore concentrate instead on the behavior of *states?* Or, could we remove ourselves even further from individuals and examine international politics from the perspective of entire *systems* of states? Each level of analysis—individual, state, or systemic—will make us look at different things, so the reader must be aware of the differences among them. For example, the classical theory of balance of power is an attempt to explain the behavior of many states over a lengthy period of time. It proposes that states will form coalitions and countercoalitions to fend off hegemonic drives, and that a "balancer" will intervene on behalf of the weaker side in order to redress the balance or restore the old equilibrium. The behavior of *individual* political units is thus explained in terms of the state of the whole system (balanced or imbalanced) and the presence or absence of one aggressive state and a balancer. This type of analysis makes no reference to personalities, domestic pressures, or ideologies *within* states. Foreign policy behavior is conceived as a reaction to the external environment, the state of balance or imbalance among *all* the units in the system.

If we look at international politics from the perspective of individual states, rather than from the state of the system in which they exist, quite different questions arise. We can attempt to explain the behavior of states by reference not just to the external environment (the system), but primarily to the domestic conditions that affect policy-making. Wars, alliances, imperialism, diplomatic maneuvers, isolation, and the many goals of diplomatic action can be viewed as the results of domestic political pressures, national ideologies, public opinion, or economic and social needs. This level of analysis has much to commend it, for governments do not react just to the external environment or to some mythical balance or imbalance. Their actions also express the needs and values of their own populations and political leaders.

Finally, we may study international politics and foreign policy by concentrating on the actions and behavior of individual statesmen. This is the usual approach of diplomatic historians, based on the sound point that when we say "states" behave, we really mean that policy-makers are defining purposes, choosing among courses of action, and utilizing national capabilities to achieve objectives in the name of the state. This level of analysis focuses upon the ideologies, motivations, ideals, perceptions, values, or idiosyncrasies of those who are empowered to make decisions for the state.

Which level of analysis should we employ as the most useful perspective from which to explain or understand politics among nations? Each makes a contribution, but each fails to account for certain aspects of reality that must be considered. We cannot understand Soviet foreign policy adequately by studying only the attitudes and values of its foreign minister, nor is it sufficient to analyze Soviet social and economic needs. We must have some knowledge as well of ideological considerations and of the general configuration of power, influence, domination, and subordination throughout the world. The main characteristics of the external environment are no less important than those of the state's internal environment. Therefore, all three levels of analysis will be employed at different times, depending upon the type of problem which must be analyzed. The perspective of international systems is very broad, though not comprehensive, and provides the best approach for delineating the *main* features and characteristics of international political processes over a relatively long period of time. The essence of the types of relations among Greek city states can be described without examining the character of each city state or the motives, ideals, and goals of each statesman in each city state. Today, the structure of alliances, power, and domination in the world sets limits upon the actions of states and policy-makers, no matter what their ideological persuasion, the state of domestic opinion, or individual ideals. The next three chapters will concentrate on the description of historic international systems with a view to illustrating the general nature of relationships among their component political units. At the same time, ways can be suggested in which the main characteristics of the system affect the behavior of individual states. Subsequently, the focus will shift so that foreign policy behavior will be explained primarily by reference to domestic national needs and values, and individual variables.

## A Framework for Analysis

The purpose of the framework for analysis outlined below and spelled out in the remainder of the book is to develop a way of looking at and thinking about international politics. It attempts to increase understanding of the great variety of phenomena in the field of study by defining concepts, establishing classification schemes, and describing some of the variables which affect policy-making and relations between nations. We are interested primarily in *types* of foreign policies, bargaining processes, and means of wielding influence, not with the activities of any one state or group of states.

As with most approaches, the framework for this book requires a certain amount of abstraction, and thus simplification of reality. Not all the facts, events, issues, or conditions of international relationships can be considered. Hopefully, however, those which are included can be made more meaningful when related to each other, as well as to concepts and schemes of classification. The test of the framework is the extent to which it helps explain the most important facts, and how adequately it leads to generalizations of reasonable validity. The framework, it should be remembered, is only an organizing device and not a theory of international politics. Any theory should have axioms, propositions, and formal hypotheses which can be verified both logically and empirically. This kind of theory has not yet been developed in most of the social sciences, perhaps least of all in the field of international relations. We must be content to engage in relatively modest theoretical activity which defines concepts, establishes taxonomies, and suggests some of the variables which affect behavior at the international level—in short, activity which creates some order out of an immense field of knowledge.

The framework begins with an examination of several historical international systems. Keeping in mind that the purpose of the first part of the book is to explain the nature of, and the reasons and conditions behind, the actions and interactions of independent political units towards each other, these three chapters are based on the assumption that the external behavior of these units is partly a function of the system in which they operate. A state's *general* orientation (but not specific actions) toward the external environment can best be assessed and understood from a macroscopic point of view, where the total structure of power, influence, and domination in the system, as well as the major social and technological characteristics within the political units, serve as the main influences on policy-making and state behavior. To look at actions and interactions in terms of historical systems requires analysis of *gross* patterns of relationships and general foreign policy orientations, not individual historical events or specific policies pursued in particular situations.

However, the main characteristics of an international system can account for only part of the conditions underlying the actions and policies of states. The structure of the system, as well as technological and geographic characteristics, place limitations on what a state, through its policy-makers, can reasonably hope to achieve. However, since most political behavior is goal oriented—toward the extension or protection of certain values, interests, or objectives—it is also necessary to examine what types of external goals political units of various types have traditionally sought to achieve. Thus, Chapters II, III, and IV will analyze foreign policy behavior by referring to the main characteristics of international systems, and the subsequent two chapters will examine policy as primarily a response to domestic needs and values. In Chapter VI, for instance, we will analyze conditions *within* political units—ideologies, doctrines, economic needs, and public opinion—which influence or determine the objectives of states.

While Chapters V and VI are concerned with the formulation of objectives, Chapter VII begins the third part of the framework by analyzing the general techniques political units employ toward each other in attempting to achieve or defend those objectives. Here, the concepts developed in the first six chapters will be of less use since we will no longer be concerned with gross patterns of behavior or general foreign policy orientations which can be understood by reference to the nature of an international system. We will be interested in assessing how states influence each others' behavior through promises, rewards, threats, and punishments, and in specifying the types of conditions and situations in which power can be wielded effectively. Chapter VII delineates a quasi-theory of power that serves as the background to the subsequent five chapters, which examine in detail the political, military, and economic techniques states employ recurrently in achieving or defending their objectives. These range from traditional forms of persuasion through diplomatic bargaining, to techniques involving force and violence. Though many of the illustrations will be taken from the relations between major powers, techniques of political action at the international level are universal: all states use diplomacy, propaganda, economic embargoes, boycotts, and threats of military force against other states.

A framework which helps to explain the nature of relations between states and the conditions affecting state behavior is incomplete without reference to the kinds of *limitations,* or restraints, that affect policy formulation and implementation. We often forget that governments, through their policy-makers, are not entirely free to act as they might wish in all circumstances. It has already been noted that the structure of the international system imposes limitations on what a state would likely attempt to do. Treaty commitments, general principles of international law, weak capabilities, domestic and external public opinions, and ethical norms also act as restraints on state behavior. Many observers have claimed that legal and ethical principles are largely irrelevant in international politics, or that power and prestige are the values that always precede or supersede others. One only has to look at a variety of policy-making situations to see that such conclusions are overly pessimistic. While some governments frequently violate legal principles and treaty commitments, in most types of transactions between states they are observed rigorously. We want to suggest, therefore, the kinds of situations in which legal and ethical restraints *are* effective in controlling action, and under what circumstances other values, such as security or power, take precedence.

Saved for the last section is a problem which will be introduced briefly in the chapter on objectives. There, it will be suggested that there are basically four types of international relationships—collaborative, conflict-ful, competitive, and dominant—depending upon the degree to which the objectives, values, and interests of two or more states are compatible. Chapters XV and XVI will examine in more detail the kinds of behavior typical of conflict and collaboration—how states resolve conflicts, the forms of behavior most conducive to compromise and peaceful settle-ment, the types of international institutions which have been created to cope with dangerous conflicts, and the extent to which these institutions have been employed. The final chapter will examine a peculiar type of collaboration which is becoming increasingly important and significant in international relations. This is often observed in the "security commu-nity," any group of states whose mutual relations are conducted as if war between them would be almost inconceivable. Sweden and Norway may have some incompatible objectives, but the possibility that they would use force against each other to reconcile those incompatibilities seems very remote. The most dramatic types of security communities involve a degree of supranational integration of economic, military, or political institutions, but groupings of states which remain institutionally uninte-grated are of interest as well. There are many types of conflicts within such security communities, but as will be seen, the methods of resolving them tend to be quite different from those employed by states which maintain normally hostile relations. We will be concerned in the last chapter, then, with conflict that takes place within a context of over-all collaboration.

This framework attempts to emphasize the differences and similarities of political processes at the international level in different historical contexts, and to illustrate how the disparate data of the study can be put into meaningful relationships with each other. The key concepts, to summarize, are the *systems*, or environments, in which state behavior occurs, the *objectives* of states in these systems, the variables affect-ing the *formulation* of objectives and actions, the *methods* and *processes* which political units employ or become involved in when attempt-ing to achieve or defend their objectives, the *limitations* or restraints they encounter in employing these techniques, and the typical forms of behavior they adopt when their objectives are more or less incompatible.

## International Politics, Foreign Policy, and International Relations

If by now the reader is confused over the use of the terms international relations, international politics, and foreign policy, he joins the company of most experts in the field. Many definitions of these terms exist, but there is little agreement upon which are the most adequate or where the distinctions between them lie. The reason for this lack of consensus is no doubt related to the problem of organizing devices. How one defines these terms is largely influenced by what one wants to investigate, and what one investigates is largely a function of his particular approach, model, or theory of the subject.

Most studies in "world politics" or international politics have in fact been studies of foreign policy, where policy is defined as the decisions that define goals, set precedents, or lay down courses of action, and the actions taken to implement those decisions. They have concentrated on describing the interests, actions, and elements of power of the great powers. But at what point, if any, does foreign policy become international politics? Distinction between the terms may be more academic than real, but it is roughly the difference between the *actions* (decisions and policies) of a state or states, and the *interactions* between two or more states.[8] The student who analyzes the actions of a state toward external environment and the conditions—usually domestic—under which those actions are formulated is concerned essentially with foreign policy; the person who conceives of those actions as only one aspect of a pattern of actions by one state and reactions or responses by others is looking at international politics, or the processes of interaction between two or more states. The distinction is illustrated in the figure.

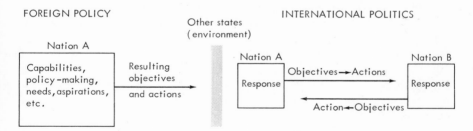

This book will apply both perspectives, depending upon the problem under analysis. A discussion of state objectives, variables affecting their choice, and some techniques employed to achieve them is related closely to the study of foreign policy, while consideration of international systems, diplomatic bargaining, and behavior in conflict situations comes closer to the idea of interactions between states.

As distinct from international politics and foreign policy, the term

[8] See Fred A. Sondermann, "The Linkage Between Foreign Policy and International Politics," in *International Politics and Foreign Policy: A Reader in Research and Theory*, ed. James N. Rosenau (New York: The Free Press of Glencoe, Inc., 1961), pp. 8–17.

international relations may refer to *all* forms of interaction between the members of separate societies, whether government-sponsored or not. International relations would include the analysis of foreign policies or political processes between nations, but with its interest in *all* facets of relations between distinct societies, it would include as well studies of international trade unions, the International Red Cross, tourism, international trade, transportation, communication, and the development of international values and ethics. The student of international politics is not concerned with these types of relationships or phenomena, *except where they impinge upon official government objectives, or where they are employed by governments as instruments of inducement to achieve military or political objectives.* The student of international relations is interested in all aspects of international trade. In the field of international politics, we are concerned with international trade only to the extent that governments may employ economic threats, rewards, or punishments for political purposes, as when they promise to lower tariffs *vis-a-vis* another country in return for the right to establish a military base in that country.

### Some Biases in the Study of International Politics

No observer in a field so replete with complexities, ethical problems, and historical consequences could fail to reflect certain biases in his analysis. Even the most objective scholar is partly a prisoner of his experiences, the values predominant in his society, and the myths, traditions, and stereotypes which permeate his nation and environment. A general analysis of international politics presented by an Indian or Egyptian author, even if it employed a similar organizing device or frame of reference, would likely be very different than that in the succeeding chapters. One cannot avoid some distortion caused by different cultural perspectives. However, there are other sorts of biases that permeate the field, and the reader should remain aware of these.

First, most analyses of foreign policy and international politics reflect a preoccupation with essentially national problems. This is not so much a case of authors making value judgments which suggest that their country is right while others are wrong (this shortcoming is prominent in high school history texts, however) as it is a tendency to regard the most important problems and conflicts in the world as those in which their country is involved. No one can deny the importance of the post-war Soviet-American rivalry, but in many American texts there is a tendency to view almost all international political problems in terms of this rivalry.

Hence, international politics become almost synonymous with the cold war, and solutions become identified with effective nuclear deterrents, the cohesion of NATO, and effective foreign aid programs. Threats all seem to emanate from the Communist nations, and all Western actions appear only as responses to those threats.[9] By using such concepts as objectives, capabilities, threats, punishments, and rewards—which all states have or employ—we are able to avoid much of the slanted phraseology of the cold war ("Communist imperialism," "free world," and "aggression") which can only hinder understanding of the techniques of statecraft commonly used by all states, no matter what their ideological commit ments. One can still have a strong attachment to liberal or conservative values and at the same time recognize that nuclear threats are no less threats just because they emanate from Washington or London instead of Moscow; nor are "information programs" any less propaganda just because Western countries have somewhat higher scruples than the Communists about presenting a reasonably balanced analysis of a foreign policy situation.

A second prominent bias derives from the common obsession with the unusual, the dramatic, and the violent. Anyone who reads newspapers regularly can see the tremendous distortion of reality in favor of violence and sensationalism. News media focus our attention on great international crises while they systematically neglect to mention relations between states when they are in a tranquil state. In fact, the vast majority of transactions between states are peaceful, unexciting, stable, predictable, and conducted with strict regard to treaty obligations. These transactions do not make news. The average North American man on the street has plenty of opinions on the Suez crisis, Cuba, or Southeast Asia, even though his level of *knowledge* on these dramatic issues is often appallingly low. But how many know anything about the nature of relations between the Scandinavian states, or the forms of cooperation between the Central American republics? An unceasing emphasis on violence and conflict naturally leads to perspectives which take "power politics" and cold warfare as the *norms* of inter-state behavior, whereas they are really the exception.

Although attempts will be made to call attention to cooperative types of relationships and to the large number of social, political, and economic

[9] Preoccupation with the cold war or the relations among the great powers has had alarming effects on scholarly research in international politics. Most research and literature in the field examines the many facets of Soviet, American, British, French, or Chinese foreign policy, but there is practically no English-language literature concerning, for example, the relationship between public opinion and foreign policy in Indonesia, the propaganda techniques of Ghana, the diplomatic practices of India, or the subversive activities of dozens of small states.

state objectives that can be achieved through collaboration, peaceful competition, and quiet diplomatic persuasion, this book will reflect in part the bias toward the conflictful aspects of international politics. There are, as justification for this bias, practical obstacles against overcoming it. While a great amount of research and writing has been done on alliances, war-making capacity, violence, the cold war, and deterrence, apart from studies of international technical organizations and international trade, relatively little has been written on unexciting types of relationships. All facets of American-Soviet relations have been covered in a voluminous literature; but one can scan English-language bibliographies for a long time before uncovering systematic studies of Canadian-American relations, or Belgium's diplomacy towards the Netherlands. Hopefully, as we become more alert to our biases, these great gaps of knowledge in the field of international politics will be filled.

## SELECTED BIBLIOGRAPHY

Algosaibi, Ghazi A. R., "The Theory of International Relations: Hans J. Morgenthau and His Critics." *Background,* VIII (1965), 221–56.

Barber, Arthur, "The Citizen, the Scholar, and the Policymaker," *Background,* VIII (1964), 79–86.

Boasson, Charles, *Approaches to the Study of International Relations.* Assen: Van Gorcum & Company, 1963.

Boulding, Kenneth E., "Is Peace Researchable?," *Background,* VI (1963), 70–77.

―――, "Theoretical Systems and Political Realities," *Journal of Conflict Resolution,* II (1958), 329–34.

Brody, Richard, "Three Conceptual Schemes for the Study of International Relations," in *Foreign Policy Decision-Making: An Approach to the Study of International Politics,* ed. Richard Snyder, H. W. Bruck, and Burton Sapin. New York: Free Press of Glencoe, Inc., 1962.

Bull, Hedley, "International Theory: The Case for a Classical Approach," *World Politics,* XVIII (1966), 361–77.

Burns, Arthur L., "Prospects for a General Theory of International Relations," in *The International System: Theoretical Essays,* ed. Klaus Knorr and Sidney Verba. Princeton: Princeton University Press, 1961.

Burton, J. W., *International Relations: A General Theory.* Cambridge: Cambridge University Press, 1965.

Fox, W. T. R., ed., *Theoretical Aspects of International Relations.* Notre Dame, Indiana: Notre Dame University Press, 1959.

―――, and Annette Baker Fox, "The Teaching of International Relations in the United States," *World Politics,* XIII (1961), 339–59.

Glaser, William A., "The Types and Uses of Political Theory," *Social Research,* XXII (1955), 275–96.

Guetzkow, Harold, *et al., Simulation in International Relations: Developments for Research and Teaching.* Englewood Cliffs, N.J.: Prentice-Hall, Inc., 1963.

Harrison, Horace V., ed., *The Role of Theory in International Relations.* Princeton: D. Van Nostrand Company, Inc., 1964.

Hempel, C. G., "Typclogical Methods in the Social Sciences," in *Philosophy of the Social Science: A Reader,* ed. M. Nathanson. New York: Random House, Inc., 1963.

Herzog, Arthur, *The War-Peace Establishment.* New York: Harper & Row, Publishers, 1963.

Hoffmann, Stanley, *Contemporary Theory in International Relations.* Englewood Cliffs, N.J.: Prentice-Hall, Inc., 1960.

————, "International Relations: The Long Road to Theory," *World Politics,* XII (1959), 346–77.

Holsti, Ole R., "The Citizen, the Scholar and the Policy-Maker: Some Dissenting Views," *Background,* VIII (1964), 93–100.

Kaplan, Morton A., "Is International Relations a Discipline?," *Journal of Politics,* XXIII (1961), 462–76.

————, "Problems of Theory Building and Theory Confirmation," in *The International System: Theoretical Essays,* ed. Klaus Knorr and Sidney Verba. Princeton: Princeton University Press, 1961.

————, *System and Process in International Politics.* New York: John Wiley & Sons, Inc., 1957.

Kelman, Herbert C., "Social-Psychological Approaches to the Study of International Relations: Definition of Scope," and "Social-Psychological Approaches to the Study of International Relations: The Question of Relevance," in *International Behavior: A Social-Psychological Analysis,* ed. Herbert C. Kelman. New York: Holt, Rinehart & Winston, Inc., 1965.

Kindelberger, Charles P., "Scientific International Politics," *World Politics,* X (1958), 83–98.

Kreith, Kurt, "Peace Research and Government Policy," *Background,* VIII (1965), 269–78.

Lyons, Gene M., and Louis Morton, *Schools For Strategy: Education and Research in National Security Affairs.* New York: Frederick A. Praeger, Inc., 1965.

McClelland, Charles A., "The Function of Theory in International Relations," *Journal of Conflict Resolution,* IV (1960), 303–36.

————, *Theory and the International System.* New York: The Macmillan Company, 1966.

Meehan, Eugene J., *The Theory and Method of Political Analysis.* Homewood, Ill.: The Dorsey Press, 1965.

Morgenthau, Hans J., *Politics Among Nations* (3rd ed.). New York: Alfred A. Knopf, Inc., 1960.

Oppenheimer, Martin, "The Directions of Peace Research: Conflict or Consensus," *Journal of Human Relations,* XIII (1965), 314–19.

Röling, Bert V. A., "National and International Peace Research," *International Social Science Journal,* XVII (1965), 487–504.

Rosecrance, Richard, "Categories, Concepts and Reasoning in the Study of International Relations," *Behavioral Science,* VI (1961), 221–31.

Rosenau, James N., ed., *International Politics and Foreign Policy: A Reader in Research and Theory.* New York: Free Press of Glencoe, Inc., 1961.

Russell, Frank M., *Theories of International Relations.* New York: Appleton-Century-Crofts, 1936.

Singer, J. David, "The Level-of-Analysis Problem in International Relations," in *The International System: Theoretical Essays,* ed. Klaus Knorr and Sidney Verba. Princeton: Princeton University Press, 1961.

———, "The Relevance of the Behavioral Sciences to the Study of International Relations," *Behavioral Science,* VI (1961), 324–35.

Snyder, Richard, H. W. Bruck, and Burton Sapin, eds., *Foreign Policy Decision-Making: An Approach to the Study of International Politics.* New York: Free Press of Glencoe, Inc., 1962.

———, "Some Recent Trends in International Relations Theory and Research," in *Essays in the Behavioral Study of Politics,* ed. Austin Ranney. Urbana, Ill.: University of Illinois Press, 1962.

Waltz, Kenneth N., *Man, the State and War.* New York: Columbia University Press, 1959.

Wright, Quincy, *The Study of International Relations.* New York: Appleton-Century-Crofts, 1955.

Zawodny, J. K., *Guide to the Study of International Relations.* San Francisco: Chandler Publishing Company, 1966.

# INTERNATIONAL
# SYSTEMS

An international system can be defined as any collection of independent political entities—tribes, city states, nations, or empires—which interact with considerable frequency and according to regularized processes. The analyst is concerned with the typical or characteristic behavior of these political units toward each other and their general foreign policy orientations.[1] While observers of international affairs have traditionally explained the behavior of states in terms of national attributes, needs, or individual characteristics of policymakers, the external environment and particularly the

[1] The concept of "system" as it has been employed in "general systems analysis" is a formal method of analysis that can be used for studying social systems. We use the term in two ways: (1) as a description of regular patterns of interaction among independent political units, and (2) as a variable which helps explain the behavior of the units comprising the system. For the difference between the usages of the concept, see Jay S. Goodman, "The Concept of System in International Relations Theory," *Background,* VIII (1965), 257–68.

# CHAPTER II

structure of power and influence in an international system may have profound effects on the general orientations of a state toward the rest of the world. Thus the major characteristics of any international system can be used as one set of variables to help explain the typical actions of that system's component political units. This chapter will focus on international structures and political processes of selected historical civilizations without, however, including lengthy descriptions of individual historical events or personalities, except where these had such a great impact on the system that they changed its major characteristics. Historical detail is sacrificed in order to emphasize typical or recurring patterns of behavior among interacting political units, permit greater understanding of comparative international politics, and assess the effects of structures and processes on the behavior of component political units.

Each historical system will be analyzed from five aspects. First the *boundaries* of the system—the line between interaction and environment—will be designated. Any international system has identifiable boundaries—geographic, cultural, or issue lines beyond which actions and transactions between the component political units have no effect on environment, and where events or conditions in the environment have no effect on the political units. Though the Chinese states and the Greek city states existed simultaneously in the fifth century B.C., there was no interaction between them; to the Chinese, the Greek political units were merely part of an unknown environment. While the Greeks conducted exploration and trade that brought them into contact with many peoples in Eurasia, the political life of these people had little effect on Greek politics.

Second, what are the main characteristics of the political units whose interactions form an international system? We are concerned with the types of governments and administrations political units developed, the role of the average citizen or subject in the political unit's external relations, and the methods by which resources of the unit were mobilized to achieve external objectives.

Third, any international system has a definable *structure,* a characteristic configuration of power and influence or persisting forms of dominant and subordinate relationships. Sometimes a system's structure is typified by power being concentrated in one state which then dominates others; in other eras, power may be diffused quite equally among a large number of states so that none is capable of dominating or leading the others for any period of time; or, the structure may be "polar," where two antagonistic blocs of states, each led by states of superior strength, array against each other. We also want to identify the "great powers" of each era, analyze how they acquired their position, and describe the situation of the lesser political entities—whether they were satellites, neutrals, or reluctant alliance partners. This analysis also requires discussion of the *stratification* within each system, and the criteria commonly employed to distinguish between "great powers" and lesser units. Descriptions of the structure of each system also include identification of the major "subsystems," such as the most important rivalries, issues, alliances, blocs, or international organizations.

Fourth, each international system will be analyzed in terms of the most common forms of *interaction* among the component units—diplomatic contacts, trade, types of rivalries, and organized violence or warfare.

Finally, interactions and processes in most systems are regulated or governed by explicit or implicit rules or customs, the major assumptions or values upon which all relations are based. As regulators of each system, the techniques and institutions used to resolve major conflicts between the political units will also be considered. More detailed discussion of the major rules and institutions regulating contemporary foreign policy behavior will be found in Chapter XIII.

It would be impossible in two chapters to describe the main characteristics of these five categories for all international systems that have arisen and declined in history. This chapter will concentrate instead on three civilizations for which there is considerable historical evidence on interstate relations: the Chinese state system under the Chou dynasty, the Greek system of city states, and the international politics of Renaissance Italy during the fifteenth century. The succeeding chapter will conclude with a discussion of the more familiar western European state systems during the eighteenth, nineteenth, and twentieth centuries.

## International Politics
## in the Chou Dynasty, 1122 B.C.–221 B.C.

Though scholars on the Orient usually classify these nine centuries of Chinese history under the Chou title, there were at least two and possibly three fundamentally different structures in which international political processes took place. One was the feudal order which lasted from 1122 B.C., with establishment of the dynasty, until approximately 771 B.C., when the central Chou monarchy was defeated by insurgent feudal lords and "barbarians" and forced to move its capital from Hao (near the present city of Sian) to Loyang, further east. This feudal epoch has been called the "Western Chou" period. The era from 771 to 483 B.C., known as the "Spring and Autumn" period, developed a system of large independent states, sometimes arranged into two antagonistic blocs, replacing the small, hierarchical feudal order of the Western Chou period. The period of the "Warring States" (403 to 221 B.C.) was noted politically for conflict and competition among the larger states, decline of stable alliances and the polar power structure, and eventual destruction of the system itself.

## Boundaries of the Chou System

During the Western Chou (feudal) period, the political influence of the Chou dynasts extended only to the territory of the lower Huang Ho basin, roughly the area between the Huang Ho and Yangtze rivers in central China. There were, of course, inhabitants throughout the territory which comprises modern China, and the Chou authorities had contacts with some of them, even though they were regarded as barbarians (*wu*). Aside from these sporadic involvements with the *wu*, the Chou political units developed in isolation from the rest of the world. As the system of large independent states replaced the feudal structure, contacts were made with people on the Indian subcontinent, but there is no evidence that these interactions had any immediate political significance to the Chinese states. During the Warring States period the larger political units extended their domain and sinicized many of the areas populated by the *wu*, so that by 221 B.C. parts of present-day Manchuria, the eastern tip of the Shantung Peninsula, and some territory south and east of the Yangtze River were organized politically and became components of the system.

## Nature of the Political Units

In the feudal era the main political unit was the Chou monarchy, which dispensed land, titles, and favors upon its vassals. The bureaucratic organization of the monarchy was already well developed in this period, and differentiated to serve a large variety of governmental functions.

In addition to the central monarchy, which theoretically held title over all the known territory of China, a number of small feudal units, created and sustained by the central monarchy, also played an important political role. The Chou kings donated tracts of land, including towns and villages, to feudal lords and retiring civil servants in return for the payment of taxes. Vassals were also obligated to carry out certain other duties, such as following the king in wars and expeditions against the *wu*, guarding the frontiers of Chou lands, and supplying manpower to the king for his armies. The territorial extent of these feudal units varied considerably. Most consisted of walled cities and surrounding lands, extending a radius of up to 60 miles,[2] but in some instances the monarch would reward a

2 Owen and Eleanor Lattimore, *China: A Short History* (New York: W. W. Norton & Company, Inc., 1944), p. 66.

deserving noble with a tract of land the size of New York State. The noble could then subdivide the land into fiefs ranging in size from several fields to several hundred square miles, an area comparable to a large Texas ranch.[3] The literature of the period indicates that there were at least 130 large feudal states subservient to the central monarchy during the Western Chou period, although some authorities mention as many as 1,800.[4]

In theory, nobles and vassals were not allowed to expand their territory at the expense of neighboring feudatories without royal sanction. But even during the height of Chou power feudal lords maintained some relations with each other (rather than directly through the monarchy) and in some cases fought wars over territorial spoils.

Within their own states the nobles maintained considerable autonomy, appointing their own officials and levying taxes in accordance with their own needs. They maintained their own armies (partly for purposes of internal security) and, if they desired, could split up their land among relatives and sub-vassals, creating even smaller political units (fiefs). During the early parts of the Spring and Autumn period (771 to 483 B.C.), the strength and independence of feudal lords grew rapidly at the expense of the central Chou authority. Emulating the administrative mechanisms within the Chou domains, the vassals themselves created regular governmental organizations as state functions expanded and became more pervasive in the lives of ordinary people. Large-scale irrigation and construction projects, collection and storage of grain, construction of walled cities, and organization and maintenance of armed forces required the establishment of coherent administrative structures and processes.[5] With the aid of administrative mechanisms which made them independent and self-sufficient, the feudal lords and royal princes were able not only to maintain control over their own expanding territories, but to resist the influence of the central monarchy as well.

Another development which strengthened the independence of the feudal states was the growth of rudimentary forms of nationalism. In the Western Chou period, popular patriotism had been directed toward

[3] Dun J. Li, *The Ageless Chinese: A History* (New York: Charles Scribner's Sons, 1965), p. 47.

[4] There seems to be little agreement regarding the number of units in the feudal system. Richard L. Walker, in *The Multi-State System of Ancient China* (Hamden, Conn.: The Shoe String Press, 1953), mentions that in 722 B.C., when the feudal order was declining rapidly, there were 170 states (p. 20). Edward T. Williams, in *A Short History of China* (New York: Harper & Row, 1928), mentions the existence of about 1800 states during the height of the Chou dynasty (p. 56); and Friedrich Hirth, in *The Ancient History of China to the End of the Chou Dynasty* (New York: Columbia University Press, 1923), claims that about 130 states were noted in the Chou literature (p. 11).

[5] Walker, *The Multi-State System of Ancient China*, p. 37.

village chiefs and the "Son of Heaven," the Chou monarch, and only occasionally to the feudal lord. But after 771 B.C. ordinary people began to recognize and emphasize the differences in dialects, customs, religion, and cults among the states as their contacts with others began to proliferate and the position of the Chou monarch—the symbol of unity— eroded. Pride in local distinctions and loyalty to the prince of the state became much more pronounced toward the end of the Spring and Autumn period. The significance of this development was that during the period of the Warring States princes could more easily organize peasant militias and armies to fight their wars for them. In turn, peasants and townsmen believed that they were fighting not just as a duty to a feudal lord but for the sovereignty, independence, and honor of their own state.[6]

In addition to the Chou monarchy, the feudal realms of the early Chou period, and the large independent states that developed in the Spring and Autumn period, a fourth type of political unit also existed in the Chinese system. This was the attached state (*fu-yung*), independent only in relation to some purely local affairs. These attached states were mostly holdovers from the feudal era, small bits of territory which had not been conquered and absorbed by the larger feudal rulers as they developed their administrative mechanisms and armed forces. In external relations the attached states were almost totally dependent upon their neighbors.[7]

## The Structure of the Chou System

The center of influence during the Western Chou period resided with the political unit—the central monarchy—which could create or extinguish lesser political entities. The structure of the system in the feudal era was hierarchical. Most feudal lords were dependent upon the Chou monarchy for lands, subsidies, and protection against each other, but because of the difficulty of transportation and communication between units on the territorial fringes of the system, as well as the development of administrative mechanisms within the feudal units, there were different degrees of dependence and subservience between the small political units and the monarchy. The Chou kings ruled directly over extensive tracts of territory near the present city of Sian. Next to this, they created a circle of small states, each ruled by a direct relative of the king's family. Because of close family and geographical relationships, these local rulers—usually princes—were in a weak position to increase their authority at the expense of the Chou monarch. Another circle of states further from the

---

[6] Walker, *The Multi-State System of Ancient China,* p. 36.

[7] Cf. Derk Bodde, "Feudalism in China," in *Feudalism in History,* ed. Rushton Coulborn (Princeton: Princeton University Press, 1956), p. 56.

capital was ruled by other nobles who had also received their territory from the king, but who were distant members of the ruling house or relatives by marriage. Toward the fringes of the system (called the "region of tranquil tenure") the monarchs created a multitude of small states governed by former military or civil officials who were awarded territory, villages, and towns in return for services to the Chou kings. The function of these states (termed *kuo*) was to watch over the activities of hostile tribes beyond the borders of the system. For this service the vassals received special royal subsidies. At the farthest region of the system stood the area of "wild domain," land inhabited by barbarian tribes, Chou vassals whose loyalty was doubtful, and groups which retained sporadic connections with the Chou but which were not wholly sinicized.

In part, this feudal structure was held together for several centuries by obligations which the vassals and members of the royal family had to fulfill toward the central monarchy or their immediate superiors. The relationships of dominance and subordination were also sustained by an official mythology which held the king to be the "Son of Heaven," ruling by divine decree. A challenge to his power could thus be interpreted as a form of sacrilege.

But the Chou dynasts were incapable of preventing the eventual growth of power among the many vassals. The feudal lords through the centuries had consolidated political, military, and administrative power over ever-larger pieces of territory, and had succeeded in creating self-sufficient states. By the beginning of the Spring and Autumn period, many of them had acquired or conquered enough territory to make it possible for them not to rely on the royal family for subsidies or grants of land. When ambitious nobles went to war and defeated a neighbor, they no longer turned the conquered rulers into sub-vassals, but incorporated them and their land as integral parts of their own territory.[8] The smaller units were simply swallowed up by the larger.

Moreover, the rulers of these territories increasingly derived their authority from inheritance, rather than from the central monarchy. Regardless of lineage, they called themselves princes, and by the fifth century many were known as kings.[9] By the beginning of the eighth century, successors of the original vassals and princes were already going to battle against each other and even against the Chou monarchy itself. In 707 B.C., a vassal actually defeated the Chou monarch's army,[10] and 50 years later a group of leaders from the more powerful states determined

[8] Li, *The Ageless Chinese*, p. 59.
[9] Williams, *A Short History of China*, p. 62.
[10] Li, *The Ageless Chinese*, p. 50.

the succession of the Chou throne.[11] Increasingly the central monarchy had to rely for its prestige and power on those theoretically subordinate to it. Between the eighth and seventh centuries, therefore, the patterns of dependency had become reversed. While the monarch retained a certain ceremonial importance, leaders of independent states in no way felt compelled to observe the wishes of the king.

In four centuries the structure of the Chou system changed from one in which the characteristic relationship was of a feudal type, with clearly established patterns of dominance and subordination, to a system in which a small number of independent states interacted with each other, with no permanent hierarchy of power and influence. The most important conditions which made this development possible were the relative isolation of many of the feudal units from the central authority,[12] their aggrandizement at each others' expense (thereby creating larger territorial units), growth of popular loyalties, and establishment of administrative mechanisms which made the political units more self-sufficient.[13] The number of units in the late Spring and Autumn and Warring States periods varied with each new conquest or absorption, but fluctuated normally between ten and fifteen. By 230 B.C. there were only seven major states and three smaller entities remaining as independent units.

The processes by which smaller states were absorbed into larger ones normally involved the use of force. The state of Ch'i, for example, was particularly successful in expanding its territory at the expense of smaller neighbors. Chronicles of the period record that in 664 B.C. Ch'i "brought Chang to terms"; four years later it "removed" Yang. In 567 Ch'i "extinguished" Lai and T'ang; and in 549 it "seized" Chieh-ken.[14] In other cases the rulers of small states voluntarily sought the protection of larger units and ended up as protectorates, attached states, or quasi-independent provinces. In 645 the government of the state of Chin lost territory when it paid a ransom of eight cities in order to obtain the return of its ruler, who had been seized by the people of Ch'in. In some other cases states either bartered or sold territory to others. This process of absorption could not go on indefinitely, since there was no rapid movement to expand at the expense of the *wu* beyond the original frontiers of the early Chou empire.

As unoccupied territory available for absorption declined, states warred

---

[11] Walker, *The Multi-State System of Ancient China*, p. 27.

[12] Cf. Wolfram Eberhard, *A History of China* (London: Routledge & Kegan Paul, Ltd., 1950), p. 34.

[13] The economic reasons for the decline of feudalism are discussed in Li, *The Ageless Chinese*, pp. 60–61.

[14] Walker, *The Multi-State System of Ancient China*, p. 29.

increasingly among themselves. One result was a tendency toward the polarization of power between the states of the north, which (for ceremonial purposes only) still identified themselves with the Chou monarchy but were under the effective leadership or domination of Ch'i, and the several states of the south under the domination of Ch'u. While these two groupings constituted crude collective security subsystems, they were also the instrumentalities of Ch'i and Ch'u, used partly for their own purposes. These two blocs were roughly analogous to the Western and Soviet blocs after World War II, except that they were never very stable. The period of the Warring States, for example, saw members of both blocs fight vigorously against their own "allies."

In a system where territorial expansion became a prime objective of state policy, and power was distributed among ten or fifteen large states, there was no role for neutrals. Those units which attempted to remain outside the quarrels of other states or alliances ultimately faced extinction, absorption by another state or bloc, or, in the case of the Chou (northern) alliance, a type of quasi-independence which allowed for considerable cultural and political autonomy, but not military neutrality.[15]

By the third century, whatever was left of Chinese unity dissipated as all states began to wage war against each other, regardless of alliance commitments or traditional friendships. Wars became great campaigns of massacre and annihilation, with serious consequences to the political and economic stability of both victors and defeated. Between 230 and 221 B.C., the westernmost state of Ch'in, a semi-barbarian and partly isolated political unit, conquered Han, Chao, Wei, Ch'u, Yen, and finally Chi bringing to an end the Chou dynasty and the system of independent states. The system was replaced by the Chin empire, ruled by the Han dynasty, which successfully destroyed all symbolic vestiges of feudalism and the political independence of separate territorial units.[16]

Aside from several traditional rivalries the leagues of states which operated during parts of the Spring and Autumn and Warring States periods could be classified as important subsystems. The states of the Chou league, for example, created a semblance of order in their mutual relations, and adopted privileges and rules of interaction which they did not extend or observe in their relations with states outside the league. These rules, which included procedures for the pacific settlement of conflicts among member states, also helped sustain the solidarity of the alliance. The other major subsystem, the southern league of states under Ch'u leadership, did not develop any tradition of solidarity as was found

[15] Walker, *The Multi-State System of Acient China,* p. 101.
[16] Li, *The Ageless Chinese,* p. 56.

in the Chou league. It was held together primarily by the use or threat of force applied by Ch'u, and eventually dissolved as Ch'u conquered all of its allies and simply incorporated them into its own territory. The standards of conduct within this alliance were not significantly different from those in the relations between the two blocs.

The forms and criteria of stratification during the Western Chou period were similar to those in the European medieval order: the status and prestige of each political unit was based upon the personal relationship between the central dynast and his vassals. Thus, each political unit was ranked at diplomatic and ceremonial functions according to the original title conferred to its leader by the monarch, corresponding approximately to the titles of prince, duke, marquis, earl, viscount, and baron. By the Spring and Autumn period stratification became established upon the visible elements of a state's power and prestige; rulers who attended international conferences in the eighth century B.C. no longer ranked themselves according to the official titles of their feudal ancestors. Prestige and status in the system after 771 B.C. were based primarily upon a state's available military resources, and secondarily upon the prestige, wealth, and family connections of its rulers. The number of four-horse military chariots was the most conspicuous indicator of a state's power.[17] Another indicator of a state's prestige and status was the number and quality of allies it could count upon for military assistance.

Since the Chinese were very conscious about their "international" ranking, they frequently attempted to impress neighbors, allies, and enemies by winning spectacular military victories or, if warfare was wanting, by conducting large military reviews before visiting dignitaries from other states. In 529 B.C., for example, the government of Ch'i organized a military performance in which it displayed over 4,000 chariots.[18] Since the largest army mobilized for battle during the early Chou dynasty contained only 3,000 chariots,[19] it is clear that this state exhibited almost its entire military capability in an effort to impress others with its might.

Whether measured by available military forces, family connections, wealth, or allies, there was no persistent hierarchy of status or power after the strength of the Chou monarchy had declined to symbolic proportions. Military power and diplomatic status were diffused among a number of relatively large and equal states. These could be considered the great powers of the epoch, states which, though roughly equal with each other,

---

[17] Cf. Cheng Te-k'un, *Shang China* (Cambridge: W. Heffer and Sons, Ltd., 1960), p. 295. Richard Walker points out that even today the translation of the term "great power" is commonly rendered in Chinese as a "country of ten-thousand four-horse chariots."

[18] Walker, *The Multi-State System of Ancient China*, p. 48.

[19] Cheng, *Shang China*, p. 295.

determined the fate of lesser political units either by absorption or through leadership of alliances. During the early part of the Spring and Autumn period no one state was predominant in the system, as alliance patterns shifted rapidly and leadership passed back and forth among Ch'i, Chin, and Ch'un in the north, and Ch'u, Wu, and Yueh in the south. During the latter portion of this period and throughout the Warring States period, however, power and status gravitated primarily to the leaders of the two main alliance systems, Ch'i and Ch'u, and ultimately to Ch'in, which conquered all of the other states.

Below these great powers were smaller states, political units which maintained all the requisites of independence but which, for lack of military capabilities, economic resources, family connections, or defense establishments (such as walled cities), had to rely for their survival upon the great powers and their alliances. A third tier of states included the *fu-yung*, or attached states, and smaller protectorates which owed their independence to the goodwill of their protectors. These units were seldom over eight square miles in size and, as the lowest units in the political order, did not have direct diplomatic access to the ceremonial center of the system, the Chou monarchy, but had to communicate indirectly through their protectors.[20]

Distinct from the real order of stratification was the theoretical hierarchy which persisted for centuries after it had ceased to have any political or military significance. Even when the states of the system had dwindled in number to ten or fifteen and banded together into two warring alliances, the house of Chou maintained vestiges of ceremonial and symbolic importance. The dynastic capital was still considered the center of the system of states and the monarch was officially deemed the ceremonial head of his "empire," much as European dynasts and princes continued to pay lip service to the Holy Roman Emperor long after he had lost his political and military power. The leaders of most of the Chinese states continued to offer ceremonial deference to the Chou monarch, and if they could obtain his presence at meetings of heads of state or conferences of alliance partners they would willingly pay tribute to him and emphasize the myths of the "empire" in order to secure his blessing on their own schemes.

## Forms of Interaction

During the feudal period levels of political and commercial interaction among the units were low, except when formal diplomatic and ceremonial exchanges were arranged between the dukes, princes, and other nobility

[20] Walker, *The Multi-State System of Ancient China*, p. 38.

and the central Chou monarchy. Interaction and communication followed closely the hierarchical pattern of authority in the system, although feudal units in close proximity naturally had many relations with each other.

In the Spring and Autumn and Warring States periods each of the independent states conducted its external relations without reference to the official center of the empire. There was a proliferation of contacts between states, not only formal and diplomatic, but trade and commercial as well. The Chinese states never established permanent diplomatic organizations, but recurring occasions for arranging alliances, declaring war, making peace, or maintaining prestige in the system through ceremonial or military displays led to almost constant diplomatic exchanges between the units. Chinese sources of this period list such diplomatic exchanges as *ch'ao*, a court visit paid by one ruler to another; *hui*, meetings between permanent government officials of two or more states; *p'in*, friendly missions of information or inquiry; *shih*, exchange of emissaries; and *shou*, hunting parties where government representatives combined diplomatic affairs with recreation.[21] The ceremonies attending these types of exchanges were so lengthy that many states did have, in effect, permanent diplomatic communication with each other.

These exchanges often had a direct connection with a state's security or expansionist objectives, even when contacts ostensibly had ceremonial purposes. Almost all of the major events in the life of a ruling family—assumption of a throne, burial of a former ruler, marriages between families of rulers, or even birth of children into a ruler's family—required diplomatic representation from other friendly states, and these occasions were used for bargaining over state interests.[22] Marriages between ruling families were a means of creating and sustaining alliances, a practice familiar to students of early European diplomatic history.

A unique aspect of transactions within the Chinese system was the extent to which they occurred between states with different religious or cultural traditions. Though Ch'u and Ch'in were not fully sinified states, they were able to interact with the others essentially on a basis of equality. Apparently wars, alliances, and peace were made in the light of a state's immediate objectives and interests, while ideological or cultural distinctions remained largely irrelevant to a state's orientation toward others. Hence, if a state found it in its own interest to conclude an alliance with even the most uncultured barbarians at the fringes of the system, it would not hesitate to do so.[23]

[21] Walker, *The Multi-State System of Ancient China*, p. 75.
[22] *Ibid.*, p. 78.
[23] *Ibid.*, p. 99.

Commercial exchange was another form of interaction. Normally this was a private affair of merchants who were free to travel from state to state and conduct their transactions without administrative interference. However, in so far as grain and other commodities were necessary to feed armies, governments maintained an interest in having sufficient stores to support their forces in times of poor harvest. Since they could not always obtain adequate supplies from their own peasants, occasionally they had to send out economic missions to purchase agricultural products from other states.[24]

War was a frequent form of interaction between states during the Spring and Autumn and Warring States periods. It is recorded, for example, that Duke Huan of Ch'in went to war 28 times in a reign lasting 43 years.[25] In the feudal order, force (provided partly by the vassals) was used primarily by the Chou dynasts against the *wu* and occasionally against errant nobles whose actions were deemed damaging to the interests of the empire. In the system of independent states all of the units used organized violence as a method of achieving objectives—whether territory, slaves, "honor," or allies. During the feudal era, engagements were seldom fought as battles of annihilation, but more as trials of strength, finesse, and glory.[26] Fairly rigid rules of warfare prevailed (for example, a charioteer could not fight against anyone of lower or higher rank) and helped to moderate the destructiveness of battle. By the period of Warring States, however, wars had become great contests, fought brutally by huge armies numbering in the hundreds of thousands. Mass slaughter replaced duelling by charioteers, and the casualties of battle reached proportions enormous even by contemporary standards. In 274 B.C. a Ch'in general reportedly killed 150,000 enemy soldiers, and the massacre of prisoners of war was a common occurrence.[27]

The Chinese also used various forms of subversion and intervention in other states' internal affairs as methods of achieving their objectives. The number of dynastic quarrels and marriages arranged between families of different states led to situations in which one government could support certain claimants to the throne in a neighboring territory, and if it succeeded in creating disloyal factions or cliques could then help foment revolutions or *coups d'état* and place a subservient, or at least friendly, ruler on the throne. According to one authority,[28] the Chinese states

[24] *Ibid.*, p. 80.
[25] Li, *The Ageless Chinese*, p. 50.
[26] Kenneth S. Latourette, *The Chinese: Their History and Culture* (New York: The Macmillan Company, 1959), p. 61; Marcel Granet, *Chinese Civilization* (New York: Meridian Books, Inc., 1951), p. 290.
[27] Cf. Eberhard, *A History of China*, p. 57; Li, *The Ageless Chinese*, p. 56.
[28] Walker, *The Multi-State System of Ancient China*, p. 86.

persistently employed the techniques of subversion to expand their influence into other areas. In the Spring and Autumn period, for example,
there were at least 36 instances of successful subversion, frequently
brought to a conclusion when the intervening state made a show of force
at the last moment in order to assure the victory of rebel elements.

## The Rules of the System

In the latter periods of the Chou dynasty there was considerable
discrepancy between the official rules, traditions, and myths which were
supposed to govern relations between political units, and the actual
behavior of independent states. The official mythology and customary
rules of behavior, buttressed by the writings of philosophers such as Con-
fucius, emphasized unity, obedience to the "Son of Heaven," harmony
among all parts of the political order, and the obligation of all lower
entities—whether sons to fathers or vassals to lords—to higher authorities.

But practice during the Spring and Autumn and Warring States periods
did not accord with the myths and customs appropriate to the feudal
order. In a system of many powerful, ambitious, and independent states
such rules were anachronisms. Instead, the main units developed rules or
customs which reflected the major political and military characteristics of
the system. The official theories of hierarchy, imperial rule over all subjects, and attending patterns of superior-subordinate relationships, were
belied by the assumptions of later periods which recognized that the great
powers, at least, were more or less sovereign equals, free from all restraints imposed by the Chou monarchy. Treaties concluded after 771 B.C.
were treaties between equals, even where the Chou authorities were
involved. Obligations were entered into only by the consent of both
parties to the treaty and, unlike the Western Chou era, no authority had
legal or customary rights in another independent state's territories. Even
compacts between the Chinese states and various barbarian groups were
concluded on a basis of equality. There was, however, no belief in the
sanctity of independence, for throughout the Spring and Autumn and
Warring States periods the larger units conquered and amalgamated
lesser territories, with no intention of returning their independence after a
short period of occupation. Conquered territories were simply annexed.

More explicit rules were formulated into treaties which contained the
specific obligations of states toward each other and provided means for
enforcement. One guarantee of compliance with treaties was the practice
of exchanging hostages. A state would concede several cities or members
of the ruling family as hostages, to be kept—or destroyed—by the other
treaty partner if the first broke its obligations. Among customary rules

were those demanding that states send envoys to each other at frequent intervals, that members of the two main alliance systems send a minimum of one mission every three years to the court of the league president, and that "summit" meetings be held at least every five years.[29] Other rules prescribed in detail the types of conduct and behavior appropriate in warfare, though towards the end of the system the rules of warfare were systematically violated in great campaigns of annihilation.

Most conflicts during the feudal era were mediated directly by the Chou monarchy—except those on the periphery of the system, where central influence was at a minimum. With the decline of the Chou dynasty's effective position among the newly-arising independent states, conflicts had to be resolved directly by those involved. During the early Spring and Autumn period there were no institutions which could provide mediatory or conciliatory services, but as the two alliance systems developed they did establish techniques for resolving conflicts arising *within* the alliance. It was in the interest of the alliance—or at least to the advantage of the predominant powers in each alliance—to maintain peace and collaboration between alliance members. When disputes broke out among them, therefore, other members often found it necessary to intervene, either to secure a mediated resolution or, if that was impossible or improbable, to threaten or force one or both parties to terminate their quarrel. In 546 B.C., moreover, some of the smaller states which had been increasingly victimized by larger neighbors called a conference of states which successfully drafted a multilateral treaty of non-aggression. This resulted in 40 years of relative stability and non-violence in inter-state relations. Whatever techniques were employed by the Chinese states in the Spring and Autumn period were quickly cast aside, however, in the period of Warring States, when conflicts were resolved almost entirely by the use of force.[30]

The influence of the international structure on political units' foreign policies can be discerned from this discussion of the Chinese international systems. In the feudal era, the units were weak in relation to the central monarchy and had little freedom to maneuver in their external relations. Bound to the center by traditional, mythical, and contractual obligations, the lesser units seldom had a choice but to conduct their relations with each other in accordance with the policies and rules set forth by the emperor. In parts of the Spring and Autumn and Warring States periods, however, when military capabilities and diplomatic influence were widely

---

[29] *Ibid.,* p. 81.
[30] Li, *The Ageless Chinese,* p. 53; Walker, *The Multi-State System of Ancient China,* p. 88.

diffused among a number of relatively equal political units, and when the blocs were not operating, the structure placed fewer limitations on external actions and objectives. To be sure, the smaller states were virtual satellites or protectorates, but the medium and large states enjoyed considerable freedom of action. They could forge or destroy alliances, seek security through isolation, or attempt, though usually unsuccessfully, to defend themselves by remaining neutral. The Chinese example thus suggests that if power is diffused the latitude for choice of foreign policy orientations is substantial, while security from outside attack may be low. Strategy, alliance-making, war, and rapid shifts in orientation toward neighbors and more distant states are characteristic features of the diffuse system. In the feudal system, on the contrary, most action is confined to court intrigues and secret bargaining, while major objectives are determined for the units by the emperor. Freedom of action is limited, but security from outside attack may be enhanced. Generalizations such as these seem to be confirmed from other historical international systems as well.

### The External Politics
### of the Greek City States, 800 B.C.–322 B.C.

The Greek world was geographically more extensive than its Chinese counterpart. While the Chinese remained isolated from most other cultural groups, Greek merchants and travellers found their way to India, the shores of the Baltic, Spain, and the north coast of Africa. Most of the famous city states were located on the Greek peninsula and on islands of the Aegean Sea, but the Greeks also colonized locations throughout the shores of the Mediterranean, establishing their political organizations and culture in the areas on which the cities of Nice, Marseilles, and Naples are presently found. Since these people maintained commercial and diplomatic relations with the Phoenicians, Persians, Arabs, Indians, and various tribes in Europe and Southern Russia, the geographical boundaries of the system are difficult to establish. Persian expansion in the Aegean was a major threat to the interests of all Greek city states on the peninsula; while the activities of the Phoenicians had little impact on relations between most Greek city states, they determined the fate of several Greek colonies on the Italian peninsula. Non-Greek political units thus played an important, though sporadic, role in Greek life. Since the relations among city states and colonies constituted the majority of interactions and transactions in the system, however, we will describe these rather than emphasize the Greeks' relations with the "barbarians," people of non-Hellenic culture on the fringes of the Greek world.

## Nature of the Political Units

The city state (*polis*) was the main form of political organization throughout the Greek world from the eighth century until Philip of Macedonia conquered the peninsula in the late fourth century B.C. Most of these units were comprised of a group of towns or small cities, usually walled, surrounded by relatively small areas of agricultural territory. Attica, for example, was the area occupied by the Athenian people. It included many small agricultural villages, but the city of Athens was the center of political life and administration and the people throughout Attica were called Athenians. The population of the city states varied from the largest, such as Syracuse, Acragas, and Athens, with about 25,000 male citizens, to the smallest, such as Siris and Thourioi in Sicily, which contained only several thousand inhabitants. In size the city states ranged from several hundred square miles, including outlying agricultural territory, to small towns built on the shores of the Mediterranean Sea comprising only several hundred acres. Most *poleis* were about 100 square miles.

The forms of government in the city states varied from priest-kings ruling over tribal organizations, small oligarchies of the rich, and military tyrannies, to freely elected governments where citizens (omitting peasants, merchants, and slaves), whose tenure in office rotated frequently, formulated and administered policies directly. A major distinction between the Chinese and Greek political organizations was that in the former the majority of the population was neither involved in nor called upon to play a political role, while in some Greek city states citizen participation was extensive.

The city state cannot be understood adequately when described only in terms of its political institutions, for the Greeks considered the *polis* the *ideal* social organization for liberating man from his natural state, and for providing justice, promoting fellowship and harmony, and training personal character. Despite the many economic, cultural, and linguistic ties among Greek city states, there was no struggle to create a common framework for uniting all the Hellenic people into a more viable empire. The Greeks emphasized the virtue of limited political organizations— small enough to allow for the assembly of all free citizens to help make political decisions and small enough for government and administration to never seem impersonal influences over the lives of citizens. The state and society were thus indistinguishable concepts among the Greeks.

Aside from the *poleis,* three other types of political units played roles in the Greek international system. One was the tributary state, a *polis* which came under the hegemony of another city state but was allowed to maintain some degree of autonomy in internal affairs. During the fifth century, when Athens dominated the Delian League, a number of the smaller members of the alliance became tributary states. Most of these were obliged—ostensibly as alliance partners—to accept Athenian domination over their external relations, contribute to the Athenian treasury (officially, a contribution to the alliance), and make war and peace according to the interests of Athens. Failure to follow Athenian leadership resulted in serious punishment, including occupation of the recalcitrant city state by Athenian troops and construction of permanent Athenian garrisons.

The second type of political unit was the military colony, *cleruchy,* which some city states established to guard strategic territories, waterways, and trade routes. The *cleruchy* also served as an outlet for surplus population from the mother city state, particularly after these cities grew to the point where their own agriculture could not provide adequate food supplies for the population.

Finally, many city states also established non-military colonies throughout the Aegean and Mediterranean Seas. They erected these towns and cities primarily as new sources of food supply and areas for relieving population congestion at home. Many city states also sent politically unreliable citizens and unwanted aspirants for public office to their colonies, sometimes in exile, sometimes to fill honorific positions. Though the original connection between the city state and its colonies was one of dependence, after several decades most colonies became independent of their mother city states and retained only formal religious ties. Otherwise, the colonies organized their own political administration and conducted their own external affairs.[31]

### The Structure of the System

As each city developed during its formative years in relative isolation, the system originally displayed a highly diffuse structure of influence and power. Each unit was independent. Although frequent wars over territory, personal rivalries, and frontiers ended in the total destruction of some city states, there were few permanent hierarchies of dominance-dependence. Some city states had wider-ranging interests and activities

[31] For description of some of the city states, see Kathleen Freeman, *Greek City States* (London: Methuen & Co., Ltd., 1948); for the colonies, Johannes Hasebrook, *Trade and Politics in Ancient Greece* (London: G. Bell & Sons, Ltd., 1933), pp. 106–08.

than others, and consequently gained more prestige. By the fifth century, however, the structure of the system became more stratified and rigid, with city states such as Athens, Sparta, Acragas, Corinth, Argus, and Thebes increasingly dominating the actions and transactions of the smaller units around them. The main sources of change from a diffuse to a "polar" international system, where power and influence coagulated around two blocs of states, were the rapid growth and extension of Athenian naval and commercial strength, and the threat of Persian penetration into the Ionian islands, Thrace, and Macedon.

As a response to this external danger, the Greeks established the Hellenic League into a military alliance and placed it under the leadership of Sparta and Athens. Despite the semblance of Greek unity during the Persian Wars (492–477 B.C.), there were serious conflicts between members of the League, mostly occasioned by the smaller city states' fear of Athenian imperialism and expansion. Thus, after the Greek victories over the Persians, Athens' competitors, led by Sparta, formed a rival organization, the Peloponnesian League, an intricate alliance and collective security system designed to deter further Athenian expansion, and in some cases to "liberate" areas already under Athenian domination. A bitter competition over trade and naval supremacy between Corinth and Athens led ultimately to the Peloponnesian Wars involving the two military alliances.

By the outbreak of these wars in 431 B.C., Athens had already become an empire, ruling directly or indirectly (ostensibly through a new multilateral alliance, the Delian League) over a number of independent and tributary city states. But this hegemony was not created solely by Athens' commercial superiority or even by the imperialism of Cimon and Pericles. Many city states voluntarily accepted Athenian laws, courts, and currency simply because these Athenian institutions were more admirable than their own arrangements.[32] Athens also provided many services for other city states, such as leading the alliance against Persia, clearing the seas of pirates, and organizing trade connections with non-Hellenic peoples.

By 431 B.C., then, the Greek city state system had become partly polarized into two large blocs. The Athenian empire led one bloc and was followed by its voluntary or tributary allies, including the prominent city states of Rhodes, Miletus, Corcyra (a formidable naval power), as well as other units located in the eastern Aegean and northern and western Greece. Sparta led the Peloponnesian League, with Elis, Arcadia, and Corinth as its most important allies. Unlike the Chinese system, where

---

[32] Adda B. Bozeman, *Politics and Culture in International History* (Princeton: Princeton University Press, 1960), p. 86.

neutral status was not condoned, many city states and colonies on the Greek peninsula and throughout the shores of the Mediterranean Sea remained free from direct involvement in the Peloponnesian Wars. The system was not, therefore, organized completely around the two blocs.

By the middle of the fifth century an identifiable order of stratification had replaced the more diffuse, egalitarian distribution of power, status, and prestige found in the era when the city states were relatively isolated from each other. The criteria according to which states were ranked during and after the fifth century were primarily military, commercial, and cultural. Sparta and Athens assumed leadership of the two blocs because of their military or commercial capabilities. Sparta gained respect and prestige from the fighting efficiency, bravery, and loyalty of its soldiers. Even those who abhorred Sparta's authoritarian political and social institutions admired the greatness of its armies.[33] Athens, on the other hand, wielded considerable influence over other city states by virtue of its citizens' aggressive commercial practices. When it had achieved a position of trading predominance it could easily reduce smaller states to subservience by applying boycotts and embargoes on their trade. Other states moved voluntarily towards Athens, expecting profitable trade relations and protection of commercial routes by the Athenian fleet. Sparta, which possessed only one colony and few commercial connections, had to rely essentially on military force to achieve its objectives.

Also contributing to Athens' prestige and status were the cultural and political contributions of its citizens. Many city states accepted direct Athenian rule or political leadership in external affairs in order to obtain the advantages of Athenian political institutions, laws, culture, and commercial practices. Above all, perhaps, cultural excellence was a criterion of greatness. Athens was to the Greeks what Paris was to Europe in the eighteenth century, the cultural center of the system, in Pericles' words, "the educator of Hellas."[34]

### Forms of Interaction Among the City States

Prior to the fifth century the city states conducted little trade among themselves, as each unit was virtually self-sufficient in the few necessities of life and the commodities needed to sustain a fairly simple technology. Governments generally took no part in trading activities (except in some cases to obtain revenues) and merchants faced numerous obstacles to successful transactions, including land and sea pirates, non-convertible

[33] H.D.F. Kitto, *The Greeks* (Edinburgh: R. Clark Ltd., 1951), p. 94.
[34] *Ibid.*, p. 76.

monies, and non-enforcement of debts among citizens of different city states.[35] By the fifth century, however, the growth of population and merchant classes and the need to obtain military supplies prompted rapid development in commercial activity among the units. Commercial transactions aided the city states in their internal development, but also led to important rivalries. By the time of the Peloponnesian Wars private merchants no longer operated on their own, but relied extensively on governments to provide protection and open new sources of raw materials and markets. Simultaneously, many governments used trade to build up military resources, and employed their merchants as agents through which they could place diplomatic pressure by threatening boycotts and embargoes on other city states. The tradesmen of Athens, backed by the powerful Athenian fleet, were particularly aggressive in developing markets abroad, while the Athenian government occasionally helped them exclude the trade of rival city states, such as Corinth, from sources of supply. By the time Athens dominated large parts of the Aegean Sea and the Gulf of Corinth, no city state could conduct extensive overseas trade without the tacit approval of Athenian authorities.

One form of interaction which prevailed even in the early period of the city states was the meetings of Greeks at religious festivals and councils. The Greeks observed one basic religious form and created a number of institutions (called *amphyctyonies*) to maintain the purity of the religion and provide means for organizing common festivals and sacrifices. The shrines at Olympia and Delphi offered centers for interaction of all Greeks. Religion, then, was one of the unifying elements in the system (truces were always declared during the Olympic games) and helped the Greeks appreciate their common inheritance and distinguish themselves from the "barbarians" with whom they had developed many contacts. The religion did not, however, lead to any political unification among the many units; indeed, as each city state had its own deities, religious symbols were often the basis for violence and conflict, not political cooperation. One of the major problems of the system was that despite the Greeks' propensity to fraternize with each other in social, religious, recreational, intellectual, and aesthetic matters, they were unable to carry these forms of cooperative behavior into political and military relationships.

If the political units could cooperate on some questions of common concern, generally their interests conflicted and their governments resorted to the use of force to resolve those conflicts. War was a recurrent phenomenon of the system, and most peace treaties were drafted to

[35] Hasebrook, *Trade and Politics in Ancient Greece*, p. 85.

remain in effect only during a specific period of time. Part of the explanation for the frequency of violence lies in the coupling of religious and political symbolism within the city states. In the early period of the Greek system, wars arising over territorial quarrels often developed into ideological crusades involving the honor and glory not only of the city state, but also of its particular deities. For this reason, many wars were fought with terrible brutality, resulting in complete destruction of the defeated city state and sale of its inhabitants into slavery.

The sources of war varied. In the early period wars over religious issues were numerous; one example was the conflict between Athens and Crissa which erupted into armed violence after the Crissans destroyed Apollo's temple at Delphi. Border conflicts frequently led to warfare, while conflicts arising out of internal revolts and civil wars, in which outside city states intervened, were not uncommon after the fifth century. War was also used to obtain control over strategic waterways and mountain passes. Athens used force several times to punish recalcitrant allies or city states which had attempted to defect from the empire or Delian League to join the league of states led by Sparta. Finally, the search for booty and commercial advantage were important sources of military violence. Throughout the period economic interaction became more prominent, but this did not always lead to cooperative forms of behavior. On the contrary, wars, conflicts, and rivalries tended to become more intense as the economic stakes involved in a quarrel increased. However, not every divisive issue could become a cause for a contest of arms, since wars were costly, destructive, and often indecisive. Other means of wielding influence had to be employed as well.

Among these was the practice of diplomacy, formal efforts by the government of one city state to induce another city state, through oral persuasion, to act in the interests of the first. Diplomacy was conducted through the medium of the ambassador, usually an honored citizen with oratorical skills, who was sent to persuade governing officials of another city state to make formal decisions by concluding treaties of friendship, alliance, or commerce. In wartime ambassadors—including those sent by the "barbarians"—normally enjoyed diplomatic immunities and were used primarily at the end of hostilities to negotiate the terms of peace, deliver prisoners, and make arrangements for burial of war victims. The Greeks did not organize permanent diplomatic missions headed by resident ambassadors, but they did establish the institution of *proxenos*, roughly analogous to our contemporary consul-general, an agent of one state with permanent residence in another whose main function is to provide services, protection, and commercial contacts for travellers and merchants in foreign countries.

Major Rules of the Greek System

The Greeks developed a number of rules, observed in treaties or custom, which regulated diplomatic relations and the conduct of warfare. These gave recognition to the independence and equality of the units and defined the limits of immunities for both diplomats and religious shrines in time of war; other rules pronounced standard procedures for declaring war, providing asylum, and conferring citizenship.[36] Since wars were often costly and indecisive, the Greeks also developed procedures for resolving conflicts short of force. Arbitration and conciliation, two procedures for interjecting third parties into diplomatic bargaining situations, were among the important contributions the Greeks made to subsequent diplomatic practices.[37] They occasionally employed these procedures for handling recurring boundary disputes, conflicts involving public debts, and quarrels arising from differing interpretations of treaties.[38] Normally parties to a dispute honored the decisions of arbitrators, particularly since the arbitrators enjoyed great public prestige. Despite arbitral procedures, war and violence continued to be employed as means of settling conflicts, leading ultimately to the exhaustion of the most important city states.

The fate of the Greek system was analogous to that of the Chinese: both succumbed, after a long period of bitter strife between two major blocs, to a superior force which, though part of the system, was considered to be "barbarian" and alien. For the Chinese states, Ch'in was the danger lurking behind the Wei River; for the Greeks, Macedonia was the external threat. The demise of the Greek city state system has been a focus of interest for historians, many of whom have proposed hypotheses about the inability of the Greeks to modify their political structures in the face of internal instability and external threat.

One hypothesis explaining the decline of the Greek system asserts that independent city states were a feasible form of political organization as long as the units were relatively isolated from each other and economically self-sufficient. Aristotle had claimed that the first law of existence for

[36] Arthur Nussbaum, *A Concise History of the Law of Nations* (New York: The Macmillan Company, 1961); Coleman Phillipson, *The International Law and Custom of Ancient Greece and Rome* (London: Macmillan & Co., Ltd., 1911).

[37] The Greeks did not invent these procedures. Many primitive tribes and more extensive empires had developed procedures and institutions by which disinterested third parties attempted to reconcile two feuding families, tribes, or nations. The Europeans, however, developed the practice during the eighteenth and nineteenth centuries using the Greek experience as a model.

[38] Marcus N. Tod, *International Arbitration Amongst the Greeks* (Oxford: The Clarendon Press, 1913). For further discussion of arbitral procedures, see Chapter XV.

the city state was self-sufficiency, but even then few city states could meet that requirement. With growing commerce and population, all sorts of intricate dependencies developed which were often exploited by those who sought commercial or military advantages over others.[39] In other words, the instability and recurrence of warfare in the system derived from the nature of the units of which it was comprised. A corollary assumption is that if the Greeks had been able to create large territorial states with coherent administrative mechanisms, they could have overrun the rest of the known world as Alexander, Philip of Macedon's son, eventually did.

The second hypothesis, closely related to the assumptions in the first, claims that the inability of the Greeks to unite led to their ultimate downfall. Their internecine feuds and the struggles of the Peloponnesian Wars wearied them and led to great domestic instability in many of the city states. Even when farsighted men perceived the growing strength of Macedon, the Greeks could not overcome their own quarrels to unite in self-defense.

It could be argued also that the development outside of Greece of much larger territorial and administrative units commanding extensive military power made the Greek city states obsolete, just as developing dynastic states in sixteenth and seventeenth century Europe superseded the small independent walled cities of Medieval Europe. By the third century B.C., no system based on such small units as the city states could remain isolated from the new giants. Larger political units—first the Persians, succeeded by the Macedonians and ultimately the Romans— made the city states appear weak and paltry in comparison. Either the Greeks would have had to unite into one large territorial empire, participating as just one of several larger entities in the politics of the Mediterranean area, or they would be engulfed, as they were, by new states which had previously been merely peripheral actors in Greek life. The small republics and city states of Renaissance Italy were similarly engulfed by the larger dynastic states of Europe in the fifteenth and sixteenth centuries.

## International Politics in Renaissance Italy

The unique character of politics in the Italian peninsula during the fifteenth century can be appreciated by comparing the system of Italian city states and republics with the political structure in the rest of Europe.

[39] Kitto, *The Greeks,* p. 62.

Though Europe at this time was not in its medieval period, its political organization maintained the major features of earlier centuries. Nation states did not exist, there was no concept of ethnic nationhood that had any practical significance to the form of political organizations, and though kings reigned on thrones, few ruled directly over a specified group of people inhabiting definable territories. Instead, there were many hierarchies of authority in the known areas of Europe. Some kings, to be sure, were sovereign and commanded the obedience of nobles on some questions of policy. There also existed hundreds of semi-sovereign walled cities and feudal lords, some of whom determined who would sit on the king's throne. The church hierarchy was an independent power on most ecclesiastical and moral issues of the day, and wielded considerable influence in secular politics as well. Kings made treaties with their vassals, and vassals made contracts with each other—sometimes at the expense of the king; individual churches, monasteries, or convents had special privileges and immunities; peasants and independent cities formed protective leagues; in order to keep their thrones, kings often had to mortgage or sell their rights to territory. Europe was a patchwork of small quasi-sovereignties, states within states, and overlapping hierarchies, whose powers were defined in complicated contracts and oaths.[40]

In contrast, a reasonably well-defined set of political entities had developed on the northern part of the Italian peninsula by the beginning of the fifteenth century. Venice had already existed for several centuries as an important trading state with the east. It had a regular system of administration, the rudiments of a diplomatic service, and historical interests upon which to base its diplomatic activities. The rest of northern Italy was rapidly developing into politically distinct pieces of territory.

## The Boundaries of the System

According to historians,[41] the condition which most favored development of independent city states and republics in Italy during the fourteenth and fifteenth centuries was the relative isolation of the peninsula from the rest of Europe. Not that there was any lack of contact between all areas of Europe, but the territories north of the Alps were still splintered into thousands of political authorities, and not even some of the more aggressive European kings could turn as far south as Italy in search of dynastic prestige or territory. They had too much to handle with their

[40] Gerhard Ritter, *Die Neugestaltung Europas im 16. Jahrhundert* (Berlin: Verlag des Druckhauses Tempelhof, 1950), pp. 23–25.
[41] Garrett Mattingly, *Renaissance Diplomacy* (London: Jonathan Cape, Ltd., 1955), pp. 59–61, 97.

own vassals and pretenders to their thrones to intrigue among the Italian states. In addition, a number of crises like the Hundred Years War, the fight between temporal and ecclesiastical authorities over control of the papacy, and recurrent chaos on the Iberian peninsula kept them either preoccupied or impotent. The periodic intrusion of non-Italian authorities into the system was, therefore, well within the bounds which the system could tolerate without creating fundamental changes in its structure or patterns of interaction. It was when the Milanese prevailed upon the French to intervene on their behalf in 1494 that the system collapsed; after the fifteenth century it became just another part of Europe, its politics integrally related to developments on the rest of the continent.

What distinguishes the boundaries of the Italian system from those of China and Greece is that the inhabitants on the fringes of the system were not considered barbarians. If Europe was not unified politically during the fifteenth century, at least it was a cultural and religious unit, with only linguistic and dynastic differences having any practical significance. Although the Italians did not interact extensively over political or commercial problems with other Europeans, the city states or republics on the peninsula were not isolated. The boundaries of the system were defined by the predominant direction of political-diplomatic-military interaction, not by cultural or religious forms of interaction.[42]

## Nature of the Political Units

An important political characteristic of the Italian states in the fifteenth century was lack of security and stability in their governments. Few governments, with the exception of the Venetian and papal authorities, could rule with safety of tenure, because few were established on secure foundations; most lacked any basis for legitimacy, whether historical, customary, or religious, being founded on force, fraud, and repression. The forms of government varied from outright tyrannies to rule by oligarchies. Venice was governed by a conservative aristocracy of patrician families, and the papal states were administered by a conglomeration of feudal lordships and petty tyrants, each more or less subordinate to the popes. A few of the units were genuine republics with various degrees of popular rule.[43]

Because of political instability in many of the units, governing officials could not assume much support from their own populations in either

[42] If we were to consider cultural and religious forms of interaction as defining the boundaries, the Italian political units would become merely one subsystem of the general European system.

[43] Ritter, *Die Neugestaltung Europas,* pp. 24–26; Mattingly, *Renaissance Diplomacy,* pp. 94–95.

domestic or external affairs. Though rulers attempted to build their political strength and prestige through lavish ceremonies and festivals, there was no phenomenon of nationalism or deep emotional attachment to the political unit. Most people recognized that the state's external interests were synonymous with dynastic or oligarchic interests. Citizens seldom understood these interests, nor were they particularly affected by the personal fates of their rulers. The lack of popular involvement in questions of foreign relations meant that the rulers could seldom rely upon the population as an asset or capability. Interaction among the Italian states, as it was to be in Europe during the succeeding three centuries, was essentially confined to the highest social levels and to the professional organizations (armies and diplomatic corps) created specifically for the conduct of foreign relations.

The major units in the Italian system included the papal states, Venice, Milan, Genoa, Florence, and Naples. A number of smaller political organizations—often walled cities and areas in which political power had not yet attained any regular form—lay between the important states.[44] The concept of territoriality—that political power should be based on a specific piece of territory, and sovereignty should extend only to certain natural frontiers corresponding with historical or ethnic divisions—had not yet developed, so the geographical bases of each unit were almost as ill-defined as the political bases for government and administration.[45]

The exceptional political unit of the era was Venice. Unlike its sister republics, it was not a new state, ruled by some faction or oligarchy of debatable lineage. Venice had been growing as a political and administrative unit for several centuries, and had successfully expanded its commercial and military influence to the Adriatic area and the Middle East. The objectives which its governors pursued were in many cases popularly supported; they were directly related to the welfare of the state's citizens rather than to dynastic or family interests. Consequently, Venice was one of the few states in this system which could count upon considerable support from its population in matters of war and peace.

## The Structure of the System

The distribution of power—diffuse—and the patterns of domination-subordination within the Italian Renaissance system were similar to those in China during the early portion of the Spring and Autumn period,

[44] Mattingly, *Renaissance Diplomacy*, pp. 78–79.
[45] Cf. Federico Chabod, "Was There a Renaissance State?" reprinted in, and transated by Heinz Lubasz, ed., *The Development of the Modern State* (New York: The Macmillan Company, 1964), p. 30.

except that the number of units was considerably smaller in Italy. Why, then, didn't the Italian states form permanent coalitions around the central, powerful states, as had been the result of the diffuse power structure in both China and Greece?

The Italian states did conquer and annex smaller neighbors until the peninsula contained only six "major powers" and a few lesser entities. Once the number of units in China and Greece had been reduced, relations solidified around major antagonistic blocs or leagues of states. Each system had a polarized structure in its later years, except that in Greece a number of city states remained neutral in the major bloc conflicts. But in Italy there was no polarization of power around two antagonistic centers. As the units quarrelled and fought over territorial and dynastic interests, they concluded a number of alliances, but shifted their allegiances almost annually, so that there was little time for connections between the states to assume more permanent characteristics.

The structure of the Italian system took on unique characteristics after the Peace of Lodi in 1454, when the three main antagonists in northern Italy—Venice, Milan, and Florence—created the Most Holy League, a collective security organization designed to make the *status quo* of relatively diffused power and equality among the major political units a permanent condition of the system. The Italians, unlike the Chinese and Greeks, apparently realized that continued strife and warfare among units of roughly equal capabilities and strength would ultimately endanger the independence of each; with this realization they were able to reconcile their main antagonisms adequately to bring some stability to the system in the last 40 years of its independent existence. Starting with a diffuse structure of power and influence roughly analogous to the Chinese and Greek systems in their early stages, only the Italians were able successfully to balance the many units and prevent any one from dominating the others. The Italian states thus avoided a polar structure of power, which might have led to a disastrous confrontation.

The major criterion for distinguishing the strength and prestige of the Italian states was money, for without it no government could field a professional army, establish a permanent diplomatic corps, or put on the feasts and celebrations used to impress both the local citizenry and visiting dignitaries. Lineage and historical or religious legitimacy were also noteworthy sources of a government's prestige, but since so few governments could claim these sanctions for their rule, other criteria must have been more important.

During the first half of the fifteenth century there were no permanent subsystems on the Italian peninsula. Alliance patterns shifted frequently, and historical animosities between certain states did not always prevent the conclusion of alliances of convenience when it served the interests of both antagonists. In the period 1454 to 1494, however, the Most Holy League constituted a subsystem of considerable importance. Since the three original signatories—Milan, Venice, and Florence—invited all other states on the peninsula to adhere to it, it was originally intended to be not merely a small alliance or bloc within a larger system, but a permanent organization or confederation of all the states of the system. The League never achieved this aspiration, but in providing a legal basis for a particular distribution of power it was a major source of the relative stability that ensued for 40 years after it was drafted.

## Major Forms of Interaction

Even though communications facilities within the peninsula were primitive, the small area encompassing the group of states allowed for considerable contact among them. Trade had existed for centuries and continued to be a major form of communication between the units, as well as with other areas of Europe. As in Greece, commerce led both to cooperative and conflictful types of relationships; some increased the welfare of all parties on the basis of mutual advantage, but others led to acrimonious trade wars, sometimes ending in violence.

Renaissance Italy is most noted in the history of international politics for developing permanent diplomatic institutions for conducting foreign relations. Permanent embassies staffed by career diplomats were organized partly as a matter of prestige, but also to enable governments to collect information about their allies or potential enemies on a systematic basis. Without envoys with direct access to the courts and councils of other states, how could governments, each in close proximity with the others, insecure, and vitally affected by their neighbor's diplomatic moves, obtain information about the latest intrigue, amount of money in a foreign treasury, size and morale of the army, or organization of plots and counter-plots? Diplomatic reporting became one of the primary requisites for the formulation of successful external policies in fifteenth century Italy. Aside from ceremonial and bargaining duties, the ambassador abroad served as his government's main source of information about new alliances, plans of aggression, secret agreements, and domestic strife.

After commerce and diplomatic communication, warfare was a common form of interaction. The Italian states employed violence recurrently to achieve objectives or settle conflicts. The objectives of war, aside from upholding a ruler's "honor" and prosecuting legal claims, were closely related to aspirations for increasing a state's capabilities by obtaining booty, new tax resources from an annexed province or city, or ransoms and indemnities. These were all legitimate objects of military campaigns. Kings, princes, ruling families, or elected councils often thought of foreign politics in terms of profits and losses, and since any increased source of revenue was an addition to a state's capabilities, war was well worth the small risks and costs of a military campaign.[46] Unlike the Greek wars, which were frequently fought by armed citizens and slaves and sometimes lasted for decades, the wars of the Italian peninsula during the first half of the fifteenth century were managed by professional officers (*condottieri*) and fought by mercenary troops. The forms of combat were mild by today's standards, as victory in the field normally resulted from a series of brilliant maneuvers rather than annihilation of the enemy's forces. After all, soldiers cost money and represented an investment not to be wasted. Machiavelli could report of some battles in the fifteenth century in which casualties were limited to several horses and men.[47]

Another common technique for obtaining political and economic objectives was subversion of the political processes of a neighboring city or state. The prevalence of clandestine political operations can be accounted for by two characteristics of the Italian system. First, since the units were geographically and linguistically so close to each other, it was relatively easy for subversive agents to operate abroad as sources of information or links with plotting factions. Second, because the bases of political power and legitimacy in many of the units were so weak, the resulting domestic turmoil (with the exception of Venice and the papal states) presented opportunities for outside powers to intervene in an attempt to place their own men in power. Political instability and insecurity of regimes, a characteristic equally prevalent in many nations today, thus had numerous consequences on international affairs. As today, the Italians in each small political unit could not isolate internal problems from the external environment. It was this feature of the system which gave rise to so much diplomatic intrigue, conspiracy, and betrayal, and set the standards of amorality often associated with the "Italian" diplomatic style, or "Machiavellianism."[48]

### The Major Rules of the System

Since the works of Machiavelli are often cited as proof of the amorality or "power politics" of the fifteenth century, one would not expect the Italians to have developed explicit rules and principles which effectively

[46] Mattingly, *Renaissance Diplomacy*, p. 134.

[47] Hans Morgenthau, *Politics Among Nations* (New York: Alfred A. Knopf, Inc., 1950), p. 288.

[48] Bozeman, *Politics and Culture in International History*, p. 479.

restrained their behavior towards each other. Historians do not, in fact, assign credit to the republics and city states for developing ethical or legal restraints to their actions. The medieval concept of "just war," which had established criteria under which force could be used legitimately, had no application in Renaissance Italy; no authority in the fifteenth century, either ecclesiastical or temporal, sought to judge the righteousness of a state's behavior. War was an accepted means of achieving objectives or resolving conflicts, and few questioned the right of governing authorities to engage in it. Since the turmoil of many republics' domestic affairs created opportunities for subversion, there was no strict rule against intervention in other states' internal affairs. Assassination, bribery, and betrayal were common occurrences in diplomatic relations. Nor do we find evidence of the strong value placed on political independence that was so evident in Greece. Instead, the larger states annexed the smaller with impunity and were prevented from expanding indefinitely primarily by the countervailing power of other states or alliances. The concepts of sovereignty, equality, and territorial integrity had not yet developed as the bases upon which to conduct interstate relations.

In diplomatic bargaining situations, standards of honesty and good faith were rather low, though it did occur to some governments that a reputation for credibility might enhance their influence and prestige. Generally, however, the governments of the Italian units failed to recognize that diplomatic effectiveness might be related to moral and ethical principles. Gerhard Ritter,[49] for example, has pointed out that all European ruling authorities in the fifteenth and sixteenth centuries regularly deceived each other in unscrupulous ways. They had not yet developed a capacity to relate diplomatic means to ends, and frequently undertook aggressive schemes and foreign conquests which they could bring off successfully only by relying on intrigue, bluff, delaying tactics, and lucky breaks. Governments spent vast sums of money to bribe influential statesmen in foreign courts, arrange lavish "summit" meetings between princes, and despatch renowned orators and ambassadors to persuade other governments to act in the sending state's interests. These tactics seldom succeeded because few governments, knowing their own standards of conduct, had any faith in the dependability of their rivals and pseudo-allies.

There were, then, no fundamental rules of the system which helped to establish limits for action; yet, whether resulting from political conditions, low-level technology, or financial considerations, a number of unwritten

[49] Ritter, *Die Neugestaltung Europas,* pp. 21–22.

understandings or rules were observed in the conduct of warfare. These helped keep organized violence between the units within tolerable bounds for the system. Unlike the Peloponnesian Wars, which drained the strength and vitality of so many city states and made them vulnerable to outside invasion, the Italians were able to regulate their violence so that it would not cause total political collapse on the peninsula. Moreover, through the medium of the Most Holy League, the cities and republics made a most important decision implying that all states in the system should accept the distribution of power essentially as it had been arranged at the Peace of Lodi in 1454.

The Most Holy League never functioned as an effective instrument for the pacific settlement of conflicts. It had no institutional basis, and during the last 40 years of the fifteenth century the Italian states did not radically alter their diplomatic style. Nevertheless, the diplomats and governments of these states apparently perceived that a treaty which sanctified the territorial *status quo* and provided a mechanism for enforcing that agreement was in their own self-interest. Thus they constructed through the Treaty of Venice (which established the Most Holy League) the ground rules for conducting inter-state relations during the remainder of the century. In that document, the signatories promised to defend each other's territory against attack from any source, and each state undertook to provide military forces for joint action. In case of threat or outbreak of war, all members were to consult immediately and continue multilateral discussions until the danger subsided. Any member of the League which broke its obligations of non-recourse to violence was to be expelled and, if necessary, disciplined by collective action.

In practice the Most Holy League never fulfilled the expectations of its originators. Instead of existing in peace and stability, the Italian states continued to quarrel, and in 1474, when the Pope and the King of Naples were implicated in a plot against the Medici rulers of Florence, they averted general war only by a narrow margin. The difference between the two halves of the century was more a diminution in the scope of violence than a growth of stability.[50] Whether the 40 year period of tension without large-scale violence was a result of the treaty or of a rough balancing of capabilities among the main units is difficult to judge. But at least after the Treaty of Venice there were no wars which transposed the system into the hegemony of one state or into two antagonistic blocs, or which led to its collapse.

Nevertheless, the Italian system was engulfed by the general European

[50] Mattingly, *Renaissance Diplomacy*, pp. 94–96.

political order in the last decade of the fifteenth century. Throughout the century Italian tyrants, princes, and ruling families had called upon Europeans north of the Alps to intervene on their behalf in factional and inter-state quarrels, and European rulers were eager to involve themselves in Italian affairs in search of crowns, lordships, and subsidies.[51]

These intrusions into peninsular affairs were not permanent and did not result in a major modification of the Italian system through coupling of European and Italian issues. Yet the habit of seeking extra-Italian involvement in alliances or domestic political quarrels eventually led to a more permanent European presence on the peninsula. In this way the Italian city states and republics became in effect just a group of smaller units in the wider European system of the sixteenth century. The French invasion of the peninsula in 1494, in response to a plea from Milan to counterbalance the House of Anjou's influence in Genoa and deter an attack on Milan's ally, Naples, was of such large scope that it amounted to a vast European intervention in Italian affairs. From that point political isolation of the Italian peninsula was no longer possible, and for the succeeding four centuries the Italian states became merely the objects of French, Spanish, and Austrian rivalry, plunder, and expansion.

As in the Chinese system during parts of the Spring and Autumn and Warring States periods, the diffuse power structure on the Italian peninsula during the fifteenth century had an important effect on general foreign policy orientations and the style of conducting relations between the units. The Italian city states and republics were free agents, uninhibited by superior temporal powers or bloc leaders. They sought their objectives by forming and breaking alliances, seeking isolation, noninvolvement, or neutrality, or by intriguing in other states' internal affairs. Unlike the alliance partners of Athens and Sparta during the fifth century B.C., or the units in feudal China whose actions were largely determined by a superior power, the Italian political units survived in a hostile environment by perfecting the art of diplomatic maneuvering. Latitude for choice among policy alternatives was wide, but security and certainty of success were scarce. If we examine international politics in Europe since the eighteenth century we can observe how international structures, stratification systems, and interaction processes, as well as technological developments, can influence the behavior of each of the component units of an international system.

[51] *Ibid.*, p. 61.

## SELECTED BIBLIOGRAPHY

Bayley, C. C., *War and Society in Renaissance Florence*. Toronto: University of Toronto Press, 1961.

Bozeman, Adda B., *Politics and Culture in International History*. Princeton, N.J.: Princeton University Press, 1960.

Eisenstadt, S. N., *The Political Systems of Empires*. New York: Free Press of Glencoe, Inc., 1963.

Ghoshal, U. N., "The System of Inter-State Relations and Foreign Policy in the Early Arthasastra State," in *India Antigua*. Leiden: E. J. Brill, Ltd., Publishers, 1947.

Goodman, Jay S., "The Concept of System in International Relations Theory," *Background*, VIII (1965), 257–68.

Graham, A. J., *Colony and Mother City in Ancient Greece*. Manchester: Manchester University Press, 1964.

Hanrieder, Wolfram, "Actor Objectives and International Systems," *Journal of Politics*, XXVII (1965), 109–32.

Hasebrook, Johannes, *Trade and Politics in Ancient Greece*. London: G. Bell and Sons, Ltd., 1933.

Korff, Baron S. A., "An Introduction to the History of International Law," *American Journal of International Law*, XVIII (1924), 246–59.

Larus, Joel, ed., *Comparative World Politics: Readings in Western and Pre-modern Non-Western International Relations*. Belmont, Calif.: Wadsworth Publishing Company, Inc., 1964.

Lubasz, Heinz, ed., *The Development of the Modern State*. New York: The Macmillan Company, 1964.

Mattingly, Garrett, *Renaissance Diplomacy*. London: Jonathan Cape, Ltd., 1955.

Modelski, George, "Agraria and Industria: Two Models of the International System," *World Politics*, XIV (1961), 118–43.

———, "Comparative International Systems," *World Politics*, XIV (1962), 662–74.

———, "Kautilya: Foreign Policy and International System in the Ancient Hindu World," *American Political Science Review*, LVIII (1964), 549–60.

Nussbaum, Arthur, *A Concise History of the Law of Nations*. New York: The Macmillan Company, 1961.

Phillipson, Coleman, *The International Law and Custom of Ancient Greece and Rome*. London: Macmillan & Co., Ltd., 1911.

Russell, Frank M., *Theories of International Relations*. New York: Appleton-Century-Crofts, 1936.

Tod, Marcus N., *International Arbitration Amongst the Greeks*. Oxford: The Clarendon Press, 1913.

Walker, Richard L., *The Multi-State System of Ancient China*. Hamden, Conn.: The Shoe String Press, 1953.

# THE WESTERN STATE SYSTEM

What had occurred in Renaissance Italy continued throughout Europe between the fifteenth and nineteenth centuries—the continent filled up with organized political power and administration. From feudal relations between the Holy Roman Empire, free cities, ecclesiastical authorities, duchies, aspiring monarchs, and small republics emerged an order of centralized political units led by dynastic families. These central monarchs eventually broke the power of lesser political authorities on their territories through bribery, coercion, or violence, and instituted nation-wide administrative and judicial organizations.

This process did not occur simultaneously throughout the continent. As early as the latter part of the sixteenth century Great Britain was a political unit with a defined territory in which a central monarchy ruled effectively over all subjects. Complex administrative mechanisms which extended to all areas and levels of society replaced the localized judicial and

# CHAPTER III

administrative organizations of the feudal period. While nobles often resisted the monarchy, they did not have independent territorial bases or armies with which to challenge royal authority effectively.

Through marriages, alliances, and domestic and external armed conflict, the monarchs of France, Spain, Russia, and Austria were eventually able to create central dynastic orders as well, but the small states and principalities of Germany and Italy did not unite until the late nineteenth century. The nationalist impulses which helped them to unite were different from those conditions which had made possible the creation of central dynastic regimes in other parts of Europe. Up to the nineteenth century most of the important states in international politics were empires and dynastic orders whose boundaries were defined through innumerable royal marriages, alliances, ancient land titles, and wars. Nationalism was not a factor in dynastic politics. The European states which arose in the nineteenth and twentieth centuries, however, *resulted* from nationalism. They were organized around the remaining ethnic, religious, and linguistic distinctions in Europe, not on dynastic interests. Prior to the nineteenth century the state created the nation, while in the last 160 years nationalism has *preceded,* and in many cases created, the state.

## The International Politics
## of Eighteenth Century Europe

A significant feature of eighteenth century European international politics was the relatively even distribution of diplomatic influence and military capabilities among the major states, a characteristic found also in China, Greece, and Renaissance Italy in certain periods of their history. England, France, Sweden, Spain, the Austrian Empire, Russia, Prussia, and Turkey (to the extent that the latter was involved in European politics) were not significantly different in their domestic political institutions, armed might, or international prestige. This relatively equal distribution of power and influence made it possible for the dynastic states to shift alliance partners without radically upsetting the structure of the whole system. Alliances were based on the juxtaposition of constantly changing dynastic, economic, and colonial interests, not on ideological principles. Flexibility within the groupings of states was the result.

The dynasts of the eighteenth century, as well as the aristocratic classes within each state, were united by strong cosmopolitan bonds and a common political culture. They commonly spoke French and identified themselves as the joint rulers of "Christendom" as well as the rulers of particular pieces of territory.[1] Royal families and many aristocrats were joined across state boundaries by marriage, while professional soldiers and diplomats, regardless of nationality, worked for the services which gave them the highest rank, salary, or prestige. There was no stigma attached to the German who commanded Russian forces, or the Italian who became one of the French court's most favored and trusted advisers. The Spanish diplomatic and military services in the eighteenth century were graced by such names as Konigsegg, Wall, O'Reilly, Fitzgerald, and Alberoni, while John Elphinstone, Sir Samuel Greig, and Peter Lacey made fine careers in the service of the Russian Tsarina. The continent was also unified through common support for the principles of royal legitimacy and dynastic succession. While radical political theories had already developed in England and France in the late seventeenth and eighteenth centuries most literate upper-class subjects adhered faithfully to the royal mystique.

The stability of political life and the consensus in support of royal legitimacy helped preclude intervention and subversion as means of achieving political objectives. There were court intrigues of various types, but if one dynast attempted to unseat another through military intervention or court subversion, he was undermining the principles of royal succession and the divine right of kings, principles upon which his own authority rested.

Wars, too, displayed conservative characteristics. They were fought by professional and mercenary armies, usually for the purpose of outmaneuvering the enemy rather than annihilating him. Destruction of lives and property was often limited (though losses attributed to disease were high) because of the low level of military technology, high cost of maintaining a professional army, high rate of desertion, and also because the objectives for which force was used—to obtain strategic territory, generate prestige for a dynast, or secure colonies—were limited. War was to be used, according to philosophers of violence such as Clausewitz, to impose the will of one sovereign upon another by defeating the latter's capacity to resist.[2] This purpose did not require annihilation, occupation, or the forcible imposition of alien social institutions onto other populations.

International politics of the eighteenth century have thus been characterized under various terms, each designed to illustrate the essence of the system. To some, it has been known as the period when the "balance of

---

[1] The Holy Roman Empire, though of little practical consequence, still symbolized the cultural unity of the continent.

[2] Karl von Clausewitz, *War, Politics, and Power,* ed. and trans. Edward M. Collins (Chicago: Henry Regnery Co., 1962), p. 63.

power" operated, when kings and their advisers conducted foreign affairs as if they were playing a game of chess or strategy, where they could easily calculate the power of their adversaries and adjust their foreign policy orientation through alliances or neutrality to achieve or defend their interests. If conflicts on the continent threatened to become too violent, the dynasts could play out their quarrels in the New World, where vast lands and commercial opportunities could be traded back and forth in wars and peace treaties. Others have called this era the "golden age of diplomacy," emphasizing the consensus of political values that prevailed in Europe, the cosmopolitanism of the upper classes, the regard for principles of royal authority and Christianity, and the propensity to resolve conflicts through skillful diplomatic bargaining, territorial exchanges, or alliance-making rather than through large-scale violence, propaganda, or subversion.[3]

But lying behind those conditions which helped to create stability and moderation in the politics of the eighteenth century European state system were some characteristics which led to conflict. The religious wars of the previous century were not easily forgotten, and their memory sustained international hostilities and suspicions. Strongly-held national sentiments did not exist at the grassroots level, but many peasants and townspeople were not entirely indifferent toward the policies of their rulers—particularly not toward those whom they regarded as alien in nationality or religion; insurrection against "foreign" rule was an occasional consequence of a system in which land and peoples were traded back and forth to satisfy the strategic or prestige requirements of dynasts. Although monarchs were sensitive to the rules of etiquette and their prestige among foreign courts, this did not prevent them from occasionally employing deceit and fraud as diplomatic tactics. Wars, though less destructive by today's standards, were limited more by the crude military technology of the day than by any great concern over humanitarian principles. In other words, the elements of stability—cosmopolitanism, the principles of dynastic legitimacy, limited wars, shifting alliances, and a roughly equal distribution of power—did not prevent the occurrence of sharply contentious issues and frequent recourse to the use of force.[4] But various diplomatic procedures and mechanisms, operating within a common political culture, were adequate for the kinds of conflicts that arose. No one state conquered Europe; Europe did not collapse into chaos,

[3] For a characterization of eighteenth century diplomatic relations which emphasizes the elements of stability in the system, see Richard Rosecrance, *Action and Reaction in World Politics* (Boston: Little, Brown and Company, 1963), pp. 17–30.

[4] Cf. George Liska, "Continuity and Change in International Systems," *World Politics,* XVI (1963), 118–36.

inviting invasion from the east; no technological developments fundamentally changed the main characteristics of political and economic life;
and there were no important ideological incompatibilities which made
divisions between states deep and rigid. If the eighteenth century system
was not entirely peaceful and stable, neither was it inflexible or unable to
cope with the main issues of the day.

### The International System
### of the Nineteenth Century

The periods from 1789 to 1939 and from 1945 to the present can be
considered as containing distinct international systems. Though both have
retained some of the features of the eighteenth century, several developments in the nineteenth and twentieth centuries have caused fundamental
changes in the structure and processes of international politics. The first
was the rise of nationalism—development of strong emotional attach-
ments to the central state (adding to the traditional loyalties to provinces
or towns) and involvement of the average citizen or subject in his
government's political life. This has had several important consequences.
During the eighteenth century statesmen and dynasts had been able to
trade European and colonial territories with considerable ease, using
ancient titles to land and strategic considerations as the predominant
criteria for determining frontiers. In the succeeding century nationalist
leaders held that the only legitimate basis for political organization was a
distinct ethnic or linguistic group; the state should be based, therefore, on
nationality. The results of this doctrine were the rise of nationalist
movements in the areas of Europe where the state did not correspond to
ethnic distinctions, and the subsequent collapse of such multinational
states as Russia, Austria-Hungary, and Sweden-Norway under the pressure of war and nationalist insurrection. A new type of European political
phenomenon—movements for national independence—arose during the
nineteenth century to supplement the more traditional concerns over
which statesmen quarreled.

A second consequence of nationalism was that mass public involvement
could be used by governments as a military and diplomatic bargaining
capability. By invoking the theme of "sacred national honor," governments in the nineteenth century could mobilize their populations to
support their diplomacy or wars, while previously dynasts had found it
difficult to generate popular enthusiasm for objectives not rooted deeply
in social and economic aspirations. While armies in the eighteenth

century—taking personal oaths of loyalty to the king, queen, or prince—
had numbered between ten and seventy thousand, during the wars of the
French revolution they were counted by the hundreds of thousands, and
during World War I by the millions. The symbolic break from the
eighteenth century tradition of dynastic diplomacy came in 1791 when
the French revolutionary regime instituted the *levée en masse,* a system of
nationwide conscription designed to build a citizens' army to replace the
older professional armed forces of the Bourbons. This army was sent
abroad to "liberate" Europe from dynasticism, and to conquer Belgian,
German, and Italian territory for the greater glory of the French *nation,*
not for the prestige of the French king.

Modern governments can create national fervor for their causes, but the
greater involvement of the average citizen or subject also imposes restrictions on the policy-makers' freedom of action. Foreign relations in the
eighteenth century were never as simple as a game of checkers, even
though dynasts and their advisers were relatively free to shift policies,
objectives, and alliance partners without worrying about domestic reactions.[5] By the late nineteenth century, however, even the more auto-
cratic regimes had to anticipate public reactions to their diplomatic
maneuvers, while others had to accommodate pestering opposition parties
in parliaments or worry about embarrassing newspaper editorials.

The second development of the nineteenth century which had important consequences on international politics was the application of scientific and industrial technology to the conduct of warfare. Public enthusiasm over diplomatic and military questions enabled governments to
conscript large armies, while improvements in military technology enabled them to prosecute their military plans more quickly and violently.
Starting with the wars of the French revolution, armed conflicts tended to
become increasingly wars of annihilation in which violence could not be
confined to military targets. Rising casualty figures, military and civilian,
indicate the revolutionary developments in the art of warfare. In France,
for instance, casualty rates in wars between 1630 and the outbreak of the
revolution in 1789 fluctuated between one out of every 1,000 population
and one out of every 200. During the wars of the French revolution and
the Napoleonic period, approximately one of every 75 French citizens was
a victim of fighting.[6] In World War I about one of every 18 Frenchmen
was either killed or wounded as a result of the conflict, and in World War

[5] In England, however, Parliament in the eighteenth century did impose important
controls over the king's prerogatives in the conduct of foreign relations.

[6] Similar figures are cited in Hans Morgenthau, *Politics Among Nations* (New
York: Alfred A. Knopf, Inc., 1950), p. 293.

II, one out of every 10 Russians suffered injury or loss of life. If international systems can be distinguished from each other in part by major changes in the processes of interaction and methods of resolving conflicts, then the nineteenth and twentieth centuries are markedly different from the eighteenth century in this one aspect alone: major wars have become great social undertakings involving extensive civilian mobilization and destruction, fought for the purpose of annihilating the enemy and imposing political and social institutions upon the defeated nation.

The development of nuclear weapons has been the most revolutionary contribution of science and technology to war. While in the past some strategists argued that the invention of the machine gun, tank, or airplane made war "obsolete," the perfection of fission and fusion weapons has indeed made total war irrational, even if nuclear weapons could be used in a limited fashion for specific ends. No bank of heavy artillery or wing of airplanes can crush a nation's economy. Even the massive Allied incendiary strategic raids on Germany during World War II had only minor effects on Germany's capacity to produce war matériel. Strategic nuclear weapons, on the other hand, can destroy the economic capacity of a nation (if it is reasonably concentrated in large urban centers), and most of its population, as well as endanger the lives and health of citizens in countries not directly involved in the nuclear salvo. While there are means to reduce nuclear destruction, the only safety mechanism strategists have yet devised is the deterrent—the threat to retaliate instantly in case of a first strike. As Robert Oppenheimer has pointed out, the nuclear giants are analogous to two scorpions in a bottle; if one attacks the other, it can do so only at the price of its own destruction.[7] Nuclear weapons have thus added a new characteristic of vulnerability to international politics. Whatever protection could be afforded in the past by national frontiers or territorial fortresses, such contrivances are of no significance today if war fought with nuclear weapons should break out in Europe or directly between the Soviet Union and the United States. As a unit of protection, the modern nation state is as vulnerable to nuclear destruction as was the walled city or moated castle to the modern cannon.[8]

---

[7] "Atomic Weapons and American Policy," *Foreign Affairs,* LI (1953), 529. Even optimistic military planners in NATO argue that a nuclear war in Europe would be over in at least 30 days.

[8] This is the thesis argued by John Herz in his *International Politics in the Atomic Age* (New York: Columbia University Press, 1959), Intro. and Chap. 8. For further discussion of the effects of nuclear weapons on contemporary international politics, see Chapters IV and XII, this volume.

The third development in the nineteenth century with major consequences on the structure and processes of the European state system was the rise of ideological principles and political doctrines as a major motive or guide to foreign policy behavior. Though the wars of the French Revolution had territorial objectives, they were undertaken in the name of the universal principles of "Liberty, Equality, and Fraternity." Similarly, those who led the grand coalition against the French revolutionary and Napoleonic armies were partly motivated by a desire to safeguard the principles of royal legitimacy against radical French doctrines. Thus, many of the conflicts within Europe during the nineteenth century were fought in a context of the incompatible values represented by French revolutionary republicanism and royal legitimacy and conservatism. In this century, different and incompatible images of a world order have derived from the doctrines of Nazism, Communism, and liberal democracy.

The international politics of the nineteenth century were thus uniquely affected by the growth of ideological issues, the increasing destructiveness of warfare, and the rise of nationalism and popular involvement in foreign relations. A development with equally great consequence on the structure and processes of international politics occurred in the latter part of the century, and all of its implications are becoming clear only today. This was the extension of the European state system into the rest of the world and the subsequent rise of nearly 80 new political units, mostly former colonial territories, as important actors in the modern international system. The European continent was the primary arena for international politics during the nineteenth century, and aside from the weak Latin American republics and several feudal leftovers, there were only about 20 important states which interacted regularly. Today there are over 130 independent states, all conducting transactions through unprecedented levels of trade, diplomatic communication, travel, and occasional subversion and warfare. Contentious issues no longer arise predominantly in Europe, but appear most frequently in Asia, the Middle East, Africa, and Latin America. They no longer involve the major powers of the nineteenth century—Great Britain, France, Prussia, Germany, Austria-Hungary, and Turkey—but attract instead the involvement of extra-European powers, primarily the United States, the Soviet Union, and Communist China. In short, the geographical boundaries of the nineteenth century and contemporary systems have been extended from the European continent to the whole world, and the number of political units in these systems has trebled in the last 50 years.

## The Contemporary International System

The contemporary international system is in some ways similar to its nineteenth century predecessor. Most main issues and *characteristic* forms of interaction are not significantly different from those in the European states system. Contemporary ideological issues trace their origins to nineteenth century Europe; the question of nationhood and national independence still raises serious international problems; and the search for economic modernization that took place on the continent during the nineteenth century is only beginning in the underdeveloped countries. Diplomatic forms and procedures developed in Europe have extended to all areas of the world, though they are almost unrecognizable when compared to eighteenth century practices. The main rules governing international transactions are also an extension, development, and refinement of those which arose during the eighteenth and nineteenth centuries in Europe.

It is not difficult to understand why these characteristics of European international politics are still predominant in a world-wide system. In 1875 less than one-tenth of Africa had been colonized by Europeans; 25 years later only one-tenth of the area remained free of colonial administration. In the last three decades of the nineteenth century Great Britain acquired over four million square miles of territory, France acquired three and one-half million square miles, Belgium colonized almost one million square miles, and the Tsarist regime in Russia extended its control over territory amounting to one-half million square miles. The processes of establishing colonial administration and control differed in various areas, but in each case the administering powers unwittingly created aspirations among indigenous populations for all of the values that they themselves cherished: independence in political life, industrialization of the economy, and international prestige. Despite the great variety of cultural contexts in which relations between states occur today, some important characteristics of the system represent merely an extension into new areas of the diplomatic, economic, ideological, and military traditions of the Europeans. What sets off the contemporary international system from its European predecessors is the rise in number of states, great capacity for destruction, vulnerability of states to destruction and subversion, and predominant position of influence that has been achieved by three essentially non-European states, the Soviet Union, Communist China, and the United States. Other similarities and differences between the contemporary system and the European states systems up to 1945 can be assessed by employing four of the categories of the previous chapter—the nature of the political units, the types of stratification and structures of power and influence, the major forms of interaction, and the rules governing relations between the units.

## The Nature of the Units

A major characteristic of the political units comprising the contemporary international system is their territorial basis. States today maintain systematic administrative control over people living in a well-defined territory. Some territorial divisions are artificial—particularly in Africa— in the sense that frontiers do not correspond to ethnic, linguistic, or geographic distinctions, but in most cases the territorial boundaries of modern states are closely related to such distinctions. The unique and frequently permanent territorial bases of each state thus not only give the state its economic, technological, and military advantages and problems, but in many cases also provide the state with legitimacy, since the territory incorporates a distinct ethnic, linguistic, or religious group. England can have no claim to continental French territory as long as language and culture serve as a basis for differentiating legitimate frontiers; but when ethnic and linguistic differences did not matter in international politics, it was perfectly conceivable for the English to own territory in France, as they did until the seventeenth century. While the units in many historical international systems derived their identity, strengths, and weaknesses from the territory they occupied, and while some even developed a concept of a frontier or boundary setting them off from other political units, not until modern times have the boundaries of states been so carefully defined, permanent, and immune from encroachment by outsiders.[9]

In the ancient Chinese, Greek, or Renaissance Italian systems, the political units approximated each other in administrative development and general economic and technological levels. There were variations, of course, in government procedures, public participation in political life, religious forms, and economic institutions, but generally the variations were not so great as to make comparisons between the units difficult. Today, despite common characteristics of territoriality and national independence, diversity among political units is great. One could classify

[9] Herz emphasizes, however, that the unique characteristic of the nation state, its "impermeability," (the ability of governments to administer their policies on defined territories free of outside or internal interference) is declining. For a detailed discussion of the rise of "territoriality" and "impermeability," their significance to inter-state relations, and their decline in contemporary conditions, see his *International Politics in the Atomic Age,* Parts I and II.

states according to size and population and the differences among them would be much greater than the corresponding variations in the political units of other international systems. The Soviet Union covers one-sixth of the world's land surface; six states—Canada, the United States, the Soviet Union, Brazil, China, and Australia—comprise over one-half of the world's land territory. On the other hand, there are political units— Luxembourg, Lebanon, Singapore and Trinidad, for example—smaller in size than some metropolitan areas in the United States. Population variations are even more extreme: less than 100,000 people inhabit the Maldive Islands, a member of the United Nations; several states have fewer than one million inhabitants, while China has a population of over 700 million. The physical and population differences between the Soviet Union and Togo are infinitely greater than the differences between Athens and one of the smaller city states in Greece, or between Prussia and Schleswig-Holstein in the eighteenth century.

Political, social, and economic variations among contemporary nation states are equally dramatic. While no general categorization can accurately describe the diversity of nation states today, it is one way to approach comprehension. There is a group of highly industrialized states, with relatively stable political systems in which major conflicts over constitutional arrangements, the place of minorities, civil liberties, and fundamental economic arrangements have been resolved. These units are also typified by high literacy rates, high per capita income (often 20 or more times as great as in underdeveloped countries), broad public participation in political life, social mobility between classes, low death rates, and high density of communications media.

Another group of states is rapidly achieving the industrial and technological levels found in most of western Europe and North America, but still faces problems of illiteracy, poor health and, in some cases, overpopulation, as well as low agricultural productivity and political instability. Many of these states are ruled by authoritarian figures, and few provide orderly procedures for changing political elites. Others feature rule by "dictatorships of the proletariat," meaning rule by charismatic leaders or single-party bureaucracies. Many have totalitarian political systems in the sense that they condone neither public apathy nor free discussion, and systematically inculcate an ideology or group of doctrines at the exclusion of all others. There is a semblance of popular involvement in foreign policy problems, but in the absence of political freedoms and uncensored news media, it is difficult to assess public sentiments on foreign issues.

A third group of states incorporating a large segment of the world's population displays characteristics of high illiteracy, poor communication, low agricultural productivity, rapidly growing populations, unimaginable poverty, and little social mobility. Though these states normally maintain administrative mechanisms providing a variety of governmental functions for the citizenry, their influence may barely reach the grass-roots level, where life is conducted according to tribal, village, or other traditional patterns. Political instability is rife; few of these states have resolved their major constitutional issues or developed political "rules of the game" which command widespread support. Political stability depends more on the influence or coercion of key personalities or groups—often the armed forces—than on widely accepted constitutional or legal principles. When these personalities change, or ruling groups become politically weak, corrupt, or demoralized, rebellion and civil war are often the result. Moreover, many of these states are mere geographic expressions, corresponding neither to ethnic, linguistic, or religious distinctions. Most of the frontiers of the present African states were drafted by colonial administrations in terms of their own political interests rather than in accordance with the natural divisions of the continent. Indonesia, Vietnam, India, the Sudan, Iraq, Kenya, Somaliland, and Nigeria all have important religious, linguistic, and ethnic minorities which add inestimable complications to their political life.

Finally, there are still a few states whose predominant socio-economic-political characteristics are comparable to those found in seventeenth century Europe. These comprise the territories ruled by dynastic families as private realms. Though some of these societies appear to go through the motions of modernization, their economic and political life is dominated by the personal whims of dynasts or theocratic oligarchies. The Dominican Republic under the Trujillo regime is one example, and a few of the sheikdoms on the Arabian peninsula, as well as Saudi Arabia and Haiti, might be placed in this category.

The modern international system also differs from its European predecessors in having several supranational and international political units, organizations of states which, on certain issues, develop a common policy. The only comparable institutions were the church in Renaissance Italy and the leagues of states in Greece. Some, like the Common Market, possess a degree of supranational authority; they can make a limited range of decisions independently of the desires of member states, and possess the authority to enforce those decisions. Most, however, are intergovernmental agencies which cannot act except with the consent of their membership. Still, on some issues they have traditional policies which usually elicit the membership's support, and they maintain bureaucratic mechanisms to carry out the policies. Technical experts rather than professional diplomats formulate the decisions of many of these organizations. If we specify carefully the issue under consideration, it makes sense to speak of the Common Market's "policy," the "action" of the United Nations, the "work" of the Food and Agricultural Organization, or the "reaction" of NATO. These political units, though comprised of states, seek to achieve or defend certain common objectives in the international environment. The major difference between them and nation states is that (1) they are unifunctional agencies designed to promote or defend one specific program, and (2) they do not possess independent means to enforce their policies or decisions through the threat or use of force.

### International Stratification

Observers of contemporary international politics usually make distinctions among "great powers," "middle powers," and "small powers." The basis for this type of classification is seldom explicit, but it is not difficult to place some states into each category. The United States and the Soviet Union are undoubtedly "great powers," while Costa Rica would fit easily into the "small power" class. Others, however, defy instant categorization. Should India be termed a "great power" or a "middle power"? If we employ any single criterion, such as military capability, for differentiating the status of states we may run into difficulties. The United States is militarily much more powerful than France, but this does not mean that on *all* international issues or in all relationships it enjoys greater status and influence than the French. We cannot assume that a "great power" is great solely by virtue of its military strength any more than we can assume that the nation which is most powerful militarily will also wield the most influence in the world. What is important is that today policy-makers "rank" states according to different criteria in different situations. Status and prestige are not objective facts; they result from subjective estimations of worth and not everyone will agree as to what criteria constitute the bases of worth.

One study of differentiation among states[10] suggests that policy-makers today judge other countries primarily on the basis of three criteria, each reflecting values that generally command esteem throughout the world. These include (1) a nation's level of technology, which is closely related to its (2) immediately available military capabilities, and (3) the reputation it can generate abroad through its day-to-day diplomatic conduct and political, economic, and social behavior at home.

During the eighteenth century the royal family's connections and wealth and the size of the professional armed forces served as predomi-

[10] Gustavo Lagos, *International Stratification and Underdeveloped Countries* (Chapel Hill: The University of North Carolina Press, 1963), Chap. 1. Lagos uses the concept of prestige as his third basis of stratification.

nant indicators of international status. Today the primary standard of judgment is technology and all the material things which derive from its application to economic activity. Economic and technological development are among the main national objectives of underdeveloped countries, not only because they are necessary to sustain rapidly increasing population, but also because they are symbols of modernity and nationhood. We often hear of projects in both developed and underdeveloped countries which, from an economic point of view, are of questionable value—the steel mill which depends upon imported raw materials; the national jet airline which relies upon foreign personnel for its operation and maintenance; the modern highway that leads to no useful destination; and inefficient, though physically impressive, manufacturing concerns. These enterprises cannot be judged only for economic value because they serve important social and psychological needs as well. They are tangible evidence of a country's modernity and search for status and prestige among other states. Similarly, an important value—quite apart from scientific knowledge—in space programs is the opportunities they provide for displays of technical and scientific prowess.

Military capacity, unlike technological level and economic activity, has always symbolized a political unit's status among others. No "great power" in the present or past has failed to maintain a large military establishment, and those states which aspire to great power status allocate a large portion of their resources to developing an impressive military machine. Both the French and Chinese governments have claimed, for instance, that they could not hope to achieve great power status unless they developed arsenals of nuclear weapons and modern delivery systems.[11] Nuclear weapons, delivery systems, and space technology are important components or symbols of great power status. Like the displays of chariots in ancient China, these weapons and instruments are designed partly to impress others and thereby increase diplomatic bargaining influence.

In the past it was not so difficult for states to impress neighbors, allies, and enemies by developing military forces. Dynasts were limited by the quantity of funds, but if the money was available any government could build a fleet of wooden ships or train a professional army of 20,000 men, armed with cannon and carts. All states were roughly equal because all

[11] In 1963 Communist China's foreign minister claimed that nuclear weapons, missiles, and supersonic aircraft were the most important indicators of the technical level of a nation's industry. Unless China possessed the most modern weapons, he suggested, it would "degenerate" into a second or third class nation. For the direct quotation, see Alice L. Hsieh, "The Sino-Soviet Nuclear Dialogue: 1963," *Journal of Conflict Resolution,* VIII (1963), 110.

possessed basically an agricultural economy and a crude technology. Today the costs of research and development, as well as the manpower, scientific, and technological skills required to create and maintain a modern armed force, are beyond the capacity of all but a few societies. The Chinese Communists may, over a period of ten or twenty years, build the bases required of a modern military establishment, but if they succeed in this endeavor it will probably be at the cost of improving the over-all economy. Some economically and technologically advanced nations have already learned that even with highly skilled manpower and a heavy industrial base, it is extremely difficult both to create modern armed forces and maintain a reasonable level of economic growth. The governments of these nations have decided instead to obtain their most expensive equipment from the two major military arsenals, the United States and Soviet Union, and concentrate on developing less costly weapons. Certainly the underdeveloped countries cannot hope to achieve status by attempting to build military capabilities matching those of the industrialized states. In fact, as measured by military capabilities, the gap between developed and underdeveloped nations is growing wider, as is the gap between their economic levels. The cost of developing and producing the most sophisticated and destructive armaments has become prohibitive to all but a few nations. And yet, states such as Nigeria, Turkey, or India do not lack international status just because they do not possess the most modern nuclear weapons and delivery systems.

A state's status and reputation today may be based more on its diplomatic behavior and domestic socio-economic and political institutions than on its technological level or military capacity. A government may enjoy a reputation for meeting its treaty commitments, being a loyal ally, or the quality of its trained diplomats. Or it may derive prestige from adhering to a particular foreign policy orientation. Yugoslavia's prestige in the West rose immediately after Tito's government was expelled from the Soviet bloc. Today many Afro-Asian countries underscore their independence by refusing to make alliances or special military arrangements with members of the NATO or Soviet blocs, while countries which do make such commitments are often scorned by their underdeveloped brethren. Despite its economic level and military strength, the Republic of China has relatively little prestige among other Afro-Asian states because it is viewed as a close ally of the United States and a major cause of conflict between Communist China and the United States.[12] Governments and

---

[12] For example, Nationalist China belongs to few of the caucuses of underdeveloped countries in the United Nations, and has never attended the many conferences of non-aligned states, even though some of those attending had as extensive alliance commitments as those maintained by Nationalist China.

publics also tend to judge other nations by the character of their political leadership and economic and social institutions. India and Israel have a reputation in Western Europe and North America for being able to run democratic institutions successfully under adverse conditions, while Egypt's status may derive largely from the prestige of its political leaders. Sweden and Switzerland, while possessing some prestige in the under-developed world on account of their neutral foreign policy orientations, are probably better known and admired in the Western world by virtue of their high standards of living.

Because there are so many different standards for judging the status of nations, no single and permanent hierarchy of states—the great and the small, or the influential and the weak—exists. If governments generally rank each other by their armaments, technology, diplomatic behavior, and domestic institutions, this does not mean that these criteria are the most important in all issue areas or subsystems, or that all the criteria are given equal weight by different policy-makers. On the international trade issue, for example, one may find states ranked in one way, based on the general role they occupy in the international trade system, while on the issue of disarmament the configuration of status and prestige may be quite different, depending upon which states possess the largest military capa-bilities, seriously tackle disarmament problems, and display a more reasonable diplomatic bargaining style. In the Communist subsystem, the ranking of states may be based on unique criteria, such as the state's (or party's) adherence to a particular doctrinal line or even the revolutionary careers of its political leadership. Furthermore, even if the criteria of technological level, military capacity, socio-economic institutions, and diplomatic behavior determine a country's status among most policy-makers and publics, different governments may perceive the combination of these criteria in different ways. India may have status in the West because of its political leadership and democratic political institutions, but other states in Asia may place little value on these qualities and hold India in low esteem because of its weak military capacity. There is evidence that India does not enjoy much prestige in Pakistan, Burma, and Communist China.[13]

## The Structure of the System

Many observers have characterized the post-war world as "polarized." Since 1947, the United States and the Soviet Union have not only origi-nated and defined most international issues but have also taken the

[13] Charles H. Heimsath, "Nonalignment Reassessed: The Experience of India," eds. Roger Hilsman and Robert C. Good, *Foreign Policy in the Sixties: The Issues and the Instruments* (Baltimore: The Johns Hopkins Press, 1965), pp. 47–66.

diplomatic and military leadership in dealing with them. Whether concerned with military policies, the fate of Germany, security for Europe, or
disarmament, the two major actors in each case have been the Soviet
Union and the United States. But it is misleading today to view the
structure of power and influence in the world as being polarized on all
issues, for there are other problems in which quite different states are
involved and where these two great powers have not assumed or appro-
priated leadership positions. The main states in the colonial issue
subsystem are the metropolitan nations, underdeveloped countries, and
remaining colonial territories (or, more specifically, their nationalist movements), with the Soviet Union playing only a supporting role. These are
the actors which define the issues, the procedures under which they will
be handled in the United Nations, and the ultimate solutions. The United
States is not greatly involved in colonial issues (unless they become
coupled with a perceived threat of communism) and has seldom been
able to determine through its diplomatic actions the outcome of conflicts
between nationalist movements and colonial powers.[14]

In matters of foreign trade, still another configuration of power and
influence exists. Here the main actors are the nations which purchase the
bulk of the world's raw material exports, those which sell heavy machine
goods, those which can control the flow of currency between nations by
their fiscal policies, and the countries dependent upon foreign trade either
to sustain a tolerable standard of living or help develop a modern
economy. These would include the United States, Canada, most Western
European countries, Japan, and many underdeveloped nations. But until
the early 1960's the Soviet bloc was not a major factor in international
trade relationships and had little, if any, impact on the major diplomatic
decisions affecting that trade. If the world is polarized on the trade issue,
it is a north-south polarity, where producers of raw materials in most
underdeveloped countries receive low income from their export products
but must pay high prices for heavy manufactured goods imported from
industrialized nations.

In geographic, rather than issue, subsystems (the two are, of course,
related) one may also find unique structures of power and influence. The
United States may be a leader in Latin American affairs; its diplomatic
and economic resources can be used in such a way that most Latin countries will adjust their behavior and interests to correspond with those of
the United States. But the United States is certainly unable to provide
such leadership in Africa, where it has few traditional interests, relatively

---

[14] The United States played an important part in the war between Indonesian
nationalists and Dutch authorities between 1947 and 1949. Though it moved cautiously, it gave support to the independence movement.

little economic influence, and receives slight sympathy for its position on cold war issues. In brief, the structure of power and influence in the world is neither static nor universally definable. It appears under different configurations depending upon the issue and geographic subsystems involved.

Nevertheless, relations between the Soviet Union and the United States still overshadow other issues areas to such an extent that it may not be an exaggeration to characterize the world as polar. The fate of millions of people throughout Europe and in many underdeveloped areas depends upon decisions made in Moscow and Washington—and increasingly in Peking, which suggests a decline in polarity. It is difficult to conceive of any settlement over the Berlin or German problems which could be concluded against the wishes of the United States and Soviet Union; nor would any disarmament agreement without their participation be of any significance. National budgets and stock market levels of several dozen countries vary according to the state of relations between these two countries. Because of the veto, the United Nations cannot take effective action through the Security Council to impose peaceful settlements on dozens of regional conflicts without prior consent of the United States and the Soviet Union. Thus, one feature of our era is the apparent dominance of one of its diplomatic and conflict subsystems. The world system, when conceived as encompassing relations among *all* states, is affected greatly by what transpires in this one Soviet-American subsystem, whereas developments, let us say, in the Commonwealth subsystem may have little impact on either Soviet-American relations or conditions in the entire system.

## The Nature of Interaction

All indicators used to measure the amount of interaction and number of transactions between states in the contemporary international system suggest rapid and continuing expansion of both intergovernmental and private contacts. The number of people involved in formal diplomatic relationships, for example, has proliferated. Important embassies no longer contain only an ambassador and several secretaries, in contact with a limited number of the host country's officials and upper classes. Instead, they are staffed by hundreds of diplomats and experts who meet officials, groups, and private citizens at all levels of the host country's government and society. In the early 1800's, less than a dozen American diplomats worked in Paris to protect and promote the interests of the United States and its citizens in France. Today, several thousand Americans are needed to fulfill these functions. International functional organizations such as the

World Health Organization, the International Labor Organization, or the International Civil Aviation Organization bring together thousands of technical experts from over 100 countries, who coordinate national policies and present proposals for resolving issues of common concern to the membership. Perhaps the most dramatic indicators of the increasing level and scope of interaction between societies are those which reveal the number of contacts between ordinary citizens of different countries. These figures also indicate the extent to which nations have become interdependent through trade and communication.[15]

International trade and commerce statistics provide one measure of increasing interaction between societies. In 1938 the total exports of all countries in the world were worth approximately $23 billion; in 1962 the value of exports had risen to $140 billion, a gain of about 600 per cent. Even if we allow for declining value of the dollar, the increase is still outstanding. Some regions, in particular, have rapidly increased their commercial connections with other countries. Again in 1938, the colonies of Central Africa exported both to their metropolitan states and to the rest of the world only $410 million worth of goods. By 1962 these areas, now mostly independent, sold over $3 billion worth of products in international markets. The United States sold goods valued at $405 million in 1938 to all of the countries of Asia. In 1962, American exports to Asia were worth about $3.5 billion. The 21 Latin American republics sold only $26 million in Asia one year before the start of World War II, but less than 20 years after the end of that war exports from Latin America to Asia were worth almost $400 million. Eastern Europe and the Soviet Union have only recently become large customers of products shipped from outside the Communist bloc. With the exception of the United States, whose exports to the area comprising the Communist bloc were worth less in 1962 than in 1938, most other countries have increased their trade with the bloc in a dramatic fashion. Latin American exports to East Europe and the Soviet Union in 1938 were valued at $26 million; in 1962, they were worth $475 million. Africa's exports to the area in 1938 were a paltry $19 million, but had increased to $265 million by 1962.[16]

Communication between ordinary citizens of different countries is another indicator of the growing number of transactions and interactions between states. For example, international civil aviation scheduled services flew in 1948 a total of 8 billion passenger kilometers. Fourteen years later they flew 56 billion passenger kilometers, with the national airlines

[15] The problems of war and violence as a form of interaction between modern states will be considered separately in Chapter XII.

[16] These figures are extrapolated from United Nations, *Statistical Yearbook, 1963* (New York: United Nations, 1964), pp. 458–67.

of Thailand, Ireland, England, and Yugoslavia increasing their passenger kilometer loads over international routes by 1000 per cent, 800 per cent, 900 per cent, and 3000 per cent respectively.[17]

The numbers of letters sent from one country to another also attest to increasing levels of intersocial contact. To cite some figures: in 1948, the people of Madagascar sent almost 5 million letters abroad; in 1962, they sent 11.5 million letters to foreign destinations. This rise in mail flow rates can be attributed partly to increasing population and literacy, but a large portion comes from a growing number of personal contacts and commercial transactions. In 1948, Mexicans sent about 34 million letters abroad; 14 years later the figure was almost 150 million. While mail flow rates have increased rapidly in some areas, others have displayed comparatively slow growth. The people of Turkey, for example, sent more than three times as many letters abroad in 1962 as they did in 1948, while in the comparable period Americans increased the number of letters with foreign destinations by only 18 per cent.[18]

The number of travellers from one country to another, whether for purposes of study, health, touring, or business, is another useful indicator of increasing social interaction at the international level. Figures for some of the newer countries are difficult to obtain, but the incidence of travel in the Western countries and the larger states of Asia, such as India and Japan, has increased dramatically. In 1948, 149,000 people entered Austria; 14 years later five and one-half million visited that country. Only 14,000 people entered Greece in 1948; in 1962 over one-half million visitors appeared. Japan had fewer than 3,000 visitors in 1948 but almost one-quarter million by 1962. The origins and destinations of travellers are also of interest because they show the main directions and scope of private contacts. United Nations figures suggest that personal contacts are still made essentially *within* political blocs, although the number of Westerners visiting Communist countries is reasonably large. In 1962, only 1,500 Russian citizens travelled to England, while almost 30,000 British subjects visited the Soviet Union. In the same year only 40 Hungarians visited Australia, which means that interaction between these two countries was confined almost exclusively to formal diplomatic and commercial channels. In contrast, some 14,000 Americans visited Australia in 1962.[19]

All these figures suggest the same conclusion: while in historical international systems contacts between political units were made pri-

---

[17] *Ibid.*, pp. 406–11.

[18] *Ibid.*, pp. 427–33.

[19] Figures extrapolated from United Nations, *Statistical Yearbook, 1949–1950*, pp. 322–23, and *Statistical Yearbook, 1963*, pp. 416–25.

marily through formal diplomatic channels and occasionally through private trade, today the level of interaction, whether measured by diplomatic contacts, international travel, mail communication, or commerce, is very great and is growing rapidly. Although widespread personal contact between citizens of different countries is still beyond the means of most people, those who spend their entire lives in one locality are still made aware of the external environment through various media of communication to an extent that earlier generations would have found impossible.[20] If it is trite to suggest that the world is "shrinking," it is nevertheless true. A distinct characteristic of the modern era is that internal and external policies, and major domestic and foreign events in all states, have important consequences on the everyday lives of many people in other areas of the world.

One type of relationship between states, aside from those involving formal diplomatic contacts and commercial transactions, needs finally to be explored. This is the widespread employment of clandestine agents and paramilitary forces for obtaining intelligence, fomenting civil disorders, organizing subversive movements abroad, and extending a state's influence over foreign political movements. The various forms of subversion and reasons for the burgeoning of *sub rosa* forms of competition will be examined in more detail in Chapter XI. Here we should point out only that in the twentieth century internal wars have become an international event, and most domestic political systems are no longer able to isolate themselves from the effects and interventions of the external environment. Statesmen and publics of different countries tend to judge each other on the basis of internal political and social institutions; thus, when civil turmoil breaks out into violence—when two sides in a civil war symbolize two incompatible ideologies or "ways of life"—it is difficult to keep the resulting conflict isolated. The major revolutions of our era have been internal wars, fought originally for complex socio-economic, constitutional, and ideological reasons, but to outsiders they were also wars which pitted "freedom" against "anarchy," "capitalist slavery" against "socialist equality," "the Church, order, and national traditions" against "communism, atheism, and republicanism." The Bolshevik revolution, the Spanish Civil War, or at least a dozen civil wars since 1945 have all symbolized in some way the great value conflicts of our era, and attracted outside

---

[20] There are still many areas of the world, however, where knowledge of the external environment is extremely crude. In a typical Indian village, for instance, only a few people will know even the name of India's prime minister, much less the existence of some distant diplomatic crisis. See Y. B. Damle, "Communication of Modern Ideas and Knowledge in Indian Villages," *Public Opinion Quarterly,* XX (1956), 257–70.

intervention. The relatively simple forms of diplomatic and military interaction over territorial, economic, or dynastic-type disputes are still with us, but in addition we have conflicts which arise from more complicated phenomena, including those which originate as internal disorders but end as major international crises.[21]

## The Major Rules of the Modern System

Territoriality, "impermeability," and political independence, the major characteristics of the nation state as it developed in Europe during the sixteenth and seventeenth centuries, were also the bases upon which dynasts, diplomats, and lawyers of that period created the fundamental rules for conducting relations with each other. The three fundamental rules were, and continue to be, the sovereignty, territorial integrity, and legal equality of states.

By the conclusion of the seventeenth century most of the dynastic states of Europe were politically sovereign—the central governments and their creations at lower levels of administration were the only rule-making and rule-applying bodies in defined territories. On the inside, political units such as duchies or walled cities were incapable of challenging the central authorities or making treaties with "outside" powers, and neither the Holy Roman Emperor nor the church as supranational institutions could order kings and princes to undertake actions without their consent. The principle of sovereignty—that governments are the supreme law-makers in their own territories—was little more than a legal doctrine expressing a situation that prevailed politically throughout large portions of Europe by the end of the seventeenth century. The principle was established firmly in the Treaty of Westphalia (1648), which held that only sovereign (e.g., impermeable and independent) states could enter into treaty relations with each other, and that the Holy Roman Empire could no longer command the allegiance of its parts. This implied that a political unit which was not sovereign (such as a duchy *within* France) could not become a legal unit in the system; it could not make treaties, enter international organizations, or claims any other rights or duties under international law. This rule is still the basis of all interaction today, for without legal sovereignty, as recognized by other states, a political unit, be it colony, protectorate, or trust territory, has no legal standing among

[21] For a lucid discussion of various types of civil disorder and the problem of attracting outside intervention, see James N. Rosenau, "Internal War as an International Event," in *International Aspects of Civil Strife*, ed. James N. Rosenau (Princeton: Princeton University Press, 1964), pp. 45–91.

other states.[22] States are free, by virtue of their sovereignty, to govern as they wish within their own territory and to formulate their own external policies except where limited by self-approved treaty obligations.

The second major rule follows from the first. If a state is sovereign it cannot allow, without its own consent, other political entities to make or apply their own rules on its territory; it has the corresponding obligation not to intervene in the internal affairs of other states or compromise their territorial integrity. In transactions between states, therefore, governments can attempt to influence each other's behavior only through established diplomatic channels. They cannot by-pass relations with other governments and attempt to influence the domestic political processes of another country by establishing their physical presence (occupation) or laws on another's territory, or attempt to persuade, cajole, or threaten its inhabitants by direct action against them on their own territory. In an age of subversion and extensive international propaganda, where states are highly permeable to outside influences, this rule is not only violated systematically, but may be on the verge of obsolescence.

The third rule states simply that whatever divergences in size, population, location, or military capabilities, all states are equal with respect to legal rights and duties. All are, theoretically, sovereign and independent, all possess equally the rights of territorial integrity and self-defense, and all are equally obligated to avoid interfering in other states' internal affairs, observe treaty obligations, and, since adoption of the United Nations Charter, avoid the threat or use of force (except in self-defense) in relations with other states. From these three basic rules flow a number of more specific limitations on state action, as defined in treaties, international custom, and general principles of international law.

The three basic rules specify the accepted and expected forms of behavior in relations between states.[23] Through their regular observance they also constitute characteristic norms of behavior. This is not to deny

[22] There are exceptions, however. For example, two constituent republics of the Soviet Union, Byelorussia and the Ukraine, have separate representatives in the United Nations and maintain their own foreign ministries. The policies of these "states" do not, of course, diverge from those of the Soviet government. Moreover, some political units are technically sovereign, but are highly permeable and do not possess the political attributes of sovereignty. The Communist East European states during Stalin's rule were considered sovereign, but were hardly free to make their own policies against Russian demands. In a treaty of 1907 the Cuban government permitted the United States to intervene unilaterally in its affairs to preserve "life, liberty, and property," should these become endangered by domestic turmoil in the island. Cuba was thus no longer impermeable (the United States occupied Cuba from 1906 to 1909), but still retained the fiction of being a sovereign state.

[23] These rules are clearly outlined in the Inter-American Convention on the Rights and Duties of States, signed in Montevideo, Uruguay, in 1933.

occasional exceptions, particularly to the second rule of non-interference. But if these fundamental rules were not observed with reasonable consistency, the structure of the system and the nature of interstate relations would change radically. The Chinese states did not place high value on sovereignty and independence, nor did they have a concept of permanent frontiers or territoriality. Since these rules did not constitute the assumptions behind all political action, there was a diminution in the number of politically independent states as the large and powerful engulfed the small and weak. In international history since the eighteenth century, however, the number of independent states has increased, not decreased. In particular, the number of very small and economically weak states has grown rapidly. It is significant that during the last two centuries militarily aggressive states have seldom incorporated conquered states into their own territory; they have either temporarily occupied them, eventually restoring them to virtual independence, or have turned them into satellite states, political entities subservient in economic, defense, and foreign policies, but nevertheless maintaining some of the attributes of sovereignty. Despite the many wars of aggression since the seventeenth century, the only exceptions to the general rule of observance of independence have been the divisions of Poland among Prussia, Russia, and Austria in 1772, 1792, and 1795, and between the Soviet Union and Germany in 1939, the violent reincorporation of several areas such as the Caucasian Republic which had seceded from Russia in 1918, the establishment of the puppet state Manchukuo by the Japanese, the reabsorption of the Baltic states during World War II, and the Nazi "Anschluss" with Austria in 1938. In several hundred other wars or conflicts since the seventeenth century, states were not, as in the Chinese system, "removed" or "extinguished."[24]

### Factors of Stability, Instability, and Change in the Contemporary System

Over a period of several centuries the system of many small feudal states under control of the Chou monarchy became transformed into a structure in which power was diffused among several large states. Each state was independent of the others and constantly shifted alliance partners as new threats arose or subsided; these temporary alliances were the only form of political unity during the Spring and Autumn period. This structure eventually gave way to one in which power and influence

[24] These statements do not refer, of course, to European imperialism where many tribes and petty states in the Western Hemisphere, Africa, and Asia lost their independence to the white man, or to the unification of Germany and Italy.

were for the most part concentrated around two blocs or leagues of states. The Greek city state system similarly changed its structure from one in which power and influence were diffused among a large number of relatively equal units to a configuration in which power accrued to two bloc leaders. These changes could be linked to transformations within the political units and to hostile intervention of outside powers. In feudal China, for instance, the small states on the periphery of the system were relatively independent of the center and able to seize surrounding territory, develop their military capacity, and establish administrative mechanisms adequate to cope with the problems of governing a large territory and population. When size, military power, and economic welfare became values of importance, the small feudal political units incapable of change were either conquered by more powerful neighbors or lived on as insignificant anachronisms in a Chinese world of large states.

We have similarly examined some recent social and technological developments which helped transform the eighteenth century continental system of diffuse power and shifting alliances into a world-wide system of the twentieth century, in which, on most issues, the United States and the Soviet Union wield effective power and leadership. What conditions, then, tend to sustain peaceful types of competition in the contemporary world, and which are related to chaos and violence? What contemporary developments, if any, are leading to fundamental alteration of the postwar polar structure? What conditions favor perpetuation of this framework, and which help to erode or destroy it?

It may seem a paradox, but the one development in the twentieth century which has likely induced the main antagonists of the cold war to moderate their policies has been the invention and production of nuclear weapons and modern delivery systems. While weapons of mass destruction are obviously dangerous—and possibly lethal to life on earth—the system of mutual deterrence created by the Soviet Union and the United States has undoubtedly made them aware of the risks of extreme destruction in nuclear exchanges. The potential destructiveness of nuclear weapons has also forced strategists and policy-makers to become more circumspect in using conventional force, for this form of violence may also "escalate" into nuclear warfare. It may not be entirely comforting to know that those who control nuclear weapons understand the immense capabilities for destruction in their hands, but considering the great conflicts and tensions of the cold war, it is significant that both sides have so far refrained from initiating extremely serious provocations toward each other.[25] Russian and American political leaders have claimed, and through their behavior, verified, that their governments would not use

[25] The Cuban missile crisis of 1962 is one exception.

nuclear weapons for achieving or defending foreign policy objectives or interests except as response to the most extreme threats. The Russians have also avoided using conventional military techniques for promoting "revolution" since their abortive attempt, via the North Koreans, in 1950. In short, possession of instruments of massive destruction has led neither to nuclear nor conventional war, but to adoption of other techniques of achieving objectives, which employ low levels of force and involve limited risks. Religious conflicts of the sixteenth and seventeenth centuries and tensions caused by Nazi aggression in the 1930's led to horrible wars of annihilation. The cold war, though it involves analogous stakes and fundamental incompatibilities in values and interests, has been fought primarily by means of diplomacy, propaganda, nuclear threats, intervention, and subversion, not by total war.

A second characteristic of the contemporary international system which helps moderate Western-Communist conflict is the presence, since the middle 1950's, of a large number of non-aligned states. While in some ways these states serve as new battleground for Soviet-American-Chinese competition, in others they help moderate direct confrontations between these powers. They have frequently berated Western and Communist governments for inciting violence and attempting to export their own conflicts to non-aligned areas. They have made numerous appeals against imprudent actions and have on occasion proposed compromise formulas on such issues as disarmament and Vietnam. On the most serious cold war crises, such as the conflicts over Berlin in 1958 and 1961, the Quemoy issue in 1958, and the Soviet-American confrontation over Cuba in 1962, the non-aligned nations have accomplished little as mediators. On issues involving Soviet-American rivalry in underdeveloped areas, however, their views have found expression in ultimate settlements. They were particularly instrumental in achieving solutions for the Middle East crises of 1956, 1957, and 1958, and for the Congo problem in the early 1960's.

While the underdeveloped countries attempt to impose their views on East-West confrontations, their own political and economic instability creates opportunities for violence and outside intervention. In the underdeveloped countries there are strong pressures for social change, and in some, equally strong sentiments against economic development, land reform, and social equality. Innovating pressures and conservative responses, as well as the lack of ethnic, religious, or linguistic homogeneity, help create environments in which political instability and civil disturbances are likely to occur frequently.[26] Disgruntled ideological groups,

[26] For a statistical correlation between low to moderate per capita income and high incidence of domestic violence, see Bruce Russett, *Trends in World Politics* (New York: The Macmillan Company, 1965), pp. 136–37.

party factions, or ethnic minorities often seek aid from abroad, and states like the Soviet Union and Communist China, with their universalist, messianic long-range goals, are only too willing to capitalize on the discontent of these groups in order to extend their own influence into the underdeveloped areas. Their intervention helps promote counter-intervention by Western nations. Some important Western powers, including the United States, have put into power or propped up conservative and repressive regimes whose only claim to legitimacy was their vehement anti-communism. Conditions of domestic instability, combined with the revolutionary or conservative interventions of outside states, tend to transform internal wars into international conflicts.[27]

Aside from recurring crises arising over border and ethnic disputes and regional imperialism, the continuing commitment of some revolutionary states to achievement of long-range ideological goals which require fundamental transformations in the structure, processes, and rules of the international system is another characteristic of the contemporary era whose effect is to create instability, frequent diplomatic crises, and occasional military confrontations. It is impossible to create a world commonwealth of states ruled by "dictatorships of the proletariat," directed from Moscow or Peking, without compromising the most fundamental political values of the nation state system, territorial integrity and political independence. To the extent that a few Communist states proclaim world revolution as their long-range objective, they will be perceived as a threat to other states, and their revolutionary activities abroad will cause crises. Similarly, the vague long-range objective of American policy, or Western policy in general, to create a world of independent states whose economic development can be achieved through orderly and democratic procedures, may require conservative political, economic, and diplomatic programs which will conflict with the designs of those who do not have the patience or inclination to achieve domestic modernization through long-winded parliamentary debates, costly litigation, or American-style elections. The failure by Westerners to understand and accept domestic revolutionary processes in underdeveloped countries may lead just as frequently to international controversy and diplomatic crisis as does Communist subversion.

Which contemporary conditions help perpetuate or dissolve the polar structure of power in the world? Rigid distinctions between ideologies and social institutions, for one, distinguish bloc actors from each other and help create inflexible alliance systems. In the eighteenth century

[27] Cf. Samuel P. Huntington, "Patterns of Violence in World Politics," in *Changing Pattern of Military Politics,* ed. Samuel P. Huntington (New York: Free Press of Glencoe, Inc., 1962), pp. 17–50.

states shifted military allegiances back and forth as dynastic or national interests coincided or conflicted. But in our era a Communist state does not easily become a potential alliance partner among Western nations, even when its national interests are being threatened or frustrated by another Communist state. This does not mean that realignments are, or will be, impossible; but ideological differentiation makes it difficult for members of one bloc to threaten leaving it in order to obtain membership in another.[28]

Inequalities in military capabilities may also be linked to the rise and continuation of a polar structure of power and influence in the world. After World War II all the European states were economically and militarily incapable of providing the means for safeguarding their own security. European states on both sides of the iron curtain were more or less dependent upon the United States and the Soviet Union for military aid and for providing a deterrent. By depending upon a nuclear power for a deterrent, each lost some of its freedom of diplomatic action—much as the allies of Athens and Sparta did in the fifth century. Great discrepancies in economic resources also help to create and sustain a polarized power structure. Even before the European states faced an immediate military threat from the Soviet Union after 1945, they were already dependent upon the United States for the supplies, food, and manpower necessary to defeat Nazi Germany. After the war their needs for outside assistance remained in order to reconstruct their war-ruined economies. Though the Soviet Union exploited rather than reconstructed the Eastern European countries after the war, once the bloc had become united around ideological principles, military needs, and Soviet domination, it was sustained by the economic dependency of countries on the periphery of the Soviet Union.

Another phenomenon which tends to create and sustain a two bloc power configuration is the common perception by a large group of states of a single, strong threat to their security and interests. Perhaps the most important factor in the Western Europeans' ability to overcome traditional hostilities, prejudices, and conflicts has been their common fear of the Soviet Union. As long as this fear of Russia has persisted, the coalition of Western European states, Britain, and Canada under American leadership has remained reasonably solid. But as the possibility of a direct Soviet invasion of Western Europe has become more remote, and traditional rivalries again appear—as between Turkey and Greece—pressures

---

[28] After the Yugoslav government was expelled from the Soviet bloc, it signed a treaty of friendship and cooperation with Greece and Turkey, thereby linking it at least indirectly with NATO. By 1955, however, it was clear that Yugoslavia would not become a member of the Western alliance.

to promote "independent" foreign policies, divorced from the needs of the alliance, have arisen. Similarly, in the European portion of the Communist bloc, the common fear of West Germany[29] (constantly reinforced by domestic propaganda) is an important factor creating cohesiveness of the bloc, while in the Far East the perception of American "imperialism" helped for over a decade to maintain solidarity among such disparate states as Communist China, the Soviet Union, North Vietnam, and North Korea. As European members of the Communist bloc increasingly perceive China as an ideological heretic, if not a direct military threat, the singular preoccupation with West Germany as a source of threat may decline. In other words, when a group of states perceives multiple threats, including some *within* an existing alliance, the cohesiveness of the bloc is likely to show signs of disintegration.

Since the late 1950's many of the conditions which supported or perpetuated the polar structure of power and influence in the post-war world have undergone considerable change. The Soviet threat to Western Europe does not seem so imminent as it once did, except when the Berlin problem erupts periodically. The Turks appear more concerned with the fate of their brethren on Cyprus than with any Soviet designs on their territory, and the Western European states have reached impressive economic growth rates and even dominant positions in some sectors of international trade and finance. Whether a cause or result of diffusion of power in the Communist bloc, the economies of the Eastern European states have also become less dependent upon the bloc leader, and East European governments have increasingly attempted to reorient their trade patterns toward Western markets and sources of supply.

On the military level, the same disintegrating pressures can be observed. The British have possessed a nuclear capability since 1957, and although their government has been increasingly inclined to view the costs of maintaining a meaningful and independent nuclear force as prohibitive, their military strength remains a factor which lends them international prestige and the possibility of conducting policies independently of the United States. Similarly, the regeneration of France's economic and political life under the Fifth Republic has enabled that nation to pursue increasingly independent strategic and foreign policies.

The trend toward disintegration in the Soviet bloc is even more pronounced because the bloc originally displayed such a highly monolithic structure. Any rebellion against Soviet leadership or domination

---

[29] Most security and alliance treaties drafted in 1947–1948 between the Soviet Union and the East European nations specifically mention Germany ("and states allied with it") as the power they are attempting to deter from aggression.

would be particularly dramatic given the nature of controls the Russians have maintained over their allies since 1948. By 1956 both the Poles and Hungarians had rebelled, not necessarily against communism, but at least against Soviet domination. The friction between China and the Soviet Union was even more important because it led to great ideological divergences which could not be reconciled through military means. By the middle 1960's there were at least two major centers of power in the Communist world, each arrayed against the other over ideological issues such as appropriate revolutionary strategies to employ around the world, but also quarreling over purely national objectives. The Soviet government displayed increasing displeasure over Chinese policies in Southeast Asia, India, and Africa, while in return the Chinese accused Soviet leadership of making bargains with the "imperialists" at the expense of both Marxist-Leninist revolutionary principles and Chinese national interests. With the invasion across parts of India's frontiers in 1962 and the explosion of nuclear devices in 1965—without Soviet assistance—the Chinese signified to the world that henceforth they would formulate their revolutionary and foreign policies independent of Moscow's desires. For some security and economic purposes, the Soviet bloc remains reasonably cohesive; but in many other ways, power within the bloc has become diffused among several centers. The individual states have gained some freedom of action both domestically and in their external relations.

Another development which has helped modify the post-war structure of power has been the formation of over 50 new independent states through the process of de-colonization. Until 1955 their number was so small that they had little impact on most east-west issues or proceedings within the United Nations. Today, though the non-aligned nations do not constitute any permanent bloc, their growth in influence on many international political issues has fundamentally changed the polar bloc structure that existed through the 1950's. In diplomatic crises where their own interests are involved they have been able to impose restraints on the actions of the United States and the Soviet Union; certainly the Soviet Union has not been able to conduct diplomatic relations with the non-aligned states in the same manner that it ordered its relations with the East European countries. Nor has the United States government found the non-aligned states as pliable as many of its own allies. There are, of course, certain issues, such as Berlin, in which the non-aligned states are not directly involved and where, therefore, the major antagonists are reasonably free to develop their own diplomatic strategies. But cold war conflicts, such as the Congo, fought out in underdeveloped areas, display the imprint of the needs and interests of the non-aligned states. In other words, some non-aligned states are influential in imposing limitations on the actions of major powers, and in the United Nations, where they command almost a majority of votes, their position is likely to be particularly effective.

## Types of International Systems

By comparing historical descriptions of international systems, it is possible to construct typologies of political orders at the international level. But which criteria should be used to differentiate among the systems? The nature of the units which interact provides one basis of differentiation, but evidence is insufficient to suggest that the *forms* of political organization—whether feudal units, city states, agricultural states, or nation states—determine the unique characteristics of international politics in a given era. International systems could also be classified according to the types of issues which bring political units into conflict. But the most meaningful distinction may relate to the types of structures—the general patterns of power, dominance, and influence— that persist among units comprising the system. The significance of a system's structure lies in its influence on the general orientation of constituent units' external policies, and on the restraints it can impose on the units' freedom of action.[30]

If a system's structure is used as the differentiating criterion, we can outline models, based on the historical descriptions above, of at least four different kinds of international systems: (1) the "hierarchical," (2) the "diffuse," (3) the "diffuse-bloc," and (4) the "polar." China in the Western Chou period (from 1122 until approximately 771 B.C.) is the only example of a hierarchical structure discussed in these chapters, but further historical examination would uncover other systems with similar features.[31] In this type of system, power and influence are concentrated in one unit which has the authority to create lesser units and chastise errant units if they attempt to challenge the central authority's leadership and domination. The central authority maintains order and stability by offering rewards and subsidies such as grants of land or honorific titles, making threats of punishment, and vigorously inculcating official myths and ceremonies which emphasize the sanctity of superior-subordinate relationships. Interaction and communication within the system also

[30] See Chapters IV and VI for further discussion of this point.
[31] Some features analogous to those of the Chinese system in the Western Chou period would be found in the Moslem empire and in the Holy Roman Empire before the seventeenth century.

follow the hierarchical principle. They are conducted primarily between the central authority and immediately subordinate units; units at the bottom of the hierarchy usually communicate with the central authority only through mediating states. Communication between the lesser units is at best sporadic, and non-existent in most cases. Alliances theoretically cannot exist since all power flows from the top down. In the process of disintegration, however, ambitious subordinate units may secretly ally with each other to challenge the position of the central authority.

Power and influence in the diffuse system are distributed widely among the interacting units. There is an ill-defined hierarchy of status among states, established according to various criteria of stratification, but a comparatively large number of political units are of roughly equal size and military capability. None permanently dominates the others, although there may be some leaders of regional alliances. Diplomatic and military coalitions form frequently, are open-ended, and disintegrate rapidly once mutual objectives have been achieved. They do not form into stable blocs. These coalitions are unstable because the interests underlying them tend to shift quickly, members are not economically or ideologically dependent upon each other, and there are no ideological issues dividing the alliances. Communication and interaction among the units is widespread, although geographic proximity and logistic factors undoubtedly make some units more involved than others in the major issue areas. China in the Spring and Autumn period and occasionally in the period of Warring States, Greece between the ninth and fifth centuries B.C., the Italian city states in the first half of the fifteenth century, and Europe during the eighteenth century, most of the nineteenth, and part of the twentieth century would fit the model of the diffuse system.

The diffuse-bloc system existed in the Greek period when the Athenian empire and the Peloponnesian League constituted powerful and relatively permanent blocs with surrounding allies or satellites, but many other city states remained independent of bloc affiliations, pursuing their objectives with considerable freedom of action. The same general pattern was repeated in Europe in the last two decades of the nineteenth century, again in the four or five years preceding the outbreak of World War II, and has reappeared since 1955 when an increasing number of non-aligned states has successfully broken the military-diplomatic supremacy of the two bloc leaders. Patterns of communication and interaction in the diffuse-bloc system are similar to those in the diffuse system—they go in all directions, except that bloc members tend to become dependent upon, or subservient to, bloc leaders, and conduct relatively few relations with opposing bloc members or non-involved states.

The polar model constitutes a generalization of the main features of power, influence, and patterns of communication and interaction found in China during portions of the period of Warring States (after the northern and southern leagues were formed), in Europe at the time of the French revolutionary and Napoleonic wars, immediately prior to World War I, and again in the period following World War II until approximately 1955. In this type of system military power and diplomatic authority center around two bloc leaders which dominate or lead lesser units by combining rewards—such as providing security and economic assistance—with implicit or explicit threats of punishment against recalcitrant allies. Interaction and communication seem to be primarily between the two antagonistic bloc leaders and between each of the bloc leaders and their respective client states. In the post-World War II period, however, interaction and communication *among* the lesser states of the Western bloc has been consistently high, while prior to 1956 it was largely absent within the Soviet bloc.

Conflicts and issues within the polar model seem to contain strong ideological overtones, although territorial issues and questions of spheres of influence may be mixed in with the competition over values. Strong value incompatibilities between blocs thus sustain cohesiveness within blocs. In ancient China it was the "legitimate" league of Chou states against the partly "barbarian" southern bloc; in the years between 1789 and 1815 it was conflict not only between France and the rest of Europe, but also between the universal principles of republicanism and royal legitimacy; in our day, the principles of Marxism-Leninism conflict in many ways with democratic liberalism.

These categories of international systems emphasize the recurrence of various power structures and interaction patterns in different historical contexts. Were there any other similarities between these systems? Each of the historical examples at some stage became transformed from the diffuse type to either the diffuse-bloc or polar types. Diverse conditions might be responsible for this phenomenon, but the trend is unmistakable. No system originally comprised of a large number of roughly equal units, with power diffused among them, retained that structure for a very long period, and the usual direction of development was toward a polar structure.

Even polar structures were not very stable. Starting with the anti-French coalition between the eighteenth and nineteenth centuries, polar structures have developed into diffuse structures, only to turn into polar structures again. In China and Greece, however, once power and influence were distributed between two bloc leaders, the wars that followed led ultimately to complete destruction of the systems. The descriptions of the systems thus suggest no patterns as to the types of system more conducive to stability among independent political units. The scope of violence in the hierarchical and diffuse systems, as well as during the last 40 years of the unique Italian system, was limited. But this may be attributed as much to a crude military technology, small territorial basis of political organizations, and absence of overriding ideological issues, as to the structure of the system. Also, in most of the historical diffuse systems there was ample unorganized territory into which the states could expand. In China and Greece, eighteenth and nineteenth century Europe, and to a lesser extent in the first half of the fifteenth century in Italy, the political units could increase their territorial holdings without necessarily depriving other politically organized centers of their own territory. Africa, the Middle East, and Asia served more than once as convenient outlets for imperialist pressures in Europe. On the other hand, in polar systems, the amount of space available for political expansion was usually limited, so improvement of one state's territorial position could be secured only at the expense of others.[32] Aside from these differences, war and violence seem to have been typical forms of interaction in all of the systems.

An examination of these systems suggests that processes which lead to changes in their structures are occurring much more rapidly in the Western cultural context. Almost four centuries elapsed between the establishment of the hierarchical Chou system and its transformation into a diffuse structure during the Spring and Autumn period. The main characteristics of the Greek system when it had a diffuse structure remained essentially unchanged for almost three centuries. Today, technological innovation, economic development, and the effects of total war create rapid and radical changes in the world's power structure. England's decline as a major power in international politics occurred in less than two decades, while the rise of the Soviet Union and the United States took place virtually within the period of time that they were involved in World War II. Communist China's rise to prominence and diplomatic influence has occured in little more than a decade. Nuclear war, major scientific discoveries, or continuation of disintegrating tendencies in the two major military blocs could bring about even more radical shifts in the structure of power and influence in the near future.

## SELECTED BIBLIOGRAPHY

Albrecht-Carré, René, *A Diplomatic History of Europe Since the Congress of Vienna.* New York: Harper & Row, Publishers, 1958.

Aron, Raymond, *The Century of Total War.* New York: Doubleday & Company, Inc., 1954.

[32] Cf. Rosecrance, *Action and Reaction in World Politics,* p. 239.

Brzezinski, Zbigniew K., *The Soviet Bloc: Unity and Conflict.* Cambridge: Harvard University Press, 1960.

Carr, Edward H., *The Twenty Years' Crisis, 1919–1939.* London: Macmillan & Co., Ltd., 1946.

Claude, Inis L., Jr., *Power and International Relations.* New York: Random House, Inc., 1962.

Deutsch, Karl W., "The Future of World Politics," *The Political Quarterly,* XXXVII (1966), 9–32.

————, *Nationalism and Social Communication.* New York: John Wiley & Sons, Inc., 1953.

Dorn, Walter L., *Competition for Empire, 1740–1763.* New York: Harper & Row, Publishers, 1940.

Emerson, Rupert, *From Empire to Nation.* Cambridge: Harvard University Press, 1960.

Gross, Leo, "The Peace of Westphalia, 1648–1948," *American Journal of International Law,* XLII (1948), 20–41.

Gulick, Edward V., *Europe's Classical Balance of Power.* Ithaca, New York: Cornell University Press, 1955.

Heilbroner, Robert L., *The Great Ascent: The Struggle for Economic Development in our Time.* New York: Harper & Row, Publishers, 1963.

Hekhuis, Dale J., Charles G. McClintock, and Arthur L. Burns, eds., *International Stability: Military, Economic and Political Dimensions.* New York: John Wiley & Sons, Inc., 1964.

Herz, John H., *International Politics in the Atomic Age.* New York: Columbia University Press, 1959.

Holborn, Hajo, *The Political Collapse of Europe.* New York: Alfred A. Knopf, Inc., 1951.

Horowitz, Irving L., *Three Worlds of Development: The Theory and Practice of International Stratification.* New York: Oxford University Press, 1966.

Jouvenel, Bertrand de, *Sovereignty: An Inquiry into the Political Good,* trans. J. F. Huntington. Chicago: University of Chicago Press, 1957.

Kaplan, Morton A., ed., *The Revolution in World Politics.* New York: John Wiley & Sons, Inc., 1962.

Krabbe, Hugo, *The Modern Idea of the State,* trans. George Sabine. New York: Appleton-Century-Crofts, 1922.

Kulski, W. W., *International Politics in a Revolutionary Age.* New York and Philadelphia: J. B. Lippincott Co., 1964.

Lagos, Gustavo, *International Stratification and Underdeveloped Countries.* Chapel Hill: The University of North Carolina Press, 1963.

Millikan, Max, and D. L. M. Blackmer, eds., *The Emerging Nations.* Boston: Little, Brown and Company, Inc., 1961.

Moussa, Pierre, *The Underprivileged Nations,* trans. Alan Braley. Boston: Beacon Press, 1963.

Mowat, Robert B., *The European State System.* London: H. Milford, 1923.

Nadel, George H. and Perry Curtis, eds., *Imperialism and Colonialism*. New York: The Macmillan Company, 1964.

Niebuhr, Reinhold, *The Structure of Nations and Empires*. New York: Charles Scribner's Sons, 1959.

Northrop, F. S. C., *The Taming of the Nations*. New York: The Macmillan Company, 1952.

Organski, A. F. K., *World Politics*. New York: Alfred A. Knopf, Inc., 1960.

Pounds, Norman, and Sue Simons Ball, "Core Areas and the Development of the European States System," *Annals of the Association of American Geographers*, LIV (1964), 24–40.

Rosecrance, Richard N., *Action and Reaction in World Politics*. Boston: Little, Brown and Company, 1963.

————, "Bipolarity, Multipolarity, and the Future," *Journal of Conflict Resolution*, X (1966), 314–27.

Russett, Bruce M., *Trends in World Politics*. New York: The Macmillan Company, 1965.

Seabury, Paul, *Power, Freedom, and Diplomacy: The Foreign Policy of the United States of America*. New York: Random House, Inc., 1963.

Seaman, Lewis C. B., *From Vienna to Versailles*. London: Methuen & Co., Ltd., 1955.

Seton-Watson, Hugh, *Neither War Nor Peace: The Struggle for Power in the Postwar World*. New York: Frederick A. Praeger, Inc., 1960.

Staley, Eugene, *The Future of Underdeveloped Countries*. New York: Harper & Row, Publishers, 1954.

Stoessinger, John G., *The Might of Nations: World Politics in Our Time*, rev. ed. New York: Random House, Inc., 1965.

Strachey, John, *The End of Empire*. New York: Random House, Inc., 1960.

Taylor, Alan J. P., *The Struggle for Mastery in Europe, 1848–1914*. Oxford: The Clarendon Press, 1957.

Wolfers, Arnold, ed., *Changing East-West Relations and the Unity of the West*. Baltimore: The Johns Hopkins Press, 1964.

# FOREIGN POLICY ORIENTATIONS

The main characteristics of international systems may have important effects on how policy-makers of constituent political units seek to achieve or defend their objectives, their latitude of choice in adjusting to external conditions, and the different degrees of involvement they display in major issues of the system. This chapter will continue to explore the various ways that systemic conditions affect nations' foreign policy behavior and indicate how other variables relate to levels of involvement and basic foreign policy strategies such as isolation, non-alignment, and alliances.

Few states are at any given time concerned with direct threats to their security or "core" values. Some states are so weak in capabilities—the means by which they can influence the behavior of other states—that even if they were vitally interested in a problem, there would be little they could do directly to affect its outcome. The government of Malawi may have well-formulated views on American-Cuban relations, but

# CHAPTER IV

aside from occasional diplomatic statements there is little its government can do by itself to influence the state of these relations. Moreover, some states are so geographically remote from the major scenes of international conflict or areas of collaboration that interest on the part of the government or the population as a whole may be difficult to generate. One would not expect the people of Iceland to be particularly interested in the problems of Central Africa, and their government would not likely be directly involved in Central African affairs. Many Europeans and Americans, whose governments maintain extensive commitments around the world and whose foreign policy objectives and aspirations impinge upon the interests and values of many other societies, often forget that all countries are not equally interested in the great collaborative ventures and conflicts of our era. Many governments have few international concerns outside of advancing or protecting the private interests of their own citizens through routine trade and cultural contacts. Degrees of involvement in affairs of the system thus may vary from the maximum levels attained by major powers to the low number of official international transactions in which Iceland, Gabon, Bhutan, or Mauritania are involved. Even the level of involvement of the great powers varies with different issue areas. The United States is a prime actor in many issue subsystems, from disarmament to international trade, but it is not an active participant in the issue of colonialism.

A country's level of involvement in various international issue areas is often the expression of its general orientation toward the rest of the world. By orientation we mean a state's general attitudes and commitments toward the external environment, its fundamental strategy for accomplishing its domestic and external objectives and aspirations. A nation's general strategy or orientation is seldom revealed in any one decision, but results from a series of cumulative decisions made in an effort to adjust objectives, values, and interests to conditions and characteristics of the domestic and external environments.

By examining the structure of power and influence and the actions of political units in diverse international systems, it is possible to identify at least three fundamental orientations that have been adopted recurrently, regardless of historical context. These are (1) isolation, (2) non-alignment, and (3) coalition-making and alliance construction. Ministers in the ancient Chinese system under the Chou dynasty recommended these strategies to their leaders, choice depending upon geographic location of the state and its position between other powers. Kautilya, the philosopher of inter-state relations during the Chandragupta period in ancient India, also referred to these fundamental orientations as means of increasing power, gaining security, or conducting successful policies of imperialism. Even today, any state's general orientation and strategy toward the external environment can be described by one of these three terms.

Under what circumstances have governments adopted these strategies? What domestic and external conditions help make these strategies or orientations successful, and when do they fail? At least four conditions or variables can help account for the selection of any particular strategy. First is the structure of the international system. The patterns of dominance, subordination, and leadership of an international system establish some limits on the freedom of action of the component units. By definition it would be impossible for a state in a truly polar system to seek its objectives or defend its interests by isolating itself, nor would a political unit in a hierarchical system attempt to build coalitions against the center. Second, a state's general foreign policy strategy can be linked to the nature of its domestic social and economic needs. Third, the degree to which policy-makers perceive a *persisting* external threat to their own values and interests will have great bearing on their strategy toward the external environment. Finally, a state's geographic location, topographical characteristics, and endowment in natural resources can often be linked to its choice of orientations.

## Isolation

A strategy of political and military isolation is indicated by a low level of involvement in most issue areas of the system, a low number of diplomatic or commercial transactions with other political units and societies, and an unwillingness to commit any military capabilities to, or allow any military privileges for, outside states. Isolationist orientations are based on the assumption that security and independence can best be accomplished by cutting off most transactions with other units in the system, or by maintaining diplomatic and commercial contacts abroad while handling all perceived or potential threats by building deterrents solely on the home base. How are the four variables of system structure, domestic needs, threats, and geographic features related to isolationist strategies?

Logically, at least, an isolationist orientation would only be adopted, or could only succeed, in a system with a reasonably diffuse structure of power, where military, economic, or ideological threats do not persist, and where other states are regularly shifting alliances. A polar system is defined as an international structure in which all states, voluntarily or through compulsion, commit their military capabilities to the purposes of a bloc or bloc leader. In a hierarchical system, isolation might be possible only if the power of the central unit was so weak that it could not reach effectively to every vassal state. This was the case in China during the Western Chou period, when many of the smaller political units on the geographic periphery of the system were so physically isolated from the Chou capital that they were able to develop into powerful states with a minimum of interference from the emperor. They paid lip service to the "Son of Heaven," but politically remained independent while their strength grew to the point where they could effectively challenge not only other rising states, but the central monarchy itself. Throughout the Greek period, a number of city states and former colonies deliberately isolated themselves behind the barriers of the Mediterranean Sea as a way of escaping commitments to either side during the Peloponnesian Wars. In the first three centuries of the Greek city state system, many smaller units in mountainous regions remained isolated simply because they could not overcome the divisive effects of topographical features. Isolation in this case was not so much a strategy chosen to cope with external threats as a response to certain geographical limitations.

Political units which adopt an orientation of isolation are usually self-sufficient in most basic economic and social needs. In order to maintain a "way of life," including social values, political structures, or economic patterns, the political unit does not have to change the external environment in its favor. Nor, in many cases, does it depend upon others to fulfill its social and economic needs. The reverse of this situation is that activities of other units in the system also fail to have appreciable impact on the isolated state's internal developments. This does not mean that an isolated state necessarily fails to conduct commercial or diplomatic relations with other states. It may do so, but not to such an extent that conflicts in those relations could lead to unpleasant military consequences or military threats from abroad.

Isolation orientations cannot be linked directly to the absence or presence of perceived threats, whether military, economic, or cultural. Some political units have remained isolated for centuries because geographic barriers prevented foreign incursions. Others have adopted isolation strategies as a means of coping with an actual or potential threat— not by meeting it in battle, but by withdrawing behind the frontiers and erecting defenses which would make the state impermeable to military attack or cultural infiltration.

Geographic and topographic characteristics are related in many ways to a strategy of isolation. Surrounding high mountains, wide seas, or uninhabitable plains or deserts will afford protection to political units, provided that other states in the system do not possess means for easily by-passing these features. Geographic remoteness reduces the number of potential threats while protective topographical features provide natural shields behind which to hide, reducing further the number of potential threats. Until the nineteenth century, for instance, the high mountain barriers and lack of access routes were conditions favoring the sustained isolation of Nepal. Nepal was not, in terms of distance, located far from the great centers of British military, economic, and political influence on the Indian subcontinent, but the natural barriers surrounding Nepal were adequate to cope with most massive foreign intrusions. The British were diplomatically and commercially active in Nepal, but not to the extent that they were in other colonial or semi-colonial areas. China invaded Tibet in 1950 and began building military roads in the Himalayan valleys, thus making Nepal's position much less secure. Because it is now much more accessible, it is more open to external influences, particularly to the effects of competition between Communist China and India over the frontiers of the two countries. In other words, given the level of contemporary technology and military potential, Nepal's isolation strategy depends more on the state of Chinese-Indian relations than on geographic features.

The deliberate isolation of Japan for several centuries after the first Japanese contacts with Europeans is one illustration of a state adopting this strategy in response to a perceived threat. In this case the Japanese emperors sealed off the islands (though they tolerated a minimum of trade with some Europeans) to prevent "barbarian" infiltration, meaning either territorial conquest or the more subtle pollution of Japanese culture and values by alien practices. By the middle of the nineteenth century, however, Western naval power in the Pacific had become so formidable that it could easily breach Japan's "impermeability." In 1854, Japan was isolated. Only five decades later it was making commercial and military coalitions with Great Britain, the United States, and several European countries, and was acting as one of the important units in major conflicts of the Far East.

The United States in the nineteenth century, for different reasons, also successfully followed strategies of isolation from the conflicts of the European powers. America was certainly part of the European system, if interaction was measured in terms of commercial and cultural contacts. But the United States was not directly involved in most of the ideological, national, and dynastic issues separating the European powers. President Washington's advice regarding "no entangling alliances" was adopted as

CARL A. RUDISILL LIBRARY
LENOIR RHYNE COLLEGE

official American policy, in part because American policy-makers saw no immediate European threat directed against their continent. The Americans had to decide whether to become involved in Europe's problems, not whether the Europeans were about to meddle in America's problems.

The absence of a European threat to the Americas can be linked to geographic conditions, particularly the broad expanse of the Atlantic Ocean which constituted a considerable barrier to communication and any potential naval invasion embarking from the continent. Moreover, the British navy helped to protect North America from incursions by other European powers. Another condition favoring an isolation strategy was the high degree of self-sufficiency in land, raw materials, and natural resources. British and European capital and labor came voluntarily to North America to help economic expansion and exploitation of extensive resources. There was enough land available for agricultural self-sufficiency, and most manufactured goods were obtainable through trade. Finally, international conflicts of the nineteenth century raged over the continent, in the Mediterranean Sea and the Balkans, and later in Africa and the Middle East, while the great imperial rivalries in the New World between Spain, France, and England had been resolved for the most part by the end of the Napoleonic Wars. All of these political, economic, and geographic conditions led most Americans to conclude that isolation was the best available strategy to provide security and allow the country to concentrate on internal expansion and development.

These historic examples indicate that there may be strong incentives for governments to choose strategies of isolation. Those who support these strategies are not, as many have argued, indifferent to the world around them; on the contrary, they may possess very adequate pictures of international conditions and potential threats. Political units remote from scenes of conflict in the system, relatively independent economically and militarily, and which perceive that involvement would only jeopardize their social, economic, and political values, often find that they can best maintain their values and achieve their aspirations through isolationist foreign policy orientations.[1]

---

[1] Ethiopia is another example of successful nineteenth century isolation. Prior to World War I, the monarchs of Ethiopia sought to protect their throne and their society's religion by keeping European influence to a minimum. They were aided by the rough topography of the country. Several European expeditions had attempted to invade the Ethiopian highlands but found it almost impossible because of the long marches and high mountain passes. In 1906, wishing to avoid colonial competition over the territory and recognizing that in any event occupation of the country would be extremely costly, the European powers signed a treaty agreeing to respect Ethiopia's independence.

## Strategies of Non-Alignment

Traditionally there has been confusion over the differences among such terms as "neutrality," "neutralism," and "non-alignment." In one sense they all signify the same type of foreign policy orientation, where a state will not commit its military capabilities, and sometimes its diplomatic support, to the purposes of another state. Unwillingness to commit military capabilities to others' purposes is the hallmark of non-alignment as a foreign policy strategy, but there are some variations in the circumstances by which a state adopts a non-aligned policy; it is here that neutrality and neutralism have distinct meanings.

Neutrality refers to the *legal status* of a state during armed hostilities. Under the international laws of neutrality, a non-belligerent in wartime has certain rights and obligations not extended to the belligerents.[2] These rules state, for example, that a neutral may not permit use of its territory as a base for military operations by one of the belligerents, may not furnish military assistance to the belligerents, and may enjoy free passage of its non-military goods on the open seas and, under certain conditions, through belligerent blockades.

A neutralized state is one which must observe these rules during armed conflict but which, during peace, must also refrain from making military alliances with other states. The major difference between a neutralized state and a non-aligned state is that the former has achieved its position by virtue of the actions of others, while the latter chooses its orientation by itself and has no guarantees that its position will be honored by others. A state is often neutralized when the great powers agree to guarantee its non-aligned position through a multilateral treaty. The European powers neutralized Switzerland in 1815, Belgium in 1831, and Luxembourg in 1867. More recently, Austria (1955) and Laos (1962) were neutralized by agreement between the major Western governments and the Soviet Union. Under neutralization treaties, the state in question binds itself not to allow foreign troops on its soil or in any way to compromise its status by making military agreements or giving military privileges to other states on its own territory. In turn, the guaranteeing powers undertake not to violate the territorial integrity or rights of the neutral in both wartime and peace.

What motivates the great powers to establish and guarantee the neu-

---

[2] Neutral status and alliance commitments are not necessarily incompatible. For example, if state A makes an agreement to assist state B only if state C attacks, it could still remain neutral if any state other than C attacked B.

trality of certain states? Sometimes, as in Laos, their own rivalry over the territory in question may lead to undesired results, or, more simply, the area under contention may not be worth a possible military confrontation. A solution to this situation is for both sides to withdraw and make an agreement that neither will again seek to gain military advantages in the territory. In other cases a state may perform functions of value to the major powers, and it is understood that these functions can only be carried out if all nations observe its neutrality. For instance, Swiss diplomatic establishments have frequently taken over minimal tasks of communication and representation for countries that have severed diplomatic relations. During both world wars the Swiss performed many additional services for the belligerents: they cared for prisoners of war, arranged for transfer of stranded diplomatic personnel, and served as the main liaison agents for the small amount of secret diplomatic communication between governments at war with each other. Finally, the Swiss government, or the International Red Cross headquarters in Switzerland, has acted as a mediator or channel of communication in preliminary armistice or peace negotiations.

The most common form of non-alignment today is found among those states which, on their own initiative and without the guarantee of other states, refuse to commit themselves *militarily* to the goals and objectives of others states. Though they lend diplomatic support to blocs or bloc leaders on particular issues, they refrain from siding diplomatically with any bloc on *all* issues. The non-aligned states of Europe—Ireland, Sweden, and Finland—are usually sympathetic to Western diplomatic or economic projects, but do not formally join these except when the projects or organizations contain no conditions that might compromise their non-alignment. They attempt to remain uninvolved in the major bloc conflicts, though on occasion they promote plans for non-violent settlements. The non-aligned countries in the underdeveloped areas similarly avoid formal commitments to blocs, but they show a greater inclination to distrust the major Western powers, criticize publicly the actions of any state, and give vocal support to bloc actions when they are deemed in their own interests.

The propensity of underdeveloped non-aligned states to shift from supporting one bloc to the other on different issues stems from a conception of the blocs quite different from the one that the two blocs have of themselves and of each other. Western statesmen like to regard their countries as democratic bulwarks against communism, aggression, slavery, and subversion. Soviet leaders and citizens see themselves as threatened by imperialists and military regimes which are preparing for nuclear war against the young Socialist states. Foreign military bases, the support of "reactionary" regimes, and nuclear threats emanating from Washington are all taken as evidence of the basically evil intentions of the West. To attentive citizens of the non-aligned states, however, both blocs may appear equally bad, each attempting to dominate the new states for their own economic and strategic interests. To them, the term "free world" may sound ludicrous in so far as it includes references to Spain, Portugal, and South Africa; in the face of rebellion in East Germany, Poland, and Hungary, the term "peoples' democracies" may seem equally absurd. In short, these people and their governments make their own evaluations of which side is right or wrong in different circumstances, and the conclusions are not always flattering to either side. By following independent paths of judgement, their diplomatic support does not reside with one bloc permanently.[3]

In the present international context, non-alignment strategies are mostly confined to military matters, for on a certain range of issues nations which consider themselves non-aligned do, in fact, create temporary blocs and diplomatic coalitions. They have certain common interests, such as supporting anti-colonial movements and organizing attempts to obtain better terms of trade from industrialized nations. In international trade conferences and on some types of issues in the United Nations, the non-aligned states combine to increase their influence vis-à-vis the industrialized nations and bloc leaders.

Aside from refusal to give military support to blocs by joining alliances or permitting other nations to maintain bases on their territories, what other indicators can be used to judge whether a state is in fact non-aligned? Recent diplomatic practice does not provide much evidence. Some states are non-aligned more by virtue of public declarations than their foreign policy actions. Others are non-aligned because the governments of some leading non-aligned states say they are. For example, Cuba, which has an implied military alliance with the Soviet Union, was invited to attend the conference of non-aligned countries that convened in Cairo in October, 1964. One year later, Malaysia, which relies heavily upon Great Britain for military support, was similarly invited to the abortive non-aligned conference in Algeria. Yet states like Sweden and Ireland, which have no external military commitments, are usually left off the invitation lists to these gatherings of non-aligned states. Another indicator of non-alignment—public commitment to the principles of peaceful coexistence—is sometimes cited. But here, too, the actions of many non-aligned states have violated these principles. Indonesia, India,

---

[3] John W. Burton, *International Relations: A General Theory* (Cambridge: Cambridge University Press, 1965), p. 201.

and Egypt—all commonly identified as leading non-aligned states—have handled conflicts with neighbors in a manner hardly consistent with the concept of peaceful coexistence. If they believe in peaceful coexistence between East and West, they do not appear to believe in it so strongly when their relations with states like Malaysia, Pakistan, and Israel are concerned.

Some leaders have conceived of a non-aligned strategy (sometimes called "positive neutralism") as requiring more than avoidance of commitments to military blocs. In their view, non-aligned nations should actively promote world peace by mediating East-West bloc conflicts, and by organizing a "third force" which can help balance and cushion the damaging effects of East-West rivalry. India during the 1950's was perhaps the most active non-aligned state in cold war conflicts. It undertook mediating functions in the Korean and Laotian conflicts, and aided in the peace supervisory activities of the United Nations in the Suez crisis of 1956 and the Congo imbroglio during the early 1960's.

Successful strategies of non-alignment would seem possible in international systems with diffuse or diffuse-bloc structures. Theoretically, the military capabilities of member units in a hierarchical system are bound, by hereditary and contractual obligations, to the center unit. If the Chou monarchy was under attack from the "barbarians," or if it waged war to punish a recalcitrant vassal, the other units were obligated to come to its support by supplying foot soldiers and money. In the polar system where all states belong to antagonistic blocs, there is similarly no room for, or tolerance of, states which attempt to remain neutral or non-involved in bloc conflicts. In the Chinese system during parts of the Spring and Autumn and Warring States periods, units which attempted to maintain complete autonomy in foreign relations were either forced into alliances or annexed by more powerful neighbors.

Non-alignment strategies can be linked to a number of domestic considerations and pressures. Some political units have adopted this orientation as a means of obtaining maximum economic concessions from both blocs, recognizing that to make permanent military arrangements with one bloc would close off the other as a possible source of supply, markets, and foreign aid. Given the strong commitment of many governments in the underdeveloped world to achieve adequate economic growth rates as fast as possible, few can afford to restrict their international trade to any one area of the world. Much less can they afford to restrict their sources of economic aid. Some non-aligned governments feel that because of the political implications of aid agreements, the more sources of aid that are available, the more the nation can effectively counter threats to cut off aid by the donors. To be non-aligned is to maximize opportunities to meet domestic economic needs, while minimizing dependencies.

Non-alignment, it is often argued by its practitioners, also increases the diplomatic influence of those who adopt it as a foreign policy strategy. They suggest that through alliances, nations give up freedom of action and lose the opportunity to formulate their policies in terms of their own needs. In too many instances an alliance forces weak states to sacrifice their own interests for the needs of the great powers, and when tensions turn into crises, the small alliance partners are usually unable to affect the outcomes, even though these may have serious consequences on their interests. As independent states, however, non-aligned nations have room to maneuver and may be able to influence the behavior and actions of *both* blocks.[4]

A strategy of non-alignment is particularly well suited to the domestic *political* conditions and needs of underdeveloped countries. By being expressed sometimes in anti-Western terms, it accords with the anti-colonial attitudes of indigenous elites and mass political parties. By emphasizing dangers to the nation from the machinations of the great powers, it helps create national unity, a commodity sorely needed in societies torn apart by religious, tribal, or linguistic conflicts. To many African and Asian nationalist leaders (most represent the first generation of native leaders), non-alignment foreign policy strategies express and emphasize the independence of their countries. Understandably, they find that it pays political dividends at home and abroad not to give any impression of making military or ideological commitments to their former colonial overlords or to states which might compromise their independence in the future.

Non-alignment may be a response to perceptions of threat as well as to domestic economic and political pressures. Nations have traditionally sought to maintain their independence and territorial integrity by withdrawing or avoiding involvement in conflict areas. The reverse of "positive neutralism," this type of strategy is based on isolationist impulses. In the present international context, however, the fear is not so much of a *direct* threat to independence—except perhaps by way of "neo-colonialism"—as it is concern that bloc conflicts will spill over into non-aligned areas, or that regional conflicts in the underdeveloped world will attract great power intervention. The non-aligned states have had few concrete interests in the outcome of great cold war crises such as Berlin, Hungary, or Vietnam. They have always expressed a fear, however, that such confrontations could escalate into nuclear warfare which would eventually engulf them. Those non-aligned states which have perceived a *direct* threat emanating from one of the great powers have also con-

---

[4] This type of argument is ably presented by Alex Quaison-Sackey in his *Africa Unbound* (New York: Frederick A. Praeger, Inc., 1963), pp. 105–11.

sidered abandoning the non-aligned strategy in favor of military alliances with those who could offer them protection.

Non-alignment as a strategy to defend independence and secure economic and social needs can usually be expected to succeed if the state in question is reasonably distant from the main areas of international conflict. States like Switzerland and Sweden managed to stay outside of both world conflicts in the twentieth century in part because of their geographic and strategic position. Though neither was very distant from the main scenes of battle, both enjoyed favorable topographical and geographic features: the high mountains surrounding Switzerland constituted barriers which would have made Nazi invasion of the country extremely costly. The Germans could control both the Baltic Sea and parts of the North Atlantic by occupying Denmark and Norway, while control of Sweden was not crucial to either of these objectives. In other words, a strategy of non-alignment may be sustained successfully even in wartime if the area is of little strategic value to bloc leaders or various belligerents.

What other conditions can be linked to the success or failure of non-alignment strategies? Successful non-alignment is also basically a problem of credibility—convincing other states that the strategy is actually advantageous to their own interests. It is when a non-aligned or neutralized state compromises its independent position, or is forced to compromise it by outside pressures, that the strategy will fail. Actions, not just words, have to conform to the expectations of other states.

To safeguard its position, particularly when crisis or conflict develops around or near its frontiers, the non-aligned state must avoid any kind of military engagements with third parties. Usually this means that it must also have the capacity to resist incursions upon its territory or pressures by outside powers to use its land for military purposes. If the non-aligned or neutralized state cannot resist such pressures, it can no longer expect others to respect its special position.

Another factor in making the strategy credible abroad is the general condition of politics within the country. The non-alignment of Sweden, Ireland, and Burma are credible in part because most of the important political parties in those countries support the strategy. There are no powerful political groupings which, if in control of the government, could drastically change the foreign policy orientations of their nation. One reason why the Soviet Union has supported Finland's participation in Western and Scandinavian cultural and economic organizations is because it has recognized that few Finns would want to break off friendly relations with the Soviet Union in order to join NATO. It has been willing, in other words, to allow a certain amount of Finnish-Western collaboration as long as that collaboration did not extend to military matters or promote the development of anti-Russian political parties in Finland. Similarly, Western powers have for many years donated aid to, and provided favorable trade arrangements for, Yugoslavia on the expectation that the Yugoslavs would not identify themselves completely with the Soviet position on world affairs or join the Warsaw alliance system.

For a strategy of non-alignment to succeed, there must be reasonable political stability in the non-aligned country so that conditions which would possibly attract outside intervention or subversion do not develop. If there are divisive political, ethnic, or ideological groupings which sap the internal coherence of the state, foreign powers are likely to meddle through subversion, infiltration, or outright military intervention. In this case, neutrality becomes merely a formality and is no longer credible. The neutrality of Laos, for example, rests on a precarious base, even if guaranteed by international treaty. Laotian politics are turbulent, political elites do not accept non-alignment with unanimity, and dissident factions, such as the Communist Pathet Lao with the aid of North Vietnamese allies, undermine the stability of the neutralist regime, thus calling into question the ability of the government to fulfill its obligations as a non-aligned state. If the weak state has to call in foreign troops to help quell domestic or externally supported uprisings, its position of non-alignment or neutrality would be seriously compromised.[5]

The most difficult time to maintain a non-aligned orientation is during large-scale war. Throughout history, non-aligned and neutralized states have proclaimed their intention of remaining uninvolved in great power conflicts, only to be invaded or forced into alliances by those who respected their position in peacetime. Leopold III declared Belgium neutral in 1936, but the Belgians hardly had the capacity to enforce this position against the Nazi war machine, whose most direct route to France lay through Belgian territory. Norway, too, declared its neutrality prior to the outbreak of World War II, but as its geographic location was of importance to German military operations against Great Britain in the North Atlantic, it was invaded in 1940. Even where non-aligned or neutralized states are not invaded at the beginning of military operations, wars have a tendency to "spill over" into areas originally uninvolved. A neutral state such as Laos was unable to maintain its territorial integrity during the war in Vietnam because its territory was useful to the North Vietnamese for infiltrating guerrilla troops and matériel into South Vietnam.

[5] The conditions which help sustain a policy of non-alignment are discussed by Risto Hyvärinen, "Neutrality in International Politics," an unpublished paper prepared for the Center for International Affairs, Harvard University (April, 1964), p. 71.

Successful strategies of non-alignment thus require the juxtaposition of many conditions, including favorable structure of power and influence in the system, national capacity to defend independence and territorial integrity against those who do not honor a neutral position, the benevolent attitude or indifference of the great powers, reasonable remoteness from the main centers of international conflict, and a reasonable amount of internal political stability. In times of great international conflict or widespread war, however, most nations gravitate either voluntarily or through coercion toward alliances.

## Diplomatic Coalitions and Military Alliances

Governments which seek to construct permanent diplomatic coalitions or military alliances assume that they cannot achieve their objectives, defend their interests, or deter perceived threats by mobilizing their own capabilities. They thus rely upon, and make commitments to, other states which face similar external problems or share similar objectives.

Of the four types of international systems, alliance strategies appear commonly in all but the hierarchical variety. In the Western Chou era the feudal units were subservient to the central monarchy, and the only coalitions sanctioned by the leader of the system were those between itself and the subordinate units. Secret coalitions between the vassal states were deemed treasonable, but as the superior-subordinate, contractual relations of the system decayed due to the growth of power among feudal units on the periphery, alliances became commonplace. In the diffuse system, alliances appear regularly, but tend to be temporary in so far as state objectives derive from specific needs and interests rather than ideological aspirations. In the polar and diffuse-bloc systems, alliances tend to be closely-knit structures in which the smaller alliance partners do not easily remove themselves from the bloc. Bloc alliances persist over a period of time, because they usually express deep ideological cleavages between bloc leaders, not just dynastic or commercial rivalries.

Alliance strategies are closely linked to domestic needs. States which share common economic problems are likely to form economic blocs, trading groups, or diplomatic coalitions which maintain solidarity on trade issues. Thus, while on many problems today the underdeveloped countries do not constitute a bloc in the military-diplomatic sense, they have joined together on the question of obtaining more favorable terms of trade from industrialized countries. Nations which decide for various domestic or ideological reasons to undertake programs of territorial or revolutionary expansion may combine to form aggressive military alliances. Alliances have also bolstered weak regimes and served essentially domestic political purposes rather than defense against external threats. Throughout history political units have offered their military capabilities to other states in order to help maintain friendly governments in power or perpetuate a particular dynasty against internal and externally supported rebellion or subversion. Though most alliances today are initially formulated for defense against a common external enemy, their effect may be to protect weak regimes against internal dissidence and revolution. Military aid given under alliance agreements may be used by the recipient to quell rebellions, while the military training assistance it receives often comes in the form of instruction in riot control techniques and counter-insurgency warfare. In both Communist and Western alliance systems, some partners have joined basically out of the need to secure external protection against internal unrest.

Common perceptions of threat are probably the most frequent sources of alliance strategies. As Thucydides noted over 2,000 years ago, mutual fear is the only solid basis upon which to organize an alliance.[6] States construct economic blocs, defensive alliances, or temporary diplomatic coalitions usually to act as deterrents against those that are making demands against their interests or posing immediate military threats. NATO was the primary Western response to the Berlin blockade, the Communist *coup d'état* in Czechoslovakia in 1948, and the expectation that similar actions, backed by the Red Army, would take place in France and Italy. The Warsaw alliance was formed in 1955 in response to the rapid recovery of West Germany during the early 1950's, its incorporation into NATO in the winter of 1954–1955, and the Communist expectation of a possible German "war of revenge" against East Europe. Most bilateral security treaties of 1948 between the Soviet Union and the Eastern European Communist nations were also directed specifically against a perceived threat from a resurgent Germany.

Geographic conditions do not appear to play a significant role in alliance-making or the formation of diplomatic or economic coalitions. Common threats or common advantages seem to be more important considerations. Military agreements have been concluded between states separated by great distances, where geographic characteristics made actual military cooperation very difficult, yet there are probably as many examples of alliances or blocs between neighboring states: the members of the Common Market, for instance, are all located in the western portion of the European continent. Alliances in eighteenth century Eu-

---

[6] Thucydides, *A History of the Peloponnesian War,* trans. Benjamin Jowett (Oxford: Ashendene Press, 1930), Book III, Par. 11.

rope also do not reveal any relationship between location and coalition. In some cases, a dynastic regime would make an alliance with a distant nation against its immediate neighbors; in others, neighbors would form defensive groups against threats emanating from the other side of the continent.

## Types of Alliances

All diplomatic coalitions and alliances have one common characteristic—they attempt to increase diplomatic influence on some issue or problem or create a deterrent effect by combining capabilities. But aside from this feature, there are many different types of groupings. Diplomatic coalitions within the United Nations tend to form around specific issues or types of issues (such as colonialism) and break up when other problems are being considered. Economic and trade blocs are usually more permanent because the needs they are designed to fulfill usually persist. In other circumstances, governments may best meet their domestic economic needs or increase their diplomatic advantages by forming supranational institutions or international organizations, in which case coalitions initially designed for specific purposes become permanent subsystems leading to collaboration on a wide range of problems.

Military alliances can be classified and compared according to four main criteria: (1) the nature of the *casus foederis* (the situation in which mutual commitments are to become operational); (2) the type of commitments undertaken by the treaty signatories; (3) the degree of cooperation or military integration of the military forces of the alliance partners; and (4) the geographic *scope* of the treaty.

Although partners to an alliance have some similar or overlapping foreign policy objectives, negotiators of the treaty are usually very cautions in defining the *casus foederis*. Some treaties, particularly those in recent years which have been used for offensive purposes, contain a very vague definition of the situation which will bring the alliance into operation. Because of universal condemnation of outright aggressive military alliances, offensive treaties seldom express their real purpose. The 1939 German-Italian "Pact of Steel," for example, provided that "If it should happen, against the wishes and hopes of the contracting parties, that one of them should become involved in warlike complications . . . the other contracting party will come to its aid as an ally and will support it with all its military forces." The term "warlike complications" is so vague that it could (and did) commit Italy to assist Hitler in almost any situation. Soviet mutual assistance treaties with Bulgaria and Romania (1948) also have such obscure definitions of the *casus foederis* ("drawn into military activities") that it is difficult to predict when and under what exact circumstances the Soviet, Romanian, and Bulgarian armies would begin military operations. In contrast to the vague *casus foederis* are those which contain a very precise definition of the situation in which the alliance is to be put into effect militarily. The NATO treaty, in Article 5, states that military measures can only be taken in response to an actual *armed attack* on one of the signatories.

Alliance treaties also differ according to the type of responses and responsibilities required once the situation calling for action develops. The Soviet-Bulgarian treaty of 1948 unequivocally provides that if one of the parties is "drawn into military activities," the other will *immediately give . . .* military and other help by all means at its disposal." This type of commitment is called a "hair-trigger" clause because it automatically commits the signatories to military action if the *casus foederis* occurs. A similar clause is found in the Brussels pact among Great Britain, France, Belgium, the Netherlands, and Luxembourg. Since the clause establishes automatic commitments, it leaves little leeway for decision-makers and diplomats to decide what to do once the *casus foederis* arises.

In contrast, some treaties only spell out vaguely the type of responses the treaty partners will make. The ANZUS treaty which ties Australia, New Zealand, and the United States into a defensive alliance system provides that each party will "act to meet the danger . . . in accordance with its constitutional processes." This treaty contains no precise military commitments, nor does it prescribe any course of action to which the parties commit themselves if one of them is attacked. Similarly, the Japanese-American security treaty of 1960 provides only for "consultations" between the parties if Japan is attacked.

Alliance responsibilities may be mutual or one-sided. Mutual defense treaties theoretically require all the signatories to assume equal commitments toward each other. According to the principles in the NATO and Warsaw treaties, an attack on any one of the signatories is to be considered an attack on all, requiring every signatory to come to the aid of the victim of aggression or armed attack. Other alliance treaties impose unequal burdens on the signatories. After "consultations," the United States may become obligated to defend Japan against external attack, but the Japanese are *not* obligated under the 1960 security treaty to assist in the defense of North America if war or invasion should occur there.

A variation of the unequal-burden treaty is the *guarantee* treaty, whereby one or more states receive guarantees for their security from a third party or parties, while the guaranteeing power or powers receive nothing in return except perhaps the possibility of enhancing stability and peace. Guarantee treaties of this variety were popular in the 1920's; one prominent example was the Locarno treaty of 1925, in which Great Britain and Italy undertook to come to the assistance of France, Belgium, or Germany, depending on which was attacked or the target of a violation of the Franco-Belgian-German frontiers. For guaranteeing these frontiers, Italy and Great Britain received in return no tangible commitments from the beneficiaries.

Alliances may also be distinguished according to the degree of integration of military forces. Alliance treaties in historic international systems seldom provided for more than casual coordination of military planning, while national forces remained organizationally and administratively distinct. European alliances in the eighteenth century typically required signatories to provide a specified number of men and/or funds for the common effort, but otherwise set forth no plans for coordinated military operations or integrating forces or commands. Any coordination that did take place was the result of *ad hoc* decisions made after hostilities began. In one of the most enduring alliances of the nineteenth century, the Austro-German Dual Alliance of 1879, rudimentary military coordination was carried out only through the services of military attachés in Vienna and Berlin, and when the alliance was put to the test in 1914, German military and political leaders knew very little about Austria's mobilization plans.

Since World War II the major leaders of both coalitions have sought to increase military integration to the extent that allied forces would operate, if war came, almost as one unified armed force. Integration may be accomplished by establishing a supreme commander of all allied forces (such as the Supreme Allied Commander, Europe, in NATO), standardizing weapons systems for all national forces, integrating military personnel of different countries into one command structure (as proposed in the ill-fated European Defense Community), or permitting one of the major alliance partners to organize, draft, and direct all strategic and tactical war plans for the other partners. Major alliances today also have permanent headquarters, continuous political and military consultants, innumerable meetings of technical experts, and a continuing avalanche of memoranda and staff studies. Alliances have become inter-governmental institutions with permanent bureaucracies.

Not only have alliances become large organizations, but the manner in which they operate has changed since the eighteenth century. In that period alliances were often concluded only *after* an armed attack had occurred, so that commitments were undertaken only for a very limited range of objectives. Today, however, alliances have a greater deterrence function. The purpose of the alliance is to prevent crises and increase diplomatic influence, not just to fight a war. Major contemporary alliances are built on the assumption of *bloc* politics, and on the presence of almost permanently congruent foreign policy objectives or permanent external threats. The lengthy sequence of threat perception-crisis-mobilization-declaration of war—a sequence that in the eighteenth century often lasted several months—can no longer be assumed with the new technology of warfare. The elements of speed and surprise vital to military success require that alliance commitments and war plans be agreed upon and drafted *before* any crisis occurs. In comparison to 200 years ago, alliance systems today are less flexible, more permanent, and more highly organized.

Finally, alliances differ with respect to the scope of their coverage. Soviet mutual aid treaties are designed to cover only the territory of the state that is attacked or "drawn into military activities," but one of the major problems in drafting and interpreting the NATO treaty concerned whether the signatories could be committed to defend the overseas colonies or territories of France or Great Britain. The French and British governments insisted that NATO obligations extend to at least some of their overseas territories, so Article 5 of the treaty was drafted to read: ". . . an armed attack on one or more of the parties is deemed to include an attack on the territory of any of the Parties . . . , on the Algerian department of France, on the occupation forces of any Party in Europe, on the islands under the jurisdiction of any Party in the North Atlantic area north of the Tropic of Cancer, or on the vessels or aircraft in this area of any of the parties." In 1965, coverage of the Treaty was extended to Malta, which had received protection under Article 5 by virtue of being "an island under the jurisdiction of" Great Britain, but which received its independence in 1964.

Although these distinctions relating to the forms and types of alliances may seem quite technical, they are important because precise definitions of scope, *casus foederis,* and obligations lend predictability to the responses alliance partners will make in crisis situations. Predictability is an important element in international stability and may become crucial in crisis situations. One of the main objections against secret treaties and alliances is that decision-makers cannot plan actions and predict responses of both friends and potential enemies if they are not familiar with treaty commitments and obligations. However, it must be acknowledged that treaties do not provide complete predictability, and that the circumstances of the moment will largely determine the types of responses which alliance partners make in critical times. The NATO treaty, for example, stipulates that the parties will decide how to commit themselves only at the time an "armed attack" takes place against one of the signatories. Yet, if the Soviets launched a massive invasion of Western Europe, there is little doubt that previously drafted retaliatory plans of the NATO bureaucracy would come into effect almost instantaneously, with slight latitude for negotiations and discussions among the treaty partners. In such a situation, even when alliance commitments are common knowledge, do alliance strategies succeed?

No generalizations can be offered as to whether defensive alliances successfully deter aggression or provide stability for the international system. Presumably a potential aggressor faced with an overwhelming coalition against it will not risk destruction of its society when it possesses foreknowledge of certain defeat. Yet, decision-makers do not always behave rationally in crisis situations, and there are enough examples (discussed in more detail in Chapter XII) of their going to war knowing that the probability of success was low to disprove this presumption. All we can say is that alliances probably inject a factor of caution among decision-makers with aggressive designs; defensive alliances increase greatly the risks and costs to the aggressor, but do not necessarily prevent organized violence. We can only speculate on the wars that did not begin because alliances effectively performed the deterrence function, but both past and present reveal occasions when defensive alliances failed to deter, lower tensions, or promote stability in the system.

### Strains in Alliances

Aside from poor military coordination or planning, one reason that alliances may fail to deter potential aggressors is because they lack political cohesiveness or are riven by internal quarrels and political disagreements. Presumably any military coalition will be more effective to the extent that its members agree on the major objectives to be achieved, help each other diplomatically, and trust that once the *casus foederis* arises, the partners will in fact meet their commitments. In any international system comprised of independent and sovereign states, however, there is no automatic guarantee that even the most solemn undertakings will be fulfilled if those commitments are in conflict with the prevailing interests of different governments. Several situations can cause strains in alliances, impairing their effectiveness both as deterrents and as fighting organizations.

The first is when two or more parties create an alliance for essentially different purposes. If all partners of a defensive military coalition perceive a common enemy or threat, the alliance is likely to withstand strains caused by ideological incompatibilities or distrust arising from personality differences between political leaders. But if the objectives are incongruent, or the potential enemy of one alliance partner is not the enemy of the other, serious problems of cooperation and coordination arise and make the alliance more formal than real. The Franco-Prussian alliance of 1741, for instance, lasted only several years before the diverging objectives of the signatories led to bitter quarrels over the prosecution of military campaigns. Frederick the Great was interested above all in destroying Austria and detaching Bohemia from Maria Theresa's realm, while French policy-makers, less interested in dealing a blow to Austria, wanted to drive the English from the continent in general, and from Flanders in particular. The Prussians were hardly interested in these French objectives, with the result that there was no coordination of military operations, no trust in each other's diplomatic maneuvers, and ultimately, no alliance. Similarly, the Anglo-Austrian alliance of the 1740's suffered serious strains when it became increasingly clear that Britain's major interest was in protecting its Hanoverian territories, while Austria's predominant foreign policy objective was to crush Prussia.

More recently, the American-Pakistan alliance organized through SEATO has been more a means through which Pakistan has received arms than a coalition leading to meaningful diplomatic cooperation. When the United States induced Pakistan to join SEATO in 1954, it regarded the Moslem country as a bulwark against communism. The purpose of the alliance, as seen from Washington, was to prevent Russia or Communist China from moving into South Asia. Pakistan, however, concluded the alliance primarily to obtain American arms and diplomatic support against India, its traditional enemy. Diplomatic relations between the United States and Pakistan reached a low point in the 1960's when Pakistan criticized the United States for failure to lend it support on the Kashmir issue and, as the Pakistan government saw it, for giving comfort to the Indians. Left virtually isolated on the Kashmir problem, Pakistan turned increasingly to Communist China, which was also embroiled in a border conflict with India. The American response to Pakistan's flirtation with China was manifested in reduction of economic and military aid. American diplomats desperately tried to induce the government of Pakistan to reiterate that the "common enemy" was China, a view the Pakistanis could not easily accept so long as their only diplomatic support against India came from Peking.[7]

A second factor which leads to strains in military alliances is incompatibility of the major social and political values of allying states. By themselves, ideological incompatibilities seldom prevent formation of military coalitions so long as the parties face a common enemy. But such

[7] Cf., Mohammed Ayub Kahn, "The Pakistan-American Alliance: Stresses and Strains," *Foreign Affairs*, XLII (1964), 195–209.

alliances are constantly confronted with misunderstandings and suspicion, usually expressed in unwillingness to share military secrets, coordinate military programs and campaigns, and a decided feeling that the other alliance partner is failing to live up to its commitments. During World War II, the Soviet Union, which for two decades had urged and worked for the overthrow of "decadent" bourgeois regimes in Western Europe, eagerly formed an alliance with these regimes once it was attacked by Germany. The threat posed by Nazi Germany to the rest of the world was so apparent that even Western liberal democrats and conservatives supported the alliance with the Communists. On the other hand, the wartime alliance operated with many irritations because of deep-seated attitudes of distrust and ideological differences. Stalin feared that the Western Allies would make a separate peace with Germany, leaving the Nazis free to crush Bolshevism; alternately, he interpreted the failure of the Allies to invade France before 1944 as evidence of their intention to let the Nazis and Communists bleed each other to death so that the capitalists could come in later to pick up the pieces. Even at the administrative level, distrust was reflected in Stalin's refusal to allow British and American military officials observe Russian operations in the field, let the Western Allies establish air bases on Russian territory, or permit Lend-lease officers to investigate Russian military and matériel requirements. The allied wartime coalition was only a temporary marriage of convenience.

Even more unlikely was the Nazi-Soviet non-aggression treaty of 1939, concluded after six years of unprecedented vituperation and hysterical propaganda between Russia and Germany, in which each side tried to demonstrate that the enemy's ideology was the incarnation of evil. And yet, certain common interests did arise in the diplomatic situation preceding the outbreak of war in the fall of 1939, interests that united the two countries into a semblance of alliance for almost two years. Hitler desired to avoid a two-front war, and the only way he felt he could accomplish this was to ensure that the Soviet government would not form an anti-German coalition with the Western powers. The Soviet government also wanted something that could be obtained only with German acquiescence—territory in the Baltic states and Poland which would provide the Russians with better defenses against Germany. The famous non-aggression treaty of 1939 was thus based on the overlapping of strategic interests. Relations between the two countries following conclusion of the treaty were not cordial, even though the Russians, at the expense of Communist parties throughout the world, seriously attempted to fulfill their commitments. The Germans, however, did not concede their ultimate objective of conquering Russia, and the preparations they took for final invasion to the East did not fail to arouse suspicions in Moscow.

Since World War II, the United States has entered into military alliances with several states whose internal political institutions offer a contrast with American preferences. Though often justified as necessary to "defend freedom," the American security treaties with Nationalist China and, through NATO, with Portugal, can hardly be justified on ideological grounds. These alliances are based, rather, on common perceptions of threat and overlapping strategic interests. If anything, the differences in social and political values between the alliance partners create friction and public embarrassment. On the other hand, the Anglo-American alliance is strong and withstands frequent disagreements between the two partners not just because the over-all interests of the two countries coincide, but also because the two countries represent similar cultural, political, and social traditions.

Development of nuclear weapons may, finally, have divisive effects on modern alliances. In the post-World War II period, most states of Western Europe were eager to receive the protection of the American "nuclear umbrella." Militarily weak, they had no capacity to deter a possible Soviet invasion carried out by the massive Red Army in Eastern Europe, and had to allocate their scarce resources for rebuilding their war-torn economies. By the 1960's the situation had changed. Europe was recovered economically and entering a period of unprecedented prosperity. The Russians no longer possessed a military manpower advantage as compared to NATO. Most important, the nuclear monopoly held by the United States in the late 1940's and early 1950's had come to an end. Washington, New York, and Houston were as vulnerable to Russian nuclear attack as Leningrad, Moscow, and Baku were to an American nuclear salvo. In a system of Soviet-American *mutual* deterrence, some observers—particularly French military officials—questioned whether the United States would be willing to destroy itself in order to protect Western Europe from the Soviet Union.

These officials underlined their doubts by publicizing simple hypothetical situations. Suppose the Soviet government decided to take over West Berlin, an action the Russian army in East Germany could carry out with a minimum of immediate Western military resistance. Would the United States retaliate with nuclear weapons against the Russians, knowing the Russians would respond immediately against American cities? In citing such situations, these observers have raised a fundamental question of military planning in the nuclear age. Is a deterrent really credible if the guaranteeing power—in this case the United States—knows beforehand that it must destroy itself to save others? During the 1960's the French government has argued that though it finds no fault with American *intentions* to defend Europe, it is not convinced that in all possible crisis situations the Americans could be expected to live up to their commitments. This is not a uniquely American weakness, they point out. It is a fact of international life that no state will likely invite its own destruction in order to defend others. In this kind of nuclear stalemate situation, the "others" must be armed with nuclear weapons so that if the "nuclear umbrella" fails to operate, smaller allies would still have independent means of deterring possible moves against their vital interests. It is to cover the 5 per cent of hypothetical cases when the United States might not retaliate, the French argue, that Europeans must have their own nuclear weapons.

By itself, this type of reasoning would not create serious strains in an alliance—unless the holder of the "nuclear umbrella" does not want its allies to possess such weapons. This, indeed, has been the case in NATO, for just as the French have been concerned that the United States deterrent may not be totally reliable, so American planners have expressed a fear that if the French develop an independent nuclear capacity —as they have—they might use the weapons in a manner contrary to American interests. It is assumed in Washington that if the French ever use their nuclear weapons, the situation would automatically drag the United States into the war. American strategists also point out that if the French should have independent nuclear weapons, why shouldn't the Germans, Dutch, Belgians, and Italians have them as well? An alliance in which each nation is independently drafting plans to fight *its* kind of war for *its* political objectives is an alliance bound to lack coordination and common purpose. It is one of the paradoxes of nuclear weapons that though they are supposed to provide increased security for alliances, they may create political dissension instead. Because the consequences of nuclear war are potentially so terrible, a doubt must be raised about any alliance commitments in the atomic age: in the crisis, will any state risk its own destruction to save others?

### Summary

Levels of interaction and involvement among states in any international system vary widely. Some units are highly involved in world or regional affairs and make formal commitments of resources in many areas in order to achieve or protect their values and interests. Other states are isolated in many ways from the rest of the world. Their domestic policies have little impact on the fate of other societies and events abroad have little effect on their internal conditions. The level of involvement of a given state is related to systemic and domestic conditions, social and economic needs, and capabilities. Levels of involvement also vary from issue to issue.

All states adopt through cumulative decisions one of several basic foreign policy strategies or orientations. These also reflect a government's major external objectives and its general level of involvement in international politics. Isolation is the most difficult strategy to sustain today because many conditions which formerly made it an attractive alternative no longer exist. Non-alignment displays some of the characteristics of isolation, but it is designed primarily to avoid the "spill over" effects of bloc rivalries and meet domestic economic and political needs. Non-alignment is characterized by unwillingness to make any military commitments to, or provide any military privileges for, the major blocs. It does not, however, require states to avoid all types of coalitions; in fact, non-aligned states constantly form diplomatic and economic coalitions among themselves to achieve certain common objectives. Among conditions necessary or helpful to sustain a strategy or orientation of non-alignment are the benevolent disposition of the major powers, domestic political stability, capacity to resist those who would compromise a state's neutrality, and reasonable distance from the main areas of bloc conflict. Alliance strategies are prominent among those states which have a relatively high level of involvement in international problems and which perceive a common threat to their interests and values. Alliances are also concluded occasionally to help bolster weak regimes from internal rather than external threats.

This and the preceding chapters have examined how political units orient themselves toward the external environment. Gross patterns of behavior and types of relationships have been accounted for in part by the structure of the system in which the units operate, as well as by major economic, technological, and social changes and needs.

When we want to assess more specific aspects of international politics, we must concentrate more heavily on the individual characteristics and peculiarities of each state and its governing officials, remembering that even the day-to-day actions of political units are influenced by the structure of the system, its major rules, and a state's general orientation to the outside world. In the next chapter we begin by exploring some of the common types of objectives which political units typically seek to achieve or defend.

## SELECTED BIBLIOGRAPHY

Anabtawi, Samir N., "Neutralists and Neutralism," *Journal of Politics,* XXVII (1965), 351–61.

Bowie, Robert, "Tensions Within the Alliance," *Foreign Affairs,* XLII (1963), 49–69.

Brecher, Michael, "Neutralism: An Analysis," *International Journal*, XVII (1962), 224–36.

Buchan, Alastair, *NATO in the 1960's*. New York: Frederick A. Praeger, Inc., 1960.

Claude, Inis, Jr., *Power and International Relations*. New York: Random House, Inc., 1962.

Cotrell, Alvin J., and James E. Dougherty, *The Politics of the Atlantic Alliance*. New York: Frederick A. Praeger, Inc., 1964.

Crabb, Cecil V., Jr., *The Elephants and the Grass: A Study of Nonalignment*. New York: Frederick A. Praeger, Inc., 1965.

Deane, John R., *The Strange Alliance*. New York: The Viking Press, Inc., 1947.

de Rose, François, "Atlantic Relationships and Nuclear Problems," *Foreign Affairs*, XLI (1963), 479–90.

Dinerstein, Herbert S., "The Transformation of Alliance Systems," *American Political Science Review*, LIX (1965), 589–601.

Freymond, Jacques, "The European Neutrals and the Atlantic Community," in *The Atlantic Community: Progress and Prospects*, eds. Francis O. Wilcox and H. Field Haviland, Jr. New York: Frederick A. Praeger, Inc., 1963.

Haas, Ernst B., "The Balance of Power as A Guide to Policy-Making," *Journal of Politics*, XV (1953), 370–98.

———, "The Balance of Power: Prescription, Concept, or Propaganda?" *World Politics*, V (1953), 442–77.

Hoffmann, Stanley, "De Gaulle, Europe, and the Atlantic Alliance," *International Organization*, XIII (1964), 1–28.

Holsti, K. J., "Strategy and Techniques of Influence in Soviet-Finnish Relations," *The Western Political Quarterly*, XVII (1964), 63–82.

Knorr, Klaus, ed., *NATO and American Security*. Princeton: Princeton University Press, 1959.

Leifer, Michael, *Cambodia and Neutrality*. Canberra: Australian National University Press, 1962.

Liska, George, *Nations in Alliance: The Limits of Interdependence*. Baltimore: Johns Hopkins Press, 1962.

Low-Beer, Francis, "The Concept of Neutralism," *American Political Science Review*, LVIII (1964), 383–91.

Lyon, Peter, *Neutralism*. Leicester: Leicester University Press, 1964.

Martin, Laurance, ed., *Neutralism and Non-Alignment: The New States in World Affairs*. New York: Frederick A. Praeger, Inc., 1962.

Modelski, George, ed., *SEATO: Six Studies*. Melbourne, Australia: Cheshire, 1962.

Nayer, N. P., "Non-Alignment in World Affairs," *India Quarterly*, XVIII (1962), 28–57.

Osgood, Robert E., *NATO: The Entangling Alliance*. Chicago: University of Chicago Press, 1962.

Power, Paul F., ed., *Neutralism and Disengagement.* New York: Charles Scribner's Sons, 1964.

Sayegh, Fayez A., ed., *The Dynamics of Neutralism in the Arab World: A Symposium.* San Francisco: Howard Chandler, Publisher, 1964.

Sen, Chanakya, pseud., *Against the Cold War: A Study of Asian-African Policies Since World War II.* New York: Asia Publishing House, 1962.

Singer, J. David, and Melvin Small, "Formal Alliances, 1815–1939," *Journal of Peace Research,* No. 1 (1966), pp. 1–32.

Stehlin, Paul, "The Evolution of Western Defense," *Foreign Affairs,* XLII (1963), 70–83.

Wolfers, Arnold, ed., *Alliance Policy and the Cold War.* Baltimore: Johns Hopkins Press, 1959.

# Foreign Policy Objectives

Some aspects of international politics and foreign policy, such as general foreign policy orientations and latitude of choice, can be accounted for by reference to systemic conditions. But political units do not just react or adjust to limitations imposed by the external environment. Societies have *purposes,* many of which can only be achieved by influencing the behavior of other states. To understand state behavior adequately, we must, in addition to systemic conditions, discuss general types of objectives which are the basis of many foreign policy actions. Here we move from the systemic, or macroscopic, level of analysis, to concentrate on characteristics of individual states.

Surprisingly little attention has been devoted to the types of collective interests and values political units seek to achieve in different international systems. Libraries abound with ancient and modern diplomatic histories which describe the motives and objectives of statesmen, but these usually emphasize the unique

# Chapter V

aspects of objectives, rather than the similarities or the domestic and international needs which helped shape them. Perhaps statesmen themselves are partly to blame for the lack of systematic analyses of collective interests and values as expressed in foreign policies, for except in some crisis situations, they seldom explain in detail what it is they are attempting to achieve. When a prime minister claims, for instance, that "our objectives are peace, security, and the fulfillment of our legitimate aspirations," he has not really enlightened anyone about what his policies are designed to accomplish. Another reason, perhaps, is the popularity of simple theories concerning the external objectives of states. Some have argued that all states seek to increase their power at the expense of others, or that the only objective of Soviet Russia's foreign policy is to conquer the world. Communists claim that by virtue of the laws of economic development, capitalist societies pursue only imperialist objectives. Though there may be elements of reality in such assertions, these simplistic theories fail to provide explanations or descriptions of the variety of contemporary collective interests and values. Nation states are *multi-purpose* entities, whose objectives express no single factor such as a "desire for power." Their behavior is conditioned by a combination of environmental (systemic) characteristics, immediate actions by other states which impinge on the interests or values of the state in question, and domestic social and economic needs.

Sometimes the term "national interest" has been used (or abused) as a device for analyzing nations' objectives. There has developed in the United States, in fact, a prolonged scholarly debate on the meaning of this concept, but little agreement has arisen. The vagueness of the concept is its main shortcoming. As Paul Seabury has noted,

> The idea of national interest may refer to some *ideal* set of purposes which a nation . . . *should* seek to realize in the conduct of its foreign relations. Wanting a better word, we might call this a *normative,* civic concept of national interest. . . . A second meaning of equal importance might be called *descriptive.* In this sense the national interest may be regarded as those purposes which the nation, through its leadership, appears to pursue persistently through time. When we speak of the national interest in this descriptive sense, we move out of the metaphysical into the realms of facts. . . . It might similarly be said that the national interest is what foreign policy-makers say it is. A third definition might make the meaning of national interest somewhat clearer. The American national interest has often been an arena for conflict amongst individuals and groups whose conceptions of it . . . have differed widely. Disagreement about policy and action may arise even among men who are essentially in agreement about the general aims of their country in the world. But policy disagreements are usually due to differences

among policy-makers about conceptions both of what the United States is and what its role in world politics, even its mission, should be.[1]

Though there may be some immutable national interests such as self-preservation, to which everyone will agree, no one can claim with certainty that any other specific goal or set of goals is in the national interest.

Therefore, we will avoid the term and substitute the concept of *objective,* which is essentially an "image" of a future state of affairs and future set of conditions which governments through individual policy-makers aspire to bring about by wielding influence abroad and by changing or sustaining the behavior of other states.[2] The future state of affairs may refer to concrete conditions, such as passing a resolution in the General Assembly or annexing territory, or to values, such as the promotion and achievement of popularity, prestige, or democracy abroad, or to a combination of the two. Some objectives remain constant over centuries and directly involve the lives and welfare of all members of a national society. Others change almost daily and concern only a handful of government personnel and citizens (e.g., tariffs on strawberries). These types of objectives are the interests of private individuals and groups, promoted by governments for the welfare of a few citizens. They are private interests translated into public policy.

Even if we use the concept of objective to describe the great variety of collective interests and values that operate in international politics, we should not assume that foreign ministers and diplomats spend all of their time carefully formulating logical and coherent sets of collective and/or private goals to pursue systematically through the rational ordering of means to ends. Some statesmen or governments have, of course, spent time and resources to define the ultimate goals of their actions. Charles de Gaulle has formulated a set of goals for France which, even if described in fairly mystical terms, has been carefully thought out in accordance with his interpretations of historical development and France's "destiny" in that development. Not all his policies have been compatible with achievement of the goals, but generally he has persisted in his plans despite widespread criticism from France's major allies.

If there are examples where governments operate to fulfill a series of

[1] Paul Seabury, *Power, Freedom, and Diplomacy: The Foreign Policy of the United States of America* (New York: Random House, Inc., 1963), p. 86.
[2] Richard C. Snyder, H. W. Bruck, and Burton Sapin, "Decision-Making As An Approach to International Politics," in *Foreign Policy Decision-Making,* eds. Richard C. Snyder, H. W. Bruck, and Burton Sapin (New York: Free Press of Glencoe, Inc., 1962), p. 82; see also George Modelski, *A Theory of Foreign Policy* (New York: Frederick A. Praeger, Inc., 1962), pp. 8–11, 50.

logically consistent goals, there are many more where they do not seem to be working toward the achievement of any specific objective or where, at best, they improvise policies to meet specific domestic or external crises or commitments. This is not surprising, for most transactions between governments are routine and unplanned, and serve primarily the interests and needs of a few private citizens. The work of a foreign office frequently appears to develop in a completely random fashion, with no discernible relationship between decisions arrived at and policies conducive to the achievement of collective goals. As one British diplomat has claimed, "most important decisions are often made, not as part of a concerted and far-sighted policy, but under the urgent pressure of some immediate crisis."[3] His comment is typical of criticisms aimed at the foreign policies of many countries, namely that these governments have no real policies but only respond to the initiatives of others. They are concerned with solving problems as they arise, not with defining long-range objectives and formulating the means to achieve them. Some of the great foreign policies of the United States, such as the European Recovery Program, were products of planning, delineation of objectives, and assessment of costs. But, as Paul Seabury points out:

> All too often policy is the product of random, haphazard, or even irrational forces and events. Equally often it is the result of dead-locked judgements, an uneasy compromise formula. Often what appears on the surface as a nation's settled course of action may be due to indecision, unwillingness or inability to act. It may be no policy at all but simply a drift with events. Sometimes foreign policies are the products of statesmen's passive compliance with strong domestic political pressure—and thus products of contending political forces within the nation itself. Finally, policy may be due to statesmen's abdication of choice and rational judgement in the face of ruthless and strong external pressures.[4]

A second point we must remember when using the concept of objective is that governments often pursue incompatible private and collective interest and value objectives simultaneously. It is the task of policy-makers to rank and choose among conflicting objectives, and determine which are feasible within a specific set of circumstances. Disarmament, for example, has been conceived by many governments as both an end in itself and a means to achieve increased national security from foreign military threats. Yet, the implementation of any disarmament scheme would incur serious short-term risks to any nation's security. Many

---

[3] Quoted in Anthony Sampson, *Anatomy of Britain* (New York: Harper & Row, Publishers, 1962), p. 311.

[4] Seabury, *Power, Freedom, and Diplomacy*, p. 5.

objectives of Soviet foreign policy seem to be similarly incompatible. Lenin often claimed that the interests of both the Russian nation and the Soviet state should be subordinated to the goals of proletarian internationalism, that is, to the victory of world revolution. But Stalin reversed Lenin's thesis and followed policies which promoted Soviet strength, often at the expense of foreign Communist parties. More recently the Soviet government has distributed foreign aid to regimes—as in Iraq and Egypt—which persecute Communists. There is almost constant conflict among Soviet policy-makers who must attempt to reconcile short-run political and diplomatic goals with an ideological commitment to support the "international proletarian movement." Americans, too, have had their share of difficulties in reconciling policy objectives. For over four decades the United States has publicly proclaimed its support for the principle of self-determination, national independence, and its sympathy for anticolonial movements; but it has also had to support NATO allies which were attempting to retain their overseas territories by using American-supplied arms against native independence movements.

## Types of Objectives in Historical Systems

Among primitive tribes, distinction between collective interests of the political unit and private interests of its members is not always clear. Anthropological investigations of such groups as the Veddas, Australian aborigines, the Fuegians, and some North American Indians have revealed that, with the exception of common grazing rights, these people developed few *collective* interests which they had to achieve or protect in relations with other groups or tribes. Yet, when one member of the collectivity was harmed in any way by outsiders, it became the collective duty of his own people to inflict revenge on the wrongdoer or his tribe. External objectives became more complex as tribal units achieved a higher level of civilization. Many groups became more sedentary and based their existence on a particular piece of territory which they had to defend or extend against others to survive. Other important collective objectives were access to, and rights over, water and communication routes. Independent political groups learned later the value of goods and slaves, which eventually became the objects of group conquest. Further economic and social development brought awareness of the needs or advantages of imperialism. In addition to plundering and robbing neighbors for goods and slaves, such groups as the Vikings, the early Anglo-Saxons, and the Danes systematically *occupied* and settled regions formerly held by militarily inferior peoples.

The promotion of value objectives through religious expansion or cultural imperialism is also typical of political units with concepts of collective interests. Drives for expansion in the Chou empire were often motivated by a desire to bring the "barbarians" the benefits of Chinese culture. Forced conversion of the "heathen" to the Islamic religion was a major objective in the Saracen campaigns across North Africa and into Spain and France in the seventh and eighth centuries, while appeals to regain the Holy Land to destroy the Islamic "infidel" led to a series of crusades from Europe during the Middle Ages. Although in later years commercial agents used the crusades to destroy the influence of economic competitors in the Mediterranean area, these mass journeys were essentially motivated by Christian zeal. Plunder, booty, or territorial annexation were not objectives; on the contrary, the crusades often cost their leaders personal wealth and sometimes their fiefdoms as well. Religious conversion was also one of the major goals in construction of Spain's overseas empire.

In the fifteenth and sixteenth centuries, Europe was composed of a complex of political units, including the largely symbolic Holy Roman Empire, dynastic states covering large and often non-contiguous areas, and hundreds of small dukedoms, religious states, and walled cities. The range of objectives among these units was equally wide. The Italian city states were in almost constant warfare over issues of papal succession or objectives of territorial expansion and plunder. Conflicts also developed from the personal rivalries and ambitions of princes and were settled, like feuds, by private armies. International politics were typified by the conflicting private interests of dynasts and princes. And yet, higher purposes reflecting prevailing social and religious values were also to be observed. The policies of Charles V, Holy Roman Emperor, King of Spain, ruler of the Austrian territories, the Netherlands, and various Italian holdings, were directed both toward extending his personal Hapsburg empire and creating a unified, Christian Europe. While he committed money and men to pursuit of his own glory and expansion of his personal wealth, he also led crusades against Islam in the Mediterranean area and Hungary.

In the early seventeenth century, international politics became particularly violent as extreme religious differences between Protestants and Catholics exacerbated the international tensions already caused by dynastic ambitions. Religious ideology became identified in the person of each dynast; whereas ordinary people in the various realms could not be counted upon to support the territorial or family interests of their kings and princes, once religious issue became involved, they committed themselves fully to the great conflicts. The Thirty Years' War (1618–1648), for example, involved a degree of violence, devastation, and ideological fervor that was not to be seen again until the wars of the French Revolution. As in our own age, friends and foes were identified more by what they believed than by what they sought.

The European state system in the eighteenth century is particularly interesting because its members pursued in their external relations a combination of personal, dynastic, religious, private, commercial, and *national* objectives. Since monarchs believed (with the exception of Frederick the Great) that they ruled by divine right, and attributed their sovereignty and absolutism to the Lord of Creation, they considered their own family interests their most important concerns. The state served primarily as a vehicle for protecting the wealth, security, and patrimony of a particular dynastic line.[5] Among Louis XIV's main objectives, to which he committed the skills of his diplomats, were to place a Bourbon on the throne of Spain and obtain his own election as Holy Roman Emperor. In the same period the English kings were as much concerned with family interests in Hanover as with various threats to England posed by Spain or France. Some of the important diplomatic crises and wars between states in the eighteenth century arose from conflicting claims of private families.

Eighteenth century states in Europe also pursued objectives which had little relationship to private dynastic interests—except that often they reflected on the prestige of monarchs. These included colonial ventures and expansion of trade and commerce. Statesmen such as Cardinal Fleury and Sir Robert Walpole exemplified those ministers who were increasingly organizing their policy objectives around other than religious or dynastic considerations. They had to respond to rising commercial interests and demands, and thought in terms of national capabilities and national prestige. In addition to safeguarding dynastic objectives, these men quarreled over trade routes, rules governing navigation, strategic frontiers, colonies, and naval proficiency, all of which came to be regarded—not only in the courts but also among the developing middle classes—as vital collective interests to be secured, extended, or defended. The major wars of the eighteenth century illustrate the rise of national objectives: the War of the Austrian Succession, as its name implies, concerned dynastic interests, but Frederick the Great's invasion of Silesia, trade rivalry, and the lure of colonial empire were important issues as well; and in the Seven Years' War (1757–1763), commercial and colonial objectives reflecting middle class interests, as well as the British desire to

---

[5] Cf., Walter L. Dorn, *Competition for Empire, 1740–1763* (New York: Harper & Row, Publishers, 1940), p. 10.

obtain a monopoly of sea power, far outweighed dynastic concerns as factors in the conflict.

Even in our own era political units seek to achieve a complete range of private and collective, concrete and value objectives. In some areas, state interests are still indistinguishable from dynastic interests. It is questionable, for example, whether the former King of Saudi Arabia or some recently bygone Latin American dictators perceived that the interests of their country might be distinct from their private family interests. To them, the primary objectives of foreign policy were to protect their ruling position and secure quantities of personal wealth and prestige. On the other extreme we find governments which commit national resources to the expansion of messianic philosophies, regardless of what the effects will be on the personal lives, prestige, and fortunes of those who formulate these objectives. Between these extremes exist the vast majority of modern states which seek to achieve collective objectives of national security, welfare of citizens, access to trade routes, markets, and vital resources, and sometimes the territory of their neighbors. Given the wide range of objectives that exist today, then, how can they be classified?

One method might be to distinguish among military, economic, political, and ideological objectives, but divisions between such categories are not at all clear and it is doubtful whether policy-makers operate in terms of these criteria—even if most governments contain separate departments dealing with the military, economic, political, and ideological aspects of foreign policy. A second scheme might classify objectives according to geographic area: what are a particular state's objectives toward its immediate neighbors? the states in a neighboring continent? or areas on the other side of the world? This scheme would correspond to actual government organization, since most foreign offices are subdivided into geographic bureaus and sections. But if we wish to make general statements about *types* of objectives, then the nation-by-nation description of policies would be largely repetitive. Instead, we will employ a combination of three criteria: (1) the *value* placed on the objective, or the extent to which policy-makers commit themselves and their countries' resources to achieving a particular objective; (2) the *time element* placed on its achievement; and (3) the kinds of *demands* the objective imposes on other states in the system. From these we can construct categories of objectives such as the following: (1) "core" values and interests, to which governments and nations commit their very existence and which must be preserved or extended at all times (achievement of these values or interests may or may not impose demands on others); (2) middle-range goals which normally impose demands on several other states (commitments to their achievement are serious and some time limits are usually

attached to them); and (3) universal long-range goals, which seldom
have definite time limits.[6] In practice statesmen rarely place the highest
value on long-range goals and do not, consequently, commit many
national capabilities or policies to their achievement—unless the goals
are central to a political philosophy or ideology, in which case they
may be considered "core" or middle-range interests. Those states which
work actively toward achieving universal long-range goals usually
make radical demands on *all* other units in the system and thus create
great instability.

### "Core" Interests and Values

"Core" values and interests can be described as those kinds of goals for
which most people are willing to make ultimate sacrifices. They are
usually stated in the form of basic "principles" of foreign policy and
become the articles of faith which a society accepts uncritically.[7] Such
terms as "command of the sea," a "frontier on the Rhine," and the
"Monroe Doctrine" suggest basic foreign policy orientations, attitudes
towards others, or goals which at one time were held sacrosanct by entire
communities.

"Core" interests and values are most frequently related to the self-
preservation of a political unit. These are short-range objectives because
other goals obviously cannot be achieved unless the political units pursuing them maintain their own existence. The exact definition of a "core"
value or interest in any given country depends on the attitudes of those
who make policy. There are, for example, many different interpretations
of self-preservation. Some disagree over definitions of self—that is, what
constitutes an integrated polity. Others will disagree equally on what
policies contribute best to preservation. Some colonial regimes have been
willing to grant independence to indigenous peoples voluntarily, while
others have considered that overseas holdings constitute an integral part
of the nation which must be defended at all costs. Nevertheless, most
policy-makers in our era assume that the most essential objective of any

---

[6] Arnold Wolfers has outlined an alternative scheme for classifying goals. He
distinguishes between *aspirations* and genuine *policy goals,* which correspond roughly
to the distinction between long-range goals and others of more immediate importance.
*Possession goals* refer to the achievement of national values and needs, while *milieu
goals* are those conditions outside of the nation state itself which a state seeks to
change. Wolfers also distinguishes between *national goals* and *indirect goals* which
correspond roughly to my concepts of "collective interests" and "private interests." See
Arnold Wolfers, "The Goals of Foreign Policy," in his *Discord and Collaboration:
Essays in International Politics* (Baltimore: The Johns Hopkins Press, 1962), Chap. 5.
[7] Modelski, *A Theory of Foreign Policy,* p. 86.

foreign policy is to ensure defense of the *home* territory and perpetuate a particular political, social, and economic system based on that territory.

Some governments place equally great value on controlling or defending neighboring territories because these areas contain assets such as manpower and raw materials which can increase a state's capabilities, or because they believe that the major threat to their own territorial integrity might materialize through adjacent lands. Achievement of favorable strategic frontiers has been a traditional short-run policy objective to which states have been willing to commit great resources. Fearing repeated invasions from Germany, the French for many years placed more value on securing the Rhine River frontier than on defending some of the less important French provinces against Italian encroachment. Russians have traditionally attempted to dominate the areas between themselves and Western Europe, and the Soviets today are fully committed to the defense of Eastern Europe. They would probably react, as the Warsaw Treaty stipulates, to an attack on this territory as if it were an attack on the Soviet Union itself. The United States has similarly pledged through the NATO treaty to consider an attack on one of its European allies as an attack on itself. The objective of safeguarding American security by defending Western Europe has persisted since 1949 despite changes in administration in Washington. There is, then, almost unanimous agreement in the United States that the territorial integrity and independence of the Western European countries constitute a "core" interest of the United States.

After self-preservation and defense of strategically vital areas, another prominent "core" value or interest is ethnic, religious, or linguistic unity. Today, no less than in the great era of nationalism in the nineteenth century, the most legitimate bases of frontiers correspond to ethnic, linguistic, or religious divisions. Territories carved up according to historical or strategic criteria, where ethnic groups are arbitrarily divided between sovereignties, are likely to become areas of conflict as neighboring states attempt to "liberate" their own kin from foreign rule. Irredentist movements, subversion, and sometimes racial warfare are often the products of frontiers which divide ethnic, linguistic, or religious groups. In almost all areas where such arbitrary divisions occur, governments make reunification a major objective of foreign policies, and sometimes place such a high value upon it that they are willing to employ large-scale force to achieve it. The Aaland Island dispute between Finland and Sweden, the Karelian war of 1921–1922 between Finland and the Soviet Union, several conflicts in central Europe and the Balkans in the interwar period, the Sudetenland crisis of 1937–1938, as well as the serious problem between the Netherlands and Indonesia over West Irian, the Kashmir wars, intermittent crises in Germany, arguments between

Austria and Italy over the Tyrol, and tensions between Kenya and Somaliland, and Somaliland and Ethiopia have arisen since World War II essentially because one government attempted through threats, subversion, or outright military attack to incorporate into its own territory ethnically related people living in neighboring states.

The kinds of demands that pursuit of these "core" values or interests require of other actors in the system vary. States with well-established frontiers corresponding to ethnic divisions, which protect their territories and social orders through ordinary defense policies, are not likely to disturb even their immediate neighbors. Those which seek more favorable strategic frontiers or ethnic unity normally do so at the expense of the "core" values and interests of their neighbors, and thus create dangerous conflicts.

Such conflicts may not always lead to violence or war because interpretations of "core" values or "vital interests" may change under different circumstances. The British were willing for decades to fight against any internal or external assaults on their empire as if they were fighting for the city of London. But in 1945 the economic and military strains of maintaining the empire were so great that many British leaders recognized they could no longer consider the colonies as "core" interests to be preserved at all costs. A bizarre interpretation of "core" values and interests was the view propounded by Lenin that the development of world revolution was more important than saving either his Bolshevik regime or the independence of the Russian nation.[8] It was partly because of his exceptional commitment to world revolution that he was willing to concede to Germany in the Brest-Litovsk treaty almost one-quarter of Russia's traditional territory and one-half of its population. In this case, although the objective of world revolution was a middle-range goal if we are using the criterion of time, in terms of the value Lenin placed on its achievement it was a "core" interest. Lenin's successors have displayed quite different—and more traditional—attitudes, however, through their claims that the defense of Russian territory and the Soviet state, rather than promotion of revolution, is the first foreign policy priority.[9] Lenin's

---

[8] Lenin's priority on the "world revolution" is illustrated by comments he made shortly after the Bolshevik revolution to a group of his friends: "We are creating a socialist state. From now on Russia will be the first state in which a socialist regime has been established. Ah, you are shrugging your shoulders. Well, you have still more surprises coming! It isn't a question of Russia. No, gentlemen, I spit on Russia! That's only one stage we have to pass through on our way to world revolution!" Quoted in Robert S. Payne, *The Life and Death of Lenin* (New York: Simon and Schuster, Inc., 1964), p. 418.

[9] As, for example, when former Premier Khrushchev, in reply to Chinese claims to certain Soviet territory, announced: "Our borders are sacred and inviolable and any attempt to change them by force means war." UPI release from Moscow, September 13, 1964.

priorities were exceptional; in most cases, policy-makers explicitly state or reveal through their actions that the basic objective, to which any degree of sacrifice may be required, is defense of the home territory plus any other territory deemed necessary to self-preservation, and perpetuation of a particular political, social, and economic order, or as some call it, a "way of life."

## Middle-Range Objectives

Since there is such a variety of middle-range objectives, it would be useful to divide this category into four further types and illustrate each with contemporary examples. The first type of middle-range objective would include the attempts of governments to meet public and private demands and needs through international action. Social welfare and economic development—a primary goal of all governments in our era—cannot be achieved through self-help, as most states have only limited resources, administrative services, and technical skills. Interdependence means that to satisfy domestic needs and aspirations, states have to interact with others. Trade, foreign aid, access to communications facilities, sources of supply, and foreign markets are for most states absolutely necessary to enable them to provide for increasing social welfare.

A variation of this type of objective occurs when governments commit themselves to promote private citizens' interests abroad, whether or not these relate to broad social needs. Instead of encouraging general expansion of trade or access to foreign markets, they might, under pressure from specific domestic groups or economic interests, undertake certain foreign policy initiatives that have little connection with the interests of society in general. The American government in the early twentieth century, for instance, committed its power and resources to protect the foreign investments of private firms operating in Latin America. It intervened frequently, sometimes with force, in the internal affairs of Caribbean and Central American states essentially to guarantee the profits of these firms. It was thus translating private business interests into middle-range government objectives, even though the interests had little to do with the general level of social welfare in the United States.

Today, the Scandinavian states, Belgium, the Netherlands, Ireland, Canada, Australia, New Zealand, and even some of the major powers hold no territorial or imperial ambitions, their international prestige is established, their "core" interests have been secured, and they do not seek to promote or impose their cultural, religious, or ideological values abroad —though they might wish to expand their economic influence. Most international transactions in which they are involved concern technical and economic matters, including such problems as tariffs, taxes, trade expansion, and inter-state transportation. These problems relate primarily to the interests of private business organizations and voluntary associations, and their promotion by government agencies seldom raises demands that conflict with the "core" values or interests of other states. Indeed, a vast majority of transactions between governments are today concerned with advancing and regulating what are essentially private concerns and relationships between individuals and groups in separate nations.

A second type of middle-range objective is to increase a state's prestige in the system. In the past, as today, this was done primarily through diplomatic ceremonial and displays of military capabilities, but increasingly in our era prestige is measured by levels of industrial development and scientific and technological skills. In addition to responding to domestic pressures for higher living standards, political elites of underdeveloped states who are acutely sensitive to their material poverty may undertake massive development programs primarily to raise international prestige. Development has become one of the great national goals of our times and is sought with almost as much commitment of resources as the securing of some "core" values and interests. This middle-range goal has no particular time element, but most of today's leaders in underdeveloped countries hope that they can begin to catch up with more economically advanced countries within their own lifetimes.[10]

Industrialized countries and major powers can increase their international prestige through a number of policies and actions, including expansion of military capabilities, distribution of foreign aid (in which both the donor and recipient raise their prestige), diplomatic ceremonial, including reciprocal visits by heads of state, industrial and scientific exhibitions, and particularly through development of nuclear weapons and the capacity to explore outer space. An independent nuclear capability is probably the most important single indicator of a nation's military and diplomatic status today.

[10] The value placed on economic development may be so great that in some cases a country is willing to forego its independence by merging itself into a more viable economic-political community. Modernization thus becomes a "core" value and replaces sovereignty, territorial integrity, and nationhood as a priority. This is one interpretation behind various proposals for political and economic unification of some African countries. The goal of economic development has also been prominent in simulations of international politics. American students, State Department officials, and foreign students who have played foreign policy "games" concentrated heavily on problems of economic development for their own country. See Robert C. Noel, "Evolution of Inter-Nation Simulation" in Harold Guetzkow, et al., Simulation in International Relations (Englewood Cliffs, N.J.: Prentice-Hall, Inc., 1963), pp. 88–97.

The demands which the goal of increasing prestige may require are extensive, but they do not seem, at least in our age, to conflict with the "core" interests or values of other states. While underdeveloped countries make requests for foreign aid, technical assistance, investment capital, and more favorable terms of trade, industrialized countries realize that these are legitimate demands and in many cases voluntarily commit impressive quantities of capabilities in the form of loans and technical instruction.

A third category of middle-range objectives would include the many different forms of self-extension or imperialism. Some states make demands for neighboring territory even if that territory does not satisfy any important security or ethnic requirements. Territorial expansion becomes an end in itself, whether or not it fulfills any strategic, economic, or social needs. Others do not *occupy* foreign territory, but seek advantages, including access to raw materials, markets, and trade routes, which they cannot achieve through ordinary trade or diplomacy. Exclusive control and access may be obtained through establishment of colonies, protectorates, "satellites," or "spheres of influence." Ideological self-extension is also prevalent in many forms, where agents of a state undertake to promote its own socio-economic-political values abroad or "convert" other peoples to a particular religious, cultural, or political faith.

European imperialism in Africa between 1870 and 1900 was a mixture of all of these public and private, economic and ideological, purposes. Often private citizens journeyed to the "dark continent" to seek fortunes, put an end to the Arab slave trade, or convert "savages" to Christianity; later they prevailed upon their governments to establish colonies and regular administrative services so that they could pursue their activities more easily and with greater security. Once a government had established such a colony to help its private citizens, it committed itself to maintain exclusive control over the area in question. In such cases, the interests of private citizens were converted to middle-range objectives of governments and, once the empires or colonies were established, developed into collective "core" interests to be defended at all costs.

More recently Stalin's Russia, Mussolini's Italy, Sukarno's Indonesia, Nasser's Egypt, and Communist China have served as examples of states practicing regional imperialism for economic or strategic purposes, while simultaneously promoting an ideology or political value system abroad. Russian expansion into central Asia—a process started by the Tsars for religious, economic, and military purposes—was revived after 1917 as the drive to convert the indigenous peoples to socialism gave the objective new urgency. The Chinese Communists similarly expanded into Tibet in 1950–1951 for both strategic and ideological reasons. Indonesia under

Sukarno's leadership was a good illustration of a nation pursuing incompatible middle-range objectives. As an underdeveloped country it was committed to modernization and industrialization; at the same time it sought to extend its territory at the expense of others and combat with armed force and propaganda all forms of "neo-colonialism." But to achieve the latter objectives, it had to convert scarce domestic resources and foreign credits into military capabilities, slowing down or halting its economic development. Evidently, it placed a higher value and a shorter time limit on achieving the aims of territorial expansion and promotion of anti-"neo-colonialism" doctrines than on economic development. Egypt has reversed the priorities. Its commitments to the ideal of Arab unity and extermination of Israel are well known; but the Egyptians have not set definite time limits for achieving these goals, nor have they been willing to commit so many resources to these tasks that the other middle-range goal of economic development would be seriously compromised.

### Long-Range Goals

Long-range goals are those plans, dreams, and visions concerning the ultimate political and/or ideological organization of the international system, rules governing relations in that system, and the role of particular nations within it. The difference between middle-range and long-range goals relates not only to different time elements inherent in them; there is also a significant difference in scope. In pressing for middle-range goals, states make *particular* demands against *particular* states; in pursuing long-range goals, states normally make *universal* demands, for their purpose is no less than to reconstruct an entire international system according to a universally applicable plan or vision. As Lenin, one of the great modern visionaries, wrote in 1920:

> We have always known, and shall never forget, that our task is an international one, and that our victory [in Russia] is only half a victory, perhaps less, until an upheaval takes place in all states, including the wealthiest and most civilized.[11]

Since destruction and reconstitution of an established international order obviously conflicts with the middle-range and "core" objectives of its members, any system which contains one or more actors committed to such plans will be unstable and typified by violent international conflict.

[11] V. I. Lenin, *Collected Works* (Moscow: Foreign Languages Publishing House, 1961), Vol. XXXI, p. 371.

Some of these visions may be delineated explicitly, deriving from a coherent political or religious philosophy. Others, such as Hitler's concepts of the "Thousand Year Reich" and the European "New Order," are merely vague images of a future state of affairs. But it is not the explicitness or rationality of a vision which creates international tensions and conflict; it is the degree to which a political unit is willing to commit capabilities and resources to its achievement. Whereas in recent years the Soviet government has been relatively cautious in seeking to promote its long-range objectives,[12] Hitler mobilized tremendous material and manpower resources in pursuit of his vision. Indeed, he was perfectly willing to destroy Germany and sacrifice all of his middle-range objectives for the sake of creating the "New Order."

### Contemporary Long-Range Objectives

Messianic plans for reorganization of continents or the entire world seldom succeed because the threatened states coalesce, where otherwise their interests might not coincide, to build a preponderance of military capacity and eventually destroy the revolutionary state in violent wars. Recent examples are the wars of the French Revolution, the Napoleonic Wars, Hitler's defeat in Europe, and Japan's defeat in Asia after it had almost succeeded in building its "Greater East Asia Co-Prosperity Sphere." In the case of Soviet long-range goals, however, there is a new element in the vision. Although the Soviets conceive it their duty to promote and support revolution abroad, they are not required by their political doctrines to press too hard, for Marx claimed that the goal of world communism would be reached in any event through the inexorable laws of historical development. This element of determinism in Marxism allows Soviet policy-makers a flexibility not found in other universalistic philosophies. They can either export revolution and support indigenous Communist movements through massive aid, or save their resources for economic development, secure in the knowledge that history will in any case develop according to the Marxist pattern. Napoleon, Hitler, and the Japanese imperialists did not believe that they had "history" on their side, and only through aggressive actions could they achieve their long-range objectives.

---

[12] This is undoubtedly one aspect of the conflict between Soviet Russia and Communist China. The Soviet government appears to be reluctant to pursue an aggressive foreign policy, the costs of which might slow down Soviet industrial and agricultural development. The Chinese, on the other hand, seem to place greater value on supporting violent revolution abroad, even if the costs to the Chinese population are substantial.

Even if Russian Communist leaders have perceived the possibility of choosing between giving historical processes a push or letting them take their course toward the predetermined end, they have attempted to draw pictures of the world as it would develop after the world proletarian revolution was completed. Since the Russian Revolution inaugurated the first enduring Socialist order, it was natural that Bolshevik theoreticians would use the organization of their own society as a model for the entire world. Thus, the new world would be organized, at least initially, on the principles of federalism for the constituent units, a socialist economy, and government (or "dictatorship of the proletariat") by soviets (councils) of workers and peasants. But what was to be the position of nation states in the new order—and particularly, what was to be the role of the first Socialist nation state?

There is room for disagreement on the nature of the Soviet image of ultimate Communist world order. Some Western experts, citing Russia's relations with the satellites through the 1950's, the propensity of the Russian Communist Party to define the goals, strategy, and tactics of the international Communist movement, and its domination of many revolutionary movements, argue that the vision is one of a communized world subservient to the interests of the Russian center—a Communist version of the Roman Empire.

Lenin's early pronouncements on the subject did not hint that the ultimate world federation of socialist states was to be dominated by Russians, but subsequent statements and actions by Communist leaders increasingly identified the Soviet Union as the nucleus of the new order. Progress toward the ultimate goal was thus closely linked to the aggrandizement and fortunes of the Russian state. Meanwhile, the original principle of voluntary accession of Socialist states into one great federation was increasingly belied by the Soviet interpretation of federalism within its own borders. Non-Russian parts of the Soviet Union were theoretically allowed autonomy in many political, social, and cultural affairs, but in Stalin's era the entire Union was ruled firmly from Moscow. Manifestations of "bourgeois nationalism" in constituent units of the Union were met with purges, mass executions, incarcerations, and forced migration of "unreliable elements." Soviet policy toward its Eastern European neighbors after World War II also contradicted the idea of voluntary federalism which was to be one of the underlying principles of the new order under communism.

According to some Soviet theorists, even the principle of federalism was to be transitory. Federation was only a *method* designed to allow diverse peoples and cultures to unite politically. What Communists should strive for ultimately, they proclaimed, was construction of a genuine world economy which would be directed and planned in one center—presumably Moscow. The Comintern Theses of 1920 declared that it would be necessary to strive for an ever closer federal union, but that federation would be only a transition form toward complete unity. Federation, it was hoped, would foster the tendency toward creation of a single world economy regulated by the proletariat of all nations according to one common plan.[13] The expectation was that Soviet Russia would be joined (by force, if necessary, according to Stalin) by other Soviet Republics in a federation that would eventually develop into a World Soviet Federation. This, in turn, would be transformed into a unitary, highly centralized world state. As Premier Khrushchev told a Czechoslovakian audience in 1957, the Soviet Russian brand of socialism was the only Socialist system possible, and was therefore appropriate for the Czechs, the French, and even the Americans.[14] Even in the world Socialist state, Moscow would lay down the basic ideological, economic, political, and cultural standards for all other peoples to follow.

Other observers of communism note a more egalitarian vision in Communist literature and philosophy.[15] Emphasizing the concept of a Communist "Commonwealth of Nations" based on fraternal relations among sovereign and equal parties and states, they argue that aside from organizing and supporting the violent overthrow of bourgeois regimes, Moscow would not necessarily be the center of an empire. As the oldest Socialist state, it would simply provide leadership and act as an example to other revolutionary states. Hence the vision is one of ever-expanding revolution to build a world order of sovereign states—not so different from the present system, except that all states would adhere to a common socio-economic system and political philosophy.

The vision, no matter how interpreted, is explicit and has persisted as the ultimate goal of communism for over a century. But how long will Soviet policy-makers continue to regard the Communist world state or commonwealth as the long-range objective of their policies? What time limits and how many national resources are they willing to commit to its achievement? Lenin anticipated the universal victory of socialism in his own lifetime, believing that the German proletariat would gain power either in 1918 or 1919 and the collapse of bourgeois regimes in the rest of Europe would follow shortly thereafter. To him, world revolution was a

[13] Cf., Elliott R. Goodman, *The Soviet Design for a World State* (New York: Columbia University Press, 1960), p. 233.

[14] Goodman, *The Soviet Design for a World State*, p. 349.

[15] Cf., William Welch, "The Sources of Soviet Conduct: A Note on Method," *Background*, VI (1963), 17–28.

"core" value or at least a middle-range goal to be achieved even at the expense of Russian territorial integrity. In 1919, for example, he declared that it would not be long before communism had become victorious in the entire world, before he would see the founding of a world-wide Federal Republic of Soviets.[16] Later that year he even predicted that by July, 1920, all Communists would greet the victory of the "International Soviet Republic."[17] Since Lenin believed these developments would occur inevitably as a result of contradictions within capitalism and collapse of public order in many nations following World War I, the Soviet government could confine its activities to exploiting "revolutionary situations" abroad through agitation and propaganda. Unlike Stalin, Lenin did not believe, with the important exception of the Soviet campaign against Poland in 1920, that the Soviet state should use its military capabilities to impose Communist regimes abroad.

Stalin recognized that the new order could not be achieved unless the Soviet state used its national power, influence, and resources to this end. Construction of the new order became the objective not only of communism, but of Russian foreign policy as well. Stalin also did not hold to Lenin's optimistic predictions about imminent world revolution. Instead of anticipating the downfall of capitalism in the next year or even during the next decade, Stalin's theoreticians spoke of long "historical stages" to which they could arbitrarily attach almost any period of time. As the tenets of Marxism-Leninism became embarrassingly irrelevant to the problems of modern society, the ultimate objective receded even further into the future. In 1935, for example, one Communist veteran told the Seventh World Comintern Congress that it would take communism a shorter time to achieve world victory than it did for the bourgeoisie to replace feudalism with capitalism. His estimate would place the world victory of communism somewhere around 1960. In 1952, however, a Soviet economist predicted that capitalism was undergoing its second stage of crisis (the first existed between the world wars) and that during this stage there would be a "lengthy" period of coexistence between capitalism and communism. Coexistence would no longer be necessary by the end of the present century, because by then communism would be victorious throughout the world.[18] To Lenin, the long-range goal was defined in terms of months; to Stalin it was an objective which Soviet diplomats and the Red Army should pursue for two or more decades; and today, the achievement of the mission is placed several generations

[16] Goodman, *The Soviet Design for a World State*, p. 32.
[17] *Ibid.*
[18] Goodman, *The Soviet Design for a World State*, pp. 188–89.

ahead.[19] As the time limit passes into the remote future, middle-range goals such as construction of communism within Soviet Russia and development of Soviet diplomatic prestige around the world seem to occupy an increasing portion of Soviet policy-makers' time and Russia's resources.

Among the Western countries, only France under Charles de Gaulle has recently pursued a long-range foreign policy goal which compares in explicitness to the Soviet vision for the new order. De Gaulle's vision of the future is based on his understanding of the past. Two ideas in particular stand out in his historical interpretations: the importance of the nation state (to him, it represents the "will" or "soul" of a people) in international politics, and the role of France as a leading force in European civilization. De Gaulle recognizes the recent emergence of the United States, the Soviet Union, and Communist China as major powers, but does not concede that Europe's role is to be merely a pawn in the struggles between these giants. He conceives of Russia as a permanent member of the European family whose historic interests lie in preserving a continental balance of power, not in spreading a false philosophy indiscriminately around the world. The Communist leaders of Russia are, he believes, an aberration, and their policies in no way conform to the "true" interests of Russia. He claims that communism in general is becoming an increasingly irrelevant factor in international politics, while traditional forms of nationalism are emerging once again as the main motive force of the nation state. He cites the growing independence of the Eastern European states from Moscow as proof of his thesis. De Gaulle envisages for the future a world of independent nation states, each pursuing its traditional national interests, but coalescing around continental or hemispheric leaders. The newer states of the world, though he is not very explicit on this point, will create their own orders, but will remain dependent upon the traditional major powers for developing and sustaining their economies.

De Gaulle is most explicit when he describes his image of the future of Europe and France. On the continent, France and Germany will provide leadership for others. Russia and the East European states will eventually become reconciled with their historical destiny, providing that their policy-makers renounce Communist ideological objectives and adhere only to the traditional interests of their nations. Europe will also be independent of any extra-continental powers, but because of historical ties, it will

---

[19] Khrushchev suggested that in the United States, the present generation's *grandchildren* will live under socialism. This could mean anywhere between 1985 and 2020.

cooperate with the United States and the "Anglo-Saxon" world. Plans for complete integration of Europe must, however, be abandoned. Supranational federations, he claims, do not conform to political reality because they cannot reflect the "national will" of diverse peoples. Europe will become a "federation of fatherlands," where each member will cooperate with the others but not fully integrate politically or militarily and thus lose separate identity.

France's role in Europe, he argues, must be one of leadership. To resume its position as a traditional leader in European military, political, or cultural affairs, France must destroy its post-war political malaise and dependency upon the United States. This can only be done by increasing French prestige, developing an independent nuclear capability, and adhering to its own objectives no matter how much criticism they may evoke abroad. The most important requirement—after French resurgence —for a stable European order must be solidarity between France and Germany. From this belief de Gaulle has consistently and successfully devoted his energies to reconciling ancient Franco-German enmities. Toward the general long-range objective of creating an independent Europe of all European states, including the Soviet Union, he has devoted national resources and the talents of French diplomats. He does not believe that the objectives can be achieved through force or subversion.

Such a brief sketch of de Gaulle's concept of a world order cannot do justice to all of his assumptions and logic, and sometimes, illogic; here it is only important to point out that no other contemporary Western statesman, including Churchill and Roosevelt, has worked so consistently according to such a large architectural design. In the United States some leading public figures have thought about the long-range goals of American foreign policy, but none has developed so coherent a scheme as the French president. Some Americans have spoken of a world of independent, and preferably democratic and affluent, states whose transactions would be conducted according to the rules of international law and the Charter of the United Nations. To this vision, many have added the features of universal disarmament and an effective international organization which would control a powerful international police force to deter potential aggressors. Other Americans have been more concerned in their long-range visions with extending into the future the world as it appears to them in the present. To them, a desirable system of international politics would be an American-centered one. The United States would create a network of alliances, alignments, and economic agreements to protect the "free world" from the Soviet Union; the world would remain polarized between two irreconcilable civilizations. In the "free" portion of the world there would be economic, cultural, and political diversity; but whatever the character of any particular country's internal institutions, it could—or should—not maneuver between blocs or proclaim itself a neutral between the two contending forces.[20]

Another popular American image of the future international system emphasizes the concept of Atlantic community. The nations of Europe and North America, all supporting common religious, historical, cultural, and philosophical traditions, would unite to provide for their common defense and economic advancement. This image appears as a persistent theme in the foreign policies of post-war administrations, where both Democratic and Republican presidents have desired to bring Europe to a position of greater equality with the United States. But none of these long-range objectives has been formulated in detail and from them not very many distinctive policies—except toward Europe—have flowed.

Though leaders of a state may define long-range objectives such as those discussed above, the objectives do not necessarily determine the actions which will be used to achieve them. One of the frequent mistakes of armchair analysts is to assume that the only American objective abroad is to promote its liberal and free enterprise values, or that every Russian diplomatic maneuver is part of a carefully formulated plan to communize the world. Certainly in many of its actions, the United States actively seeks to promote abroad its own domestic values. This is one American middle-range goal. It rewards states with liberal political institutions; it has on occasion withheld recognition of governments—particularly in Latin America—that have not come into being through, or observed, constitutional processes; it has cut off foreign aid to governments which were constituted through violence; it has occasionally insisted that recipients of aid not use funds to build nationalized industries to compete against private entrepreneurs; and through its propaganda programs it has emphasized the virtues of its own political and social values. On the other hand, where other interests and objectives have been more important, it has not attempted to promote its own "way of life" abroad. It has conducted transactions and formed alliances with all types of regimes; it has rewarded conservative groups, ignored the principle of self-determination, or remained officially indifferent to the values expressed in the economic and political life of other countries. It has intervened in the internal affairs of other states, sometimes to support conservative regimes against liberal factions, sometimes to save liberal governments against plots on the right. The Soviet Union similarly pursues *all* ranges of foreign policy objectives and commits varying resources to their realization. But

---

[20] See the discussion of these views in Seabury, *Power, Freedom, and Diplomacy,* p. 357.

these objectives, no matter how diverse, do not contain within them specific courses of action.

If a state wishes to secure more strategically advantageous frontiers at the expense of its neighbors, it can do so using almost any technique from persuasion to aggression. To persuade, it can offer a piece of its own territory as compensation, promise a friendship treaty, foreign aid, or a hundred other types of rewards. To coerce, it can build alliances or subvert the neighboring regimes and establish puppet governments which would then cede the desired territory. Certainly the Soviet goal of a world Communist state, or a Commonwealth of Socialist societies, does not prescribe any immutable strategic or tactical foreign policy principles. With the exception of the Bolshevik war against Poland in 1920, Lenin did not believe that communism should be imposed abroad by the Red Army; but Stalin did appreciate the possibilities of using military power and succeeded in expanding communism by unleashing the Red Army. Though each man held approximately the same long-range goal, each sought to achieve it through different methods.

How a nation secures its "core" values and interests and pursues or defends its middle- and (if any) long-range goals cannot, therefore, be predicted easily. A conservative, trade-oriented society will adhere to different standards when it seeks to influence the behavior of other states than will a young, revolutionary, and nationalistic society. Selection of goals and means to achieve them is influenced partly by system-wide values and rules, by the initiating actions of other nations, and perhaps more profoundly by the needs, values, myths, and ideologies found within a national society, as well as the idiosyncrasies of individual statesmen or revolutionary leaders. In the following chapter, we will see how these phenomena are related to the formulation of foreign policy.


### The Interaction of Objectives:
### Collaboration, Conflict, and Competition


International politics arise when states seek to change or sustain the behavior of other political units in the system in order to achieve, defend, or extend their private or collective interests, values, and objectives. Some types of objectives can be achieved by making few demands on other states; others require substantial changes in the policies, actions, and interests of neighboring states if they are to be fulfilled. In many instances, objectives of states are so similar that if one government successfully pursues its interests it will bring common advantages. This is the basis for international cooperative enterprises ranging from formation of alliances to organization of multilateral technical assistance programs or programs to control international narcotics traffic. When objectives are incompatible, one state's gain is at the expense of others; when they are compatible, one state's gain may involve advantages to others as well.

Most behavior resulting from interaction of states can be classified as conflictful, collaborative, or competitive. In Chapters XV and XVI we will spell out in detail the various ways that states resolve conflicts or undertake collaborative ventures. Here we may, however, describe the main characteristics of conflictful, competitive, and collaborative relationships, since these types of relationships derive essentially from the degree to which objectives, interests, and values between states coincide or are incompatible.

The concept of collaboration may create an image of an international organization hard at work resolving common problems or of technical experts in the field teaching others how to improve agricultural productivity. When we use the term conflict, we may mean certain facets of violence or simply a disagreement over some issue. Whatever our common understanding for these terms, we often assume that collaboration and conflict are opposites and that international politics (often defined as the search for power at the expense of others) is primarily a conflictful process. This view is understandable because our attention is frequently called to the great world crises, while we are less often made aware of the tacit or overt collaboration—even in conflict situations—which exists in the world. We should hesitate to identify collaboration as the core of only "good" types of relationships such as those observed in international technical organizations. After all, construction of an aggressive alliance may involve as much collaboration as an international program to raise health and literacy standards, where governments may disagree seriously about its purposes, organization, and financing. The reason we assume that such programs represent collaboration is that the conflictful content in them seldom leads to violence or military threats. But the reason they do not lead to violence is not because there is less conflict; it is only because the interests involved are not vital and therefore not worth the risks and costs of military action. Whenever interests and objectives are inconsistent or incompatible, conflictful types of relationships will arise; whenever they are compatible, they are likely to lead to collaborative types of transactions. International politics is always a mix of these types of relationships, as well as of competition. As we will see below, it is virtually impossible to find examples of pure conflict, or of collaboration which does not involve some conflict.

In dissecting the concepts of collaboration, competition, and conflict, we find that they may include several different characteristics or forms of behavior. We can define collaboration as:

1. Perception that two or more interests, values, or objectives coincide and can be achieved, promoted, or satisfied by both parties simultaneously. As an example, assume that two neighboring states, (A) and (B), perceive a threat from a common enemy (C). Each state, through its policy-makers, recognizes that, like itself, its neighbor wishes to increase its defensive capacity (or standard of living, territory, security, or any other value or interest) and that once accomplished this increased defensive capacity will be used to deter the common enemy;

2. Perception or expectation by one state that the policies of the other in seeking to achieve its objectives might help it realize its own interests or values. In our example, state (A) expects that state (B)'s mobilization program will not hinder (A)'s own program but, on the contrary, will help it. This expectation of mutual benefit through collaborative transactions will usually lead at least one of the states to initiate proposals for discussing, coordinating, or planning the acts needed to secure the coinciding objectives;

3. Agreement on the substance of the transactions between two or more states to achieve their common or coinciding objectives. States (A) and (B) might agree, for example, to exchange defense secrets, provide each other with technical assistance, or divide up military functions, each assuming the role for which it is best fitted;

4. Official or unofficial rules that will govern all future transactions which will be taken to implement the agreement. In the case cited, it might be an understanding that the two states will exchange military missions of a certain rank, that neither side will share its secrets with a third party, or even such an assumed procedural rule as observing common diplomatic etiquette in all transactions;

5. The transactions between the states to fulfill their agreement.

The example cited might seem to constitute a fairly exceptional case of collaboration, where the two interests coincide to such an extent that no disagreement on their implementation arises. In reality even the most cooperative types of transactions may involve some disagreement—hence conflict. Perhaps state (A) did not really wish to reveal its defense secrets to (B) until (B) had given guarantees that it would not sell them to a third party. If the two governments had a long tradition of friendship and collaboration, (A) might conclude that the costs of holding out for such guarantees would be greater than the advantages of having them. Or it might feel that the costs of disagreement were so trivial that it might as well compromise on the issue. In relations between traditionally friendly countries, good manners, custom, habit, and the desire to maintain friendly relations often forces one side to absorb small costs where it might not do so with a traditionally hostile state. In a sense, there is a procedural disagreement (conflict) between (A) and (B), but the strong desire to reach agreement makes compromise or absorption of costs relatively easy.[21]

Conflict, as we might expect, contains behavioral characteristics opposite to those found in collaboration, including:

1. Perception that two or more states' objectives are more or less incompatible;

2. Perception or expectation by one state, through its policy-makers, that the policies, demands, or acts committed by another state to achieve its objectives are depriving or will threaten to deprive the first of its own interests and values. Using the case from the discussion of collaboration, assume that although both states perceive a common enemy (C), state (A) also fears that state (B)'s military buildup might be used to invade its own territory. Although both have a similar objective in providing defense against a perceived threat from (C), the acts of state (B) to increase its military capacity are seen by (A) to be threatening its own interests;

3. Rules that govern or influence transactions between two states when they perceive that their objectives are more or less incompatible. Even when two states go to war, they normally accept and sometimes even announce publicly the "rules" which will govern their hostilities. In the Korean War, for example, both sides kept the conflict limited to the Korean peninsula, even though each was capable of extending the war to the other's main staging areas in China and Japan. These "rules of the game" (usually voluntary and understood rather than the subject of a formal communication or agreement) place at least some limitations on the manner in which the conflict is handled;

4. Acts or transactions which one state undertakes to protect its interests against the demands and actions of the other, or acts or transactions which one state takes to change the behavior of the other, after it is recognized that objectives are more or less incompatible. Where the transactions will lead is, of course, difficult to predict. This is a problem where policy-makers must weigh costs and advantages.

The characteristics of competition are different from collaboration and conflict primarily because they do not involve interaction of objectives. In conflict and collaboration states must alter or sustain the interests, actions,

---

[21] A general discussion of the costs, risks, and advantages of compromise is in Alfred Kuhn, *The Study of Society: A Unified Approach* (Homewood, Illinois: The Dorsey Press, 1964), p. 370.

and values of other states. Fulfillment of their own objectives *depends upon* the behavior of other states. The United States cannot sustain its alliance with France if France is unwilling to remain an alliance partner; the Soviet Union cannot maintain the solidarity of the world Communist movement—an important middle-range goal—unless it can change Chinese attitudes and policies; and the Scandinavian countries cannot continue their programs of social and intellectual cooperation unless members of the Nordic association sustain their present relationships. But in competitive situations, objectives can be achieved—within certain bounds, of course—regardless of the behavior of others. The United States and the Soviet Union are competing in space exploration, but do not have to change each other's policies and actions in order to conduct the competition. Since both countries have the same objectives, there is an obvious basis for collaborative efforts, but as long as they do not choose to collaborate through pooling resources and scientific talent, they can still pursue their objectives without threatening each other. Unlike conflict, in a competitive situation one's gain is not necessarily the other's loss; both can be advancing simultaneously.

Many types of foreign policy objectives thus do not lead necessarily either to cooperation or conflict with others. If prestige is an important objective, it can be achieved through building up military capabilities, economic development, raising literacy rates, or building industrial show-pieces. None of these actions necessarily involves threats or deprivations of other states' interests, or cooperative efforts with other states. In the eighteenth and nineteenth centuries, when there were still great tracts of land in the Western Hemisphere and Africa available for colonization and exploitation, governments could compete with each other to establish empires. Once the land became scarce or when two or more governments made claims to the same territory, then the *competition for* empire turned into *conflict over* empires.

### The Interaction of Objectives:
### Domination and Dependence

In the relations between some political units, collaboration may be forced by one state upon the other. The dominant nation imposes its own objectives, usually through explicit or implicit threats of violent punishment against refusal to accept them. This is the typical situation with satellites, colonies, and protectorates; in the latter, ruling authorities maintain their formal positions but transfer to the "protector" the right to conduct foreign relations, defense policies, and sometimes even domestic policies. The dominant nation then sets limits to the freedom of choice for the subordinate unit's policy-makers.

There are historical cases where the dependent unit at first freely accepted the subordinate position on some policy goals in order to realize some other value or interest. In some protectorates, for example, local authorities willingly accepted British economic domination and exploitation in return for the security and prestige the British could provide them. Elsewhere, as in the relations between Great Britain and many of its colonies or between the United States and some Caribbean countries until 1933, the dominant nation permitted the subordinate policy-makers considerable latitude in formulating domestic policies, reserving for itself only an ultimate veto as well as the right to regulate the dependency's relations with other nations. In other examples, such as the relations between the Soviet Union and the East European countries between 1947 and 1956, the dominant nation wielded controls over almost every aspect of the satellites' domestic and foreign policies. There was some genuine collaboration arising out of truly compatible objectives, but in many cases policy-makers in the "satellites" had no feasible alternatives which they could consider. Any deviance from the objectives established in Moscow was considered subversive of "working class solidarity" and its perpetrators were quickly purged or exterminated. Thus, the risks and costs of positing goals or policies which conflicted with those established by the Soviet Union were so great—as the Hungarians and Poles learned in 1956—that they were seldom considered seriously.

Put in the context of the (A)-(B) relationship used above, the behavioral characteristics of dominant-dependent relationships would include:

1. Perception by dominant (A) that (B)'s interests and values are not compatible with its own, and consequent policies incorporating rewards, threats, and punishments which (A) uses to impose new and compatible objectives on (B);

2. Perception by (B) either that it can achieve peripheral values or interests by accepting (A)'s demands, or that there are no feasible (e.g., low risk or cost) alternatives except to adopt the goals established for it by (A). It recognizes that deviant behavior or any challenge of the dominant country's policies might lead to total destruction of its own "core" values and interests, including outright annexation to (A), imposition of a military occupation, or annihilation of segments of the population;

3. The conclusion by (B) that it is, therefore, better to accept the

position of subordination and to conduct all transactions in accordance with the official or unofficial rules and expectations established by (A).

All the relations and interactions between any two given states constitute a mix of collaboration, conflict, and competition, depending on the extent to which their objectives, interests and values coincide or are incompatible. In some subsystems, such as that of the United States and Soviet Union, conflictful behavior in handling transactions is prominent, while the elements of collaboration are less obvious. The long-range and some of the middle-range goals of the Soviet Union are incompatible with those of the United States, and neither side can compromise its values and interests except at very high costs. When one achieves its objectives, the other usually perceives it as a setback for its own aspirations. Even some of the "core" interests of the two states are perceived to be incompatible: many of the military policies, for example, which each side formulates to safeguard its own security are deemed by the other to constitute a threat to its own vital interests. But important areas of collaboration coexist with the many incompatible goals and hostile attitudes in the Soviet-American subsystem. Both sides have tacitly or implicitly collaborated to restrain Communist Chinese foreign policy, help prevent the spread of nuclear weapons, or raise the economic levels of underdeveloped countries.

We will return in Chapter VII to the problem of conflictful and cooperative relations, as seen in the context of the techniques that states use to influence each other's behavior. Before proceeding, however, we must examine further the question of *why* certain states choose certain types of objectives.

## SELECTED BIBLIOGRAPHY

Aspaturian, Vernon V., "The Challenge of Soviet Foreign Policy," in *The Revolution in World Politics,* ed. Morton A. Kaplan. New York: John Wiley & Sons, Inc., 1962.

Aubert, Wilhelm, "Competition and Dissensus: Two Types of Conflict and of Conflict Resolution," *Journal of Conflict Resolution,* VII (1963), 26–42.

Beard, Charles A., and G. H. E. Smith, *The Idea of National Interest: An Analytical Study in American Foreign Policy.* New York: The Macmillan Company, 1934.

Boulding, Kenneth E., *Conflict and Defense: A General Theory.* New York: Harper & Row, Publishers, 1962.

Caroe, Sir Olaf, "Soviet Colonialism in Central Asia," *Foreign Affairs,* XXXII (1953), 135–44.

Deutsch, Morton, "A Theory of Cooperation and Competition, *Human Relations,* II (1949), 129–51.

Gallo, Philip S., Jr., and Charles G. McClintock, "Cooperative and Competitive Behavior in Mixed-motive Games," *Journal of Conflict Resolution,* IX (1965), 68–78.

Good, Robert C., "National Interest and Moral Theory: The 'Debate' Among Contemporary Political Realists," in *Foreign Policy in the Sixties: The Issues and the Instruments,* ed. Roger Hilsman and Robert C. Good. Baltimore: The Johns Hopkins Press, 1965.

Goodman, Elliott R., *The Sovet Design For A World State.* New York: Columbia University Press, 1960.

Handman, Max, "War, Economic Motives, and Economic Symbols," *American Journal of Sociology,* XLIV (1939), 629–48.

"The Idea of National Interest," Symposium, *American Perspective,* IV (1960), 335–401.

Kaplan, Morton A., *System and Process in International Politics.* New York: John Wiley & Sons, Inc., 1957, Chap. 8.

Knorr, Klaus, "Theories of Imperialism," *World Politics,* IV (1952), 402–31.

Marshall, Charles Burton, *The Exercise of Sovereignty: Papers on Foreign Policy.* Baltimore: The Johns Hopkins Press, 1965.

Modelski, George A., *A Theory of Foreign Policy.* New York: Frederick A. Praeger, Inc., 1962.

Moon, Parker T., *Imperialism and World Politics.* New York: The Macmillan Company, 1926.

Morgenthau, Hans J., "Another 'Great Debate': The National Interest of the United States," *The American Political Science Review,* XLVI (1952), 961–88.

———, *In Defense of the National Interest.* New York: Alfred A. Knopf, Inc., 1951.

Osgood, Robert E., *Ideals and Self-Interest in American Foreign Relations.* Chicago: University of Chicago Press, 1953.

Oskamp, Stuart, and Daniel Perlman, "Factors Affecting Cooperation in a Prisoner's Dilemma Game," *Journal of Conflict Resolution,* IX (1965), 360–74.

Robbins, Lionel C., *The Economic Problem in Peace and War: Some Reflections on Objectives and Mechanisms.* London: Macmillan & Co., Ltd., 1947.

Schellenberg, James A., "Distributive Justice and Collaboration in Non-zero-sum Games," *Journal of Conflict Resolution,* VIII (1964), 147–50.

Schumpeter, Joseph, *The Sociology of Imperialism.* New York: Meridian Books, 1955.

Seabury, Paul, *Power, Freedom, and Diplomacy.* New York: Random House, Inc., 1963. Chaps. 4, 11.

Shelling, Warner R., "The Clarification of Ends, or, Which Interest is the National," *World Politics,* VIII (1956), 566–78.

Welch, William, "The Sources of Soviet Conduct: A Note on Method," *Background*, IV (1963), 17–28.

Wolfe, Bertram D., "Communist Ideology and Soviet Foreign Policy," *Foreign Affairs*, XLI (1962), 152–70.

Wolfers, Arnold, *Discord and Collaboration: Essays on International Politics.* Baltimore: The Johns Hopkins Press, 1962. Chaps. 2, 5, 6, 10.

Yalem, Ronald J., "The 'Theory of Ends' of Arnold Wolfers," *Journal of Conflict Resolution,* IV (1960), 421–25.

# The Formulation
# of Foreign Policy
# Objectives

An outline of the types of objectives governments seek reveals little about the genesis of those goals. Nor does it explain why two states with roughly similar objectives pursue them in different ways, one using customary techniques of diplomatic bargaining, the other employing threats of force or organized violence. How do we account for shifts in objectives or the different actions undertaken to achieve them? Though some states have purposes, needs, and values which are relatively fixed throughout several centuries, others change their policies frequently, shifting with each political or economic development abroad. Partly through accident, but sometimes with considerable foresight and planning, the United States in the nineteenth century made territorial expansion a primary external objective. It either seized or purchased parts of Florida and the Southwest from France, Spain, and Mexico, and gained the Oregon territories through threats against the British. While the United States

# Chapter VI

attempted to preclude further European colonial expansion into Latin America, the American government loaned its power to protect private economic interests with established spheres of influence throughout the Caribbean and Central America. The United States also seized the Philippines from Spain and gained control over the Hawaiian Islands in a fashion similar to that employed by European imperialists in Africa. Today, however, territorial expansion and economic imperialism are no longer among the middle- or long-range goals of American policy-makers. Are these shifts in general objectives the result of new paths charted by strong presidents or secretaries of state? If so, we are explaining foreign policies in terms of the personalities and values of a few key statesmen. Do the changes reflect, on the other hand, fundamental modifications in American social values? Can they be explained by the world-wide demise of colonialism? Has the changing structure of the international system, from diffuse to polar, prompted the United States to adjust its foreign policy objectives?

One explanation can be given by referring to fundamental changes in the structure of the international system between the nineteenth and twentieth centuries. It could be argued, for example, that American expansion into areas under weak political administration was comparatively easy during the nineteenth century, but as the world's territory became fully organized into nation states and empires, and the structure of power and influence in the world changed from a diffuse to polar configuration, widespread territorial expansion became almost impossible without meeting strong armed resistance. In other words, the *general orientation* (the cumulative decisions of many policy-makers) of a state's policies can be deduced or even predicted from the system's structure. It is much more difficult to explain individual foreign policy decisions or specific objectives in systemic terms. The structure of the system is always the environment within which policy decisions are made, but it may not be the most salient aspect of the environment, as far as policy-makers are concerned, in *all* situations. To help understand the reasons for specific actions and objectives, rather than general orientations, we have to employ techniques of analysis, which focus on individual policy-makers' behavior or national needs and opinion rather than on the general distribution of power and influence in the system.

One way to account for specific foreign policy objectives is to emphasize the perceptions, images, attitudes, values, and beliefs of those responsible for formulating policy objectives. We may combine the diverse factors which affect the choice of policy goals under the concept of "definition of the situation."[1] The definition of the situation would include

[1] This concept is introduced and discussed in Richard C. Snyder, H. W. Bruck, and Burton Sapin, eds., *Foreign Policy Decision Making* (New York: Free Press of

all external and domestic, historical and contemporary, conditions which policy-makers consider relevant to any given foreign policy problem. These might include important events abroad, domestic political needs, social values or ideological imperatives, state of public opinion, availability of capabilities, degree of threat or opportunity perceived in a situation, predicted consequences and costs of proposed courses of action, and the time element or "requiredness" of a situation. It is difficult to generalize about which factors are most important in each situation, since policy-makers seldom draw up careful lists assessing the relative weight of each component of the definition of the situation. But for analytical purposes we can break down the components of any definition of a situation and examine those conditions in the external and domestic environments which are *usually* considered relevant in formulation of objectives and actions. Foreign policy objectives and behavior thus can be linked to: (1) the images, values, beliefs, and personality or political needs of those individuals responsible for establishing goals, priorities among them, and actions needed to achieve them; (2) the structure and conditions in the international system; (3) national role; (4) domestic needs; (5) capabilities; (6) general social values, public opinion, and specific group interests; and (7) organizational needs, values, and traditions.[2] The relevance of these factors will depend largely upon the attitudes, judgments, and purposes of individual policy-makers operating within policy-making organizations that have traditional goals, functions, and rules.

## Images, Attitudes, Values, Beliefs, and Personal Needs as Components of a Definition of the Situation

While for some purposes it may be useful to analyze the "behavior of nations" in terms of structure of a system, this is only an analytical device designed to make comprehensible the thousands of decisions and actions of those in a position to commit the state and its capabilities. Even if we gain some understanding of general characteristics of international politics in an historical era by relating the behavior of political units to the structure of an international system, we must also look at the behavior of policy-makers to explain particular decisions, actions, or objectives. We have to explain why different policy-makers respond to the same condi-

---

Glencoe, Inc., 1962), pp. 65–68, 80–85. For an application of the concept see the article by Snyder and Glenn Paige entitled "The United States Decision to Resist Aggression in Korea," in the same volume, esp. pp. 239–46.

[2] Some of the other components, such as perception of threat, degree of urgency, and perceptions of alternatives will be considered in Chapter XII, where policy-making in crisis situations is discussed.

tions in different ways, or why some statesmen, despite different ideological orientations and entirely different national constituencies, respond in some instances in a very similar manner. Though separated by great differences in historical circumstances, geography, culture, and diplomatic situation, the leaders of Pakistan and India during the war over Kashmir in 1965 displayed neither unique forms of behavior nor uncommon attitudes when compared with the behavior and attitudes of those leaders who plunged Europe into war in 1914. But most government leaders to not have to make decisions regarding peace or war. Despite frequent rhetoric to the effect that they have "no choice" but to take certain action, policy-makers are confronted with situations abroad and demands by other states which permit many alternative responses, including acquiescence, inaction, threats, or commission of various acts of punishment. When a prime minister says he was "compelled" to do something, he means only that he has rejected other alternatives. There is always an element of choice in policy-making. In situations perceived as containing only slight threat, will different people in different historical and cultural circumstances behave the same way? Probably not, since so many factors other than immediate stimulus may be considered relevant in the definition of this type of situation.

### Images

Any delineation of objectives, choice among courses of action, or response to a situation in the environment may be explained partly in terms of policy-makers' perceptions of reality. Man acts and reacts according to his *images* of the environment. In policy-making, it is not the state of the environment that matters so much as what government officials believe to be that state. By image we mean an individual's *perceptions* of an object, fact, or condition, his *evaluation* of that object, fact, or condition in terms of its goodness or badness, friendliness or hostility, or value, and the *meaning* ascribed to, or deduced from, that object, fact, or condition. Consider a trained fishing expert and the city-bred novice fisherman with no previous experience. The expert can deduce valid conclusions about fishing conditions from a variety of facts, conditions, or "clues," such as water temperature, depth or color, weather, and time of day. The novice, even though he sees the water, feels its temperature, and knows it is late afternoon, is unable to draw any particular conclusions from these indicators because by themselves they have no meaning in terms of his past experience. Because the same conditions or facts are seen and interpreted in different ways (in the case of the novice, hardly interpreted at all), the two men will react and behave differently. The expert will go where the fish are and work his tackle in such a way as to catch them. Barring beginner's luck, the novice will struggle up and down a stream, flail the water with an assortment of useless lures, scare the fish, and catch nothing. Similarly in foreign policy, different policy-makers can read different meanings into a situation, and because they characterize a situation differently and deduce different conclusions from it, will behave differently. In particular, complex situations involving many interests, historical, economic, or social factors, and value positions, are likely to be perceived differently.

Even the most well-informed expert in a policy-making agency cannot know *all* of the relevant factors in a situation; his images of reality will always be different from reality. The discrepancy between image and reality is partly a result of physical impediments to the flow of information due to lack of time, faulty communications, censorship, or lack of competent advisors or intelligence sources. It is also a problem of the distortion of reality caused by attitudes, values, beliefs, or faulty expectations. Any individual is bombarded constantly by messages about the environment, but he selects and interprets only a fraction of what he "sees" because only a part of it may be relevant to a particular situation. Sometimes the person also "sees" only information which conforms to his values, beliefs, or expectations. There are both physical and psychological factors which can distort the information upon which policy-makers' images of reality are based.

If the policy-maker relies on faulty information, misinterprets cues, twists the meaning of messages to fit his own preferences, or disregards information which contradicts his values and preferences, his psychological environment—upon which he will act—is quite different from the physical environment—in which his policies have to be executed. The distinction between psychological environment, or definition of the situation, and physical environment, or "reality," must be kept in mind in all analyses of foreign policy. One can readily see the distinction in the case of the attack on Pearl Harbor. In early December, 1941, President Roosevelt and American diplomats were attempting to arrange high level negotiations with the Japanese government to resolve some issues separating the two countries. At this time American officials had predicted an impending military attack by the Japanese, but they expected it to occur somewhere in Southeast Asia. They could not imagine a direct attack on the American fleet at Pearl Harbor and so took no precautionary measures; they had facts about impending Japanese military actions but could not deduce or predict the correct "meaning" from those facts. The American definition of the situation was thus at odds with reality, and actions designed to cope with the expected Japanese moves were in-effective.

This example illustrates the problem of discrepancies between images and physical environment which arise from faulty or inadequate informa-tion and unwarranted expectations.[3] But how do we account for differing interpretations and characterizations of reality when easily verifiable facts are available? Here the problem of attitudes, values, beliefs, doctrines, and analogies becomes important, for they help determine the meanings ascribed to a set of facts about internal and external conditions. Though distinctions among the concepts of attitude, value, belief, and doctrines are not always clear, they can be defined as follows for the analysis of foreign policy-making.

### Attitudes

Attitudes can be conceived as general evaluative propositions about some object, fact, or condition: more or less friendly, desirable, danger-ous, or hostile. In any international relationship policy-makers operate—usually implicitly—within some framework of evaluative assumptions of hostility or friendship, trust or distrust, and fear or confidence toward other governments and peoples. These attitudes may have important consequences on how policy-makers react to the actions and demands of other states, perceive the *intentions* of other governments, and define their own objectives towards others. If a Swiss military airplane crosses over the French frontier, we would not expect French officials to behave the same way as if a Soviet aircraft unexpectedly flew over Paris. Atti-tudes of hostility and suspicion would probably become operative imme-diately upon identification of the Soviet aircraft, while these attitudes would most likely be absent in any definition of the situation created by the Swiss border violation. In the former case there would likely be serious apprehension about the intention of the Russian action. Similarly, if a high level policy-maker receives a conciliatory message from the government of a state he perceives to be hostile, his attitudes of distrust and hostility may lead him to interpret the message in a different manner than if he had received even a less conciliatory message from the leader of a non-hostile state. Threats that are only potential may be viewed as actual because hostile attitudes predispose policy-makers to distort the evidence. Particularly where evidence of intention is ambiguous, policy-makers may have to fall back upon traditional attitudes of distrust and

---

[3] See the careful analysis of this problem by Harold and Margaret Sprout, "En-vironmental Factors in the Study of International Politics," *Journal of Conflict Resolu-tion*, I (1957), 309–28.

hostility. One of the primary purposes of intelligence gathering is thus to provide reasonably accurate data about other nations' intentions (as well as their capabilities) so that policy-makers will *not* have to rely on intuition or hunches.

## Values

Our values are the result of upbringing, political socialization in various group contexts, indoctrination, and personal experience. They serve as standards against which our own actions and those of others are judged, and are thus the bases of many of our attitudes. Values point out the general direction toward which our actions should be directed (wealth, power, prestige, happiness, isolation) and for policy-makers they also serve as reasons and justifications for goals and actions. For example, in Western societies the values of individual freedom, civil liberties, national self-determination, independence, and economic well-being are frequently cited as reasons behind certain policy objectives or as the objectives toward which actions are directed. To the policy-maker and the public in general, actions which support these values are good; those which do not are to be avoided or resisted if undertaken by other states. In many underdeveloped countries the values of rapid economic development, national unity, freedom from foreign control, and national prestige serve as the main criteria against which to judge one's own policies and those of other states. In socialist societies the values of working class solidarity, the struggle against "imperialism," and support for "national liberation movements" would be observed frequently in policy statements. Such values as these do not necessarily prescribe specific responses for particular situations, but they do establish attitudes toward the situation and provide both justifications for and guides to the policies designed to cope with them.

## Beliefs

Beliefs can be defined as propositions which policy-makers hold to be true, even if they cannot be verified. They are the foundation of national "myths" and ideologies, and efforts to question or examine them systematically are often met with hostility or even persecution. Some beliefs which are widespread in societies and expressed in the behavior of policy-makers include those claiming that a particular nation, "way of life," or ethnic group is superior to any other, that a particular political system or economic order is superior to others, that human progress and moral improvement are inevitable, that communism is inevitable, or that a particular country will always be a "threat." Some more specific Western beliefs (closely related to liberal values) claim that all conflicts can be resolved through negotiation, that the use or threat of force is unethical except for purposes of self-defense, that foreign aid will produce stability and democracy, and the corollary belief that hunger and poverty create communism.[4]

In a foreign policy-making context such beliefs are important, for they often become the unexamined assumptions upon which numerous policy choices are made—for instance, Woodrow Wilson's belief that secret diplomacy, autocracy, and the balance of power caused war; the common Western belief that the Communist threat is basically a military threat; President Eisenhower's belief that all political leaders were essentially reasonable and peace could be secured by frank discussion;[5] and the Chinese Communist belief in the implacable hostility of all "imperialists."

Like most people, policy-makers do not like to be told that their beliefs are wrong, or that the images upon which their actions are based are not consonant with reality. Social scientists have repeatedly observed the human's resistance to "uncomfortable" facts, the stability of his images in the face of rapidly changing events in the environment, and his ability to distort or ignore facts and deny important aspects of reality.[6] Foreign policy experts seem to be no exception to these observations. The story of the diplomat in the field whose warnings and advice were shunted aside or ignored by a foreign minister because they contradicted the minister's pet beliefs is a recurring complaint in diplomatic memoirs. To take two examples, a study of President Eisenhower's Secretary of State, John Foster Dulles, illustrated how he interpreted facts about, and incoming messages from, the Soviet Union to make them fit his own beliefs about that country, which always emphasized its aggressiveness and great hostility toward the West. In some instances Dulles interpreted information —often ingeniously—in such a way as to reinforce a previously held belief.[7] Even more clearcut was Hitler's sensitivity to all information which suggested the imminent defeat of Germany's armed forces. German intelligence sources provided Hitler with accurate statistics of Ameri-

[4] Stanley Hoffmann, "Restraints and Choices in American Foreign Policy," *Daedalus* (Fall 1962), p. 682.

[5] Paul C. Davis, "The New Diplomacy: The 1955 Geneva Summit Meeting," in *Foreign Policy in the Sixties,* eds. Roger Hilsman and Robert C. Good (Baltimore: The Johns Hopkins University Press, 1965), pp. 166–67.

[6] For a summary of these findings, see Karl W. Deutsch and Richard L. Merritt, "Effects of Events on National and International Images," in *International Behavior: A Social-Psychological Analysis,* ed. Herbert C. Kelman (New York: Holt, Rinehart & Winston, Inc., 1965), pp. 132–87.

[7] Ole R. Holsti, "The Belief System and National Images: A Case Study," *Journal of Conflict Resolution,* VI (1962), 244–52.

can industrial and military production, but in the last two years of the war, the Führer became increasingly annoyed at these figures because they suggested pessimistic conclusions. Finally Hitler ordered that no more statistics be quoted to him, and forbade his officials to believe them or even to discuss them among themselves. Other officials who suggested that the morale of German citizenry was lagging by late 1944 were dismissed from their positions.[8]

## Doctrines and Ideologies

A doctrine can be defined as any explicit set of beliefs which purports to explain reality and usually prescribes goals for political action. Foreign policy objectives which derive from political doctrines are often put into slogan forms, such as "extending freedom," "trade follows the flag," "he who holds the land will hold the sea," "the throne and the altar," "the white man's burden," "make the world safe for democracy," "the New Order," or "world revolution." In some political systems the leadership inculcates into the society a comprehensive framework of doctrines, known also as an ideology. Ideologies not only establish foreign policy goals, evaluative criteria, and justifications for actions, but have important effects on perceptual processes as well. Marxism-Leninism as an ideology has great consequences in Soviet foreign policy. It can be related to political goals and action in at least five ways.

First, it establishes the intellectual framework through which policy-makers observe reality. All messages and cues from the external environment are given meaning, or interpreted, within the categories, predictions, and definitions provided by doctrines comprising the ideology. A Soviet policy-maker would interpret a foreign civil war as manifestation of a class struggle (as during the Spanish civil war); he would see conflicts among "capitalist" states as a fight between their ruling classes over markets (as in the official Soviet interpretation of World War I); and he would regard any recession in a free enterprise economy as evidence of Marx' predictions regarding the laws of economic development.

In its second function, the ideology prescribes for policy-makers an image of the future state of the world; it establishes the long-range goals of a state's external behavior, to be promoted through diplomacy, propaganda, revolution, or force. Third, the ideology serves as a rationalization, justification, and guide for the choice of more specific foreign policy tactics. As in Western countries where foreign policies are often justified in terms of such popular values as "preserving freedom," so in the Soviet

[8] John K. Galbraith, "Germany Was Badly Run," *Fortune* (December 1945), p. 200.

Union various foreign policy actions can be justified as being consistent with the general values inherent in the Communist ideology.

Fourth, the set of doctrines in communism defines for policy-makers the main stages in historical development within which specific foreign policy strategies can be enunciated. For example, when the Soviet Union was weak and the only Socialist state in existence, Soviet theoreticians could define the epoch as one in which the "forces of imperialism" were vastly superior. Defining the world situation as a period of "capitalist encirclement" made certain objectives attractive, namely building up Russian capabilities, rather than concentrating on promoting the "world revolution." But by 1956, Soviet theoreticians could explain that an entirely new epoch, involving a new "balance of forces," had developed, and that Soviet foreign and defense policies would have to change accordingly. Now that the Soviet Union was, they claimed, as strong as the imperialist bloc, it no longer had to fear capitalist encirclement; in the new epoch of "peaceful coexistence" victories could be gained by ideological proseletyzing and revolutionary activities, particularly in underdeveloped countries. In short, the ideology of Marxism-Leninism provides general outlines for defining the basic characteristics of a given historical era. From these characteristics Soviet officials can make certain deductions about appropriate foreign policy goals.

Finally, the Communist ideology posits a moral and ethical system which helps prescribe the correct attitudes and evaluative criteria for judging one's own actions and those of others. Communism is distinguished from other ideologies primarily because it claims to be an entirely objective and scientific ideology and moral system, rather than merely the preferred ideology of particular leaders. Communist theoreticians maintain that Marxism-Leninism is all powerful because it is correct, and because only Marxist-Leninists are "armed with the truth," only they have a legitimate claim to power in the world. They are on the side of history, they maintain, and all other doctrines or economic systems are retrograde. Good people are those who swim with the current of history, building communism and fighting imperialism and fascism, while bad people (or states) are those that are fighting history by clinging to outmoded (capitalist, feudal, and so on) economic systems and their colonies. Capitalism is immoral, according to the evaluative criteria of Marxist doctrines, because it is a barrier to human progress. Any technique used to fight capitalism or imperialism is *ipso facto* moral and justified because it is in accord with the laws of historical development. When people are observing reality through the lenses of such beliefs and doctrines, it is little wonder that their interpretations of international affairs are unique.[9]

[9] The great discrepancies between images of reality in the Soviet Union and the West has led some social scientists to imply that most cold war conflicts are caused by

In American foreign policy liberal values and doctrines play a similar role, though they are much less evident as guides to social and political analysis. Many American foreign policy actions are organized to promote liberal institutions and private enterprise abroad. When major threats to American economic or security interests are not involved, for instance, policy-makers often undertake programs to encourage development of democratic political institutions and discourage authoritarian political practices. In Latin America in particular, American diplomats and propaganda agencies have in recent years attempted to promote free elections and observance of civil liberties.[10] When military regimes have taken command, a frequent American response has been to withhold diplomatic recognition and terminate foreign aid unless the government promised to establish a date for holding free elections in the future. On other occasions, the United States government has made a show of force or actually intervened militarily to prevent uprisings against legally constituted governments. However, in instances where democratic political procedures led to corruption, increase in indigenous Communist or radical political strength, economic decay, or threats to American private interests, the United States has been equally prepared to support authoritarian regimes which could more effectively handle these "problems." The promotion of liberal values is thus not an absolute or persistent objective in American foreign policy, but is tempered by such other objectives and needs as defending security and economic interests and maintaining the solidarity of alliances.

## Analogies

We have all experienced attempts to clarify and understand a phenomenon by making analogies. The physiology instructor may make an analogy between the heart and a pump, the eye and a camera, or the brain and a computer. In each case the object under study is not analyzed in terms of its own properties or characteristics, but with reference to

---

incongruent images rather than by irreconcilable objectives. See, for example, Urie Bronfenbrenner, "Allowing for Soviet Perceptions," in *International Conflict and Behavioral Science,* ed. Roger Fisher (New York: Basic Books, Inc., 1964), pp. 161–78, and the critical discussion by Ralph K. White, "Images in the Context of International Conflict: Soviet Perceptions of the U.S. and the U.S.S.R.," in *International Behavior,* ed. Kelman, pp. 236–76.

[10] Cf. Theodore Wright, "Free Elections in the Latin American Policy of the United States," *Political Science Quarterly,* LXXIV (1959), 89–112. Active promotion of liberal values abroad was perhaps most pronounced in Woodrow Wilson's foreign policies. During his presidency he frequently refused to recognize any Latin American regime which came into being through unconstitutional processes. In the case of Mexico, Wilson not only refused to recognize a revolutionary government, but took active steps to overthrow it by getting all major powers to withhold recognition.

some other object. Similarly, in formulating policy goals and responses to conditions abroad, diplomats and government officials frequently characterize a situation and deduce appropriate actions to cope with it by reference to a different, though analogous, set of historical circumstances. The image of reality is based on, or compared to, a past situation, though of course current information must be available in order to suggest the comparison or analogy in the first place. For example, Prime Minister Eden of England found a close analogy between Hitler's foreign policy objectives and diplomacy in 1938 and President Nasser's behavior in the Middle East in 1956. As a British foreign secretary during the late 1930's, Eden had questioned his government's appeasement policy against the Nazis. Convinced that Nasser presented a threat similar to that posed by Hitler, he deduced that the only way to handle the analogous situation was through a show of force. Though the decision to invade Egypt in 1956 was formulated in the light of careful intelligence estimates (which were faulty in many ways), Eden did not consult most members of his government to see if they thought his image of the situation and the assumptions of his decision were correct.

During the Vietnam crisis in the 1960's American policy-makers frequently justified their actions and helped characterize the situation by citing the appeasement analogy of the 1930's: if you let aggressors achieve their objectives, you only whet their appetite for more. Appeasement, they maintained, only leads to general war, usually fought at some disadvantage by the democracies; but a strong display of force and determination can discourage aggressors and save the peace in the long run. In what respects the situation in Southeast Asia in the 1960's was really analogous to Europe in the 1930's can be debated, but the analogy was an important part of the psychological environment in which policy-makers formulated their goals and actions.

Foreign policy goals and actions are largely a response to domestic and external conditions, but no two people perceive the environment in exactly the same way. Sometimes knowledge is faulty or sparse because of lack of information or experience; more important, characterizations of the environment and responses to changing events are heavily influenced by established attitudes, values, beliefs, doctrines, and analogies. It is these that give shape and meaning to our perceptions of reality, resulting in images upon which our actions are based. But these actions can only lead to successful achievement of objectives if the images from which they derive are more or less accurate reflections of reality. Foreign policy decisions on goals or actions thus result from combining values and attitudes with perceptions provided by various sources of information.

Under what circumstances are the attitudes, values, images, or ideologies of several key policy-makers crucial to a country's foreign policy? Can we best explain or understand contemporary Swedish, Canadian, Belgian, or Philippine foreign policies by carefully examining these countries' prime ministers or foreign ministers? Many would argue that traditional policies, national roles, or the state of public opinion would be more important factors. But what of Nazi Germany, Stalin's Russia, Castro's Cuba, or France under de Gaulle? Would the United States have responded to the war in Europe in a significantly different manner had Alfred Landon been elected president instead of Franklin Roosevelt? If we attempt to provide an answer in each case, we must make some judgment about the effect of one individual, his values and beliefs, on a state's external relations; either it is an important explanatory variable or it is not. Clearly if we want to explain or understand German foreign policy in the Nazi era, we would not necessarily need to make careful examinations of Germany's traditional policies, its treaty commitments, the state of German public opinion, or even Germany's military capabilities. We would, however, be interested in the German foreign ministry (depending on the issue involved) and particularly in Adolf Hitler—his personality, ideology, beliefs, and how these affected his perceptions of reality and his selection of "core" values and interests, middle-range goals, and long-range goals. Similarly, almost every serious analysis of French foreign policy in the Fifth Republic has focused on de Gaulle's personal values and beliefs rather than on other factors which may be important in his characterization of a situation.

One problem of stressing individual values, images, or ideological commitments is that a leader's views of reality may be mediated by his political role or important organizational influences in the policy-making process. Is the leader relatively free to make policy without consulting others, or is he restricted by constitutional, bureaucratic, or political limitations? There are, for example, important consequences on decision-making procedures in parliamentary democracies that are not found in strong presidential systems or in dictatorships. To what extent can a prime minister act in the areas of foreign policy as a strong president might act? If foreign policy decisions are the result of considerable debate and discussion within a cabinet meeting—as they often are in countries with a parliamentary system—one would expect personal views to be less evident than in situations where a policy-maker does not have to consult broadly.[11] In this case, the definition of the situation would comprise the

[11] Some hypotheses regarding personality variables in policy-making in an organizational setting are discussed by Sidney Verba in his "Assumptions of Rationality and Non-Rationality in Models of the International System," *World Politics*, XIV (1961), 93–117.

consensus arrived at by many different people, and it would be difficult to assume that any one person's images, whether accurate or distorted, were crucial.

Studies also reveal that the personal political position or prestige of a leader may be an important component of a definition of the situation, and that some foreign policy actions are geared primarily to solve some internal political problem, such as a leader's lagging prestige, rather than to cope with an issue arising in the external environment. To the extent that the policy-maker is cognizant of his domestic political position as being a motivation for action (or non-action), individual variables again become important for foreign policy analysis. This is the case where *private motives* are translated into public policies.[12]

If we believe that any explanation of a country's objectives or actions in terms of the leaders' images, values, ideological commitments, or private motives is insufficient, we might be tempted to seek a psychological explanation for his policies. We would then try to establish a link between a policy-maker's psychological needs and his public actions. A wide range of psychological characteristics is at least potentially relevant to policy-making styles. These would include propensity to take risks, intelligence, image inflexibility, desire for self-esteem and domination, achievement, as well as any serious mental imbalances. Attempts to relate personality characteristics to public policies have not yet been very fruitful except where policy was clearly identified as the result of one man's will, or where the policy-maker displayed obvious abnormal characteristics.[13] Psychoanalytical studies of Napoleon's, Hitler's, or Stalin's key foreign policy decisions might uncover interesting subconscious motivations, but such inquiry would probably not help us understand the foreign policy behavior of many other political leaders. In short, psychological variables

---

[12] This situation raises serious problems for the historian. A policy-maker may give as reasons for his actions the state of public opinion, conditions abroad, or commitments which have to be fulfilled, whereas privately the most important consideration or component of a definition of the situation is his concern for his own political prestige and reputation. Since such considerations are seldom confessed even in memoirs, it is difficult to establish with certainty the relevance of private motives to public policies. There is also the problem of statesmen giving different reasons for their actions to different audiences at different times. For example, Mussolini emphasized on different occasions at least three reasons—his personal prestige, anti-communism, and strategic advantages—for his decision to intervene in the Spanish Civil War. Hugh Thomas, *The Spanish Civil War* (London: Eyre & Spotiswoode, 1961), pp. 226–27.

[13] Among the attempts at this kind of analysis are Alexander and Juliette George, *Woodrow Wilson and Colonel House: A Personality Study* (New York: The John Day Company, Inc., 1956); Arnold Rogow, *James Forrestal: A Study of Personality, Politics, and Policy* (New York: The Macmillan Company, 1963); and Harold D. Lasswell, *Psychopathology and Politics* (Chicago: University of Chicago Press, 1930).

or characteristics may be important explanatory devices for analyzing those leaders who are in a constitutional or political position single-handedly to formulate objectives and who can command the obedience of others to implement them. But where policy, often undramatic, is the result of consultation, compromise, and bargaining among many individuals and advisers, the impact of subconscious psychological needs will be almost impossible to measure and identify, and may not help explain decisions in any case.[14]

### The Structure of the International System, Conditions Abroad, and Systemic Values as Components of a Definition of the Situation

In Chapter II it was suggested that general foreign policy orientations and strategies, if not specific decisions, are partly a function of the structure of power and influence among the units comprising the system. The major characteristics of the systems are therefore one important component of any perceptions of "reality." This is simply a shorthand way of stating that policy-makers of diverse states perceive major structural aspects of the external environment in approximately the same way, and through a series of cumulative decisions tend to orient their state's policies to fit that structure. In a "polar" structure, for example, policy-makers of small states may all recognize that their security can best be achieved by alliances with one of the bloc leaders, regardless of other variables such as the policy-makers' private preferences, state of public opinion within a country, or traditional policies. Or, as in the Chinese and Athenian leagues, smaller members may perceive that they have "no choice" but to adhere to the bloc leaders' policies. Europe's collapse during World War II and the attending rise of the United States and the Soviet Union had a profound impact on the types of security systems considered feasible in the post-war world. Governments of weak European states observed that they could not provide for their own security either by creating a European alliance or attempting to remain neutral. They realized that they would have to rely on the United States or the Soviet Union to provide them with security. Once the smaller European states were committed to their respective alliance systems they partly abandoned their freedom to formulate policies outside of those sanctioned by the bloc leader. The power structure, in other words, established certain

[14] Verba, "Assumptions of Rationality and Non-Rationality." For another type of psychological approach, see Arthur Gladstone, "Relationship Orientation and the Processes Leading Toward War," *Background,* VI (1962), 13–26.

conditions over which the smaller states had little control; it was a "given" in any definition of a situation, the most basic perception of the external environment. To put it in another way, the structure of the system establishes limits on what general foreign policy orientations are feasible.

On the other hand, if the structure is not hierarchical in both blocs, and if there is a large number of relatively noninvolved states on the periphery of the major subsystem (as was the case in Greece during the fifth century and in the post-World War II period), various forms of nonalignment may appear as feasible foreign policy orientations. In a diffuse structure, policy-makers are more likely to try a number of different alignments because no one state or group exists as a permanent threat to the others. The power structure is fluid and even small states may affect its configuration by different foreign policy maneuvers or alliance commitments.

The influence of systemic structure on foreign policy is also prominent when the structure is undergoing fundamental changes. Only the policy-makers of an isolated state would fail to take seriously an important change in international politics, whether it was the breakup of a bloc, the rise of a number of new political units, or the creation of new blocs. New power configurations create new opportunities for some states by casting off old limitations on their actions; or they create, as the term "an unfavorable shift in the balance of power" indicates, new threats which must be deterred by constructing countervailing balances.

Any government's external goals and actions are also a response to rapidly changing conditions and developments abroad—a new treaty or alliance, a foreign civil war or *coup d'état,* a depression, or a war. Even political units which subscribe to vague long-range objectives must solve problems on a day-to-day basis. They must react to situations which are not of their own making and which may seem unrelated to their long-range plans, but which nevertheless impinge on some of their immediate interests. Thus, policy-making in *particular* situations involves a process where government officials gauge the intentions of other states, examine various alternative courses of action in response, and speculate about the possible consequences of those courses of action. In making policy to respond to the placement of Soviet intermediate range missiles in Cuba during 1962, for instance, the 15 American policy-makers responsible for advising President Kennedy spent the better part of two weeks trying to decide what Premier Khrushchev's motives for placing the missiles had been, and then carefully weighing the costs and possible consequences (e.g., the probable Soviet response) of various alternatives, including doing nothing, making a diplomatic protest, blockading Cuba against import of more weapons, conducting an air strike against the missile emplacements, or invading the island. Each proposal was fraught with dangerous consequences, either in the long-run or immediately, and the blockade was finally selected because it seemed to involve fewer risks and allowed the Russians a wider range of options for their own response. In making this decision, anticipated Russian responses (based on memories of past Soviet behavior) bore much more weight than considerations of domestic public reaction, the state of the system, ideological imperatives, or organizational needs and traditions. In short, any government's particular objectives are largely a function of the actions and objectives of other states.

We must emphasize, however, that those actions are interpreted in an intellectual framework of attitudes, expectations, and values. Against their ideological background, Soviet perceptions of American intentions and actions would appear most unfamiliar to us. There is evidence that Soviet policy-makers sincerely believe that most American actions express a desire to dominate the world through direct application of force, political and military subversion, and economic penetration. Soviet expectations regarding American objectives are strikingly similar to American interpretations of most of Russia's external objectives.

Events in the external environment can also have a more subtle impact on a state's objectives, for any international system possesses certain values or doctrines which transcend purely local or national values. For example, in the eighteenth century the doctrine of divine right and the values associated with royal authority were accepted by the European upper classes irrespective of nationality; hence, certain external objectives and actions relating to the preservation or extension of royal authority were highly valued. If dynastic prestige was a goal to which all monarchs aspired, then the various methods of achieving status, such as alliances and marriages, were also considered legitimate. Today it would appear absurd if Great Britain made an alliance with Sweden in order to enhance the prestige of both countries' royal families. In the late nineteenth century establishment of empires became a "legitimate" national objective, providing increased international influence, economic rewards, and considerable prestige. In the contemporary setting one of the great trans-national values is self-determination and political independence, while the value placed on colonies is almost nonexistent. The predominant system-wide value today is economic development. A nation's status is closely related to the level of its technology, military forces, and industrialization, no longer to the personal prestige of dynasts, to colonies, or to royal palaces. Since all the major Western states have placed such high value on industrialization and have achieved so many social goals (including international influence) through industrializing policies, it is little wonder that this objective would have a great impact on the values of newer states as well. While there are some important indigenous pressures for economic development and modernization—as well as strong resistances—the objective of industrialization is adopted by many governments in part because other states have adopted it as their own goal.

## National Role

In response partly to the general structure of power within an international system, governments adopt general orientations toward the outside world, as neutrals, bloc leaders, faithful alliance partners, international mediators, or carriers of an ideology. In each instance the role creates certain obligations and commitments which policy-makers will usually attempt to fulfill. Foreign policy objectives and actions of a government within an alliance will normally display characteristics compatible with the purposes and expectations of the alliance partners. Thus, the *expectations* of other states become an important component of a definition of the situation and help sustain a state's international role. The margin of choice for American policy-makers is not very great considering its military power because, as Stanley Hoffmann points out,[15] a leader of several alliances has to maintain its leadership by meeting commitments and expectations. To do this it might have to undertake some actions which are popular neither from the point of view of its own taxpayers nor from the expectations of states not in the alliance. Certain objectives and policies also devolve upon the Soviet government by virtue of its role as professed leader of the Communist bloc. Some obligations, such as an appropriate degree of ideological and revolutionary activity, may conflict with Soviet aspirations to gain influence among underdeveloped countries. Governments which have formally declared their foreign policy orientation as non-aligned also feel strong compulsions to conform to patterns of behavior consistent with the role of a non-aligned state, lest they be branded as satellites or "puppets" of former colonial powers. Indeed, policy-makers may place such heavy emphasis on meeting expectations of other states or observing specific treaty obligations that they are willing to undergo considerable criticism from the domestic public.

A nation's traditional role may also have cumulative effects on the perceptions and attitudes of both policy-makers and the public in general. If they conceive of their nation as a "free world leader," as the "outpost of

[15] Hoffmann, "Restraints and Choices in American Foreign Policy," p. 670.

democracy," or as an "honest broker" between the East and West, certain beliefs and attitudes toward international affairs are likely to become an established part of their definition of any situation, and will be reflected in their responses to developing conditions abroad. The interaction of national role and perceptions might be tested by examining the attitudes and images of policy-makers who are faced with similar conditions abroad, but govern countries with different roles in the system.[16] For example, Finland and Burma are both countries with analogous geographical situations (located next to powerful Communist neighbors) and traditional non-aligned or neutral foreign policy orientations. Do their leaders then perceive potential threats from their neighbors in the same way that the leaders of West Germany and Pakistan do, two countries also with potentially hostile neighbors, but which belong to alliances? Why did many Americans believe that Communist Cuba, a small nation in terms of military and economic capabilities, could pose a threat to the security of the United States? This characterization of Cuba formed the basis of American objectives of isolating the island through embargoes and boycotts and, if possible, overthrowing the Castro regime. Most Mexicans did not believe that Cuba represented a threat to their independence or security. The different interpretations of reality may be explained by the sensitivity to communism that America's role as a leader of the Western alliance has engendered in policy-makers and the general public.

### Domestic Needs

A number of foreign policy objectives are formulated to fulfill general social needs and advance more specific interests of domestic groups, political parties, and economic organizations. In the middle of the nineteenth century, for example, the British government had little interest in establishing new colonies. But by the 1890's missionary societies, explorers, commercial firms, and military adventurers had prevailed upon the political parties and government to create colonies and protectorates to provide security under which they could conduct activities in Africa with safety. Partly in response to competition from France and Germany, considerations of prestige, and importuning of pressure groups, the

[16] The implications of national role on perceptions and definitions of situations are analyzed in Richard Brody, "Cognition and Behavior: A Model of Inter-State Relations," Stanford Studies in International Conflict and Integration, July 1964 (mimeo.), pp. 32–33.

British government ultimately made expansion of the empire an official policy objective.[17] The interests of some types of private groups can only be secured by governmental actions toward other states. If such groups are successful in their agitation, they may obtain official recognition of their interests by policy-makers who will raise these private interests into collective objectives, demanding official time and attention, diplomatic representation, spending of public money, and occasional use of armed force. Typical examples occur when a government negotiates a tariff agreement with another state to benefit one of its own business enterprises or industries, or intervenes diplomatically or militarily in another country to protect the property and investments of its own citizens or business enterprises.

More important, the main geographic, demographic, and economic characteristics of a country help create *general* social needs that can be fulfilled only through transactions with other states. The conditions may be so obvious that they are not openly acknowledged as crucial elements in a definition of a situation, but almost every political objective and diplomatic action implicitly gives recognition to their importance. Of the components in many definitions of situations, a country's geographic location and topographical features may be the most important because they are the most permanent.[18] While modern technology can alter the political and economic significance of geographic characteristics, many of these characteristics still influence policies by providing opportunities or by placing limitations on what is feasible in both domestic and foreign policy programs. A country's size, population, distribution of natural resources, climate, and topography will have an important bearing on its socio-economic development, needs vis-à-vis other nations, and access to other areas of the world. These conditions also have the greatest relevance to military and defense policies. Topographical features create avenues for invasion and suggest the best lines of defense; economic characteristics and distribution of natural resources determine a nation's self-reliance or dependency on others in wartime as well as during peace; and climate imposes restrictions on the types of warfare that can be conducted in a particular area or the kinds of agricultural products that can be grown.

Any British or Japanese foreign minister is aware that his country is a small island, heavily populated, unable to grow adequate food supplies and, therefore, highly dependent upon foreign trade to maintain an

---

[17] Cf. H. A. C. Cairns, *Prelude to Empire* (London: Routledge & Kegan Paul, Ltd., 1965).

[18] Nicholas J. Spykman, "Geography and Foreign Policy, I," *American Political Science Review*, XXXII (1938), 28.

acceptable standard of living. Given the general goal of maintaining living standards, some foreign policy objectives, such as trade expansion, naturally proceed from the economic and geographic situation. Lack of raw materials and food within the islands makes it necessary for the British and Japanese to import these commodities; in order to import they have to manufacture export goods which can compete successfully against the products of other exporting nations. The geographical characteristics of Japan and England thus help create persisting interests and objectives no matter what the circumstances abroad or which political party or foreign minister is in power. This does not mean that all people similarly interpret the significance of geographic and economic conditions, or that any government will defend or achieve persisting interests in exactly the same way. The British Conservative Party, responding to the need to expand trade, may promote this expansion by subsidizing exports; the Labour Party may try to accomplish the same goal by lowering the volume of imports. In the 1930's the Japanese sought to meet their economic needs and population pressures by creating the "Greater East Asia Co-Prosperity Sphere," a semi-colonial region which would provide cheap raw materials, expanding markets, and a region for settling Japan's surplus population. In the 1950's and 1960's, however, the Japanese have sought to satisfy their persisting socio-economic needs by modernizing industrial capacity, rationalizing agriculture, and conducting vigorous export sales programs in international markets.

## Objectives and Capabilities

Foreign policy decision-making is always carried out with some knowledge of a country's immediate or potential capacity to achieve its objectives. Rational behavior implies some correspondence between means and ends, and in many instances the means available will influence the types of ends selected. The quantities and types of available capabilities, whether diplomatic personnel, economic goods, transportation facilities, or military forces, indicate what is possible to accomplish in a given situation.

Long-range goals—vague images of a future state of affairs—may require such radical demands and alterations of the international system's structure that their achievement would require types and quantities of capabilities which most states lack. Nevertheless, the policy-makers may persist, at least symbolically, in pursuing that goal. In its early years the Soviet regime (rather untypically of a weak government) formulated a long-range goal of world revolution, but was itself quite incapable of creating, much less directing, this revolution. The lack of capabilities did not force the Russians to denounce world revolution as an ultimate goal; they turned their attention instead to more immediate objectives. Similarly, neither France nor the United States today possesses the means or inclination to create the kind of world or regional orders they might desire, yet the long-range goals still point the general direction for their day-to-day actions and policies.

## Foreign Policy Objectives as a Function of Public Opinion

Probably no aspect of the study of international politics or foreign policy is more difficult to generalize about than the relationship of public opinion to a government's external objectives and diplomatic behavior. More research on this area, particularly in non-Western countries, needs to be completed before students of international relations can offer generalizations with much confidence. The characteristics of political systems in the world today vary so immensely—from primitive, patriarchal, or religious oligarchies to modern industrial democracies and totalitarian dictatorships—that any proposition would have to be qualified in terms of the type of society being considered. Our comments will refer, therefore, primarily to those societies in which the public has relatively free access to information from abroad, where there is a general awareness of the external environment, and where formal political institutions are maintained by widespread political support.

First, we should eliminate those hypotheses which suggest either that foreign policy goals and diplomatic behavior are merely a response to domestic opinions, or that public attitudes are virtually ignored as important components of a definition of a situation. Some government officials have claimed frankly that their decisions could not be influenced by fickle public attitudes; it is also easy to cite examples where officials yielded to public pressures despite their own preferred policies. Instead of assuming a simple or direct relationship between public opinions on foreign affairs and government policies, we should distinguish (1) *who* is expressing opinions concerning (2) *what* issues in (3) *which* situations. The characteristics of these three qualifiers may have important effects on the ultimate influence of public opinion on the formulation of objectives and actions.

Studies of public attitudes conclude that the vast majority of population —even in highly literate societies—is unknowledgeable, uninterested, and apathetic with regard to most issues of world affairs.[19] They also reveal that public images and attitudes toward foreign countries are highly resistant to change even when dramatic events radically alter the main issues of international politics.[20] Other studies suggest that government, university, and private programs which have sought to create wider public knowledge and appreciation of the complexities of international politics have seldom met with success.[21]

For purposes of analysis, any society has a small top layer of the "attentive"[22] public which is reasonably well-informed, articulate, and interested, though not necessarily more prone to change basic attitudes when subjected to new information, propaganda, or dramatic events abroad. In most Western countries the attentive public is closely correlated with higher education, urban domicile, professional occupation, higher income, middle age, and male sex. Estimates of the size of the attentive public range from 1 to 15 per cent, depending on how the category is defined. Next to the attentive public in developed countries exists a layer of the population normally comprising 30 to 50 per cent of the total, which possesses established attitudes toward, and images of, foreign countries and their actions, some knowledge of a limited range of issues, and some capacity to express opinions if asked. Their views are seldom the result of independent inquiry, but are usually inculcated by parents, leaders of voluntary associations, political parties, or the individual's preferred media of communication. Finally, the rest of a society, in some cases comprising 70 per cent or more of the population, can be characterized on *most* issues as apathetic, uninformed, and non-expressive, although in certain circumstances these people can display considerable interest in some issue areas and, if properly mobilized, can express great hostility or loyalty to foreign nations or their political leaders.

On what kinds of issues are the opinions found in different layers or groups within society expressed as demands to establish certain foreign

[19] For example, Gabriel Almond, *The American People and Foreign Policy* (New York: Harcourt, Brace & World, Inc., 1950); Gabriel Almond and Sidney Verba, *The Civic Culture* (Princeton: Princeton University Press, 1963), esp. Part II regarding knowledge of, and interest in, domestic politics; Warren E. Miller and Donald E. Stokes, "Constituency Influence in Congress," *American Political Science Review*, LVII (1963), 45–56; Milton J. Rosenberg, "Images in Relation to the Policy Process: American Public Opinion on Cold-War Issues," in *International Behavior*, ed. Kelman, pp. 277–334.

[20] Deutsch and Merritt, "Effects of Events on National and International Images," in *International Behavior*, ed. Kelman, pp. 132–87.

[21] Joseph Frankel, *The Making of Foreign Policy* (New York: Oxford University Press, 1963), p. 72.

[22] The concept is introduced by Almond in *The American People and Foreign Policy*.

policy goals or to undertake certain actions vis-à-vis other states? The attentive public is likely to be concerned with a wide range of foreign policy problems and to express opinions on them either directly to policy-makers or simply to friends and associates. They are also likely to have adequate information on a number of foreign countries, well-defined opinions, and preferred solutions to contemporary problems. While the bottom layer may be generally apathetic, on *certain* issues it may become highly involved and express views through diverse channels. Consider one hypothetical example. Wheat farmers in the Midwest may not have much general interest in world affairs, may possess little knowledge about foreign countries and their problems, and have unrefined attitudes and images based more on family or regional traditions than on a careful examination of contemporary information. But if a problem relating to wheat export programs arises, the farmers will probably become highly involved, express their views in most vigorous terms to friends, associates, and policy-makers, and suggest preferred solutions. In other words, apathy and ignorance end when a problem is perceived as having a *direct* impact on the life of the individual. The *scope* of public expression is thus related to the nature of the issue or problem under consideration.

It would still be an oversimplification to argue that those in the bottom layer of a society (in terms of interest and knowledge, not class) become involved only on issues of direct relevance to their private lives, while those of the attentive public are interested in a much broader scope of affairs. No matter what the level of interest or knowledge among people, they all hold some notions about appropriate and inappropriate foreign policy goals and actions. Gabriel Almond has used the term foreign policy "mood" to suggest those very *general* attitudes or predispositions which prevail in a nation at any given time. In the nineteenth and early twentieth centuries in the United States, the predominant public mood was isolation and indifference to European affairs. In the 1950's, it was a mood of pronounced fear of, and hostility toward, the Soviet Union. War weariness in Great Britain during the 1930's was an important basis for England's appeasement policy toward Hitler and Mussolini. Such moods, while not suggesting concrete foreign policy objectives, at least *set limits* around the theoretical policy alternatives of policy-makers. The Prime Minister of neutral Sweden could not, for example, announce one day that he had concluded a military alliance, unless large segments of the population also believed that neutrality was outmoded, ineffective, or incompatible with some value such as national survival. Nor would the President of the United States be likely to proclaim that he would withdraw all American commitments abroad and turn the country into an isolated "Fortress America." On the major questions of a country's general orientation to the rest of the world, war and peace, and general style of diplomacy, everyone has opinions and is likely to express them when challenged. When the *scope* of public opinion is so broad, it is likely to have great influence on the alternatives which policy-makers would regard seriously.

The impact of public attitudes and opinions on the selection of objectives can be related, then, to the scope of the public, which in turn is related to the type of issue at stake. A third variable would be the general situation in which opinions are being expressed. Is the role of opinion in times of crisis the same as it is during a period of relative stability and non-involvement in international affairs? We would expect the *scope* of the opinion-expressing public to vary directly with the degree of urgency or threat in a situation. More people are probably aroused to take interest in foreign affairs when a crisis develops than when diplomatic conditions are "normal," and there is much historical and experimental evidence which suggests that even societies strongly divided among themselves tend to become united in times of crisis. If a diplomatic-military crisis creates a public consensus, this opinion is likely to restrict the number of options which diplomatic officials would seriously consider.[23]

On the other hand, deep-seated attitudes of distrust toward other countries are not easily changed simply by the development of new circumstances. During the critical period after the outbreak of World War II, President Roosevelt was cautious in making too many commitments in support of England because of the presence of a strong isolationist mood and anti-British sentiments. When the United States joined the war against Germany in late December, 1941, it took considerable efforts at persuasion by the government before a large proportion of the American public would accept the need to create an alliance with the Soviet Union, a nation towards which Americans had directed considerable hostility since the Bolshevik revolution. Similarly, the French government could withdraw from Indochina in 1954 because the French population was weary of supporting a distant military effort which was accomplishing little and involved great sacrifices; but no French government from 1954 to 1958 could have survived in office had it tried to negotiate a withdrawal agreement providing independence for Algeria. In this case, it was not so much that the French population was overwhelmingly in favor of "pacifying" Algeria, but that opinions were split among many different groups, none of which could command a convincing majority. Finally, when the government of Ireland had to decide in 1939 whether to remain

[23] Cf. Morton A. Kaplan, *System and Process in International Politics* (New York: John Wiley & Sons, Inc., 1957), p. 55.

neutral or join England against Nazi Germany, the government felt compelled to accept the neutrality option because that choice was supported by most of the articulate population—despite some feelings among officials that the other course would have been preferable. Many similar cases could be cited, but they all suggest one conclusion: public opinion in these critical situations, while it does not prescribe exact policies or responses, establishes limits beyond which few policy-makers would normally dare to act.[24]

It would be omitting an important part of the relationship between opinion and foreign policy if we suggested that policy-makers only *respond* to public pressures. In fact, the relationship in democratic societies involves complex interaction in which officials and the public or its component groups react to each others' behavior, values, and interests. If in some cases government officials feel constrained to choose policy goals and actions consistent with prevailing public moods, it is no less true that they spend considerable time advocating their own position and characterization of a situation to the population. Because of superior knowledge and access to information, governments occupy a position from which they can interpret reality to the population and actually create attitudes, opinions, and images where none existed before. While independent communications media may express differing views, a prime minister or president can be very persuasive by virtue of his political prestige and expertise. It has often been observed that information or propaganda emanating from a reliable or prestigious source has more impact on opinions than information dispersed by less credible sources.[25] Thus, what many people know of, or feel about, a critical situation abroad and its own government's actions and responses to it may originate from the government itself—from press conferences, parliamentary debates, or political speeches. As much as they respond to public opinions, governments also help create those opinions. Public opinion, rather than controlling or restricting policy choices, may serve primarily to support government actions.[26]

In political systems where all information is controlled by the government, public opinion plays predominantly a supporting function. A

[24] In examining a non-critical issue, however, one study suggests that policy-makers in the United States enjoy considerable freedom from any restraints imposed on their decisions by public groups. See Raymond Bauer, Ithiel Pool, and L. A. Dexter, *American Business and Public Policy: The Politics of Foreign Trade* (New York: The Atherton Press, 1963).

[25] Cf. C. I. Hovland, I. L. Janis, and H. H. Kelley, *Communication and Persuasion* (New Haven: Yale University Press, 1953), pp. 19–55.

[26] Cf. James Rosenau, *National Leadership and Foreign Policy: A Case Study in the Mobilization of Public Support* (Princeton: Princeton University Press, 1963).

person whose sources of information on the outside world are restricted to a government-controlled newspaper must have considerable initiative and access to unusual resources in order to develop attitudes and opinions contrary to those prescribed for him by his government.[27] Since members of such societies normally have no independent sources of information and are not allowed channels of communication through which to express opposition to a government's foreign policies, the government is free to change its objectives, withdraw from untenable positions, or change allies without having to worry about domestic reactions. Domestic attitudes are not, therefore, a salient aspect of the definition of the situation. President Roosevelt, collaborating with Congressmen, executive officers, and many members of the press, labored many months to convince the American public that it should support an alliance with the Soviet Union against Nazi Germany. But Joseph Stalin could easily switch from a policy and propaganda line which emphasized great hostility toward Nazi Germany to one of collaboration with Hitler. Clearly, considerations about the state of public opinion in the Soviet Union played little role in Stalin's leadership; Stalin could never quite comprehend that governments in the Western democracies were not similarly free to alter policies with impunity.

## Organizational Values, Needs, and Traditions

Students of international politics or diplomatic history often cite cases in which foreign offices, military organizations, or intelligence agencies took actions formulated independently of the top political leadership, or a president or prime minister was unable to persuade bureaucrats to implement his own policy objectives. "Departmental policy" refers to those actions which lower officials determine in accordance with their own needs and values. Of the many cases in modern history where those with formal policy-making authority were kept ignorant of the actions of lower personnel, perhaps none led to more fatal consequences than the occasion in 1914 when German military and diplomatic officials took steps to goad Austria into war against Serbia, and deliberately kept the Kaiser uninformed of their own activities as well as of several British diplomatic moves aimed at reducing tensions and preserving peace.

The relevant factors in a definition of a situation may become extraordinarily complex and diverse because they involve the interests and

[27] Irving L. Janis and M. Brewster Smith, "Effects of Education and Persuasion on National and International Images," in *International Behavior,* ed. Kelman, p. 193.

attitudes of many competing government agencies. In the United States, for example, many external issues and foreign situations touch upon the interests and jurisdictions of the Departments of Defense, Agriculture, Commerce, and Treasury, in addition to the Department of State. Before decisions can be made, all of the people concerned have to be consulted and a policy must be designed to accommodate all of those interests. In states deeply involved in the affairs of the system, recurrence of external problems which impinge upon the interests of many government agencies requires establishment of formal interdepartmental machinery, which may very well formulate and administer policies of which the top political leadership has only slight knowledge.[28] Another factor which may complicate the definition of objectives and implementation of policies is the rivalry and suspicion among personalities in different agencies, where some may not accept others' definition of a situation or resent the intrusion of other agencies in problems they feel to be within their exclusive competence.

Even where top policy-makers are fully consulted about all major decisions, bureaucratic values will tend to impinge upon individual beliefs, attitudes, and images. A foreign minister is restrained in his actions and prerogatives partly by constitutional and customary limitations, partly by his general political position vis-à-vis other policy-makers, and by their expectations of what constitutes proper conduct for a foreign minister. No matter how strong the personality, he will always be subjected to influences from the bureaucracy, whether the need to maintain policies consistent with traditional forms of behavior, reliance on organizational sources of information, or more specific resistance by lower-level policy-makers against attempted procedural or substantive innovation by the foreign minister. Anyone who has worked in a large organization has learned that whatever his personal views and beliefs, he faces strong pressures to conform with group norms.

Under what circumstances are administrative processes and organizational values, needs, and traditions likely to have an important role in the definition and implementation of objectives? First, where political leadership at the top is weak or unstable, the main administrative organs of the state may have to make policy in the light of their own needs, values, and traditions. Second, most non-critical transactions between states are carried out by the lower echelons of policy-making organizations, often

---

[28] There are over 160 formal interdepartmental and interagency committees on foreign affairs in the United States government. Kenneth Thompson, *Political Realism and the Crisis of World Politics* (Princeton: Princeton University Press, 1960), p. 124.

without the explicit direction of a foreign minister or head of government. For routine problems, traditional departmental policies rather than direction from above serve as the main guidelines for action. The American State Department in any one day receives about 1,300 cables from American diplomatic and consular officials abroad providing information, requesting directions, or seeking permission to make certain decisions in the field. But of that large number of communications the Secretary of State will read only 20 to 30—about 2 per cent of the total. The State Department also sends out approximately 1,000 cables daily, many of which elucidate objectives and provide directions on policies designed to implement them; of these the Secretary of State may see only six, while the President will have only one or two of the most important communications referred to his office.[29] The implication of this type of communications system is clear: on routine and non-vital matters (though if a bad decision is made on these, it may result in a diplomatic crisis) the experts and lower officials of policy-making organizations define specific objectives in the light of their own values, needs, and traditions. High officials are generally concerned only with suggesting the main outlines of objectives, not with their specifics nor with the detailed means by which to implement them. As Joseph Frankel points out,[30] high-ranking officials within policy-making hierarchies are far removed from information which describes the external environment in detail. They become captives of advisers, oversimplifications, and all the prejudices, established attitudes, and procedures of large bureaucratic organizations. It is little wonder that diplomatic history is replete with cases of top policy-makers choosing disastrous courses of action because their images of reality and expectations were at odds with real conditions in the environment.

In a crisis situation, where decisions of great consequence have to be made rapidly, the effect of bureaucratic processes may be reduced considerably.[31] In these circumstances a few key individuals at the highest level of responsibility and authority usually congregate to map strategy and responses to the problem or threat they are confronting. There is no time for detailed consultations, preparation of position papers, or thorough analysis of the situation and its background. Since urgency is the most salient aspect of the definition of the situation, decisions have to be made largely upon the basis of immediately available information,

[29] Testimony of Secretary of State Dean Rusk to a Senate Subcommittee, reported in *Time*, LXXXIII, No. 4 (January 24, 1964), 19.

[30] Frankel, *The Making of Foreign Policy*, p. 96.

[31] For a discussion of this hypothesis, see Brody, "Cognition and Behavior," p. 37.

unverified rumors, and the views of upper-level advisers.[32] Under such conditions, individual attitudes, values, beliefs, and images of the highest policy-makers become particularly important in defining the situation, choosing responses and goals, and implementing policies.

### Relationships Among the Components[33]

The analysis of policy-makers' attitudes, values, beliefs, and personality needs implied that their relevance to a definition of a situation is related to factors of political role and various administrative procedures. In another section it was suggested that, in crisis situations, public opinion can impose restrictions on the options available to policy-makers in a democratic political system, while public opinion in authoritarian political systems, no matter what the situation, plays little or no role in helping to shape foreign policy objectives and actions. We also argued that organizational needs, values, and traditions are less important in influencing policy-making during times of crisis than during consideration of routine problems. All of these statements are really *hypotheses* about relationships among the various factors which may influence foreign policy behavior. It may be useful to know that the state of domestic opinion, the structure of the system, and traditional policies are important aspects, let us say, of the Danish foreign minister's view of a situation towards which he must respond. But ideally we would also want to know *under what conditions* these are more important than organizational values or personality variables. Too often we assume that only one component of a definition of the situation can explain the behavior of states in their relations with other states.

The problem of assessing the relative importance of different components—and the relationship among them—is well illustrated in analyses of Soviet foreign policy. Some observers of Russian politics claim that ideological imperatives are the paramount consideration in formulation of Soviet foreign policy. They argue that the Soviet Union, as any other state, has certain core values and interests such as national independence and territorial security, but all middle-range and long-range objectives

[32] Cf. Snyder and Paige, "The United States Decision to Resist Aggression in Korea," in *Foreign Policy Decision-Making*, ed. Snyder, Bruck, and Sapin.

[33] One of the few systematic attempts to grapple with the problem of relating various influences on policy-making is the paper by James Rosenau, "Pre-Theories and Theories of Foreign Policy," in *Approaches to Comparative and International Politics,* ed. R. Barry Farrell (Evanston: Northwestern University Press, 1966), pp. 27–92. Some of the remaining comments in this chapter are based on his analysis. See also Kaplan, *System and Process in International Politics,* pp. 54–74.

and the diplomatic strategies used to achieve them are deduced from Marxism-Leninism. Others have emphasized the persistence of purely "national" themes in Soviet foreign policy; they claim that by virtue of its geographic position (which creates certain weaknesses and strengths from a military point of view), the Soviet Union is primarily continuing Tsarist foreign policies, albeit under Communist slogans. This type of analysis suggests that Soviet policy-makers define their environment and perceive Russian needs and interests much as their predecessors did, except that they place more emphasis on doctrinaire justifications for their actions. A third type of analysis of Soviet foreign policy emphasizes contemporary leadership qualities and role rather than ideology or traditional policies as the most important elements in Russia's external behavior. Diplomatic maneuvers and major policy decisions are thus seen not as tactics designed to implement some grandiose ideological plan, but as a means of establishing or safeguarding the position of the top leadership or a way of fulfilling certain psychological needs. Finally, another generalization explaining Soviet actions abroad claims that the leadership is increasingly concerned with fulfilling domestic needs and responding to consumer demands. Thus, domestic needs and expectations will loom as important components of any definition of a situation.

Which of these interpretations is correct? All would seem at least partially valid since ideology, traditional policies, personal and political needs, and domestic needs would likely be relevant to many policy-making situations.[34] But this tells us very little about the relative importance of each component in different circumstances. We can use historical data to test our propositions and perhaps even make predictions for the future. For example, an analysis of Soviet foreign policy made in terms of the components listed in this chapter would probably reveal that during the 1930's the structure of the system (as interpreted in Marxist terms), national needs, traditional policies, and Stalin's personality and political role were the most important aspects of reality considered by Soviet policy-makers in selecting goals and diplomatic strategies.

In the absence of systematic, comparative analyses of foreign policies in different countries, it is difficult to make verified statements concerning which phenomena might be considered relevant or significant under different circumstances. Instead we can suggest some hypotheses about which components (personal attitudes, beliefs, and political or personality needs, system structure and values, national role, domestic needs, capa-

---

[34] Cf. William Welch, "The Sources of Soviet Conduct: A Note on Method," *Background,* VI (1963), 17–28.

bilities, social values and public opinion, and organizational needs, values, and traditions) are likely to constitute the most salient aspects of a definition of the situation, and under what conditions.

1. The more critical or urgent a situation is perceived, the fewer people will become directly involved in defining the situation, choosing responses, and selecting goals.

2. The fewer people making these decisions, the more likely that their actions will reflect personal idiosyncrasies, attitudes, beliefs, and personal political needs.[35]

3. The more people involved in defining a situation, formulating goals, or choosing alternatives, the more the decisions will reflect group and organizational values, needs, and traditions, and the less they will reveal the attitudes, beliefs, or images of any single person.[36]

4. National role (e.g. status, alliance commitments, expectations of other states, historical policies) is most likely to be an important factor in the formulation of objectives when (a) the structure of the system is polarized, (b) the leadership is responsive to public opinion, (c) policies are largely defined by bureaucratic organizations, (d) the state is a member of an alliance all of whose members perceive a common threat, (e) the state is a leader of a bloc, group, or alliance of states, and (f) the situation is non-critical.

5. Conversely, a government's foreign policy objectives are *least* likely to be influenced by national role when (a) the international system has a diffuse structure, (b) the situation is defined essentially by one man who can effectively control his domestic resources, including popular attitudes and opinions, (c) personal values, personality needs, or political needs can be achieved through foreign policies, (e) the state is neither a leader nor a member of an alliance or coalition, and (f) the situation is deemed critical.

6. Domestic needs will be salient aspects of a definition of a situation when (a) the state is dependent upon external sources of food and supply, (b) policy-makers are responsive to expressions of domestic opinion, and (c) a territory is perceived to be highly vulnerable to attack from abroad.

7. Capabilities establish limits on objectives for all states, no matter what other internal or external conditions prevail.

8. Capabilities are a less important consideration for governments which subscribe to long-range, revolutionary objectives.

[35] Cf. Snyder and Paige, "The United States Decision to Resist Aggression in Korea," in *Foreign Policy Decision Making*, ed. Snyder, Bruck, and Sapin.
[36] Verba, "Assumptions of Rationality and Non-Rationality."

9. The availability of capabilities may be a less important component of a definition of the situation in crisis situations.[37]

10. Doctrines and ideologies are more important in defining situations in political systems or governments (a) which subscribe to an official set of doctrines, (b) where the top leadership is not responsive to expressions of public opinion or domestic needs, and (c) during non-critical situations. In conditions of crisis (e.g., attack, major threat), responses are seldom deduced from, or closely related to, doctrines or ideologies.

11. Policy-makers in states which are highly involved in the affairs of the system and in a condition of internal turmoil and insecure top leadership will formulate their policy goals primarily on (a) ideological principles and revolutionary values, (b) personal values and political needs, (c) immediate conditions abroad, and (d) role. Organizational values, needs, and traditions, domestic needs, capabilities, system-wide values, and public opinion play a relatively insignificant role.

To summarize, making foreign policy decisions and formulation of goals and objectives involve complex processes in which values, attitudes, and images mediate perceptions of reality provided by various sources of information. The resulting images or definitions of the situation form the reality and expectations upon which decisions are formulated. The components of any definition of a situation will vary with conditions in the system, internal political structure, degree of urgency in a situation, and political roles of policy-makers, but most definitions of a situation include estimations of capabilities, domestic reactions, and national role. How important each component may be in a given situation is difficult to predict, although some hypotheses have been presented. In the absence of a verified theory of foreign policy, these statements will have to remain as crude generalizations or untested hypotheses, subject always to qualifications and exceptions provided by new developments in international politics.

## SELECTED BIBLIOGRAPHY

Almond, Gabriel, *The American People and Foreign Policy*. New York: Harcourt, Brace & World, Inc., 1950.

Armstrong, John A., *Ideology, Politics and Government in the Soviet Union*. New York: Frederick A. Praeger, Publisher, Inc., 1962.

---

[37] Dina A. Zinnes, Robert C. North, and Howard E. Koch, Jr., "Capability, Threat, and the Outbreak of War," in *International Politics and Foreign Policy: A Reader in Research and Theory*, ed. James Rosenau (New York: Free Press of Glencoe, Inc., 1961), pp. 469–82.

Baldwin, Hanson W., "Managed News: Our Peacetime Censorship," *Atlantic Monthly* (April 1963), pp. 53–59.

Bauer, Raymond E., Ithiel Pool, and L. A. Dexter, *American Business and Public Policy: The Politics of Foreign Trade*. New York: The Atherton Press, 1963.

Beloff, Max, *New Dimensions in Foreign Policy: A Study in British Administrative Experience, 1947–1959*. New York: The Macmillan Company, 1961.

Bishop, Donald G., *The Administration of Foreign Affairs*. Syracuse: Syracuse University Press, 1961.

Boulding, Kenneth E., *The Image*. Ann Arbor: University of Michigan Press, 1956.

Bronfenbrenner, Urie, "The Mirror Image in Soviet-American Relations: A Social Psychologist's Report," *Journal of Social Issues*, XVII (1961), 45–56.

Buchanan, William, and Hadley Cantril, *How Nations See Each Other*. Urbana: University of Illinois Press, 1953.

Byrnes, Robert F., "Attitudes Toward the West," in *Russian Foreign Policy: Essays in Historical Perspective*, ed. Ivo J. Lederer. New Haven: Yale University Press, 1962.

Christiansen, Bjorn, *Attitudes Toward Foreign Affairs as a Function of Personality*. Oslo: Oslo University Press, 1959.

Cohen, Bernard C., *The Political Process and Foreign Policy: The Making of the Japanese Peace Settlement*. Princeton: Princeton University Press, 1957.

————, *The Press and Foreign Policy*. Princeton: Princeton University Press, 1963.

Dawson, R. H., *The Decision to Aid Russia, 1941: Foreign Policy and Domestic Politics*. Chapel Hill: University of North Carolina Press, 1959.

Deutsch, Karl W., and Richard L. Merritt, "Effects of Events on National and International Images," in *International Behavior: A Social-Psychological Analysis*, ed. Herbert C. Kelman. New York: Holt, Rinehart, Winston, Inc., 1965.

Doob, Leonard W., "South Tyrol: An Introduction to the Psychological Syndrome of Nationalism," *Public Opinion Quarterly*, XXVI (1962), 172–84.

Duijker, H. C. J., and N. H. Frijda, *National Character and National Stereotypes*. Amsterdam: North-Holland Publishing Co., 1960.

Elder, Robert, "The Public Studies Division of the Department of State: Public Opinion Analysts in the Formulation and Conduct of American Foreign Policy," *Western Political Quarterly*, X (1957), 783–92.

Fensterwald, Bernard, Jr., "The Anatomy of American 'Isolationism' and Expansionism," *Journal of Conflict Resolution*, II (1958), 111–39, 280–309.

Frankel, Joseph, *The Making of Foreign Policy*. New York: Oxford University Press, 1963.

Guetzkow, Harold, *Multiple Loyalties*. Princeton: Princeton University Press, 1955.

Hayes, Carleton J. H., *Essays on Nationalism*. New York: The Macmillan Company, 1926.

Hero, Alfred O., "Americans in World Affairs," Vol. I, "Mass Media and World Affairs," Vol. IV, and "Opinion Leaders in American Communities," Vol. VI, in *Studies in Citizen Participation in International Relations*. Boston: World Peace Foundation, 1959.

Hilsman, Roger, Jr., "Intelligence and Policy-Making in Foreign Affairs," *World Politics*, V (1952), 1–45.

Holsti, Ole R., "The Belief System and National Images: A Case Study," *Journal of Conflict Resolution*, VI (1962), 244–52.

Huntington, Samuel P., "Strategy and the Political Process," *Foreign Affairs*, XXXVIII (1960), 285–99.

Inkeles, Alex, and Raymond Bauer, *The Soviet Citizen*. Cambridge: Harvard University Press, 1959.

James, Alan, "Power Politics," *Political Studies*, XII (1964), 307–26.

Kedourie, Elie, *Nationalism*. London: Hutchinson & Co., Ltd., 1961.

Klineberg, Otto, *The Human Dimension in International Relations*. New York: Holt, Rinehart & Winston, Inc., 1964.

Kohn, Hans, *Nationalism: Its Meaning and History*. Princeton: D. Van Nostrand Co., Inc., 1955.

Levinson, Daniel J., "Authoritarian Personality and Foreign Policy," *Journal of Conflict Resolution*, I (1957), 37–47.

Lippmann, Walter, *Public Opinion*. New York: The Macmillan Company, 1922.

London, Kurt, *How Foreign Policy Is Made* (2nd ed.). New York: D. Van Nostrand Co., Inc., 1950.

Markel, Lester, *et al.*, *Public Opinion and Foreign Policy*. New York: Harper & Row, Publishers, 1949.

McCamy, James L., *The Conduct of the New Diplomacy*. New York: Harper & Row, Publishers, 1964.

Miller, Warren E., and Donald E. Stokes, "Constituency Influence in Congress," *American Political Science Review*, LVII (1963), 45–56.

Ogburn, Charlton, Jr., "The Flow of Policy-Making in the Department of State," in *International Politics and Foreign Policy: A Reader in Research and Theory*, ed. James N. Rosenau. New York: Free Press of Glencoe, Inc., 1961, pp. 229–33.

Östgaard, Einar, "Factors Influencing the Flow of News," *Journal of Peace Research*, No. 1 (1965), 39-63.

Pruitt, Dean G., "Definition of the Situation as a Determinant of International Action," in *International Behavior: A Social-Psychological Analysis*, ed. Herbert C. Kelman. New York: Holt, Rinehart & Winston, Inc. 1965.

Rosenau, James N., *National Leadership and Foreign Policy: A Case Study in the Mobilization of Public Support*. Princeton: Princeton University Press, 1963.

————, "Pre-Theories and Theories of Foreign Policy," in *Approaches to Comparative and International Politics,* ed. R. Barry Farrell. Evanston: Northwestern University Press, 1966.

————, *Public Opinion and Foreign Policy.* New York: Random House, Inc., 1961.

Scott, William A., "Psychological and Social Correlates of International Images," in *International Behavior: A Social-Psychological Analysis,* ed. Herbert C. Kelman. New York: Holt, Rinehart & Winston, Inc., 1965.

Shafer, Boyd C., *Nationalism: Myth and Reality.* New York: Harcourt, Brace & World, Inc., 1955.

Singer, J. David, "Content Analysis of Elite Articulations," *Journal of Conflict Resolution,* VIII (1964), 424–85.

Snyder, Richard C., H. W. Bruck, and Burton Sapin, "Decision Making as an Approach to the Study of International Politics," in *Foreign Policy Decision Making,* ed. Richard C. Snyder, H. W. Bruck, and Burton Sapin. New York: Free Press of Glencoe, Inc., 1962.

Snyder, Richard C., and Glenn D. Paige, "The United States Decision to Resist Aggression in Korea," in *Foreign Policy Decision Making,* ed. Richard C. Snyder, H. W. Bruck, and Burton Sapin. New York: Free Press of Glencoe, Inc., 1962.

Sorenson, Theodore C., *Decision-Making in The White House: The Olive Branch or the Arrows.* New York: Columbia University Press, 1963.

Sprout, Harold and Margaret, "Environmental Factors in the Study of International Politics," *Journal of Conflict Resolution,* I (1957), 309–28.

Spykman, Nicholas J., "Geography and Foreign Policy, I," *American Political Science Review,* XXXII (1938), 28–50.

Tucker, Robert C., *The Soviet Political Mind.* New York: Frederick A. Praeger, Publisher, Inc., 1963.

Verba, Sidney, "Assumptions of Rationality and Non-Rationality in Models of the International System," *World Politics,* XIV (1961), 93–117.

White, Ralph K., "Images in the Context of International Conflict: Soviet Perceptions of the U.S. and the U.S.S.R.," in *International Behavior: A Social-Psychological Analysis,* ed. Herbert C. Kelman. New York: Holt, Rinehart & Winston, Inc., 1965.

# Power and the Achievement of Objectives

The previous five chapters have been concerned with the types of objectives and interests which states pursue, the role that various domestic and systemic factors play in the formulation of those objectives and interests, and the way that the main features of an international system, such as its structure and stratification, influence a political unit's general orientation to the outside world. In some cases, we attempted to account for the behavior of states by reference to the nature and characteristics of the international system; in others we concentrated on the internal needs of states and their populations, as well as on the particular objectives and values of individual political leaders and policy-makers. We have employed three different levels of analysis to answer three central questions in the study of international politics and foreign policy: what kinds of goals do political units seek, what was the genesis of those goals, and what general orientations toward the external environment are possible or

# Chapter VII

probable as means of securing the basic goals of security and independence?

This and the following five chapters will be concerned with a different problem. We will assume that objectives, interests, and orientations are given, and concentrate instead on the major techniques that political units employ to achieve or defend those objectives, interests, or orientations. To cope with this problem, we have less need to make reference to types of international systems, because with the exception of hierarchical systems in which most actions of the constituent units are prescribed or regulated from the center, political units generally use similar techniques for accomplishing and defending their goals. To be sure, "revolutionary" states may display unique forms of statecraft when compared to small states with a low level of involvement in the affairs of the system. But basically any political unit, the achievement or defense of whose interests and objectives depends upon the actions of other nations, must use techniques of *bargaining*, ranging from oral efforts at persuasion to threats or use of force.

Some social objectives can be achieved through a state's own domestic policies; they are not dependent upon the actions of other states in the system.[1] But as states are increasingly unable to satisfy all the needs, values, and aspirations of their populations and sub-groups, they have to turn to other nations. Most underdeveloped countries and many industrial nations as well could not maintain even a minimum standard of living without conducting extensive foreign trade; others cannot hope to industrialize unless they receive an influx of development capital and technical skills; a number of states believe that they cannot protect even core values such as national independence without the active assistance and support of alliance partners. In short, in the contemporary international system, most of a nation's collective domestic and external goals cannot be defended or achieved without influencing the behavior of other states. Goal achievement is thus contingent upon the reactions and actions of others. It is here that the concept of power comes into the study of international politics, for power includes the means by which all states influence the behavior of others so as to protect and extend their own interests. Though some observers have argued that governments have a choice between using "power politics" and other means to gain their objectives, this kind of dichotomy is at best a crude normative generalization. Some governments may be more prone than others to use military threats to influence the behavior of foreign nations, but no government,

---

[1] This chapter is a modified version of my article, "The Concept of Power in the Study of International Relations," *Background,* VII (1964), 179–94.

unless it is isolated from the external environment and essentially self-sufficient, fails to seek to influence the behavior of the nations surrounding it. In so doing it makes threats (not necessarily military), offers rewards, and commits various actions of punishment to induce behavior consonant with its own interests. International politics occurs between all states, all but the most routine administrative transactions involve the use of power, and therefore all international politics are in a sense power politics.

In order to gain or defend their objectives, states must undertake various *acts* or actions towards others. When these acts or actions take on a pattern and are systematically directed toward the achievement of some specified objective, value, or interest, we can say that they constitute a foreign policy. An act is basically a form of communication intended to change or sustain the behavior of those upon whom the acting government is dependent for achieving its objectives. In international politics, acts may take many different forms. A diplomatic note asking another state to cease its military provocations is an act designed to change behavior. The promise of granting foreign aid is an act, as are propaganda appeals, displays of military strength, subversion, raising tariffs, instituting embargoes or boycotts, wielding a veto in the Security Council, or intervening in another country with military force. These types of acts and the circumstances in which they are likely to be successful will be discussed in the following chapters. To help understand the concept of power, however, we may use here any hypothetical act which is used as a means of influencing the behavior of other states.

Once objectives have been formulated as a response to the acts of other states, images, domestic pressures, ideological imperatives, organizational values, or personality needs, the international political process continues as any state—let us say state A—seeks through various acts to change or sustain the behavior (e.g. the acts and policies) of other states. Power can thus be defined as the general capacity of a state to control the behavior of others. This definition can be illustrated as follows, where the solid line represents various acts:

A seeks to influence B because it has established certain objectives which cannot be achieved (it is perceived) unless B (and perhaps many other states as well) does X. If this is the basis of all international political processes, the capacity to control behavior can be viewed several different ways.

1. Influence (an aspect of power) is essentially a *means* to an end. Some governments or statesmen may seek influence for its own sake, but for most it is instrumental, just like money. They use it primarily for achieving or defending other goals, which may include prestige, territory, souls, raw materials, security, or alliances.

2. State *A*, in its acts toward state *B*, uses or mobilizes certain *capabilities*. A capability is any physical or mental object or quality available as an instrument of inducement, to reward, threaten, or punish. The concept of capability may be illustrated in the following example. Suppose an unarmed man walks into a bank and asks the clerk to give him all her money. The clerk observes clearly that the man has no weapon and refuses to comply with his order. The man has sought to influence the behavior of the clerk, but has failed. The next time, however, he walks in armed with a pistol and threatens to shoot if the clerk does not give him the money. This time, the clerk complies. In this instance the man has mobilized certain resources or capabilities (the gun) and succeeds in influencing the clerk to do as he wished. The gun, just like a nation's military forces, *is not synonymous with the act of influencing;* it is the instrument used to induce the clerk to change her behavior to comply with the robber's objectives.

3. The act of influencing *B* obviously involves a *relationship* between *A* and *B*, though as will be seen later, the relationship may not even involve overt communication. If the relationship covers any period of time, we can also say that it is a *process*.

4. If *A* can get *B* to do something, but *B* cannot get *A* to do a similar thing, then we can say that *A* has more power than *B* regarding that particular issue. Power, therefore, can also be viewed as a *quantity*, but as a quantity it is only meaningful when compared to the power of others. Power is therefore relative.

To summarize, power may be viewed from several aspects: it is a means, it is based on capabilities, it is a relationship and a process, and can also be a quantity.

For purposes of analyzing international politics, we can break down the concept of power into three distinct analytic elements: power comprises (1) the *acts* (process, relationship) of influencing other states; (2) the *capabilities* used to make the wielding of influence successful; and (3) the *responses* to the acts. The three elements must be kept distinct. Since this definition may seem too abstract, we can define the concept in the more operational terms of policy-makers. In formulating policy and the strategy to achieve certain goals, they would explicitly or implicity ask the four following questions:

1. Given our goals, what do we wish $B$ to do or not to do? ($X$)
2. How shall we get $B$ to do or not to do $X$? (implies a relationship and process)
3. What capabilities are at our disposal so that we can induce $B$ to do or not to do $X$?
4. What is $B$'s probable response to our attempts to influence its behavior?

Before discussing the problem of capabilities and responses we have to fill out our model of the influence act to account for the many patterns of behavior that may be involved in an international relationship. First, the exercise of influence implies more than merely $A$'s ability to *change* the behavior of $B$. Influence may also be seen when $A$ attempts to get $B$ to *continue* a course of action or policy which is useful to, or in the interests of, $A$.[2] The exercise of influence does not always cease, therefore, after $B$ does $X$. It is often a continuing process of reinforcing $B$'s behavior.

Second, it is almost impossible to find a situation where $B$ does not also have some influence over $A$. Our model has suggested that influence is exercised only in one direction, by $A$ over $B$. In reality, influence is multilateral. State $A$, for example, would seldom seek a particular goal unless it had been influenced in a particular direction by the actions of other states in the system. At a minimum, there is the problem of feedback in any relationship: if $B$ complies with $A$'s wishes and does $X$, that behavior may subsequently prompt $A$ to change its own behavior, perhaps in the interest of $B$. Suppose that state $A$, after making threats, persuades $B$ to lower its tariffs on the goods of state $A$. This would seem to be influence travelling only in one direction. But when state $B$ does lower its tariffs, that action may prompt state $A$ to reward state $B$ in some manner. The phenomenon of feedback may be illustrated as follows:

[2] J. David Singer, "Inter-Nation Influence: A Formal Model," *American Political Science Review*, LVII (1963), 420–30. State $A$ might also wish state $B$ to do $w$, $y$, and $z$, which may be incompatible with the achievement of $X$.

Third, the number of times a state becomes involved in acts of influence depends upon the general level of involvement of its government in the system. The first requisite for attempting to wield influence is a perception that somehow state B (or any other) is related to the achievement of state A's goals and that there is, or will be, some kind of relationship of interdependence. If the relationship covers only inconsequential matters, few acts of influence may be necessary; but the greater the involvement, dependence, or interdependence, the greater the necessity to wield influence over other nations. Except for limited trade relations, for instance, there is little perception of interdependence between Iceland and Uganda, hence little need for the government of Iceland to attempt to influence the domestic or external policies of the African country.

Fourth, there is the type of relationship which includes "anticipated reaction."[3] This is the situation, frequently found in international politics, in which A might wish B to do X, but does not try to influence B for fear that B will do Y instead, which is an unfavorable response from A's point of view. In a hypothetical situation, the government of India might wish to obtain arms from the United States to build up its own defenses, but does not request such arms because it fears that the United States would insist on certain conditions for the sale of arms which might compromise India's non-alignment. This anticipated reaction may also be multilateral, where A wishes B to do X, but will not try to get B to do it because it fears that C, a third state, will do Y, which is unfavorable to A's interests. India wants to purchase American arms, but does not seek to influence the United States to sell them for fear that Pakistan (C) will then build up its own armaments and thus accelerate the arms race between the two countries. In this situation, Pakistan (C) has influence over the actions of the Indian government even though it has not deliberately sought to influence India on this particular matter or even communicated its position in any way. The Indian government has simply perceived that there is a relatively high probability that if it seeks to influence the United States, Pakistan will react in a manner contrary to India's interests.

Fifth, power and influence may be measured quite objectively by scholars, but what is important in international politics is the *perceptions* of influence and capabilities held by policy-makers. The reason that governments invest millions of dollars for gathering intelligence is to develop a relatively accurate picture of other states' capabilities and intentions. Where there is a great discrepancy between perceptions and

[3] Herbert A. Simon, "Notes on the Observation and Measurement of Political Power," *The Journal of Politics*, XV (1953), 500–16.

reality, the results to a country's foreign policy may be disastrous. To take our example of the bank robber again, suppose that the man held a harmless toy pistol and threatened the clerk. The clerk perceived the gun to be real and deduced the robber's intention to use it. As a result, she complied with his demand. In this case the robber's influence was far greater than the "objective" character of his capabilities and intentions, and distorted perception by the clerk led her to act in a manner unfavorable to her and her employers.

Finally, as our original model suggests, A may try to influence B *not to do X*. Sometimes this is called negative power, or deterrence, where A acts in a manner to *prevent* a certain action it deems undesirable to its interests. This is a typical relationship in international politics. By signing the Munich treaty, the British and French governments hoped to prevent Germany from invading Czechoslovakia; the Soviet government, by using a variety of threats, has sought to prevent West Germany from obtaining control over nuclear weapons; by organizing the European Recovery Program and NATO, the United States sought to prevent the growth of communism in western Europe and/or a Soviet military invasion of this area.

## Capabilities

The second element of the concept of power consists of those capabilities that are mobilized in support of the acts taken to influence state B's behavior. It is difficult to assess the general capacity of a state to control the actions and policies of others unless we also have some knowledge of the capabilities involved.[4] Nevertheless, it should be acknowledged that social scientists do not understand all the reasons why some actors— whether people, groups, governments, or states—wield influence successfully, while others do not.

It is clear that in political relationships not everyone possesses equal influence. We frequently use the terms "great powers" and "small powers" as a shorthand way of suggesting that some nations make commitments abroad and have the capacity to meet them that others lack. The distinction between the "great powers" and the "small powers" is usually based on some rough estimation of tangible and intangible factors which we have called capabilities. In domestic politics it is possible to construct a lengthy list of capabilities and attributes which seemingly permit some

[4] We might assess influence for historical situations solely on the basis of whether A got B to do X, without having knowledge of either A's or B's capabilities.

to wield influence over large numbers of people and important public decisions. Robert Dahl lists[5] such tangibles as money, wealth, information, time, political allies, official position, and control over jobs, and such intangibles as personality and leadership qualities. But not everyone who possesses these capabilities can command the obedience of other people. What is crucial in relating capabilities to influence, according to Dahl, is that the person *mobilize these capabilities for his political purposes,* and that he possess skill in mobilizing them. A person who uses his wealth, time, information, friends, and personality for political purposes will likely be able to influence others on public issues. A person, on the other hand, who possesses the same capabilities but uses them to invent a new mousetrap is not likely to be important in politics. The same propositions also hold true in international politics. The amount of influence a state wields over others can be related to the capabilities *mobilized* in support of foreign policy objectives. To put this proposition in another way, we can argue that a capability does not itself determine the uses to which it will be put. Nuclear power can be used to provide electricity or to coerce and perhaps destroy other nations. The use of capabilities depends less on their quality and quantity than on the external objectives a government formulates for itself.

The *variety* of foreign policy instruments available to a nation for influencing others is partly a function of the quantity and quality of capabilities. What a government seeks to do—the type of objectives it formulates—and how it attempts to do it will depend at least partially on the resources it finds available. A country such as Thailand, which possesses relatively few and underdeveloped resources, cannot, even if it desired, construct nuclear weapons with which to intimidate others, establish a world-wide propaganda network, or dispense several billion dollars annually of foreign aid to try to influence other countries. We can conclude, therefore, that how states *use* their capabilities depends on their external objectives, but the choice of objectives and the instruments to achieve those objectives are limited or influenced by the quality and quantity of available capabilities.

### The Measurement of Capabilities

For many years students of international politics have made meticulous comparisons of the mobilized and potential capabilities of various nations, assuming that a nation was powerful, or capable of achieving its objec-

[5] Robert A. Dahl, *Who Governs?* (New Haven: Yale University Press, 1961).

tives, to the extent that it possessed certain "elements of power." Comparative data relating to production of iron ore, coal, hydroelectricity, economic growth rates, educational levels, population growth rates, military resources, transportation systems, and sources of raw materials are presented as indicators of a nation's power. Few have acknowledged that these comparisons do not measure a state's power or influence, but only its base. Our previous discussion would suggest that such measurements and assessments are not particularly useful unless they are related to the foreign policy objectives of the various states. Capability is always the capability to do something; its assessment is most meaningful when carried on within a framework of certain goals and foreign policy objectives.

The deduction of actual influence from the quantity and quality of potential and mobilized capabilities may, in some cases, give an approximation of reality, but historically there have been too many discrepancies between the basis of power and the amount of influence to warrant adopting this practice as a useful approach to international relations. One could have assumed, for example, on the basis of a comparative study of technological and educational levels and general standards of living in the 1920's and 1930's that the United States would have been one of the most influential states in international politics. A careful comparison of certain resources, called the "great essentials,"[6] revealed the United States to be in an enviable position. In the period 1925 to 1930, it was the only major country in the world that produced from its own resources adequate supplies of food, power, iron, machinery, chemicals, coal, iron ore, and petroleum. If actual diplomatic influence had been deduced from the quantities of "great essentials" possessed by the major nations the following ranking of states would have resulted: (1) United States, (2) Germany, (3) Great Britain, (4) France, (5) Russia, (6) Italy, (7) Japan. However, the diplomatic history of the world from 1925 to 1930 would suggest that there was little correlation between the *capabilities* of these countries and their *actual influence*. If we measure influence by the impact these states made on the system and by the responses they could invoke when they sought to charge the behavior of other states, we would find for this period quite a different ranking, such as the following: (1) France, (2) Great Britain, (3) Italy, (4) Germany, (5) Russia, (6) Japan, (7) United States.

Indeed, many contemporary international relationships reveal how often the "strong" states do not achieve their objectives—or at least have

[6] Frank H. Simonds and Brooks Emeny, *The Great Powers in World Politics* (New York: The American Book Company, 1939).

to settle for poor substitutes—even when attempting to influence the behavior of "weak" states. How, for instance, did Marshal Tito's Yugoslavia effectively resist all sorts of pressures and threats by the powerful Soviet Union after it was expelled from the Communist bloc? Why, despite its overwhelming superiority in capabilities, was the United States unable in the 1960's to achieve its major objectives against a weak Cuba? How have "small" states gained trading privileges and all sorts of diplomatic concessions from those nations with great economic wealth and military power? The ability of state A to change the behavior of state B is, we would assume, enhanced if it possesses physical capabilities to use in the influence act; but B is by no means defenseless or vulnerable to diplomatic, economic, or military pressures because it fails to own a large modern army, raw materials, and money for foreign aid. The successful exercise of influence is also dependent upon such factors as personality, perceptions, friendships, and traditions, and these have a way of rendering power calculations and equations difficult. Aside from these situational factors we may specify certain other conditions which help determine, regardless of military and economic capabilities, whether or not acts of influencing will succeed. These conditions, or variables, also help explain why states with very weak capabilities are often able to resist the demands of the strong, and sometimes achieve their own demands at the expense of the interests of major powers.

### Variables Affecting the Exercise of Influence

One reason that gross quantities of capabilities cannot be equated with effective influence relates to the distinction between a state's capabilities and the perceptions others have of those capabilities. A nuclear force, for example, is often thought to increase the diplomatic influence of those who possess it. No doubt nuclear weaponry is an important element in a state's general prestige abroad, and those who control this weaponry may very well display more confidence in their diplomatic style. One only has to look at the difference in Soviet diplomacy between the period when it had no nuclear capacity and was highly vulnerable to American nuclear retaliation, and its posture today, when it too can threaten instant retaliation. When it was militarily weak, the Soviet government's diplomacy was defensive, hypersensitive, brusque, and rigid. With nuclear weapons, its diplomatic behavior shows evidence of more confidence and flexibility.[7]

[7] Alastair Buchan, *NATO in the Sixties* (rev. ed.) (New York: Frederick A. Praeger, Publisher, Inc., 1963), p. 21.

Yet the most important aspect of a nuclear capability—or any military capability—is not its possession, but the willingness to use it if necessary. Other governments must know that the capability is not of mere symbolic significance. The Cuban government possesses a particular advantage over the United States (hence, influence) because it knows that in almost all circumstances the American government would not use strategic nuclear weapons against its country. It has therefore effectively broken through the significance of the American nuclear capability as far as Cuban-American relations are concerned. A capability is useless unless it is both mobilized in support of foreign policy objectives and made credible.

A second variable which determines the success or failure of acts of influence is the extent to which there are *needs* between the two countries in any influence relationship. In general, a country which needs something from another is vulnerable to its acts of influence. This is the primary reason that states which are "weak" in many capabilities can nevertheless obtain concessions from "strong" countries. Consider the case of France and England and some of the "weak" states in the Middle East. Both European countries are highly dependent upon Arab lands for oil supplies. They have an important need which only the Arab countries can satisfy at a reasonable cost. On the other hand, the Middle Eastern countries which control these oil resources may not be so dependent upon Britain and France, particularly if they can sell their oil easily elsewhere. Because in this situation needs are not equal on both sides, the independent states (in terms of needs) can make demands (or resist demands made against them) on the dependent great powers, and obtain important concessions. The British and French governments know that if they do not make these concessions or press their own demands too hard, the Arab states can threaten to cut off oil supplies. Their dependency thus makes them vulnerable to the demands and influence acts of what would otherwise be considered "weak" states.

Of course there are few relationships where need goes only one way. Venezuela needs American oil markets and is therefore potentially vulnerable to an American threat to reduce or close those markets should some contentious issue arise between those two countries. But the United States might also find it difficult to obtain adequate alternative sources of oil and, in any case, would probably not want all of Venezuela's oil to be sold, for instance, to the Communist countries. In the form of a general hypothesis, we can suggest that regardless of the quantity, quality, and credibility of a state's capabilities, the more state $B$ needs, or is dependent upon, state $A$, the more likely state $A$'s acts—threats, promises, rewards, or punishments—will succeed in changing or sustaining $B$'s behavior.

Understanding the dynamics of power relationships at the international level would be relatively easy if capabilities, credibility, and need were the only variables involved. Unfortunately, political actions do not always conform to simple hypotheses because human characteristics of pride, stubbornness, prestige, and friendship enter into all acts of influence as well. A government may be highly dependent upon some other state and still resist its demands; it may be willing to suffer all sorts of privations and even physical destruction and loss of independence simply for the sake of pride. British policy-makers, we could imagine, might at some time rather do without oil for a while than make concessions to certain governments in the Middle East.

Additional variables affecting the exercise of influence can be observed in the situation where two small states of approximately equal capabilities make similar demands upon a "major" power and neither of the small states is dependent upon the large—or vice versa. Which will achieve its objectives? Will both exercise influence equally? Hypothetically, suppose that the ambassadors of Belgium and Albania go to the British Foreign Office on the same day and ask the British government to lower tariffs on bicycles, a product which the two countries would like to export to England. Assume that the quality and price of the bicycles is approximately the same and that the British government does not wish to allow too many imports for fear of damaging the domestic bicycle industry. Assume further that both the Belgian and Albanian ambassadors offer roughly equal concessions if the British will lower their tariffs on bicycles. Both Albania and Belgium, they claim, will lower their own tariffs on English automobiles. Which ambassador is most likely to have his request complied with—that is, to achieve his government's objectives? Chances are that the British government would favor the request of the Belgian ambassador and turn down the representation by the diplomat from Tirana. The explanation of this decision can probably not be found in the capabilities of either of the small countries (both offered approximately equal rewards) or in need, since in this hypothetical situation Britain needs neither of the small countries' automobile markets. Belgium would get the favorable decision because British policy-makers are more *responsive* to Belgian interests than to those of Albania. Albania represents a Communist state whose government normally displays through its diplomacy and propaganda strong hostility toward England.

The fourth variable, after capabilities, credibility, and need, which determines the effectiveness of acts of influence is thus the ephemeral quality of responsiveness.[8] Responsiveness can be seen as a disposition to

[8] The concept of responsiveness is introduced by Karl W. Deutsch *et al.*, *Political Community and the North Atlantic Area* (Princeton: Princeton University Press,

receive another's requests with sympathy, even to the point where a government is willing to sacrifice some of its own values and interests in order to fulfill those requests; responsiveness is the willingness to be influenced. In one study, it was shown that members of the State Department in the United States may take considerable pains to promote the requests and interests of other governments among their superiors and in other government agencies, provided that the requesting government feels that the issue is important or that the need must be fulfilled.[9] In our hypothetical case, if the quality of responsiveness is present in the case of the Belgian request, members of the British Foreign Office would likely work for the Belgians and try to persuade other government agencies concerned with trade and commerce to agree to a lowering of the tariff on bicycles. In the British reaction to the Albanian request, it is not likely that the government would display much responsiveness. Suspicion, traditional animosities, lack of trust, and years of unfavorable diplomatic experience would probably prevent the development of much British sympathy for Albania's needs or interests. Though Albania and Belgium made similar requests and similar counter-offers, the lack of responsiveness on the part of the British officials toward Albania's government and its policies would probably account for their rejection of the Albanian request. When the other variables of capabilities, credibility, and need are held constant or made equal, the degree of responsiveness will determine the success or failure of acts taken to influence other states' behavior.

If effective influence cannot be deduced solely from the quantity and quality of physical capabilities, how do we proceed to measure influence? Assessments of physical capabilities may be adequate for rough estimations of influence or war potential, but to be precise, we have to refer to the actual processes of international politics, not to charts or indices of raw materials and military might. We can best measure influence by studying the *responses* of those in the influence relationship.[10] If *A* can get *B* to do *X*, but *C* cannot get *B* to do the same thing, then in that particular issue, *A* has more influence. If *B* does *X* despite the protestations of *A*, then we can assume that *A*, in this circumstance, did not enjoy much influence over *B*. It is meaningless to argue that the Soviet Union is more powerful than the United States unless we cite how, for what

1957) and developed by Dean G. Pruitt, "National Power and International Responsiveness," *Background*, VII (1964), 165–78. See also Dean G. Pruitt, "Definition of the Situation as a Determinant of International Action," in *International Behavior: A Social-Psychological Analysis*, ed. Herbert C. Kelman (New York: Holt, Rinehart & Winston, Inc., 1965), pp. 393–432.

[9] Pruitt, "National Power," 175–76.

[10] Robert A. Dahl, "The Concept of Power," *Behavioral Science*, II (1957), 201–15.

purposes, and in relation to whom, the Soviet Union and the United States are exerting influence. We may conclude that capabilities themselves do not always lead to the successful wielding of influence, and other variables have to be considered as well. In general, the successful wielding of influence varies with (1) the type of goals a state pursues, (2) the quality and quantity of capabilities at its disposal, (3) the skill in mobilizing these capabilities in support of the goals, (4) the credibility of threats and rewards, (5) the degree of need or dependence, and (6) the degree of responsiveness among the policy-makers of the target country.

## How Influence Is Exercised

Social scientists have noted several fundamental techniques that individuals and groups use to influence each other. In a political system which contains no one legitimate center of authority (such as a government, or a father in a family) that can command the members of the group or society, bargaining has to be used among the sovereign entities to achieve or defend their objectives. Recalling that $A$ seeks one of three courses of conduct from $B$ (e.g., $B$ to do $X$ in the future, $B$ not to do $X$ in the future, or $B$ to continue doing $X$), it may use six different tactics, involving acts of:

1. *Persuasion.* Persuasion may include threats, rewards, and actual punishments, but we mean here situations in which a government simply initiates or discusses a proposal with another and elicits a favorable response without explicitly holding out the possibility of rewards or punishments. We cannot assume that the exercise of influence is always *against* the wishes of others and that there are only two possible outcomes of the act, one favoring $A$, the other favoring $B$. For example, state $A$ asks $B$ to support it at a coming international conference on the control of narcotics. State $B$ might not originally have any particular interest in the conference or its outcome, but decides, on the basis of $A$'s initiative, that something positive might be gained not only by supporting $A$'s proposals, but also by attending the conference. In this case there might also be the expectation of gaining some type of reward in the future, though not necessarily from $A$.

2. *The offer of rewards.* This is the situation where $A$ promises to do something favorable to $B$ if $B$ complies with the wishes of $A$. Rewards may be of almost any type in international relations. To gain the diplomatic support of $B$ at the narcotics conference, $A$ may offer to increase foreign aid payments, lower tariffs on goods imported from $B$,

support *B* at a later conference on communications facilities, or promise to remove a previous punishment. The last tactic is used often by Soviet negotiators. After having created an unfavorable situation, they promise to remove it in return for some concessions by their opponents.

3. *The granting of rewards.* In some instances, the credibility of a government is not very high and state *B*, before complying with *A*'s wishes, may insist that *A* actually give the reward in advance. Frequently in armistice negotiations neither side will unilaterally take steps to demilitarize an area or demobilize troops until the other shows evidence of complying with the agreements. One of the clichés of cold war diplomacy holds that deeds, not words, are required for the granting of rewards and concessions.

4. *The threat of punishment.* Threats of punishment may be further subdivided into two types: (a) positive threats, where, for example, state *A* threatens to increase tariffs, institute a boycott or embargo against trade with *B*, or use force, (b) threats of deprivation, where *A* threatens to withdraw foreign aid or in other ways withhold rewards or other advantages that it already grants to *B*.

5. *The infliction of non-violent punishment.* In this situation, threats are carried out in the hope of altering *B*'s behavior which, in most cases, could not be altered by other means. The problem with this tactic is that it usually results in reciprocal measures by the other side, thus inflicting damage on both, though not necessarily bringing about a desired state of affairs. If, for example, *A* threatens to increase its military capabilities if *B* does *X* and then proceeds to implement the threat, it is not often that *B* will comply with *A*'s wishes because it, too, can increase its military capabilities. In this type of situation, both sides indulge in the application of punishments which may escalate into more serious forms unless the conflict is resolved.

6. *Force.* In previous eras, when governments did not possess the variety of foreign policy instruments available today, they frequently had to rely upon the use of force in the bargaining process. Force and violence were not only the most efficient tactics, but in many cases the only means possible for influencing. Today, the situation is different. As technological levels rise and dependencies develop, other means of inducement become available and can serve as substitutes for force.[11]

---

[11] François de Callières, a renowned French diplomat of the eighteenth century, also suggested the utility of these techniques when he wrote: "Every Christian prince must take as his chief maxim not to employ arms to support or vindicate his rights until he has employed and exhausted the way of reason and persuasion. It is to his interest also, to add to reason and persuasion the influence of benefits conferred, which indeed is one of the surest ways to make his own power secure, and to increase it." *On the Manner of Negotiating with Princes,* trans. A. F. Whyte (Boston: Houghton

## Patterns of Influence
## in the International System

Most governments at some time use all of these techniques for influencing others, but probably over 90 per cent of all relations between states are based on simple persuasion and deal with relatively unimportant technical matters. Since such interactions seldom make the headlines, we often assume that most relations between states involve the making or carrying out of threats. But whether a government is communicating with another over an unimportant technical matter or over a subject of great consequence, it is likely to use a particular type of tactic in its attempts to influence, depending on the past tradition of friendship or hostility between those two governments and the amount of compatibility between their objectives and interests. Allies, for example, seldom threaten each other with force or even make blatant threats of punishment, but governments which disagree over a wide range of policy objectives and hold attitudes of suspicion and hostility toward each other are more likely to resort to threats and imposition of punishments. We can suggest, therefore, that just as there are observable patterns of relations between states in terms of conflict, collaboration, competition and domination-dependence, there are also general patterns of relations between states with reference to the methods used to influence each other. The methods of exerting influence between Great Britain and the United States are *typically* persuasion and rewards, while the methods of exerting influence between the Soviet Union and the United States in the early post-World War II era were typically threatening and inflicting punishments of various types. We can construct rough typologies of international relationships as identified by the typical techniques used in the act of influence.

1. *Relations of consensus.* Relations of consensus would be typical between those states that have few disagreements over foreign policy objectives, a high degree of mutual responsiveness, or a very low level of interaction and involvement in each other's affairs. An example of the first would be Anglo-American relations, and of the last, the relations between

---

Mifflin Company, 1919), p. 7. In a treatise on foreign policy written approximately 300 B.C., Kautilya noted four fundamental techniques for obtaining the desired results from other Indian states: conciliation (sama), gifts (dana), dissension (bheda), and punishment (danda). Cf. George Modelski, "Kaultilya: Foreign Policy and International System in the Ancient Hindu World," *American Political Science Review,* LVIII (1964), 353.

Thailand and Bolivia. In the relations of consensus, influence is exercised primarily by the technique of persuasion and through the subtle offering of rewards. Since violence as a form of punishment is almost inconceivable between two countries, the military capabilities of neither actor are organized, mobilized, and "targeted" toward the other.

2. *Relations of overt manipulation.* Here there may be some disagreement or conflict over foreign policy objectives, or state A might undertake some domestic policy which was disapproved by state B, such as a form of racial discrimination. Since there is some conflict, there will also be at least a modest degree of involvement between the two actors, or a perception that A and B are in some kind of a relationship of interdependence. The techniques used to influence will include, if normal persuasion fails, (a) offers of rewards, (b) granting of rewards, (c) threats to withhold rewards (e.g., not to give foreign aid in the future), or (d) threats of non-violent punishment including, for instance, the raising of tariffs against B's products. Militarily, in relations of overt manipulation there is still no mobilization or targeting of military capabilities toward state B. Military capabilities are thus of little relevance to the power of each state toward the other. Examples of overt manipulation would include relations between China and the Soviet Union, 1960–1963, and relations between France and the United States during this same period.

3. *Relations of coercion.* In relations of coercion, there are fundamental disagreements over foreign policy objectives. Almost all actions that A takes externally are perceived by B to be a threat to its own interests. Involvement is, therefore, high, and the degree of mutual responsiveness is usually very low if it exists at all. A seeks to influence B's behavior typically by (a) making warnings and threatening punishments, (b) inflicting non-violent punishments, and, under extreme provocation, (c) the selective and limited use of force as, for example, in a peacetime blockade. Military capabilities are likely to be targeted toward each other and become a relevant factor in power relationships, since they are often mobilized for threats and the policy-makers labor under the assumption that they might have to be used. Examples would include relations between the Soviet Union and the Western coalition for most of the period since 1947, Cuba and the United States between 1960 and the present, Nazi Germany and Czechoslovakia between 1937 and 1939, and Egypt and Israel since 1948.

4. *Relations of force.* Here there is almost total disagreement on foreign policy objectives and the areas of consensus are limited to a few necessities such as communications. The degree of involvement is obviously extremely high. The typical form of exercising influence is through the

infliction of violent punishment, though in some instances rewards (e.g., peace offers) might be proffered. National capabilities are mobilized primarily with a view to conducting the policy of punishment. However, the quantity of military capabilities used will vary with the geographic and force-level boundaries which the disputants place on the conflict.

Though most relations between states could be placed in one of the previous categories, it should also be apparent that, under changing circumstances, governments are required to resort to techniques of influence toward others that they would normally avoid. The cold war represents a curious phenomenon in the history of international politics because in the relations between east and west *all* of the techniques of influence are being used simultaneously. There are several issue areas of policy where objectives are perceived by both sides as being compatible and where agreements—either in treaties or through "understandings"— can be reached without making threats or imposing punishment.[12] There are also areas of great controversy where the antagonists commit military capabilities and seek to influence each other's behavior most of the time by making threats and carrying out various forms of punishment. Similarly, in the bitter cold war between Israel and the Arab states, all ranges of relationships are to be observed. Both sides have deep distrust toward the other and display almost no mutual responsiveness. Their objectives are in almost all cases incompatible. Both sides have used propaganda, bribery, subversion, diplomacy, boycotts, embargoes, displays of military strength, and espionage as means of building up their capabilities and making threats. At the same time, on a very narrow range of issues, Israel and the Arab states have displayed almost cooperative forms of behavior.

To summarize this analysis of power, we can suggest that power is an integral part of all political relationships, but in international politics we are interested primarily in one process: how one state influences the behavior of another in its own interests. The act of influencing becomes a central focus for the study of international politics, and it is from this act that we can best deduce a definition of power. If we observe the act of influencing we can see that power is a process, a relationship, a means to an end, and even a quantity. Moreover, we can make an analytical distinction among the act of influencing, the basis, or capabilities, upon which the act relies, and the response to the act. Capabilities are an important determinant of how successful the wielding of influence will

[12] Areas of agreement between the Soviet Union and the West which have resulted either in treaties or "understandings" would include cessation of nuclear tests, demilitarization of the Antarctic and outer space, renouncing of nuclear war as an instrument of policy, and efforts to prevent the spread of nuclear weapons.

be, but they are by no means the only determinant. The nature of a country's foreign policy objectives, the skill with which a state mobilizes its capabilities for foreign policy purposes, needs, and responsiveness are equally important. Acts of influencing may take many forms, the most important of which are the offer and granting of rewards, the threat and imposition of punishments, and the application of force. The choice of means used to induce will depend, in turn, upon the general nature of relations between any two given governments, the degree of involvement between them, and the extent of their mutual responsiveness. Having analyzed the general techniques of wielding influence and the conditions under which power is likely to succeed, we may now turn to the specific instruments of inducement used to achieve objectives, ranging from simple diplomatic persuasion to the use of violence on a massive scale.

## SELECTED BIBLIOGRAPHY

Algosaibi, Ghazi A. R., "The Theory of International Relations: Hans J. Morgenthau and His Critics," *Background*, VIII (1965), 221–56.

Ash, Maurice A., "An Analysis of Power, with Special Reference to International Politics," *World Politics*, III (1951), 218–37.

Bachrach, Peter, and Morton S. Baratz, "The Two Faces of Power," *American Political Science Review*, LVI (1962), 947–52.

Burns, Arthur Lee, *Power Politics and the Growing Nuclear Club*. Princeton: Princeton University Press, 1959.

Dahl, Robert, "The Concept of Power," *Behavioral Science*, II (1957), 201–15.

Fox, Annette B., *The Power of Small States: Diplomacy in World War II*. Chicago: The University of Chicago Press, 1959.

German, Clifford, "A Tentative Evaluation of World Power," *Journal of Conflict Resolution*, IV (1960), 138–44.

Gross, Ernest A., "Moral Power in International Relations," *Journal of International Affairs*, XII (1958), 132–37.

Jones, Stephen B., "The Power Inventory and National Strategy," *World Politics*, VI (1954), 421–52.

Knorr, Klaus, *The War Potential of Nations*. Princeton: Princeton University Press, 1956.

McClelland, Charles A., *Theory and the International System*. New York: The Macmillan Company, 1966, chap. III.

Morgenthau, Hans J., *Politics Among Nations*, 3rd ed. New York: Alfred A. Knopf, Inc., 1960.

Organski, A. F. K. and Katherine F., *Population and World Power*. New York: Alfred A. Knopf, Inc., 1961.

———, *World Politics*. New York: Alfred A. Knopf, Inc., 1958.

Pruitt, Dean, "National Power and International Responsiveness," *Background,* VIII (1964), 165–78.

Riker, William H., "Some Ambiguities in the Notion of Power," *American Political Science Review,* LVIII (1964), 341–79.

Simon, Herbert A., "Notes on the Observation and Measurement of Political Power," *The Journal of Politics,* XV (1953), 500–16.

Singer, J. David, "Inter-Nation Influence: A Formal Model," *American Political Science Review,* LVII (1963), 420–30.

Sprout, Harold and Margaret, eds., *Foundations of National Power: Readings on World Politics and American Security* (2nd ed.). New York: D. Van Nostrand Co., Inc., 1951.

Van Der Kroef, Justus M., "The Sociology of Confrontation," *The Southwestern Social Science Quarterly,* XLV (1964), 226–38.

Wasserman, Benno, "The Scientific Pretensions of Professor Morgenthau's Theory of Power Politics," *Australian Outlook,* XIII (1959), 55–70.

Wolfers, Arnold, *Discord and Collaboration: Essays on International Politics.* Baltimore: The Johns Hopkins University Press, 1962, Chap. VII.

# The Instruments
# of Policy:
# Diplomatic Bargaining

In seeking to achieve objectives, realize values, or defend interests, governments must communicate with those whose actions and behavior they wish to deter, alter, or reinforce. Today there are many occasions and media of communication which may be employed for conveying hopes, wishes, or threats to others. At the press conference, political rally, or banquet, government officials make statements directed not just to domestic audiences but to foreign governments and peoples as well. Nevertheless, most official attempts to wield influence abroad are carried out through formal diplomatic channels or by direct communication between foreign ministers and heads of state.

The subjects of interstate communication include definitions of a government's objectives, rationalizations for them, threats, promises, and holding out possibilities for concluding agreements on contentious issues. As will be seen, the function of the diplomat is not so much to formulate his government's goals as to

# Chapter VIII

explain them abroad and attempt to persuade others to adjust their own policies to conform to those objectives. A diplomat is partially successful when he can get the government to which he is accredited to see a particular situation as his own government perceives it; he is totally successful when he is able to alter or maintain the actions of a foreign government in a manner favorable to the interests of his own government. Normally during the process of communication, those who formulate policy will reassess their objectives in the light of changing circumstances and varying foreign responses. Diplomats then convey the modified objectives to foreign governments, and the whole routine continues until consensus is reached through bargaining, is imposed by the use of force, or one government abandons or withdraws from its objectives if they meet resistance abroad.

Objectives and diplomatic bargaining strategies are thus subject to constant reformulation on the basis of information and assessments provided by diplomats abroad. When mutual interest and consensus on a problem exist, the policy-formulating and implementing processes may require only the length of time needed to fill in details on a piece of paper. When there is disagreement, misunderstanding, or incompatibility between two or more governments' values, objectives, and interests, the process may involve long periods of time. Both India and Pakistan, for instance, have maintained their basic objectives with regard to the states of Kashmir and Jammu for more than two decades while all of their diplomatic bargaining, threats, rewards, and use of force to resolve the issue have not succeeded in changing each others' position. The main purposes of this chapter are to illustrate some of the techniques of diplomatic bargaining, and to discuss some of the contemporary problems attending diplomatic action. Before discussing these processes, however, it is necessary to examine some of the basic rules and traditions of diplomatic communication between independent states and analyze the position of the main medium for interstate communication, the ambassador.

## The Institutions, Rules, and Personnel of Diplomacy

The emissary is among the first political roles established in human society. Between primitive tribes, whether friendly or antagonistic, communication was necessary, and special personnel with certain religious, bargaining, or linguistic skills were appointed to conduct discussions on a variety of issues. Emissaries bargained over the allocation of hunting territory, settling of family or clan disputes, or planning of an inter-tribal marriage. Today diplomats seek to extend national interests in foreign territories, protect the national society from a perceived threat, increase the volume of trade, resolve a conflict over contested territory, or regulate traffic in drugs.

It was not until the fifteenth century that the concept of a permanent mission, or legation, was instituted in Europe. Italian city states during the late Renaissance period first developed a systematic diplomatic service and recognized the need for establishing a corps of professional diplomats. The functions of these early diplomats included obtaining information, safeguarding political and military interests, and extending commerce. Indeed, organized diplomacy may have owed as much for its origins to the development of extensive trade networks in Europe and the middle east as to political and military matters. The Venetian diplomatic service, for example, was originally a commercial organization. The new dynastic regimes emerging in Europe later emulated the diplomatic institutions established on the Italian peninsula, and by the eighteenth century diplomacy was recognized as an important and honorable profession, even if its methods were not always so reputable.

Classical diplomacy operated among few political units: in 1648, for example, there were only 12 well-defined sovereign states in Europe, and the affairs of one did not frequently impinge on the interests of the other In the present international system not only are there over 120 sovereign states, but their economic, political, and military interdependence means that almost any major domestic or foreign policy decision in one will have repercussions on the interests of many others. In this setting the problem of achieving mutually acceptable solutions to all issues is difficult and usually cannot be resolved through the relatively slow and cumbersome procedures of bilateral negotiations. Thus, a correlation between economic, scientific, and technological development and the growth of multilateral diplomacy can be observed. It is no accident that the most rapid growth of permanent multilateral diplomatic institutions occurred simultaneously with the fastest period of industrial and technological development in Europe. The bilateral patterns of diplomatic communication of the eighteenth century gave way first to *ad hoc* multilateral conferences, and more recently to permanent multilateral diplomatic and technical organizations.

Until the latter part of the nineteenth century, most multilateral conferences dealt with the terms of peace following major European wars, but after the Franco-Prussian war of 1870–1871 governments began to send delegates to conferences dealing with the codification of international law (the Hague Conferences of 1899 and 1907) and the more technical economic problems which European governments commonly faced.[1] In 1875 a group of governments established the Universal Postal Union, the first permanent international machinery involving the membership of most of the states in the world. The idea of a permanent conference machinery was also put into practice in the League of Nations, and during the 1920's other important *ad hoc* conferences were held in Genoa, Brussels, Geneva, and London to deal with economic reconstruction, German reparations, and disarmament. The machinery for Allied economic cooperation during World War I (The Inter-Allied Maritime Transport Council) was copied and expanded considerably during the war against Nazi Germany and Japan. There were also momentous meetings between the heads of state of the major powers at Ottawa, Cairo, Teheran, and Yalta, and the Allies created a series of interlocking conference systems to coordinate all aspects of the war effort and to plan for the post-war organization of the world.

Today the concept of multilateral conference diplomacy is institutionalized in the United Nations and its specialized agencies. These organizations are widely known, but multilateral diplomacy also occurs constantly in thousands of *ad hoc* conferences and less formal meetings between diplomats or government officials. During the nineteenth century, for example, the American government sent diplomatic representatives to 100 conferences, or an average of one per year; in the period 1956–1958, American diplomats, specialists, and politicians attended 1,027 international conferences, an average of one conference per day.[2]

Not only has a large portion of diplomatic communication become channeled through multilateral institutions and organizations, but even in bilateral relations, the institutional framework of communication has become increasingly complex as the range of issues common to any pair of states has expanded. During the eighteenth century, when foreign relations were concerned primarily with military, political, and dynastic problems, a country could be represented adequately in each major capital by an ambassador or minister and several secretaries. An envoy could perform his duties satisfactorily by keeping up on political developments in the country to which he was accredited and by applying tact,

[1] These conferences considered such disparate subjects as agriculture, regulation and production of sugar, international standards of sanitation, tariffs, international telegraphy, navigation on the Danube, the prime meridian, liquor traffic, statistics, maritime signalling, and weights and measures.

[2] Elmer Plischke, *The Conduct of American Diplomacy* (2nd ed.; Princeton: D. Van Nostrand Co., Inc., 1961), p. 474.

common sense, and intelligence to his contacts with foreign officials. Today, if the diplomat at the ambassadorial rank is to achieve success in his efforts to influence the government to which he is accredited, he must command knowledge of a wide variety of affairs and subjects, including economics, propaganda techniques, labor relations, and all facets of political analysis. He frequently administers an embassy with a staff of several hundred specialists and secretaries. Office routine, expertise, and discipline within a bureaucratic organization have replaced the glamor and leisure of eighteenth century salons and courts.

The last development of significance in diplomatic procedures has been the rapid increase in direct communication between heads of state. As modes of transportation have made travel a simple affair, high ranking officials and policy-makers can by-pass the traditional diplomatic intermediary and maintain direct communication among themselves. These face-to-face confrontations may raise problems since many presidents and prime ministers are not trained in diplomatic skills, but they have the compensating advantage of allowing constitutionally responsible officials to make decisions on the basis of their broad authority and to by-pass the bureaucratic resistances or impediments to easy communication between governments. These officials often enjoy foreign travel because it raises their personal prestige at home and abroad and enables them to clarify their views personally to other heads of state. It is little wonder, then, that European leaders visit Washington or Moscow as often as twice each year, that most American presidents make at least several major trips abroad, and that leaders of non-aligned states are in almost constant personal communication with each other and with the major leaders of the Western and Communist blocs.

Whether conducted through trained diplomats or by heads of state, communication between governments representing widely diverse social, economic, and political systems is naturally liable to all sorts of distortion due to cultural differences, ideological cleavages, and plain misunderstandings. Since permanent diplomatic institutions were established in Italy during the fifteenth century, governments have commonly recognized that it is to their mutual advantage to observe certain rules of procedure which help make communication easier to conduct and less liable to distortion. Diplomatic bargaining processes become impaired if no one agrees as to whom is entitled to represent a state, or if diplomatic envoys are subject to harassment or intimidation by those to whom they are accredited. Three sets of rules concerning protocol, immunities, and non-interference have therefore been developed in western international law and custom to facilitate communication between states.

## Protocol

Diplomatic protocol is of considerable importance in assisting diplomats to pursue their tasks in an effective manner. Although the rituals of protocol may seem merely ceremonial leftovers of a previous era, they have a definite function even today. Rank, for example, was a matter which constantly added irritants to international relations in the eighteenth century, and solution of the problem at the Congress of Vienna in 1815 has helped in many ways to reduce little frictions that may lead to poor relations and communication between governments. In the early years of modern diplomacy, the Pope claimed the right to decide the ceremonial order of the various dynasts' representatives, but as the influence of the church in secular affairs declined, diplomats and their governments were left to their own devices—sometimes with disastrous results. Rank, protocol, and precedence had great symbolic significance; ambassadors and envoys frequently received orders not to permit other courts' envoys to precede them in ceremonial processions, for such acts could reflect adversely on the prestige and honor of their own dynast. In formal processions, for example, diplomats would plan strategies enabling them to gain favorable positions in the line. Several incidents have been recorded where coachmen were killed attempting to gain advantages over their rivals. It was not uncommon, moreover, for ambassadors to engage in duels to vindicate their honor and prestige when it was questioned by another envoy. In such circumstances, the candor and friendly personal relations necessary to successful diplomacy were not always easy to display.[3]

In 1815 four diplomatic ranks were established and universally adopted by European courts and foreign offices. The highest rank was assigned to ambassadors and papal nuncios, followed by envoys extraordinary and ministers plenipotentiary, ministers resident, and *chargés d'affaires*. These titles are still in use today and determine the ranking of diplomatic officials at ceremonial and political functions. The question of precedence was not, however, completely solved by agreement on the question of rank. Therefore, the delegates to the Congress of Aix-la-Chapelle in 1818 agreed that among members of the same rank precedence should be established no longer on the prestige or power of the diplomat's government, but solely on the length of time the diplomat had served as ambassador in one country. Thus, if the ambassador of Luxembourg to the United States has held his position in Washington, D.C., longer than

[3] Cf. Hans Morgenthau, *Politics Among Nations* (3rd ed.; New York: Alfred A. Knopf, Inc., 1960).

the Soviet ambassador, he always precedes the Soviet ambassador. The diplomat who has served the longest period in a foreign capital is normally referred to as the *doyen,* or dean, of the diplomatic corps, and on ceremonial occasions always precedes other ambassadors.

Another aspect of protocol which influences the efficiency of diplomatic processes is language, for precision in communication is one of the major requirements of effective diplomacy. To many outside government serv-ice, the style of written diplomatic communication seems at best specious and at worst, hypocritical. Diplomatic correspondence today is largely devoid of the circuitous and gentlemanly phrases in use a generation ago, but it is still not unusual to see notes stating that "I have the honor to acknowledge your excellency's note . . ." or "I feel constrained to advise you that my government cannot but acquiesce in the view that. . . ." The use of such rhetoric is declining and there is an increasing tendency in diplomatic communication to be frank and avoid any impression of being dilatory.

Formerly, by adhering to strict rules of etiquette, diplomats could phrase statements which gave precise meaning without creating the impression of impoliteness or belligerence. Gordon Craig cites the ex-ample of a meeting in 1859 between Napoleon III and the Austrian ambassador to France, when the Emperor in the politest terms expressed his regret that Franco-Austrian relations were not more cordial. If the Austrian ambassador was alert, he realized that Napoleon had really meant that unless the Austrians changed their foreign policy, a Franco-Austrian war was likely to ensue.[4] While diplomats were aware of the meaning between the lines, at least the diplomatic environment *seemed* to be one of amity, courtesy, and common understanding. As will be seen below, much of the formality of diplomatic communication has been replaced by frankness and, in some cases, vulgarity, polemics, and in-temperate name-calling.

## Immunities

If governments are to seek to influence each others' policies and actions through effective communication, they must assume that their diplomatic agents abroad will not be abused or placed under conditions that would prevent them from engaging freely in bargaining and persuasion. Even among primitive people, envoys or messengers were usually regarded as sacrosanct and enjoyed special privileges and immunities when travelling abroad. Communication would have been impossible if emissaries had

[4] Gordon A. Craig, "On the Diplomatic Revolution of Our Times" (The Haynes Foundation Lectures, University of California, Riverside, April, 1961), p. 9.

been treated as "heathen," burned, tortured, or eaten before delivering their messages. In ancient China, Greece, and India, as well as in the Muslim Empire, diplomatic immunities were regularly accorded to envoys and messengers from "barbarian" communities. On occasion, ambassadors were imprisoned or slain because they were suspected of trickery, but in most cases (as indicated in the ancient Indian *Mahabharata*, "The King who slays an envoy sinks into hell with all his ministers") there were strong ethical sanctions and reasons of self-interest against violating diplomatic immunities.[5]

It is still the general rule of international law that a diplomat and his embassy are to be treated as if they were on their native soil. They are immune from prosecution under the laws, customs, rules, or regulations of the government to which they are accredited. Those who enjoy diplomatic status (usually all the full-time foreign staff of the embassy) may not be molested by national police officials, nor may the premises of an embassy be visited by local law-enforcement agents without the invitation of the embassy staff. If an American official enjoying diplomatic status parks his auto in a restricted zone in Teheran, for instance, he is not liable to fine, trial, or imprisonment by Iranian officials. However, if diplomatic officials commit serious crimes abroad the host government may either demand that the official be recalled or request that his immunities be lifted so that he can be indicted and tried in the receiving country's courts of law. In a recent case a member of a foreign embassy in Copenhagen was apprehended by local officials for organizing and deriving profits from a call-girl establishment. He could not be tried under Danish laws because he enjoyed diplomatic immunity, but the Danish foreign ministry protested to the guilty diplomat's government and obtained his immediate recall. A Central American diplomat, in a similar situation, was arrested upon his arrival in New York when police apprehended him attempting to smuggle a large amount of heroin into the United States. The State Department requested the foreign government to strip the man of his diplomatic status, which it consented to do, and he was eventually tried, convicted, and imprisoned according to American legal procedures.

If in this case the Central American government had refused to recall the ambassador or lift his diplomatic status, the United States could have declared him *persona non grata*, thus forcing the Central American government to recall him. In most cases governments do recall their

---

[5] Cf. Frank M. Russell, *Theories of International Relations* (New York: Appleton-Century-Crofts, Inc., 1936), p. 42. In several recent instances the Soviet government has promised immunity and safety to emissaries and delegations, only to imprison or execute them upon arrival. The cases in question involved a group representing the Polish underground, in 1945, and the military and political leaders of the Hungarian revolution in 1956.

diplomats when requested to do so, and designating a diplomat *persona non grata* usually results from a diplomat's political actions, not from breaking a local law. Ambassadors and other diplomatic officials are usually declared *persona non grata* only when their efficiency has been impaired by indiscreet political statements, interference in internal affairs of the host country, or taking advantage of their status to indulge in espionage activities. During the cold war, there has been rather rapid turnover of diplomatic personnel in the Western embassies in Moscow and the Soviet embassy in Washington, as numerous diplomats (many were intelligence agents posing as diplomats) have been apprehended while conducting illegal intelligence activities. Retaliation has also become an accepted practice; for example, if a British diplomat is expelled from the Soviet Union, the British government will normally request the immediate recall of a Soviet diplomat in London. Although the activities of diplomats during the cold war have taxed the laws and customs of immunity, they are still recognized as essential to effective diplomacy, and there has been surprisingly little discussion over the merits of either abandoning or proscribing them.[6]

### Non-interference

If diplomatic officials ordinarily enjoy immunities from the laws of the country to which they are accredited, other customs have developed which limit the types of actions they can undertake in attempting to influence the policies of foreign governments. Chief among these is the stricture that they cannot in any way interfere in the internal political processes of another country. Normally, they are expected to confine official discussions to government personnel. Certainly they may defend their own government's policies to the foreign public by addressing private groups, but they must not make appeals to these people asking them to put pressures on their own government; nor can they provide funds to political parties, or provide leadership or other services to insurgents, political factions, or economic organizations.

These rules of non-interference are well-established in law and customary practice, but as the domestic affairs of countries have increasingly important foreign policy implications, the rules are in many cases circumvented. In 1919, President Wilson toured Italy exhorting the Italian people to press their government to make concessions at the Paris Peace Conference; foreign aid and technical personnel frequently "suggest" how foreign governments should reform their economy, organize a military

[6] Most Communist governments and the United States restrict the travel privileges of each others' diplomats. Certain areas of the United States, for instance, cannot be visited by Russian diplomats.

force, or put down civil rebellion.[7] As will be discussed in Chapter XI, Nazi, Western, and Communist diplomats have amassed an impressive record of intervention in other countries' internal affairs by fomenting civil disorders, subsidizing subversive political factions, and disseminating covert propaganda.

## The Functions of Diplomats

Aside from the main role of diplomats in bargaining and communicating information between governments, they perform several other duties which should be mentioned briefly. These can be classified under the headings of (1) protection of nationals and their property abroad, (2) symbolic representation, (3) obtaining information, and (4) providing advice and making over-all policies.

### Protection of Nationals

This function, which involves protecting the lives and promoting the interests of nationals residing or travelling abroad, is a routine task, although during catastrophes or civil disorders the role of diplomats in this capacity may become very important. Nationals have to be protected or evacuated if necessary, they must be represented by legal counsel if jailed, and their property or other interests abroad must be protected if the local government does not provide such service. It is the general practice among major powers to assign consular agents rather than embassy personnel to perform these duties. Consulates, which may be established in many cities in a country, are diplomatic substations that serve travellers to and from the host country with regard to visas and other information, protect the interests of their own citizens when on foreign soil, and assist in commercial transactions. Consular agents occasionally perform the other three major functions of diplomats, but only when normal diplomatic communication has been disrupted.

### Symbolic Representation

In his role as a symbolic representative, the diplomat of other eras seldom did more than attend court ceremonies; today, however, the ambassador, in addition to attending ceremonial and social occasions, must address foreign groups and be present at all events with which his

[7] For an analysis of the shoddiness of contemporary diplomatic practices in comparison to the nineteenth century, see Lord Vansittart, "The Decline of Diplomacy," *Foreign Affairs*, XXVIII (1950), 177–88.

country is somehow connected, no matter how remotely. If a Soviet ballet group visits the United States, the Russian ambassador is expected to be on hand for the opening performance; if the United States has constructed a medical center for children in some underdeveloped country, the American ambassador must not only attend its opening but also display a continuing interest in its activities. Whether in agriculture, medicine, music, physics, or military policies, if his government has some stake in a project, the diplomat must symbolize that stake by his physical presence and continuing concern. In his symbolic capacity, the ambassador is concerned with the totality of relations—whether political or not—between his own country and the one to which he has been sent.

## Obtaining Information

Because information and data are the raw materials of foreign policy, the gathering of information—by official acts, at cocktail parties, or by covert means—is the most important task of the diplomat, aside from his bargaining activities. Precise information must be made available to those who formulate policy if there is to be a minimum discrepancy between the objective environment and the image of the environment held by policy-makers. Data concerning military potential, personalities, and economic trends or problems may be supplied by intelligence units abroad, but intelligence experts work under limitations when it comes to assessment of trends, intentions, responses, attitudes, and motivations. While the diplomat may also provide a large quantity of raw data in his reports, his main role in providing information is to use his skill and familiarity with the foreign society to interpret the data and make reliable assessments and forecasts of responses of the receiving government toward his own government's policies. He might be asked to predict answers to some of the following questions: What are the implications for the host government's foreign policy if a new party is elected to power or a military junta gains control through a *coup d'état?* What is the influence of a certain columnist or radio commentator upon official policy and public opinion? What tactics are likely to be adopted by the foreign government in forthcoming negotiations over the allocation of foreign aid grants? How would the foreign government react to a major diplomatic maneuver by the diplomat's government in another area of the world? What position might the foreign government take in a future international conference on tariffs, or on the regulation of narcotics, or on an issue before the General Assembly of the United Nations?

The success of a diplomat in answering and assessing such questions will depend upon the scope and variety of sources of information he is able to cultivate among party leaders, government officials, trade unions, the press, and the military. The ambassador or diplomat who relies too heavily upon one official source of information is likely to obtain only a distorted version of reality.

How do diplomatic officials obtain vital information? Most of it comes from reading and examining reports, debates, and newspaper articles published in the country where they are stationed. Since the volume of information in these sources is normally beyond the capacity of any one individual to assess, ambassadors rely on extensive staff assistance and full-time specialists concerned with a particular range of problems. Commercial attachés not only negotiate trade agreements and promote trade relations, but also have the responsibility for knowing in detail the development, structure, problems, and leaders of the foreign country's economy. Cultural, agricultural, labor, scientific, and military attachés perform the same duties within their respective areas of competence, while intelligence officials attached to the embassy have the responsibility for obtaining more covert information.

Information is also obtained through informal means. "Entertainment," one diplomat claimed, "oils the hinges of a man's office door." Though legislators and taxpayers frequently disparage diplomats for the time and money they spend on cocktail parties and dinners, there are definite advantages to these informal occasions. In a light setting it is often easier to persuade and obtain vital information. The strain of rigid protocol is removed and unofficial views can be exchanged, while the element of personal acquaintance—and sometimes plentiful quantities of liquor—may increase confidence and trust. Rumors can be assessed and verified, personal reactions elicited, and all types of interesting information obtained more easily at social functions than during official calls and in official communications.

### Providing Advice and Making Over-all Policies

The final important function of diplomats, aside from bargaining and negotiation, is to provide advice to those who formulate goals and plans of action, and occasionally to make important policy decisions themselves. All diplomats serve in a sense as policy-makers because they provide a large portion of the information upon which policy is based. A principal contribution of the diplomat in the policy-making process thus comes from his skill of interpretation and judgment about conditions in the country to which he is accredited. But even if a diplomat is particularly useful in this capacity, it does not mean that his judgments will always be considered or that his advice or warnings will be heeded. A diplomat's influence in the formulation of a nation's goals will depend on a number of different considerations. If he enjoys political prestige among the top policy experts at the home foreign office, if he has a reputation for reliability, initiative, and resourcefulness, and refrains from attempting to sabotage official policy in its execution, he may be called upon frequently to make policy recommendations—his functions will include advice as well as providing information. He will probably not have any role in formulating the broad objectives of governmental policy abroad, but given those objectives, he may be asked to suggest the best ways to achieve them. On the other hand, if the diplomat is new in his post or career, if he vigorously questions official policy, and if his assessments are not reliable, it is unlikely that he will have much influence in policy formulation.

Beyond such general considerations there are a number of conditions peculiar to modern diplomatic organizations which diminish the influence of career diplomats in the policy-making process. One is the ease with which bureaucratic officials can combine policy-making and diplomatic roles. Prior to World War I, the prevailing practice was for government officials to formulate external goals and strategies and then direct their diplomatic agents abroad to attempt to achieve them. With the modern means of travel at their disposal, foreign ministers can now visit foreign capitals and obtain their information firsthand; they can similarly become negotiators and perform the task of diplomatic bargaining as well as policy-making. While they must still rely on ambassadors abroad for some information, there are few impediments, aside from the rush of business, which prevent foreign ministers from being policy-maker, administrator, and negotiator simultaneously. John Foster Dulles, Secretary of State in the Eisenhower administration, flew over 400,000 miles in six years of office to attend meetings of the NATO Council, the United Nations, and SEATO, and to conduct delicate negotiations with the Russians and many other governments.

Another impediment against a significant role in policy-making for diplomats is the limited environment within which they operate. Ambassadors generally develop considerable competence in handling bilateral relations between governments, but it is more difficult for them to perceive these relations in the broader context of over-all foreign policy. Though political officials at the highest level of government lack detailed knowledge of conditions abroad, they act upon a broad understanding of situations, of which bilateral relations are only a part. What to the ambassador may seem a logical and desirable policy to pursue in the bilateral system may be the wrong policy in view of the total substance of a country's foreign policy. Moreover, foreign ministers and high political officials also view policy in terms of the domestic political environment and requirements. The definition of the situation that operates in foreign policy decision-making includes an important domestic sector that is not always understood by the diplomatic agent who has lived abroad for a long period of time.

In an effort to improve relations between the Soviet and American governments, for instance, the American ambassador in Moscow may recommend that the United States sell one million tons of surplus wheat to the Russians. In the environment in which the American ambassador operates, this may be a perfectly logical and desirable proposition, but the Secretary of State, whose operational environment is necessarily larger, will not make the decision merely on the basis of the ambassador's recommendation. He is alert to the views of Congressmen on the proposal, and if these are hostile, may not wish to endanger his relations with the legislature for the sake of selling a million tons of wheat to the Russians. Moreover, by selling the wheat he might offend the interests of several key allies who depend heavily upon the Soviet Union as a market for their own surplus wheat. Thus, different perspectives in the field and at home will prevent, in many instances, the ambassador from wielding great influence where policy is formulated.

The bureaucratic structure and organization of foreign offices hinders many reports and recommendations from ambassadors abroad from reaching those who make policy at the highest level. In the eighteenth and nineteenth centuries communications were slow, there were only approximately 20 states in the European system, and foreign contacts were limited to a few political or commercial affairs, so foreign ministers could keep abreast of all the activities of their diplomats. Today, most dispatches—including some potentially important ones—never get beyond the "desk officer" in the foreign ministry. High-level officials who formulate major policy decisions within the context of large organizations tend to become further and further removed from the environment in which their diplomats operate. In a period of crisis between two countries, the ambassador may play a more significant role in recommending courses of action, but even in this situation he is merely an expert whose advice may or may not be followed.

Finally, there are personal and social reasons which prevent diplomats in the field from initiating proposals on major policy decisions. Occasionally diplomats are so afraid of being accused of lack of judgment by their superiors that they may prefer to avoid making any recommendations at all. Evading responsibility in this way may not be solely their fault, since most bureaucratic organizations have established policies, persisting by the sanction of time and tradition, which can only be changed by those with the greatest political strength. The diplomat who challenges these traditions is in many cases likely to become suspect. As suggested in Chapter VI, persons with highly structured belief systems tend to select and rely on information and recommendations which reinforce or sustain their own images, prejudices, and stereotypes. High-level officials in organizations which hold strong commitments to certain policies tend to overlook or downgrade information provided by ambassadors which contradicts or questions the validity of these policies.

One example is provided in a detailed study of the crisis preceding the outbreak of World War I. In the summer of 1914 Kaiser Wilhelm dismissed the accurate warnings of Prince Lichnowsky, his ambassador in London, as utter nonsense coming from "that old goat." Prince Lichnowsky's reports, the study reveals, did not conform to the Kaiser's view that England would remain neutral if war broke out between the major antagonists of the crisis. On the other hand, the highly inaccurate reports of the German ambassador in St. Petersburg supported the Kaiser's expectations that the Tsar's government was bluffing in its announced policy of supporting Serbia, and were thus accepted uncritically.[8] When diplomats are faced with circumstances where their advice is either rejected or ignored, it is little wonder that they judge their policy-making role to be insignificant. It is a fact, nevertheless, that most foreign offices suffer from rigid procedures and established policies which impel policy-makers to downgrade "uncomfortable" information. As a former Secretary in the Australian Department of External Affairs has written:

> The only facts and opinions regarded [in foreign offices] as relevant will be those which fall within the framework of broad government policy, and which are compatible with the basic assumptions on which government policy is conceived. There will be "reliable" sources, those which support government policy, and "suspect" sources, which have the unfriendly habit of producing facts which do not support government policy. Very important human factors, of course, creep into activities of this nature. The desire for promotion, the need not to offend by producing embarrassing facts, the reluctance to report from overseas events which would suggest policy was wrongly based, are all most relevant influences in the final formulation of national policy.[9]

Although the problems of bureaucratic resistance and individual rigidity may exist in any foreign office, totalitarian diplomatic establishments are particularly vulnerable to them. It has long been suspected that Soviet diplomats operate under great pressure to report only what the Soviet government wants to hear. Since only the upper echelons of the Soviet

[8] Robert C. North, "Fact and Value in the 1914 Crisis" (Stanford Studies in International Conflict and Integration, 1961).

[9] John W. Burton, *Peace Theory: Preconditions of Disarmament* (New York: Alfred A. Knopf, Inc., 1962), pp. 184–85.

decision-making machinery can formulate the official "line," a diplomat seriously jeopardizes his career and integrity by suggesting that those who formulate policy may be mistaken, or ought to listen to unorthodox views. Alexandr Kaznacheev, a Soviet diplomat who defected from service in the Russian embassy in Rangoon during 1959, verified in part these suspicions. He suggests in his book, *Inside a Soviet Embassy*, that only Soviet intelligence agents were able to send accurate and objective information to Moscow, and that the diplomatic personnel were precluded from proposing policy alternatives. According to his account of arriving at the Soviet embassy in Rangoon, he was told by Soviet officials only to use insignificant words and the usual doctrinaire clichés—all supporting the official line—in his reports. They further warned him against making any independent judgments or straightforward statements. His conclusion after several years of service was that not even the Soviet ambassador in Burma could propose policy changes or suggest alterations of official attitudes in Moscow.[10]

### The Purposes of Diplomatic Communication

In most cases the purpose of negotiation between two or more governments is to change or sustain each other's objectives and policies or to reach agreement over some contentious issue. While this is ordinarily the case, entering into discussions through diplomatic intermediaries may have other purposes as well. Before analyzing the techniques diplomats employ in bargaining and securing agreements, these other objectives should be noted.

First, a large amount of diplomatic communication between governments is undertaken primarily for exchanging views, probing intentions, and attempting to convince other governments that certain actions, such as attending a conference, lowering tariffs, or proffering diplomatic support on a particular international issue, would be in their interest. Here there is no hard bargaining, and diplomats or government officials do not ordinarily employ threats or offer rewards. The majority of routine diplomatic contacts between governments is of this nature, and almost all visits by heads of states are undertaken not for bargaining, but simply for "exchanging views" and "consulting."

Second, bilateral diplomatic meetings or multilateral conferences may be arranged for the purpose of stalling or creating a decoy which gives

[10] Alexandr Kaznacheev, *Inside a Soviet Embassy: Experiences of a Russian Diplomat in Burma* (Philadelphia: J. B. Lippincott Co., 1962), pp. 45, 84, 192.

the illusion that a government is seriously interested in bargaining, while it really desires no agreement. During the conduct of warfare, one state may agree to armistice negotiations to assuage public opinion, while it simultaneously steps up its military campaigns. By agreeing to negotiate, it may be able to draw attention away from its other activities.

Third, a government may enter into diplomatic negotiations primarily for the purpose of making propaganda; it uses a conference not so much to reach agreement over a limited range of issues as to make broad appeals to the outside public, partly to undermine the bargaining position of its opponents. In an age when "secret diplomacy" is viewed with suspicion and many diplomatic negotiations are open both to the press and public, a conference which is certain to receive extensive publicity around the world offers an excellent forum for influencing public attitudes. Soviet negotiators have earned a reputation for employing international conferences for propaganda purposes, but any time two or more governments cannot agree—or do not wish to agree—upon the issues under consideration and yet desire to gain some advantages from their efforts, they are likely to use the proceedings primarily to embarrass their opponents and extoll their own actions and attitudes. The open forum of the General Assembly offers one important arena for attempting to influence non-diplomatic opinion. Indeed, many observers of United Nations affairs note that most speeches made in that body are designed primarily for public domestic and international consumption, not for the information of other delegates. The many conferences on disarmament and arms control since World War II have similarly been exploited for propaganda purposes. In these instances the Soviet Union has not been the only participant. When Western diplomats found that the Soviet government would not accept their proposals, rather than break up the proceedings they would spend their time attempting to embarrass the Soviet delegates or publicizing the righteousness of their own cause.[11]

The trained observer can readily discern when a party to diplomatic negotiations is exploiting a conference or meeting *primarily* (since all "open" diplomacy involves some propaganda) for the purposes of influencing the attitudes of the general public rather than for changing the bargaining positions of its opponents. Persistent use of slogans, epithets, vague phrases (such as "general and complete disarmament") and repetition of totally unacceptable positions indicates that bargaining is not the real purpose of the discussions. Other techniques include repeated attempts to discredit the opposition, deliberate and frequent misrepresenta-

[11] Cf. Joseph L. Nogee, "Propaganda and Negotiation: The Case of the Ten-Nation Disarmament Committee," *Journal of Conflict Resolution,* VII (1963), 510–21.

tion of the other party's positions, widespread discussion of subjects not on the agenda, or inconsistent statements. John Foster Dulles remembered when attending the Moscow Minister's Conference in 1947 as an observer how Soviet Foreign Minister Molotov would make lengthy speeches at the meetings, each inconsistent with its predecessor. In one instance he would proffer friendship to the defeated Germans and promise them help in reconstructing their economy; in the next he would please the anti-German sentiments of the Soviet population by demanding stiff reparations from the Germans; and to the Poles, he promised generous portions of German territory.[12] Anthony Eden pointed out that Molotov also enjoyed using the device of repetition to ensure maximum international publicity for the Soviet point of view. At a meeting of Foreign Ministers in Berlin during 1954, Molotov took up the better part of 13 meetings to repeat incessantly the Soviet government's case, as well as to launch attacks on Western policies. At no time during these 13 meetings would the Soviet foreign minister allow the conference to begin discussions of the items on the agenda.[13] An American delegate at one series of disarmament meetings in 1960 noted to the Soviet negotiators that they had employed the vague phrase "general and complete disarmament" 135 times in about two hours of speechmaking.[14]

Diplomacy, however, is used primarily to reach agreements, compromises, and settlements where government objectives conflict. It involves, whether in private meetings or publicized conferences, the attempt to change the policies, actions, objectives, and attitudes of other governments and their diplomats by persuasion, offering rewards, exchanging concessions, or making threats.

### The Negotiating Process:
### Bargaining and Capabilities

One of the points emphasized in the previous chapter held that the quantity and quality of capabilities does not necessarily indicate a state's effective influence over other governments. Many observers have assumed that one can only bargain effectively "from a position of strength," or that a "great power" can always achieve its objectives against "small powers" by virtue of its greater capacity to inflict punishment. In diplomatic negotiations, however, capabilities are important (1) *in so far as they are*

[12] John Foster Dulles, *War or Peace* (New York: The Macmillan Company, 1950), p. 67.
[13] Anthony Eden, *Full Circle* (London: Cassell & Company, Ltd., 1960), p. 65.
[14] Nogee, "Propaganda and Negotiation," p. 515.

*relevant to the bargaining situation,* and (2) if they are mobilized to be used as threats, rewards, or instruments of exchange. Many capabilities are irrelevant to bargaining situations and probably would not be mobilized for making threats or rewards. Consider the hypothetical case of negotiations between the Soviet Union and Iran for certain rectifications of the frontier between the two countries. The Soviet Union could offer foreign aid agreements as one inducement to gain favorable frontier lines, but unless the issue was crucial to the Soviet government it could hardly threaten to use its nuclear weapons against Iran. In this type of negotiation, the Soviet Union's great capabilities in nuclear weapons, to say nothing of its vast territory, large population, or extensive literacy, are unimportant. Another example would be where the United States and Egypt were at odds over their respective positions on such issues as colonialism or aid to "national liberation" movements in Africa. The United States could not use its nuclear capability to induce a change in Egypt's policies and attitudes, nor would Egypt's lack of certain capabilities as compared to the United States place it in a weak bargaining position. But in negotiations over a trade treaty with Egypt, the United States could very effectively use its superior *economic* capabilities as a lever for achieving its objectives. It could offer generous financing terms, threaten, without damage to itself, to cut off Egyptian markets in America if the Egyptians refused to lower tariffs on certain goods, or select from a wide variety of products those most likely to be useful to the Egyptians in exchange for their export commodities. Similarly, military capabilities are most important in bargaining situations which involve a military confrontation of some sort, or where one side is trying to induce the other to agree to peace discussions or armistice negotiations. By no means, therefore, is the side which is relatively weak in most capabilities necessarily weak in all bargaining situations. If, as suggested in the previous chapter, the strong partner is somehow dependent upon the weak—if he *needs* something the weaker side possesses or controls—the weak state may actually have a much stronger bargaining position.

Other factors influencing the strength of the parties to a series of negotiations are also involved. The personality and negotiating skills of diplomats are certainly important, though it should not be assumed that governments can maintain friendly relations with each other just because their ambassadors get along socially. A negotiator who has a reputation for bargaining skill and personal reasonableness may be able to obtain concessions that an obnoxious personality could not. In other instances, the qualities of evasiveness, deceit, and vulgarity might be assets to negotiations, particularly if the purpose is to *avoid* agreement or to induce the other side, through exasperation, to make concessions.

Another factor in bargaining strength is the general reputation of a nation's diplomats and their negotiating techniques. If one party gains a reputation for bluffing (making threats without carrying them through), future threats will be less credible. Or, as in the case of the Soviet Union during Stalin's era, if it earns a reputation for breaking agreements, others may be unwilling to negotiate even when that government seriously wants an agreement. Finally, a negotiating team's "strength" can be related to the amount of responsiveness or public international sympathy its government is able to generate for its position. During the middle stages of World War II, when the Soviet Union was militarily weaker than the other allies, Stalin was able to gain concessions from the West regarding Russia's role in Eastern Europe that he could not have obtained once the cold war started, when Western sympathy for Russia's objectives had cooled considerably.

### The Negotiating Process:
### Inducing Agreement

The choice of techniques and tactics to employ in diplomatic negotiation depends generally upon the degree of incompatibility between two or more nations' objectives and interests, the extent to which they are committed to them, and the degree to which they want to reach agreement. Diplomatic negotiations between friends and allies seldom display the same characteristics as those between hostile governments. Where there is already considerable agreement about the principles of an issue, negotiation may involve only working out the details, or deducing the consequences from the principles.[15] When governments are responsive to each others' interests, moreover, they have a good basis for arranging compromises and exchanging concessions. In negotiations within the Common Market, for instance, the parties agree widely on the objectives of the organization and have intimate knowledge of each others' economic needs and interests. To a large extent they can negotiate over essentially technical matters and do not have to worry about reconciling great principles. A common desire to reach agreement may also induce the bargaining agents to make concessions. The alternative is to adhere inflexibly to a position, prevent agreement, and accept the adverse publicity for adopting such a position.

Where objectives are fundamentally incompatible and both sides maintain strong commitments to their respective positions, the problem of

[15] Fred C. Iklé, *How Nations Negotiate* (New York: Harper & Row, Publishers, 1964), Chap. 11.

influencing behavior, actions, and objectives through diplomatic bargaining becomes much more complex. Two stages toward reaching a settlement in such conditions are involved. First, one party must get the other to *want* an agreement of some sort; he must somehow make the other realize that any agreement or settlement is preferable to the *status quo* of incompatible positions or non-agreement, or conversely that the consequences of non-agreement are more unfavorable to him than the consequences of agreement. Second, once the stage of "agreeing to an agreement" has been reached, the two parties must still bargain over the specific terms of the final agreement.

Of the two steps, the first is probably more difficult to achieve when commitments to incompatible objectives are strong; so long as one or both parties believe they can achieve their objectives through actions other than negotiations, diplomatic bargaining cannot lead to settlement. In the post-war negotiations over the status of Austria, negotiators from the Western allies and the Soviet Union met over 400 times before an agreement was worked out. It was clear that, with the exception of the last several meetings, the Soviet government did not wish to make an agreement or change its objectives toward Austria but was content to maintain the occupied status of the country. Negotiations were not used to bargain, but to mark time, discuss other issues, make propaganda, and give the impression that serious talks were proceeding. Only after other developments had occurred within the Soviet government and throughout Europe did the Russian government, over Foreign Minister Molotov's objections, decide that it wanted to conclude a permanent settlement of the Austrian issue. Once that decision was made, negotiations were completed in a matter of weeks.

If both sides have made the prior decision that agreement is more desirable than non-agreement or maintenance of the *status quo,* it remains for them to bargain over the specific details of settlement. Diplomats can employ a great variety of bargaining techniques. Basically, they present their conditions, define their own objectives, use threats and offers of rewards to try to obtain their acceptance or recognition by the other party, and, if this fails, reassess their original positions in terms of possible concessions which they hope will elicit agreement or a change in the objectives of the other side. All the time, they must simultaneously reveal their *commitment* to their bargaining positions lest the other party assume that they do not feel very strongly about their conditions and would be willing to compromise them without significant compensations.

Promise of a reward is in a sense a bribe or inducement which offers some future advantage in return for agreement on a specific point under contention. These may range from promises of "soft" peace terms, monetary loans, or diplomatic support at some future conference, to such symbolic acts as unilaterally releasing prisoners of war or suspending hostilities. One common ploy of governments which make extensive demands on the territorial *status quo* is to offer the reward of a permanent settlement of all other issues dividing two or more states if the other side will just give in on one specific territorial demand. Hitler promised that he would make no more territorial demands in Europe if only the Western powers would assist him in inducing the Czechs to cede the Sudetenland to him. He held out the possibility of a permanent settlement of all outstanding issues if this last problem could be resolved in his favor. Similarly, during the dispute between Indonesia and the Netherlands over West Irian in the early 1960's, Indonesian officials claimed that this would be their last territorial demand and that once it was met, stability could return to the region. Shortly after achieving their objectives in West Irian, the Indonesians began a systematic policy of "confrontation" against Malaysia, and attempted to break off Sabah and Brunei from the Federation.

Threats can be conceived as the opposite of rewards, where state A announces that if state B does not do X, it will do Y, which will hurt or damage B's interests. In a general setting where objectives between two or more states conflict, this can include a threat to start war, break diplomatic relations, impose economic embargoes or boycotts, institute a blockade, withdraw a foreign aid program, or in other ways punish state B. In addition, threats more peculiar to a particular diplomatic negotiating situation can be employed. The negotiators of one side might threaten to break off discussions (implying that they would prefer non-agreement to continued stalemate or acceptance of B's conditions), reveal secret agreements, increase their terms of agreement, or "let the military take over."

The effectiveness of threatening actions depends above all on their *credibility*.[16] State B has to believe that the threat will be carried out if it does not meet state A's demands. Credibility would seem to be established when B realizes that A can fulfill the threat and thereby damage B, without seriously harming its own interests. If, for instance, state A's diplomats threaten to walk out of a conference, and B knows that such action would seriously jeopardize the chances of obtaining an agreement it wants, it might very well be willing to make last-minute concessions to prevent a breakdown of negotiation.

The effectiveness and credibility of a threat would also seem to require that there be some symmetry between the *magnitude* of the threat and the issue under contention. If the Soviet Union threatens to start a nuclear

---

[16] The problem of credibility in military threats, introduced briefly in Chapter VII, will be discussed fully in Chapter XII.

war with Iran because the latter will not concede some relatively minor point in frontier negotiations, the threat will not seem credible; it is out of proportion to the issue at stake. This was one of the major problems with the doctrine of massive retaliation espoused by American strategists in the 1950's. They claimed that the United States would respond with a massive nuclear attack against the Soviet Union at a time and place of its own choosing if the Soviet government employed even low levels of force in its efforts to promote communism. Because there was at best only a very low probability that the United States would actually launch nuclear weapons against the Soviet Union in case of a war of "national liberation" in Southeast Asia, the threat had little credibility. Or, as Kenneth Boulding has summarized it, beyond a certain point, the higher the magnitude of a threat, the lower is the subjective probability that it will be believed.[17]

To be credible, threats must also appear to be one-sided. State *A* has to make it clear that if the threat is fulfilled it will not damage its own interests—in other words, the costs to the target of the threat will be much greater than to the party that makes the threat.[18]

In some instances those who make threats may also have to take certain actions which demonstrate that they have the *capacity* to fulfill them. This might involve mobilizing troops, cutting off foreign aid or trade for a short period, ordering a reduction in embassy personnel, or staging a short walk-out from a conference—all actions designed to indicate that the "real thing" can be done if necessary.

Finally, it may be advantageous to make deliberately vague threats or, as some might put it, ominous warnings. While these may not be entirely credible, they have the advantage of giving the threatening side many alternative forms of punishing actions—or inaction—if the other side does not take heed. The common diplomatic phrases "we will not stand (or sit) idly by" while state *B* does something, or state *B* "must bear complete responsibility for the consequences of its actions" are threats of this kind. They do not commit the threatener to specific actions, but indicate that state *B*'s actions are perceived as dangerous and could lead to various forms of counter-action or reprisal.

The problem with making threats in diplomatic negotiations is that even if they are reasonably credible, the other side might test them. In this case the threatener has to act and perhaps damage his own interests, or back down and earn the reputation of being a bluffer. In other words, if the threat is actually challenged, it has failed its purpose. Between 1958

---

[17] Kenneth E. Boulding, *Conflict and Defense: A General Theory* (New York: Harper & Row, Publishers, 1962), p. 255.

[18] In certain circumstances a threat may be more credible if it would damage both sides. Cf. Thomas C. Schelling, *The Strategy of Conflict* (Cambridge, Mass.: Harvard University Press, 1960), pp. 124–31.

and 1962 the Soviet government threatened several times to sign a peace treaty with East Germany, in effect giving the Communist regime there control over Allied access routes to West Berlin. In each instance the Russians gave the three Western Allies a time limit to join the negotiations or otherwise be left out altogether. The Allies refused to act, and instead built up their military capabilities in West Germany and West Berlin to signify that if the Soviet Union fulfilled its threat the Allies would fight, if necessary, to keep the access routes open. Each time the Soviet government failed, as threatened, to sign a treaty with the East German regime, the credibility of its threats declined further.

A problem partly related to that of making threats credible is establishing a *commitment* to a bargaining position. Diplomatic negotiations normally start with all sides presenting their "maximum" demands, usually the positions they would like ideally to achieve in the negotiations. Since diplomats realize that initial positions are maximum positions, they must probe to find out how far their opponents are willing to pull back from such positions. During the negotiating process itself they bargain over various proposals until some point of compromise has been reached. But *where* that point is located depends on the effectiveness of threats and rewards and also on the extent to which a diplomat can convince others that he and his government are committed to certain points, principles, and values. If the opponents know or suspect that a government is not deeply committed to one of its proposals or bargaining positions, they will be inclined to demand extensive concessions, hoping to attain a point of compromise much more advantageous to themselves. Compromise, after all, does not require that the parties place the point of agreement exactly half-way between the initial positions. An important part of diplomatic negotiating strategy thus concerns the efforts of bargaining agents to show each other, as convincingly as possible, *why* a position cannot be compromised beyond a certain point.

One way is to argue that as much as the government or diplomatic delegation would like to make further concessions, it cannot do so for fear of alienating the public at home and jeopardizing the chances that any treaty or agreement would be approved by a legislative body. This is the ploy (often sincere, of course) that "public opinion" or parliamentary opinion is committed to certain positions, principles, or values, and that no agreement which compromises them could be concluded. In other words, diplomats try to create the impression that neither they nor their government has the authority to make concessions.[19] Another way is to transform a dispute over a relatively concrete issue such as a piece of

[19] Schelling, *The Strategy of Conflict,* p. 28.

territory into a matter of principle. This strategy, sometimes called "issue escalation," is also designed to illustrate commitment, for it is generally understood that concessions over principles are harder to make than concessions over trivia. Instead of treating the problem of access to West Berlin or defense of the offshore islands of Communist China and Formosa as narrow territorial issues, the United States has chosen to characterize them in terms of freedom versus communism. This has the effect of displaying commitment to the cause, and at the same time it enables the government to incite public enthusiasm for the principle, thus further displaying its commitment. Both citizens and allies can be rallied, whereas if the issue were characterized in legal or technical terminology, little public or international support could be generated. When one side has firmly displayed a commitment to a position, it is in a better position to resist demands for concessions.

The problem with this strategy is that in mobilizing domestic and foreign enthusiasm for a position, governments and diplomats decrease their bargaining flexibility and in effect cut off the possibility of backing down in case the opponent seriously presses his demands.[20] If both sides remain committed—particularly publicly committed—to fundamentally incompatible positions of principle, then little room remains for effective bargaining. By attempting to establish commitment or credibility to a position, negotiators and their governments may create such inflexibility that the possibilities of reaching agreement are closed out.

Offering rewards, making threats, and establishing commitments are thus the major techniques employed in the process of diplomatic bargaining between nations. Though some of the problems common to these techniques are listed above, each bargaining situation is unique and no one can predict with certainty which methods of inducement will work. We can only suggest the conditions under which they would be more likely to succeed. In addition to the basic strategies involving threats, rewards, and commitments, a number of more specific techniques have been used recurrently by diplomats, and need to be mentioned briefly.

One is to exploit the impatience of the opponents—particularly when they want an agreement quickly—and induce them to make concessions they might otherwise avoid were they content to engage in lengthy bargaining processes. As suggested by innumerable instances in which Soviet negotiators stalled and obstructed negotiating sessions, the foremost ploys for exploiting impatience are haggling over minor details, introducing new and unexpected topics for the agenda, and evading

[20] E. James Liebermann, "Threat and Assurance in the Conduct of Conflict," in *International Conflict and Behavioral Science,* ed. Roger Fisher (New York: Basic Books, Inc., 1964), p. 105.

crucial points. Conversely, over-all settlements may be reached more quickly by starting with quick agreements on small and minor issues where considerable consensus already prevails, and subsequently exploiting this "momentum" to obtain concessions on important issues. A further technique is to offer large concessions at first on the assumption that if you show your goodwill the other side will feel compelled to reciprocate. This is a calculated gamble, for if the other side does not come through with important concessions, you are left with either having to maintain your initial concessions and continue making even more until some point of compromise is found, or retracting concessions, an action which, though frequently performed in disarmament negotiations, leaves you open to the charge of not negotiating in "good faith."

Finally, a government and its diplomats can threaten to increase its terms later on if the opponents do not take what is offered now.[21] A familiar gambit by shopkeepers, this may be extremely effective if the opponent is, in terms of the specific issue under contention, much weaker. In the summer and fall of 1939, the Soviet government made territorial and other demands on Finland. When Finnish diplomats rejected most of the Soviet demands and proposals, Stalin and Molotov let it be known that once the Red Army had its say in the matter, the demands would increase. After the Soviet Union attacked Finland that winter and its armies made some headway against the Finns, Soviet demands did in fact grow stiffer, and the peace signed in March, 1940, was considerably more disadvantageous to Finland than the original Soviet demands of 1939. The situation in wartime when one side is on the verge of defeat is also a propitious moment to employ this technique for inducing the opponent to agree to surrender or armistice terms.

### The Negotiating Process: Diplomatic Styles

Many of the techniques of inducement outlined above are commonly practiced by the diplomats and governments of all states, large and small, Western and Communist, developed and underdeveloped. But nations differ considerably in their general approach to diplomatic bargaining and the value orientations which their bargaining behavior expresses. Perusing diplomatic historical accounts of conferences, conference records, and memoirs of retired diplomats can provide an appreciation of the differences in diplomatic negotiating styles extant in the world today.

[21] Iklé, *How Nations Negotiate,* p. 72.

Diplomats are naturally inclined to see their own negotiating styles as the epitome of courtesy, cooperation, and goodwill, but contrasts between national bargaining styles are not always very clear. In outlining the major or typical characteristics of Anglo-American, Nazi, and Soviet diplomacy, it should not be assumed that the most unsavory aspects of the latter two are never adopted by the former, or that Soviet and Nazi diplomats were never courteous, frank, and inclined toward compromise.

Nevertheless, British and American diplomats have, over the years, approached their tasks with certain assumptions about the proper forms of behavior and the best techniques for reaching agreement. In many respects these assumptions differ from those upon which Russian or Nazi German diplomacy are or were based. One important bias, perhaps reflecting typical Anglo-American domestic political and commercial values, is that any agreement can be reached through compromise. Compromise among Westerners is considered a sensible, fair, and rational way of reaching agreement over contentious issues. Each side gives up something, but in the process goodwill and harmony develop. It is assumed that dilution of a bargaining position (if not of an ideological principle) is well worth an agreement and, moreover, that the process of compromise leads to quick solutions. Both British and American diplomats are frequently observed to start negotiations by immediate offers of concessions in the hope that the other side will feel a moral obligation to reciprocate.[22]

Another characteristic assumption of the Anglo-American approach to negotiations is that expressions of goodwill toward the opponent, as well as frankness and candor in discussions, will produce an atmosphere conducive to compromise and similar pronouncements of goodwill on the part of the opponents. Many American diplomats have observed how they made strenuous efforts to be personable, friendly, and scrupulously honest with foreign officials in the hope of inducing cooperative forms of behavior. Admiral Standley, a wartime American ambassador to the Soviet Union, recalled in his memoirs how he had planned to meet the Russians on a "man-to-man" basis and get to know them, their likes and dislikes, hobbies and avocations—in short, to cultivate personal friendships—in the expectation that these good personal relations would lead to friendly forms of diplomatic bargaining. He learned soon after arrival in Moscow that this approach was more likely to lead him to lose his shirt.[23]

[22] Cf. "Negotiating from Hope," *The Economist* (May 1955), p. 447; Edward R. Stettinius, Jr., *Roosevelt and the Russians* (New York: Doubleday and Company, 1949), pp. 6, 157, 325.

[23] William H. Standley and Arthur A. Ageton, *Admiral Ambassador to Russia* (Chicago: Henry Regnery Co., 1955), pp. 131, 163, 194.

Cordell Hull, American Secretary of State under President Roosevelt, believed that only friendly methods of persuasion, and avoidance of the use of threats, would win Russia's friendship, but American diplomats who dealt directly with Russian officials found that friendly approaches and repetitious pleas of goodwill seldom accomplished their objectives.[24] Another American ambassador in Moscow was convinced that Soviet authorities interpreted gestures of friendly cooperation or goodwill as evidence of weakness or some sort of plot. He argued that the only thing they respected from foreign diplomats was firmness, power, and force.[25]

Sir Harold Nicolson, a historian and former British diplomat, has observed that the British and Americans typically adhere to what he calls the "shopkeeper" approach to diplomacy. It is based on the theory that compromise and subsequent reconciliation are preferable to total victory and vindictiveness, that negotiating is essentially a technique used to reach agreement and durable understanding, not a method of carrying on warfare, and that in all disputes there is some middle point and all that is needed to find it is frank discussion.[26] Of the British and American diplomats who have offered advice regarding the attitudes and qualities most likely to lead to successful diplomatic careers and negotiations, most have emphasized a willingness to compromise, desire for fairness, sincerity, honesty, goodwill, and cooperation.

Not all Anglo-American diplomats have put into practice all of these attitudes and qualities in negotiations with foreign officials. Governments of other states have pointed out that British and American diplomats have on occasion betrayed trust by leaking information, stalled interminably when they did not wish to compromise, used abusive language, questioned the motives and integrity of their opponents, turned serious negotiations into propaganda or morality plays, employed crude threats against weak states, and made agreements in principle only to fail to implement them in subsequent actions.[27] Such actions, however, do not seem to constitute a typical style of negotiation, nor do they reflect any ideological approach or strategy to foreign relations. They would appear

[24] Cf. Cordell Hull, *The Memoirs of Cordell Hull,* Vol. II (New York: The Macmillan Company, 1948), pp. 1465, 1467.

[25] See the report of Laurence Steinhardt to Washington in United States, Department of State, *Foreign Relations of the United States: Diplomatic Papers, 1941,* Vol. I: *The Soviet Union* (Washington, D.C.: Government Printing Office, 1958), p. 765.

[26] Sir Harold Nicolson, *Diplomacy* (New York: Oxford University Press, 1939), pp. 52–54.

[27] Examples would include the long British procrastination after agreeing to give full independence to Egypt and Charles de Gaulle's complaint that President Eisenhower failed to implement several proposals after agreeing to them in principle. Theodore Sorenson, *Kennedy* (New York: Harper & Row, Publishers, 1965), p. 561.

to be, rather, individual blunders or ploys useful for very particular bargaining situations. In some cases, they were no more than an expression of extreme frustration with the bargaining practices of opponents. Indeed, when placing Anglo-American diplomatic behavior in the context of many frustrating negotiations with the Soviet Union since the end of World War II, it is to be wondered how the negotiators have maintained decorum as long as they have.

Unique styles of diplomacy have been introduced by the great totalitarian powers of the twentieth century. They have, on the whole, challenged classical European traditions of diplomacy by propounding and putting into effect a diplomacy which is designed to be not only a method of communication and bargaining, but also an instrument for propaganda, revolutionary agitation, and intimidation. Revolutionary diplomatic style derives not just from totalitarian political values and ethics; it is also a result of the commitment of these states to the destruction of an international system and its reconstitution according to their own concept of a world order. It is, finally, based on the recognition that, given the types of demands revolutionary states make on the *status quo*, the only way to succeed is through unconventional methods. The extreme objectives which they represent cannot be achieved in most cases by moderate methods of frank discussion and commercial-type bargaining.

The first common characteristic of the diplomacy of revolutionary states is the use of intemperate language. While often appearing dilatory and equivocal, traditional European diplomatic communication adhered closely to set phrases, courteous tone, and subtlety. In contrast, totalitarian regimes—desiring perhaps to create the maximum propaganda and emotional impact on foreign publics—have consistently employed epithets, crudities, and vulgarisms to denounce opponents. Instead of referring to other governments by their proper names, they frequently employ such terms of derision as "fascists," "warmongers," "lackeys," "stooges," or, in the case of the Communist Chinese characterization of several statesmen attempting to act as mediators to the Vietnamese war, as "freaks," "monsters," and "nitwits." Not all use of threats, insults, and abuse is for the purpose of propaganda. Often it is a carefully planned move to throw the other side off balance, and particularly to induce the opponent's negotiators to make ill-considered or intemperate responses.[28]

A second characteristic of totalitarian diplomatic style is its frequent use of conferences and diplomatic exchanges for propaganda purposes

---

[28] Gordon A. Craig, "Techniques of Negotiation," in *Russian Foreign Policy: Essays in Historical Perspective,* ed. Ivo Lederer (New Haven, Conn.: Yale University Press, 1962), p. 370.

rather than negotiation. Western diplomats and politicians have emulated the totalitarians in this regard, but seldom on a systematic basis. The Soviet government, on the other hand, announced early in its life that revolutionary diplomacy was not to be confined to the traditional functions of reporting, representation, and negotiation. As the first Soviet Commissar for Foreign Affairs, Leon Trotsky announced in 1917 that he would issue a few revolutionary proclamations to the people of the world and then shut his foreign ministry. When the expected world revolution failed to materialize after World War I, Soviet diplomats (known as "peoples' representatives;" they had no diplomatic ranks or titles until the late 1920's) were sent abroad primarily to help organize and finance local Communist parties, distribute revolutionary literature and, where possible, subvert established governments. No less than the Bolsheviks, the Nazis also used their diplomats for these purposes, while Hitler and other leading Nazi officials made innumerable speeches directed toward foreign audiences. In some cases they insulted foreign governments publicly; in others they attempted to demoralize foreign populations by making blatant threats; on several occasions they openly appealed to foreign pro-German elements to rise up against their own governments.

Arbitrary interpretations or violations of agreements are another common characteristic of totalitarian diplomatic style. One of the persistent themes of Western governments in attempts to justify a cautious attitude toward entering into diplomatic conversations with totalitarian regimes has been that these governments seldom take agreements seriously and have no scruples about breaking them when they are of no further advantage. Lenin frequently pointed out in his writings that in matters of promoting revolution, "It would be mad and criminal to tie one's hands by entering into an agreement of any permanence with anybody. . . ."[29] It was also Lenin who, in his best known commentary on agreements, argued that "promises are like pie crusts, made to be broken. . . ." The historical record, aside from Lenin's admonitions, confirms at least partly that totalitarian regimes have few qualms about abrogating or violating treaties. Hitler's promises of "just one more demand" meant little except as a ploy to induce other states to make concessions, nor did many of the treaties or agreements into which he entered mean that their provisions would be observed. The Nazi agreement with Poland in 1934, the Anglo-German naval agreement of 1935, the Munich agreement, and the Nazi-Soviet agreement of 1939 were all systematically violated by the Germans. Experienced Western negotiators have learned that Soviet agreements

[29] Quoted in Nathan Leites, *A Study of Bolshevism* (New York: Free Press of Glencoe, Inc., 1953), pp. 531–32.

"in principle" are not to be construed as signifying an impending agreement on all matters of detail, nor are promises not put into writing to be construed as secure.[30]

Closely related to the previous characteristic of violating agreements or failing to implement prior commitments is the ease with which totalitarian regimes employ deception in diplomatic negotiations. The basis for such tactics is well-established in Communist and Nazi philosophies, which hold that anything advancing the cause of the "revolution" is moral no matter how immoral those actions may appear according to "bourgeois" standards. In the case of the Soviet Union, the tactics of deception are also based on the assumption that "bourgeois" diplomacy is itself immoral and deceitful. In the Soviet view, their own devious actions may be justified as a necessary response to previous duplicity by "imperialists." Since Soviet officials are trained in an atmosphere where politics are partly conspiratorial and bluffs, threats, and maneuvering thrive, it is probable that they project similar experiences onto their opponents. Finally, since Soviet negotiators and political leaders believe that the Western states seek to destroy their own societies, they assume that Western efforts at promoting goodwill, frankness, and friendly personal relations are merely clever devices for pulling them into diplomatic traps. They regard Western attitudes toward negotiations not so much the expression of cultural traits as deliberate ploys used to gain concessions.[31]

Techniques of deception and duplicity vary, but they involve such things as making false promises, granting concessions to induce the other side to reciprocate and subsequently rescinding the original concessions, violating secrecy arrangements, or simply making statements with no relation to the truth. The propensity to indulge in meaningless diplomatic talk is illustrated in an incident at the United Nations, when an exasperated Australian diplomat penned a note to one of Andrei Gromyko's assistants complaining that Mr. Gromyko's speech was hardly consonant with the truth and seemed, on the contrary, completely hypocritical. A member of the Soviet delegation later cornered the Australian and asked him with candor whether he himself actually believed what his own government said in its speeches.[32]

[30] Cf. John Foster Dulles, "The Atlantic Alliance," *Department of State Bulletin*, XXXVII (December 1957), 989; Robert Murphy, *Diplomat Among Warriors* (Garden City, N.Y.: Doubleday & Company, 1964), p. 434.

[31] Cf. William Hayter, *The Diplomacy of the Great Powers* (London: Hamish Hamilton, 1960), p. 117; Edward Crankshaw, "Suspicion is a Great Kremlin Wall," *The New York Times Magazine*, November 25, 1962, p. 133; for various quotations of Lenin and Stalin justifying duplicity, see Vernon V. Aspaturian, "Dialectics and Duplicity in Soviet Diplomacy," *Journal of International Affairs*, XVII (1963), 42–60.

[32] Nancy MacLennan, "Russia's Iakov Malik," *United Nations World* (March 1949), p. 57.

The most blatant cases of Soviet duplicity, usually involving deliberate lying, failure to implement agreements already reached, or direct violation of agreements, occurred prior to, during, and shortly after World War II, when the Soviet Union was ostensibly an ally of the Western democracies. Examples of violations of agreements and promises would include the agreement to let each allied nation allow others to send military missions behind its lines to deal with their own liberated prisoners; the agreement to let Western allied air forces use an airbase near Budapest in the closing stages of the war; the agreement to let Western scientists visit the German submarine experimental station at Gdynia; the agreement to include pro-Western elements in the Bulgarian and Romanian governments at the end of the war; and the agreement to reorganize the Polish government as stipulated by the Yalta pact. A more recent case occurred in 1962 when Soviet Foreign Minister Gromyko assured President Kennedy that Soviet missiles in Cuba were short-range, defensive missiles. They turned out to be intermediate range ballistic missiles, capable of hitting almost any target in the United States.[33]

Since Stalin's death, the Soviet government has infrequently resorted to the most blatant forms of deception. This development can be accounted for by the decreasing number of Western-Soviet diplomatic negotiations as compared to the period of World War II, and increased sensitivity of the Russian government toward opinion in underdeveloped and non-aligned countries. To employ the negotiating tactics commonly used by Stalin, Molotov, and Vyshinsky would only alienate governments whose good relations with the Soviet Union are an advantage to the Russians.

A final noteworthy characteristic of Soviet diplomatic style is its inflexibility. Many Western diplomats have noted the extent to which their Russian counterparts endlessly repeat negotiating positions and proposals and refuse to make the slightest changes without prior approval from Moscow. These traits can be understood in part by the peculiar position Soviet diplomats occupy as negotiators. Western bargaining agents are normally instructed to carry out general proposals, but are given some latitude to decide on their own authority when and how to concede a minor point, introduce a compromise formula, or draft a phrase in an agreement. Soviet diplomats are seriously restricted in their bargaining activities by the requirement that they refer the most miniscule change

[33] During the Bay of Pigs invasion in 1961, Ambassador Stevenson stated in the Security Council that B-29 bombers which had attacked Cuba were flown by Cuban defectors. This was the "cover story" he had been given by the State Department, whereas in fact the bombers were flown from Guatemala by Cuban exiles to destroy the Cuban air force prior to invasion of the island. Stevenson was greatly embarrassed when the facts were learned, even though he was ignorant of his government's duplicity when he had made the statement.

under contention to appropriate authorities in Moscow. They have little or no authority to respond immediately to their opponents' proposals or to make any changes to their own bargaining positions—even to the point where they have refused to agree to the punctuation on a communiqué summarizing the day's proceedings. In those instances where Soviet diplomats have exercised some discretion without full instructions, they were seriously reprimanded or expelled from the diplomatic service.[34]

There is considerable evidence that in the past decade Soviet diplomatic style has been changing. Russian theoreticians and political leaders no longer boast about employing deception or breaking agreements with the "imperialists," and the old Leninist aversion to compromise (in the Soviet vocabulary, compromise is often viewed as an evil word)[35] is crumbling against the need for the Soviet Union to make political and commercial compromises if it wishes to maintain any diplomatic influence abroad. In Stalin's era, the Soviet Union was largely isolated from the rest of the world; today, with interests and influence spread around the globe, it cannot afford to indulge in the type of diplomacy which almost automatically creates hostility among all of those against whom it is practiced. Propaganda, stalling, threats, and an inflexible assumption of the correctness of their own bargaining positions[36] remain integral aspects of typical Soviet diplomatic behavior, but the vulgarity, bluster, and rigidity of Molotov or Vyshinsky are for the most part absent in the diplomacy of their successors. Soviet diplomats appear to have become more sensitive to the opinions of foreign colleagues and have, indeed, made concerted and successful efforts to ingratiate themselves personally with colleagues from other countries. Perhaps the new Soviet regime has become more aware of public relations, realizing that the most offensive aspects of revolutionary diplomatic style create more enemies than friends.[37]

---

[34] Philip E. Mosely, *The Kremlin and World Politics* (New York: Vintage Books, 1960), pp. 4–41; Dulles, *War or Peace*, p. 24.

[35] Mosely, *The Kremlin and World Politics,* pp. 32, 296.

[36] For example, Premier Khrushchev argued on the eve of a Foreign Ministers Conference in 1959: "They say that with the U.S.S.R. you must negotiate in the following fashion: 'concession for concession!' But that is a huckster's approach! . . . We do not have any concessions to make because our proposals have not been made for bartering. . . ." United States, Department of State, *Geneva Foreign Ministers Meeting, May–August, 1959. International Organization and Conference Series 8* (Washington, D.C.: Government Printing Office, 1959), p. 307.

[37] A distinction should perhaps be made between Soviet diplomatic style in closed meetings and in open conferences. The worst features commonly appear in the open meetings, perhaps because they are used for propaganda, because they fear appearing weak before a public audience, or because they have to show Communists that they are sufficiently "tough" with the imperialists. In quiet negotiations, these external pressures are not present, thus allowing Russian diplomats to adopt more moderate styles.

Although public interest in diplomatic affairs and the modern media of communication have made nineteenth century modes of inter-governmental communication obsolete, there is growing awareness among many governments of the world that some aspects of traditional European diplomatic style (such as secrecy), which have hitherto been considered evil or wicked, have advantages. An increasing number of observers have also noted that the type of diplomacy so popular after both world wars, where publicity and open debate were actually sought, has corresponding disadvantages. Winning points in a debate, whether in the League of Nations or in the United Nations, may not be the best way to obtain agreement on a contentious issue; as debates are often designed to make propaganda or embarrass the opponent, their effect is usually to make the opponents less flexible, not more amenable to compromise. Thus, more bargaining occurs today in the corridors and salons of the United Nations than in debates in the General Assembly and Security Council. Two Secretaries-General, Dag Hammarskjöld and U Thant, have pleaded for a return to traditional techniques, avoiding the *reductio ad absurdum* of public diplomacy, "open threats openly arrived at," and have set impressive examples themselves by accomplishing major settlements through unpublicized bargaining and discussion. Diplomatic communication is an obvious necessity in any international system and presumably the more precise, unemotional, and unpublicized it is, the more chances it has to succeed as a method for reaching objectives and settling conflicts.

## SELECTED BIBLIOGRAPHY

Acheson, Dean, *Meetings at the Summit: A Study in Diplomatic Method*. Durham, New Hampshire: University of New Hampshire Press, 1958.

Aspaturian, Vernon V., "Dialectics and Duplicity in Soviet Diplomacy," *Journal of International Affairs*, XVII (1963), 42–60.

Bell, Coral, *Negotiating From Strength*. London: Chatto and Windus, 1962.

Campbell, John C., "Negotiating with the Soviets: Some Lessons of the War Period," *Foreign Affairs*, XXXIV (1956), 305–19.

Cardozo, Michael H., *Diplomats in International Cooperation: Stepchildren of the Foreign Service*. Ithaca: Cornell University Press, 1962.

Claude, Inis L., Jr., "Multilateralism: Diplomatic and Otherwise," *International Organization*, XII (1958), 43–52.

Craig, Gordon A., and Felix Gilbert, eds., *The Diplomats: 1919–1939*. Princeton: Princeton University Press, 1953.

————, "On the Diplomatic Revolution of Our Times," The Haynes Foundation Lectures, University of California, Riverside (April 1961).

————, "Totalitarian Approaches to Diplomatic Negotiations," in *Studies in Diplomatic History and Historiography in Honour of G. P. Gooch,* ed. A. O. Sarkissian. London: Longmans, Green, 1961.

Dennet, Raymond, and Joseph Johnson, eds., *Negotiating with the Russians.* Boston: World Peace Foundation, 1951.

Fedder, Edwin H., "Communication and American-Soviet Negotiating Behavior," *Background,* VIII (1964), 105–20.

Fox, Annette Baker, *The Power of Small States: Diplomacy in World War II.* Chicago: University of Chicago Press, 1959.

Harries, O., "Faith in the Summit: Some British Attitudes," *Foreign Affairs,* XL (1961), 58–70.

Hayter, William, *The Diplomacy of the Great Powers.* London: Hamish Hamilton, 1960.

Hovet, Thomas, Jr., "United Nations Diplomacy," *Journal of International Affairs,* XVII (1963), 29–41.

Iklé, Fred C., *How Nations Negotiate.* New York: Harper & Row, Publishers, 1964.

Jensen, Lloyd, "Soviet-American Bargaining Behavior in the Postwar Disarmament Negotiations," *Journal of Conflict Resolution,* VII (1963), 522–41.

Kertesz, Stephen D., and M. A. Fitzsimmons, eds., *Diplomacy in a Changing World.* Notre Dame, Indiana: University of Notre Dame Press, 1959.

————, "Reflections on Soviet and American Negotiating Behavior," *The Review of Politics,* XIX (1957), 3–36.

Lall, Arthur S., *Modern International Negotiation: Principles and Practice.* New York: Columbia University Press, 1966.

McKenna, Joseph F., *Diplomatic Protest in Foreign Policy.* Chicago: Loyola University Press, 1962.

Meeker, R. J., G. H. Shure, and W. H. Moore, Jr., "Real-time Computer Studies of Bargaining Behavior: The Effects of Threat Upon Bargaining," *Proceedings, American Federation of Information Processing Societies Conference,* XXV (1964), 115–23.

Mosely, Philip E., *The Kremlin and World Politics.* New York: Vintage Books, 1960.

Nicolson, Sir Harold George, *Diplomacy* (2nd ed.). London, New York: Oxford University Press, Inc., 1952.

————, "Diplomacy Then and Now," *Foreign Affairs,* XL (1961), 39–49.

Nogee, Joseph L., "Propaganda and Negotiation: The Case of the Ten-Nation Disarmament Committee," *Journal of Conflict Resolution,* VII (1963), 604–15.

Pearson, Lester B., *Diplomacy in the Nuclear Age.* Toronto: S. J. Reginald Saunders and Company, 1959.

Pen, J., "A General Theory of Bargaining," *American Economic Review,* XLII (1952), 24–42.

Regala, Roberto, *Trends in Modern Diplomatic Practice*. Milan: A. Giuffre, 1959.

Rubin, Seymour J., "American Diplomacy: The Case For Amateurism," *The Yale Review*, XVL (1946), 321–35.

Rusk, Dean, "Parliamentary Diplomacy: Debate versus Negotiation," *World Affairs Interpreter*, XXVI (1955), 121–38.

Sawyer, Jack, and Harold Guetzkow, "Bargaining and Negotiation in International Relations," in *International Behavior: A Social-Psychological Analysis*, ed. Herbert C. Kelman. New York: Holt, Rinehart & Winston, Inc., 1965.

Schelling, Thomas C., *The Strategy of Conflict*. Cambridge, Mass.: Harvard University Press, 1960.

Spanier, John W., and Joseph L. Nogee, *The Politics of Disarmament: A Study in Soviet-American Gamesmanship*. New York: Frederick A. Praeger, Publisher, Inc., 1962.

Strang, William, *The Diplomatic Career*. London: A. Deutsch, 1962.

Thayer, Charles W. *Diplomat*. New York: Harper & Row, Publishers, 1959.

Thompson, Kenneth W., *American Diplomacy and Emergent Patterns*. New York: New York University Press, 1962.

Vansittart, R. G., "The Decline of Diplomacy," *Foreign Affairs*, XXVIII (1950), 177–88.

Vatcher, William H., *Panmunjom: The Story of the Korean Military Armistice Negotiation*. New York: Frederick A. Praeger, Publisher, Inc., 1958.

Wriston, Henry M., *Diplomacy in A Democracy*. New York: Harper & Row, Publishers, 1956.

# The Instruments of Policy: Propaganda

International political relationships have traditionally been conducted by government officials. Prior to the development of political democracy and modern totalitarianism, the conduct of foreign affairs was the exclusive province of royal emissaries and professional diplomats. Louis XIV's famous phrase, "l'état, c'est moi," may seem strange to those who think of government in impersonal terms, but until the nineteenth century the interests of any political unit were usually closely related to the personal and dynastic interests of its rulers. The wielding of influence was limited to direct contacts between those who made policy for the state. Diplomats bargained and court officials made policy decisions, but all were relatively indifferent to the public response abroad, if any, to their actions. They had to impress their foreign counterparts, not foreign populations.

Communications across the boundaries of political units were in any case sporadic. Travel was limited

# Chapter IX

and few people had any first-hand knowledge even of their own country-men. In most societies non-aristocratic people were illiterate, unknowl-edgeable about affairs outside of their town or valley, and generally apathetic toward any political issue that did not directly concern their everyday life. The instruments of communication were so crude as to permit only a small quantity and languorous flow of information from abroad. Populations were isolated from outside influences; if a diplomat could not achieve his government's designs through straightforward bar-gaining, it would not avail him to appeal to the foreign population, which had no decisive influence in policy-making.

With the development of mass politics—widespread involvement of the average citizen or subject in political affairs—and a widening scope of private contacts between people of different nationalities, the psychologi-cal and public opinion dimensions of foreign policy have become increas-ingly important. In so far as people, combined into various social classes, movements, and interests groups, play a role in determining policy objectives and the means used to achieve or defend them, they themselves become a target of persuasion. Governments no longer just make prom-ises of rewards or threats of punishment to foreign diplomats and foreign office officials; they make them to entire societies. One of the unique aspects of modern international political relationships is the deliberate attempt by governments, through diplomats and propagandists, to influ-ence the attitudes and behavior of foreign populations, or of specific ethnic, class, religious, economic, or linguistic groups within those popula-tions. The officials making propaganda hope that these foreign groups or the entire population will in turn influence the attitudes and actions of their own government. To cite some illustrations: Soviet propaganda agencies would disseminate anti-war propaganda among certain groups of Japanese, who would in turn protest against their own government's diplomatic support of the United States on certain international issues. The protest might be so strong that the Japanese government would feel obligated to play down its support of the United States. Or the Egyptian government would disseminate propaganda in Jordan, characterizing the Jordanian regime as reactionary and anti-Arab unity, thus hoping that the Jordanian population would overthrow the regime and substitute a government dedicated to Arab unity and socialism. In any case, the propagandist makes a careful distinction between the government of the target country and the social groups and political movements of the country. The propagandist's model for wielding influence would appear as in the figure.

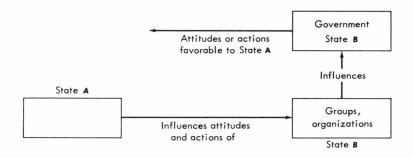

## What Is Propaganda?

Definitions of propaganda are as plentiful as the books and articles that have been written on the subject. Obviously not all communication is propaganda, nor are all diplomatic exchanges undertaken to modify foreign attitudes and actions. After a careful review of various definitions, Terence Qualter suggests that propaganda is the

> . . . deliberate attempt by some individual or group to form, control, or alter the attitudes of other groups by the use of the instruments of communication, with the intention that in any given situation the reaction of those so influenced will be that desired by the propagandist. . . . In the phrase "the deliberate attempt" lies the key to the idea of propaganda. This is the one thing that marks propaganda from non-propaganda. . . . It seems clear, therefore, that any act of promotion can be propaganda only if and when it becomes part of a deliberate campaign to induce action through the control of attitudes.[1]

Kimball Young uses a similar definition, but places more emphasis on action. He sees propaganda as

> . . . the more or less deliberately planned and systematic use of symbols, chiefly through suggestion and related psychological techniques, with a view to altering and controlling opinions, ideas, and values, and ultimately to changing overt actions along predetermined lines.[2]

Both definitions have four common elements: (1) a communicator with the *intention* of changing attitudes, opinions, and behavior of others, (2) the symbols—written, spoken, or behavioral—used by the communicator,

[1] Terence H. Qualter, *Propaganda and Psychological Warfare* (New York: Random House, Inc., 1962), p. 27.
[2] Quoted in J. A. C. Brown, *Techniques of Persuasion: From Propaganda to Brainwashing* (Middlesex: Penguin Books, 1963), p. 19.

(3) the media of communication, and (4) the audience or, as it is often called in the terminology of public opinion studies, the "target."

Since propaganda, according to these definitions, involves essentially a process of persuasion, it cannot be equated with scientific efforts to arrive at some truth. It is not logical discourse or dialectical investigation. It relies more on selection of facts, partial explanations, and predetermined answers. The content of propaganda is therefore seldom completely "true," but neither is it wholly false, as is so often assumed. The propagandist is concerned with maximizing persuasiveness, not with adhering to some standard of scholarship or uncovering some new fact. The common tendency to equate propaganda with falsehood may itself be a result of propaganda. Western newspaper editorials frequently brand Communist speeches or diplomatic maneuvers as "propaganda," while the activities of their own governments abroad are known as "information programs." The implication is usually quite clear: the Soviet version of reality is false, while Western versions are true. In the context of our own values, beliefs, and perceptions of reality, foreign information may indeed seem a deliberate distortion of the truth. Soviet propagandists have in many instances told deliberate lies, but from the point of view of their images of aggressive Western intentions, and their culture and values, much of their work involves the dissemination of legitimate information. Similarly, to Soviet audiences who are taught to think in the framework of Marxist-Leninist concepts, information sponsored by Western governments may also be seen as involving distortions of reality.

### Selecting the Target:
### Whose Attitudes Can Be Changed?

Soviet and Nazi efforts to institute foreign propaganda programs (they were the first systematic peacetime propaganda programs) were based on intuition, experiment, and revolutionary experience. Some aspects of the programs were self-defeating, and yet, few professional propagandists today could match the skills and insights of Trotsky, Lenin, and Goebbels. During the course of their revolutionary activities these men developed propaganda techniques based on perceptive analyses of the psychological traits of human beings in their political roles. Soviet propagandists carefully selected targets and attempted to formulate messages that would appeal specifically to particular groups of people.[3] In a new nation

[3] The Soviets make an important distinction between propaganda and "agitation." To them, propaganda refers to the intensive instruction and elucidation of the tenets of Marxist-Leninist philosophy to a small audience. Agitation refers to the presentation

in Southeast Asia, for example, they understood that an appeal to the politically active, Western-educated elites would have to be couched in terms entirely different from those used in an appeal to peasants at the village level. In a country where social distinctions are rigid, communication between urban elites and rural peasants almost non-existent, and important values and symbols among various groups, strata, and classes differ widely, propaganda appeals have to be differentiated according to the attitudes, desires, loyalties, and hatreds of each group.

In contrast, once World War II had ended, Western governments generally failed to appreciate the effectiveness of propaganda as an instrument for wielding influence in international politics. They assumed that disseminating the "truth" would change any clear-thinking person's attitudes toward Western policy, and that the best way to counter Communist propaganda was to demonstrate its falsehood. Many believed that propaganda should be directed primarily toward audiences which held opinions hostile to the West. In other words, propaganda should be used primarily to "convert" Communists and other anti-Western elements in a foreign population.[4]

Western governments which use propaganda as an instrument of foreign policy have since 1948 developed different approaches and attitudes toward foreign communications. Today, they are quite convinced that diplomatic positions need to be buttressed by favorable foreign attitudes, and rely on studies made by social psychologists which examine scientifically the problem of attitude formation and change. Whether Soviet propagandists are using such studies is not known, but, as will be discussed, they do display sophistication in selecting targets and propaganda themes. Before turning to the question of propaganda techniques, or *how* attitudes and actions are changed, we must consider first some of the implications of studies on attitudes and look at the question first posed by the modern propagandist: *Whose* attitudes can be changed?

Some psychologists and sociologists make a distinction between the "nuclear" personality and the "social" personality. The former includes basic attitudes towards objects, ideas, and people which are usually formed in infancy and reinforced during childhood. These attitudes may or may not relate to political phenomena. In some families, politics are not a matter of general discussion, so the child is left in later years to form his own opinions, based on his own experiences and social relationships

---

of one or several ideas, usually slogans, to the masses of people. Thus, their definition of propaganda resembles our term indoctrination, while agitation resembles our definition of propaganda.

[4] W. Phillips Davison, "Political Communication as an Instrument of Foreign Policy," *Public Opinion Quarterly*, XXVII (1963), 29–30.

outside the family. Still, any child develops general liberal or authoritarian attitudes, whether they have a political content or not. In other families, fundamental political attitudes—in addition to liberal or authoritarian predispositions—are instilled into the child to the extent that no amount of propaganda, or even experience, is likely to change them. Children born and raised in homes where the parents are vocally prejudiced against specific minorities normally grow up with the same prejudices and do not alter them until they move to a different environment. Some attitudes are so deeply ingrained that even a new environment will not prompt an examination of them. The "nuclear" personality and the attitudes central to that personality thus are not amenable to change simply by being subjected to propaganda. This is one reason that people who have been brought up in homes and schools where traditional liberal values were systematically inculcated are seldom converted to any totalitarian organization or faith. For the same reason, Western efforts to convert dedicated Communists who have lived their entire life in a Communist society are not likely to succeed unless these people have already become alienated from the Communist society.[5]

Following the early childhood years, as the individual becomes a part of larger associations (schools, boy scouts), he forms attitudes on new ideas, objects, and people; often these conform to the prevailing attitudes of peer groups. The strength of these group-established attitudes and opinions can be seen in experiments which failed to modify attitudes of individuals contrary to predominating views within the groups to which those individuals belonged. The significance of the "social" personality is that one's political attitudes tend to be functional to the groups to which one belongs. Or, as one of the consistent findings of voting behavior studies indicates, an individual's political preferences are likely to be similar to those of his closest associates.

The implications of these findings are important for the propagandist. They suggest that it is easier to change the attitudes of small associational groups or categorical groups, such as classes, which already share similar attitudes, than of an entire national population which does not constitute a likely target unless all the members of the national society are united strongly on some value such as the maintenance of national prestige or independence. It is the propagandist's job to find the key groups in society and determine what kinds of appeals will arouse the desired response in the selected targets. To summarize, (1) many people have

[5] One study reveals that people who lack totalitarian predispositions but who still adhere to totalitarian political parties in democratic societies are likely to be suffering from personality disorders. See Gabriel A. Almond, *The Appeals of Communism* (Princeton: Princeton University Press, 1954), Chap. 10.

deep-seated attitudes with political implications and which become over the years fixed character traits, sometimes liberally disposed or sometimes radically disposed, and seldom amenable to change; (2) other attitudes are also a function of the group and can be changed most easily by altering group attitudes collectively; and (3) a person's attitudes may also be changed by moving an individual into a new milieu.

The next question is: How does the individual handle information and experience which directly contradicts his established attitudes? People are resourceful in resisting information which does not fit their own pictures of reality. Voting behavior studies in the United States indicate that the more partisan a voter before the election, the less likely he is to subject himself to the campaign appeals of the party for which he will not vote. Those who do subject themselves to information that contradicts their views may lose confidence in their opinions, but will frequently go out of their way to seek any information which substantiates their original position. Others, when exposed to "unfriendly" information, may reject it or perhaps distort its meaning and significance. Or they might question the credibility of the information or its source and pass it off as mere "propaganda." Certainly the individual's initial attitude toward the communicator will have an important bearing on his reception of the information.[6]

We can see these mechanisms operating frequently when we are confronted with information emanating from a hostile country or political party. How often have we failed to read a speech made by a Soviet leader simply because it came from a hostile source or because we assumed it was mere "propaganda"? Yet we will read carefully a speech by a prime minister of a friendly country or by the candidate of "our" political party because the substance of the speech is not embarrassing to our attitudes.

The presence of these and other mechanisms which insulate us from hostile propaganda would indicate that the propaganda instrument is not equally effective against all types of targets. If there are such resistances, who is susceptible and what kinds of targets are most likely to respond in a desired fashion? The experience of government propagandists and the conclusions of the social sciences seem to point to some answers.

First, propaganda may successfully arouse or create desired attitudes and opinions if it is a major or sole source of information for a particular target. The propagandist has an advantage if he provides information on a new subject or issue, where public attitudes are not already crystallized

[6] Percy H. Tannenbaum, "Initial Attitude Toward Source and Content as Factors in Attitude Change Through Communications," *Public Opinion Quarterly*, XX (1956), 414.

and prior information was spotty. Soviet propagandists have been quite effective in parts of Africa because they can send information to people who, for the first time, are becoming aware of the outside world. Their image of the Soviet Union is not based on direct experience with Stalinist foreign policy or intimate knowledge of Soviet history. Information which the Soviet propagandists make available to these people may be decisive in creating initial attitudes. By focusing attention on the favorable aspects of Soviet life, they are likely to make some impact and create images that did not exist before. This conclusion has been explored in experimental situations, where audiences were subjected to very slanted information on a topic about which they knew very little or possessed few preconceptions. Even when the participants had access to other sources of information they readily accepted as true the bias of the news media most easily accessible to them.[7]

Second, propaganda is likely to be effective when directed toward people who share at least partially the attitudes of the communicator.[8] It is more successful in strengthening *existing* attitudes or crystallizing predispositions than in converting those already hostile. Soviet foreign propaganda does not try to create more Marxist-Leninists all over the world. It seeks, rather, to elicit specific attitudes toward the Soviet Union and its policies—or toward vague symbols such as "peace" or complete disarmament—among people who are neither in a Communist party nor likely to join one as a recruit, but who nevertheless hold some favorable attitudes toward these symbols or Soviet policies.[9] Similarly, the United States Information Agency currently spends more money trying to reinforce the pro-American attitudes of various people around the world than it does in attempting to convert Communists to Western values.

Third, propaganda is likely to be effective among youths and apathetic people. Youths are more vulnerable to suggestion and persuasion, because they are the least likely to hold rigid beliefs or attitudes. Results of research projects suggest that children are particularly open to persuasion between the ages of four and eight, and that their suggestibility declines steadily with increasing age. Revolutionary parties which create youth

[7] For one experiment which establishes this point, see A. D. Annis and Norman C. Meier, "The Induction of Opinion Through Suggestion by Means of Planted Content," *Journal of Social Psychology*, V (1934), 65–81.

[8] Thus, one of the standard ploys of propagandists sending messages to a hostile audience is not to reveal their own identity. Nazi propagandists frequently used this "black" propaganda, either by failing to mention the source altogether, or by creating some fictitious cover name that would seem legitimate to the audience.

[9] Paul Kecskemeti, "The Soviet Approach to International Political Communication," *Public Opinion Quarterly*, XX (1956), 304–5.

groups, religious organizations, as well as manufacturers of clothing, cigarettes, and cars, are all aware of this conclusion and design their propaganda programs accordingly. Apathetic people are also likely targets for the same reason: they do not hold rigid views and tend to be unsure of the political opinions they do adopt. Where such uncertainty persists, persuasion is facilitated, although arousing interest may be difficult.

Finally, propaganda seems to be most effective when directed toward groups whose members share similar attitudes, and toward crowds. We have already suggested that attitudes and beliefs are mechanisms which satisfy social adjustment. A person is not a likely propaganda target if the content of the propaganda conflicts strongly with the values and opinions which circulate among his closest social connections. We are all wary of adopting and articulating unpopular views—not just because they are unusual, but because we might face social ostracism for expressing them. Crowds, on the other hand, do not necessarily contain an effective network of personal contacts. They are particularly susceptible to propaganda appeals but, as the following statement by J. A. C. Brown suggests, only if there is already some shared attitude between the propagandist and target.

> The study of crowd psychology . . . has shown that, although people do many things whilst in a crowd that they might not otherwise, . . . new attitudes spring . . . from the individual members of the crowd and not, as was formerly thought, from a mysterious entity described as the "crowd" mind. Because of . . . intensification of emotion [in crowds] it is possible to cause disorganized masses of people to behave in other than their everyday manner, to stimulate and lead them more easily than an organized public which is prepared to listen to reason and discuss a problem. But it is not possible to make them do anything. Negro lynching crowds exist because anti-Negro feelings already exist; the crowd intensifies the feeling to the point of action but does not create it.[10]

It is not clear why people are more suggestible in the crowd, but many observers have noted that individual credulity tends to fall to a low level when emotions are raised in a large gathering. In their domestic propaganda the Nazis were well aware of this characteristic and put on fantastic parades and party rallies to impress the people. There is some evidence which indicates that the arousal of any strong emotion may make the individual in the crowd more suggestible, sometimes even when that emotion is directed initially *against* the leader of the crowd.[11]

[10] Brown, *Techniques of Persuasion*, p. 68.
[11] Brown, *Techniques of Persuasion*, p. 24.

### Creating Impact

Having selected appropriate targets, the second task of the propagandist is to catch the attention of those to whom he will direct his message. Attention-getting may be a difficult endeavor, particularly among people apathetic or hostile to the communicator. Therefore, the devices used by the propagandist tend to be spectacular, colorful, or unusual, and may not even be related to the substance of the message. When attention is elicited, propagandists then attempt to evoke and play on emotions. This cannot be done, obviously, by presenting a calm catalogue of facts (except where the facts "speak for themselves"). Rather, symbols are used to bring about an emotional response, from anxiety and guilt to hatred, which is probably the most potent of all unifying emotions. The common conception that propaganda is synonymous with lying probably arose from efforts of the Allies and Germans during World War I to create hatred toward the enemy by fabricating stories about atrocities and inhumane behavior. Propagandists frequently appeal to hatreds, or try to create them, during times of great international tension and in the actual conduct of war, when a maximum number of people and allies have to be mobilized to support a government. In these circumstances hatred of a national enemy becomes a virtue, while the emotions of love, anxiety, and guilt are seldom included in the various propaganda themes.

These emotions can be raised through almost any communication medium: orators can inspire a crowd to violent acts simply by giving information, displays of military strength can create fear, and pictures of atrocities create revulsion and, subsequently, hatred. Probably the most effective technique for foreign propaganda is the coordination of message content with the actual policies and actions of the government.

The adage "actions speak louder than words" undoubtedly applies in international propaganda efforts. The images which foreign populations possess of other countries are usually based on news reports, movies, and cultural events rather than on direct experience. Since most people are uninformed of foreign affairs, their conceptions and attitudes toward foreign countries are seldom detailed. Spectacular, news-making foreign policy actions will be noticed by a relatively broad cross-section of the foreign population, whereas regular governmental information programs abroad will reach a much smaller audience. Few Americans read *Pravda*, or the Soviet journal *International Affairs*, or listen to Radio Moscow. But a great number of Americans know immediately when the Soviet government has achieved a spectacular space success. In short, people are likely to be more impressed with what governments do than with what propagandists say they do.

Where a great discrepancy between the words and actions of a government exists, either people abroad become disillusioned or the credibility of the propagandist is compromised, thus making the target populations wary of incoming information. Whatever impressions Soviet propagandists had made in Western Europe through their years of anti-colonial appeals in the United Nations were probably destroyed after the Soviets put down the Hungarian revolt of 1956. Similarly, American propaganda toward Eastern Europe which implied American support of anti-Communist uprisings had less effect after the United States failed to intervene in Hungary. Finally, the credibility of North Korean propaganda which claimed that the United States had used germ warfare was reduced (except among those who really *wanted* to believe the charges) after the Communists refused to admit an impartial Red Cross investigation. In these instances, all the emotions and expectations which had been raised and attitudes which had been crystallized through verbal and pictorial messages were compromised by the self-defeating actions of the governments which sent the propaganda.

## Techniques of the Propagandist

So far we have discussed the problem of selecting targets and some aspects of attitude formation and change. Now we can analyze specific propaganda strategies and techniques that have been used in foreign policy during the last several decades. One of the purposes of external propaganda is to modify the loyalty of particular groups of citizens toward their own government—either to destroy it, or to create it if it did not previously exist. When the Nazis, and often the Soviet government, were attempting through ordinary diplomatic means to achieve their foreign policy objectives, they simultaneously used propaganda for purposes of subversion. To "soften up" the foreign population they identified their governments as "cliques," "puppets," and "oppressors," made charges of corruption against them, and, in general, used any means which could discredit the established authorities. If various groups' loyalties to their own government could be shaken or destroyed, it became an easier task to substitute another loyalty, such as to a Nazi party, or create apathy. Those groups or individuals in a society which were already alienated from the government were of course a prime target for external propaganda, and constituted the material out of which "fifth columns" and subversive Communist elements developed. By playing upon their hatred or revulsion toward the legitimate government, the propagandist could lead them to take political action—riots, mass meetings, or boycotts—which created confusion and embarrassed the regime in power, thus furthering the interests of Nazi Germany or Soviet Russia.

Another strategy exploits potential or actual divisions within a society, often leading to violent action in the form of pogroms, strikes, and riots. This violence damages the international prestige of the government, undermines local confidence in it, and may force it to take unpopular repressive measures. For example, the Nazis directed propaganda toward the Sudeten Germans, urging them to violent action against the majority Czechs. When the Czech government sought to put down Nazi-inspired riots, German propagandists accused it of persecuting a minority. A number of influential Europeans, sympathetic to the position of the Sudeten Germans, consequently made little effort to protest the Munich settlement in 1938 and subsequent Nazi takeover of Czechoslovakia.

A similar strategy attempts to split allies from each other. But instead of provoking class, religious, or ethnic hatreds *within* a society, this type of propaganda tries to *unite* the society by suggesting that a country's allies are unreliable, scheming, or ready to "sell out" the interests of friends. A frequent theme of Nazi propaganda during World War II held that while British soldiers were on the front lines, American troops were in England seducing their wives and girl friends. Post-war American propaganda behind the Iron Curtain has also attempted to arouse Eastern European nationalism by arguing—with some truth—that the Soviet government was exploiting the satellite economies for its own purposes.

Having established a target and appropriate strategy, propagandists then may use a variety of specific techniques in delivering the messages. Among the more prominent are:[12]

1. *Name calling.* The propagandist attaches an emotion-laden symbol to a person or country. Targets are expected to respond favorably, from the propagandist's point of view, to the label without examining any evidence. Propagandists relate their appeals to stereotypes that already exist in the audience. Thus, Communists become "reds," labor leaders become "union bosses," and constitutional governments become "capitalist cliques."

2. *Glittering generality.* This is similar to the previous technique, but is used to describe an idea or policy rather than individuals. The term "free

---

[12] These categories are adapted from Alfred McClung Lee and Elizabeth Bryant Lee, *The Fine Art of Propaganda: A Study of Father Coughlin's Speeches* (New York: Harcourt, Brace & World, Inc., 1939), pp. 22–25.

world" is a favorite generality of Western propagandists. "Socialist solidarity" is used in the Communist world to describe the complex relations
among Communist states and parties, while "the African soul" is supposed
to create a similar image of strength and unity.

3. *Transfer.* The propagandist attempts to identify one idea, person,
country, or policy with another to make the target approve or disapprove
it. One way to evoke a particularly hostile attitude among religious people
against communism is to equate it with atheism. Communists regularly
equate capitalism with decadence, and anti-Semites hope to create public
support for their bigotry by associating Jews with Communists.

4. *"Plain folks."* Any propagandist is aware that his problems are
compounded if he appears to the audience as a "foreigner" or stranger.
He seeks, therefore, to identify as closely as possible with the values and
style of life of the targets by using local slang, accent, and idiom.

5. *Testimonial.* Here, the propagandist uses an esteemed person or
institution to endorse or criticize an idea or political entity. A variation of
this is the "appeal to authority," where the target is asked to believe
something simply because some "authority" says it is true.

6. *Selection.* Almost all propaganda, even when it uses the other
techniques discussed above, relies on the selection of facts, though it is
seldom very specific in its factual content. When a detailed presentation is
given, the propagandist uses only those facts required to "prove" his
predetermined objectives.

7. *Bandwagon.* This technique plays on the audience's desire to "belong" or be in accord with the crowd. It is similar to the testimonial,
except that a mass of people, rather than a single esteemed person or
institution, serves as the attraction. The messages of Communist propagandists frequently use such phrases as "the whole world knows that
. . . ," "all peace-loving people recognize that . . . ," or "all progressive
people demand that . . . ," This technique implies that the target is in a
minority—if he opposes the substance of the message—and should join
the majority. Or, if the target is sympathetic to the propagandist, this
technique will reinforce his attitudes by demonstrating that he is on the
"right" side, along with everyone else.

8. *Frustration-scapegoat.* One easy way to create hatred and relieve
frustrations is to create a scapegoat. Revolutionary regimes faced with
complex internal economic and social disorders and popular frustrations
frequently create an internal or external "spook" to account for the
peoples' miseries. The most famous example was the myth created by
Hitler that Germany's internal and foreign problems were created by the
"Jews"—who were often equated with Communists.

The reader will have noticed that these techniques are used not only in foreign propaganda, but in all organized efforts to persuade, including political campaigns and particularly in commercial advertising. Several of these techniques may be used simultaneously to create the maximum effect.

To this point, the discussion of propaganda as an instrument of foreign policy has been theoretical. To understand better some of the strategies, techniques, and problems which governments face in attempting to influence others, it will be useful to discuss in some detail recent American, Soviet, and Egyptian foreign information programs, though these are by no means the only governments which use propaganda as an instrument of foreign policy.

## American Propaganda

The theoretical discussion should not suggest that if the propagandist correctly gauges his audience, carefully selects his targets, and skillfully combines his techniques, he will always succeed in "winning men's minds." A review of American and Soviet propaganda policies indicates that in both governments there remains considerable uncertainty regarding the kinds of philosophies and techniques that should guide their foreign information programs.

The American propaganda program is formulated by the United States Information Agency (USIA, known in the field as the United States Information Service), an organization created in 1954 by President Eisenhower. The agency organizes the activities of over 100 libraries and information service offices abroad, a world-wide radio service (the Voice of America), television, film, and news services, and numerous special programs. The State Department handles student and cultural exchanges, which are an important aspect of the American propaganda effort. The guiding philosophy of the USIA is included in the statement of purposes:

1. To explain and interpret to people overseas the meaning and purposes of American foreign policies.
2. To serve as a source of accurate non-sensational news abroad without competing with private American news sources.
3. To present the full sweep of American life and culture to the people of the world in order to correct misconceptions and to combat false or distorted pictures of the United States.[13]

[13] President's Advisory Committee on Information, *Sixteenth Annual Report to Congress* (Washington, D.C.: Government Printing Office, 1961), p. 3.

While this is a fairly clear statement of purposes, the actual programs needed to implement them have never been easy to formulate. The philosophy of the USIA places heavy emphasis on creating a favorable image of the United States and its policies abroad, but in practice the agency has devoted much time and effort attempting to counteract Soviet propaganda. This defensive policy, while understandable, is negative in character and has achieved few spectacular successes. Perhaps the most serious difficulties have arisen in connection with the choice of targets and types of themes to be used for certain populations in underdeveloped countries. There have been instances, for example, where the themes of "democracy" and "private enterprise" were used among landless peasants whose only experience with private enterprise was one of exploitation and degradation, and where "democracy" meant, at least in their own experience, corrupt rule by closed oligarchies. Similarly, to display visual evidence of the American standard of living—a frequent American propaganda technique—to uneducated and often illiterate peasants often creates either incredulity or outright antagonism.

On the other hand, American propaganda programs have been successful in reinforcing the pro-American attitudes of certain segments of foreign populations, including key economic, cultural, and political elites. People who already have a favorable predisposition toward the United States do visit USIA libraries, take free English language lessons, or avail themselves of the various recreational and educational programs offered by the Service. It is questionable, however, whether these programs extend to a large majority of the population, or whether they make any impact, in the long run, on those who are anti-American or apathetic.

American propaganda has also made a major attempt to create abroad an unfavorable image of the Soviet Union in particular, and communism in general. American propagandists have created out of the Berlin Wall a potent anti-Communist symbol which can easily evoke a desired response among those who understand the human suffering that the Wall has created. Soviet defections, anti-Semitism, lack of individual freedom, and Russian economic difficulties constitute other themes for American anti-Communist propaganda.

In underdeveloped areas of the world anti-Communist propaganda is less likely to succeed. These areas are usually far removed from the Soviet Union, the people have seldom experienced unfavorable Soviet policies directly, and communism does not seem a salient problem in their lives. Though some American propaganda in these areas is decidedly anti-Communist in its main themes—particularly when directed to local elites and property owners—it usually emphasizes that the objectives of American foreign policy are compatible with the interests of the underdeveloped country, and that the United States can be very helpful in assisting in the process of industrialization. Where such themes are coupled with displays of effective foreign aid programs, the impact may be considerable. American propaganda in underdeveloped areas also argues that free enterprise and economic, social, and scientific advancement go together, and that the aspirations of less fortunate people can be achieved within a framework of democratic reform rather than totalitarianism.

The USIA has used all of the traditional propaganda techniques, though deliberate distortion has been avoided. In addition, instead of relying exclusively on the dissemination of ideas, symbols, information, and messages designed to create some unfavorable image of the Soviet Union or favorable image of the United States and its policies, the USIA has also found it effective to render *services* which have a *direct and immediate benefit to the targets' personal or economic life*. While the Voice of America uses all of the traditional techniques of propaganda in its news analyses, it also provides free lessons in the English language. The USIA *Bulletin* is a news-teletype production which reaches over 100 countries and is available to local newspapers at ¼ cent per word, compared with the much higher prices that regular wire services charge. Through this service the USIA disseminates full texts of important speeches by American public officials so that foreign editors can draw their own conclusions and, in some cases, reprint entire sections of the speech at a very low cost. This service benefits both the propagandist and the target. For the United States, it means wide coverage of those speeches and news items which it wants publicized around the world; for the foreign newspapers it means inexpensive information and news copy. In addition to providing books, periodicals, films, and magazines in USIA libraries around the world, the Agency also provides technical and information services to foreign businessmen, labor organizers, educators, and farmers. In other words, the Agency seeks to provide information and assistance relevant to the activities of foreign groups and individuals. As one former USIA official has argued, if American propagandists can provide information that is useful to existing foreign organizations, or can help new organizations to form, they are much more likely to have a significant political impact than if they focus their attention on influencing isolated individuals.[14]

People frequently lament the comparatively small amount of money available to the USIA, and assume that because the Russians spend so much more, their diplomacy will be more effective and they will eventually win what has become known as the "war for the minds of men."

---

[14] Davison, "Political Communication," p. 35.

What these critics overlook is that private individuals who go abroad for business, study, or tourism provide more propaganda for the United States than does the USIA. Although the Soviets spend greater quantities of money than Americans to disseminate radio broadcasts, publications, and films, they do not encourage Russian people to travel abroad, nor do they invite thousands of foreigners to travel freely around the Soviet Union. Over three million Americans go abroad each year. Many see little except the insides of hotels, museums, and churches, but others reside abroad, meet people, and are able to convey more effectively than any propaganda medium how Americans live, what they value, and how they react to foreign people and their values. An increasing number of Western Europeans, Asians, and Africans also visit the United States, enter private homes, and are not prevented from travelling wherever they wish to go. No less important are the thousands of international business, professional, and scholarly contacts that constitute a vast framework for non-official international communication. The free flow of information, goods, and people between societies may be more important in creating peoples' attitudes toward other countries than the words, symbols, and clichés of propagandists. Perhaps it is the realization of such facts that has prompted the Soviet regime in recent years to expand and adopt more flexible and bold approaches to its foreign information programs.

### Soviet Propaganda

The long-range objectives of the Soviet Union have for many years been closely associated with destruction of the contemporary international system and substitution of a world of socialist states. Whereas the Soviet government has core and middle-range objectives similar to those of many other states, one long-range external purpose, as it has often claimed, is that of promoting revolution abroad. Clearly, the Soviet government cannot achieve its long-range objectives simply through diplomatic bargaining or deliberate aggression. Soviet governments from the time of the Bolshevik revolution have thus recognized that both the advocacy of revolution and the promotion of Russian middle-range objectives could be enhanced by formulating systematic propaganda programs which would by-pass foreign governments and influence foreign populations instead. These populations, it was hoped, would in turn force their governments to act in a manner consistent with Soviet interests. Propaganda is thus both a technique to assist Soviet diplomats in conferences and bargaining sessions and a means of promoting revolutionary activity abroad.

Soviet propaganda still relies extensively on Marxist-Leninist terminology and traditional Russian demonology, but today it is infused with a pragmatism that was lacking prior to 1953. The new flexibility of Soviet propaganda is perhaps nowhere more evident than in the current emphasis on increasing face-to-face contacts. In addition to touring cultural and entertainment troupes, the Soviet government regularly sends abroad scientific, technical, and artistic delegates, and willingly invites foreign tourists and delegates to visit some parts of the Soviet Union. In a thorough analysis of recent Soviet foreign propaganda, Frederick Barghoorn points out that in 1953 only 42 private tourists visited the Soviet Union, while a decade later over 100,000 visitors made the trip. Similarly, over 40,000 Soviet tourists travelled in non-Communist countries in 1960, while during the Stalin period only a handful of trusted Communist officials ever left the Soviet Union.[15] Soviet visiting delegations are still under strict scrutiny by security officials and do not have the freedom to roam around foreign countries as their Western counterparts do. They are not in a position, therefore, to make those private contacts which are so important in creating favorable attitudes and images.

Premier Khrushchev emphasized at the Twentieth Congress of the Soviet Communist Party in 1956 that Russian propaganda must not be concerned too much with inculcating abstract principles of communism, but must become increasingly practical.[16] While Stalin conceived of the world as divided into two rigid and unalterably hostile camps—the socialist and capitalist—present Soviet leadership has recognized the opportunities available for cultivating underdeveloped countries through appeals to nationalism and anti-colonialism. As Soviet propagandists appeal to broader and more diverse targets abroad, they have replaced the old clichés of Marxism-Leninism with newer slogans. Instead of using such terms as "proletariat" and "working class," which elicited desired attitudes and behavior among only a limited segment of any society, Soviet slogans today include the terms "masses," "all peace-loving people," and, most broadly, simply "the peoples." Instead of "violent revolution," "class struggle," "imperialist hyenas," and "bloodsuckers of the people," they talk of the "national interest," the "interests of peace-loving peoples," and "aggressive circles."[17]

Increased use of non-doctrinal themes in Soviet propaganda reflects important changes in the strategy of Soviet foreign policy since Stalin's

[15] Frederick C. Barghoorn, *Soviet Foreign Propaganda* (Princeton: Princeton University Press, 1964), p. 277.
[16] Barghoorn, *Soviet Foreign Propaganda*, p. 30.
[17] John H. Kautsky, ed., *Political Change in Underdeveloped Countries: Nationalism and Communism* (New York: John Wiley & Sons, Inc., 1962), p. 79.

death. Current Soviet middle-range objectives include, among others, reduction of Western influence in underdeveloped countries, support of wars of "national liberation," whether or not they are Communist-inspired, and withdrawal of American military power from around the world.

If Soviet propaganda is to support such objectives, it must seek to influence the attitudes and behavior of diverse populations, including non-Communists, liberals, pacifists, peasants, intellectuals, and foreign military establishments. In other words, in their attempts to influence governments through manipulating indigenous populations, Soviet propagandists are attempting to arouse favorable attitudes among a variety of non-Communist "progressive" groups, regardless of the class origins of their members.

Russian propaganda employs three interrelated strategies in support of middle- and long-range Soviet foreign policy objectives: (1) it capitalizes on international situations which are embarrassing to the West (splitting allies from each other and neutrals from the West); (2) it utilizes the reputation and prestige of "front" groups to help publicize and find support for Soviet positions on international questions among non-Communists; (3) it creates goodwill abroad for the Soviet Union and its policies by using modern and meaningful themes which will appeal to specific targets in terms of their needs, frustrations, and aspirations.

Throughout the world millions of people have latent or expressed anti-Western predispositions. In the new countries it derives from nationalism and anti-colonialism. In Western Europe and North America it can be found among intellectuals who are convinced that the West is the main source of antagonism in the cold war. These people may not be Communists or supporters of Soviet foreign policy, but some of their political attitudes, if activated, can be useful in undermining pro-Western governments and Western influence in these areas. Soviet propaganda exploitation of the Suez invasion was so effective, for example, that most people in Asia, Africa, and the Middle East were more agitated with British "imperialism" than with Soviet activity in crushing the Hungarian rebellion which was occurring simultaneously in the autumn of 1956. Anti-Western propaganda is likely to be effective in these underdeveloped areas because it gives structure, content, and rationalization to sentiments that are already widespread. Soviet propaganda exploits a problem—"neo-colonialism"—that is salient in the underdeveloped areas of the world. It successfully crystallizes opinion and occasionally turns anti-Western attitudes into political action, often strikes and riots, which is embarrassing to the West and sometimes overturns regimes that support Western military alliances.

In addition to exploiting anti-Western sentiments around the world the Soviets, even during Stalin's period, reached non-Communist targets through the use of "front" organizations. The "front" strategy enables Soviet propagandists to influence people who would not normally be drawn into an openly confessed Communist organization.[18] These groups appeal not just to Marxist-Leninists in terms of Communist dogma, but to all "progressive" people through such symbols as "peace," "better understanding," or "friendship." Among the many front organizations active today are the World Federation of Trade Unions, the World Federation of Democratic Youth, The International Union of Students, the many bilateral Soviet friendship societies (e.g., the Soviet-French Friendship Society), and the World Peace Movement. The last organization has been particularly important as a disseminator of Soviet propaganda and is, therefore, worth discussing in some detail.

The Peace Movement arose in France during 1948 as a spontaneous organization of liberals and pacifists concerned over the implications of nuclear weapons and the cold war.[19] Although Soviet theoreticians had traditionally regarded pacifists with disdain, Russian and European Communist parties eventually gained influence over the Movement and made it an outlet for Soviet propaganda. It was not, however, formally identified as a Communist organization, and among the leaders of the Movement were many prominent non-Communist intellectuals. The Communist parties in Western Europe urged any individual to join, regardless of class origin or political party preference. The Movement had as its general objective prevention of all forms of military development in Western Europe, an objective obviously in accord with Soviet foreign policy interests. In mass meetings and annual conferences, members and delegates expressed opinions against the creation of NATO, rearming of West Germany, building of American bases overseas and, in general, against any Western activity designed to deter Soviet military actions and Russian-sponsored revolutionary activity. Propaganda themes were closely related to the attitudes or fears of broad segments of the Western European population. In France, for example, the Movement used the symbols of nationalism and American cultural domination to creat opinion against the formation of NATO and the building of American bases in France. In its attempts to prevent the creation of a German post-war army, the Bundeswehr, it reminded the French of the occupation years

[18] Kecskemeti, "The Soviet Approach," p. 302.
[19] For details on the Peace Movement, see Marshall D. Shulman, *Stalin's Foreign Policy Reappraised* (Cambridge: Harvard University Press, 1963), pp. 80–103, 199–221.

under the Nazis and the prominent role of "Nazi generals" in the new West German army.

Through its activities, the Peace Movement was able to mobilize a body of opinion which had some impact on those who formulated French foreign and defense policies. The group was fairly successful in creating the impression that its members and the Soviet government genuinely wanted peace, whereas Western militarists, through NATO, were planning to unleash new aggressions. This view, which in some ways nullified the credibility of Western nuclear superiority over Russia, was most cogently revealed in the Stockholm Peace Appeal of 1951, a vague document calling for "peace" in terms generally suitable to Soviet foreign policy. The appeal collected over 500 million signatures, though a large majority came from the Soviet Union and the Eastern European Communist states.

The history of the Peace Movement indicates the extent to which the Soviets, as early as 1949, were able to capitalize on legitimate fears of nuclear war and use broad propaganda themes to appeal to diverse segments of the European population. The present Soviet regime has continued employing flexible propaganda strategies aimed at gaining support for Soviet foreign policy among non-Communist audiences. By using "front" organizations and by creating themes of broad appeal designed, nevertheless, for specific targets, it has succeeded in building an image of the Soviet Union, particularly in the underdeveloped countries, as a modern, industrialized, peaceful, and progressive nation.[20] To create this image and seek favorable attitudes toward Soviet foreign policy objectives, Russian propagandists have in recent years relied on three general themes: (1) nationalism, (2) modernization, and (3) peace.[21]

Most of the propaganda which exploits nationalism is not couched in the orthodox phraseology of Marxism-Leninism, for one of the most difficult tasks of Communist theoreticians has been to reconcile Marx' disdain for "bourgeois nationalism" with the obvious importance of nationalism in the contemporary world. Thus, while in intra-bloc propaganda the Soviet government decries manifestations of Eastern European nationalism (though it promotes Russian "patriotism"), propaganda directed to underdeveloped areas fully supports policies expressing nationalist attitudes, whether they take the form of territorial claims (e.g.,

[20] For a discussion of non-Western images of the Soviet Union, see Vernon V. Aspaturian, "The Challenge of Soviet Foreign Policy," in *The Revolution in World Politics,* ed. Morton A. Kaplan (New York: John Wiley & Sons, Inc., 1962), pp. 209–32.

[21] These themes are discussed in detail in Barghoorn, *Soviet Foreign Propaganda,* Chaps. 3–6.

Soviet support for Indonesia's claim to West Irian), wars of "national liberation," expropriation of Western property, or elimination of Western military bases. Soviet propaganda to Asia, Africa, and the Middle East also emphasizes that any ties with the "imperialists" will jeopardize the independence of the new states and subject them to "neo-colonialism."[22] If successful, these appeals based on symbols of nationalism will promote the decline of Western influence and, presumably, simultaneously create goodwill for the Soviet Union.[23] For European targets, the theme of nationalism is usually put in the form of anti-Americanism, suggesting that America's decadent culture is invading Europe and that the United States supports NATO militarily only to protect itself and maintain domination over weaker NATO members.

Since Soviet leaders have recently argued that other societies, especially the underdeveloped countries, will adopt the Communist example if they see the impressive achievements of Soviet science, welfare, and technology, it is natural that Soviet propagandists would use the theme of modernization. This theme is also effective in creating prestige for the Soviet Union. A steady stream of statements, charts, diagrams, and statistics goes via the radio and various publications to the newer countries. These figures emphasize that the Soviet Union has achieved the status of a major power in less than 50 years and that it is winning the "battle of growth rates" over the United States. Soviet space achievements are also acknowledged to be the result of the superiority of communism. Accomplishments of Russian writers and artists, and the level of interest in cultural affairs among the Russian people in general, are frequently compared with the salacious literature that seems to be so popular in Western countries.[24]

Soviet propaganda in underdeveloped countries also places special emphasis on development of the Soviet Union's Asiatic areas, particularly Uzbekistan, where natural and economic conditions are in many respects similar to those in other Asian areas. Articles, pictures, and news reports describe the difference between the Central Asian republics during the Tsarist period, when indigenous populations lived in ignorance and poverty, and today, when there has been spectacular technological, educational, and cultural progress. The relative religious freedom of Moslems in the area is heavily emphasized in Soviet information directed to the Middle Eastern countries. In propaganda of this sort, the Soviet

[22] Note that this idea is almost the same as the American propaganda theme which claims that diplomatic, commercial, and foreign aid ties with the Soviet Union or Communist China will lead to the subversion of non-aligned states.

[23] Barghoorn, *Soviet Foreign Propaganda*, p. 162.

[24] Barghoorn, *Soviet Foreign Propaganda*, Chap. 6.

government is careful to point out that the problems it has faced in building up the Central Asian republics are similar to the problems faced by the people in underdeveloped areas today. It creates an impact by being applicable to the concerns of the target populations.[25]

Peace themes are among the most prominent in Soviet propaganda. These, too, are effective because they play upon rational fears and well-established and widespread attitudes against war. Moreover, these themes appeal to broad groups of people in almost any country, though somewhat different emphasis must be given for each specific target. For Communists and their supporters, classical Leninist strictures about the rapacity and aggressiveness of "imperialists" will be used, while for audiences in non-aligned and pro-Western states the slogans of peaceful coexistence and "normalization of relations" are more prominent.[26] In either case the objective is to create the assumption that Soviet diplomatic programs are motivated by a sincere desire to create peace, while Western diplomatic intransigence prevents this objective from being achieved. Soviet disarmament propaganda is also closely related to the peace theme. Soviet diplomats present grandiose schemes of complete and general disarmament, but are notably reticent to spell out details or explain in depth the great technical difficulties involved in disarmament measures. Indeed, many postwar Soviet disarmament proposals could not be considered seriously outside of their propaganda value. The propaganda objective of Russian disarmament diplomacy was admitted by the Soviet leadership in a document which circulated at the Third Congress of the Romanian Communist Party in June, 1960. In this document, Russian officials stated that whatever other objectives might be involved, their propaganda for disarmament created broad popular fronts and mass movements in favor of peace. These groups would, it was expected, embarrass "aggressive" circles in the West and create public pressures against the maintenance of American overseas military bases.[27]

In attempting to propagate the three main themes of nationalism, modernization, and peace in the most effective manner, Soviet propagandists may use all of the techniques discussed earlier in this chapter. While not averse to using "plants," forgeries, and other surreptitious techniques, they normally employ three or four standard methods of propaganda and persuasion, along with several others which are unique. Of the ordinary methods, they rely frequently on the "testimonial,"

[25] Alexandr Kaznacheev, *Inside a Soviet Embassy* (Philadelphia: J. B. Lippincott Co., 1962), p. 104.
[26] Barghoorn, *Soviet Foreign Propaganda*, p. 87.
[27] Edward Crankshaw, *The New Cold War: Moscow v. Pekin* (Middlesex: Penguin Books, 1963), p. 102.

quoting well-known Western personalities or selections from the Western press, though often out of context. By associating respected non-Communist political, business, scientific, or cultural leadership with Soviet causes, they attract attention among people who would otherwise fail to respond to messages clearly emanating from a Communist source. The "glittering generality" or reliance on symbols of very low specificity is also found frequently in Communist messages. For example, instead of representing a "national liberation movement" as a band of revolutionaries, Russian propagandists will portray it as a mass revolt of *all* the people against a reactionary, puppet government propped up by the "imperialists."

Of the unique approaches, Paul Kecskemeti notes one which he calls the "universal trauma" approach: there is a manifest evil in the world. All right-thinking people, regardless of party, abhor that evil. The main exponents of the evil are enemies of the Soviet Union or the Communist Party. The Soviet regime, or party, unflinchingly combats it. Hence, all right-thinking people, regardless of party, must count the Soviet Union as an ally and act accordingly.[28] An example of this technique can be seen in the following statement by Mrs. Janos Kadar, wife of Hungary's leading Communist, to Radio Budapest's Foreign Language Broadcasting Service for a forum entitled "Women Can Save the Peace."

> Women, who are responsible for life, can save the peace. This is an idea with deep content. . . . To all mothers who have worried and suffered for their loved ones, each fellow human being is the beloved child of an anxious mother. The barbarous destruction of human life that is the consequence of war belies the suffering and labor with which mothers rear their children. . . . Women can do much more for peace than ever before. The role of women in economic and social life is undergoing a profound and decisive change. In the Socialist countries we are advancing with great strides on the road to full equality. This is an inevitable process in all countries, regardless of retrograde elements who oppose women's progress. Women must be mobilized to save the peace. The tasks are universally known, for the Peace Council [a Communist front organization] has already set down realistic demands in many public documents. The government of the Soviet Union and its delegations have tabled their proposals at many conferences. The realization of these aims would fulfill the desires of the women's movement to save the peace. To put an end to the possibility of war means to realize peaceful coexistence . . . this is the aim of all mankind. . . .

The Soviet government has at its disposal all the modern communication media to disseminate propaganda themes. Face-to-face contacts are emphasized increasingly to supplement the traditional media of books,

[28] Kecskemeti, "The Soviet Approach," p. 305.

pamphlets, magazines, and radio. Soviet films, once of such a thoroughly ideological character that no one outside—and few inside—the Soviet Union would pay to watch them, are rated today among the world's artistic achievements. Trade fairs, exhibits, visiting sports teams, circuses, ballets, and technological displays create generally favorable attitudes among a wide variety of people toward the Soviet Union and its economic and cultural achievements.

But the largest amount of money is still spent on radio and books. Radio Moscow broadcasts to every area of the world in native languages, and possesses the most powerful transmitting equipment available. Though the estimated audience of this service is smaller than either that of the Voice of America or the British Broadcasting Corporation's Overseas Service, it can shift attention rapidly to areas suitable for exploitation, and can broadcast messages which would not be acceptable for domestic Russian consumption.[29] Soviet propagandists do not have to be concerned with irate legislators or voluntary associations which do not fully agree with the themes or messages being disseminated. The Soviets also publish, at subsidized prices, thousands of foreign language books and hundreds of magazines and journals. These range from inexpensive editions of Russian literary classics to inflammatory propaganda appeals; every publication is directed toward a particular market. Soviet information officials abroad request local newspapers to reprint or simply to sell space in their publications for Soviet articles, news, and photographs. Finally, the Russians possess a unique propaganda medium in the various Communist parties in foreign countries. All local Communist parties maintain mass communication media in countries where the party is legal, and since Soviet leadership in some cases directs the general political and propaganda strategies of these parties, they in turn perform a considerable amount of the international communication that would otherwise have to be borne alone by the Soviet government.

### Egypt's Radio Propaganda

One of Egypt's long-range objectives during the last decade has been to promote the formation of an Arab empire stretching from the Gulf of Arabia to the Atlantic Ocean, with Egypt at its head. The purpose of this empire would be, aside from fulfilling sentimental aspirations for Arab unity, to divide up the assets of the region more equitably. Egypt in particular suffers from overpopulation, while other Arab states possess

[29] Barghoorn, *Soviet Foreign Propaganda*, p. 285.

extensive oil revenues and uninhabited lands that could be put to agricultural use. In other words, the empire could help solve many of Egypt's most pressing economic and social problems.

Since the objective of creating an Arab empire conflicts with some of the core interests and values of other Middle Eastern states, the Egyptian government under President Nasser could not hope to attain its goals merely through diplomatic persuasion. Propaganda, particularly through radio broadcasting, has thus supplemented Egypt's other instruments of foreign policy. For several reasons, the Egyptian government has employed radio broadcasting almost exclusively as the medium for disseminating its information.[30] First, the rate of illiteracy in the Middle Eastern countries is very high, and radio is the only medium which could reach a large number of people. Second, radio ownership is widespread among Arab populations, making one of the primary modes of communication. Finally, the Egyptian government can use almost all types of programs— thus ensuring maximum impact—to carry the political messages needed to create favorable attitudes abroad toward the idea of Arab unity. News commentaries, speeches, plays, and light programs all contain political messages. Songs emphasize lyrics which carry political themes, and most of Egypt's popular singers have broadcast songs with political verses.

The strategy of Egyptian radio propaganda has been primarily to divide the societies of Arab states which have not been favorably disposed to support the Arab empire idea and, in a more positive vein, to build up support abroad for President Nasser and his pan-Arab ideals. The first strategy has been fulfilled mainly by disseminating inflammatory information which would set various segments of a foreign society against each other or against the government. In Jordan, for instance, Egyptian radio propaganda has tried to create antagonisms within the officer corps of the Jordanian army by suggesting the existence of widespread nepotism and favoritism in promotion policies; it has tried to set the general population against the government by characterizing the royal authority as corrupt, reactionary, and a puppet of "imperialist" forces; it has disseminated propaganda that would alienate the young generation from the old generation, the rural peasants from urban dwellers, and Palestinians from Jordanians. In each case, the propaganda attempts to make the target feel that he is constantly being cheated, misled, or discriminated against by his own fellow citizens or government.

[30] The information on Egypt's radio propaganda comes from A. Loya, "Radio Propaganda of the United Arab Republic—An Analysis," *Middle Eastern Affairs*, XIII (1962), 98–110.

While in some instances this strategy has succeeded—certainly it has broken down loyalties toward certain governments—it has not been without failures, particularly those caused by sudden shifts in Egypt's official foreign policy. On occasion Egyptian propaganda in Saudi Arabia has portrayed King Saud or King Faisal as a "great lion of the desert," a brother of President Nasser, and a man of dignity. When the Saudi Arabian government has resisted proposals for Arab unity, King Saud and his successor have been characterized in Egyptian broadcasts as corrupt rulers, feudalists, friends of American oil imperialists, and old, weak, and degenerate.

In trying to obtain more positive support for Egypt's long-range foreign policy objectives, propagandists have emphasized the idea that Arab unity is "inevitable," ordained by God for President Nasser to fulfill, and that the Egyptian president is a very popular leader at home.

Egyptian radio propaganda has employed several basic themes in attempting to overthrow recalcitrant neighboring regimes and build up more favorable attitudes among Arab publics for the idea of empire. One theme has attempted to arouse hate, particularly against established governments not sympathetic with Egypt's objectives. This has been done by uncovering scandalous information about rulers, particularly by identying them as "lackeys of imperialism," or, even worse, as "agents of Israel." A second theme has been to arouse pride by reminding the Arabs of their glorious past. It emphasizes that these past glories were achieved only because of Arab unity and that, therefore, a new unity, under President Nasser's leadership, would bring new glories to the Arab peoples. Since 1961 and the failure of the attempt to unite Syria with Egypt in the United Arab Republic, Egyptian propaganda has made serious attempts to build a more solid basis for pro-unity sentiments among the Arabs. Rather than merely creating hatreds or inculcating a "mystique" for President Nasser, this information has stressed the ideological aspects of unity—Arab socialism—and the importance of creating appropriate economic and social bases for unification. Though it is too early to gauge the long-range impact of this theme, at least it is less likely to alienate governments in the Middle East which had hitherto regarded President Nasser's plan for Arab unity as basically a form of Egyptian imperialism to be implemented at their expense. Moreover, emphasis on the positive aspects of Arab unity has helped to make this in many cases a very popular issue among broad segments of the Arab population. The fact that Middle Eastern governments and diplomats frequently make reference to the ideal of Arab unity can be traced at least in part to the efforts of the Egyptian government's external propaganda.

### The Effectiveness of Propaganda
### in International Politics

Comparisons of amounts spent by the United States, Egypt, and the Soviet Union for propaganda do not indicate the relative success of their programs. But they do suggest the extent to which these governments rely upon the propaganda instrument as a means of seeking foreign influence and prestige. Professor Barghoorn estimates that the Soviet Union spends more than twice as much on its foreign information program as does the United States, and others estimate the Russian superiority to be much larger.[31] The Voice of America probably has a larger international audience than its Russian counterpart, but the Soviets hold a significant advantage in the quantity of books and magazines sold abroad. Egypt's program is less costly because it is confined essentially to broadcasting and to a limited geographic area. But quantity, and even quality, does not indicate the impact of propaganda in changing attitudes and creating desirable political actions.

There are no published case studies which have scientifically assessed the impact of propaganda programs in international relations. There is little doubt, however, that the United States, Britain, Egypt, China, and the Soviet Union have been able in certain circumstances to create definite attitudes out of latent predispositions and to motivate some people to behave politically in a manner consistent with the objectives of the propagandist. For the Russians, this conclusion should apply to many people in underdeveloped countries and among some leftist and pacifist groups in the West. Kecskemeti believes that Soviet propaganda has been most successful when it has sought to project the image of Russia as combatting a major evil, such as Nazism, "imperialism," or nuclear war.[32] In many areas of the world, social, political, and economic conditions are so unfavorable that any advocate of violent change will get at least a sympathetic hearing. Peasant poverty, land hunger, oppressive political regimes, and unemployment are all conditions which, in an era of high expectations, can easily be exploited for political purposes.

The main shortcoming of a good deal of the information designed to change attitudes of foreign audiences is its lack of subtlety—or the inability of propagandists to see reality as others do. Incongruence of images between communicator and target often results in messages which

[31] Barghoorn, *Soviet Foreign Propaganda,* p. 306.
[32] Kecskemeti, "The Soviet Approach," pp. 305–8.

create responses of incredulity, amusement, or irritation. Propagandists often fail to realize that it is difficult to create new fears or expectations where there is no realistic basis for them. Issues of the greatest importance to the propagandist may be of only peripheral interest to the foreign audience. American propaganda in Pakistan, for instance, has repeatedly attempted to create the impression that Communist China is the only threat to South Asia. Many Pakistanis do not perceive such a threat; on the contrary, they regard India as the primary threat to Pakistan's objectives and independence, a view hardly in keeping with the American government's perceptions of the situation in Asia. Since the Chinese issue is not important to most Pakistanis, there is little that American propagandists can do about it no matter how hard they try.

Soviet propaganda against "imperialist exploitation" is similarly inexpedient among populations that cannot see any evidence of this supposed exploitation. No matter how relevent the themes of nationalism, modernization, and peace to wide audiences in the world, the Russian propensity to fall back on Marxist-Leninist demonology, where everyone is placed into neat stereotypes of good and evil, alienates many who are intelligent enough to see that issues are more complex than that. Thus, despite the development of new propaganda techniques and the careful tailoring of messages to audiences, many governments have failed to crystallize foreign opinions or change attitudes because they have failed to divest themselves of clichés, stereotypes, and concern over issues that are not salient to foreign targets.

The effectiveness of propaganda as an instrument of foreign policy and a means of influencing others thus probably depends on the circumstances or nature of the issue under dispute between two or more states. We have already suggested how resistant some people are to messages that challenge their own picture of the world and how others, through apathy, indifference, or resignation, will not respond to any political appeal which emanates from a foreign source. Yet the skillful propagandist can exploit tense situations and motivate some people to take desired political action. Hitler's propagandists were quite successful in increasing—if not creating —social tensions in Austria and Czechoslovakia and in generating suspicion abroad toward legitimate Austrian and Czech governments. If propaganda by itself did not achieve Nazi foreign policy objectives, at least it created a psychological mood in the victim countries and throughout Europe which helped lead the Czechs, Austrians, British, and French to capitulate to German diplomacy and subversion. But the circumstances in Europe and North America in the 1960's are quite different from those of Europe in the 1930's. Accordingly, Soviet propaganda in this area has made little difference in the major conflicts of the cold war. The Europeans are not generally more responsive to Soviet diplomatic bids because of the activities of Soviet propagandists. In underdeveloped areas, however, propaganda competition is vigorous, and Western and Soviet diplomatic influence may very well be related to the success or failure of their respective foreign propaganda programs. There is already ample proof that the citizens of underdeveloped countries view the Soviet Union and its diplomatic objectives in a different light than most Western publics do.

Whether or not propaganda is effective as an instrument of policy in all circumstances, governments will be likely to use it increasingly as modern media of communication become easily available. States with aggressive, expansionist, or revolutionary foreign policy objectives—which often cannot be achieved through normal diplomatic persuasion—will no doubt pursue vigorous policies of external communication, agitation, and propaganda. Alliance partners and major powers which maintain a high level of involvement in the affairs of the international system, and must seek to legitimize their policies through foreign diplomatic support, will also continue to develop means by which they can influence the attitudes of populations abroad. It is no accident that such states as Egypt, Communist China, the Soviet Union, the United States, France, Great Britain, and many smaller powers—all nations with widespread alliance commitments or revolutionary, expansionist foreign policy objectives—possess highly developed propaganda programs. Even small states with a low level of involvement in the system use propaganda for at least limited purposes, such as attracting tourists, raising their prestige in the international community, or increasing trade. In an era when popular attitudes and behavior can vitally affect diplomatic relations between states, the use of psychological instruments of policy will become increasingly important for creating the framework of attitudes in which responsiveness grows and the exercise of influence through punishments and rewards either succeeds or fails.

## SELECTED BIBLIOGRAPHY

Abelson, H. J., *Persuasion: How Opinions and Attitudes Are Changed*. New York: Springer Publishing Co., Inc., 1959.

Alba, Victor, "The Chinese in Latin America," *The China Quarterly*, No. 5 (1961), 53–61.

Aronson, Elliott, Judith A. Turner, and J. Merrill Carlsmith, "Communicator Credibility and Communication Discrepancy as Determinants of Opinion Change," *Journal of Abnormal and Social Psychology*, LXVII (1963), 31–37.

Barghoorn, Frederick C., *The Soviet Cultural Offensive*. Princeton: Princeton University Press, 1960.

———, *Soviet Foreign Propaganda*. Princeton: Princeton University Press, 1964.

Biryukov, N., "Broadcasting and Diplomacy," *International Affairs* (Moscow), X (1964), 63–68.

Brown, J. A. C., *Techniques of Persuasion: From Propaganda to Brainwashing*. Middlesex: Penguin Books, 1963.

Clews, John C., *Communist Propaganda Techniques*. New York: Frederick A. Praeger, Publisher, Inc., 1964.

Davison, W. Phillips, *International Political Communication*. New York: Frederick A. Praeger, Publisher, Inc., 1965.

———, "Political Communication as an Instrument of Foreign Policy," *Public Opinion Quarterly*, XXVII (1963), 28–36.

Deutsch, Karl W., and Richard L. Merritt, "Effects of Events on National and International Images," in *International Behavior: A Social-Psychological Analysis*, ed. Herbert C. Kelman. New York: Holt, Rinehart & Winston, Inc., 1965.

Greene, Felix, *A Curtain of Ignorance: How the American Public Has Been Misinformed About China*. Garden City, N.Y.: Doubleday & Company, Inc., 1964.

Janis, Irving L., and M. Brewster Smith, "Effects of Education and Persuasion on National and International Images," in *International Behavior: A Social-Psychological Analysis*, ed. Herbert C. Kelman. New York: Holt, Rinehart & Winston, Inc., 1965.

Jordan, Alexander T., "Political Communication: The Third Dimension of Strategy," *Orbis*, VIII (1964), 670–85.

Joyce, Walter, *The Propaganda Gap*. New York: Harper & Row, Publishers, 1963.

Kecskemeti, Paul, "The Soviet Approach to International Political Communication," *Public Opinion Quarterly*, XX (1956), 299–308.

Kirkpatrick, Evron, ed., *Target: The World*. New York: The Macmillan Company, 1956.

Laves, Walter H. C., and Charles A. Thomson, *Cultural Relations and U.S. Foreign Policy*. Bloomington: University of Indiana Press, 1963.

Loya, A., "Radio Propaganda of the United Arab Republic—An Analysis," *Middle Eastern Affairs*, XIII (1962), 98–110.

McGuire, William J., and Demetrios Papageorgis, "The Relative Efficacy of Various Types of Prior Belief-Defense in Producing Immunity Against Persuasion," *Journal of Abnormal and Social Psychology*, LXII (1961), 327–37.

Moody, Mary Jane, "Tourists in Russia and Russians Abroad," *Problems of Communism*, XIII (1964), 3–13.

Passin, Herbert, *China's Cultural Diplomacy*. New York: Frederick A. Praeger, Publisher, Inc., 1963.

Qualter, Terence H., *Propaganda and Psychological Warfare*. New York: Random House, Inc., 1962.

Whitaker, Urban G., Jr., ed. and comp., *Propaganda and International Relations*. San Francisco: Howard Chandler, Publisher, 1963.

Zeman, Z. A. B., *Nazi Propaganda*. New York: Oxford University Press, 1964.

# Economic Instruments of Policy

Just as modern nations are politically and technologically interdependent, so do they rely upon each other
for those resources and commodities which enable
them to develop and sustain viable economies. Some
economic systems are particularly dependent upon
external markets and sources of supply and could not
function for more than a few weeks if they were cut
off from the rest of the world. British farmers, for
example, could produce enough food by themselves
to support only 12 million of Britain's 53 million
people. The British people would starve to death
within six months if they could not import food and
raw materials; their economy would collapse within
several months if they could not sell manufactured
products abroad. For almost any national endeavor,
whether it is to establish or increase standards of living or to produce capabilities and resources which can
be used for domestic or foreign policy purposes,
reliance on others has become one of the paramount

## Chapter X

conditions affecting the exercise of influence in international relations.

Needs which are not capable of being filled within national frontiers help create dependencies on other states. As we have suggested, degree of need is one variable element in the successful exercise of influence in international politics. Because economic resources are often scarce—but necessary to fulfill national values and aspirations—needs in the modern world are frequently of an economic nature. Possession of these resources can be transformed easily into political influence. It is the need for key raw materials by industrial powers that helps explain how "weak" countries, as measured by military or economic capabilities, are able to influence the actions of the "strong." Economic resources are among the major capabilities that can be mobilized for political purposes.

Today some underdeveloped countries use their possession of rare minerals or other commodities to wield effective international influence. But the underdeveloped countries badly need capital, machinery, and technical help to develop their economies. They lack a variety of export products, and for these reasons are vulnerable to economic pressure from industrialized countries. When a country relies on the export of a few commodities to earn foreign exchange, any drop in the price of these exports can have disastrous effects on the economy. If, for example, the United States were suddenly to cease purchasing Venezuelan oil, it could quickly ruin the Venezuelan economy, which must finance its imports through the sale of oil in North America. Until the Venezuelans develop a diversified line of export goods, their position of economic dependency can be used by the United States—if necessary—to wield influence over Venezuelan domestic or foreign policies. Such forms of dependency are not uncommon between underdeveloped and industrialized countries, and can be exploited for political purposes, provided that alternative markets are not available. If influence is to be created out of economic need, the need must be genuine.

## Objectives of International Economic Policies

Since this book is concerned with the wielding of political influence and the instruments used in the influence act, the problem of private international trade is of no immediate interest to us. We must distinguish normal international trade, which has as its purpose private profits or, in the case of state trading, merely seeks to obtain needed commodities, from trade which is manipulated clearly for a political purpose, by a government. If two businessmen in different countries make a contract to import or export a certain type of commodity, this is not a political act; nor is it a political act if a government raises tariffs in order to obtain revenue. The distinction we are concerned with is the purpose of the trade: is it entirely economic, or is it political? This is not a question of state trading versus private transactions. In fact, those governments which do not engage in state trading impose a wide range of regulations on the transactions of private businessmen. Some newer countries have established foreign trade monopolies to protect young domestic industries, improve their balance of payments situation, or more effectively plan and direct the growth of their economies. The government of the United States—which indulges in very limited state trading—may impose regulations on private commercial transactions to bring about a desired political result in another country. In this case, there is no state trade, but the government has imposed certain restrictions on private economic decision-making in order to influence the political behavior of another country. The criteria for the restrictions are political, not economic. The distinction between normal international trade and trade for political purposes thus comes to this: the private businessman, even when he acquires considerable economic resources through international trade, cannot translate these resources into governmental political influence unless he becomes an agent of the state, or unless he can, through various pressures, get his government to act on his behalf, for his private interest. The state, on the other hand, can overlook the profit motive and use the economic need or dependency of another country to wield political influence over it, whether through state trading or regulation of private international commercial transactions.

Government monopoly over foreign trade does provide some advantages if economic instruments of policy are to be used extensively for political reasons. It means, for example, that the government is in possession of all relevant information about domestic and foreign economies and can act more quickly in commercial transactions than if it has to manipulate such controls over economic life as tariffs, quotas, licenses, or exchange rates. Moreover, the state trader can overlook the economic feasibility of commercial transactions. A Soviet state trading organization can easily purchase a large portion of the Burmese export rice production at 20 per cent above world prices (even if the Soviet people do not eat rice), thus creating some desired impact on the Burmese economy. But it is ,much more difficult for, let us say, the French government to order French businessmen to buy more rice than the French population will eat, at a price that will make it extremely unprofitable for the importers. Those governments which most often exploit the economic need and dependency of other countries for their own political purposes frequently create state trading monopolies.

Trade instruments of foreign policy are normally used for three purposes: (1) to achieve any foreign policy objective by exploiting need and dependency and offering economic rewards or threatening or imposing economic punishments; (2) to increase a state's capabilities or deprive a potential enemy of capabilities; and (3) to create economic satellites (e.g., guaranteed markets and sources of supply) or help maintain political obedience in satellites or "spheres of influence" by creating a relationship of economic dependency.

Economic instruments of foreign policy are most often used for purposes of persuasion, reward, or punishment in order to influence the behavior of another state. For example, in 1964 the Soviet government promised to finance a large portion of Egypt's economic development program in return for Egyptian support of the Soviet diplomatic position on colonialism, disarmament, and the Russian-Chinese conflict. Similarly, the Soviet government granted several loans to Afghanistan during the 1950's on the implicit condition that the government of Afghanistan would sign a treaty of neutrality and maintain a foreign policy of benevolent neutrality toward the Soviet Union. In 1966, the American government offered to resume large-scale aid to Pakistan if it would reduce its hostility toward India and at the same time recognize that the main threat to South Asia was Communist China.

Historically, economic forms of punishment have been used more frequently than rewards. Once a position of economic dependency or need has been established in another country, a government may threaten to stop making purchases, cut off vital supplies, or refuse to pay a loan in order to obtain some military or political concession. As will be seen, there are many modern examples where economic reprisals have been used in attempting to influence the behavior of other nations.

Finally, both the carrot and the stick may be used simultaneously in attempts to wield influence. What particular combination of rewards or punishments is employed depends upon the circumstances of the situation, the type of economic need or dependency, and sometimes even upon estimations of economic profits and losses.

The second main objective in using economic instruments of policy is to acquire resources to develop a country's military strength or deprive a potential enemy of those same resources. This objective may be achieved through normal trade, but most governments seeking to improve their military position actively engage in the stockpiling of scarce raw materials, and frequently attempt to manipulate international markets in order to deprive potential enemies of the same commodities.[1] Resources may be

---

[1] Small states which have only limited military hopes or objectives normally purchase their arms from the major powers and do not undertake massive stockpiling programs. These comments apply mainly to the major powers.

accumulated through a variety of means: normal trade, manipulation of foreign exchange rates and gold holdings to create irresistible markets for foreign producers of needed materials, or simply creating economic satellites whose economies are specifically organized to serve the military and industrial requirements of the state to which the satellite is bound.

The third objective is to create such satellites or to bind satellites politically by establishing a high degree of economic dependency. The Soviets exploited the Eastern European countries after World War II not only to help reconstruct their own war-torn economy, but also to make these countries so dependent upon the Soviet Union for both exports and imports that they could not hope to break politically from the Communist bloc.

Of course these three main objectives may appear simultaneously in any foreign policy. The Nazis, for example, combined all three objectives, although the overriding consideration of Nazi foreign economic policy was to maximize the Reich's military capabilities. According to Hjalmar Schacht's "New Plan" of 1934 and Walther Funk's "Four Year Plan" of 1936, the German foreign trade program was designed to make Germany as self-sufficient as possible so that in war-time it would not have to rely on foreign sources to sustain the military machine. To achieve this goal, the Germans constantly used economic rewards and punishments against their neighbors and cleverly created economic satellites and dependencies in the Balkans and Eastern Europe.

In the case of the Soviet Union, the objectives are also combined; the rationale behind the state trading program is a mixture of economic *and* political considerations. Indeed, the impulses behind Soviet foreign trade often seem to contradict each other. During the 1920's and 1930's official Soviet doctrine on foreign trade emphasized self-sufficiency (autarky), but Stalin's programs for heavy industrial development and increased military strength could not be achieved without extensive foreign trade and a certain degree of dependence upon outside sources of machinery and technical advice. The conflict of policies was illustrated in the acute Soviet need for Western goods and technology and the small role of foreign trade (before Stalin's death) in total Soviet economic activity.

Since 1945, the Soviets have used their economic strength to secure the satellites firmly to the Socialist camp. As Anastas Mikoyan frankly admitted in 1949, the aim of Soviet trade was not just to defend the Soviet economy from "imperialist" penetration, but to bind others to it.[2] Since the late 1950's, the Soviet government has increasingly played down the

[2] Noted in Stanley J. Zyzniewski, "Soviet Foreign Economic Policy," *Political Science Quarterly,* LXXIII (1958), 217.

theme of autarky, realizing that it could increase its potential for influencing other nations by expanding trade with them. It has engaged in an extensive effort to increase trade with some selected Western and underdeveloped countries, and has in some cases created degrees of economic dependency which it could exploit effectively by offering economic blandishments or threatening punishments.

Economic considerations in Soviet trade should not be overlooked. Soviet trade with Western Europe is conducted primarily for procuring machinery and equipment which the Soviet economy can not yet produce at satisfactory economic costs. Soviet exports to Europe are generally composed of commodities which are plentiful in the Soviet Union and which the Soviet economy can produce at genuinely low prices. Yet this type of "normal" trade—which the Soviets have sought to increase rapidly—has a partial political objective as well: by breaking into European markets and establishing extensive trade relations, the Soviet government can pressure the NATO countries to relax their embargo of strategic goods to the Soviet Union. Moreover, the prestige of even moderate scale trade with Europe and the United States would substantially assist Soviet trade efforts in other countries. If these Western nations would extend credits to the Soviet Union, then other countries would no doubt follow the example.[3]

Other countries also combine the three political objectives of foreign economic policies. The British, French, and Americans today, and the Japanese in the past, frequently use economic rewards and punishments for political purposes (though they do not engage in state trading), and during periods of international crisis have regulated private international transactions to build up their military capabilities. British and French colonies and protectorates were sometimes maintained primarily to assure access to uncompetitive sources of raw materials. Economic instruments were also used to maintain the loyalty of the colonies and protectorates.

### Techniques of Economic Reward and Punishment

When offering rewards or threatening economic punishments, at least two conditions must be satisfied to make the exercise of influence effective: (1) the target of the influence act must perceive that there is a genuine need for the reward or for avoidance of the punishment, and (2) there must be no easily available alternative market or source of supply to the target. The specific techniques which can be used to reward or punish

[3] Robert Loring Allen, "What Are the Goals of Soviet Foreign Trade?" *Foreign Policy Bulletin,* XXXVIII (April 15, 1959), 115.

constitute various controls over the flow of goods between countries: tariffs, quotas, boycotts, and embargoes. Loans, credits, and currency manipulations can be used for rewards as well.

1. *Tariffs*. Almost all foreign-made products coming into a country are taxed for the purpose of raising revenue, protecting domestic producers from foreign competition, or other domestic economic reasons. The tariff structure can be used effectively as an inducement or punishment when a country stands to gain or lose important markets for its products by its upward or downward manipulation. The United States government, for example, has accorded both Poland and Yugoslavia preferential tariff treatment in an effort to keep these two countries as independent of Moscow as possible. However, the President is authorized by an act of Congress to withdraw this favorable tariff structure any time he deems it to be in the "national interest," that is, at any time that either Poland or Yugoslavia begins to conduct policies which are too vigorously anti-American.

2. *Quotas*. To control imports of some commodities, governments may establish quotas rather than tariffs (tariffs may of course be applied to the items that enter under quotas). Under such arrangements the supplier usually sends his goods into the country at a favorable price, but is allowed to sell only a certain amount in a given time period. The United States government maintains quotas on the import of sugar from Cuba (before 1960), the Dominican Republic, and other sugar-producing nations. Since these countries sell a large portion of sugar (their major export crop) to the United States, any shift in the size of the quotas could either assist or severely damage their economies.

3. *Boycott*. A trade boycott organized by a government eliminates the import of either a specific commodity or the total range of export products sold by the country against which the boycott is organized. Governments which do not engage in state trading normally enforce boycotts by requiring private importers to secure licenses to purchase any commodities from the boycotted country. If the importer does not comply with this requirement, any goods purchased abroad can be confiscated and he can be prosecuted.

4. *Embargo*. A government which seeks to *deprive* another country of goods prohibits its own businessmen from concluding any transactions with commercial organizations in the country against which the embargo is organized. An embargo may be enforced either on a specific category of goods, such as strategic materials, or may cover the total range of goods that private businessmen normally send to the country being punished.

5. *Loans, credits, and currency manipulations*. Rewards may include

favorable tariff rates and quotas, granting loans (a favorite reward offered by the major powers today to underdeveloped countries), or extending credits. The manipulation of currency rates is also used to create more or less favorable terms of trade between countries.

The choice of techniques or combination of techniques to be used will be influenced by the goals being pursued, the type of economic vulnerability or need that exists in the country being rewarded or punished, the estimated effectiveness of alternative techniques, and, since dependency is usually a bilateral proposition, assessment of the possibility of countermeasures. A government will not seriously consider applying an embargo against another country if that country supplies badly needed resources; restrictions on imports through high tariffs or a boycott will not be very effective in damaging the competitor if it sells most of its products in another market; and an embargo will not deprive a competitor if it can easily purchase the commodities elsewhere at comparable prices. Some of the techniques and problems of applying economic rewards and sanctions in attempting to influence the behavior of other nations can best be seen by illustrations from the recent history of international politics.

### Economic Rewards and Punishments in Operation

The post-war history of Soviet-Yugoslav relations provides an excellent example of economic instruments, along with propaganda, military threats, and diplomacy, playing an important role in Soviet attempts to influence developments in Yugoslav foreign and domestic policies. Shortly after World War II the Soviet Union began to assist the new Communist regime in Yugoslavia by enlarging trade and providing small amounts of economic assistance. In 1948, however, Tito was expelled from the Communist bloc because of his unorthodox domestic policies and unwillingness to submit to Soviet domination in ideological and political matters. The Yugoslav heresy resulted in threats of military action by Hungary, Romania, and Bulgaria, vituperation in Communist propaganda organs, and excommunication of the Yugoslav Communist Party from the Cominform. The Soviet Union also organized a Communist bloc embargo and boycott against Yugoslavia. The embargo was potentially an effective technique of punishment because in 1948 Yugoslavia sold over 50 per cent of its exports to the bloc and received 95 per cent of its imports from the same source.[4] The unfavorable economic impact of the embargo and

[4] Harold J. Berman, "The Legal Framework of Trade Between Planned and Market Economies: The Soviet-American Example," *Law and Contemporary Problems*, XXIV (1959), 504.

boycott on Yugoslavia was short-lived, however, because Tito was able to turn to Italy and Great Britain for compensating trade agreements, and to the International Bank for Reconstruction and Development for development loans.

After Stalin's death, Soviet-Yugoslav relations intermittently deteriorated and improved. In 1955 the Soviet government signed a barter pact for the exchange of commodities worth over $79 million annually. In the same year Russia cancelled a $90 million Yugoslav debt and attempted to get other Eastern European countries to expand trade with the former heretic. Between 1955 and 1958 the bloc countries committed themselves to loans of nearly $500 million in attempting to win back Tito's loyalty and subservience to Moscow on ideological matters. Tito continued to vacillate, however, and each time in 1957 and 1958 that he emphasized his independent Communist line, the Soviet government either threatened to cut off assistance or conveniently "delayed" the granting of new loans. In May, 1958, Premier Khrushchev suspended negotiations on loans that amounted to nearly $300 million. By 1963 Tito had mended relations with Soviet Russia—without compromising his independence—and was amply rewarded through new trade agreements and increased Soviet loans.[5]

Considering Yugoslavia's economic dependency on the Soviet bloc, Communist economic punishments and rewards should have succeeded; they failed simply because Yugoslavia turned to the West and found alternative supply and market sources.

A case where alternatives were not available and economic sanctions succeeded occurred in the relations between Finland and the Soviet Union in 1958. After parliamentary elections in 1958, in which Finnish Communists won over one quarter of the seats, a coalition government headed by a Social Democrat was formed. This government did not include among its ministers any Communists, however. The Soviet government has held a traditional enmity against all Finnish Socialists, and the Soviet Premier wasted no time in announcing his displeasure and distrust of the new Finnish Prime Minister. The Soviet government also objected to inclusion of Conservatives in the new cabinet. Various articles in the Soviet press pointed to the "rightist" government as symptomatic of a general resurgence of "reactionary" forces in Finland, and criticized these "rightists" for attempting to destroy friendly Soviet-Finnish relations and planning to increase Finnish trade with the West at the expense of Soviet-Finnish trade. To indicate that it would not tolerate such political leadership in a neighboring country, the Soviet government began to apply a number of diplomatic and economic pressures:

[5] Figures are provided in Berman, "The Legal Framework of Trade," and in Robert Loring Allen, *Soviet Economic Warfare* (Washington, D.C.: Public Affairs Press, 1960), pp. 16, 41.

1. The Soviet ambassador in Helsinki returned to Moscow and was not replaced. The ambassador left without paying the usual courtesy and farewell visit to the Finnish President.

2. The Communist Chinese ambassador left Helsinki for Peking for "consultations."

3. The Soviet government refused on "technical grounds" to sign an agreement with Finland covering fishing rights in the Gulf of Finland.

4. Talks which had proceeded smoothly on the Finnish lease of a Soviet canal (in former Finnish territory) for shipping logs to the Gulf of Finland were suspended.

5. A Finnish trade delegation scheduled to travel to Moscow to negotiate the 1959 trade agreement was left waiting without a Soviet invitation.

6. In November, 1958, the Soviet government abruptly halted all trade with Finland, including goods which had already been ordered. This action had the most serious effect, since many Finnish metal and machinery products sold in the Soviet Union could not be sold in Western markets because their prices were not competitive. In other words, since no alternative markets existed, the Soviet cancellation of trade threw many Finnish workers out of jobs, adding to an already severe winter unemployment problem.

Recognizing that such economic pressures could seriously damage the Finnish economy and worsen an already large unemployment problem, several members of the cabinet resigned and a new government more to the liking of the Kremlin eventually formed. The Soviet economic pressures in this case worked very efficiently.[6]

The Chinese Communists, although they do not possess the economic capabilities of the Russians, have used their vast potential markets as a lure to gain political concessions from Western governments, and particularly from Japan. Japanese businessmen have been eager to sell their products on the mainland, as is indicated in the 600 per cent increase of Japanese-Chinese trade between 1952 and 1960.[7] Since the Japanese government does not recognize Communist China, this trade has been organized through a series of unofficial agreements between Chinese state trading corporations and groups of Japanese companies. In 1958, a Japanese election year, the Chinese capitalized on Japanese businessmen's

[6] K. J. Holsti, "Strategy and Techniques of Influence in Soviet-Finnish Relations," *The Western Political Quarterly*, XVII (1964), 63–84.

[7] One source suggests that trade between Japan and China increased 1000 per cent between 1952 and 1956. A. Doak Barnett, *Communist China and Asia* (New York: Vintage Books, 1960), p. 236.

desire for trade by offering new markets for their goods—but only at a political price. A trade agreement worth almost $300 million and offering great attractions to Japanese industry was drafted in Peking. The Chinese let it be known that such an agreement would have to be ratified by the Japanese government, an act tantamount to Japanese recognition of Communist China. Although the Kishi government (which was fighting for re-election) was committed to a policy of non-recognition of the Peking regime, the Chinese formally offered to conclude the deal, clearly implying that the Japanese could enjoy the vast mainland markets if they elected a government willing to sign such a treaty. The Kishi government was re-elected and subsequently refused to make any commitment on the treaty, whereupon China broke off all direct trade relations and cancelled all outstanding contracts.[8]

The use of controls over trade to deprive potential or actual enemies of goods which could increase their military capabilities is illustrated in the NATO strategic embargo on the Soviet Union and Communist China. In the late 1940's Western governments individually began to impose restrictions on exports of military matériel and certain raw materials and manufactured goods which had a military potential. During the Korean war NATO members (except Iceland) coordinated their individual embargo efforts so that one country could not profit by the sale of commodities to the Soviet bloc while others voluntarily abstained from such trade. They drafted a series of strategic embargo lists which governed the sale of 120 items and commodities to the Soviet bloc, including electronic equipment, chemicals, petroleum products, transportation equipment, synthetic rubber, and various heavy machinery components. In addition to its participation as a director on the NATO embargo coordinating committee, the United States also restricts (under the 1951 Battle Act) the sale of other items to the Communist bloc, even though these do not have any clear military potential.

Effectiveness of the embargo has often been a source of controversy among NATO members. Some have argued that while it has undoubtedly deprived Communist nations of needed equipment, the controls have also forced them to become militarily self-sufficient and thus potentially stronger. Other critics point to the alternative sources of supply which have become available to the Soviet Union and China in recent years. An example occurred in 1963, when the NATO Advisory Council agreed that no NATO member should sell large diameter steel pipes to help the

[8] A. Boone, "The Foreign Trade of China," *China Quarterly*, No. 11 (September 1962), p. 172. A different version, though it also emphasizes the use of trade to gain political concessions, is in Barnett, *Communist China and Asia*, pp. 237–38.

Soviet Union build its "friendship pipeline" for shipping natural gas from the Soviet Union to the Eastern European countries. The Soviet government attempted to purchase the pipe in West Germany and Japan, but was unsuccessful because, it claimed, the American government had placed pressure on the suppliers not to make the pipe available to the USSR. Sweden did sell some pipe, however, thus depriving the NATO members of a potentially lucrative sale. Another problem is that some business organizations in NATO countries are urging their governments to ease the embargo restrictions so that they can develop markets in the Soviet bloc. The experience with the embargo has not been entirely satisfactory, and if relations between the Soviet Union and the West continue to relax, more conflicts may arise over the definition of strategic items.

Cuban-American relations during the period of the Castro regime provide many examples of American efforts to use economic instruments of policy for foreign policy objectives. When Dr. Castro began to expropriate American-owned property in Cuba, the State Department and Congress retaliated by ordering reduction of quotas on the import of Cuban sugar. This hardly subtle measure of punishment failed to deter the Cuban government from adopting an increasingly anti-American foreign policy. Since American officials feared that Premier Castro might also seek to spread revolution beyond the confines of the island, they formulated measures to isolate the regime diplomatically and economically from the rest of the Caribbean and Central American regions. This involved an American embargo on sale of weapons to Cuba; the State Department simultaneously implored other Western governments to control shipments of military goods to the Castro regime. Later, when the Cubans had made explicit their association with the Communist bloc, the American government instituted a complete economic and travel boycott of Cuba. Since the United States had traditionally purchased a majority of Cuba's exports, this punishment seriously crippled the Cuban economy until the Cubans found alternate markets for their products (mainly sugar) in the Soviet Union, Eastern Europe, and Communist China. Although these measures helped to isolate Cuba, they did not bring down the Castro regime, so more pressures were applied. First, the United States imposed almost a complete embargo on exports to Cuba, excluding only food and medicines. Next, American diplomatic officials continued to urge other governments to reduce their exports to the island. To help enforce this policy, the State Department prohibited all foreign vessels carrying goods to Cuba from stopping in American ports to pick up new cargoes on their return voyage. This policy was not received with enthusiasm among foreign shipping companies, but did reduce further trade between Europe and Cuba. As a final measure, the American government in 1964 imposed controls even on the export of food and medicine to the island.

How effective was the application of these economic punishments? Cuba briefly became economically isolated from its traditional trading partners, and its economy suffered seriously. Spare parts for automobiles, trucks, boats, and industrial plants became unavailable, and most economic indicators (except unemployment) moved steadily downward. Food rationing was also imposed. Combined with several poor sugar harvests, the punishments created almost disastrous effects on the Cuban economy.

But, as in the case of Yugoslavia, the Cubans were eventually able to find alternative markets for their exports and some sources of supply to keep the economy running. By granting large loans and providing shipping facilities, the Communist bloc countries prevented the total collapse of Cuba's economy. At times Dr. Castro might have wondered whether he could keep his regime in power, but the punishments did not modify his aggressively anti-American behavior. The economic isolation of Cuba from the West might have succeeded in one respect, however: since the Cuban government had to allocate so many resources and so much human energy into keeping the economy from collapsing, it may not have had either the time or resources to undertake major programs of external expansion, revolutionary agitation, or subversion in Latin America.

Another problem with the policy of punishment was that it failed to get total support from European countries. As with many international embargoes and boycotts, unless all of the participating countries perceive the target as a threat to their own security or economic interests, they are not likely to sympathize completely with policies which deprive their businessmen of economic opportunities. In the case of the embargo on Cuba, many NATO allies and non-aligned governments thought that the United States was too sensitive to Castro's presence in Cuba. They did not greet the embargo with much enthusiasm and when, for example, British and French companies made major sales to Cuba their governments made no attempts to prevent the fulfillment of the trade contracts.

We can cite, finally, one case of the exploitation of economic need and dependency which originally involved two minor powers. Afghanistan is a land-locked Asian country which, in the early 1950's, had at its disposal only two feasible trade routes to the outside world: the first went through Pakistan, the second through the Soviet Union. In 1950 Afghanistan began to make territorial claims on Pakistan, demanding the Pakhtoonistan area and a port city on the Indian Ocean in Pakistan territory. As a reprisal against Afghan diplomatic pressures, propaganda, and political intrigues among the Pakhtu tribes, Pakistan threatened and finally closed the principal overland transit routes available to Afghanistan through Pakistani territory. Later in the same year Pakistan prohibited shipment of oil destined for Afghanistan through its territory. Because Afghanistan was effectively blockaded in the south, it turned to the Soviet Union and signed a four year trade treaty in which the Soviet government agreed to meet Afghanistan's oil requirements. In addition, the Soviet Union offered to prospect for oil in Afghanistan. But when the Afghan government requested an oil exploration team from the United Nations, Soviet objections forced the Afghans to drop the invitation. Pakistan subsequently lifted its blockade as Afghanistan temporarily lost interest in its territorial claims.

A similar situation arose in 1955 when Pakistan again closed its borders to Afghan trade. Now air transportation and a route through Iran were available, but the costs of these alternatives were almost prohibitive. Once again the Afghans turned to the Soviet Union. In return for an agreement permitting duty-free export and import transit across the Soviet Union, Afghanistan increased its trade with the northern neighbor and permitted a sizable increase in the number of Soviet technicians coming to the country. All these agreements have, of course, significantly increased Soviet influence in Afghanistan.[9]

## Economic Penetration
## and Establishment of Dependencies

In addition to using economic instruments of reward and punishment, some states have sought through economic penetration to create virtual colonies or economic satellites. Nazi trade policies in the Balkans and Eastern Europe during the late 1930's illustrate some of the objectives and techniques for creating dependencies. In these examples, economic relations were subject to such manipulation by the Nazi government that weaker countries—or more properly, their economies—were molded to serve German interests.

The objectives of German trade policy were to maximize economic self-sufficiency and increase German military capabilities. These objectives required some expansion of foreign trade, but the Germans did not wish to remain dependent upon the highly industrialized countries of Europe for imports. Accordingly, they placed first priority on developing self-

[9] Details in Allen, *Soviet Economic Warfare*, p. 182; also, Hugh Tinker, *India and Pakistan: A Political Analysis* (New York: Frederick A. Praeger, Publisher, Inc., 1962), pp. 142–43, 215–16.

sufficiency in heavy industrial goods. Foreign trade would be used primarily to purchase raw materials unavailable in Germany and to import some food supplies, especially wheat and tobacco. As this plan was implemented, German trade patterns shifted from their traditional configuration: trade with Western Europe declined while imports from the Balkans, Eastern Europe, and Latin America increased.

Controls on imports and exports were effected through "exchange permits," licenses, and complicated manipulations of exchange rates. German businessmen were required to secure exchange permits or licenses for transactions with foreign firms. These controls enabled the German government to channel all essential commodities into various war industries, and to make certain that foreign exchange earnings were not spent for frivolous imports. Through their various control programs, the Nazis formed virtual government monopolies which collectivized German buying power and enabled them to place large, concentrated demands on prospective trade partners.

The Nazi regime began its penetration of the Balkans and Eastern Europe by offering a large German market for the smaller countries' exports, at prices sometimes as high as 30 per cent above world market levels. The Romanians, Bulgarians, Yugoslavs, and Greeks were of course pleased to sell their products to a guaranteed market at such high prices. German trade terms would have held strong attractions to businessmen operating under stable economic conditions, but as the Balkan states were in the midst of an economic depression and were gaining little attention from international markets, they were particularly attracted.

By selling at very high prices to the Germans, these countries quickly lost their traditional markets in the rest of Europe. To increase economic dependency, German trade agreements often offered credits for payment rather than convertible currency or gold, forcing the Balkan countries to purchase a large share of their imports from Germany. As a typical example of trade manipulation, Germany would purchase the entire Bulgarian wheat export crop at favorable prices. It would then sell the wheat on the world market at a low price and still earn valuable foreign exchange and gold with which to purchase heavy machinery and items necessary for military development. Through this transaction Germany would undercut any market for Bulgarian wheat elsewhere, and, by paying the Bulgarians for the wheat in credits, make the Bulgarians purchase a variety of expendable German goods, some of which were useless in Bulgarian markets. In addition, by paying unduly high prices for the wheat, the Germans helped create local inflation, further reducing Bulgarian exports to other countries. Nevertheless, German prestige among Bulgarian wheat farmers rose high. Indeed, several major trade transactions were completed in this fashion before the Bulgarians discovered their adverse effects on the economy.

When the Balkan governments protested against certain trade practices the Germans threatened to stop purchasing their exports or to block all credits with which these countries could purchase needed imports. By 1938, Yugoslavia, Hungary, and Romania sold over 45 per cent of their exports to Germany and purchased about 50 per cent of their imports from the Third Reich. Bulgaria sold 58 per cent of its exports in this one market and bought 63 per cent of its imports from it.[10] By the time World War II broke out, the economies of these countries had been carefully readjusted to fit German military requirements.

Romania's economy received the most benefits from the German policy of economic penetration, at least in the short run. The Romanians possessed the largest oil resources in Europe and were able to extract advantageous economic agreements from the Germans by promising to fill the Germans' petroleum needs. As in the other Balkan countries, the Germans promised Romania an extensive oil market at high prices. Untypically, however, they were also willing to sell armaments, machinery, and other heavy goods the Romanians needed for developing their economy. In return, Romania signed an agreement for mutual exploitation of mineral (mostly oil) resources, permitted German economic "advisers" to enter the country, and granted various privileges to German-owned enterprises in the country. By 1939, however, most of Romania's production was geared to German needs, not for Romanian economic development. German economic pressures (and Himmler's intrigues) were also evident in the appointment of the Fascist Ion Antonescu to head the government in September, 1940. With such a "connection" Romania's dependency on Germany soon became complete: by the end of the year over 80 per cent of Romania's exports went to the Third Reich, and a large proportion of its imports came from there as well. German troops entered Romania to protect the oil sources later in 1940, and until 1944 Romania fought as an ally of the Germans.[11]

In the present era, such economic dependencies are seldom found even in the Communist bloc. Most countries have developed a range of markets which makes them less vulnerable to economic take-over. Nevertheless, the Eastern European economies are still highly dependent upon the Soviet Union, and former French colonies in Africa and certain states in Latin America are very dependent upon France and the United States

[10] Figures and details from Howard S. Ellis, *Exchange Control in Central Europe* (Cambridge: Harvard University Press, 1941), p. 268.

[11] Figures and details from Antonin Basch, *The Danube Basin and the German Economic Sphere* (London: Routledge & Kegan Paul, Ltd., 1944), pp. 209–12.

for sale of their export commodities. Iceland, Finland, Egypt, and Afghanistan sell large portions of their exports in the Soviet bloc or import from it key commodities such as petroleum. These countries are not in any sense economic satellites, but the degree of economic dependency on one major power makes them at least vulnerable to economic blandishments and punishments.

## Economic Warfare

Economic warfare refers to those economic policies used as an adjunct to military operations during wartime. The objective is either to hold or conquer strategic resources so that military forces can operate at maximum strength, or deprive the enemy of these resources so that his capacity to fight will be weakened. Economic warfare was used extensively by all the major combatants in both world wars, as none of the belligerents except the United States could raise and sustain a modern army and feed a civilian population by relying solely on its own resources. Mutual dependence thus becomes even more crucial during wartime. The techniques that have been used can be summarized as follows, using examples primarily from World War II.

1. *Blockade.* In both wars the Allies established blockades around Germany in an attempt to "starve" it of materials necessary to prosecute the war. Although rules of international law specifically prescribe the nature and extent of legitimate blockades, the Allies frequently disregarded these rules and blockaded even neutral vessels carrying non-military goods to Germany. In World War II the Allied blockade was applied at first only to Germany, but as the European neutrals—Sweden, Switzerland, Portugal, Turkey, and Spain—were able to sell and ship valuable raw materials and manufactured goods to the Third Reich, the blockade authorities also threatened to impose strict controls over them. Two American economic warfare officials have described the function and problems of blockades as follows:

> It was theoretically possible for us to cut off all imports from overseas [to the neutrals] in order to force a neutral country to cease its trade with Germany, or to use our blockade controls as a club to compel a neutral citizen to follow a pro-Ally line. In practice, however, the situation was seldom so simple, and open pressure of this sort was rare. Some of the reasons for Allied hesitation . . . involved complex considerations of international law, political and diplomatic expediency, and military strategy, as well as economic warfare pure and simple.
> The possibility of such sanctions was always there, however, implicit in all

our relations with the neutrals. It was our major source of bargaining power, and in the later stages of the war, as our military and diplomatic position became stronger, it was used more and more effectively to curb neutral aid to our enemies. We prevented Spain from importing essential petroleum products until the Franco government curbed exports of tungsten to the Axis and made other concessions. We employed similar pressure less dramatically against Sweden and Switzerland, to force cuts in their economic aid to Germany.[12]

2. *Blacklist.* Since much of the trade between the neutrals and Germany was conducted by private firms, Allied pressures were exerted directly on them. One device which has been used effectively by governments (sometimes in peacetime as well) against private traders is the blacklist. During World War II these lists, drafted by British and American economic warfare authorities, included the names of Axis nationals or agents located outside enemy territory, as well as neutral or even Allied citizens who were conducting trade with the Axis states. Persons on the list were considered enemies of the United States or Great Britain; their property was subject to seizure; no American or Briton could deal commercially with them in any way; and they could not travel or ship any of their commodities to occupied Europe through any routes or facilities under Allied control. These people could carry on trade with the Axis only if they were prepared to lose all markets in the Allied countries and face the confiscation of their goods during shipment to Europe.

3. *Pre-emptive buying.* Most of the Allied program was concentrated on trying to outbid German agents for materials which the neutrals were willing to export to either side. Where the blacklist was not feasible, the Allies paid greatly inflated prices for commodities in order to keep the Germans from purchasing them. With combined American and British financial resources, the Germans were hard pressed to match the exorbitant prices the Allies were willing to pay. But pre-emption did not always take the form of legal market operations. Sometimes it involved smuggling, highjacking, flooding mines, tying up transportation, sabotage, or any other means that would deprive the Axis of needed supplies.[13]

4. *Rewards.* Economic warfare during World War II also used rewards as well as threats and punishments, though it was normally a combination of the two. Sweden, for example, was promised access to Allied oil and other products which its armed forces desperately needed when it agreed to reduce the export of bearings to Germany. By selling Spain the

[12] David L. Gordon and Royden Dangerfield, *The Hidden Weapon: The Story of Economic Warfare* (New York: Harper & Row, Publishers, 1947), p. 13.
[13] Gordon and Dangerfield, *The Hidden Weapon*, p. 99.

materials it needed to maintain its economy, the Allies succeeded at least partially in reducing Spanish economic dependency upon Germany.

The success of economic warfare, according to Gordon and Dangerfield, has been difficult to assess. Certainly the German armies did not collapse as a result of shortages created by Allied pre-emptive buying and the blockade. But the Germans did have to pay high prices for some needed items, and they had to invest other material and human resources in creating substitutes. Had the materials been readily available, the Germans could have freed thousands of people and millions of dollars for other purposes.

### Foreign Aid as an Economic Instrument of Policy

Foreign aid—the transfer of money, goods, or technical advice from a donor to recipient—is an instrument of policy that has been used in foreign relations for centuries. In the past it was used primarily for short-run political advantages rather than for humanitarian principles or long-range economic development. In the eighteenth century statesmen regularly offered their foreign counterparts "pensions" or bribes of cash for the performance of certain services. Governments also used military aid in the form of subsidies and donations of men and equipment. Throughout the eighteenth and nineteenth centuries the British were often unwilling to sustain the costs of maintaining large standing armies; instead they provided money, matériel, and naval power while their allies raised troops and fought most of the land battles. Most eighteenth century alliances included provisions for financial subsidies. In the Treaty of Worms of 1743, for instance, Britain pledged Austria a subsidy of £300,-000 in addition to 12,000 troops.

Economic needs and expectations today are widespread and acute among more than 65 per cent of the world's population. Economic development and industrialization are among the main objectives of public policy in all countries, but underdeveloped nations cannot hope to achieve these goals without the assistance of those societies which can provide development capital and technological skills. Aid programs benefit simultaneously the donors and the recipients: recipients receive money, loans, materials, and knowledge from which they hope to fashion a modern economy, political stability, or military security; the donors, regardless of the types of "strings" they attach to their aid, always hope to receive some political or commercial dividend either immediately or in the long run.

The British were the first to formulate aid policies designed primarily to foster long-range economic development. Through the Colonial Development and Welfare programs beginning in the 1930's, they sought to diversify the economies of their colonies and prepare them for both political and economic independence. After World War II, the United States displaced Britain as the main dispenser of foreign aid, first to help reconstruct war-damaged European economies—for which the Americans spent nearly $33 billion in the European Recovery Program—and later to assist the underdeveloped countries in creating modern military forces and begin the long road to economic viability and industrialization. After Stalin's death in 1953, the Soviet Union joined the expanding group of states which was donating funds and technological advice to underdeveloped regions. Today, almost all industrialized states of the world contribute at least some of their wealth and skills. Most of the programs are bilateral undertakings negotiated directly between donors and recipients, but in addition there are multilateral aid organizations and programs, such as the International Bank for Reconstruction and Development and the United Nations Technical Assistance Program, through which industrialized members of the organization make available personnel with special skills to the underdeveloped members. Although these multilateral programs have grown rapidly during the last decade, their value still constitutes less than 10 per cent of the aid which flows from industrialized countries to underdeveloped regions.

Of the bilateral programs, only the major powers are able to use foreign aid as an effective instrument of policy to support their diplomacy, and even these do not dispense aid in large quantities to *all* underdeveloped countries. West Germany, Sweden, Italy, Japan, Canada, and Australia, among others, provide grants, loans, and technical assistance to a few selected countries, but the amounts involved are not normally great enough to permit them to exploit the needs of the recipients for their own political purposes. They give aid primarily out of humanitarian considerations and also to promote the commercial interests of their own citizens. Among the major powers, France gives the greatest amount of aid measured as a per capita contribution, but it is directed primarily to the former French colonies in Africa. Although the Soviet Union currently has about 35 recipients of its aid programs, most of it goes to a few key countries such as China (until the early 1960's), India, Indonesia, Afghanistan, and Egypt. American economic or military aid has reached more than 75 countries of the non-Communist regions since World War II, but most of it has also been concentrated among a few recipients. In 1966, about 80 per cent of American economic aid went to a few important allies or neutrals such as Brazil, Chile, India, South Korea, South Vietnam, Pakistan, Nigeria, and Turkey. In our discussion of foreign aid as an instrument of policy, therefore, we will be referring primarily to the programs of the major powers which are directed toward key recipients.

## Types of Foreign Aid

There are four main types of aid programs: (1) military aid, (2) technical assistance, (3) grants, and (4) development loans. The first is also probably the oldest, for military aid is a traditional technique for buttressing alliances. In the last century, both France and Great Britain spent millions of francs and pounds to strengthen their continental allies. The donors supplied money and matériel, while the recipients provided most of the manpower.[14] Since World War II the United States and the Soviet Union have spent more resources on military aid than on their foreign economic programs—and the objective has been the traditional one of safeguarding their own security by strengthening the military capabilities of allies. By helping the recipients to build modern armed forces, the donors feel less need to station their own troops abroad.

Most forms of military aid have the advantages of built-in controls. Not only are the recipients dependent upon the donors for creating a modern military force, but they cannot operate the force effectively unless the donor is willing to provide the necessary support, replacement parts, and maintenance. Thus, the controls provide a partial guarantee that the recipient will use its military forces in a manner compatible with the interests of the donor—unless the recipient can obtain ammunition, spare parts, and training from alternative sources. In 1954, for example, Syngman Rhee's government in South Korea threatened to break the armistice ending the Korean War and invade North Korea to reunify the country by force. The American government strongly opposed the scheme and threatened to cease all military aid to the Republic of Korea if Rhee carried out is plans. Since the South Koreans were almost totally dependent upon the United States for their military equipment, the Korean government had little choice but to abandon the proposal.

Technical assistance, the least costly of all types of aid programs, is designed to disseminate knowledge and skills rather than goods or funds. Personnel with special skills from industrialized countries go abroad to

---

[14] Hans Morgenthau, "A Political Theory of Foreign Aid," *The American Political Science Review*, LVI (1962), 303. Monetary and honorific rewards—or bribes—were also used extensively as a means of achieving diplomatic objectives in the eighteenth century. For a humorous lesson on how to use diplomatic bribes and a description of the various European "customs" for proffering and receiving such bribes, see the essay by François de Callières, *On the Manner of Negotiating with Princes,* trans. A. F. Whyte (South Bend, Indiana: University of Notre Dame Press, 1963), pp. 24–26.

advise on a wide variety of projects. Some famous American programs and organizations such as "Point Four" and the Peace Corps have been associated with such projects as malaria control, agricultural mechanization, public administration, development of fisheries, teaching programs, land reclamation, road construction, and development of medical and sanitary facilities. The impact of these programs can be very great, particularly in rural areas, while the costs are relatively modest except when they are associated with major development projects.

Until the late 1950's the preferred method of transferring capital and goods was to donate outright grants or gifts for which no economic repayment was expected. This was the form in which most American funds for the European Recovery Program and the Mutual Security Program were dispensed. But outright gifts of this type always create problems for the donor and recipient, and lately the governments of the major powers have replaced grants with long-term loans. Grants of military equipment are still dispensed regularly, and special economic grants are frequently made available when countries face such emergencies as an immediate military threat, famine, or floods. Under Public Law 480, also known as the "Food for Peace" program, the United States has annually distributed abroad several million tons of surplus food for which the recipients pay low prices in their own currencies rather than in dollars. The payments are usually kept in special funds which are loaned back to the receiving country for economic development projects. These transactions constitute at once grants, subsidies, and loans.

The major powers thus provide a number of foreign aid programs, each of which is supposed to fulfill somewhat different objectives. Military aid is used to achieve short-run security interests. Technical assistance is used more for the long-run purpose of economic development, particularly for the social aspects of development. Military and economic grants can be used as bribes for specific political purposes, humanitarian relief, or programs for long-range economic development. Loans, too, can be used in a flexible manner, either as a reward for some immediate political concession or as part of a long-range strategy to help develop a country's economy.

What proportion each dispensing country devotes to these types of programs will reflect its over-all foreign policy objectives. During and immediately after the Korean War the United States, fearing military invasions from Communist Russia and China, emphasized military aid and defense support for its main allies. In 1953, for example, the United States allocated $4.2 billion for military grants and only $2.6 billion for economic aid. In the later years of the Eisenhower administration and during John F. Kennedy's presidency, the American government reduced military aid and increased lending facilities to support long-range development projects for non-aligned as well as allied countries. In 1961, a typical year of post-Korean War aid programs, the United States spent $5.9 billion on foreign assistance, divided almost equally between grants and loans. But over 75 per cent of the sum was made available for economic development loans, technical assistance, emergency relief, and surplus food grants, with the remainder devoted to military grants.[15]

## Political Objectives of Foreign Aid

Given the dependency of many underdeveloped countries on industrialized nations for capital, advice, and occasionally military assistance, how is foreign aid used as an instrument of policy to influence the behavior of recipients? What criteria do governments use in dispensing aid? Are they purely economic and humanitarian, or do military and political considerations dominate the foreign aid policy-making processes?

Most aid programs are obviously not undertaken solely for humanitarian purposes, for a vast portion of the aid goes to a few countries—and sometimes not the countries which have the most pressing needs. India, Pakistan, and Egypt, for instance, are large recipients because of their strategic and symbolic importance in world politics. On the other hand, all aid policies and commitments do not have an immediate or exclusive political or security objective behind them. Many aid programs are formulated by trained economists, on the basis of economic criteria. Others are designed to relieve immediate suffering or forestall some economic catastrophe. Yet, aside from relieving emergencies, economic development is seldom considered by the donors as an end in itself. Even in the long run, it is designed to help secure certain of the donors' political objectives which it cannot achieve solely through diplomacy, propaganda, or military policies.

It is not solely for humanitarian sentiments or a profound sense of duty to the underdeveloped countries, for example, that the United States has committed itself to provide $20 billion over a ten year period for the Alliance for Progress. The assumption behind this program, as in most Western economic development programs, is that successful economic development in underdeveloped countries will create political stability and reduce the threat of violent revolution and unrest which can be exploited by Communists. Some also assume, though there is little evidence to support the view, that economic development will help bring liberal democratic regimes into power and prevent the recipients from

[15] Agency for International Development, *U.S. Foreign Assistance and Assistance from International Organizations: Obligations and Loan Authorizations, July 1, 1945–June 30, 1961 (revised)* (Washington, D.C.: Agency for International Development, n.d.), p. 1.

pursuing adventurous foreign policies. A healthy economy, they argue, brings about a pacific foreign policy.[16]

Another prominent theme governments use to justify their aid programs is that economic development helps buttress the independence of the recipients, enabling them to resist dependency on any one state or group of states. The stronger they are economically and militarily, the less vulnerable they become to external diplomatic and economic pressures and to subversion. From the American point of view in particular, the presence of a group of genuinely independent states is perceived to have a direct relation to United States security interests. It reduces the number of military commitments—including interventions—which the United States must make, and also precludes the necessity for stationing even more troops and bases abroad. From the French and British perspectives, foreign aid programs are also regarded as a continuing commitment to improvement of former colonial holdings, and a method of maintaining some diplomatic and commercial influence in regions formerly under their exclusive control.

The Soviet Union, though it often claims the opposite in its propaganda, dispenses aid to help support its political objectives, and like some Western countries, occasionally threatens to cut off aid as a punishment. Not only can the aid be used for short-run political advantages as a reward or punishment and means for increasing Soviet prestige among underdeveloped countries, but the Soviet government also conceives of aid as a method by which it can speed up the process of industrialization, create an urban proletariat, and pave the way for eventual liquidation of capitalism and transformation of the underdeveloped countries into socialism.[17]

No matter what the original objective of an aid program, whether

---

[16] As Hans Morgenthau has argued, "The popular mind . . . and much of the practice of foreign aid have proceeded from certain unexamined assumptions, no less doubtful for being deeply embedded in the American folklore of politics. Thus the popular mind has established correlations between the infusion of capital and technology into a primitive society and its domestic development, between economic development and social stability, between social stability and democratic institutions, between democratic institutions and a peaceful foreign policy. However attractive and reassuring these correlations may sound to American ears, they are borne out neither by the experiences we have had with our policies of foreign aid nor by general historic experience." "A Political Theory," 304–305.

[17] See, for example, Friedrich Ebert Institute, *The Soviet Bloc and the Developing Countries* (Hanover: Verlag für Literatur und Zeitgeschehen, 1962). Both the American and Soviet governments view each others' aid programs as motivated by short-run political considerations—particularly to "enslave" the new nations—whereas they commonly refer to their own humanitarian motivations in undertaking aid programs. For the similarity of their views, see J. David Singer, "Soviet and American Foreign Policy Attitudes: Content Analysis of Elite Articulations," *Journal of Conflict Resolution,* VIII (1964), 446, 450, 461.

economic development or human betterment, *it can be used* for rewarding, threatening, or punishing—that is, for wielding influence over the
behavior of recipients in such a manner as to help the donor achieve
certain short-run political objectives. When donors manipulate aid programs for immediate political advantages, economic and humanitarian
criteria, though still relevant, give way to political desiderata. We cannot
discuss the many ways in which foreign aid can be used as an instrument
of policy for wielding influence over the internal and external policies of
recipients, but we can point out some of the prominent short-run objectives which can be achieved by manipulating aid programs.

## Aid to Create Political Stability in the Recipient

Major donor countries have supplied millions of dollars of aid designed
to stabilize foreign governments, and through them, their own security
interests. Military aid, for example, can have three functions: to help
create a modern military force to deter *external* aggression, establish
special military forces trained to put down *internal* riots and disorders
against established authorities, and raise the prestige of local regimes and
military elites. A portion of Soviet, British, French, and American military
aid to respective alliance partners and to some underdeveloped countries
can be understood best in terms of the latter two functions. When the
United States sends jet fighters and other modern weapons to a small
Latin American country, it is playing on the desire for prestige among the
military leaders who, in most cases, wield great influence in Latin
American politics. The armaments have little external military utility, but
they increase the military's prestige and the recipient government's ability
to cope with civil disorders.

Some economic aid policies are designed primarily to elevate the
internal and foreign prestige of a regime, without simultaneously making
any significant contribution to the long-range economic development of
the country as a whole. Gaudy projects spread around the country illustrate to the indigenous people that their government is pursuing modernization and is capable of possessing the symbols of an industrialized,
powerful nation. In Hans Morgenthau's words,

> Prestige aid has in common with modern bribes the fact that its true pur-
> pose, too, is concealed by the ostensible purpose of economic development
> or military aid. The unprofitable or idle steel mill, the highway without
> traffic and leading nowhere, the airline operating with foreign personnel
> and at a loss but under the flag of the recipient country—all ostensibly
> serve the purposes of economic development and under different circum-
> stances might do so. Actually, however, they perform no positive economic

function. They owe their existence to the penchant, prevalent in many underdeveloped nations, for what might be called conspicuous industrialization, spectacular symbols of, and monuments to, industrial advancement rather than investments satisfying any objective economic needs of the country. . . . They perform a function similar to that which the cathedral performed for the medieval city and the feudal castle or the monarch's palace for the absolute state.[18]

Finally, some regimes are so weak and the nations they attempt to govern so fractionalized—or even nonexistent—that they must be propped up by the contributions of foreign governments. This subsistence aid, both economic and military, is designed to provide the basic minimal services which keep a political order intact. Jordan, for example, corresponds to no geographic entity and is based on no traditional political, social, or economic system. A creation of the British Government after World War I, it has remained a nominally independent nation largely because the British, and later the Americans, were willing to provide the aid necessary to keep the Hashemite kings on their throne. Without the aid, Jordan probably would have ceased to exist years ago, a victim of social disintegration (or lack of integration) or external subversion. Similarly, a large portion of American aid to South Vietnam in the 1960's has had the major purpose of helping established authorities maintain enough social order for them to prosecute effectively the war against the Viet Cong. Even India, which does not possess many spare resources, distributes economic and military aid to Nepal for the purpose of creating a viable buffer state between itself and China. Though this aid might make only a small contribution to economic development in Nepal, its main effect is to create political and religious strength for the Nepalese government, thereby reducing the possibility of Chinese-inspired disorders.

### Aid Designed to Change the Recipient's Domestic or Foreign Policies

Donors can also manipulate economic and military aid programs to change the internal politics of recipients. A regime can be rewarded through increased aid allotments if it promises to institute political reforms, or it can be threatened with a reduction in aid if the reforms are not carried out. In 1963 the American government decided that the war against the Viet Cong could not be prosecuted satisfactorily so long as the Diem regime in Saigon continued to behave as an arbitrary dictatorship. American diplomatic representatives frequently asked Diem and his

[18] Morgenthau, "A Political Theory," 303, 304.

advisers to observe basic civil liberties in the country and permit other political groups a voice in policy-making. When Diem consistently refused to accept the American advice, the United States quietly began to apply pressures by reducing its foreign assistance program. First it halted the financing of commercial exports to South Vietnam, and later refused to continue payments to Vietnamese Special Forces engaged in persecuting anti-Diem groups rather than fighting against the Viet Cong. It finally "postponed" renewal of the annual agreement on grants of surplus food. By the end of the year, American aid to the Southeast Asian country had been reduced by 75 per cent. These steps, which were coordinated with a diplomatic and propaganda campaign against the Diem regime, undoubtedly had an important bearing on the subsequent *coup d'état* by the Vietnamese army which threw out the Diem regime. Other post-war examples of countries where the United States exerted pressures to induce internal political reforms by threatening or actually halting aid payments include Greece, Haiti, the Dominican Republic, Brazil, and Zanzibar.

Examples of aid manipulation designed to change a recipient's foreign policies are equally plentiful. In 1963 the United States decided to cut off almost all economic and military aid to Indonesia after the Indonesian government mobilized resources to achieve its goal of "crushing" Malaysia. Similarly, the Soviet Union quietly withdrew thousands of technicians and millions of rubles worth of aid after the Chinese began to criticize Soviet leadership in the world Communist movement. Though the Russians claimed that their aid personnel were requested to leave by the Chinese, it is likely that the Soviet government took the initiative to reduce its economic aid program as an attempted means of inducing the Chinese to change their domestic and foreign policies, as well as their position on certain ideological issues. In 1960 the Soviet Union also seriously curtailed its military aid to China, thus depriving the Chinese of needed modern weapons, spare parts, and, in particular, slowing down the Chinese program to build nuclear weapons.[19]

## Aid as a Reward for Becoming an Alliance Partner

Promises of large quantities of military and economic aid are also used to obtain allies. In return for committing its resources and manpower to the development of a large, modern military capability, targeted toward the main potential enemy of the donor, the alliance partner will receive aid with which to fashion a program for economic development. Since

[19] Alice Langley Hsieh, "The Sino-Soviet Nuclear Dialogue: 1963," *The Journal of Conflict Resolution*, VIII (1964), 106–14.

World War II, the largest share of American, British, and Soviet aid has been devoted to obtaining and supporting allies.

### Aid to Help the Recipient Achieve
### Its External Objectives

Donors may grant economic or military aid enabling the recipients more easily to fulfill their foreign policy goals. This would include military aid to help deter a threat from an external enemy, enhance the recipient's international prestige, or build up its military capabilities to prosecute expansionist policies. Of the last type, a good example was Soviet military aid to Indonesia which was used by the Indonesians to acquire West Irian under threats of force, and to prosecute its policy of confrontation against Malaysia. Though the Soviet Union made few outright grants of military equipment to Indonesia, it provided extensive credits with which the Indonesian armed forces could secure new equipment.

### The Problem of "Strings" in Foreign Aid

As the examples cited suggest, almost all aid used to sustain or change internal and foreign policies of recipients has "strings," or certain expectations and conditions, attached to it. Any regime which receives large quantities of economic and military goods to help it remain in power will obviously feel that it must coordinate at least some of its policies to fulfill the expectations—implicit or explicit—of the donor. Even long-range development aid contains a wide variety of economic "strings" or technical standards which the recipient must meet if it wishes to receive grants, loans, and technical assistance. Despite what they claim in their propaganda, donors—including multilateral agencies—always insist that their goods and funds be used in a manner consistent with their own purposes. As a minimum, donors maintain rigorous economic and technical requirements which potential recipients must satisfy if they wish to qualify for assistance. Policy-makers seldom pose the question whether their aid should or should not have "strings" attached to it; they are only concerned with defining the *types* of mutual expectations, commitments, and obligations which any aid agreement will impose on both parties.

Since the elites of underdeveloped nations place such emphasis on industrialization and modernization, they need the resources and assistance of major industrial countries. In turn, the donors of aid can use these needs for their own purposes and can, in many cases, use aid as an effective instrument for supplementing their diplomacy, propaganda, and military programs. But the recipients are not without influence in their relationships with the donors. Occasionally they are able to obtain external assistance without making explicit commitments to any particular actions or policies. Ruling regimes can also argue that if they do not receive more aid, domestic tranquility will be jeopardized and local Communists will take over. In what has become a frequent bargaining tactic, the potential recipient can always threaten to go to another major power to receive aid if one donor is unwilling to grant it on favorable terms. Any donor, if asked to terminate his aid policies, will suffer a blow to its prestige in the recipient country, while the regime, if it succeeds in obtaining goods and services from an alternative source, can demonstrate to both domestic political groups and other nations that the country is independent enough to obtain aid and concessions from a variety of sources. As in any economic transactions where an alternative supply is available, the donor-recipient relationship can be exploited by the recipient for its own purposes. There are, therefore, definite limitations on the use of foreign aid as an instrument of foreign policy to achieve short-run political and military advantages.

The examples of economic rewards and punishments that have been cited suggest that these instruments of policy do not inevitably succeed. Even where real economic dependencies exist, economic pressures can be resisted if alternative markets and sources of supply are available. On the other hand, economic development and industrialization in the contemporary international system have achieved very high value as national goals and indicators of national prestige. Sometimes these needs and the value placed on them will create more responsiveness between countries, and governments will become increasingly sensitive to the economic requirements of their neighbors. Many governments have come to view economic competition as not like a zero-sum game, where the gain of one is the loss of the other. On the contrary, they commonly assume that economic development of underdeveloped countries provides not only economic dividends, but political gains as well. Yet out of need and strong commitments to rapid economic betterment arise vulnerabilities to economic-type rewards and punishments. It is likely, therefore, that economic instruments of persuasion will assume a growing role in the wielding of influence in international politics.

## SELECTED BIBLIOGRAPHY

Allen, Robert Loring, *Soviet Economic Warfare*. Washington, D.C.: Public Affairs Press, 1960.

Asher, Robert E., "Multilateral versus Bilateral Aid: An Old Controversy Revisited," *International Organization*, XVI (1962), 697–719.

Banfield, Edward C., *American Foreign Aid Doctrines*. Washington, D.C.: American Enterprise Institute for Public Policy, 1963.

Beim, David, "The Communist Bloc and the Foreign Aid Game," *The Western Political Quarterly*, XVII (1964), 84–99.

Berliner, Joseph S., *Soviet Economic Aid: The Aid and Trade Policy in Underdeveloped Countries*. New York: Frederick A. Praeger, Publisher, Inc., 1958.

Feis, Herbert, *Foreign Aid and Foreign Policy*. New York: St. Martin's Press, 1964.

Goldman, Marshall L., "The Balance Sheet of Soviet Foreign Aid," *Foreign Affairs*, XLIII (1965), 349–61.

Gordon, David L., and Royden Dangerfield, *The Hidden Weapon: The Story of Economic Warfare*. New York: Harper & Row, Publishers, 1947.

Graber, Doris A., "Are Foreign Aid Objectives Attainable?" *The Western Political Quarterly*, XIX (1966), 68–84.

Horvath, Janus, "Moscow's Aid Program: The Performance So Far," *East Europe*, XII (1963), 2–9.

Keyfitz, Nathan, "Foreign Aid Can Be Rational," *International Journal*, XVII (1962), 237–50.

Kovner, Milton, "Soviet Aid Strategy in Developing Countries," *Orbis*, VIII (1964), 624–40.

Lewin, Pauline, *The Foreign Trade of Communist China*. New York: Frederick A. Praeger, Publisher, Inc., 1964.

Liska, George, *The New Statecraft: Foreign Aid in Foreign Policy*. Chicago: University of Chicago Press, 1960.

Mahajani, Usha, "Kennedy and the Strategy of Aid: The Clay Report and After," *The Western Political Quarterly*, XVIII (1965), 656–68.

Mason, Edward S., *Foreign Aid and Foreign Policy*. New York: Harper & Row, Publishers, 1964.

Mead, W. J., "Some Political-Economic Issues Determining U.S. Tariff Policy," *The American Journal of Economics and Sociology*, XXI (1962), 131–44.

Montgomery, John Dickey, *The Politics of Foreign Aid: American Experience in Southeast Asia*. New York: Frederick A. Praeger, Publisher, Inc., 1962.

Morgenthau, Hans, "A Political Theory of Foreign Aid," *The American Political Science Review*, LVI (1962), 301–309.

Nehru, Braj Kumar, "Foreign Aid from the Viewpoint of the Recipient Countries," *Proceedings of the Academy of Political Science*, XXVII (1962), 135–45.

Oakeshott, Robert, "The Strategic Embargo: An Obstacle to East-West Trade," *World Today*, XIX (1963), 240–47.

Packenham, Robert A., "Political-Development Doctrines in the American Foreign Aid Program," *World Politics*, XVIII (1966), 194–235.

Prybyla, Jan S., "Communist China's Economic Relations With Africa 1960–1964," *Asian Survey,* IV (1964), 1135–43.

———, "Soviet and Chinese Economic Competition Within the Communist World," *Soviet Studies,* XV (1964), 464–74.

Pryor, Frederic L., *The Communist Foreign Trade System.* Cambridge, Mass.: Massachusetts Institute of Technology Press, 1963.

———, "Foreign Trade Theory in the Communist Bloc," *Soviet Studies,* XIV (1962), 41–61.

Pye, Lucian, "The Political Impulses and Fantasies Behind Foreign Aid," *Proceedings of the Academy of Political Science,* XXVII (1962), 92–111.

Shwadran, Benjamin, "Middle East Oil, 1962," *Middle Eastern Affairs,* XIV (1963), 194–200, 226–35.

United States Department of State, *The Communist Economic Offensive Through 1963* (Bureau of Intelligence and Research Memorandum RSB-43). Washington, D.C.: Government Printing Office, 1964.

United States Department of State, *A Survey of the Strategic Trade Control Program 1957–1960* (General Foreign Policy Series 175, Fourteenth Report to Congress). Washington, D.C.: Government Printing Office, 1960.

United States International Cooperation Administration, *The Strategic Trade Control System 1948–1956* (Ninth Report to Congress). Washington, D.C.: Government Printing Office, 1956.

Wolf, Charles Jr., *Foreign Aid: Theory and Practice in Southern Asia.* Princeton: Princeton University Press, 1960.

Zyzniewski, Stanley J., "Soviet Foreign Economic Policy," *Political Science Quarterly,* LXXXIII (1958).

# Clandestine Actions
# and Military
# Intervention

It was a theme of Chapter III that social and technological changes in the political units which make up any international system may have important consequences on the processes that occur within that system. Development of sovereign national states and simultaneous decline of other forms of political organization—such as city states—brought forth new techniques, institutions, and norms of statecraft in the seventeenth and eighteenth centuries. Just as gunpowder helped destroy the foundations of the feudal order and the growth of dynastic absolutism diminished the international political influence of the Catholic church, mass media of communication, rapid transportation, a complex and interdependent international economy, weapons technology, and mass politics have helped to diminish the "impermeability" of the nation state. The possibility of obtaining informal or non-official access to foreign societies has grown as the size of government missions abroad—

# Chapter XI

once confined to a few diplomats and consular agents—has increased. Short of building walls or iron curtains, most states have relatively few effective means of preventing outside infiltration, or the movement of funds, propaganda, or military matériel from abroad. States with lengthy frontiers passing through forests, jungles, deserts, or mountains are often incapable of preventing outside penetration.

As means of achieving objectives, defending interests, or promoting social values abroad, governments may—instead of sending diplomatic notes or making military threats—infiltrate foreign voluntary organizations, sponsor strikes and riots, create political scandals, attempt a *coup d'état*, or, on their own territory, organize, train, and arm a group of foreign dissidents and then send them home to conduct guerrilla warfare or subversion. States which are relatively weak in conventional military capabilities are able to mount campaigns of external subversion and infiltration at little cost, either in funds and matériel or in the risks of military retaliation by the target country. In our era, the capacity to penetrate politically and quasi-militarily into foreign societies may be as important as a capability to make military threats, impose naval blockades, or carry out conventional military assaults. In particular, weak states (militarily speaking) with revolutionary or expansionist objectives may attain objectives by conducting clandestine actions abroad. Certainly a state is no longer powerful *only* if it possesses a vast conventional or nuclear military establishment.[1]

Clandestine activities are not, of course, entirely a product of the modern age. They were organized as well in China during the Chou dynasty, in Greece, and particularly in fifteenth century Italy. In the dynastic international system of the eighteenth century, intervention for ideological principles seldom occurred and monarchs were not generally concerned with the domestic policies of their brethren.[2] Louis XIV occasionally conspired to interfere in British constitutional issues, but the main concern over other states' international political life was with questions of inheritance and royal family affairs. Dynasts concluded military alliances, as in the Triple Alliance of 1717, to place certain candidates on foreign thrones, and indulged in all sorts of court intrigues for the same purposes. But there were no attempts to subvert foreign societies in the name of ideological principles and governments had not yet developed the techniques of mass persuasion or guerrilla warfare

[1] Andrew M. Scott, "Internal Violence as an Instrument of Cold Warfare," in *International Aspects of Civil Strife,* ed. James N. Rosenau (Princeton: Princeton University Press, 1964), pp. 154–69.
[2] See Edward V. Gulick, *Europe's Classical Balance of Power* (Ithaca, N.Y.: Cornell University Press, 1955), pp. 62–65.

commonly observed today in international politics. States were, on the whole, "impermeable" to outside influences.

Intervention became more common in the nineteenth century, particularly as a method of promoting or putting down revolutions inspired by liberal and nationalist movements. The wars of the French Revolution were revolutionary wars, often different in objectives and techniques from the wars in the preceding century. Conservative regimes, following their victories over Napoleon, assigned themselves the obligation to intervene militarily against societies which were experiencing domestic liberal revolutions. Later in the same century, the United States frequently sent contingents of Marines to Latin American and Caribbean states to influence the course of local politics and revolutions. In general, however, the principle of non-intervention in other states' internal affairs was observed with considerable regularity.

The record of the twentieth century is a remarkable contrast. In some 200 revolutions which occurred during the first half of the century, foreign intervention took place in almost one half; in approximately 50 of these revolutions, *more* than one outside power intervened. Soviet Russia, Nazi Germany, and Fascist Italy interfered in their neighbors' domestic political life with unprecedented regularity. Since the end of World War II, the record has not improved. Most international crises of the period have started basically as *internal revolutions* or civil disturbances, in which one or more external states eventually became involved. This list would include Greece, China, Algeria, Laos, Lebanon, Jordan, Iraq, Kuwait, Yemen, the Congo, Angola, Vietnam, and the Dominican Republic.

While it may appear that the great powers most frequently promote subversion and clandestine operations abroad or direct outright military interventions, this impression is not substantiated by recent history. True, the clandestine and interventionary actions of the large states are usually the most dramatic because they are the most highly organized or the stakes are bigger, but smaller nations have not failed to use these techniques to achieve objectives or promote political values. Egypt and Saudi Arabia have frequently employed propaganda against foreign audiences in efforts to undermine support for Middle Eastern regimes; they have financed and organized assassination plots, bribed government officials in neighboring territories, and, as in the Yemen civil war in the 1960's, intervened with their own military troops. Many of the new states in Africa have been no less active. Opposition parties—often driven underground—establish headquarters in neighboring states and even accept foreign nationals in leadership positions. They are given not only sanctuary in foreign territories, but frequently funds, training, and arms as well. Tunisia and Algeria have provided platforms and headquarters for Moroccan opposition elements, while Morocco has been active in organizing guerrilla activities in Mauritania and neighboring Spanish Sahara. Until President Nkrumah was ousted in a *coup d'état* in 1966, Ghana had both party and governmental organizations charged with ideological and military training of opposition groups from Nigeria, Togoland, and the Ivory Coast. Ghana was seriously implicated in subversive attempts in both the Ivory Coast and Niger in the early 1960's. Until Premier Ben Bella's demise in 1965, the Algerian government served as perhaps the most well-organized and widespread center in Africa for financing, organizing, and training foreign nationals in the techniques of clandestine political action, subversion, and guerrilla warfare. Domestic plots and intrigues in which foreign African governments or parties have been involved thus have been and continue to be numerous. What has been distinctive about these efforts is their general ineffectiveness, which can be explained in part by lack of public support among target groups for externally-directed operations, political apathy, poor communications, and lack of experience and capabilities on the part of the sponsoring states.[3]

Extensive use of clandestine actions and direct military intervention as techniques of achieving objectives and promoting political values can be accounted for by at least five conditions widespread throughout the contemporary world. First, all the major powers—and some lesser states as well—have added to their traditional diplomatic bargaining techniques vast programs of military and economic assistance. Most of these programs, whether undertaken by a single state or by multilateral organizations such as the United Nations, affect the internal political, economic, and social development of the recipients. Often economic development cannot be achieved unless important political reforms are also implemented. This may require diplomatic pressures (by threats to withhold economic rewards) which obviously constitute interference in the internal affairs of the recipient. Sometimes foreign efforts to liberalize a regime may result in such political instability that the goal of economic development has to be forfeited. Where such problems confront the donor governments (and they appear in almost all military and economic aid programs), foreign diplomats seek to mold the internal development of a society in ways with no precedent in the eighteenth and nineteenth centuries. In some instances, governments use their large numbers of foreign aid personnel abroad to conduct propaganda, gather intelligence, and promote revolutionary or counter-revolutionary activities.

[3] For details, see I. William Zartman, *International Relations in the New Africa* (Englewood Cliffs, N.J.: Prentice-Hall, Inc., 1966), pp. 94–101.

Second, intervention is frequently *requested* by a regime in power or dissident groups seeking power. From the point of view of most policy-makers, states are composed of thousands of voluntary associations and of mass ethnic, economic, and political organizations, some of which may seek extra-national support to gain their ends. Local Communist parties have obtained funds, propaganda, training, and sometimes weapons from the Soviet Union or Communist China; ethnic minorities have sought outside assistance to help them achieve independence or a more favorable position in the state of which they are a part; groups of nationalists, such as the Algerians, obtained foreign assistance in their revolutions against colonial powers; cliques of military leaders have sought foreign support and diplomatic recognition prior to or during their attempt to seize power. Such dissident groups can be used by a foreign power for its own ends. It can intervene on behalf of the group, faction, or clique, and after it gains power, use its influence to secure foreign policy interests. Any unstable political order offers opportunities for external intervention. We can suggest the hypothesis that the greater ethnic, religious, economic, or ideological conflicts within a society, the greater the opportunities for foreign intervention through diplomatic interference, subversion, or invasion.

Third, political loyalties, which have traditionally extended to the predominant political institutions and authorities, whether clan, tribe, nation, or empire, sometimes are directed instead to external political entities or ideologies. In the seventeenth century, religious loyalties frequently superseded national or regional sentiments. Similarly, in the late eighteenth century, many European liberals welcomed French "liberation" even if it meant occupation by foreign troops and imposition of alien political institutions. Most people today accept the general proposition of primary loyalty to their own nation ("My country right or wrong"), but there are many exceptions among people who do not accept the legitimacy of a particular order under which they live. The quip that the French Communist Party is neither Right nor Left, but East, illustrates the existence of trans-national ideologies and loyalties directed essentially toward foreign states. This characteristic of modern politics naturally creates opportunities for foreign states, symbolizing these trans-national ideologies, to become involved in other nations' domestic politics.

Fourth, the current nuclear stalemate has apparently forced the major antagonists of the cold war into the sector of irregular warfare and subversion, where the possibility of uncontrolled military escalation is slight. Blatant military aggression to achieve external objectives may face both universal diplomatic condemnation in the United Nations and instant nuclear retaliation, while establishment of client regimes and satellite states through subversion and intervention may be sufficient to achieve some objectives at a minimum cost of national capabilities and resources, and with much lower risks.

Fifth, governments with revolutionary external objectives are naturally prone to use for foreign policy purposes the same kinds of techniques their leaders successfully employed in gaining domestic power. While on one level the French revolutionaries, Soviets, Nazis and others maintained "correct" diplomatic relations with foreign states, they simultaneously attempted to promote revolutionary activities against the social and political orders of those same states. Using race as the basis of political loyalty, Hitler proclaimed that a German's first duty was to the Third Reich, whether he lived in Austria, Czechoslovakia, or the United States. Communist governments have also spoken of "normalization of relations," "peaceful coexistence," and non-interference in other peoples' affairs, but their ideological pronouncements and domestic policy statements clearly reveal that when it is to their advantage, they will promote, organize, or support foreign revolutions and rebellious uprisings. In a Moscow speech of January 6, 1961, for example, former Premier Khrushchev asked rhetorically:

> What is the attitude of the Marxists toward such uprisings? A most positive one. These uprisings must not be identified with wars among states, with local wars, since in these uprisings the people are fighting for the implementation of their right for self-determination, for independent social and national development. These are uprisings against rotten reactionary regimes, against the colonizers. The Communists fully support such just wars and march in the front rank with the peoples waging liberation struggles.[4]

Liberation means that any group, no matter how small, which seeks to destroy existing institutions is qualified to receive commitments of Russian capabilities. In the case of Communist China, there has been not only moral and physical support for "wars of national liberation," but the clear expectation that the strategy of these revolutions would be based on the experience and practice of the Chinese Communist Party during its struggles prior to 1949. In view of such practices, any account of the foreign policies of revolutionary regimes would be particularly deficient were it limited to the plane of conventional diplomatic behavior—that is, to the granting of various political and economic rewards and threatening of punishments through recognized diplomatic personnel.

---

[4] Nikita Khrushchev's report on the world situation, in *Documents of the 22nd Congress of the CPSU*, Vol. I (New York: Cross Currents Press, 1961), pp. 29–30.

Many governments with revolutionary external objectives or doctrinal commitments have created a variety of extra-diplomatic agencies whose main functions are to dispense propaganda, organize agitation, train foreign revolutionaries, and direct subversion. Among the more prominent of these external-revolutionary organizations have been the Comintern, the Cominform, the German Gestapo, and various Soviet and Communist Chinese organizations and institutes which today have the function of providing revolutionary and ideological training for foreign Communist leaders. Though not concerned with doctrines of revolution, the Central Intelligence Agency of the United States has, as well, been involved in subversive activities abroad. These organizations sometimes play a major role in defining the objectives and techniques of states' foreign policies, and on occasion literally usurp the functions of more traditional diplomatic institutions. During the early 1920's, when the Soviet government was actively engaged in organizing and supporting revolutionary activities throughout Europe, a number of the most important foreign policy decisions were made within the organization of the Comintern. Soviet diplomats were frequently bypassed as intermediaries between the Soviet government and foreign groups, and had to remain content to deal with relatively unimportant aspects of Soviet foreign policy. In any event, the new revolutionary dimensions of foreign relations opened by the Bolsheviks required people with experience and outlook considerably different from that of professional diplomats. The directors of the Comintern and other external revolutionary organizations were primarily revolutionaries and agitators concerned with the mechanics of organizing violence and political support for doctrinal ends, not men engaged with such mundane matters as trade relations, diplomatic conferences, passports, and territorial treaties.[5]

Changes in the nature of political units, in the technological and social environment of the system, plus the five special conditions listed above, have had consequences not only in political and diplomatic processes but also in the norms which regulate these processes. Although the old rules concerning non-interference in internal affairs are still written into treaties and international charters, their observance in conflict situations is probably declining. The classical methods of exercising influence through quiet diplomacy, building up capabilities through alliances, offers of monetary or geographical rewards, or threats of military punishments no longer appear adequate tools for achieving all foreign policy objectives.

[5] See Theodore H. Von Laue, "Soviet Diplomacy: G. V. Chicherin, Peoples Commissar for Foreign Affairs, 1918–1930," in *The Diplomats, 1919–1939*, ed. Gordon A. Craig and Felix Gilbert (Princeton: Princeton University Press, 1953), pp. 234–81.

This is not to say that all governments indiscriminately interfere in their neighbors' affairs. States with a low level of involvement in the system and with stable political orders are less likely to be targets of external interference. In international relationships where persuasion and rewards are the traditional pattern of interaction—for example, in the relations between the United States and Great Britain, Australia and New Zealand, or the European states and Switzerland—external interference will be very slight. But when it does occur, protests are becoming less vigorous; intervention and certain types of clandestine political actions are not only expected but in many cases publicly condoned. In short, the relationship of the various forms of intervention to international law offers one example of how changes in an international system will produce modification of the official and unofficial rules which regulate interactions of states in that system.

It is almost impossible to give precise definitions of interference or intervention. Even international law, which generally prohibits attempts to change attitudes or behavior other than through formal government channels, fails to provide precise standards. Throughout the twentieth century nations have had to face the problem of political change ostensibly inspired by domestic forces but largely engineered by an external power. In addition to reasonably overt actions, where revolutionaries are trained, organized, and armed abroad, intervention may include propaganda, espionage, discriminatory trade policies, or support or denial of support to governments or their opposition in domestic crises where such foreign support might prove to be decisive. Experts do not wholly agree whether one government may give military and political support to another attempting to maintain itself against a possible or actual rebellion, or whether some kinds of economic and military assistance constitute intervention.[6] For example, does an American agreement to hold a summit conference with the Soviet Union and Great Britain constitute interference in British politics because, among other results, it might help raise the prestige of the Conservative Party? To the Labour Party, the American agreement might be so construed, but it would be difficult to prove that the American government agreed to attend a summit conference *primarily* to influence the outcome of the next British election. Was the Western democracies' decision not to intervene in the Spanish Civil War really non-intervention? It could be argued that by deciding *not* to intervene the democracies paved the way for General Franco's

[6] Louis Henkin, "Force, Intervention and Neutrality in Contemporary International Law," *Proceedings of the American Society of International Law* (April 1963), pp. 147–60.

victory.[7] Finally, how do we characterize an American program to help train foreign police in riot control techniques? Since riots and demonstrations are in some countries the most promising or only way to achieve political change, this type of training could be construed in some cases as aid designed to keep unpopular regimes in power. Many other controversial cases could be cited since they occur almost every day in modern international politics: no aid or trade program, military action, or important diplomatic communication can avoid having some impact on the public internal realm of other sovereign states. For our purposes, however, we will discuss six types of interference and intervention where there is little doubt that the activities are undertaken to influence the political and social processes of another country, *usually without the consent of the legitimate* (e.g., commonly recognized) *government*: (1) diplomatic interference, (2) clandestine political action, (3) demonstrations of force, (4) subversion, (5) guerrilla (unconventional) warfare, and (6) military intervention. Governments normally use combinations of these techniques simultaneously, but we shall keep them distinct in examining several cases below.

## Diplomatic Interference in Internal Affairs

Any time a diplomatic official publicly comments on the internal political processes (including foreign policy decisions) of another country, he is interfering in that country's internal affairs. Since attentive publics and government officials can be influenced by outside sources of information, there is always a temptation for foreign states or their diplomats to make unsolicited comments on the political affairs of other countries. Sometimes statements by ambassadors or government leaders regarding another state's domestic concerns are mere lapses in protocol; at other times, however, a discreet statement or threat may vitally affect the course of domestic events in a country. In 1954, Secretary of State Dulles threatened that the American government would have to undertake an "agonizing reappraisal" of its policy toward Europe if the French National Assembly did not vote to ratify the European Defense Community treaty. The statement was timed in such a way as to leave little doubt that Dulles hoped to swing a majority of the French parliamentarians behind the treaty. In another example ten years later, a heated debate occurred in Canada on the wisdom of accepting American nuclear arms on

[7] Manfred Halpern, *The Morality and Politics of Intervention* (New York: Council on Religion and International Affairs, 1962), p. 8.

Canadian territory, even if the arms were placed under control of the two governments. During parliamentary discussions in Ottawa, the Soviet ambassador to Canada released a note indicating that his government would look with "grave concern" on any Canadian decision to accept the nuclear arms. The Canadian government informed the ambassador that the debate was a domestic affair and that the Soviet government need not tell the Canadians what they should do.

Although the Soviet government has signed numerous treaties which include clauses prohibiting interference in other nations' internal affairs, it has frequently violated these obligations and displayed particularly acute sensitivity to the domestic politics of neighboring states. We have already recounted how the Soviet government cut off trade relations with Finland when a cabinet not to its liking was established in Helsinki during 1958. In 1962 the Soviet government again violated its pledges of non-interference by seeking through various threats to influence the outcome of the Finnish presidential election. At a diplomatic reception, former Premier Khrushchev frankly revealed his own interpretation of diplomatic non-interference:

> We understand that in various Finnish circles there are different opinions toward the Soviet Union, that there are those who hold a grudge and warn [the Finns] to be on guard against us. But try to understand that in such circumstances we too have to be on guard. You have parties in which there are representatives that do not favor friendly relations with the Soviet Union. . . . You might declare that this is your own internal affair. Naturally these are the internal affairs of the [Finnish] political parties. We recognize this. But to me, as a neighbor, it is not at all a matter of indifference what policy toward the U.S.S.R. this or that party's representatives choose to follow. . . . Naturally we do not wish to interfere in your internal affairs, but I believe we can express our opinions about certain individuals' position toward the U.S.S.R.[8]

A final example of diplomatic interference involving economic techniques of influence illustrates the problems confronting governments dispensing aid to nations managed by unrepresentative and unresponsive regimes. In this and many other post-war cases aid could not achieve its objectives unless political reforms were instituted—but the recipient governments were unwilling or unable to make the necessary reforms. When Greece became a participant in the European Recovery Program (Marshall Program), its government was commonly recognized to be dominated by wealthy landlords, aristocrats, and industrialists whose

[8] Quoted in Kalevi J. Holsti, "Strategy and Techniques of Influence in Soviet-Finnish Relations," *The Western Political Quarterly*, XVII (1964), 76–77.

economic, taxation, and fiscal policies cancelled out many of the gains made by the influx of American aid. National administration was ridden with graft and corruption, and despite the efforts of American auditors, some aid money went into the pockets of politicians and administrators. In these circumstances the American ambassador in Athens made representations for reforms, threatening to cut down the amount of aid if they were not implemented. Included in his proposals were such unpopular but necessary measures as curtailed government spending and subsidies, and enforcement of a revised tax program. American pressures were instrumental in bringing down one cabinet which had not been willing to institute such reforms. Several months later the United States announced a cut of $67 million in the aid program, a step which finally prompted another Greek government to put into effect some of the suggested policies. Two years later, in 1952, political obstacles to effective aid administration still existed. One block was the system for electing representatives to the Greek parliament, a system which discriminated strongly against certain political parties. The American ambassador in Athens, John Puerifoy (whom we will meet again in the Guatemalan episode), publicly condemned the electoral law and called upon the Greeks to institute a system which would return parliamentarians more favorable to the United States.[9] It is not known whether the staff in the American embassy actually drafted model amendments to the electoral law, but the Greek government did respond to Puerifoy's criticisms. One can sympathize with the motives of the American diplomats; the only other alternative courses would have been to cut off the aid program entirely or continue seeing it hampered by poor administration and political instability. Nevertheless, the American action was a clear violation of the rules of non-interference.

## Clandestine Political Action

Probably the oldest technique of interference in other countries' internal affairs is the offering of bribes. In the eighteenth century, granting monetary rewards to foreign diplomats and government officials was a typical means of achieving diplomatic objectives. It was the accepted custom (though not publicized) to pay another dynast's foreign minister or diplomats a "pension," that is, a bribe, for performance of certain services or maintenance of certain attitudes on key issues of the day.

[9] These events are discussed in Ernst B. Haas and Allen S. Whiting, *Dynamics of International Relations* (New York: McGraw-Hill Book Company, 1956), pp. 234–38.

Documents from the French court of Louis XV reveal that between 1757 and 1769 France subsidized Austrian statesmen by over 82 million livres.[10] In some of the cases cited below, American secret political action abroad probably included bribery, or at least the subsidy of subversive agents; British and French agents in the nineteenth century frequently gained control of future colonies by bribing native political leaders; and, of course, Nazi and Communist financing of clandestine political action in foreign countries is well documented.

Dissemination of covert propaganda—through unidentified radio transmitters, underground newspapers, or leaflets of unclear origin—can also be classified as clandestine political action which attempts to influence internal political processes in the interests of a foreign government. American propaganda in the crucial Italian elections of 1948, for example, was not always clearly identified, and various other American actions on behalf of the Christian Democratic Party were of a clandestine nature.

Alexandr Kaznacheev, a Soviet diplomat who defected in Rangoon, has revealed some of the methods his government used to influence domestic political affairs in Burma. In addition to giving directions and helping finance the underground Burmese Communist Party, the Soviet embassy in Rangoon would "plant" stories in the Burmese press and sometimes blackmail politicians. One of Kaznacheev's jobs in the Soviet embassy was to translate into English copies of articles which he received from Soviet intelligence agencies in Moscow. These articles would describe supposed American complicity in various campaigns of subversion in Asian countries (some were reasonably accurate, others pure fabrication), others contained generally anti-American materials. Soviet intelligence officials in Burma would then arrange through local agents to have the articles published in Burmese newspapers, especially pro-Communist publications. The newspaper would translate the article into the native language and sign it as coming from one of its "Special Correspondents" abroad. Thus a story conceived in Moscow became publicly identified as the testimony of on-the-spot reporters.[11]

Of the less savory methods, one was for the Russian diplomats to send anonymous letters—usually composed in Moscow—to local politicians, including accusations or scandalous material about these figures' political rivals. The purpose of these communications was to create distrust between party factions and between parties, and occasionally to disgrace

[10] Hans Morgenthau, "A Political Theory of Foreign Aid," *The American Political Science Review*, LVI (1962), 302
[11] Alexandr Kaznacheev, *Inside a Soviet Embassy* (Philadelphia: J. B. Lippincott Co., 1962), p. 172.

through scandal politicians whom Soviet intelligence agents wanted to have removed from prominent places in Burmese public life.[12]

Clandestine political action may also include assassination of government officials, diplomats, party leaders, or economic elites. Though assassination is not a prevalent form of interfering in a country's affairs, foreign governments occasionally finance or encourage local dissident elements who are willing to do the job.[13]

## Demonstrations of Force

One of the traditionally effective techniques of intervention—with low risks and costs—is to display or threaten to use force either to help or hinder a domestic rebellion in a foreign country. Two examples of forceful demonstrations—both by the United States—suggest that this technique may be more suitable than actually sending in troops or in other ways becoming physically involved in a domestic dispute. In 1957 pro-Western King Hussein of Jordan faced mounting internal strife against his regime. The opposition to Hussein was not of a purely local origin. Both the Egyptian and Syrian governments had directed anti-Hussein propaganda campaigns in Jordan, urging dissident elements in the society and government to overthrow the king and lead their nation to membership in the United Arab Republic. These governments were also involved in the activities of raiders and terrorists who infiltrated into Jordan from Egyptian and Syrian territory. According to a Jordanian diplomat's account, pro-Egyptian elements in the Jordanian government, led by the Prime Minister, received instructions from President Nasser of Egypt to prepare for the assault on the monarch.[14] But Hussein acted vigorously to save his throne and the independence of his country. He imposed martial law, arrested hundreds of oppositionists, and forced the resignation of pro-Nasser elements in the cabinet. The king simultaneously hinted that he would welcome American intervention to help him save the regime. The Eisenhower administration, never sympathetic

[12] Kaznacheev, *Inside a Soviet Embassy*, p. 170.

[13] It seems to be an unwritten rule of modern international politics—particularly in countries with a Western tradition—that assassination of leaders of hostile states is not an acceptable manner of settling conflicts or achieving objectives. Even Hitler attempted only one assassination (the Austrian Chancellor, Dollfuss, in 1934) of a government leader; it is surprising, moreover, that during World War II Allied leaders never became enthusiastic supporters of the German underground's plots on Hitler's life.

[14] United Nations, General Assembly, Third Emergency Special Session, *Official Records*, A/PV 375, August 14, 1958, p. 25.

to Nasser's designs for Arab unity, responded under the Eisenhower doctrine (Secretary of State Dulles claimed that Hussein was threatened by "international communism") by sending warnings to the Middle Eastern states not to use force against Jordan, and by ordering the American Sixth Fleet to sail for Lebanon. Several days later a number of vessels containing 1,800 Marines were anchored in Beirut harbor, close to Syria and Jordan, ready to intervene on behalf of the young king if necessary. Although only limited Egyptian intervention on behalf of the rebels might have brought down Hussein, the American show of force effectively dissuaded Nasser from conducting the final operation.

In 1961 a similar demonstration of force prevented supporters of the deposed Trujillo dictatorship from overturning the newly established provisional regime in the Dominican Republic. Throughout November rumors had circulated in Santo Domingo that Trujillo's three sons (one of whom was Commander-in-Chief of the Dominican Forces) were ready to launch an assault on the provisional government, whereupon the United States sent 22 warships to patrol off the Dominican shore. The provisional government had not asked for this show of force, but later acknowledged that the American action had prompted the Trujillos to flee the Dominican Republic and averted a *coup d'état* and possible civil war.

### Subversion

The term "subversion" has graced almost any rebellious activity in a country, but the distinguishing feature of subversion is that it is organized, supported, and/or directed by a foreign power, using for its own purposes the disaffected elements in a society. Open displays of propaganda by a foreign power would not constitute subversion unless the displays were related to a systematic campaign to help an indigenous rebel group seize power. One of the recent problems of Western policymakers relates to this distinction: is a revolt against an established regime truly serving the interests of the local population or rebels, or is it promoted abroad basically to serve the interests of a foreign power? Where to draw the line is extremely difficult because almost every revolution today involves some external power. The major Western powers have generally viewed *any* connection between a rebel movement and a Communist state as evidence of Communist subversion. The modern techniques of subversion can be illustrated by describing briefly how Nazi Germany, the Soviet Union, and the United States have enlisted and aided dissident elements in foreign countries to overthrow constituted regimes or pave the way for an outright military assault on the target state.

## Nazi Subversion of Czechoslovakia, 1938–1939

The main target of Nazi subversion of Czechoslovakia was the 3.5 million German-speaking Czechs living in the Sudetenland. Shortly after the Nazi revolution, some Sudeten Germans organized a political party (SDP—Sudeten German Party) under the leadership of Konrad Henlein. In his early political career Henlein professed no desire to turn his party into an agency for carrying out Hitler's plans to take over Czechoslovakia. In a 1935 speech he specifically declared that the German minority in Czechoslovakia would seek to protect its rights and interests only by cooperating with the Czech government and people.[15] Less than seven years later Henlein boasted publicly of the role that he and his party had played in subverting Czechoslovakia for Nazi Germany. He pointed out that his party, with the support of many Sudetenland Germans, had so completely destroyed internal stability, and created so much confusion throughout Czechoslovakia, that the entire country became "ripe for liquidation," according to Hitler's plans. He attributed his success to having turned 3.5 million Sudetenlanders into 3.5 million National Socialists.[16]

Henlein's first step in preparing for eventual Nazi "liquidation" of the Czech nation was to mobilize the Sudeten Germans, many of whom were neither Nazis nor pro-German, to his cause. He accomplished this objective by deliberately provoking incidents with Czech authorities, whose reprisals led the Sudeten Germans to believe that they were being persecuted as a minority. The SDP held mass public meetings, circulated manifestos demanding "rights" for the German minority, and issued false or exaggerated propaganda stories about Czech political outrages against the Sudeten Germans. Once a split within the society was achieved through propaganda, it was exacerbated by giving the militant side a feeling of insecurity—in this case by claiming that the Sudeten Germans had to remain vigilant lest they be completely destroyed as a distinct nationality by the Czechs. Social perceptions of threat rose to such a high level that political compromise became unacceptable and was, of course, discouraged by the subversive party. Moreover, the Henleinists systematically penetrated Sudeten German social and cultural groups and purged their leadership of anti-Nazi or Czech sympathizers. By 1938 an impor-

[15] Vincent Urban, *Hitler's Spearhead* (London: Trinity Press, n.d.), p. 16.
[16] *Ibid.*, p. 17.

tant part of the German population in Czechoslovakia had become not only anti-Czech, but pro-Nazi as well.

Because some Sudetenlanders, particularly in rural areas, were reluctant to give their support to the SDP, the party also indulged in kidnapping and terrorism. The campaign—which was executed by a corps similar to the German SS, called the Freiwilliger Schutzdienst (FS) —was directed both against uncooperative Germans and innocent Czechs. The terror against the Czechs naturally caused reprisals which permitted the Henleinists to charge the Czechs with further "atrocities" against the Sudeten Germans. While Henlein's party was active in its work of propaganda, infiltration, and terror, its leaders simultaneously wore a mask of political respectability by entering into formal negotiations with the Czech government to seek "honorable" guarantees for the rights of the Sudetenlanders.

Throughout 1937, ethnic divisions in Czechoslovakia widened as the SDP continued to manufacture incidents and incite its followers to acts of violence. During the year, moreover, Nazi support of the SDP became increasingly obvious. By 1938 it was also apparent to the Czech government—if not to foreign diplomats—that Henlein and the Nazis did not wish any real accommodation, but sought only to create a situation which would warrant German diplomatic and military intervention and ultimate cession of the Sudetenland to Germany. On August 6, 1938, Henlein released a fateful order to his followers, inviting them to organize a series of violent acts which would give Nazi Germany an excuse for intervening. His own attempt to seize power one month later failed and he was forced to flee to the Third Reich. Now without leadership in the SDP, German intervention had to proceed openly. As clashes between Czechs and Sudeten Germans increased in violence and frequency, causing repressive action by the Czech army, Hitler began a series of propaganda broadcasts throughout Europe which sought through vitriolic language and gross exaggeration to create the impression that the Sudeten Germans were indeed the subject of systematic persecution. Using a combination of military invasion threats against Czechoslovakia and reasoned appeals for "peace" against the Western governments, Hitler through the Munich settlement eventually annexed the Sudetenland to Germany; Czechoslovakia was left a rump state without viable military defenses.

German subversion and threats of military intervention did not end with the triumph at Munich. The Nazi government fostered a Slovak independence movement, using many of the subversive techniques that Henlein and the Austrian Nazis had already found successful in Vienna and the Sudetenland. In March, 1939, the Slovaks under German direction declared their independence from the Czechs. The Nazi press continued to accuse the Czechs of violence against Slovaks and declared that the lives of Germans still living in the Czech state were in danger. With the Wehrmacht poised and ready to march into what remained of Czechoslavakia, Hitler forced the unfortunate Czech president to sign a proclamation entrusting the remainder of his country to German "protection."

Thus, the Nazis and the SDP exploited ethnic divisions within the Czechoslovakian nation and brought them to the point of violence, offering a pretext for German diplomatic intervention, threats of invasion, and acts of terrorism. Although the SDP and its paramilitary SF organized and conducted most of the infiltration, propaganda, and terror, the Nazi government of Germany made the major policy decisions on the strategy of subversion. Henlein maintained contact with Himmler's SS through a German liaison officer in Czechoslovakia, and his lieutenants frequently travelled to Germany to attend festivals, fairs, and competitions where they were exhorted and instructed by Nazi officials in the techniques of subversion.[17] Henlein himself agreed in March, 1938, to coordinate and clear all policy with the German Foreign Office and submit all public statements (e.g., commands to his followers) to the Germans for approval. The Nazi government also supplied money and weapons to the FS for conducting its campaign of terror and intimidation, while members of the Gestapo occasionally crossed the frontier into Czechoslovakia to kidnap Czech citizens. Throughout the period the German government also released an avalanche of propaganda directed at three distinct targets: (1) the Sudeten Germans, to rally them behind the SDP and against the Czechs, (2) the Czechs, to undermine their morale, and (3) at other European countries to create the impression that Germany was intervening only to safeguard the rights of a minority. Finally, the German government took advantage of the violence in Czechoslovakia to threaten military intervention. Czechoslovakia did not collapse, then, solely through Henlein's activities. Subversion was used to create conditions which gave the Germans a pretext for threatening and finally carrying out annexation and military invasion.

## Communist Subversion of Czechoslovakia

After Czechoslovakia was carved up by the Nazis, most Czech party and government leaders fled either to London or Moscow. As a result of the Nazi-Soviet pact of August, 1939, Communist Party leaders remaining

[17] United States Department of State, Chief Counsel for the Prosecution of Axis Criminality, *Nazi Conspiracy and Aggression*, I (Washington, D.C.: Government Printing Office, 1946), 544, 546.

in Czechoslovakia at first cooperated with German occupation authorities, but after the German invasion of the Soviet Union in June, 1941, went underground and helped lead the anti-Nazi resistance movement. Although the underground Communists displayed bravery and effective activity against the Nazis, their record was not altogether enviable, for they attempted as well to discredit liberal resistance groups—sometimes even by leaking information on their membership to the Gestapo. A number of Communist leaders also went to Moscow to receive training and later returned to Czechoslovakia with orders to dispose of future non-Communist leaders.[18]

Nevertheless, formal diplomatic relations among the exile government of Eduard Beneš in London, the Czech Communist leaders who resided in Moscow during the war, and the Soviet government, remained cordial. In December, 1943, Stalin signed a Treaty of Friendship, Mutual Aid, and Positive Cooperation with the Beneš government. Klement Gottwald, one of the Czech Communist leaders in Moscow, also agreed with the exile government in London that pending establishment of a constitutional and freely elected government in Prague after the end of the war, all parties would work together to create "National Committees" to administer Czech territory as it was liberated from the Germans.

The National Committees were established in accordance with the agreement. But since it was the Soviet Red Army which liberated Czechoslovakia, the committees contained mostly trained Communists who came in to administer the territory after Russian troops had cleared it of Germans. These agents also flooded the zone of military operations with propaganda and agitation and marked non-Communist local leaders (some had collaborated with the Germans) for eventual liquidation. By early 1945, thanks to the Red Army, the Communists had created local strongholds from which they could begin operating as a legitimate political party and simultaneously infiltrate and gain control of social groups. Moreover, the Party enjoyed unprecedented popularity, for it was identified among many Czechs with the Soviet Union, which had liberated Czechoslovakia from the Nazis—while the Allies had abandoned the Czechs in 1938—and with a record of bravery as an underground partisan movement during the Nazi occupation.

Thus, when exile Czech leaders met in Moscow to decide the composition of the provisional government, the Communists possessed a basis of both organization and national prestige for their claims to important cabinet positions. The several portfolios they received were the most

---

[18] Josef Korbel, *The Communist Subversion of Czechoslovakia, 1938–1948* (Princeton: Princeton University Press, 1959), p. 59.

important for infiltrating and gaining control over the state's instruments of communication and coercion. The Communists took over the ministries of Interior (which controlled the court system and police), Agriculture, Schools, and Propaganda. A Communist sympathizer was named Minister of Defense.[19]

Communist subversion of Czechoslovakia culminated in the seizure of power in February, 1948. To prepare for the *coup d'état,* party leaders and cadres operated on two levels. Using their organizational base in the National Committees, local administration, and important government ministries, they systematically infiltrated and gained control of major economic and social voluntary associations. They simultaneously worked as a traditional political party in parliament, initiating and lending their weight to popular reform measures and conducting party propaganda which emphasized democracy, Czech nationalism, and social reform rather than revolution or dictatorship of the proletariat.

On the more clandestine level the Communists first gained control over the media of mass communication through which they could make their promises and sell a program to the people. Even before the war had ended the Red Army donated captured German printing presses to Czech Communists, and as early as 1945 the Ministry of Information (with the probable assistance of Soviet propaganda experts) started publishing dailies, weeklies, and monthlies disguised as organs of trade unions and other voluntary associations. By 1947 only members of the Czech Journalists' Union (Communist-controlled) were permitted employment as editors of newspapers. Non-Communist editors were either suspended or forced to retire by the Communist-controlled typesetters' union. Communist and pro-Communist ministers were given access to the national radio network as often as they desired, while other party leaders were limited to perfunctory appearances. The media of mass communication and the bogus journals were constantly used to extoll the Soviet Union and the Czech Communist Party and to embarrass non-Communist leaders.[20] Propaganda was also used to heighten social tension, and alter and control the behavior of non-Communists by changing their images of facts and values. In the Czech Communist propaganda, the Soviet Union became the symbol of anti-Fascism and liberation, the Communist Party assumed the mantle of progressive democracy and social justice, while all other parties and business classes were pictured as Nazi collaborationists.

A number of techniques were used to gain control of administrative

---

[19] Vratislav Busek and Nicolas Spulber, eds., *Czechoslovakia* (New York: Frederick A. Praeger, Publisher, Inc., 1957), p. 432.

[20] Rudolf Sturm, "Propaganda," in *Czechoslovakia,* ed. Busek and Spulber, pp. 107–13.

organs. For example, Communist ministers already in the government employed vast numbers of comrades, then recommended economy programs in which they released thousands of non-Communist civil servants. The army, too, was effectively neutralized. "Unreliable" officers were purged and their places filled by Communists or their sympathizers. The General Staff as well as the Directorate of Defense Intelligence passed into Communist hands, while political officers—patterned after the political commissars of the Red Army—systematically indoctrinated Czech troops. The Ministry of Interior organized a National Security Corps, an armed body of party adherents, and Provincial Security Departments (ZOB), both of which were staffed with reliable personnel.[21] It was one of the functions of these intelligence networks to identify all potential and actual anti-Communist leaders and subject them to various forms of intimidation. Finally, the party infiltrated the most important agricultural, labor, women's, and intellectual groups, or copied the pre-war pattern of Nazi subversion in Austria and formed various "front" organizations whose close connections to the Communist Party were not revealed. By capturing leadership in the country's most important voluntary associations and by creating "front" organizations, the Communists added an even broader base from which to disseminate propaganda and agitate among the people. Their control or major role in these organizations also helped create additional prestige for the party, and afforded them a large amount of favorable publicity.

As a parliamentary organization the Party was no less effective. In the 1946 elections it won the largest proportion of votes (38 per cent), and in alliance with other parties was able to introduce and pass social reform legislation which further increased its popularity throughout the country. Small landholders and tenant farmers, for example, delivered thousands of votes to the Communists after receiving land under agricultural reform legislation. The Communist Party, even though it had no parliamentary majority, was able to dominate the legislative branch of the government for almost three years. It enjoyed this position by creating a three-layered parliamentary alliance which it directed much as a holding company controls several nominally independent corporations. First, it entered into an alliance with the Social Democratic Party—the "Marxist Bloc"—in which it made most policy decisions by virtue of its numerical superiority. This alliance was then amalgamated into a "Socialist Bloc" of all Marxist and non-Marxist socialist parties. Finally, the Socialist Bloc

[21] Andrew C. Janos, *The Seizure of Power: A Study of Force and Popular Consent* (Princeton: Center for International Studies, Research Monograph No. 16, 1964), pp. 33–34.

represented a majority in the "National Front" which governed the country without serious opposition.[22]

By the end of 1947 Communist popularity began to wane as an increasing number of non-Communists were removed from important political and social positions and Party leaders resorted increasingly to blackmail, terror, brutality, and intimidation against the opposition.[23] The Party feared that in the elections scheduled for March, 1948, it would suffer a serious electoral defeat. Even so, the ground had been prepared carefully for the final seizure of power. The state's instruments of coercion were either neutralized or pro-Communist; most media of communication were firmly under the direction of the Party; and some of society's most important voluntary organizations could be relied upon to support a *coup d'état*. The crisis came in the winter of 1948. Communist cabinet ministers precipitated a serious government stalemate in Prague which forced several non-Communist ministers to resign. Klement Gottwald, the leader of the Communist Party in the government, called upon workers to demonstrate, and the Ministry of Interior exhorted other public spirited groups to send protests to President Beneš. The National Security Corps was ready to lead an insurrection, and in some districts workers were armed. In others, groups of workers took over factories and transportation facilities. Party and government agents conducted mass arrests of anti-Communists, while special "Action Committees" gained control of the main government administrative offices. Beneš was forced to accept a Communist-dominated cabinet under Gottwald's leadership. It only remained for the Communist-dominated cabinet and ministries to consolidate their power throughout the land. Most political parties were banned, many non-Communist political leaders jailed, and the most important symbols and institutions associated with the democratic regime destroyed. Czechoslovakia's foreign minister, Jan Masaryk, long a popular figure identified with his father's struggle for Czech independence from Austria, committed suicide—though many claim he was murdered by the Communists. With this tragedy, liberal democracy came formally to an end in Czechoslovakia.

We have defined subversion as a series of essentially clandestine actions undertaken by one state, enlisting some citizens abroad through propaganda, infiltration, and terror to overthrow the established regime in their own country. Wasn't the seizure of power in Czechoslovakia really a domestic Communist revolution? It will be years before the role of the

[22] Vlatislav Chalupa, *The Rise and Development of a Totalitarian State* (Leyden: H. E. Stenfert Kroese, 1959), p. 85.
[23] Korbel, *The Communist Subversion of Czechoslovakia*, pp. 185–87.

Soviet party and government in the Czech subversion is fully revealed, but some facts are already established with reasonable confidence. First, although the operational details of subversion were locally planned and executed, the main strategy—which had started as early as 1941—was formulated throughout the period in Moscow. Second, during the war hundreds of Czech Communists were trained in the Soviet Union to prepare the ground for the seizure of power. Third, in 1944 the Red Army played a major role in establishing the National Committees, liquidating Czech anti-Communists, and donating money, arms, and printing presses exclusively to Communist agents—all in violation of the 1943 treaty in which the Soviet government had sworn not to interfere in the internal affairs of Czechoslovakia. Fourth, every time the Beneš government attempted to resist Communist demands after the war, the Red Army would begin "maneuvers" on the Czech frontiers to intimidate non-Communist political leaders. Similar to the events of 1938, the Czech government faced an organized rebellion at home as well as the threat of external intervention. Finally, it is probably no coincidence that the Soviet Deputy Foreign Minister arrived and remained in Prague during the week of the seizure of power.[24] His exact role in the *coup d'état* has not been revealed through published documentary evidence, but most Western and former Czech authorities claim that he was not in Prague merely to offer a gift of Russian wheat to the Czechs, as the Communists claim. Soviet presence in Czechoslovakia and in the background was an important factor in the collapse of Czechoslovakia's post-war democratic government.

## American Subversion in Guatemala, 1954

Although the United States had engaged sporadically in clandestine political action during Middle Eastern revolutions and counter-revolutions in the early 1950's, the first acknowledged example of systematic American subversion occurred in Guatemala in 1954 after the regime of Captain Jacobo Arbenz had become increasingly identified with the Guatemalan Communist Party. Few government documents of the American role in Guatemala have been published, but most accounts agree on the following facts. Originally, Arbenz was not a Communist, but his vigorous reform programs, particularly in agriculture, met deter-

[24] See Ivo Duchacek, "The February Coup in Czechoslovakia," *World Politics*, II (1950), 511–33.

mined opposition for the church, large landowners, and the United Fruit Company, which owned almost one half million acres and the main railroad and port in Guatemala. Arbenz' support came mostly from peasants, workers, and particularly the local Communist Party. He managed to keep the support of the army by granting numerous honors and favors to loyal officers. He maintained, at first, a regime of unfettered civil liberties, which meant that the Communist Party was free to pursue its recruiting and organizing activities. In the late 1940's (under President Arevalo) and early 1950's (under Arbenz), the Party organized the workers of the country, gained control of some of the media of communication, and turned them into propaganda organs for the Party. Guatemalan foreign policy statements, perhaps reflecting Arbenz' need to maintain Communist support, became increasingly anti-American and pro-Soviet.

Late in 1952 the American government responded, partly to press the claims of the United Fruit Company against Guatemalan expropriation of its property, and also to try to break up the close association between Arbenz and the Guatemalan Communists. In October, 1953, the Eisenhower administration sent John Puerifoy, former ambassador to Greece, to serve as the American envoy and keep in touch with certain officials of the CIA in Guatemala. It also placed an embargo on the sale of arms to the Arbenz regime. On the diplomatic front Secretary of State Dulles attempted to alert other Latin American countries to Arbenz' increasingly pro-Soviet and pro-Communist politics. At the Tenth International Conference of American States, after much oral persuasion combined with offers of increased economic aid, Dulles obtained Latin American acquiescence to a document (the "Caracas Declaration") which declared that "the domination or control of the political institutions of any American state by the international Communist movement" would constitute a threat to the American states and would require "appropriate action." Armed with this implicit Latin American sanction for U.S. intervention, the American government moved to bring down the Arbenz regime. In this case the instrument of subversion was a group of anti-Communist Guatemalan exiles whose members had gathered in neighboring Honduras and Nicaragua. They had chosen as their leader a former Guatemalan army officer, Carlos Castillo Armas. Though no documentation is yet available, there is little doubt that Armas' group received arms and financial support from the United States. In April, 1954, the United States signed a treaty to deliver new arms to the Nicaraguan government, which in turn probably turned over its old weapons to Armas. The Armas group, perhaps with the help of American officials, also set up "Radio Liberation" on the Guatemalan-Honduran border to incite a rebellion against Arbenz.

American propaganda against the Arbenz regime was also directed throughout Latin and Central America.

Seeing the mounting pressure at home and abroad against his regime, Arbenz turned to the Soviet bloc for aid. He purchased 2,000 tons of weapons from Czechoslovakia—which made his country the strongest military power in Central America—to maintain the loyalty of the army and arm the workers and peasants in case he needed them to fend off a rebellion. He also began a reign of terror and imprisoned hundreds of his political opponents. After the CIA discovered the shipment of arms, the United States quickly signed a Military Aid Agreement with Honduras. To dramatize the agreement the American government airlifted the matériel to its destination. Some of these arms may also have gone to the Armas forces, which finally crossed the frontier into Guatemala on June 18, 1954.

Even if the United States had supplied Armas with military equipment, it was old-fashioned and of a limited quantity. Armas' men could not hope to overthrow the Arbenz regime without winning the support of the Guatemalan army, for as is usual in Guatemalan politics, the army ultimately determines the fate of any political regime. When confronted with Armas' puny invasion force, it could not decide whether to defend Arbenz or aid the rebels.

Meanwhile, Arbenz had appealed to the United Nations and claimed, with justification, that Honduras had violated international law by permitting Armas' rebels to organize and arm on its territory. Arbenz' appeal had the misfortune of going to Henry Cabot Lodge, American ambassador to the United Nations, who also happened to be President of the Security Council for the month of June. Lodge was able to stall deliberations in the Security Council for almost one week while the Guatemalan army vacillated. He used the legitimate excuse that the Security Council could not act while an investigating commission from the Organization of American States was looking for facts in Guatemala. After eight days the leadership of the Guatemalan army decided to throw in with the rebels. The military maintained control of the 2,000 tons of Communist weapons and refused to let Arbenz arm the workers and peasants. Under army pressure Arbenz resigned as president and eventually left the country. Ambassador Puerifoy played an important role in these events, reporting to Washington on developments in Arbenz' government and maintaining contacts with opposition elements. He was also active in negotiations which led to establishment of an army junta, headed by Armas, to govern the country.

After the relatively bloodless *coup d'état* was completed, the OAS ended its investigation and the episode was forgotten until 1957, when

Armas was assassinated by a disgruntled politician.[25] The United States had, however, succeeded in its objective: through diplomacy the American government effectively isolated Guatemala from the rest of Central America and prevented Soviet intervention; Armas and his followers constituted a convenient group with similar objectives whose actions gave the episode the appearance of a typical Latin American *coup d'état;* and the United States was influential in determining the complexion of the new regime. American subversion in Guatemala—and later in Laos and other nations—differed significantly from Nazi and Soviet subversion. Each government which used this instrument of policy seems to have its own particular "style" of subversive activity.

Two stages characterize the process of totalitarian subversion: (1) the *preparatory stage* in which the Nazis and Communists brought existing local parties under their direction, and through the processes of exploiting social tensions, liquidating opposition, infiltrating major centers of power and the state's apparatus of coercion, finally (2) created a government crisis and *seized power completely.* The Germans and Russians gave moral, fiscal, and material support during both stages and threatened to intervene to help the rebels.[26]

American subversion has displayed different characteristics. It has usually been motivated by a desire to forestall an imminent Communist take-over or help put into power dissident factions or military groups which promised to promote resolutely anti-Communist policies. Whatever other domestic concerns they have had has been of less interest to the United States.[27] American subversive techniques emphasize dissemination of anti-Communist propaganda among a few key targets (whereas the Communists and Nazis always emphasized a happy future state of affairs and a positive program) and the purchase of cooperation from political or military groups through offers of economic aid and future diplomatic and

[25] These events are discussed in Donald Grant, "Guatemala and United States Foreign Policy," *Journal of International Affairs*, IX (1955), 64–72; John D. Martz, *Communist Infiltration in Guatemala* (New York: Vintage Press, 1956); and Philip B. Taylor Jr., "The Guatemalan Affair: A Critique of United States Foreign Policy," *American Political Science Review*, L (1956), 787–806.

[26] Janos suggests that effective infiltration of the instruments of power in a democracy is only possible where the legitimate government faces external coercion. Janos, *The Seizure of Power*, p. 35. Stalin admitted that communism failed in Italy and France after World War II because the Red Army was not near those countries to help foment a revolution. See Elliot Goodman, *The Soviet Design for a World State* (New York: Columbia University Press, 1959), p. 311. In Finland, however, when the Communists attempted to seize power in 1948, there was no threat of Soviet military intervention, although Russian troops were quartered only 15 miles from Helsinki. The planned *coup d'état* failed because an important Communist official at the last moment warned state authorities of the plot.

[27] Halpern, *The Morality and Politics of Intervention*, p. 21.

military support. While the objective of Nazi and Soviet subversion was to create a "new order" involving social revolutions and establishment of client regimes, American policies have usually aimed at maintaining or placing in power a government of almost any political complexion as long as it was sufficiently anti-Communist. The Communists and Nazis have followed a pattern of active promotion of their long-range foreign policy goals through subversion, whereas the United States has used subversive techniques primarily to protect and safeguard already existing security and economic interests.[28]

Another important difference is that American officials have usually worked through ruling groups or dissident factions whose activities seldom affected the mass of society directly. The totalitarians, on the other hand, have attempted to influence the attitudes and behavior of a portion of each stratum and organization in society in order to give the appearance of popular support. American clandestine action has not promoted violence between ethnic, religious, and class groups, or attempted in any way to create what the Communists call a "revolutionary situation." Thus, the main difference between American and totalitarian subversion is between the promotion and support of violent social upheaval, capped by a transfer of power and establishment of satellite states, and the attempt to safeguard security interests through supporting or changing a few key government personnel, but without completely impairing or subjugating a state's independence.

## Guerrilla (Unconventional) Warfare

As the focus of the cold war has shifted from Europe to Asia, Africa, and Latin America, guerrilla warfare has supplanted some of the conventional techniques of subversion discussed above. This type of revolutionary activity, which combines terror with mobile guerrilla attacks, was used extensively in Yugoslavia and other occupied countries during World War II, and has since occurred in more than 15 countries. Of course not all guerrilla operations have been organized, supported, or directed by an outside power. Some of the longest and most tragic unconventional military operations have been purely domestic affairs, as in Colombia, where internal strife with characteristics of guerrilla warfare has killed several hundred thousand people over the last two decades. Successful guerrilla campaigns in Cyprus, China, and Cuba were basically internal

[28] S. N. Bjelajac, "Unconventional Warfare: American and Soviet Approaches," *The Annals of the American Academy of Political and Social Science,* CCCXLI (1962), 80.

rebellions conducted with a minimum of external interference. In South-east Asia, however, North Vietnam and Communist China have played major roles in organizing, training, and leading "national liberation" movements operating in Malaya, South Vietnam, Laos, Thailand, and Malaysia. This area offers particularly attractive conditions for guerrilla operations, including dense jungles and marshes in which troops can hide, a predominately rural population often cut off from direct influence from the central government, undeveloped communication facilities between villages and urban centers, and long unprotected frontiers which permit easy infiltration and supply of matériel from the "active sanctuary" (the country promoting the unconventional warfare). The romantic and ideological inspiration for guerrilla operations originated from Mao Tse-tung and the Chinese Communists who, unlike their Western comrades, who were concerned primarily with subversion and infiltration in an urban setting, engaged in protracted rural guerrilla warfare before achieving power. Because of the different environmental and historical traditions, subversion as practiced in Europe and unconventional warfare as practiced in Asia have been basically different means of gaining power and achieving foreign policy objectives.

Guerrilla units, for example, do not wait for a "revolutionary situation" to develop before they begin direct assaults on the state and society. Nor do they necessarily infiltrate voluntary organizations, organize mass demonstrations, run parliamentary candidates, or seek ministerial positions. They usually begin with a small handful of dedicated men who make no pretense of having a popular base or political legitimacy, but nevertheless organize themselves into small military-political units to launch attacks against established authorities at the village level. Although every country poses different strategic and tactical problems arising from varied political, social, economic, and geographic conditions, most of the major postwar guerrilla uprisings have displayed some common characteristics.

The main political strategy of guerrilla warfare is to win positive control over successively larger portions of the civilian population while simultaneously alienating the population from the regime in power. It may require only small groups of highly mobile guerrillas to defeat the state's military forces if the population remains apathetic. As Andrew Janos points out, "Governments fall not because they have too many enemies but because they have too few friends."[29] The military objective of guerrilla warfare is to cause the slow attrition of government forces to the point where they become concentrated in the larger cities, leaving the rebels to consolidate their control of the countryside.

[29] Janos, *The Seizure of Power*, p. 20.

A guerrilla force can be compared to an iceberg. What the observer sees is a small group of full-time guerrilla warriors which continually harasses government troops and drives them from the countryside. Sustaining this "cap" of the iceberg are thousands of civilians—usually peasants—who perform their ordinary routines during daytime and fight or conduct supporting activities for the "regulars" during the night. They provide food, shelter, transportation, and intelligence about government troop movements and the activities of anti-rebel leaders. Without this civilian base the guerrilla force could not continue to function for lack of food, supplies, and information. Yet the government, with all its troops and military resources, is little better off than a handful of guerrillas, for it cannot locate and identify the enemy, whose members submerge back into the mass of society after they have performed their services. The government's best hope is to obtain the loyalty of the peasants so they will identify the rebels and provide information on their activities.

To construct the civilian base and gain control over the civilian population, guerrilla cadres combine positive incentives with terror. The political leaders of guerrilla forces usually offer programs of land and political reform, combined with propaganda campaigns designed to alienate the masses from the government. Themes emphasizing nationalist symbols are also prominent. Rebel agents infiltrate villages and recruit adherents and supporting personnel. Other peasants and civilians are deterred from informing government officials on local guerrilla activities by the knowledge that if their activities are discovered, they will be kidnapped, mutilated, or murdered. Guerrillas and their village agents also practice selective terror against such government personnel as teachers, local administrators, and village leaders. In each village a clandestine or "shadow" government is eventually formed, ready to take over control immediately after the area has been purged of protecting government forces.

On the military front, the guerrillas start operating in the most remote areas, where government control and influence is least pervasive. Small units usually armed with crude weapons help capture small villages, cut government supply lines, sabotage communication facilities, and ambush government patrols. This type of harassment and attrition ultimately forces government troops to evacuate the rural areas and retreat into larger population centers. Only after several years, in which the guerrillas have gained control of the countryside through military and political operations, are they ready to launch a final military assault on the central political authorities. At this stage the war of attrition develops into a more conventional war, with the purpose of annihilating the government's military resources. Conventional strategies and tactical principles replace the guerrilla harassing techniques, and the war is fought with more destructive weapons systems, including artillery, tanks, and armored trucks. Mass demonstrations of public support for the revolutionaries are arranged—if at all—only when military defeat of the government appears imminent. The entire process of infiltration and construction of a new order begins only after the revolutionaries have gained power. All the main voluntary organizations still remain to be purged of their leadership, a new mass party to sustain the new regime has to be created, and all of the state administration has to be reconstituted. In short, much of the work which precedes a *coup d'état* in the more traditional forms of subversion still remains to be carried out after the guerrillas have seized power. From the point of view of international politics, once power is gained, the new regime immediately shifts the country's orientation toward the external power which has directed, organized, and supported the guerrillas throughout their struggle.

Guerrilla operations, whether purely local, anti-colonial, or serving the interests of an external power, seem to be currently the favorite technique of revolutionaries and their supporters. Successful guerrilla campaigns in Cyprus, China, and Cuba have received much publicity, and leaders such as Mao Tse-tung and Che Guevara have written popular treatises and manuals on the conduct of unconventional war which are carefully read by rebels from Angola to Indonesia. But this technique of overthrowing existing institutions does not invariably succeed unless the target regimes are so ineffective that they cannot maintain the support of the civilian population. For, just as manuals on guerrilla operations have proliferated, so have manuals on anti-guerrilla ("counter-insurgency") warfare. Governments are increasingly aware that the main threat to their existence and the independence of their countries comes less from overt military aggression across state frontiers than from rebel groups who receive assistance from foreign powers.

### Military Intervention

A final form of intervention, used when other techniques of wielding influence fail, is direct sending of troops (not just matériel) to (1) help a regime against rebels, (2) help foreign rebels against a regime, or (3) help either the rebels or the regime after a third foreign power has intervened on behalf of one side (counter-intervention). Most American interventions since 1945 have been of the third type, where troops were rushed in to protect a regime only when the Soviet Union, Communist

China, or other states had previously intervened. We can cite some recent examples of each type to make the distinctions clear.

Of the first type, the two most famous recent cases would be the Soviet intervention in Hungary in October, 1956, and the American intervention in Lebanon during 1958. There will continue to be disputes about the legality of these interventions. The Russians, for example, claim that the Communist order in Hungary was attacked by "fascist" and "reactionary" rebels, supported by imperialists, and that they intervened to put down the rebellion on the invitation of certain figures in the legal government. On the other hand, the Hungarian Premier, who had originally assumed office with Soviet acquiescence, had connived to transform his regime and openly supported the rebels; since he obviously did not seek Soviet intervention, crushing of the rebellion by Soviet forces could be seen as an illegal intervention designed to foist an unpopular Communist dictatorship on the Hungarian people. There was also some confusion during the Lebanon crisis of 1958. The Lebanese president precipitated it when, contrary to constitutional provisions, he sought a second term in office. When a rebellion of complex religious and political origins—at least partly organized in and supported by Syria—broke out, the president asked for American intervention, claiming that his country was being subverted by foreign agents and infiltrators. The Eisenhower administration ultimately sent over 14,000 troops to Lebanon, but their position was awkward. Although conditions in the Middle East were unstable (the government of Iraq had just succumbed to a rebellion), information pointing to Syrian complicity was scant. The United States had intervened, in other words, to prevent a civil war, not to save a regime from outside subversion. The intervention did have this effect and infused a note of caution on both sides in the dispute. The Lebanese president relinquished his plans to succeed himself in office and accepted the appointment of a military leader as provisional president. This agreement, along with the diplomatic intervention of the United Nations, ended the conflict, and eventually the Marines retired without having inflicted or received any casualties. The United States government justified its action on the grounds that intervention is permissible if it comes at the request of any government which enjoys general recognition among the other nations of the world—an argument similar to that offered by the Soviets after their troops entered Budapest in 1956.

Direct military intervention may also occur to help rebels. During the Spanish Civil War, for example, German and Italian soldiers and airmen, with their modern equipment, fought on the side of Franco's rebels against the legal government's forces. More recently, North Vietnamese troops and equipment have helped the local Pathet Lao (Communist) forces in Laos, thus violating the Geneva agreements of 1962 in which North Vietnam along with the major powers agreed to neutralize Laos and observe its territorial integrity.

American involvement in the Bay of Pigs invasion in 1961 was also of such magnitude that it could be classified as military intervention designed to overthrow a regime. Through the CIA, the United States provided financing for Cuban rebels and conducted much of the troop recruitment, planning of strategy, and establishment of embarkation and training bases in some Central American republics. It also donated air and sea transport from Nicaragua to Cuban territorial waters, disseminated anti-Castro propaganda from American-owned Swan Island in the Caribbean, and provided landing craft for the invasion. Several bombers which appeared during the battle contained Cuban exile crews, but were under the command of American military advisers. Except for the actual combat, the entire operation was planned, organized, and directed by the United States government. Having failed to change Castro's behavior through threats and actual punishments, it sought as a last resort to oust his regime by using Cuban exiles who wanted to achieve the same objective.

Finally, one nation may send troops in response to a prior intervention in the internal affairs of a country by a third power. Although the major powers have seldom sent combat troops (Vietnam is the exception) to fight against the troops of a third power, the *threat* of counter-intervention may dissuade the third power from prosecuting its original intervention. During the Israeli-French-British intervention against Egypt in 1956, the Soviet government threatened to send "volunteers" to assist Nasser's forces. The possibility of escalating the original limited intervention into a direct confrontation with Russian troops was at least one factor considered in the Anglo-French decision to accept a premature cease-fire. President Kennedy's fear of Soviet intervention on behalf of the Castro regime or Soviet retaliatory action elsewhere was also an important consideration in his decision not to involve American troops directly in the Bay of Pigs invasion.

## Conclusion

In the old European-centered international system (excepting the period 1791–1823, approximately), ideological consensus, impermeability of states, crude media of communication, and doctrine of non-interference helped to preclude one sovereign's attempts to influence the purely domestic affairs of another.[30] Non-interference is still accepted as one of the foundations of international law and one of the norms which governments should faithfully observe in their foreign relations. The Charter of the United Nations specifically prohibits member states (and the organization itself, in most circumstances) from interfering in each other's domestic problems. The norm does operate, of course, in most international transactions.

But today complete isolation of internal events from the external environment may be impossible. It can hardly be expected that many governments, as well as international organizations, will be completely indifferent to political, social, and economic developments in foreign countries. Conditions of economic and political instability in many nations create situations which foreign powers obviously will exploit—sometimes for their own gain and at others merely to prevent massacres and social collapse. When major internal conflicts which have serious implications for the core security or alliance interests of the major powers occur, intervention and counter-intervention will likely take place, even if these conflicts are not originally organized and directed from abroad. At the point where local political problems impinge upon the foreign policy interests, objectives, and values of external powers, some sort of relationship between the external power and domestic groups will be established. If a dissident faction or revolutionary movement is seeking domestic objectives which coincide with the interests of an external power, the likelihood that it will become dependent on that outside power is dramatically increased. If a regime in power is threatened by revolutionary forces clearly identified as being organized, supported, and perhaps directed from abroad, it will ask its allies and friends to intervene on its behalf, unless it believes it can cope with the problem by employing its own capabilities.

Although actions involving interference in the internal affairs of other states continue to constitute part of the techniques of achieving objectives for many countries, there seems to be a new set of norms developing

---

[30] Under the vague understandings comprising the Quadruple (later Quintuple) Alliance of 1815, the major powers of Europe pledged to intervene on behalf of any European monarch who was threatened by liberal revolution. At the Congress of Troppau (1820), devoted to discussion of the liberal revolution in Naples, the assembled Excellencies, Highnesses, and Majesties solemnly declared that "when political changes, brought about by illegal (e.g., without royal approval) means, produce dangers to other countries by reason of proximity, and when the Allied Powers can act effectively as regards these conditions, they shall, in order to bring back those countries to their allegiances, employ, first, amicable means, and then coercion." The Allied Powers subsequently intervened in Naples (1821) and Spain (1823) to restore absolute monarchies.

which establish somewhat less restrictive criteria to indicate when such actions are permissible. Clearly the old norms of complete non-interference in other states' internal affairs are being violated frequently, but it cannot be claimed that every case is entirely undesirable. Though it is premature to speculate on any long-term trend, many governments take the position that in certain instances intervention and interference in other states' internal affairs may be legitimate if those actions have the prior approval of some collective body or international organization, or the organization itself assumes such a task. Traditional legal principles prohibiting all forms of external interference are most clearly spelled out in Article 15 of the Charter of Bogotá (1948), in which the Latin American states and the United States solemnly pledged that

> no state or *group* of states has the right to intervene directly or indirectly, for any reason whatever, in the internal or external affairs of any other state. The foregoing principle prohibits not only armed attack but also any other form of interference or attempted threat against the personality of the state or against the political, economic, and cultural elements.

Under Article 16 the signatories further agreed that "no state may use or encourage the use of coercive measures of an economic or political character in order to force the sovereign will of another state or obtain from it advantages of any kind."

In contrast to these strict rules, the recent practice of the Organization of the American States, and unilaterally the United States, has been quite different. If unilateral intervention has been involved, the acting party has in most cases sought prior approval from the Latin American states, implying that if that approval is forthcoming, the intervention is legitimate. In both the Guatemalan and Cuban episodes, the United States government sought multilateral approval for its actions. In American intervention in the Dominican Republic during 1965, however, the United States took military action before it turned to the OAS to seek approval of its policies.

More significant, perhaps, are those occasions when the OAS itself determined to intervene collectively against one or more of its members. In 1960, for instance, the Inter-American Peace Commission of the OAS, in an action hardly compatible with the spirit of the Bogotá charter, condemned the Trujillo regime for "flagrant and widespread" violations of human rights in the Dominican Republic. Later in the same year, the foreign ministers of the Latin American states publicly condemned Trujillo for plotting against the life of Venezuela's president. The foreign ministers' resolution, which called upon members of the OAS to impose partial economic sanctions on the Trujillo regime, was the first time that truly collective action had been applied in the western hemisphere. Again, in 1964, the OAS Council voted almost unanimously to impose economic and diplomatic sanctions against the Castro regime in Cuba.

In the United Nations, collective intervention in the internal affairs of member states also seems to have become a "legitimate" method for coping with widespread domestic chaos that promises to involve external powers extensively. In 1956, the United Nations intervened in the Suez crisis to help terminate a prior invasion by France, Britain, and Israel. In 1958, it sent a group of observers to investigate the extent of Syrian intervention in the internal affairs of Lebanon. In the Congo, United Nations military intervention helped prevent social chaos, secession of Katanga from the central state, and unilateral intervention of the Soviet Union and possibly the United States. In 1964, the organization once again sent troops abroad, this time to Cyprus to establish and police a cease-fire in the civil war on the island, as well as to forestall a Turkish invasion and possible Russian intervention. All of these actions were taken in the name of the organization with the consent of the major governments involved. It is easy to speculate that if the interventions had not been organized, the internal wars and rebellions could have easily become transposed into major international crises.

Diplomatic interference, clandestine political actions, subversion, guerrilla warfare, and military intervention will remain important techniques for influencing or coercing other nations and exploiting or settling periodic domestic crises in unstable political systems. As long as the leaders of some states are committed to supporting, and in some cases organizing and directing, national "wars of liberation," counter-intervention can be expected as well. Other states committed to expansive objectives or ideological principles, but lacking the capabilities to achieve them through conventional military means, diplomatic bargaining, or economic pressures, will also be likely to emphasize clandestine techniques. These are often much less expensive, involve lower risks of escalating into a direct military confrontation, and, as the cases of Czechoslovakia and Guatemala reveal, if the internal conditions in a target state are right, can be brought to a successful conclusion. Where the internal circumstances of a state are less amenable to outside manipulation, or two or more states are confronted with incompatible objectives that have little relationship to domestic political processes, then—providing other techniques of inducement fail—the usual decision is to use military threats and violent punishments.

## SELECTED BIBLIOGRAPHY

Burchett, Wilfred, *Vietnam: Inside Story of the Guerrilla War*. New York: International Publishers, 1965.

Chinh, Truong, *Primer for Revolt*. New York: Frederick A. Praeger, Publisher, Inc., 1963.

Crozier, Brian, *The Rebels: A Study of Post-War Insurrections*. Boston: Beacon Press, 1960.

DeGramont, Sanche, *The Secret War: The Story of International Espionage Since World War II*. New York: G. P. Putnam's Sons, 1962.

Eckstein, Harry, ed., *Internal War*. New York: Free Press of Glencoe, Inc., 1964.

Falk, Richard A., "The United States and the Doctrine of Non-Intervention in the Internal Affairs of Independent States," *Howard Law Journal*, V (1959), 163–89.

Felix, Christopher, *A Short Course in the Secret War*. New York: E. P. Dutton & Company, Inc., 1963.

Giap, Vo Nguyen, *People's War, People's Army*. New York: Frederick A. Praeger, Publisher, Inc., 1962.

Guevara, Che, *Guerrilla Warfare*. New York: Monthly Review Press, 1961.

Halpern, Manfred, *The Morality and Politics of Intervention*. New York: The Council on Religion and Foreign Affairs, 1962.

Heilbrunn, Otto, *Partisan Warfare*. New York: Frederick A. Praeger, Publisher, Inc., 1962.

Henderson, William, "Diplomacy and Intervention in the Developing Countries," *The Virginia Quarterly Review*, XXXIX (1963), 26–36.

Huntington, Samuel P., ed., *The Changing Pattern of Military Politics*. New York: Free Press of Glencoe, Inc., 1962.

Janos, Andrew C., *The Seizure of Power: A Study of Force and Popular Consent*, Research Monograph No. 16, Center for International Studies, Princeton University, 1964.

————, "Unconventional Warfare: Framework and Analysis," *World Politics*, XV (1963), 636–46.

Kaznacheev, Alexandr, *Inside a Soviet Embassy*. Philadelphia: J. B. Lippincott Co., 1962.

Korbel, Joseph, *The Communist Subversion of Czechoslovakia, 1938–1948*. Princeton: Princeton University Press, 1959.

Mao Tse-tung, *On Guerrilla Warfare*. New York: Frederick A. Praeger, Publisher, Inc., 1961.

Orlov, Alexander, *Handbook of Intelligence and Guerrilla Warfare*. Ann Arbor: University of Michigan Press, 1963.

Osanka, Franklin M., ed., *Modern Guerrilla Warfare: Fighting Communist Guerrilla Movements, 1941–1961*. New York: Free Press of Glencoe, Inc., 1962.

Paret, Peter, and John W. Shy, *Guerrillas in the 1960's*. New York: Frederick A. Praeger, Publisher, Inc., 1962.

Rosenau, James N., ed., *International Aspects of Civil Strife*. Princeton: Princeton University Press, 1964.

Scott, Andrew M., *The Revolution in Statecraft: Informal Penetration*. New York: Random House, Inc., 1966.

Thorton, Thomas, and Cyril E. Black, *Communism and the Strategic Use of Political Violence*. Princeton: Princeton University Press, 1965.

Wise, David, and Thomas B. Ross, *The Invisible Government*. New York: Random House, Inc., 1964.

Wright, Quincy, "Subversive Intervention," *American Journal of International Law*, LIV (1960), 520–35.

# WEApons, WAR, And PoliticAl InfluENCE

The international system is often described as one of anarchy, a description which overlooks the fact that an overwhelming preponderance of international transactions are carried on by means of bargaining, persuasion, or reward rather than violence. Nor do the routine issues which make up a large proportion of any nation's foreign relations often provoke statesmen to use force. Nevertheless, recourse to violence has been and continues to be an important characteristic of the international system. In his classic study of war, Quincy Wright identified 278 wars which occurred between 1480 and 1941,[1] and while the major powers have been able to avoid a thermonuclear exchange during the cold war, international violence has erupted at various levels of intensity in nearly every region of the world since 1945.

* This chapter is contributed by Ole R. Holsti, Department of Political Science, University of British Columbia.

[1] Quincy Wright, A Study of War, Vol. I (Chicago: University of Chicago Press, 1942), p. 650.

# ChAPTER XII

The legitimacy of force as an instrument of foreign policy, although often denounced by philosophers and historians, has rarely been questioned by those responsible for the foreign policy decisions of their nations. Some states have traditionally maintained policies of neutrality, but no nation is "neutral" with respect to its own security, and neutrality does not imply unconditional renunciation of force; Switzerland maintains active defense forces, many Swedish leaders have advocated acquisition of nuclear weapons, and some of the staunchest adherents of an orientation of non-alignment in the cold war have maintained armed forces proportionately larger than those of either the United States or the Soviet Union. Except in the case of a "puppet regime" established by an outside power, it seems unlikely that any government could long maintain itself in power unless it were committed to the use of all possible means, including force, to preserve the existence of the nation and other interests deemed vital.

Some types of nations may be more prone to the use of force as an instrument of foreign policy. Wright found that new states were more likely to use violence than were older, more mature countries, but that democracies have been involved in war as often as autocracies. Nations with industrial economies were less warlike than those with agricultural economies, and states with socialist economies have been among the most warlike.[2] On the other hand, a more recent study based on data since World War II suggests that democracies and poorer countries are more peaceful than non-democracies and wealthy ones.[3] But the relationships in both studies are weak at best, and should not obscure the fact that even states which have consistently denounced violence in international affairs will use force to defend their interests as they define them. India, whose leaders have been outspoken opponents of violence in international relations, has used its military forces to capture the enclave of Goa from Portugal, prevent Pakistani control over the disputed area of Kashmir, and defend its northern frontier claims against incursions by Chinese forces. Many examples of other nations could be cited. The important point is that the decision to use violence ultimately rests with the nation; determination of core values and interests and the decision on appropriate means to defend or attain them have traditionally been considered inherent and legitimate attributes of sovereignty. Serious attempts to modify this aspect of sovereignty are largely a twentieth century phenomenon, but even the United Nations Charter permits nations to use force both individually and collectively for purposes of self-defense.

[2] Wright, *A Study of War*, pp. 828–41.
[3] Michael Haas, "Societal Approaches to the Study of War," *Journal of Peace Research*, No. 4 (1965), 307–323.

In summary, within an international system characterized by absence of effective institutionalized constraints on the use of force by its member countries, security is the scarcest of all values, and those responsible for national security are likely to perceive few adequate substitutes for procurement, maintenance, and deployment of military forces. While we may be able to attribute a particular war to an aggressive leader and social-political system, a more general reason for use of violence in international relations is the absence of systemic constraints on its use.[4]

## Weapons as Instruments of Policy

As instruments of national policy, weapons share one important characteristic with all other techniques: their purpose is to achieve or defend the goals of the nation by influencing the behavior of other states. As such, weapons are ethically neutral, and we must distinguish between goals sought through use of force and the instruments themselves. The same weapons used by the Soviets to defend their homeland against invading Nazi armies were also used to suppress the Hungarian revolution in November, 1956. Thus, it is the goals rather than the weapons which can properly be judged by ethical standards.

Except for students of tactics (narrowly defined), the role of weapons must be considered in a political rather than a purely military context. The validity of Clausewitz' strictures against a rigid distinction between politics and military strategy has become more evident as developments in military technology have transformed war from a diversion of monarchs to a menace against the continued existence of life on earth. In the nuclear age it has become more apparent than ever that military forces exist not solely for the purpose of inflicting damage upon enemies; they may also be used as a threat to buttress bargaining in diplomacy, or as means of communicating one's intentions to potential adversaries. In 1907 President Theodore Roosevelt, concerned about Japan's apparently expansionist goals in the Far East, sent an American fleet on an around-the-world trip to impress Japanese leaders with American intent and ability to maintain the status quo in the Far East. Military "maneuvers" near frontiers, and deployment of forces—even small, symbolic units—in a conspicuous manner have frequently been used to add credibility to one's diplomacy and indicate a high degree of commitment to a bargaining position. These are a few of the ways military power may be used without resorting to violence.

Force and threats to use force have consistently played a part in

[4] Kenneth Waltz, *Man, The State and War: A Theoretical Analysis* (New York: Columbia University Press, 1959).

bargaining among hostile states, and developments in military technology have often had great impact on structures and processes of political systems. Thermonuclear weapons and long-range ballistic missile systems are not merely quantitatively different from those that preceded them, but also possess qualitative attributes which have had, and will continue to have, significant impact on the international system, its member units, and the nature of relations between them. This is not to say that conventional armaments are totally obsolete; most nations' military forces are still limited to such weapons, and even the nuclear powers have found it expedient to maintain conventional forces to deal with limited provocations.

The most obvious characteristic of nuclear weapons is their destructive capacity. The single bombs which obliterated the Japanese cities of Hiroshima and Nagasaki at the end of World War II had an explosive power of 20 kilotons (20,000 tons of TNT). By recent standards such weapons are almost miniature. In 1961 the Soviet Union tested a bomb—rated at 61 megatons (61,000,000 tons of TNT)—which exceeded the explosive power of all weapons fired during World War II. Both Soviet and American arsenals are well stocked with bombs in the megaton range capable of virtually instantaneous delivery; some years ago President Kennedy asserted that nuclear stockpiles contain the equivalent of ten tons of TNT for every human being on earth, and they are continuing to grow. The American Defense Department has estimated that a general war between the United States and the Soviet Union might kill 149 million Americans and 100 million Russians, while other estimates have been even more pessimistic. Under these circumstances it is hardly surprising that traditional views of the function of military forces have been rendered obsolete, and nuclear war as an instrument of policy has been deemed "unthinkable," but, unfortunately, not impossible. Both Soviet and American leaders have expressed the view that there are few, if any, goals that can be served by the actual *use* of nuclear weapons; thus the threat to use these weapons, rather than their actual use, has become of paramount importance. Conventional weapons can still be used to achieve many types of objectives, including conquering strategic areas or overthrowing foreign governments; the main function of nuclear weapons is to *prevent* certain actions by hostile states.

It is not only the destructive capacity of thermonuclear weapons which has had impact on the international system. Development of accurate long-range ballistic missiles has provided the means for their delivery across continents at speeds which have reduced warning time almost to the vanishing point. Space and time, which once provided protection against devastating surprise attack, are of little defensive value in the nuclear-missile age. This is somewhat analogous to the invention of gunpowder in the late middle ages, which contributed to the decline of feudalism. With the introduction of the cannon to warfare, the feudal lord was no longer able to assure the defense of his subjects within the walls of his castle or fortified town. Out of the destruction of the feudal system a new unit of security—the nation—emerged. In a somewhat similar manner, the destructive capacity and range of nuclear missiles lays the territorial state open to total destruction.[5]

Since World War II the policies of nations armed with nuclear weapons have clearly dominated the international system, but acquisition and deployment of military instruments is by no means limited to the major powers. Nor, despite the huge defense budgets of nations such as the United States and the Soviet Union, is expenditure of vast resources for military means restricted to these nations. For example, during the early 1960's Jordan devoted over 21 per cent of its gross national product to military purposes. A similar proportion of expenditures by the United States would have resulted in a defense budget of over $150 billion, nearly three times the level of even the war-inflated 1967 budget. Other countries diverting over 10 per cent of their GNP to military spending include Libya, Saudi Arabia, Laos, South Vietnam, and the Congo (Brazzaville). At the other end of the spectrum, such nations as Kenya and Jamaica devote less than one-tenth of 1 per cent of their GNP to military items. Using another criterion, the percentage of total population in the armed forces, we find that Nationalist China, Israel, and a number of others have proportionately much larger armed forces than any of the major powers.[6] Although subsequent sections of this chapter will focus largely on the role of weapons and military strategy between nuclear powers, two important points should be kept in mind: (1) most nations continue to maintain and deploy military instruments, and (2) sources of international instability are by no means confined to the actions and conflicts between nuclear nations.

### The Spread of Nuclear Weapons

Military capability has traditionally been one of the attributes distinguishing the so-called "great powers" from "small powers." Since World War II this distinction has tended to give way to that between nuclear

[5] John Herz, "The Rise and Demise of the Territorial State," *World Politics*, IX (1957), 473–93.

[6] H. Roberts Coward, *Military Technology in Developing Countries*. (Cambridge: Massachusetts Institute of Technology, Center for International Studies, 1964), Appendix I.

powers and those not so armed. The high cost of developing and procuring nuclear capabilities initially prohibited all but a few industrial powers from developing them. The period of Soviet and American nuclear monopoly immediately after World War II coincided with a tendency of nations within the international system to group themselves into opposing alliances led by the two nuclear powers. Paradoxically, in the long run nuclear weapons may contribute to the loosening of a bipolar system. Diffusion of nuclear knowledge, reactors, and materials has dramatically reduced the cost and difficulty of developing nuclear military capabilities. At the same time, as the potential destructiveness of war increases, junior members of alliances may become more skeptical that other nations will risk devastation to honor treaty commitments, hence the incentive to develop and rely on one's own nuclear forces. In the 1960's it was authoritatively estimated that nations economically and technologically capable of supporting a nuclear military program numbered as high as 20, including Canada, Japan, West Germany, Sweden, Egypt, South Africa, and Israel. Despite some belated efforts by the United States and the Soviet Union to delay expansion of the nuclear club, the decision whether or not to acquire nuclear weapons now lies largely beyond the effective control of leaders in Moscow or Washington, and such decisions are as likely to reflect regional security problems as those of the cold war. Acquisition of nuclear weapons by Israel, India, or West Germany is almost certain to increase the pressures on Egyptian, Pakistani, or East German leaders to do likewise.

In the long run, diffusion of nuclear capabilities may tend to dilute the importance of traditional bases of power—population, territory, industrial capacity—and therefore reduce rather than expand the differential between large and small nations. To be sure, a nation with a large population, vast territory, and widely dispersed industrial capacity may be in a better position to "survive" a nuclear attack—and thus capable of employing threats more effectively—than a nation with limited population and territory. In the pre-nuclear era it was unlikely that a minor power could inflict an unacceptable level of damage on one of its large neighbors, much less threaten its existence; it is not inconceivable, however, that in the future a small nation armed with nuclear weapons may be in a position to do so.

For most states within the international system, nuclear power is currently only indirectly relevant to the conduct of their foreign policies. Although possessed of weak and crude military capabilities in comparison to the nuclear nations, these countries also enjoy the advantage of being unlikely direct targets of any nuclear exchange. It is one of many paradoxes of the nuclear age that threat of destruction hangs most heavily over those states, with the greatest military power; in some respects, security is inversely rather than directly related to military capabilities.

### Deterrence as a Form of Inter-nation Influence

The awesome destructive capacity of nuclear weapons has rendered the cost of their use prohibitive except in cases of extreme provocation. Because there are few political ends that can be gained through nuclear war, the primary function of these weapons is posing a threat to potential enemies. Deterrence, by which decision-makers in one nation seek to prevent certain actions by potential adversaries by threatening military retaliation, can be considered as one aspect of inter-group influence. By posing an extreme threat to the deteree's values, the deterrer seeks to preclude certain types of behavior—specifically, armed aggression as an instrument of policy. Deterrence can also be viewed as a process of communication; decision-makers of Nation A seek to communicate to their counterparts in Nation B that, "If you undertake activities X, Y, or Z, we shall surely respond with a high level retaliation against you." It is generally assumed that threat of nuclear retaliation is severe enough to deter direct aggression. Some deterrence theorists have also suggested that powerful nuclear capability will suffice to deter attack at lower levels of violence, such as conventional attacks and guerrilla incursions. But, as shall be discussed in more detail later, this conception of strategic deterrence has been questioned on both logical and military grounds.

The fundamental premises underlying any system of deterrence are: (1) decisions by both deterrer and deteree will be based on conscious calculations of probable costs and gains, accurate evaluations of the situation, and careful assessments of relative capabilities; (2) a high level of threat, such as that posed by nuclear weapons, inhibits rather than provokes aggressive behavior; (3) the value hierarchies of both deterrer and deteree are similar at least to the point that each places avoidance of thermonuclear exchange at or near the top; and (4) both sides maintain tight centralized control over decisions which might involve or provoke use of nuclear weapons.

Nuclear deterrence thus presupposes rational and predictable decision processes. No system of deterrence, however powerful the weapons, is likely to prove effective against a nation led by a trigger-happy paranoid, or one seeking personal or national self-destruction or martyrdom, or decision-makers willing to play a form of Russian roulette with thermonuclear weapons, or leaders whose information about and communication with an adversary is so incomplete that their decision-making processes are largely dominated by guesswork, or those who regard loss of most of their nation's population and resources as a "reasonable" cost for achievement of foreign policy goals.

### Credibility

The most evident requirement for effective deterrence is possession of sufficient military capacity to carry out threatened retaliation. But influence over the behavior of others is not merely a function of weapon characteristics, as can be illustrated by the case of the bandit who uses a realistic-looking toy pistol to convince the bank teller to hand over some money. Success should be attributed not to the robber's weapon, but rather to the teller's perception of it. Communicating to potential adversaries about one's capabilities is usually relatively easy. Because weapons and military personnel are tangible objects and their attributes (speed, range, destructive capacity) relatively easy to measure, probabilities of misperceptions are reduced and any distortions are likely to be toward overestimating rather than underestimating the adversary's capabilities. There are usually ample opportunities for communicating about military capabilities; for example, the annual May Day parade in Moscow provides Soviet leaders an opportunity to impress foreigners with the latest weapons in their arsenal.

"Objectively," the destructive capacity of modern weapons and the potentially catastrophic costs of nuclear war should insure sufficient caution in foreign policy decisions to make their use unnecessary. But success in avoiding nuclear war to date is cause for only the mildest optimism; the frequency of war indicates that the threat to use force and even possession of superior military capabilities has often failed to deter.[7] To explain these failures, as well as to understand the conditions for successful deterrence, we must look beyond merely the destructive capacities of nuclear stockpiles. First, as in many diplomatic bargaining situations, the deterrer must establish the *credibility* of the threat; potential aggressors must be impressed that in case of provocation the threatened retaliation will be carried out. Mere possession of powerful weapons, even an overwhelming superiority of capabilities, does not insure credibility, just as in a series of negotiations, threats need more than just enunciation to be believable. Consider again our example of the bank robber, who in

[7] Bernard Brodie, "The Anatomy of Deterrence." *World Politics,* XI (1959), 14–15.

this case enters the bank with a genuine weapon. If, for whatever reason, the teller were convinced that the threat was a bluff, she would not meet the bandit's demands. His failure could not be attributed to characteristics of his weapon—in fact, a more powerful weapon might more readily be seen as a bluff—but rather to the low credibility (as perceived by the teller) of his threat to use it. This simple example illustrates that credibility is not inherent in the weapon, but is a function of the deteree's perception of the weapon and of its owner's intentions. That is,

Deterrent effect = estimated capability × estimated intent[8]

Although this formula oversimplifies a complex relationship (a point to which we will return later in considering the deterrent effect of "overkill" capacity), it does indicate that if either perceived capability or intent is zero, deterrent effect is also zero.

Because credibility is an attribute of the deteree's beliefs, not those of the deterrer, the crucial problem for the latter is communicating intent. George Kennan has observed:

> In everything that can be statistically expressed—expressed, that is, in such a way as not to imply any judgment on our motivation—I believe the Soviet Government to be excellently informed about us. I am sure that their information on the development of our economies, on the state of our military preparations, on our scientific progress, etc., is absolutely first-rate. But when it comes to the analysis of our motives, to the things that make our life tick as it does, I think this whole great system of intelligence-gathering breaks down seriously.[9]

This disability is not, of course, limited to the Soviet Union. In general, the more ambiguous the information, the greater the likelihood of distortion between intent behind the sender's message and meaning assigned to it by the intended audience. It is much easier to communicate to potential adversaries about tangible objects such as weapons than about one's intent to use them.

One method of establishing credibility is through declaratory policy. Since World War II American leaders have repeatedly asserted that a Soviet attack on Western Europe will evoke the same response as a direct attack on the United States; Soviet leaders have made similar proclama-

---

[8] Adopted in somewhat modified form from J. David Singer, *Deterrence, Arms Control, and Disarmament* (Columbus: The Ohio State University Press, 1962), p. 172.

[9] George Kennan, *Russia, the Atom, and the West* (New York: Harper & Row, Publishers, 1957), pp. 21–22.

tions with respect to Eastern Europe. But it is difficult to communicate intent by words only; because "deeds speak louder than words," visible actions which convey a relatively unambiguous message are usually necessary to buttress policy declarations. During the early 1960's, when Premier Khrushchev was apparently unconvinced of the credibility of American defense commitments, President Kennedy is reported to have complained, "That son of a bitch won't pay any attention to words. He has to see you move."[10] Despite repeated American pronouncements concerning the intent to defend West Berlin against Soviet encroachment, the Berlin airlift of 1948-1949 and similar actions have been necessary to add credibility to the declaratory policy. Repeated failure to carry out a threatened retaliation rapidly erodes credibility. Assertions by British and French leaders that they would support Poland in case of Nazi attack had little deterrent effect, in part owing to their previous failure to act against Italian and German aggression in Ethiopia, Albania, Austria, and Czechoslovakia.

Credibility is enhanced if the threatened retaliation is roughly commensurate with the provocation. It is generally recognized that nuclear retaliation will evoke counter-retaliation, resulting in devastating damage to both the attacking and retaliating nations. The threat to unleash massive thermonuclear response to aggression, even if supported by the necessary capabilities, may not be credible in case of limited provocation (i.e., guerrilla raids). In January, 1954, Secretary of State John Foster Dulles announced a major change in American defense policy, declaring that henceforth Soviet-sponsored aggression on the periphery of the non-Communist world would be met not in kind (as in the Korean War), but with "massive retaliatory power" delivered "by means and at places of our own choosing."[11] In other words, limited aggression might be met with direct retaliation against its presumed sponsor—Moscow. Whatever credibility a policy of massive retaliation might have had during the period of American nuclear monopoly (1945-1949) was drastically reduced after the Soviet Union attained nuclear capabilities. By 1954 both the United States and the Soviet Union could unleash a massive nuclear attack on the other, but neither could escape the frightful costs of a retaliatory attack. Under these circumstances a threat to respond to any aggressive act with a thermonuclear strike might well be questioned. By 1957 even Secretary Dulles accepted the view that Western security would rest on local

[10] Arthur M. Schlesinger, Jr., *A Thousand Days* (Boston: Houghton Mifflin Co., 1965), p. 391.
[11] John Foster Dulles, "Massive Retaliation," speech, *U.S. Department of State Bulletin*, XXX (Jan. 25, 1954), 107–110.

defense, although he stressed the use of tactical nuclear weapons rather than conventional means.[12]

## Stability

Effective deterrence must also be *stable*. Adversaries must not only communicate a resolve to carry out a threat if provocation is severe enough; they must also impress enemy leaders of their intentions without provoking a preventive or pre-emptive strike out of fear. The possible consequences of the "reciprocal fear of surprise attack" can be illustrated by an analogy.

> If I go downstairs to investigate a noise at night, with a gun in my hand, and find myself face to face with a burglar who has a gun in his hand, there is danger of an outcome that neither of us desires. Even if he prefers just to leave quietly, and I wish him to, there is danger that he may *think* I want to shoot, and shoot first. Worse, there is danger that he may think that I think he wants to shoot. Or he may think that I think he thinks I want to shoot. And so on. "Self-defense" is ambiguous, when one is only trying to preclude being shot in self-defense.[13]

Leaders of two mutually hostile nations may find themselves in a similar situation. Each may prefer to back off, but be unable to convince the other of his preference.

In summary, an effective deterrence system requires more than mere possession of powerful nuclear or conventional military stockpiles. Before the nuclear age, effectiveness of weapons was usually measured by their performance against those of enemies. The contribution of nuclear weapons to national security is measured less by their capacity to inflict devastating damage on enemies than according to their ability to influence the behavior of potential adversaries so that the occasion for using them will not arise. The outbreak of war, necessitating actual use of military capabilities, represents a failure of deterrence.[14] An effective deterrent must be both threatening (credible enough that adversaries are not tempted to undertake prohibited actions), and stable (reassuring enough to reduce any incentives to launch a pre-emptive strike out of fear).

[12] John Foster Dulles, "Challenge and Response in United States Policy," *Foreign Affairs*, XXXVI (1957), 25–43.

[13] Thomas C. Schelling, *The Strategy of Conflict* (Cambridge: Harvard University Press, 1960), p. 207.

[14] Glenn H. Snyder and others have pointed out that deterrence may operate *in war* as well as *before* war. This does not negate the point, however, that outbreak of violence represents a failure of deterrence. Glenn H. Snyder, *Deterrence and Defense: Toward a Theory of National Security* (Princeton: Princeton University Press, 1961).

## Deterrence in Crisis Situations

No system of deterrence can be absolutely stable, if only because all weapons are to some degree provocative. Possible causes of failure include: (1) escalation of limited war into a thermonuclear holocaust; (2) a catalytic war, in which major powers are drawn into a conflict initiated by other nations; (3) war arising from an accidental military action or nuclear explosion; (4) a breakdown in discipline among subordinate military personnel, such as resulted in an unauthorized French bombing attack on a Moroccan village during the Algerian revolution; and (5) a war resulting from erroneous intelligence, faulty interpretation of radar images, or other types of communication difficulties.[15]

Some of these occurrences are highly improbable because of complex devices and procedures designed to circumvent accidents. For example, a number of airplanes armed with nuclear weapons have crashed without nuclear detonation, owing to safety devices built into the triggering mechanism. The presence of such safeguards does not, however, provide absolute insurance against errors of human perception, judgment, and performance. Even under normal conditions human error can only be reduced, not eliminated, and decisions to deploy or use strategic weapons are often made under the pressure of crisis.

Of the attributes of crisis, the time dimension may be most important. The processes of formulating policy in all nations, democratic and authoritarian, share at least one major characteristic: in crisis situations statesmen are denied the luxury of decision-making in leisure. Capacity to respond with weapons of almost incalculable speed of delivery and destructiveness has created one of the crucial paradoxes of the nuclear age: decisions which, because of their potentially awesome consequences, should be made with the greatest deliberation, must often be made under the most urgent pressure of time.

Ample experimental and historical evidence indicates that individual and organizational decision-making processes tend to become less effective with compression of decision time. Beyond a moderate level, time pressure has an adverse effect on creativity, memory, productivity, accuracy, and other factors crucial to decision-making under conditions of uncertainty. There appears to be a two-way relationship between time

---

[15] J. David Singer, *Deterrence, Arms Control, and Disarmament*. A somewhat different set of "scenarios" describing possible causes of war are presented in Herman Kahn, *On Thermonuclear War* (Princeton: Princeton University Press, 1960), pp. 524 ff.

and stress. Common use during crises of such techniques as ultimata and threats with built-in deadlines—as well as the rapid delivery time of modern weapons—is likely to increase the stress under which the recipient must operate. On the other hand, added increments to the stress level tend to distort perceptions of time. When decision time is short, estimates of multiple outcomes from a given decision are likely to be reduced, and concern for short-run consequences of decisions increases. To some extent, decisions made under stress may be more likely to deviate from the assumptions of calculated decision processes which underlie nuclear deterrence: extreme stress may increase likelihood of aggressive and reflexive behavior, and concomitantly decrease the probability of cautious and calculated policies.

The crisis leading up to World War I, a classic example of war through escalation, can be used to illustrate how weapons, time, and stress can affect decision-making. Archduke Francis Ferdinand, heir apparent to the throne of Austria-Hungary, was assassinated June 28, 1914, in Sarajevo by a young Serbian nationalist. Within a week Imperial Germany had promised "blank check" support of the Vienna government in an action perceived as likely to result in a "localized war" against Serbia. On July 23 the Austro-Hungarians presented Serbia with an ultimatum, the answer to which was regarded as unsatisfactory. Five days later Vienna declared war against its southern neighbor.

When war between Austria-Hungary and Serbia could no longer be prevented, it also became evident that efforts to localize it might fail. As late as August 1 many key decision-makers expressed the belief that if time permitted a reconvening of the concert powers, general war might be avoided. The British Foreign Minister wrote, for example: "I still believe that if only a little respite in time can be gained before any Great Power begins war it might be possible to secure Peace."[16] At the same

---

[16] Unless otherwise specified, quotations by decision-makers in 1914 are taken from the various document collections relating to the pre-World War I crisis: Austro-Hungarian Monarchy, *Ministerium des K. und K. Hauses und äussern*. Ludwig Bittner, Alfred Francis Pribram, Heinrich Srbik, und Hans Uebersberger, bearbeitet von Ludwig Bittner und Hans Uebersberger (Vienna and Leipzig: Osterreichischer bundesverlag für unterricht, wissenschaft und kunst, 1930). France, Commission for the Publication of Documents Relative to the Origins of the War of 1914–1918. *Documents Diplomatiques Français (1871–1914)*, 3rd Series, Vols. X and XI (Paris, 1936). Great Britain, Foreign Office, *British Documents on the Origins of the War, 1898–1914*, Vol. XI. G. P. Gooch and Harold Temperley, eds. (London, 1926). Max Montgelas and Walther Schucking, eds., *Outbreak of the World War: German Documents Collected by Karl Kautsky* (New York: Oxford University Press, 1924). Russia (1923-U.S.S.R.) Komîssiiă po îzdanîiŭ dokumentov ėpokhi împerîalîzma. *Mezhdunarodnye otnosheniia v ėpokhu imperializma; dokumenty iz arkhivov tsarskogo i vremennogo pravitel'stv 1878–1917 gg.*, seriia III, toma IV and V (Moscow and Leningrad, Vol. IV 1931, Vol. V 1934).

time, attention turned to the risks of being unprepared for the war which might break out.

Here was the dilemma. Time would be required if a general European war were to be averted; above all, a moratorium on military operations was necessary. On August 1 King George V wrote of his efforts "to find some solution which permits in any case the adjournment of active military operations and the granting of time to the powers to discuss among themselves calmly." It was clear that military preparations would stimulate similar actions by others. But increasingly these considerations were overshadowed by another: to permit a potential adversary any time advantage in mobilizing the military power of the state was perceived to be disastrous. Although no *official* mobilization orders except those of Austria-Hungary and Serbia were issued until July 29, there were increasing rumors and suspicions of undercover preparations.

On July 28 Nicholas II had warned, "I foresee that I will succumb very soon to the pressure put upon me and will be compelled to take extreme measures which will lead to war." Three days later, in the course of his desperate last minute correspondence with the Kaiser, the Tsar asserted, "It is technically impossible to stop our military preparations which were obligatory owing to Austria's mobilization."

The reaction of German decision-makers to the series of events leading up to mobilization and war was almost identical. They repeatedly asserted that, owing to the pressure of time, they had no choice but to take vigorous military measures against the threat to the east. At the same time, they claimed that only Russia was free to act in order to prevent war. "The responsibility for the disaster which is now threatening the whole civilized world will not be laid at my door. In this moment it still lies in your [Nicholas] power to avert it." And Wilhelm, like the Tsar, finally asserted that he had lost control of his own military, and that only the actions of the adversary could stop further escalation. Later the Kaiser added, "In view of the colossal war preparations of Russia now discovered, this is all too late, I fear. Begin! Now!"

On July 29 Russia had ordered, and then cancelled, general mobilization. Later it was predicted in St. Petersburg that mobilization of the four southern military districts would deter an Austro-Hungarian attack on Serbia. But technical difficulties caused the Russians to reverse their decision once again on July 30 in favor of general mobilization, German warnings notwithstanding.

In response to what was perceived as a mounting threat against its eastern frontiers, the German Government proclaimed a "state of threatening danger of war" on July 31 and dispatched a 12-hour ultimatum to Russia demanding cessation of military preparations. Berlin then ordered mobilization on August 1. The reason for the German decision was, "We could not sit back quietly and wait to see whether a more commonsense view would gain the upper hand at Petersburg, while at the same time the Russian mobilization was proceeding at such speed, that, if the worst came, we should be left completely outstripped in a military sense." The French Government simultaneously ordered general mobilization, on the grounds that, "any delay of twenty-four hours applied to the calling up of reserves and to the sending the telegram ordering covering troops will result in a backward movement of our troops, that is to say an initial abandonment of a part of our territory, either 15 or 20 kilometers every day of delay."

Although official British mobilization was delayed until August 2, Winston Churchill, First Lord of the Admiralty, and many others had advocated such action considerably earlier. On July 31 Under-Secretary of State for Foreign Affairs Arthur Nicolson had urged immediate military preparations.

Thus each mobilization was defended as a necessary reaction—made more urgent by pressure of time—to a previous decision within the other coalition. Gnawing awareness that the probable responses to military measures were countermeasures failed to deter, and assurances of defensive intent failed to provide stability; ten days after the small scale mobilizations by Serbia and Austria-Hungary on July 25 each of the major participants had ordered general mobilization, a decision commonly regarded in 1914 as an act of war. Armies totalling less than 400,000 troops called to fight a limited war between two nations had grown to nearly 12 million men, representing, in addition to Serbia and Austria-Hungary, Montenegro, Russia, France, Germany, Belgium, Turkey, and England.

One factor contributing to the rapid escalation was the rigidity of various mobilization plans. The Russian attempt to mobilize against only Austria was anathema to the Russian generals because no such plan had been drawn up. According to General Dobrorolski, "The whole plan of mobilization is worked out ahead to its final conclusion and in all its detail. . . . Once the moment is chosen, everything is settled; there is no going back; it determines mechanically the beginning of war."[17]

Similarly, the Kaiser's last minute attempt to reverse the Schlieffen plan by attacking to the east shattered Moltke, who replied: "That is impossible, Your Majesty. An army of a million cannot be improvised. It would be nothing but a rabble of undisciplined armed men without a commis-

---

[17] Quoted in Virginia Cowles, *The Kaiser* (New York: Harper & Row, Publishers, 1963), p. 343.

sariat. . . . It is utterly impossible to advance except according to plan; strong in the west, weak in the east."[18]

Does the 1914 case have any relevance for national security policy during an age in which weapons systems have only the slightest resemblance to those existing in 1914? Analysis of European military technology and doctrines would reveal, for example, that objectively time was of incalculably less importance than in the 1960's. Estimates of the time required for Austria-Hungary to field a full army ranged from three to four weeks, and the necessity of harvesting the summer's crops was a factor in the military calculations of all the continental powers. Russia's ability to mount a rapid offensive against Germany could be discounted; this assumption of Russia's lack of speed in fact underlay the Schlieffen plan.

Yet any analysis confined to the "objective" situation misses the crucial factor of perceptions. In an atmosphere of high tensions the decision-makers of 1914 perceived that time was of crucial importance—and acted on that assumption. In the culminating phases of the crisis, decision-makers increasingly perceived potential enemies as able to deliver a sudden punishing blow. As a result the costs of delaying immediate military action were perceived as increasingly high. Or, to use the language of modern deterrence theory, decision-makers in each coalition perceived those of the other coalition as able and willing to launch a massive first-strike, and thus hastened their own preparations. The entire concert system, which was assumed to act as an equilibrating mechanism, became instead a "runaway system."

The events of October, 1962, a crisis that escalated to the brink of war and then de-escalated, can be contrasted with decision-making during the 1914 crisis which spiraled into a world war. In October, 1962, the first nuclear confrontation in history was precipitated by establishment of Soviet missile sites in Cuba. For a period of approximately one week the likelihood of a full-scale nuclear exchange between the United States and the Soviet Union was high. Speaking of the events of the week of October 22, Attorney General Robert Kennedy recalled that all who had participated in the momentous decisions for American response agreed that if the Russians were ready to use nuclear weapons to defend their position in Cuba, they would be willing to use them in many circumstances. It would be better, then, to have the showdown now than at some later date.[19]

As in 1914, time pressure was woven inextricably into the entire crisis

---

[18] Quoted in Virginia Cowles, *The Kaiser*, pp. 348–9.
[19] Stewart Alsop and Charles Bartlett, "In Time of Crisis," *The Saturday Evening Post,* Dec. 8, 1962, p. 16.

situation. The pressure created by work on the Soviet missile sites in Cuba has been described by Theodore Sorensen, Special Counsel to the President: "For all of us knew that, once the missile sites under construction became operational, and capable of responding to any apparent threat or command with a nuclear volley, the President's options would be dramatically changed."[20] There was also the countervailing force created by the President and his advisers, who sought to minimize the probability that either side would respond by a "spasm reaction."

One important aspect of American policy-making during the crisis was deep concern for decisions based on adequate information. Despite public pressure, the Administration resisted taking action until photographic evidence of the missile sites was available. McGeorge Bundy recalled that upon receiving news of the photographic evidence, President Kennedy's first reaction was to insist that the evidence be conclusive.[21] As late as Thursday, October 18, a series of alternatives was being considered pending more accurate information, and while the decision to institute a blockade was being hammered out, open discussion of the alternatives was encouraged. The President recalled that sharp differences at the start of the discussions were regarded as valuable because they reflected different organizational responsibilities.[22] Another participant in the decision-making at the highest level wrote that President Kennedy, aware that discussions of alternatives in the National Security Council would be franker in his absence, encouraged the group to hold preliminary meetings without him. Thus, despite the very real pressure of time—the missile sites were to become operational by the end of the month—the eventual decision was reached by relatively open discussion. Group decision-making does not insure the emergence of sound policy, of course, but it does limit the probability of a decision performing a personality-oriented function.[23] In the case of Cuba, at least six different alternatives were carefully considered and argued in detail.[24]

It was not until Saturday, October 20, almost a week after photographic evidence became available, that the consensus developed. The President himself emphasized that the interim period was crucial to the

---

[20] Theodore Sorensen, *Decision-Making in the White House* (New York: Columbia University Press, 1963), p. 31.

[21] N.B.C. News, "Cuba: The Missile Crisis," (Feb. 9, 1964), p. 14. Transcript courtesy of N.B.C. News.

[22] C.B.S. News, "A Conversation with President Kennedy," (Dec. 17, 1962), p. 4. Transcript courtesy of C.B.S. News.

[23] Sidney Verba, "Assumptions of Rationality and Non-Rationality in Models of the International System," *World Politics*, XIV (1961), 103.

[24] Theodore C. Sorensen, *Kennedy* (New York: Harper & Row, Publishers, 1965), p. 682.

final decision when he acknowledged that if the decision had had to be made in the first 24 hours after verification of the missiles, the government would not have chosen as prudently as it did one week later, when it finally settled on the quarantine against introduction of further missiles.[25]

Unlike many decision-makers in the 1914 crisis, American leaders also displayed considerable concern and sensitivity for the manner in which Soviet leaders would interpret American actions. President Kennedy and others were aware of the possibility of misperception by their counterparts in the Kremlin. Kennedy, for one, even remembered that World War I had developed through a series of misjudgements about each state's intentions toward the others.[26] This concern for anticipated response is evident in Sorensen's recollection of the search for an appropriate response to the Soviet missiles. The policy-making group in Washington assessed possible Soviet reactions to any possible move by the United States, American response to that Soviet reaction, and so on, trying to predict each of the alternatives to their ultimate conclusion.[27]

Sensitivity for the position of the adversary manifested itself throughout the crisis. There were attempts to insure that Premier Khrushchev not be rushed into an irrevocable decision; it was agreed among members of the decision group that escalation of the crisis should be slowed down to give Soviet leaders time to consider their next move.[28] An interesting example of Kennedy's concern emerges from his management of the naval quarantine. The President ordered the Navy to delay intercepting a Soviet ship until the last possible moment, and sent this order in the clear rather than in code.[29] The Soviets, certain to intercept the message, would thus be assured that they had time in which to consider their decisions. There was, in addition, a conscious effort not to reduce the alternatives of *either* side to two—total surrender or total war. According to Sorensen, President Kennedy tried to assure that the initial American response left open a number of options for *both sides.* An air strike on the missile bases or invasion of the island would have left Mr. Khrushchev only two alternatives: surrender to the United States or counterattack. A blockade, on the other hand, would give the Soviet government a choice between turning back the weapons-bearing ships or running the blockade. Even the latter course would have left a non-violent option open to the United States.[30]

[25] C.B.S. News, "A Conversation with President Kennedy," pp. 2–3.
[26] C.B.S. News, "A Conversation with President Kennedy," p. 3.
[27] N.B.C. News, "Cuba: The Missile Crisis," p. 17.
[28] N.B.C. News, "Cuba: The Missile Crisis," p. 19.
[20] Roger Hilsman, "The Cuban Crisis: How Close We Were to War," *Look* (Aug. 25, 1964), p. 19.
[30] N.B.C. News, "Cuba: The Missile Crisis," p. 22.

Another characteristic of the decision process in October, 1962, was the conscious choice of response at the lowest level of violence or potential violence necessary to achieve withdrawal of the Soviet missiles. Senators J. William Fulbright and Richard B. Russell were among those who urged immediate invasion of Cuba, a suggestion against which the President stood firm.[31] According to Kennedy, the decision to impose a naval quarantine was based on the reasoning that as a minimum step, it had the advantage of allowing for further and more massive actions should the Soviet Union not retreat.[32] The Soviet leadership was thus given the time and the opportunity to reassess its policy.

Comparison of the decision process in 1914 and 1962 underscores the importance, in a crisis, of the ability to lengthen decision time. While the weapons available to the protagonists of 1962 were incalculably greater in destructive capacity, force structures were considerably more flexible, and were perceived as such. Most important was the fact that decision-makers in Moscow and Washington apparently understood that in crisis, weapon systems must be used to communicate both threat and reassurance. Aware not only of the frightful costs of miscalculation, failures in communication, or panic, but also of the consequences of reducing options to war or total surrender, they appeared to have maintained sight of the need to consider the consequences of their decisions for the adversary. Yet the ability of American and Soviet leaders to avoid a nuclear Armageddon is not assurance that even great skill in crisis management will always yield a peaceful escape from war. As President Kennedy said some months later, referring to the missile crisis, "you can't have too many of those."

### Deterrence Strategies

It is a truism that no strategy or weapon system can insure that adversaries will abstain from attack either out of aggressive intent or fear. This does not mean that all doctrines and weapons are equally credible and stable, and will contribute equally to national security and the effectiveness of military threats. Throughout the remainder of this chapter we will use these two criteria—credibility and stability—to examine a number of issues relating to strategic doctrines and characteristics of weapons systems: capability requirements, limited nuclear war, targeting doctrine, active defense, civil defense, and arms control and disarmament. Because the primary purpose of military policy today is to influence the

---

[31] N.B.C. News, "Cuba: The Missile Crisis," p. 30.
[32] C.B.S. News, "A Conversation with President Kennedy," p. 4.

behavior of potential adversaries, our discussion will focus on weapons and strategies as instruments of influence. We will be less concerned with the problems of fighting a war—the ultimate form of punishment—than with the possible consequences of various strategic doctrines on the behavior of others. In short, our focus will be political rather than purely military.

## Capability Requirements

Two related "rules" have generally dominated national security policy: the *para bellum* doctrine—"if you want peace, prepare for war"—and the view that security is a direct function of military superiority vis-à-vis prospective enemies.

Whatever the merits of the *para bellum* doctrine (the frequency of wars prior to 1945 suggests that it may not be a reliable guide in all situations), the most irresistible "conventional wisdom" which argues that deterrence is merely a matter of piling up more and better weapons than the opponent can amass must be qualified in a number of respects.

*Invulnerability.* The speed, range, and destructive capacity of modern weapons provides a potential attacker with the opportunity and temptation to destroy the adversary's retaliatory capacity with a surprise attack. If Nation *A*'s leaders believe that a surprise attack will permit quick victory without much likelihood of retaliation because Nation *B*'s weapons can be destroyed before they are used, the latter's deterrent posture is hardly credible. Weapons which are a superb and tempting target may prove to be no deterrent at all, as the Japanese attack on the American Pacific fleet at Pearl Harbor demonstrated.[33] Thus deterrent effect is not a function of *total* destructive capacity, but of those *weapons surviving a surprise attack.*

Nor do vulnerable forces satisfy the requirement of stability because they fail to provide decision-makers with the capacity to delay response. Knowledge that the opponent can launch a crippling surprise attack reduces decision time, and increases pressure to launch a pre-emptive strike at the first signal (which may turn out to be false) that such an attack is imminent. When both nations' deterrent forces are vulnerable the situation is even less stable, as neither side can afford to delay. Each may prefer to back off, but neither can be certain of not having his "rationality" exploited. A delay of hours, or even minutes, can make the

---

[33] Thomas Schelling in the Preface to Roberta Wohlstetter, *Pearl Harbor: Warning and Decision,* (Stanford: Stanford University Press, 1962). The implications of vulnerability were first spelled out by Albert Wohlstetter, "The Delicate Balance of Terror," *Foreign Affairs,* XXXVII (1959), 211–34.

difference between being able to retaliate or having one's weapons and delivery systems destroyed. Compressed decision time and the need for hair-trigger retaliatory forces significantly increase the probabilities of accidental war. Consider, for example, the situation of a single nuclear explosion over an American or Soviet city. Without adequate time for investigation of its causes, decision-makers might be unable to determine whether it was the result of an accident, the forerunner of an all-out attack, or some other cause. In these circumstances the pressures for immediate retaliation against the presumed attacker might become irresistible.[34]

If, on the other hand, both nations possess weapons systems capable of surviving even unlimited attack, both credibility and stability are increased. The temptation to launch a first strike should diminish as the certainty and probable cost of devastating retaliation increase. Equally important, when retaliatory systems are invulnerable, the incentive to undertake a pre-emptive attack in the absence of complete information (as in the example of the explosion of unknown origin) declines as the ability to delay response increases decision time.

Survival capability of deterrent forces can be enhanced by a number of methods. An *increase in numbers* can, at least temporarily, make it proportionately more difficult for the attacker to succeed in a first strike. This method is relatively crude, and will be effective only if the adversary does not increase his forces proportionately. The search for numerical superiority may decrease vulnerability in the short run, but its long-term consequence may be an arms race which leaves neither side more secure. *Dispersal* of forces in both overseas bases and at home may also provide some protection, but this alternative becomes less attractive as delivery systems become more accurate and the political costs of foreign bases increase. *Hardening* delivery systems (such as the "Minuteman" missile) by placing them in underground shelters, although relatively expensive, can provide adequate protection against all but a direct strike. Assuming a specified probable error in delivery systems, hardening requires the attacker to expend more weapons on each target, thereby reducing the probability of a crippling first strike. As delivery systems become more accurate, the effectiveness of hardening is eroded. Placing retaliatory sources at the maximum possible *distance* from a potential enemy insures their survival only as long as the gap in distance is not closed by longer-

[34] As the number of nations possessing nuclear weapons and delivery systems increases, and the size of weapons decreases, the problem of identifying the attacker will become more serious. The miniature bomb capable of delivery by a single agent is no longer in the realm of science fiction. J. I. Coffey, "The Chinese and Ballistic Missile Defense,'" *Bulletin of the Atomic Scientists*, XXI (December 1965), 17–19.

range delivery systems. A further measure of protection can be provided by *concealment*, but this method is already somewhat vulnerable to advances in the technology of detection. American U-2 flights over the Soviet Union proved that high altitude photography can yield considerable intelligence information. Orbiting "spy" satellites have been even more effective than the U-2, without incurring any of the political costs of manned overflights.

The most reliable method of decreasing vulnerability is *mobility*. Polaris missile-launching submarines have become a major component of American defense forces, and the Soviet Union has subsequently acquired similar capabilities. Important characteristics of this weapon system include: (1) it combines high mobility with capabilities for dispersal, distance, and concealment; (2) unlike missile sites or air bases located near cities, it provides the enemy with no incentive to attack major population centers; and (3) it does not require foreign bases.[35]

One point should be emphasized. The ability of the invulnerable deterrent forces to delay response may be a necessary, but is not a sufficient, factor to insure against a pre-emptive strike in crisis. None of the nations in the 1914 crisis had the ability to unleash a rapid destructive blow, crippling the retaliatory capabilities of the adversary. But in the high tension situation of the final week prior to the outbreak of general war, decision-makers in Berlin, St. Petersburg, Paris, and London increasingly attributed this *ability* and *intent* to potential enemies. The penalties for delay were perceived to be too high. Thus the capacity to delay response is not likely to be effective unless decision-makers (1) perceive the net rewards of delay to be higher than those of immediate action, and (2) are willing to attribute the same preferences to the adversary.

*Force Levels.* The theory of a linear relationship between military capabilities and deterrent effect has been questioned as nuclear arsenals have reached the "overkill" range. That the capacity of nuclear weapons to destroy any existing society has tended to make national leaders more cautious in considering decisions that might precipitate a nuclear war has been neither proved nor disproved, but is at least plausible; the proposition that the capacity to destroy any existing society five, ten, or 100 times over increases caution proportionately seems untenable. The case for overwhelming strategic superiority was more persuasive when delivery

---

[35] The Polaris may also remain beyond striking distance of its target (communicating reassurance) but can rapidly be brought into firing position (communicating threat) without losing its invulnerability. The implications of this attribute for arms control are discussed in John R. Raser, "Weapons Design and Arms Control: The Polaris Example," *Journal of Conflict Resolution*, IX (1965), 450–462.

systems were limited to manned bombers, targets which, before takeoff, are vulnerable to surprise attack. Sheer numerical superiority provided some short-run protection against a crippling and decisive first strike. But, as indicated above, greater protection at lower cost (fiscally, politically, and in stability) can be achieved by mobile invulnerable deterrent systems.

*Flexibility.* Perhaps the most serious limitation to the theory of a linear relationship between destructive capability and deterrent effect lies in the ability to deter aggression at many levels of intensity. One aspect of the issue has been discussed earlier—the credibility of threatening massive retaliation to deter limited aggression.

Prior to 1945, a single weapon system could generally be counted upon to perform multiple tasks. A strong French army could be deployed to defend the eastern frontiers against Germany; the same army could, with little change, also serve to pacify guerrilla warfare in colonial areas. Similarly, the British navy could serve as an instrument for multiple goals —deterrent against attack of the home island, protection of shipping and commerce, or destruction of an enemy fleet in war.

Whether nuclear arsenals are capable of serving multiple defense requirements is more open to question. For example, can the same weapons be used to deny territory to an adversary and to punish an aggressor?[36] The defense policy of the Eisenhower administration placed considerable emphasis on the deterrent effectiveness of strategic weapons across a broad spectrum of situations. General Curtis LeMay, an advocate of this position, asserted that any force that would deter a big war should deter a small war as well, provided that the United States proclaimed its intention to use nuclear weapons against even conventional military provocations.[37] In contrast to the policies of the Eisenhower administration, Presidents Kennedy and Johnson actively sought to restore a balance between conventional and nuclear forces.

Defense analysts have generally accepted the need for flexible forces. The credibility of a threatened nuclear response to limited provocation may be quite small, and will diminish each time limited aggression goes unchallenged. A commitment to meet *every* provocation automatically with a massive nuclear response denies the possibility for recalculating costs and gains with changed circumstances. Moreover, nuclear retaliation may prove more costly and less effective than reliance on conventional

[36] This distinction, and its implications for force structures, is examined in detail by Glenn Snyder, *Deterrence and Defense.*

[37] See William W. Kaufmann, *The McNamara Strategy* (New York: Harper & Row, Publishers, 1964), p. 14.

forces to offset a limited loss, such as faced the United States after the early days of the Korean war.

Threat of strategic retaliation may well prove effective against an unambiguous attack against targets of high value. Soviet and American strategic forces have effectively deterred the other from launching an invasion against either Eastern or Western Europe. But the threat of nuclear devastation must be regarded as of very limited credibility in areas where frontiers are ambiguous; where the credibility of commitments to allies may be suspect; where regimes are unstable; where the difference among genuine domestic revolutionary movements, private armies of dissident domestic factions, and foreign guerrilla forces is often blurred; and where clandestine aid across frontiers is difficult to identify and even harder to prevent. Inability to respond at an appropriate level to limited aggression in such areas may well be regarded by potential aggressors as an invitation to attack. Even a virtual American monopoly of nuclear weapons in 1950 did not prevent the invasion of South Korea. Once the invasion occurred, a threat made to devastate Moscow or Peking unless North Korean forces withdrew to the 38th parallel might well have been regarded as a bluff. To make the threat without carrying it out would reduce the future credibility of the strategic deterrent; to carry out the threat would have resulted in a major escalation of a limited war to an unlimited one. The American response to the Korean invasion, a limited one relying on conventional forces, did not result in complete victory, but did restore the frontier between the two Koreas to approximately the pre-1950 position without escalation of the conflict geographically (fighting remained confined to the Korean Peninsula) and militarily (both sides abstained from use of nuclear weapons).

A final aspect of the relationship between weapons and influence has been identified by Thomas Schelling, who distinguishes between (1) *deterrence*, the ability to prohibit certain policies (negative influence) on the part of enemies, and (2) *compellance*, the capacity to persuade the adversary to undertake specified actions (positive influence).[38] American strategic superiority has deterred the Soviet Union from overt large-scale aggression in Europe, but unsuccessful attempts to compel North Vietnam to cease supplying guerrilla forces in South Vietnam by bombing the former's transportation routes indicates the difficulty of achieving this type of influence even with conventional weapons. There is little reason to believe that the use of nuclear weapons would be more successful.

[38] Thomas C. Schelling, "Cuba, Korea, and Vietnam: Changing Concepts of Warfare" (October 1965). Unpublished paper.

## Limited Nuclear War

Out of the vigorous debate on the deficiencies of massive retaliation emerged the suggestion that tactical nuclear weapons be used to deter or punish limited aggression. Advocates of their use asserted that (1) they add to the deterrent credibility of ground forces, and (2) they provide the best defense against massive land armies by permitting substitution of technology for manpower. This position was generally accepted by Secretary of State John Foster Dulles in 1957, when he modified his previous views on the policy of massive retaliation. American troops stationed in Europe have been armed with tactical nuclear weapons, and on a number of occasions American leaders have indicated that defense of Western Europe against invasion from the East would not be limited to conventional forces.

While a strategy of local defense with low-yield nuclear weapons meets our criterion of credibility, its contribution to stability is open to question. More specifically, could a local war fought with such weapons remain localized? Henry Kissinger, one of the earliest and most influential advocates of this strategy, later agreed with those critics who pointed to the likelihood that once the "atomic barrier" was breached, it would be nearly impossible for combatants to agree on new limits.[39] As Thomas Schelling has shown, when the situation renders direct communication between adversaries difficult (as in limited war), limits may be established through tacit bargaining processes, characterized by a tendency for both parties to look for "prominent solutions."[40] Even in the absence of communication, both parties can use such prominent limits to mutual advantage. Once they are breached, however, even limited cooperation becomes virtually impossible.

The same process can be important in maintaining limits on a local war. If both sides desire to prevent escalation under conditions of poor communication and high stress, the limits must be clear and prominent. One of the clearest and most prominent of these is the boundary between conventional explosives and nuclear weapons. The case put forth by advocates of tactical nuclear weapons—that miniaturization may make their destructive capacity *less* than those of conventional high explosives —misses the point that the *qualitative* nuclear-conventional distinction is

[39] Henry A. Kissinger, *Nuclear Weapons and Foreign Policy* (New York: Harper & Row, Publishers, 1957); Kissinger, "Limited War: Conventional or Nuclear?" in *Arms Control, Disarmament and National Security,* ed. Donald G. Brennan (New York: George Braziller, Inc., 1961), pp. 138–52.

[40] Thomas Schelling, "Bargaining, Communication, and Limited War," *Journal of Conflict Resolution,* I (1957), 19–36.

a more prominent limit than any *quantitative* one; the difference between conventional and atomic arms is clear and obvious, but an upper ceiling on explosive power, such as 100, 500, 1,000, or even 10,000 tons of TNT, is not. Once the conventional-nuclear boundary is breached, this will be construed as a "signal" that a "new set of rules" is in operation, and neither party may be able to identify the next prominent limit on the ladder of escalation.

Moreover, the assertion that low-yield nuclear weapons increase the probabilities of victory in a limited war is something of a contradiction in terms. Limited war implies that something less than total victory must be acceptable to both sides. If not, limitations on escalation will inevitably be breached as the military tide turns against one side or the other, or as it becomes apparent that limited military instruments cannot achieve unlimited political goals.

Aside from the difficulties of controlling limited nuclear war and the political costs of initiating it, some serious questions about the military value of tactical nuclear weapons have been raised. Their use in heavily-populated and heavily-industrialized Europe might cause devastation almost equal to that of unlimited war. Advocates of limited nuclear warfare strategy for the United States have also built their case on the myth of the preponderant manpower of Soviet-bloc nations. The population base from which NATO nations can maintain conventional forces is in fact larger than that of the Soviet Union and its Eastern European allies.[41] Guerrilla and other limited operations, such as in Vietnam, offer few targets for battlefield use of such weapons, and the threat to do so may be irrelevant to the military situation. During the spring of 1954, as it became apparent that French forces in Indo-China were facing imminent defeat at the hands of the Communist-led Viet-minh rebels, Secretary Dulles reportedly offered France several American nuclear weapons.[42] Even had the offer been accepted, there seems little likelihood that the threat to use them would have deterred the Viet-minh, nor would their use have prevented the decisive French defeat at Dien Bien Phu.

## Targeting Policy

Considerable debate has been generated among strategists over what should be the target of threat. With few exceptions the debate has centered on the probable effects of threatening military targets (counter-force strategy) or population centers (countercity strategy). In assessing

[41] See the figures in Singer, *Deterrence, Arms Control and Disarmament*, p. 96.
[42] J-R. Tournoux, *Secrets D'Etat* (Paris: Librairie Plon, 1960), p. 48; Jules Roy, *The Battle of Dienbienphu* (London: Faber and Faber, 1965), p. 198.

the merits of these strategies we can again apply our criteria of effectiveness; that is, what do these targeting strategies contribute to the credibility and stability of deterrence?

Counterforce strategy received its most authoritative articulation in an address by Secretary of Defense Robert McNamara to the NATO meeting at Athens in 1962, which was summarized in a public address at Ann Arbor, Michigan, on June 16, 1962. The stated intent of counterforce is to impress upon the potential adversaries that in the event of war (1) their strategic striking forces would be destroyed, and (2) they would thus suffer a military defeat.

Counterforce strategy, according to its advocates, is a more credible deterrent than a countercity doctrine because an aggressive nation places higher value on its military forces than on the lives of its citizens. Thus, a threat to destroy its ability or will to wage war will prove more effective than a threat against other types of targets, including urban centers. Counterforce strategists further assert that should deterrence fail and a nuclear war actually break out, striking at the adversary's military targets rather than cities minimizes the loss of civilian life. Such a targeting doctrine also gives the opponent an incentive to avoid cities, thereby potentially reducing loss of life on both sides. Even if enemy leaders are unwilling to spare cities, their forces, which will have been reduced by a counterforce retaliation, will possess only limited capacity to strike at them.

Critics of counterforce emphasize that the policy cannot be totally divorced from a number of "first-strike" implications. For example, a strike at the adversary's strategic weapons will prove more effective if undertaken before the latter have been launched. While a decision to strike the enemy's cities may be delayed—as targets their value does not decrease with time—the value of a strike against military targets is highest before the enemy has launched any of its forces, and is progressively reduced until all bombers or missiles have been launched. Because both parties in a crisis will assess the situation in this manner, and as each knows that the other is making the same calculation, incentive for a first strike is significantly heightened. A nation adhering to a declaratory policy of "second strike only," as both the United States and the Soviet Union have done, will almost certainly erode the credibility of such assertions (in the eyes of the other's leaders) if it adopts a counterforce strategy. If Nation A adheres to a second-strike declaratory policy (words), but announces its intentions to pursue a counterforce strategy and deploys its forces accordingly (words and deeds), Nation B's leaders are more likely to make their own plans on the basis of the latter than the former.

Counterforce strategy may also serve as an impetus to arms races. The force level necessary for posing a credible threat to cities [assuming that they are unprotected by an effective anti-ballistic missile (ABM) system, a point which we will examine in more detail later] are finite and relatively easy to calculate. As stationary targets incapable of concealment, cities in Nation A provide Nation B's leaders with little incentive to increase their arms stockpiles indefinitely; a countercity strategy is compatible with finite deterrent capabilities. On the other hand, Nation A, if committed to a counterforce startegy, has considerable reason to build up stockpiles; the greater one's strategic superiority, the greater the likelihood of an effective strike against military targets. Nation B's most predictable response will be to increase its strategic capabilities, thereby setting off an arms race.

Counterforce doctrine runs directly contrary to the expressed hopes of American leaders that both the United States and the Soviet Union "protect" their retaliatory systems through mobility, dispersal, and hardening. An effective counterforce capability against protected strategic systems requires (1) overwhelming strategic superiority and (2) increasingly accurate intelligence and guidance systems to locate and pinpoint strikes against such targets.[43] Efforts toward achievement of this position will succeed only in the unlikely case that the adversary fails to increase his forces. By 1964 Secretary McNamara conceded that the value of striking at Soviet ICBM sites was "questionable" in the light of expected increases in Soviet missile launching submarine forces. If, however, Nation A should achieve the ability to destroy Nation B's retaliatory capabilities, the mutual deterrence system will become highly unstable. The latter may be tempted to launch a preventive attack and the former, aware of the temptation, will have added incentive to unleash a preemptive strike.

If a counterforce strategy is to accomplish its objective of saving the maximum number of lives in case of a failure in deterrence, both sides must move their military targets as far as possible from urban population centers; to assume that under conditions of a major war either side would spare military targets in order to save cities is to attribute to leaders of nations at war a degree of magnanimity rarely encountered even in less deadly circumstances. This requirement is virtually impossible to meet in densely populated areas such as Europe, and even within the United States many key military targets are located in or near major urban centers.

[43] The Polaris, in many respects the deterrent which comes closest to satisfying our criteria of credibility and stability, can be used only against cities.

Perhaps the most serious problem in counterforce strategy is that neither side believes the other will act with the necessary restraint. Secretary of Defense McNamara has expressed his belief that major population centers will be included as targets in any nuclear attack by the Soviet Union on the United States, and a Soviet spokesman has dismissed, as not believable, stated intentions to use "humane" methods of warfare which would spare Soviet cities.[44]

The debate over targeting policy amply illustrates the difficulties of trying to apply ethical criteria to questions of defense policy. Should war break out, sparing more rather than fewer lives, as envisioned by advocates of counterforce, is clearly desirable. But if adherence to such a targeting policy destabilizes deterrence through heightening the reciprocal fear of surprise attack, can such claims of greater morality be sustained?[45]

To date American leaders appear to have acquired the diversified nuclear arsenal for an "all options" policy which would permit retaliatory strikes against both an adversary's cities and military targets. The Soviets, possessed of a smaller and less diversified nuclear stockpile, appear to have adopted a countercity doctrine.

### Anti-ballistic Missile Systems (ABM)

A potentially significant component of deterrent capabilities is the ability to protect targets by destroying attacking airplanes or missiles before they reach their destination. Credibility is enhanced if, owing to an effective active defense system, the deterrer can threaten a potential aggressor in the knowledge that the costs of a counter-strike can be minimized.

Up to and during World War II, active defense could prove effective by inflicting only limited damage to the attacker. During the "Battle of Britain" in 1940, an attrition rate of 10 per cent eventually forced the Luftwaffe to abandon its policy of bombing England into submission. In heavy Allied raids on Schweinfurt during the summer and autumn of 1943, Germany's ability to down one-sixth and one-quarter of the attacking airplanes was a considerable victory for the defense.[46]

Intercontinental ballistic missiles armed with thermonuclear weapons

---

[44] Kaufmann, The McNamara Strategy, p. 93; N. Talensky, "Antimissile Systems and Disarmament," Bulletin of the Atomic Scientists, XXI (Feb. 1965), 26–29.

[45] For a thoughtful discussion of the relationship of ethics to strategy, see David B. Abernethy, "Morality and Armageddon," in John D. Montgomery and Arthur Smithies, eds., Public Policy, XIII (Cambridge: Harvard University Press, 1964).

[46] Hans. J. Morgenthau, "The Four Paradoxes of Nuclear Strategy," American Political Science Review, LVIII (1964), 123–135.

have added considerably to the burdens of defense. Identification and destruction of a missile is a considerably harder task than downing even a supersonic bomber. Missiles launched with numerous "decoys" render adequate defense even more difficult. The problem, aptly summarized by Defense Secretary Robert McNamara, is not to hit one incoming missile with a defensive missile, but to choose, among the thousand decoys, the one war-head that is real.[47] The second problem is even more serious. Destructive capabilities of thermonuclear weapons and size of existing stockpiles are such that even an attrition rate of 90 per cent (which is currently regarded as impossible) can result in utter devastation of the target. Not only is the task assigned to the defense an inherently more difficult one, but the more demanding criterion of effectiveness requires a level of success approaching perfection.

Even if an effective ABM system becomes technologically feasible, its deployment would not be without drawbacks. The cost of even a "light"[48] ABM system has been estimated at approximately ten billion dollars, and it is generally conceded that it would be effective only against relatively crude delivery systems, not against those possessed by either the United States or the Soviet Union. Secretary McNamara has spoken optimistically about the prospects for ABM's capable of coping with "small ballistic missile attacks of the sort that Chinese Communists might be capable of launching within the next decade."[49] But with respect to a potential Soviet attack he conceded that "attempting to assure with high confidence against all reasonably likely levels and types of attack is very costly, and even then the results are uncertain."[50]

A Soviet spokesman has gone even further, asserting that ABM's provide a technically feasible "absolute weapon of defense" capable of eliminating war.[51] Despite such optimistic statements and considerable research expenditures, neither the United States nor the Soviet Union has yet deployed a full-scale ABM system. Perhaps the most extensive effort to date has been the Soviet work on an anti-aircraft system. But, as in the case of the abandoned American Nike-Zeus, it is largely irrelevant to the delivery system of the 1960's.

[47] See his statement in Kaufmann, *The McNamara Strategy*, p. 230.

[48] Deployment of a partial ABM system in the United States may not be feasible politically. An administration request to protect some cities, leaving others "naked," would no doubt create a bitter battle in Congress. Consider the dilemma of a California Senator faced with a bill to protect Los Angeles but not San Francisco or San Diego, or the likely reaction of a Senator from Ohio who finds that Cleveland, Cincinnati, and Columbus are not among the cities to receive ABM's.

[49] Coffey, *Bulletin of the Atomic Scientists*, XXI, 17–19.

[50] Statement to the House Armed Services subcommittee, quoted in *The New York Times*, January 26, 1966, p. 10.

[51] Talensky, *Bulletin of the Atomic Scientists*, XXI, 26.

At best, ABM's would appear to offer only partial protection until the next generation of delivery systems is developed, and the speed with which weapons have been superseded in the nuclear age suggests that this type of protection may be short-lived. The more effective the protection offered by ABM's, the more likely are adversaries to increase their stockpiles of weapons and delivery systems to penetrate defenses by overwhelming them with sheer numbers.[52] Or the attacker may use his first salvo to destroy the ABM system; all subsequent weapons will get a "free ride."[53] Hence the paradox that unless ABM's are highly effective (perhaps in the order of over 90 per cent),[54] they add little to national security; but the more effective they become, the more likely they are to stimulate an uncontrolled arms race which would reduce their utility. Finally, as a number of defense analysts have pointed out, ABM's tend to be more useful to the initiator of a nuclear exchange; their deployment has first-strike implications which would tend to reinforce disbelief about adversaries' declaratory second-strike policies. In summary, whatever advantages ABM's appear to offer must be weighed against their huge monetary costs and potentially destabilizing effects.

### Civil Defense

Except in periods of intense international crisis, such as during the Berlin crisis of the summer of 1961, civil defense programs have received relatively little attention in most countries. Leon Gouré, a defense analyst with the RAND corporation, has claimed that the Soviet government has undertaken a widespread program, but travellers in that country have found no such evidence.[55]

Advocates of civil defense programs to protect urban population centers have based their case on two major points. The first is similar to the argument for ABM systems. Limiting the adversary's ability to threaten and destroy targets can generally serve to increase the credibility of one's own deterrent. A threat which, if it must be executed, is likely to result in

---

[52] The destabilizing effects of ABM's are described in Stone (1965) and the Committee on Arms Control and Disarmament of the White House Conference on International Cooperation, November 28, 1965. The Committee urged a three-year moratorium on deployment of ABM's; Jeremy Stone, "Containing The Arms Race," *Bulletin of the Atomic Scientists,* XXI (September 1965), 18–21.

[53] Jerome B. Wiesner and Herbert York, "National Security and the Nuclear-Test Ban," *Scientific American,* CCXI (October 1964), 33.

[54] Singer, *Deterrence, Arms Control, and Disarmament,* p. 130, indicates that 75 per cent is probably the upper limit of effectiveness.

[55] Leon Gouré, *Civil Defense in the Soviet Union* (Berkeley: University of California Press, 1962).

limited damage to the deterrer is more likely to be believed. Conversely, a nation with some protection against nuclear attack may be less vulnerable to nuclear blackmail. Proponents of civil defense programs have placed greater stress on their function of protecting at least some segments of society should nuclear war break out. Herman Kahn has asserted that the issue is simply one of numbers, and that the criterion of effectiveness is not whether they can protect everyone, but whether they can reduce casualties.[56]

Opponents of civil defense have generally questioned the premise that such a program would contribute to the credibility of deterrence. Even Kahn has asserted that the contribution of civil defense to deterrence is so small that it can be ignored.[57] Critics have also pointed to possible destabilizing effects of a massive program of shelters: owing to the short warning time available in case of a missile attack, shelters will prove more useful to the initiator than to the target of a first strike. Thus a civil defense program may lend confirmation to the adversary's suspicions that one's weapons may be used for other than merely second-strike purposes.

The debate over civil defense again illustrates the difficulty of applying ethical criteria to issues of defense policy, not because such standards are irrelevant, but because no policy can satisfy all of them. Even if non-military questions (What criteria should be used to determine who shall be protected? Is a shelter program a giant stride toward a "garrison state"?) are not considered, the case for shelters is by no means irrefutable. The cost of even a minimal program is high enough to limit resources available for other instruments of foreign policy.[58] Nor, given the accelerated rate with which weapons systems are rendered technologically obsolete, can shelters be assumed adequate indefinitely. Had the United States embarked on such a program during the late 1940's after the first successful Soviet nuclear test, the resulting structures would provide relatively little protection against thermonuclear weapons of the 1960's. Indeed, an extensive commitment to civil defense might provide an added incentive for potential adversaries to develop and stockpile the weapons necessary to neutralize the protection provided by shelters. Finally, because shelters provide no protection against blasts in the immediate vicinity, a program of civil defense loses much of its cogency unless steps are simultaneously taken to move military targets away from urban centers.

[56] Herman Kahn, "The Possible and the Necessary," in *Components of Defense Policy*, ed. Davis B. Bobrow (Chicago: Rand McNally & Co., 1965).

[57] Singer, *Deterrence, Arms Control, and Disarmament*, p. 81.

[58] The cost of a proposed grid system of tunnels under major American cities has been estimated at 38 billion dollars. *The New York Times*, Dec. 28, 1965, p. 1.

## Arms Control and Disarmament

Arms control and disarmament cannot be divorced from consideration of deterrence. Leaders responsible for national security are unlikely to evidence much interest in the limitation of weapons if the outcome may reduce their deterrent capabilities. Motives not directly related to national security, such as a desire to reduce the burden on national budgets of military spending, have only rarely proved incentive enough to produce lasting and effective disarmament measures. Neither the protracted arms races prior to 1914 and 1939, and since 1945, nor the example of many underdeveloped states which spend a vast proportion of their meager resources on military forces, suggest that purely economic motives will arrest spiralling arms races. On the other hand, fear of national, if not global, annihilation provides unprecedented incentives to stabilize deterrence by measures to reduce the fear of surprise attack, arrest the diffusion of nuclear weapons, minimize the probabilities and effects of technological breakthroughs, and diminish the likelihood of unintended war through accident or escalation.

Attempts to control or abolish the use of force are nearly as old as war itself, and have taken the form of trying to limit both the ends sought through war and the instruments of violence. Included in the former category are the medieval concept of the "just war," which implied that force could only be used for legitimate ends; the Kellogg-Briand Pact outlawing the use of war; the Nuremberg War Crimes trials, in which the doctrine of "crimes against humanity" was used to punish certain Nazi leaders; and the United Nations Charter, in which signatories renounced the use of force except in case of self-defense or by order of the Security Council.

More modest attempts have been made to limit and control the instruments of violence. During the nineteenth century a movement to "humanize" the conduct of war led to agreements at the Hague Conference of 1899 outlawing certain weapons, including expanding (dum dum) bullets. Delegates at the Washington Conference of 1922 sought to prevent renewal of a naval arms race by limiting capital ships of the five major naval powers—England, the United States, France, Japan, and Italy—according to the ratio of 5-5-3-1.75-1.75 respectively. Subsequent efforts during the interwar years to limit either naval or land forces were unsuccessful, and even the Washington Naval Convention failed to survive the arms race of the 1930's.

Since World War II, considerable activity on questions of arms control and disarmament have produced but two formal agreements, the nuclear test ban treaty and the agreement prohibiting nuclear weapons in outer space, and even these two accomplishments are diminished by a boycott of the treaties by two nuclear nations—China and France.

The tendency to equate arms control with formal international agreements may lead to overly pessimistic conclusions about the feasibility of placing limits on the procurement or deployment of arms. Self-imposed limits on violence are sometimes more enduring than those found in treaties, and have even survived wars. Whether deriving from fear of reprisal, military impracticality, or unwillingness to bear the onus of initiating its use, neither the Allies nor the Axis powers used poison gas during World War II. During the Korean war, both qualitative and geographical limitations were imposed on American and United Nations armed forces; despite considerable domestic pressure to bomb Manchuria, "unleash" Chinese forces on Taiwan, and use "tactical" nuclear weapons, these plans were firmly rejected by President Truman. Although the Soviet Union provided North Korean forces with military aid, Soviet personnel were withheld from the war and American supply lines in Japan were not attacked.

Other types of self-imposed arms control measures which have been practiced by the United States and the Soviet Union—in the absence of any formal agreements to do so—include: (1) efforts to prevent the proliferation of nuclear weapons, even at the cost of alienating important allies; (2) moratoria on nuclear tests for limited periods of time; (3) occasional reductions in military budgets;[59] and (4) restraint in deployment of certain types of weapons, such as orbiting thermonuclear bombs. While such limitations pale in comparison to existing stockpiles, they nevertheless illustrate that not all efforts to control require formal agreements.

Given the unquestionable importance of controlling international violence, why have efforts to control arms yielded such meager results? Not the least of the reasons is the lack of agreement even on the roots of the problem: are armaments the causes or the symptoms of international tensions? The answer is as elusive as that to the question, "Which came first—the chicken or the egg?" and the contribution of arms races to the outbreak of war can be debated. The arms race during the later nineteenth and early twentieth centuries contributed to the outbreak of World War I in 1914, but more vigilant French and British defense policies during the 1930's might have enabled them to deter the aggressive

[59] For example, in the fall of 1963 American officials announced a 4 per cent reduction in defense spending; within weeks Premier Khrushchev made a similar announcement with respect to the Soviet defense budget. Roswell Gilpatrick, "Our Defense Needs: The Long View," *Foreign Affairs*, XLII (1964), 370.

ambitions of German and Italian leaders. Arms have been and are among the most comprehensible instruments for making threats. In situations where objectives are incompatible and the two sides strongly committed to their objectives, they may not be able to influence each other's behavior through diplomatic persuasion or by offering economic rewards. In the absence of some central power which can authoritatively legislate change, states will always have to contemplate those situations where intolerable demands or actions are taken or made against them, and the only possibility of successful resistance lies in deterrence through the threat to retaliate. If arms are viewed not merely as instruments of destruction, but as bargaining capabilities, manipulated in various ways to influence other states' behavior in peacetime as well as during war, we can better understand why Litvinov's admonition, "the only way to disarm is to disarm," appears deceptively simple. Solution of tension-creating political issues might at least create an atmosphere in which weapons are seen as less necessary, but it is usually assumed that one can only negotiate tension-reducing agreements from a position of strength, or, to use Winston Churchill's words, one must "arm to parley."[60] In this sense, arms can be viewed as symptoms of deeper tensions.

Even though arms can be used for creating bargaining positions, they can also contribute to international tensions, thereby reducing the probabilities of settling outstanding political issues. Decision-makers tend to perceive the intent behind their own weapons programs as purely defensive, but infer aggressive intent from those of the adversary. Doubts about the purpose of the enemy's weapons are likely to be resolved on the "safe" side, by assuming the worst ("why else would they maintain such large arsenals?"). In high tension situations decision-makers are unlikely to settle for mere parity in armaments. Winston Churchill's statement to the House of Commons in 1912 on a British program for naval construction illustrates one link in a chain of interdependent decisions which constitutes an arms race.

> In this speech I laid down clearly, with the assent of the Cabinet, the principles which should govern our naval construction in the next five years, and the standards of strength we should follow in capital ships. This standard was as follows: Sixty per cent in Dreadnoughts over Germany as long as she adhered to her present declared programme, and two keels to one for every additional ship laid down by her.[61]

[60] Singer, *Deterrence, Arms Control, and Disarmament*, p. 178.
[61] Winston S. Churchill, *The World Crisis, 1911–1914* (New York: Charles Scribner's Sons, 1928), p. 110. Odhams Books Ltd., London, proprietors of the copyright.

Decisions about levels of armaments are based on estimates of the adversary's current and expected future capabilities. These estimates may or may or may not be accurate, and to the degree that they are incorrect, the error is likely to be in the direction of overestimating the capabilities of potential adversaries. Such misperceptions provide substantial fuel for arms races. One study revealed that military leaders invariably overestimated the military capabilities of potential enemies. In 1914, for example, although the French and Germans accurately calculated the capabilities of third powers, the Germans judged the French army to be larger than their own, whereas the French believed that their army was smaller than that of the Germans.[62] Following the initial Soviet space satellites in 1957, many American defense analysts predicted that Soviet superiority in missiles during the 1960's would seriously threaten American security. Despite President Eisenhower's assurances that the so-called "missile gap" was a myth, it became an important issue during the 1960 Presidential election. Subsequent events proved Eisenhower correct, but in the meanwhile an arms race sent defense spending up considerably in both the United States and the Soviet Union.[63]

Earlier we cited fears of surprise attack, technological breakthroughs, and diffusion of nuclear weapons as the primary incentives for stabilizing deterrence through arms control. Paradoxically, these fears are also among the most formidable barriers to arms control agreements. Unlike trade agreements—which are self-executing, in which violations are immediately apparent and not likely to endanger national survival—doubts that the other parties are actually carrying out the agreements in good faith are hard to allay. Especially in a cold war situation with a historical background of distrust and tensions, the tendency to expect the worst of others becomes deeply ingrained in the habits and expectations of decision-makers. Even gestures which, if taken at face value, would be regarded as conciliatory, tend to evoke suspicions of deceit. "Inherent bad faith models" of the adversary are hard to erode, and while the threats may well be taken at face value, attempts to communicate reassurance, even through unilateral arms reduction, are likely to be discounted. When Secretary of State Dulles was questioned in 1957 about the value for reducing world tensions of a Soviet plan to decrease unilaterally their armed forces by 1,200,000 men, he quickly invoked the theme of the bad

[62] S. F. Huntington, "Arms Races," in *Public Policy, Yearbook of the Graduate School of Public Administration, 1958*, ed. Carl Friedrich and Seymour Harris (Cambridge, Mass.: Harvard University Press, 1958).

[63] Richard A. Brody and John Vesecky, "Soviet Responsiveness: A Critical Evaluation of Certain Hypotheses About Soviet Foreign Policy" (read at AAAS Conference, Berkeley, Calif., December 1965).

faith of the Soviet leadership. He was asked, "Isn't it a fair conclusion from what you have said this morning that you would prefer to have the Soviet Union keep these men in their armed forces?" He replied, "Well, it's a fair conclusion that I would rather have them standing around doing guard duty than making atomic bombs."[64]

Fear of a technological breakthrough by potential adversaries is a potent inhibitor of agreements which curtail weapons research and development activities. This fear, particularly important as time between generations of weapons has become shorter, was cited more often than any other by those opposing the Nuclear Test-ban Treaty of 1963.

Finally, if a desire to arrest nuclear proliferation is an incentive for significant arms control agreements, fear of non-signatory nations may serve as a countervailing force. While the United States and the Soviet Union shared a nuclear monopoly, agreements between them would have been influenced only to a limited extent by the demands and military capabilities of other nations. As China, France, and other nations develop increasingly powerful conventional and nuclear capabilities, potential Soviet-American agreements are likely to be inhibited unless other nations can be induced to accept the same limitations. Moreover, as the diffusion of nuclear weapons accelerates, the problems of negotiation will become more complex. Identifying areas of mutual interest and converting these into acceptable arms control formulae—difficult even in bilateral negotiations—is not likely to become easier as the number of nations directly involved increases and the ability of alliance leaders to impose their wishes on junior members declines. China and France have already indicated unwillingness to follow the lead of the Soviet Union and the United States on issues involving weapons, and others may choose to follow their example.

Another obstacle to substantial arms control agreements is the problem of verification. As weapons become more powerful and the perceived ability of adversaries to alter the existing military balance in a short span of time increases, the need for verification by inspection or other methods also increases; at the same time, it will become more difficult to accomplish. Violations of the Washington Naval Convention of 1922 were neither difficult to identify nor could they suddenly shift the military balance in favor of the violating nation. On the other hand, production facilities for nuclear weapons are considerably harder to identify, proof of violations more difficult to establish, and the destabilizing consequences of successful cheating more serious. The consistent reluctance of Soviet

[64] John Foster Dulles, Transcript of News Conference, May 15, 1956, *Department of State Bulletin*, XXXIV (1956), 884–85.

leaders—a sentiment by no means restricted to the Soviet Union—to admit international inspection teams further reduces the probabilities of reaching substantial disarmament agreements. Available evidence indicates that atmospheric and underwater tests can be detected without on-site inspection, but control of production creates more difficult problems which, despite some ingenious proposals, are still likely to require the presence of inspection teams.

A further obstacle to arms control agreements is devising formulae which will not work to the advantage of any nation. Against a background of different security requirements, *qualitatively* different weapons systems present a problem of comparability. How many bombers are equivalent to a battleship? How many infantry divisions are worth a missile-launching submarine? What is the deterrent value of an intermediate range ballistic missile (IRBM) compared to that of an ICBM capable of reaching any spot on the globe? A piecemeal approach to disarmament—for example, starting first with nuclear weapons, then moving to conventional land forces—does not wholly resolve the problem. A substantial reduction in ICBM's, missile-firing submarines, or foreign bases, in which the Western powers enjoy a significant superiority, would strongly favor the Soviet Union. On the other hand, significant reductions of armored and infantry divisions, as well as most other conventional forces, would favor the West.

Even a purely *quantitative* formula for reduction of a single type of weapon is likely to create controversy. Consider the case of Nations A and B which have stockpiles of 10,000 and 5,000 nuclear weapons respectively. An across-the-board reduction of 50 per cent, although requiring Nation A to scrap twice as many weapons, might be considered by Nation B's leaders as a method of perpetuating their inferiority. This may have been a factor in the Soviet rejection of the American "Baruch Plan," introduced in 1946, to create an international monopoly on atomic energy. The Soviets probably viewed the plan as a method to preclude any future Soviet nuclear program, while insuring an American monopoly of atomic power through its domination of the United Nations and its agencies. To assert that even Nation B's smaller stockpiles may be enough to destroy any adversary's society several times over—in short, that when nuclear stockpiles become large enough, "superiority" ceases to have much significance—may not be persuasive to those responsible for national security. These two stockpiles might also be reduced to the same absolute level. Again, whatever its "mathematical equity," such a formula is unlikely to gain enthusiastic support from Nation A. A proposal to limit Soviet and American conventional ground forces to the same ceiling may be welcomed by Americans, but the Soviets—unwilling to withdraw their armies from Eastern Europe, and perhaps faced with increasing requirements for troops deployed along the long frontier with China—are likely to reject the plan.

A final factor tending to inhibit arms control agreements is that arms races and arms control may appear to involve different types of risks. Probably few foreign policy leaders are unaware that protracted arms races entail a danger of war, but this is at least a familiar risk. On the other hand, dangers associated with disarmament measures are much less familiar and may therefore appear more threatening. Acquisition of stable deterrent forces is probably a necessary, if not a sufficient, condition for significant reduction of arms. Only when finite deterrent forces are perceived capable of providing adequate security, and arms races and the proliferation of nuclear weapons are perceived to be a greater threat to security than the reduction of arms, are significant steps toward disarmament likely. Even at that point, disarmament efforts must proceed within the context of deterrence. This is summarized by Thomas C. Schelling: "If disarmament is to work, it has got to improve deterrence and to stabilize deterrence. Until a much greater community of interest exists in the world than is likely in this generation, war will have to be made unprofitable. It cannot be made impossible."[65]

### Summary

Weapons have traditionally been used by independent political units to help defend interests and values when threatened from abroad, or to achieve expansionist goals. By their conspicuous deployment or display, they are also used to make diplomatic threats credible in bargaining situations. Because of the great capacity for destruction and the probability of instant retaliation if used first, nuclear weapons may have only limited applicability to most diplomatic situations. Unlike conventional military forces, nuclear weapons are of only marginal utility in achieving such objectives as defeating a guerrilla movement, controlling strategic waterways, occupying territory, or intervening to save a foreign government from internal rebellion. Their main value lies in deterrence, or the capacity to prevent major provocations or massive attack by enemies. Even in this limited area of inter-nation influence, weapons policies and deployment must be carefully planned because effective deterrence depends upon credibility. Piling up weapons will not by itself establish credibility if the forces are vulnerable to destruction in a first strike.

[65] Thomas C. Schelling, "The Role of Deterrence in Total Disarmament," *Foreign Affairs*, XL (April 1962), 406. Copyright by the Council on Foreign Relations, Inc., New York.

Various measures such as dispersal, concealment, or protection have been used to lower vulnerability, but none has been totally successful. Defense policy leaders must also consider the consequences of their actions on the policies of their adversaries. Actions which seemingly increase security may in fact appear provocative to potential enemies and lead to greater instability or uncontrolled arms races. Arms control, civil defense, and active defense policies also have implications on the complex equations which create both stability and credibility.

## SELECTED BIBLIOGRAPHY

Aron, Raymond, *The Great Debate: Theories of Nuclear Strategy*. Garden City, New York: Doubleday & Company, Inc., 1965.

Berkowitz, Morton, and P. G. Back, eds., *American National Security: A Reader in Theory and Policy*. New York: Free Press of Glencoe, Inc., 1965.

Bobrow, Davis B., ed., *Components of Defense Policy*. Chicago: Rand McNally & Co., 1965.

Brennan, Donald G., ed., *Arms Control, Disarmament and National Security*. New York: George Braziller, Inc., 1961.

Brodie, Bernard, "The Anatomy of Deterrence," *World Politics*, XI (1959), 13–28.

Dinerstein, Herbert S., *War and the Soviet Union*, rev. ed. New York: Frederick A. Praeger, Publisher, Inc., 1962.

Garthoff, Raymond, *Soviet Strategy in the Nuclear Age*. New York: Frederick A. Praeger, Publisher, Inc., 1958.

Hsieh, Alice Langley, *Communist China's Strategy in the Nuclear Era*. Englewood Cliffs, N.J.: Prentice-Hall, Inc., 1962.

Kahn, Herman, *On Thermonuclear War*. Princeton: Princeton University Press, 1960.

Kaufmann, William W., *The McNamara Strategy*. New York: Harper & Row, Publishers, 1964.

Kissinger, Henry A., *Problems of National Strategy*. New York: Frederick A. Praeger, Publisher, Inc., 1965.

Morgenthau, Hans J., "The Four Paradoxes of Nuclear Strategy," *American Political Science Review*, LVIII (1964), 123–35.

Schelling, Thomas C., *Arms and Influence*. New Haven: Yale University Press, 1966.

————, *The Strategy of Conflict*. Cambridge: Harvard University Press, 1960.

Singer, J. David, *Deterrence, Arms Control, and Disarmament*. Columbus: The Ohio State University Press, 1962.

Snyder, Glenn H., *Deterrence and Defense: Toward a Theory of National Security*. Princeton: Princeton University Press, 1961.

Sokolovskii, V. D., *Soviet Military Strategy*, trans. Herbert S. Dinerstein, Leon Gouré, and Thomas W. Wolfe. Englewood Cliffs, N.J.: Prentice-Hall, Inc., 1963.

Waltz, Kenneth, *Man, the State and War: A Theoretical Analysis.* New York: Columbia University Press, 1959.

Wright, Quincy, *A Study of War,* 2 vols. Chicago: University of Chicago Press, 1942.

# EXTERNAL RESTRAINTS ON ACTIONS

Previous chapters have examined the various techniques states use to reward, threaten, deprive, deter, or punish others in seeking to change or sustain their behavior. States mobilize a variety of capabilities, ranging from diplomatic talents to large military forces, as means of persuading or coercing other states to undertake policies and actions which are in their own interest. But we must not assume that governments have unlimited possibilities when it comes to selecting among alternative courses of action. We claim that all governments *may* use subversion, intervention, economic embargoes, or even massive military force, to achieve or defend their objectives, but this is only a hypothetical statement. In reality, governments select their policies and the instruments they will employ abroad only after considering the risks and costs of many alternatives. Were they completely free from restraints, they would likely choose means that would most quickly and efficiently achieve a

# CHAPTER XIII

stated objective. We know, however, that governments usually adopt slow, costly, and uncertain policies when dealing with other states. For instance, when a major power is confronted with a reluctant ally—a state which does not meet its alliance obligations or is internally so weak that it is incapable of sustaining any type of military program—why does the senior partner patiently try to persuade it through quiet diplomacy or attempt to bolster its regime through the slow process of inducing economic and governmental reforms? Why not overthrow the regime through subversion and put in its place a "puppet" government that would do the senior partner's bidding? Or why not just occupy the country and turn it into a satellite or colony, if that would be a more efficient answer to the problem of maintaining an effective alliance? This hypothetical case suggests that governments do not always choose the easiest way out of a predicament, and in policy-making situations are constantly confronted with restraints and limitations on the potential range of actions. We can define a limitation or restraint as any condition in the domestic or external environment, or any self-imposed or externally imposed rule, which prevents policy-makers from choosing certain objectives or courses of action, or from using certain instruments or techniques of inducement against other states.

Some restraints or limitations are essentially within the state's own society. Most obvious is the lack of capabilities. Many governments do not do the things they might like to do simply because they do not have the capacity to do them. Other types of internal restraints or limitations include adverse domestic reactions to proposed courses of action, and the major moral and ethical principles that find widespread support within a domestic population and among groups of policy-makers. Administrative procedures, precedents, and bureaucratic traditions might also act as internal restraints on policy-making.

Of external restraints or limitations, the structure of the international system is undoubtedly the most important; this point has been examined in Chapter VI. To restate briefly, many states find their freedom of maneuver restricted by the general configuration of power and influence in the world. In diffuse systems, states are relatively free to make and break alliances and shift their general orientations toward the external environment, whereas in polarized systems the political units are so hemmed in by restrictive alliances and the domination of the major power or powers that latitude of choice is diminished. In addition to the system's structure, two other kinds of restraints arising essentially, but not entirely, from the external environment must be considered in detail. The first is the body of rules political units develop to determine the types of actions considered legitimate, and to define those situations in which exceptional forms of inducement or punishment, such as the use of force, may be used. In our present system, these rules are largely spelled out in the body of international law which has been developing for over four centuries.

The second type of external limitation or restraint on foreign policy behavior may be grouped under the term "world public opinion." Governments may be restrained from choosing certain courses of action not only by anticipated domestic responses, but also by responses and reactions of publics in other nations. In this chapter, we will examine the effectiveness of legal norms and external opinions as restraints on action; in the succeeding chapter, two of the major *internal* restraints, ethical principles and domestic public opinion, will be assessed.

## International Law as a Restraint on Policies

Technically, certain parts of international law could be considered as internal rather than external restraints because a portion of the law of nations is little more than the obligations into which states voluntarily enter through treaties with other states. We will place international law in the external limitation category, however, because many principles and customs of the law are commonly regarded as binding whether or not they are incorporated into bilateral treaties. That is, all states are obligated to fulfill certain duties and expected to refrain from certain types of actions because those duties and restraints have been established through custom or through general principles of behavior accepted by a majority of states over the years. Many other obligations are created through treaties, wherein states voluntarily and explicitly take upon themselves certain commitments. In whichever category we put international law, the important point is that all legal norms, whether arising from custom or general principles (externally derived), or from treaties (self-derived), create obligations. Any obligation is a limitation on a government's freedom of action. Some parts of international law define what states *may* or *must* do; others point out what states must *not* do; still other rules or norms attempt to define the *situations* in which positive or negative obligations become operational. Policy-makers must always consider whether their actions or proposed responses to the actions of others conform with these obligations and standards of conduct. If governments meet these obligations, even though it might be at the expense of their interests or efficient conduct of their foreign policy, the rules have acted as effective restraints. If, in other circumstances, governments interpret the rules in an arbitrary fashion, or violate their permissive, positive, or negative obligations, we must conclude that other values and interests were more important. A common view of international politics holds that despite the existence of international legal norms, governments are not normally restrained by them except perhaps where technical and commercial matters are concerned.

When our attention is drawn daily to activities of regimes which consider it their duty to incite and support upheavals and civil wars abroad, we may easily forget the role that precepts of classical European international law play in regulating actions and transactions between states. Discussion of the instruments of policy used for punishments and rewards to change the behavior of other governments and their societies suggests that legal norms restraining their use are not always effective. Contrary to custom and the general principles of international law, diplomatic bargaining is often used as a means of making propaganda appeals directed over the heads of established governments, rather than for reaching accommodation. Governments direct external propaganda programs to exploit social fissures in foreign societies, destroy traditional loyalties, and foster attitudes and opinions favorable to the disseminating state. Economic warfare and other forms of economic punishment in many cases directly contravene customs and treaties pertaining to tariff structures, freedom of the seas, and the rights of neutrals. In Chapter X, we noted that external interference in internal rebellions transforms civil wars and revolutions into international crises, and that, for many reasons, both great powers and small increasingly seek to achieve certain objectives by gaining control of the society and government of other states through economic, subversive, and interventionary means rather than by overt aggression. Despite the existence of numerous treaties, international organizations, and charters which attempt to restrict the use and threat of force as a means of resolving conflicts and achieving objectives, effective control over national military capabilities still rests with the independent political units making up the international system.

The League of Nations and the United Nations contained in their respective constitutions the principle—or hope—that force would be used by states only in two circumstances: either for self-defense or in pursuance of a decision made collectively by members of the international organization.[1] Though all states, upon becoming members of these organizations, have acknowledged the binding character of this principle, they have normally refused in crisis situations to accept the obligations flowing from it. When they have resorted unilaterally to the threat and use of force, claims by other members of the organization that such action was illegal have had little deterrent effect. Numerous and clearly-stated

[1] Richard A. Falk, *Law, Morality and War in the Contemporary World* (New York: Frederick A. Praeger, Publisher, Inc., 1963), pp. 38–39.

prohibitions on use of force as a means of achieving objectives have not yet reached the status of effective restraints. Decisions to employ force seem to be related more closely to perceptions of threat and calculations of military and political risks and costs than to considerations of legality.

Frequent violations of legal norms by states has led many observers of international affairs to point to the inconsistency between professed diplomatic aims of nations and their actual behavior. While governments frequently pay homage to the ideal of a "world ruled by law" or the principles of the United Nations Charter, and announce strong determination to organize their actions in accordance with the restraints and obligations of the law, their actual conduct of foreign policy would suggest that they frequently overlook duties imposed on them through treaties, general principles of law, and custom. It is not difficult to draft a list of cases where behavior violated such solemn vows. From 1914 to 1916, for example, the American government vigorously protested violations of the laws of neutrality and "freedom of the seas" by both the German and British navies. But when the United States entered the war in 1917, it soon began to violate the same principles it had sought to uphold only several months earlier, particularly by blockading shipment of non-military cargoes from Europe's neutrals to the Central Powers. More recently, American administrations have frequently avowed their intention to uphold "the rule of law." But the United States has also consistently violated the air space of Communist countries in order to obtain valuable intelligence data. Though President Eisenhower and Vice President Nixon admitted in 1960 that high altitude intelligence flights over the Soviet Union were of questionable legality, they claimed that such actions were necessary for reasons of "national security." Similarly, though the United States has been among the leaders in creating a special legal system covering relations between countries in the Western Hemisphere, it has more than once violated the very precepts which it sought to have included in various multilateral treaties with Latin American countries. The American-sponsored invasion of Cuba at the Bay of Pigs in 1961 was one of the more obvious cases indicating that the United States, like many other countries, would violate international obligations if it determined that observance of the relevant principles, customs, or treaties would result in a threat to its security.

In the case of the Soviet Union, Communist authorities have frankly admitted in the past that legal norms are used only as instruments of policy and as propaganda weapons against class enemies.[2] They have

2 Percy E. Corbett, *Law in Diplomacy* (Princeton: Princeton University Press, 1959), pp. 101–104.

never conceded that international law, aside from certain obligations arising out of treaties, can exist as an independent and impartial legal system to guide their own diplomatic behavior and impose limitations on their freedom of action. Like others, they have certainly used legal doctrines to defend diplomatic bargaining positions and make propaganda, but perhaps more than others, they have violated treaty obligations with impunity while simultaneously criticizing others for breaches of international law. While Soviet authorities have condemned as illegal American interventions in Lebanon, the Congo, South Vietnam, Cuba, and the Dominican Republic, they have asserted the right of the Soviet Union to support all "wars of national liberation," and in practice have intervened constantly in the affairs of other countries.

It is not only the great powers which sometimes violate in practice the legal norms they purport, in diplomatic rhetoric, to uphold. Even the government of India, which for years criticized others for failing to observe the law of the United Nations Charter, frequently broke legal commitments in its dispute with Pakistan over Kashmir, and in 1962 even invaded the Portuguese colony of Goa, which it had been unable to obtain through persuasion or other techniques of inducement. Many small nations in Asia, the Middle East, and Africa have repeatedly taken part in intrigues, subversion, and intervention against their neighbors despite solemn pronouncements in favor of the "rule of law" and strict non-alignment.

The problem of the effectiveness of legal restraints on foreign policy is not just one of observance or non-observance of clearly defined rules of law. Governments normally characterize conflicts in the legal and diplomatic terms *which are most advantageous to their interests and objectives*. This practice is not necessarily a capricious twisting of legal principle to fit facts, but arises out of different perceptions of reality. A government may claim in its attempt to punish or threaten a hostile neighbor that its own aggressive actions are legally justified as "self-defense." Hence, in 1956, when Israel invaded Egypt, it invoked the law of self-defense. A neutral observer may conclude that Israel used aggression, while Israeli policy-makers may have been quite convinced that their attack on Egypt was a legitimate act of self-defense. In this situation, can it be determined precisely whether or not legal principles and obligations effectively restrained actions? The South African government has consistently characterized its apartheid policies as purely a domestic affair, while those on the outside have insisted that these policies are a threat to peace and a violation of the Declaration of Human Rights, hence subject to outside interference. During the uprising in Algeria in the 1950's, the rebels characterized their struggle as a "war" between two states—France and Algeria—while the French maintained that it was a domestic rebellion. One could invoke quite different legal principles as applying to the actions taken in this situation, depending upon which characterization was accepted. When characterizations of one set of events vary so greatly, it becomes extremely difficult to decide which actions are in accord with, or in violation of, the rules of international law.[3] In either case, the policy-makers may have believed sincerely that their actions were legally justified, given their understanding of the facts.

Even if there are frequent inconsistencies between diplomatic rhetoric and foreign policy behavior, and governments do not in all cases consider that legal obligations should govern their actions, we should neither conclude that law and international politics are incompatible, nor that states, when they seek to alter or sustain the behavior of others, consistently remain indifferent to legal norms and obligations. In an era of violent social changes, there are many opportunities for using inflammatory propaganda, threats of force, subversion, guerrilla warfare, and economic sanctions. But as Richard Falk has pointed out, violations of the law in crisis situations do not indicate general lawlessness any more than the incidence of several murders in a city indicates social anarchy. It is precisely because states *do* observe legal obligations most of the time that our attention is drawn to obvious violations of legal norms. Unfortunately, we take legally sanctioned behavior for granted, and when violations occur, we jump to the conclusion that international law is a hoax, or is declining as an effective restraint on actions.[4]

Quantitatively, the vast majority of transactions between governments are conducted with meticulous observation of treaty obligations, general legal principles, and international custom. Many governments accept major sacrifices when attempting to achieve their objectives, for the sole purpose of keeping their policies within the boundaries established by international law. Indeed, the rapid growth of diplomatic, technical, and military international organizations, and massive movements of technical aid, capital, and social assistance, would be impossible to sustain outside of some kind of juridical framework. One can easily imagine the chaos that would ensue if there were no commonly recognized and supported rules regulating, for example, maritime trade, epidemics, civil aviation, telecommunications, taxation of foreign citizens and their property, birth and naturalization, and diplomatic immunities. While conflicts over vital collective interests may lead to use of questionable techniques of induce-

[3] See Falk, *Law, Morality and War in the Contemporary World*, p. 33.
[4] Richard A. Falk, "Janus Tormented: The International Law of Internal War," in *International Aspects of Civil Strife*, ed. James N. Rosenau (Princeton: Princeton University Press, 1964), p. 230.

ment, most international relationships are characterized by extensive
networks of technical, economic, and cultural transactions which are
conducted with scrupulous regard for law and treaty obligations.[5] This
comment applies, as the relations between the United States and the
Soviet Union illustrate, even between states that have serious conflicts of
interests. Anyone who looks carefully at the total number of transactions
between states will be struck by the extent to which most of them are
effectively regulated by formal and authoritative rules, observed even
though in many cases they impose serious restrictions on a government's
freedom of action.

In analyzing legal restraints on policy, we need not confine our attention to formal and written rules. It is true, of course, that an accepted rule
of international law can be invoked by a state to advance its interests or
protect its rights. But the fact that it is a written rule—part of a treaty, for
example—does not necessarily make it a more effective restraint than an
unwritten and implicit "understanding" between two or more countries. If
we compare the written and customary rules of international law with
unwritten understandings, we may find the latter to be more significant in
preventing certain types of actions than the former. The major antagonists in the cold war seem to have tacit understandings, for example, to
(1) attempt to prevent the proliferation of nuclear weapons, (2) use
tactical or strategic nuclear weapons only where core interests or values
are under direct attack, (3) limit their participation in internal and
limited wars to conventional weapons, and (4) refrain from orbiting
vehicles armed with nuclear weapons. The advantages to international
stability gained from observing these understandings may be greater than
those derived from meeting formal legal and treaty obligations; violations
of such understandings might also involve much greater consequences
than violations of formal treaties. The Soviet Union might, for example,
provide arms to a revolutionary movement in a country with whose
government it had a treaty obligating it not to interfere in its internal
affairs. Providing arms would clearly violate the treaty obligation, but still
might be undertaken without much consideration of the legal aspects of
the issue if the military and diplomatic costs and risks were not high. On
the other hand, the Soviet government would probably consider very
carefully the costs and risks involved in breaking the understanding with
the United States not to place nuclear weapons in outer space.

Still, there are cogent arguments which should alert us against placing
too much emphasis on legal norms or less formal understandings as

---

[5] Maxwell Cohen, "From Diversity to Unity: International Law in a Bipolar
World," *American Society of International Law, Proceedings* (April 1959), p. 104.

effective limitations on the use of foreign policy instruments, particularly in crisis situations. Conditions which help to make possible a viable and effective legal system in a domestic society do not exist yet at the international level. Formulation, interpretation, and implementation of legal norms lies essentially within the jurisdiction of the units making up the system, not in a supranational organization with enforcement powers.[6] We would not claim that an effective legal system existed in our domestic society if each citizen could interpret the law as he saw fit in each circumstance. Yet, this analogy applies to international law. Each state interprets its rights and obligations so as to make them conform with its interests, values, and objectives; each is free to decide whether legal norms are or are not relevant to a specific situation; and each still determines for itself whether or not it will use force to achieve its objectives. Invocation of legal rules by diplomats seeking to realize their government's objectives does not in itself establish the existence of a legal system, for often the rule is used for purposes of propaganda, to elicit support for a foreign policy action, and not as a guide to, or restraint on, behavior. When a state reserves for itself the discretion to determine whether or not a particular rule applies in a given situation, it is claiming subjectivity that would seem incompatible with the objective properties of a domestic legal system.[7]

In the following discussion of several historical international systems, we are confronted with two questions: first, was there a comprehensive set of norms which constituted an analogy to a body of commonly recognized international law? If so, how and to what extent did the political units of the system incorporate these rules in their policies and transactions? Were their actions restrained by the rules of the system? In other words, we cannot deduce the *observance* of norms in foreign policy decisions and actions from the fact that norms existed as custom or in treaties. It is one thing to say that a body of law exists, but quite another to say that an effective system of restraints on action exists.

## Use of Legal Norms
## in Pre-Industrial International Systems

The first generalization which can be made from a review of pre-industrial international systems is that legal or ethical norms, backed by religious sanctions, were often effective in regulating actions and transac-

[6] Richard A. Falk, "Revolutionary Nations and the Quality of International Legal Order," in *The Revolution in World Politics,* ed. Morton A. Kaplan (New York: John Wiley & Sons, Inc., 1962), p. 316.
[7] Corbett, *Law in Diplomacy,* vii.

tions between independent political units existing *within a common civilization or culture*. In many civilizations, one can find legal or religious principles which established routines to handle (1) communications between the political units (various forms of diplomatic immunity, for example) (2) commercial transactions, (3) conduct of warfare, and (4) observance of treaties.[8] There is also evidence regarding the lack of legal or religious norms in ordering the relations *between political units of two distinct civilizations or cultures*. The laws existing among the political units of one culture were seldom applied in relations with "barbarians" beyond the geographical and cultural boundaries of the system. Until the twentieth century, the Europeans, much as the Hindus, Greeks, or Moslems of earlier ages, did not consider that the legal obligations observed in relations with each other could be applied equally in transactions with "savages" or "barbarians" of entirely different cultures. Classical European international law and its historic analogies seem to have been recognized and commonly observed only within groups of political units which were integrated enough to constitute a real system.

The second point is that there are many analogies between the rules found operating effectively in historical systems and those of modern international law. Both the reports of explorers and the more recent studies of anthropologists have noted the rather sophisticated rules and ceremonies which were associated with economic, diplomatic, and military transactions between tribes, lineage groups, city states, and ancient empires. Almost all peoples used various forms of treaties—as we do—to secure peace, followed by some kind of ceremony, ritual, or sacrifice to seal obligations. The sanctions to these treaties were often religious beliefs that those who broke them would die or receive some violent punishment. But peace-making presupposes recognition of the inviolability of a belligerent tribe's representatives or of some mediating third party. Various forms of diplomatic immunities were extended to all kinds of messengers and envoys in these primitive systems, not just to those on official peace-making missions. Economic exchanges were normally consummated according to strict rules, and in many cases tribes also possessed rules and customs regulating the outbreak and conduct of warfare. Regular observance of these religious restraints helps to explain why, despite frequent wars and violence, many tribes survived for centuries.[9]

[8] See, for example, Baron S. A. Korff, "An Introduction to the History of International Law," *American Journal of International Law*, XVIII (1924), 246–59; Bronislaw Malinowski, "An Anthropological Analysis of War," *American Journal of Sociology*, XLVI (1941), 521–50; Rudolf W. Holsti, *The Relation of War to the Origin of the State* (Helsingfors, 1913), pp. 60–70.

[9] Holsti, *The Relation of War to the Origin of the State*, p. 67.

In the ancient Hindu international system, the role of law in ordering transactions between independent units was much less in evidence, and few analogies with modern international law are to be found. Princes and kings recognized neither the concept of a family of sovereign states nor a well-defined body of law.[10] Although some vague understandings pertaining to diplomatic immunities and commercial transactions seemed to exist, sovereigns did not faithfully observe them except when they feared serious reprisals. Some rulers did undertake obligations through treaties solemnized by oaths, but there is little evidence that treaties were observed for any reason other than immediate gain. Indeed, there was so little faith in treaties that the signatories often exchanged hostages as a guarantee for compliance. Lack of the most basic rules for transactions in the Hindu system is revealed in a passage of Kautilya's *Arthasastra,* in which he recommends that a king threatened by a neighboring sovereign invite him to his realm on the pretext of attending a festival, wedding, or elephant hunt, and then take him prisoner and even slay him.[11] War and use of force were accepted as normal activities of the state, whether undertaken for glory, plunder, territory, or creation of vassal states. There grew up later, with the fall of the Mauryan dynasties, a vague principle that certain forms of conquest ("demonaic conquests") involving indiscriminate annihilation and slaughter should be avoided. "Righteous" conquests to create vassal states were the ideal for which Hindu kings were expected to go to war. Other chronicles from the period claim that there were fairly strict rules governing conduct of warfare. These mention that warriors fighting from chariots could not strike those on foot, wounded enemies could not be slain, and, as a form of arms control, poisoned weapons could not be used.[12]

If the politics of the Hindu system strike us as violent and untempered by a set of commonly observed rules of behavior, relations between the Chinese empire and its surrounding vassal states in the feudal period (1122 B.C.–771 B.C.) of the Chou dynasty were a model of propriety and stability. The Chinese had not, at this time, developed a set of legal principles which established rights and duties between political units, but

[10] Adda Bozeman, "Representative Systems of Public Order Today," *American Society of International Law, Proceedings* (April 1959), p. 18.

[11] George Modelski, "Kautilya: Foreign Policy and International System in the Ancient Hindu World," *American Political Science Review,* LVIII (1964), 556. There is other evidence, however, that the ancient Indians did, on the whole, observe treaties and develop some legal norms that were observed for reasons other than immediate gain. See Frank M. Russell, *Theories of International Relations* (New York: Appleton-Century-Crofts, Inc., 1936), pp. 41–46.

[12] A. L. Basham, *The Wonder That Was India* (London: Sidgwick and Jackson, 1954), pp. 122–24, 126.

there were effective "unwritten" rules deriving partly from old customs. These, rather than treaties or legal codes, established norms and limits on what the Chou emperors could and could not do in their relations with other peoples. As was pointed out in Chapter II, the Chinese conceived of the Middle Kingdom as the center of the political universe. Ideal relations among the "barbarian" political units, the vassal states, and the Middle Kingdom were to be established on the model of relations between father and son. In the natural hierarchy of the universe, the Emperor (or the Son of Heaven) was at the top and each state on the periphery occupied an appropriate place. Order and stability between societies ensued when each political unit conducted its actions and transactions in accordance with the norms appropriate for its station in the hierarchy. The rules applied equally to the Emperor, so that his authority over other states could not be exercised capriciously. Moreover, as center of the political universe and "father" of many diverse "children," the Son of Heaven was obligated to set correct examples for all other states to follow.[13]

In the Spring and Autumn and Warring States periods, when the system had developed into a group of independent, rather than dependent, states, the old rules governing relations within the feudal hierarchy remained, but only as norms to which the states paid lip service. They broke down completely as effective restraints on the actions of states toward each other. War, intervention, subversion, and annihilation were frequently employed no matter what the old customs had required in the feudal period. Instead of a system of rules designed to maintain stability in a hierarchical system, the major rules of the late periods of the Chou dynasty were developed primarily as a means of encouraging certain types of restriction on the conduct of warfare—restrictions frequently violated in the last bloody stages of the Warring States period. It was a recognized principle, for instance, that belligerents would respect the person and property of non-combatants.[14] Other rules included the requirement that a state notify its allies of any impending military activity, and that it ask permission of neighboring states to send its troops through their territories. It was also considered inappropriate to invade a state whose ruler had the same surname, or to invade a state in the same year that its ruler had died.[15]

[13] See Bozeman, *American Society of International Law, Proceedings* (April 1959), p. 19.
[14] Russell, *Theories of International Relations,* p. 29.
[15] Winberg Chai, "International Law and Diplomacy in Ancient China (771–221 B.C.): An Introduction," *Chinese Culture,* V (1963), 55.

## The Growth of European International Law

Legal, religious, and ethical norms regulating transactions between diverse political units existed in many non-Western, pre-industrial international systems and civilizations. However, it was in Greece, the Roman Empire, and particularly in seventeenth century Europe that the first coherent legal systems, divorced from religion, developed. Among primitive tribes, and in India, China, and the Islamic empire, the norms observed in inter-unit transactions were inseparable from general precepts of morality or religion, or from ancient customs. The concepts of legal rights and obligations of sovereign governments, central to modern international law, did not come into existence until the appearance of the European nation state system in the fifteenth, sixteenth, and seventeenth centuries.[16]

What order that existed in late medieval Europe grew out of the authority of the Church to prescribe general rules of conduct and from the customary rules of chivalry. In addition, medieval society incorporated the tradition of natural law and order from Rome, from which other principles relating to the transactions between political units were derived. Generally, however, it was the Church, with its notions of hierarchy, authority, and duty, and its ultimate sanction of excommunication, which had the largest impact in moderating the politics of the period. The Peace of God, declared by the Church in the tenth century, attempted to impose restrictions on war, violence, and plundering, but the results were negligible. The Truce of God (1041) established by the Bishop of Arles and the Abbot of Cluny was more successful, and did effectively limit the scope and degree of violence in certain parts of medieval Europe. There was to be, for example, no fighting between Wednesday evening and Monday morning. Such declaratory laws were never observed with any precision, nor did they gain acceptance as custom except in some localities. Later in the medieval period the doctrine of "just war" arose and helped to deter some forms of violence. The Church considered war "illegal" and its perpetrators subject to ecclesiastical punishment if it was not properly declared by established authorities, with just causes and legitimate objectives.[17]

The basic premises and rules of modern international law—sovereignty,

[16] Quincy Wright, *The Role of International Law in the Elimination of War* (Manchester: Manchester University Press, 1961), pp. 18–19.

[17] See for details M. H. Keen, *The Laws of War in the Late Middle Ages* (Toronto: University of Toronto Press, 1965).

territorial integrity, equality, and non-interference in other states' internal affairs—developed simultaneously with the growth of centralized dynastic political units which no longer accepted the command of any authorities within or outside of their boundaries. Diplomats and dynasts might have acknowledged certain principles of justice deriving from the "law of nature," but generally their conduct in foreign relations was restrained, if at all, only by obligations undertaken with each other in treaties. Religious principles, the church, and abstract notions of "natural law" no longer effectively limited what the new sovereigns or principalities could and could not do toward their neighbors. Restraints were mostly self-imposed, voluntarily observed, and enforced primarily by the threat of counter-action and retaliation. Customs also played a role in providing criteria for distinguishing legitimate from illegitimate policies, and in some instances the writings of eminent lawyers and theologians, such as Grotius, Pufendorf, and Vattel, had an impact on restricting the actions of Europe's political units. This is not to suggest that by the eighteenth century there existed either a comprehensive set of legal norms prescribing rights and duties in all kinds of relations, or a general practice of observing treaties in conducting diplomatic and commercial relations between dynasts. Claims by dynasts that certain customs were so well established as to be part of international law were seldom met with agreement by other states.[18] Rules observed during the conduct of warfare seemed to arise more from the limitations imposed by a crude military technology than from commonly-recognized legal principles or humanitarian sentiments. Nevertheless, jurists and diplomats continued to elaborate on the "law of nations," the number of international treaties proliferated, and dynasts increasingly referred to legal advisers in conducting their policies, even if they did not consistently apply the legal advice they received.

New European needs gave the impetus for rapid development of international law in the nineteenth century. In particular, the growing volume of intra-European trade and development of sources of raw materials and markets in non-European areas created similar types of transactions and hence similar outlooks toward the rules needed to place economic relations on a stable and predictable basis. Britain's dominant naval position enabled it to establish almost unilaterally the foundations for the modern law of the sea. Of course, the norms designed to regulate maritime commerce during peace and war served British private and public interests, but these happened to coincide in many instances with the interests of other states as well. The greatest expansion of legal doctrines covered

[18] See Corbett, *Law in Diplomacy*, Chap. 1.

matters pertaining to the obligations of debtor states, sanctity of money, protection of commercial property during civil strife, and expropriation of private property.[19] These aspects of international law expressed the contemporary European doctrines of laissez-faire economics and the mutual interests of European businessmen in expanding markets and obtaining security for their foreign investments. In addition, new bilateral and multilateral treaties established legal controls over the main waterways of the world, including the Declarations of Paris on maritime law (1856), the series of conventions establishing regulations for the Turkish Straits, Black Sea, and Baltic Sounds, and new regimes for the Panama and Suez Canals (1888 and 1903). This complex network of legal regulation and obligation helped to provide for orderly, but constantly expanding, transactions of commercial nature. Thus, nineteenth century international law was the law of an expanding commercial civilization. But in regulating the use of force and tempering national and imperial rivalries, the law was much less effective.

The doctrine of "just war," which had placed some limitations on the use of force prior to the eighteenth century, was never carried through to the nineteenth century. On the contrary, governments viewed the threat and use of force as legitimate exercises of a sovereign's will. Though some publicists fought for the cause of peace and disarmament, the law of the period reflected the belief that war was a self-justifying instrument of inducement. The relative military stability of the nineteenth century and the restraints on the use of force flowed from the creation of deterrents and the operation of the Concert of Europe, not from the effectiveness of legal principles.

Nineteenth century international law did incorporate limitations on the scope and degree of violence.[20] New laws of neutrality established definite rights and obligations for both belligerents and neutrals, helping prevent the extension of bilateral military confrontations into continental or regional holocausts, and certain areas or countries such as Switzerland (1815), Belgium (1831), and the Congo Basin (1885) were permanently neutralized by the great powers, thereby removing them from the arenas

[19] See Richard A. Falk, "Historical Tendencies, Modernizing and Revolutionary Nations, and the International Legal Order," in *Legal and Political Problems of World Order* ed. Saul H. Mendlovitz, prelim. ed. (New York: The Fund for Education Concerning World Peace Through World Law, 1962), pp. 133–34; Charles De Visscher, *Theory and Reality in Public International Law,* trans. P. E. Corbett (Princeton: Princeton University Press, 1957), p. 136; Morton A. Kaplan and Nicholas de B. Katzenbach, *The Political Foundations of International Law* (New York: John Wiley & Sons, Inc., 1961), p. 28.

[20] Falk, "Revolutionary Nations and the Quality of International Legal Order," in *The Revolution in World Politics,* p. 320.

of conflict. A series of multilateral conventions and codes were also drafted to prevent undue suffering among troops and civilians alike. In most cases the laws of neutrality and warfare were observed until developments in military technology in the twentieth century made them more or less obsolete.

### Contemporary International Law: The Source and Existence of Legal Norms and Restraints

International law, based on its European origins, has continued to develop in scope and precision during the twentieth century despite the occurrence of two great world wars. An important part of our contemporary law has arisen from the *customary practices of states* over many decades and centuries. In many cases, governments have assembled to translate customary practices into multilateral *treaties or codes,* thus setting custom in a more precise framework of written rules. *International and domestic tribunals* have handled thousands of cases involving conflicts between citizens and governments of diverse states, and their decisions, though not strictly binding on subsequent cases, have established many important principles and precedents considered to be part of the modern law of nations. Finally, states have concluded thousands of *bilateral and multilateral treaties* establishing mutual rights and obligations as well as restrictions on what governments may or may not do in their external relations. Unlike the customary sources of international law, treaties can be drafted, changed, and adapted to particular needs and circumstances and can, therefore, establish immediately new principles, rights, and obligations to regulate the relations between states. For example, since there is no precedent or precise analogy to the problems presented by space exploration, the law covering this area must be *created* by governments through negotiated treaties. Treaties cannot establish new rights or obligations for those states which are not parties to them, whereas customary rules of law can be invoked by all states.

From these sources has grown a modern international law which displays, through custom and precedent, continuity with the past, but which is infinitely more complex than it was in the past. It seeks to regulate, stabilize, and make predictable types and quantities of commercial and political transactions that are largely unprecedented. In addition, the new law reflects contemporary ethical values which condemn the use of force as an instrument of inducement. The nineteenth century attitude and doctrine toward war as an instrument of policy to be unleashed by any government solely at its own discretion has been replaced by prohibitions in the United Nations Charter against recourse to force, and even the threat to use force, except in cases of self-defense or in conformity to a collective decision. The old laws of neutrality have been superseded by the obligation of *all* states to assist victims of aggression. As an outcome of the Nuremberg Trials of Nazi war criminals and the Genocide Convention, personal criminal liability can be imposed against those who launch wars of aggression. In short, as Quincy Wright points out,[21] under the new international law war is no longer viewed as a duel between legally equal belligerents to be regulated only in its scope, but rather as a crime against all nations which must be prevented.

It would be difficult to deny the existence of a comprehensive set of rules, rights, obligations, and legal doctrines which can be found in numerous treaties, in customs and codes, and in the thousands of decisions of national and international tribunals. These are designed to define rights, limit a state's freedom of action, and prescribe rules of conduct for all types of transactions—technical, commercial, diplomatic, and military. Before we investigate the extent to which these rules and customs effectively restrain action—or in some cases compel states to take certain actions—it is necessary to point out some of the shortcomings of modern international law, faults found in the body of norms rather than in the behavior of states.

In the first place, no legal norm is so precise as to convey absolutely clear meaning to all people. Though that part of international law based on custom may be more enduring because it reflects common usage and needs,[22] some aspects of it are also vague and imprecise, leaving each state to interpret the custom according to its own interests. Treaties can be formulated more precisely, but these, too, may contain phrases too vague to guide behavior in predictable fashion. Even some provisions of the United Nations Charter have been interpreted in many different ways by states. As one legal scholar has put it, "Legal norms . . . have in varying degrees an elastic or rubber-like quality, and can often be stretched to fit the objectives of a decision-maker."[23] Until the day when all conflicts arising out of different interpretations of the law are submitted to impartial tribunals, each government—as do private citizens—will usually construct the meaning of treaties and conventions in such a way as to favor its own political objectives.

---

[21] Wright, *The Role of International Law in the Elimination of War*, pp. 27–28.

[22] De Visscher, *Theory and Reality in Public International Law*, p. 155.

[23] Oliver J. Lissitzyn, "Western and Soviet Perspectives on International Law—A Comparison," *American Society of International Law, Proceedings* (April 1959), pp. 22–23.

Second, legal norms, when they are not legislated by a central political body, tend to change very slowly, with the result that some rules of international law become obsolete before governments acknowledge their obsolescence. Although some governments may feel strong pressures to violate obsolete and unjust norms, their actions are violations nevertheless until a majority of states in the system agrees, through practice or conventions, upon new norms. Is it valid, for example, to criticize or make claims against the Allies' persistent violations of the law of neutrality during World War II when the kind of warfare made possible by new industrial technology required vast sources of raw materials which the neutrals supplied to the Axis powers? The laws of neutrality were drafted in an age of relative economic independence, a condition which no longer prevails. Can the killing of civilians be prevented, as required by the laws of land and naval warfare, when antagonists use nuclear-tipped missiles, long-range artillery or conventional heavy bombs, or where military and civilian targets are inseparable? Is the traditional three-mile territorial limit—which developed originally because a state could only maintain effective control over adjacent waters as far as its cannons could fire—of use today when many states need and are capable of extending their jurisdiction to a further limit? In cases such as these, the need to modify the law may be perceived by many nations, but it is sometimes very difficult to get a majority of states to agree to new standards. On the other hand, if changing conditions excuse violations of rules and doctrines, very few norms would be entirely effective, and little predictability would be possible in the relations among states.

Closely related to the problem of obsolescence is the need to develop legal standards for regulating new phenomena and types of transactions between states. Presently, international lawyers are grappling with the problem of creating legal norms to cover the use of outer space, but whether or not they will succeed in this task before some states begin using outer space for military and espionage ventures remains in doubt. Perhaps where more precise and modern norms are most urgently required is in the realm of subversion, guerrilla warfare, and intervention. These, rather than overt aggression, are the instruments of policy used currently to achieve objectives and gain ideological victories, but the laws relating to these problems are often vague and occasionally obsolete.

Most international lawyers have acknowledged that modern international law is essentially a European law. Though some areas of the law, such as those relating to diplomatic immunities, communication, and maritime trade, are designed to benefit all states equally, other subjects express primarily the needs and interests of the developed Western countries. So far, the newer states have willingly adopted most of the classical European rules of law and the new principles in the United Nations Charter. But on some questions, such as the protection, confiscation, and indemnification of foreign owned property, and the use of force against colonial regimes, the underdeveloped countries have been less than enthusiastic in adopting traditional European standards.[24] With the rise of new states which have needs quite different from those of the Western industrial states, there is, in addition to differing interpretations of existing law, bound to be disagreement as to what the law *should be*. Some of the treaties to which the underdeveloped territories are partners were originally imposed by Western colonial powers. One can hardly expect that all new states will view one of the fundamental doctrines of international law, *pacta sunt servanda* (treaties are binding), in the same light as will the officials of long-established governments.

We should not place too much emphasis on these inadequacies of the body of legal norms, for it might lead us to conclude that the ineffectiveness of some legal restraints and limitations arises from deficiencies in the law itself. Nor should we assume that the behavior of governments in this respect will change simply by bringing the norms up to date or making them more precise. Despite the existence of hundreds of arbitration treaties between states, the League of Nations Covenant, the Geneva Protocol of 1924, the Treaty for the Renunciation of War (The Kellogg-Briand Treaty, 1928), the Anti-War Treaty of Rio de Janeiro in 1933, and the United Nations Charter, the use of force has not been effectively regulated yet. Some of these treaties and charters are not entirely clear in their details, but this should not suggest that more and better treaties or international institutions will solve the problem of war. More important is that relatively few disputes and conflicts of objectives arise out of differing interpretations of law. If international politics were defined only as the problems and processes of adjusting conflicts arising from differing conceptions of legal rights and duties, we should be concerned with studying ways to improve the content of the law. But since international politics involve, in addition to collaborative and competitive relationships, the problems and processes of adjusting conflicts arising from more or less incompatible collective objectives, then no matter how clear, precise, and logical the law is, it would not be observed in all instances. The body of the law is far from perfect, but failure to observe legal norms does not necessarily result from imperfections of the law.

[24] See, for example, J. J. G. Syatauw, *Some Newly Established Asian States and the Development of International Law* (The Hague: Martinus Nijhoff, 1961); B. V. A. Röling, *International Law in an Expanded World* (Amsterdam: Djambatan, 1960), pp. 10–12, 48.

### The Use of Law in the Pursuit
### of Foreign Policy Objectives

In analyzing the role of legal norms in the conduct of foreign policy, it is important to remember that many of the customs, treaties, and doctrines of international law are designed to regulate essentially *private* transactions between citizens of different nations. They are not necessarily concerned with the types of issues arising from conflicts over incompatible *collective* objectives. A substantial portion of existing treaties and legal principles create obligations and provide the ground rules for actions and transactions relating to foreign investment, fishing and conservation, extradition of criminals, maritime traffic, payment of damages to foreign citizens, citizenship, responsibility of minor police officials for actions against non-citizens, and so forth. Such affairs normally do not involve major collective interests, even though violations of established procedures or rules may create nasty incidents. The distinction between a routine and vital matter in foreign policy is not always clear,[25] of course, but great international crises seldom arise out of breaches of law affecting the interests of private citizens.

In dealing with the problems of private citizens and business enterprises, governments tend to rely heavily on established bureaucratic procedures. Since most governments apply approximately similar norms to these transactions, the element of opposition and conflict is reduced and in many cases completely eliminated. Even where violations of law have occurred against private citizens and their interests, governments are no longer likely to translate these problems into diplomatic conflicts, particularly where relations between the two states are relatively cordial. A great expansion of private and intergovernmental routine transactions has occurred during this century and, though we are not often reminded of the fact, the vast majority of these transactions and the decisions associated with them are based on principles of international law.[26] In these areas of foreign relations, governments have at least approached the ideal of the "rule of law." When conflicts do arise, they are often conflicts of differing interpretations of the law and are referred to governmental legal experts who negotiate agreements, using as their basis of discussion and decision not only facts, but established legal principles as well. In

[25] Richard A. Falk, "The Province of Law in International Relations," paper delivered at 1963 Annual Meeting of the American Political Science Association, New York, pp. 9–10.
[26] *Ibid.*

many other cases, the disputing parties submit their differences to arbitral tribunals or other prearranged procedures for settlement.

When we move into those areas of international politics involving conflicts between important collective objectives, the role of law in effectively prescribing the limits of action is much less predictable. Whether or not legal rules are a major consideration in the framing of policies in a conflict situation probably depends upon the general climate of relations between two countries, their mutual responsiveness, and the degree of incompatibility between their objectives. If a serious conflict arises between allies which have a tradition of responsiveness to each other's needs and interests, legal rules may very well set the limits to the policies used to change the behavior and attitudes of the other state, or in resolving the conflicts between them.

Legal norms are also likely to restrain behavior or to prompt observance of obligations if both sides perceive that their prestige might be lowered by flagrant violations of accepted international practice or of treaties. Certainly most governments are sensitive to their prestige and reputation, and one way to destroy it is deliberately to violate treaties and unwritten understandings.

The effectiveness of legal norms in restraining some types of behavior may also be related to general attitudes toward law found in various cultures. As two scholars of international politics have argued in comparing the effectiveness of legal restraints in foreign policies:

> Communist ideology . . . leaves no room for the sense of moral obligation as a distinct factor in the observance of international law. Even in the West this factor is probably less important than that of rational self-interest. But rational self-interest in the observance of law tends in the long run to be transformed into a moral imperative. In the pluralistic Western system, side by side with the idea that observance of law is a matter of expediency, there has always been another idea—that keeping the law is morally good, that law and morality have objective validity, and that they lie at the very foundation of civilized existence. There is a traditional respect for law that carries over into international affairs. The over-all Western attitude toward international law is a composite, a blend in varying proportions, of these two principles—the principle of expediency and the principle of moral obligation—re-enforced by the "law habit."[27]

This is not to suggest that all conflicts between normally friendly states are settled in accordance with the requirements of established legal norms. Many conflicts are not amenable, in any case, to legal treatment. But in their attempts to influence the attitudes and behavior of each

[27] Harold and Margaret Sprout, *Foundations of International Politics* (Princeton: D. Van Nostrand Co., Inc., 1962), p. 565.

other, these states do observe law—though often not as a conscious choice —by deliberately avoiding hostile actions, such as promoting civil disturbances, indulging in espionage, establishing boycotts, interfering in the other country's internal affairs, or threatening the use of force. It would perhaps be more accurate to say that in those types of relations, called in Chapter VII "relations of consensus" and "relations of overt manipulation," the observance of legal norms and practices is itself an important means to the achievement of objectives.

Disregard for treaty commitments and general principles of international law is often observed where (1) two or more states have incompatible objectives which can be achieved only at each other's expense, (2) the level of involvement between them is high, (3) there is no tradition of mutual needs or responsiveness, and (4) one side has already established a precedent by undertaking actions in violation of the law. When these circumstances combine, adherence to treaty obligations or norms prohibiting the use of certain instruments of inducement is often sacrificed in favor of defending or achieving an objective with higher value. Conflicts in this kind of relationship are seldom resolved by recourse to legal rules and procedures because values much more important than law-observance are at stake.

Whether or not legal norms effectively inhibit or restrain certain types of behavior in a conflict situation depends on an assessment by policy-makers of the value of observing legal norms versus the value of achieving or defending the stated objectives of the government, when obligations and proposed action are incompatible. In relationships typified by great hostility, incompatibility of objectives, and commission of force by the other side, no statesman could be expected to attach absolute value to law-observance if by doing so he would sacrifice all his other objectives, including the security of his country. It is in this kind of a situation that even the most legally-minded statesmen choose to use whatever techniques of statecraft or actions are necessary to achieve or defend stated objectives, even when they are fully aware that to do so involves deliberate violation of treaties or legal principles. In 1939, for example, Winston Churchill, as First Lord of the Admiralty, recommended that the Royal Navy plant mines in the territorial waters of neutral Norway in order to prevent the shipment of iron ore from Sweden to Nazi Germany. Churchill knew that such action would violate Norway's neutrality and territorial waters, but defended his recommendation on the ground that "the letter of the law must not in supreme emergency obstruct those who are charged with its preservation and enforcement. . . . Humanity, rather than legality, must be our guide."[28] It is not

[28] Quoted in Lissitzyn, "Western and Soviet Perspectives on International Law," *American Society of International Law, Proceedings* (April 1959), p. 25.

difficult to find instances where even legal scholars have defended the legal violations of governments on the grounds that there were more compelling moral imperatives—particularly the demands of "national security"—than strict adherence to legal norms and treaty obligations. Thus, when advancement of one nation's objectives seriously threatens those of another, military and strategic criteria rather than legal desiderata tend to dominate the making and execution of foreign policy decisions. The inhibiting role of law is still seen frequently when governments, confronted with a situation in which they cannot reconcile policy alternatives with legal obligations, still choose a course of action which is *least* blatantly a violation of obligations, or which is of only debatable legality.

Law tends to be used in crisis situations as a theme of propaganda and self-rectitude rather than as a set of norms prescribing effectively what governments can or should not do. Governments whose interests and rights are being pressured or violated by opponents protest these violations of recognized standards of practice, treaties, or doctrines, while those taking actions clearly in violation of established rules can usually find *some* legal principle, no matter how obsolete or disreputable, to justify their behavior. For example, the Soviet government repeatedly proclaims its support for the principle of non-interference in the internal affairs of other countries and lets loose a barrage of propaganda, based on legal themes, when any Western nation intervenes militarily in an underdeveloped country. But when the Soviet Union intervenes, either through outright military assaults or subversive activities, it appeals to such lofty principles as "self-determination" or "national liberation" to rally support for its actions. Similarly, while the United States violated rules in the Charters of the United Nations and the Organization of American States, as well as in its own Neutrality Acts, to support and direct the Bay of Pigs invasion in 1961, it sanctified its actions by invoking the Monroe Doctrine, a doctrine of very questionable legal status. In these and many other cases involving small and great nations, law was used essentially for self-justification or to gain diplomatic and domestic support.

One way of discerning the extent to which legal norms actually guide or restrain behavior in policy-making and execution is to study the role of legal advisers in foreign offices, particularly during important conflicts and crises. It would not be surprising to find that, in most of these situations, legal advisers are neither consulted nor brought actively into the decision-making process. In other cases, legal advisers may be consulted only with a view to having them construct a *post facto* justification for propaganda purposes. Occasionally, legal advisers have played the role of counsellors, impartially examining a situation in which important objectives were at stake and actually instructing the policy-makers as to the limits within which their actions should be maintained.[29] In still other instances, governments have suspended action pending inquiry by the legal experts of their foreign offices. This does not mean that the advice given will ultimately be followed, but it does suggest at least a willingness to accept legal criteria as factors in making foreign policy decisions. International law would probably become even more important in regulating behavior during conflicts if legal advisers were in a position to tell policy-makers what the rules were and what types of behavior they would require.

The attitude of the Soviet Union toward international law has changed in recent years. During the 35 years following the Bolshevik revolution, the Soviet regime systematically violated treaties and broke almost every traditional European diplomatic and legal standard. International lawyers were clearly apologists for the regime and had little, if any, influence on formulation of foreign policies. Until shortly after Stalin's death, Soviet international lawyers and party theorists viewed all law as simply an instrument of a particular class. The Soviet Union, they argued, could not be bound in its actions by the classical principles or customs of the law of nations because these were merely the rules that European and American merchants had developed in order to exploit their own working classes and colonial peoples. Since the socialist and imperialist states were locked in a lengthy combat for superiority (irreconcilable objectives were assumed), there could be no moral obligation to abide by agreements and rules made with or by the "enemy." Soviet authorities viewed international law as a weapon of the class struggle, to be used only if it served the interests of the revolution.[30]

In recent years, however, Soviet international lawyers, while not playing any important role in foreign policy-making, have come closer to accepting Western attitudes toward the law. That they use the law for purposes of propaganda is obvious; but this does not mean, contrary to frequent statements in the West, that the Soviet government is totally unreliable in meeting legal obligations, as it was, perhaps, in the past. On the contrary, with a much wider network of relations throughout the world, the Soviet government can no longer afford to create a reputation of unreliability, as Stalin did. Soviet policy-makers no doubt realize today that in order to have any relations with the West and the underdeveloped

[29] For historical examples where some important British actions were based on the views of legal advisers, see Corbett, *Law in Diplomacy*, Chap. 1.

[30] See, for example, Lissitzyn, *American Society of International Law, Proceedings* (April 1959), p. 27; Corbett, *Law in Diplomacy*, pp. 101–104; and John N. Hazard, "Soviet Socialism as a Public Order System," *American Society of International Law, Proceedings* (April 1959), p. 39.

countries, including diplomatic connections, trade, and cultural exchanges, they must abide by the rules which have come to be associated throughout the world with these kinds of transactions. Not to observe these rules and customs would mean the end of such relationships and, hence, the decline of Soviet influence in the world. The changing role of law in Soviet actions does not necessarily imply a new attitude toward the law, but does indicate that international law can be observed with considerable regularity if that law is consonant with a state's own interests.

Any review of actual cases of policy-making by governments would reveal, in summary, that international law performs several functions in foreign policy, depending upon the type of action being considered, the form and content of a conflict with another state, and the values placed on observing established rules versus achieving other objectives, when the two are incompatible. Law establishes rights and obligations, some of which are observed all the time, and others which are violated more or less regularly; it inhibits certain kinds of actions and promotes others; its doctrines are used for propaganda purposes; it can help to define areas of a dispute which are amenable to legal procedures; and it helps to make routine many types of transactions between governments and between the private citizens of different nations. Certainly in most routine transactions legal rules are all-important, but in great conflicts they tend to become more peripheral considerations in the making of decisions.

### Observing Legal Restraints:
### The Sanctions of International Law

How do we reconcile the argument that a true international legal system does not exist because the individual states decide for themselves what constitutes the norms of the system, how they should be interpreted, and how they should be applied, with the fact that governments often feel compelled to order their policies according to international rules and that often they do consult legal advisers before initiating actions? The further argument that law is used primarily for rhetorical and propaganda purposes during crisis situations does not repudiate the observation that an extensive body of usage, custom, and law does help to regulate the day-to-day business of governments. Is this to suggest that governments generally observe legal norms relating to routine transactions but neglect the rules when vital interests conflict? Such a thesis would be an over-simplification, for it is possible to cite many cases where the reverse situation prevailed. Moreover, it is difficult to determine the line between "vital" and "routine" transactions. The problem is an empirical one, requiring careful investigation: if, regardless of the importance of the issue involved, conduct is in accordance with legal doctrines and customary practices, and all parties to the transactions in question recognize and comply with the same norms, then we can say that international law, as found in custom, treaties, and court decisions, is an effective guide and restraint in the formulation and choice among policy alternatives.

In order to understand why governments do *not* capriciously and arbitrarily interpret or violate the law for short-run advantages, we have to examine briefly the sanctions of international law.

In most legal systems, rules and customs are normally observed for four distinct, though similar, reasons: (1) self-advantage, (2) habit, (3) prestige, and (4) fear of reprisal. Legal norms are a suitable basis for conducting transactions, particularly where they can help advance the values and interests of one party and where the other party, by observing the rules, can also expect some benefit. The expectation of *reciprocity*, for example, is an important factor in the observance of legal norms and obligations. A government accepts the obligations and restrictions imposed by law because it expects, or hopes, that the partners with whom it is in a relationship will base their decisions and responses on similar legal criteria. Self-advantage is mutual. This does not mean that all other considerations are irrelevant to the making of foreign policy decisions; it means, rather, that governments in most situations recognize and acknowledge the long-run advantages—particularly reciprocity—of conforming their actions to legal norms. This realization tempers considerations of expediency, military "necessity," and short-run political advantages. When the advantages of law-observation are clear and persistent, a habit or custom of conducting transactions according to certain principles and routines may also arise.

In addition to reciprocity and habit, another advantage of law-observance is that a government may effectively raise its international prestige, and thus its diplomatic influence with other states, if it develops a reputation in the community as a "law abiding" state. A reputation for meeting treaty obligations and observing well-established legal principles in many types of transactions may be an important asset in the daily dealings of diplomats. Small states, in particular, may be able to obtain a sympathetic hearing from the governments of major powers if their reputation for observing legal obligations is well established.[31] A govern-

---

[31] We can cite the case of Finland in the 1930's and 1940's to illustrate this generalization. The American government and people were very sympathetic to Finland's interests during this period largely because Finland had earned a reputation for honesty as a result of being the only country in the world to repay the United States

ment which persistently breaks treaties, defies resolutions of international organizations, and capriciously twists the accepted meaning of legal doctrines will lower its credibility in diplomatic negotiations, and hence its influence. One need point only to the poor reputation of the Soviet Union until Stalin's death. For many years Western governments were reluctant to enter into any trade or cultural negotiations with his regime on the ground that the Soviet government had violated the letter or spirit of almost every important political and commercial treaty to which it had been a signatory.

Negative sanctions, or fear of various forms of reprisal, may also prompt governments to observe their obligations. Development of norms relating to diplomatic immunities is a good example. It was common among new dynastic regimes in Europe not to accord immunities to foreign diplomats, with the result that sometimes foreign diplomats were abused, jailed, and even executed by the government to which they were accredited. But this situation did not prevail, because these governments quickly recognized that if they treated foreign diplomats in this manner, their own representatives abroad could be—and were—treated similarly.

In addition to self-interest, habit, prestige factors, and fear of reprisal, two other considerations must be mentioned as reasons why governments, when faced wth alternative courses of action, often choose the one most closely in accord with legal obligations and established practice. First, all governments, whether they explicitly acknowledge it or not, desire at least some convenience, stability, and predictability in their external relations. The ordinary transactions between nations which are necessary to maintain economic viability, communications, and even security, are based on routines protected by legal doctrines or treaties. If these transactions were made completely unpredictable by lack of law-observance, chaos and the impossibility of orderly policy-making would ensue. Even revolutionary regimes during their years of external aggressiveness willingly comply with many of the rules of law adhered to by their enemies simply in order to exist. For states with more modest external objectives, law-observance for many types of transactions becomes so routine that policy-makers would consider other alternatives only in great conflicts or emergencies. The desire for stability and predictability can also be seen when governments convene after great wars or periods of instability to make permanent changes that had been achieved through political and military actions. The peace treaty—as many other types of

---

every dollar it had previously borrowed. This one act of meeting obligations created inestimable goodwill and responsiveness toward Finland, and hence increased Finnish diplomatic influence vis-á-vis the United States. Juhani Paasivirta, *Suomen kuva Yhdsvalloissa* (Helsinki: Werner Söderström, 1962), Chap. 10.

treaties—creates a new order out of chaos, stability out of rapid change, and preditability out of uncertainty.

Governments may or may not accept the limitations on actions imposed by legal norms. Certainly it is not difficult to cite obvious violations of international law. But diplomatic history also reveals abundant evidence that many statesmen do place high value on at least appearing to comply with written and unwritten rules, legal doctrines, and treaties, and that in so doing they display not only concern over their prestige or possible retaliation, but demonstrate their belief in the ethical value of law-observance. In selecting among alternative courses of action, policy-makers do not always adopt a Machiavellian approach, thinking: "This time I will observe the law because I fear retaliation, or a lowering of my prestige, if I do not; but perhaps next time, if I think I can get away with it, I will disregard legal prohibitions and seek to achieve my objectives the quickest way possible and at least material cost." Law is, after all, more than a set of arbitrary rules derived from custom and treaties. In so far as legal norms and doctrines prevent governments from doing certain things, punish others, or prescribe certain courses of action, they reflect values and moral judgments. The provisions of the United Nations Charter prohibiting the threat or use of force, or the principles of the Genocide Convention, do not arise from custom, prior treaties, or court decisions. These rules—and many unwritten understandings—emanate directly from a widespread belief that the use of force or the systematic slaying of religious or ethnic groups is inherently immoral and ethically reprehensible.

The observance of these and many other types of rules thus derives from considerations other than convenience. Although policy-makers often excuse certain illegal actions as being dictated by the demands of "national security" or "national interest," they do not consistently break rules and norms just because they are acting in the name of the state. Men are usually anxious to do not only what is practical and convenient, but also what they believe is right. Policy-makers, just as private citizens, will frequently respect a rule, or choose that course of action most consistent with legal norms, because they believe that the norms are intrinsically correct and ought to be observed regardless of some particular disadvantage derived from their observance. An eminent international jurist, Charles De Visscher, has written that the observance of international law is ultimately a problem of individual attitudes and morality, and not a question of the existence of lack of perfection in legal doctrines.

> The problem of obligation in international law is part of the problem of obligation in general and this in turn is a moral problem. The distinction be-

tween ethical and legal categories, reasonable in itself and in many ways necessary, must not be pushed to the point of completely separating law from the primary moral notions to which all the normative disciplines are attached as to a common stem. Between States as within the State, law belongs to morals insofar as the idea of the just, which forms its specific content, is inseparable from the idea of the good, which is a moral idea. What, then, in the international sphere, is the order of facts, interests, ideas, or sentiments that can provide the moral substratum of obligation? Merely to invoke the idea of an international community . . . is immediately to move into a vicious circle, for it is to postulate in men, shut in their national compartments, something that they will largely lack, namely the community spirit, the deliberate adherence to supranational values. No society has any legal foundation unless men believe in its necessity. The ultimate explanation of society as of law is found beyond society, in individual consciences.[32]

## Foreign Expectations and "World Public Opinion" as External Restraints

Through treaties, declarations, and traditional methods of dealing with other states, most governments create abroad certain expectations that future actions will conform with past patterns of behavior. American officials expect that the British will conduct their foreign relations according to certain standards, and when these standards are not met or are violated, both governmental and public protests may ensue. Part of the unfavorable American reaction to the British invasion of the Suez Canal and Egypt in 1956 derived from the widespread expectation that the British did not, as a matter of style and tradition, resolve their international conflicts by military aggression. On the other hand, American policy-makers for many years held an "image" of the Soviet government as untrustworthy, deceitful, aggressive, and an unreliable partner to treaties and other international commitments.[33] When Soviet behavior did conform to this image, indignation was not so strong because the behavior was expected and predictable.

Opinions expressed by governments and peoples toward the actions of foreign states do not vary solely because of different expectations. There

[32] De Visscher, *Theory and Reality in Public International Law,* p. 98.

[33] This "image" is remarkably consistent in the memoirs of American statesmen who have dealt with Soviet officials since 1933, and in various writings and documents concerning American-Soviet relations in this period. See for example, Harry S. Truman, *Memoirs,* Vol. I. (Garden City, N.Y.: Doubleday & Company, Inc., 1955), p. 320; John R. Beal, *John Foster Dulles, 1888–1959* (New York: Harper & Row, Publishers, 1959), pp. 199 ff.; James Byrnes, *Speaking Frankly* (New York: Harper & Row, Publishers, 1947); Robert Murphy, *Diplomat Among Warriors* (Garden City, N.Y.: Doubleday & Co., Inc., 1964), pp. 435 ff.

exists also the problem of different perceptions by peoples with different experiences. Many forms of Soviet behavior which Westerners have considered unethical may be similar to types of behavior their own governments have practiced. The predominant American public "image" of Great Britain is that of a loyal ally, courageous, and magnanimous in voluntarily adapting its colonial empire into a free commonwealth of nations. To an African nationalist, however, the concept of Britain arising from his personal experience may be that of a rapacious imperial power which exploited his people, practiced the most blatant forms of discrimination, and supressed legitimate political movements. The same African, who has no experience with Soviet diplomacy and foreign policy, may look upon the Soviet Union as just another great power which has successfully industrialized in a short period of time and risen to a position capable of challenging the United States for world leadership. In turn, this "image" of the Soviet Union is not likely to be similar to that held by a refugee from the Hungarian revolution of 1956. Different historical experiences greatly affect our perceptions of reality and our expectations concerning the behavior of other governments. It is unlikely, therefore, that when one nation undertakes efforts of rewards or threats of punishment, its actions will be interpreted in a similar way in different areas of the world.

Aside from obvious cases such as overt aggression or genocide, it is difficult to believe that such a thing as "world public opinion" exists today, if by that we mean a fundamental and popular consensus as to what constitutes legitimate, legal, or ethical behavior in international relationships. Unlike the European international system of the eighteenth century, where a small cosmopolitan aristocracy possessed similar cultural traits and social values, the people who make judgments on international events today do so from the vantage of diverse traditions, ideologies, and ethical standards. With such diverse values, and therefore perceptions, the people in question may not only differ as to what constitutes moral and immoral behavior, but the meanings they ascribe to a set of commonly-perceived facts may be so diverse as to preclude development of any common world-wide opinion on a situation. No better examples could be cited than those international crises in which one or more Western powers was involved in a conflict with a non-aligned nation.

In 1964, for example, the United States and Belgium intervened in the Congo to rescue several thousand white civilians being held as hostages and threatened with massacre by a band of Congolese rebels. The operation was completed with some success by a surprise airlift and military operation against the rebels in Stanleyville. Though many civilians were slain by the rebels, most, including many Congolese citizens, were saved. There was little divergence in reporting the facts in the various newspapers of the world (except in the Communist press), but the meanings ascribed to those facts differed greatly. The operation was characterized in the Western press as a humanitarian mission to save innocent civilians who were being held, contrary to international conventions, as hostages and threatened with death. But the press in most African countries viewed the operation as an ugly imperialist adventure taken under the cloak of humanitarian slogans, with the real purpose of re-establishing imperialist domination of the Congo. When judgments on even a simple set of facts vary this widely it is difficult to say that any "world public opinion" exists at all.

We must also approach cautiously the concept of "world public opinion" as an effective restraint on action because often the demonstrations condemning a foreign government's external policies are not spontaneous expressions of attitudes, but organized incidents led by government officials or professional agitators who wish to embarrass the target government for their own purposes. Caution is also warranted when we are reminded that freedom of the press is not practiced in most countries and that, through governmental restrictions and censorship, citizens of many countries are able to get only their own government's version of a particular set of events. These governments usually characterize events in the light of their own ideological predilections and foreign policy interests. Even in those countries where press freedom is observed, reporting of news may be so slanted by stereotypes and omissions, or by under- or over-emphasis, that the people who obtain information solely from these news sources may express opinions not congruent with the facts of a situation.[34]

If governments do not place too much credence on expressions of hostile opinion abroad, perhaps, some would argue, they are at least sensitive to, and constrained by, opinions expressed in the General Assembly of the United Nations. This body has been characterized by some as the "organized conscience of mankind," the court which ultimately judges the conduct of all governments. While opinions expressed in the General Assembly are no doubt brought to the attention of all governments, it would be misleading to assume that governments nor-

---

[34] Some social scientists would argue that hostile attitudes directed toward another country do not arise simply out of one or two isolated cases of "immoral" international behavior that may be reported in the media of communication. Rather, there may be important psychological and social sources of the hostile attitude and the perceived "immoral" behavior is used only to confirm and reinforce latent predispositions. As we pointed out in the chapter on propaganda, attitudes which derive from the nuclear personality and are sustained by social connections are seldom amenable to change by propaganda or example. Hence, many people in the West will remain unalterably hostile to the Soviet Union, no matter how "moral" its behavior. Similarly, there will always be important groups of people around the world who are strongly anti-American, no matter how "moral" or "immoral" American policy appears to them.

mally conduct their foreign relations to accord with the sentiments of the majority, as expressed in the debates and votes of the General Assembly. In some cases, of course, the General Assembly votes overwhelmingly to condemn a particular course of action or to ask a government to cease behaving in a certain way, and the government in question, noting the diplomatic coalition arrayed against it, will comply with that vote. In these instances members of the General Assembly have been able to induce what they consider more ethical or legal behavior. It should be added, however, that in most of these instances opinions and protests voiced in the General Assembly were backed up by diplomatic pressures which individual states exerted outside of the United Nations. During the 1956 Suez invasion, for example, the British and French agreed to a cease-fire not so much because of the General Assembly's condemnation of their invasion of Egypt, but because their major ally, the United States, failed to support them in their actions and also because the Soviet Union threatened to intervene on Egypt's behalf.

What, then, are we to conclude about the role of "world public opinion" and expectations of other governments as external limitations on the conduct of a government's foreign relations? Because there are historical examples which indicate both the effectiveness and impotence of foreign opinion as influences on a government's behavior, it is difficult to generalize. However, some conclusions or hypotheses might be suggested. First, most governments *are* sensitive to the opinions expressed abroad about their policies and how they execute them. Otherwise they would not spend such large sums in trying, through diplomacy and propaganda programs, to create favorable impressions abroad. But they are not equally sensitive to all sources of opinion. Where, for example, perceptions of reality vary greatly, the government being condemned will probably not count hostile opinions as important. If the Soviet Union characterized American intervention in South Vietnam as imperialism and aggression, this is so different from the American government's understanding of the situation that Soviet hostility would probably be discounted. Also, governments are no doubt much more sensitive to opinions expressed by their closest friends and allies than those emanating from non-involved or hostile countries. Similarly, they are more concerned with conforming their actions to their allies' expectations than to those of states with whom they are not so directly involved.

Second, most governments are concerned with their prestige, an important, though intangible, aspect of their diplomatic effectiveness. No government could anticipate with pleasure a resolution in the General Assembly condemning its actions abroad. But in some crises, policy-makers place such high value on achieving or defending their objectives that they are willing to break commitments, violate rules to which they normally adhere, and, in short, follow strictly national imperatives. In many other instances policy-makers *anticipate* the reactions of other governments and choose policy alternatives which are least likely to meet with hostile reactions. We can cite cases where resolutions in international organizations both failed and succeeded in persuading governments to observe legal and moral obligations; it is more difficult to know of all those cases where governments did *not* choose a particular course of action because their policy-makers anticipated unfavorable responses abroad. If we conceive of "world public opinion" as being both the spontaneous and organized expressions of attentive publics on particular situations, often communicated through propaganda channels, it can be an effective restraint on policy, provided there is some agreement among the publics, the attitudes are also expressed by friendly governments and are not merely the expected hostility of unfriendly states, and defiance of those attitudes would lower a state's prestige and diplomatic influence.

## SELECTED BIBLIOGRAPHY

Anamd, R. P., "The Role of the New Asian-African Countries in the Present International Legal Order," *American Journal of International Law,* LVI (1962), 383–406.

Barkun, Michael, "International Norms: An Interdisciplinary Approach," *Background,* VIII (1964), 121–29.

Brierly, James L., *The Basis of Obligation in International Law, and Other Papers.* Selected and edited by Hersch Lauterpacht and C. H. M. Waldock. Oxford: The Clarendon Press, 1958.

———, *The Law of Nations,* 6th ed., rev. by Sir Humphrey Waldock. New York: Oxford University Press, 1963.

Corbett, Percy E., *Law in Diplomacy.* Princeton: Princeton University Press, 1959.

———, *Law and Society in the Relation of States.* New York: Harcourt, Brace & World, Inc., 1951.

De Visscher, Charles, *Theory and Reality in Public International Law,* trans. Percy E. Corbett. Princeton: Princeton University Press, 1957.

Falk, Richard A., *Law, Morality and War in the Contemporary World.* New York: Frederick A. Praeger, Publisher, Inc., 1963.

———, "The Reality of International Law," *World Politics,* XIV (1962), 353–63.

Fitzmaurice, Gerald G., "The Foundations of the Authority of International Law and the Problem of Enforcement," *Modern Law Review,* XIX (1956), 1–13.

Friedmann, Wolfgang, *The Changing Structure of International Law.* New York: Columbia University Press, 1964.

————, "Half A Century of International Law," *Virginia Law Review,* L (1964), 1333–58.

————, "The Uses of 'General Principles' in the Development of International Law," *American Journal of International Law,* LVII (1963), 279–99.

Higgins, Rosalyn, *The Development of International Law Through the Political Organs of the United Nations.* London: Oxford University Press, 1963.

Hoffmann, Stanley, "International Systems and International Law," *World Politics,* XIV (1961), 205–37.

Jessup, Philip C., "Diversity and Uniformity in the Law of Nations," *American Journal of International Law,* LVIII (1964), 341–58.

————, *Transnational Law.* New Haven: Yale University Press, 1956.

Kaplan, Morton A., and Nicholas de B. Katzenbach, *The Political Foundations of International Law.* New York: John Wiley & Sons, Inc., 1961.

Khadduri, Majid, and Herbert J. Liebesny, eds., *Law in the Middle East.* Washington, D.C.: Middle East Institute, 1955.

Korff, Baron S. A., "An Introduction to the History of International Law," *American Journal of International Law,* XVIII (1924), 246–59.

Lissitzyn, Oliver, "International Law in a Divided World," *International Conciliation,* No. 542 (March 1963), 1–69.

McDougal, Myres S., and Florentino P. Feliciano, *Law and Minimum World Public Order: The Legal Regulation of International Coercion.* New Haven: Yale University Press, 1961.

McWhinney, Edward, "Peaceful Coexistence and Soviet-Western International Law," *American Journal of International Law,* LVI (1962), 951–70.

Northedge, I. S., "Law and Politics Between Nations," *International Relations,* I (1957), 291–302.

Nussbaum, Arthur, *A Concise History of the Law of Nations,* rev. ed. New York: The Macmillan Company, 1954.

Ramundo, B. A., and A. Rusis, *The Soviet Socialist Theory of International Law.* Washington: George Washington University, Institute for Sino-Soviet Studies, 1964.

Stone, Julius, *Legal Controls of International Conflict: A Treatise on the Dynamics of Disputes and War-Law.* New York: Holt, Rinehart & Winston, Inc., 1954.

Syatauw, J. J. G., *Some Newly Established Asian States and the Development of International Law.* The Hague: Martinus Nijhoff, 1961.

Triska, Jan F., and Robert M. Slusser, "Treaties and Other Sources of Order in International Relations: The Soviet View," *American Journal of International Law,* LII (1958), 699–726.

Wright, Quincy, *Contemporary International Law: A Balance Sheet.* Garden City, N. Y. Doubleday & Company, Inc., 1955.

# Internal Restraints on Actions

In formulating policies and taking actions, governments often observe restraints imposed by legal principles and treaty obligations. While they anticipate foreign reactions to their plans, the configuration of power and influence throughout the international system also sets limits on their freedom of action. These types of restraints derive essentially from the external environment in which nations operate. Governments also operate under restraints which derive basically from the domestic environment. The quantity and quality of capabilities that can be employed as instruments of persuasion, inducement, or coercion act as restraints. Others would include domestic public reactions to projected and actual policies, and ethical and moral restraints.

# Chapter XIV

## Capabilities as Restraints and Limitations
## on Decisions and Actions

Many governments rule out certain types of aspirations, objectives, and actions because they are impossible, given the resources and capabilities at their disposal, to achieve. A lack of capabilities is perhaps the most explicit restraint in decision-making situations. Although governments frequently set for themselves objectives which they do not have the capacity to achieve, in formulating policies officials always make some sort of means-ends analysis. If adequate capabilities are not available either in the form of manpower, economic strength, military matériel, or diplomatic support from abroad, in most cases the objective has to be scaled down or abandoned altogether. After World War II, for instance, the British—and more reluctantly the French, Dutch, and Belgians—had to dissolve their empires because they did not possess the means, considering other social objectives their governments had to achieve, with which to hold on to them in the face of the demands of indigenous independence movements. Before 1958 the French could not seriously aspire to a position of leadership in Western Europe because of their lack of diplomatic prestige, military strength, and political stability.

Influence, as we have suggested, is always a relationship. Capabilities act as restraints on actions only to the extent that those capabilities are perceived in a particular situation to be significantly *weaker* than those whose behavior must be changed or reinforced. State A may decide not to attack state B over a disputed boundary because state B's capacity to retaliate is overwhelming. But state A might attempt to subvert B's government because the risks and costs of this type of policy might be slight. In other words, lack of capabilities as a restraint might also be conceived as the superior deterrent capacity of other states. A government is restrained in its objectives and actions not only by its internal weakness, but also by the relative strength of actual and potential opponents.

### Domestic Public Opinion as an Internal Restraint

In addition to anticipated responses of foreign governments and populations, policy-makers—at least in reasonably free societies—must measure their proposed actions against reactions of domestic groups, the "attentive public," and in some cases of the entire population. As we pointed out in Chapter VI, the influence of domestic attitudes on policy choices varies from issue to issue. Policy-makers confront some situations which will have only slight effects on domestic groups. Here, presumably, they can make their choices with little reference to the reactions of those outside the government. In questions of peace and war, or basic economic interest, however, government officials may feel constrained to take only those actions with a reasonable chance of eliciting widespread public support or which, at least, will not give rise to broad condemnation. Domestic political popularity, prestige, and the possibility of maintaining elective office are always considerations high level policy-makers keep in mind when they have to decide on some course of action. To the extent that in any situation requiring some kind of response, some actions are ruled out because of anticipated unfavorable domestic reaction, we can say that public opinion has acted as an effective restraint.

## The Role of Ethics and Morality as Internal Restraints

In the past, much of the public and scholarly debate on the place of ethics in a society's foreign relations has assumed that policy-makers have a choice between posing as "realists" or "moralists"—that ethical restraints are in a sense *voluntary* or optional. There is, in fact, an intellectual tradition in American diplomatic history reflecting the realist and moralist approaches to foreign policy. The moralists often list among their heroes Jefferson, Wilson, Hull, and some lesser figures; Hamilton, Calhoun, and Theodore Roosevelt are often cited as exponents of a realist approach to foreign relations. Looking at the speeches—though not actions—of these men, one can see the distinction between the two approaches. In the early 1790's, for instance, Jefferson and Hamilton conducted a debate over the young republic's obligations to revolutionary France. Jefferson claimed that the United States was committed to assist the French in their wars because the Franco-American alliance signed during the War of Independence was still in effect. He asserted that a country had to meet its commitments even if it was not in its direct interest to do so. Hamilton claimed the contrary, arguing that a nation's self-interest can be its only guide to policy. One cannot, he suggested, apply ethical principles to problems of foreign policy.

Regardless of historical context, commitments to self-interest or ethical principles have, to most observers, appeared incompatible. A clear expression of this supposed incompatibility can be found in one of Woodrow Wilson's campaign speeches, when he claimed that:

It is a very perilous thing to determine the foreign policy of a nation in the terms of material interests. . . . We dare not turn from the principle that morality and not expediency is the thing that must guide us, and that we will never condone iniquity because it is most convenient to do so.[1]

The difficulty with this sort of view is that it oversimplifies reality. Both moralists and realists assert that there is a choice between following policies of self-interest or of principle. The moralists imply that pursuit of self-interest at the expense of principle leads to immoral, or amoral, diplomatic and military behavior. The realists reply by declaring that self-interest, when prudently pursued, is ethically justifiable in itself, and that the pursuit of ideals only causes great ideological crusades which end in tragedy. Some would add, quoting Machiavelli, that "A man who wishes to make a profession of goodness in everything must necessarily come to grief among so many who are not good."[2] A review of diplomatic history would not support such extreme views of reality. It may be true that, in Machiavelli's day, typical forms of diplomatic conduct were notoriously low when judged by today's standards. Diplomats commonly lied, and many took their own cooks abroad for fear that local servants would poison them. The record of assassination, intrigue, and duplicity in Renaissance diplomacy is will documented.

Today, the instruments of violence are capable of destruction and misery far beyond the imagination of Renaissance military officials. But this does not mean that the *general standards* of conduct between states are low, or that ethical principles are totally absent as restraints on action. No society, after all, can achieve or defend its objectives solely through uninhibited use of force, or by breaking all commitments and obligations when it might be advantageous to do so. If the moralists argue that it is so easy to observe ethical restraints, why is it that Woodrow Wilson, one of the great moralists in twentieth century diplomacy, found it necessary to compromise his principles in the conduct of relations with Mexico in 1914, or in negotiating the various peace settlements after World War I? The complex relationship between ethical restraints and policy can be understood first by abandoning the simple dichotomy between expediency and morality, and then examining the role of values and ethics as revealed in several historical decision-making situations.

[1] Quoted in Hans Morgenthau and Kenneth W. Thompson, *Principles and Problems of International Politics* (New York: Alfred A. Knopf, Inc., 1950), p. 24.
[2] N. Machiavelli, *The Prince*, trans. Luigi Ricci, rev. by E. R. P. Vincent (London: Oxford University Press, 1935), Chap. 15.

## Ethics, Morality, and Values as Psychological and Cultural Restraints

One way of relating ethical considerations to diplomacy is to conceive of ethics as a combination of cultural, psychological, and ideological "value structures" which inhibit consideration of all possible policy alternatives in a given situation. They establish limits beyond which certain types of behavior become inconceivable. In the framework of Communist ethics and Stalin's personal values, there is nothing unusual in his suggestion to Churchill in 1944 that one way of permanently resolving the German threat would be to capture the German officer corps of 50,000 men and liquidate all of them. To Churchill, the product of an entirely different political culture, the plan seemed totally abhorrent. He rejected it not only because he knew that the British public would not stand for it (anticipated domestic reaction), but also because he found it personally repugnant.[3] Such a scheme had never occurred to Churchill in the first place, and it is in this sense that social values and individual ethical principles limit our perceptions of alternatives. The example also suggests that there is likely to be close correspondence between the ethics, belief systems, and value orientations of policy-makers and those held generally in the political culture in which they operate. If a government consistently breaks treaty obligations, practices duplicity in its diplomacy, and uses force and violence without inhibition, it is probable that the society in general and the domestic political system in particular condones such behavior. But how are we to account for decisions and policy actions which *are* beyond the boundaries of normal social or individual value systems?

Churchill could not imagine exterminating 50,000 German officers, but he ordered, apparently with public acquiescence, Allied bombers to kill hundreds of thousands of German civilians in mass incendiary raids which had only indirect consequences on Germany's military strength. An even more dramatic instance of the seeming absence of ethical restraints occurred in the summer of 1945, when the United States government decided to drop the newly-developed atomic bomb on Japan. Considering that this weapon was known to be unusually destructive of life, what possible justification could be offered as necessitating its use? How could

[3] Winston Churchill, *Closing the Ring* (Boston: Houghton Mifflin Company, 1951), pp. 373–74.

the government consider such an alternative if it meant so much suffering? The decision to use atomic weapons on Japan is instructive because it illustrates the subtle and complex role of ethics in foreign policy-making.

Three groups of people were involved in the decision. First were the scientists who had been working on perfecting the instrument. More than others, they were able to foresee both the frightening and spectacular implications of the weapon. Many scientists were deeply concerned that such an instrument of destruction should be used at all, while others saw it as the most efficient way of ending the war quickly. The second group was composed of professional military men directly connected with the bomb project. They regarded the bomb project as just another administrative task which had to be completed in the shortest time possible so that it could be used against the Japanese to force them to surrender. The third group, composed of high-level civilian policy-makers, including the Secretaries of War, State, and Navy, as well as President Truman, also regarded the weapon as a means of forcing the Japanese to surrender as well as a method of ending the war before the Soviet Union could become deeply involved in military actions against the Japanese. It was commonly anticipated that if the war dragged on and Russian troops participated in an invasion of the Japanese islands, the Soviet government would insist upon being rewarded with a zone of occupation such as it had received in defeated Germany.

How did these three groups react to the situation in which they had to decide between employing or avoiding the use of this weapon of unprecedented destructiveness? Aside from some of the scientists working on the project, the choice of using the bomb was never viewed as posing essentially a moral or ethical problem. All the policy-makers understood that a bomb dropped on a city would cause tens of thousands of deaths and as many injuries, to say nothing of the total devastation of the target cities. The Army Air Force had already been conducting massive fire bomb (napalm) raids on Japanese cities, causing a loss of life and level of destruction only slightly less than that resulting from some of the most dramatic strategic raids on German cities. In one raid on Tokyo, fire bombs destroyed several square miles of the city and caused the death of 83,000 people—considerably more than were to die several months later at Hiroshima. The Secretary of War, Henry Stimson, was the only high-level policy-maker to question the morality of these raids. They were destroying Japan's capacity to wage the war, to be sure; but at a fantastically high cost in civilian lives.

When it came to make the decision to use atomic weapons, then, ample precedents for slaughter on a massive scale already existed. Both sides had fought World War II with widespread brutality, and there was no expectation that the atomic bomb would introduce any new dimension in suffering. Widespread death would just occur more rapidly. Neither the scientists, the armed forces officials, nor the civilian policy-makers argued against using the bomb on the grounds that it would involve a large loss of life.[4]

In fact, very few of those participating in the bomb project ever questioned that the weapon would be used; this, it seems, was taken pretty much for granted. It was easily rationalized on the ground that the Japanese would never surrender without some dramatic demonstration of force. An invasion of Japan had already been scheduled for the autumn of 1945, and it was anticipated that from one-half to one million American casualties would result from such an operation, plus an even heavier toll of Japanese lives. The alternatives were either to avoid using the bomb and accept an extremely high loss of life on *both* sides, or to use the weapon, at a *relatively* low cost in Japanese lives, hoping that the destruction of one or two cities would induce the Japanese government to surrender. A third alternative—a compromise negotiated peace—was never considered in Washington after the formula of "unconditional surrender" had been agreed upon by the Allied governments in 1943. It was also ruled out because neither Congress nor the American people would have accepted less than total victory.

The main arguments concerning the bomb thus revolved around two subsidiary questions, and it is here that ethical considerations became more apparent in the making of decisions. Calculation of deaths occurring by atomic bombing as compared to an invasion of Japan was relatively easy to predict; even on hindsight the decision to use the bomb seems to have been correct, provided that the alternative of a negotiated peace is left out. The first question flowing from the decision to use the weapon was whether or not the Japanese should be warned in some way about the destructiveness of the bomb. Among the civilian policy-makers and the scientists, many argued that the United States should first demonstrate the bomb to the Japanese, either in a test in the United States or by exploding it over some unpopulated area in Japan. Those who argued along these lines felt that the United States was morally obligated to give the Japanese a clear warning and visual evidence of what fate should befall them if they did not surrender. In this way the basic moral choice

[4] Many interesting memoirs regarding Japan's surrender have been published. The facts discussed below are derived from Len Giovannitti and Fred Freed, *The Decision to Drop the Bomb* (New York: Coward-McCann, Inc., 1965). This study is based on written memoirs, diaries, and interviews of those who were involved in the decision to use atomic weapons against Japan.

would pass from the Americans to the leaders of the Japanese government. If they did not surrender, it could not be argued that they had not been given clear warning.

This point of view was not accepted. The counter-argument was based essentially on the American image of the decision-making process in Tokyo, an image which stressed the fanatic zeal of the military leaders in control of the Japanese government. This image was not far off the mark, for subsequent events in Tokyo revealed that even after the two atomic weapons had been dropped, Russia had entered the war, and the United States had instituted an effective blockade of the Japanese islands, Japanese military leaders were willing to surrender only because the emperor ordered them to do so. Most of the Japanese military group had been trained in the view that the only honorable course of action was to fight to the last man. One officer had suggested that Japan might be willing to sacrifice 20 million lives to prevent an Allied occupation and destruction of the emperorship. Indeed, after the decision to surrender had been made, some military officials attempted a *coup d'état* in Tokyo, hoping to take over the government and continue the war. The American government did not know all these details, of course, but it had ample intelligence information indicating that the Japanese would continue to resist no matter how near defeat they were, and that the peace faction within the Japanese government could not overturn or overrule the military. It was argued in Washington, therefore, that in all probability no demonstration of the bomb in a New Mexico desert or even in some relatively uninhabited areas of Japan would adequately indicate to the Japanese the destructiveness of the weapon. This position was supported by the chief scientist on the project in New Mexico, Dr. Robert Oppenheimer.

A further consideration was that the United States only possessed two bombs and, since it would take several weeks to produce others, the more that were used for purposes of demonstration and warning, the longer the war would continue, with a high American casualty rate in the Pacific Islands campaign.

Once the decision to drop one bomb had been made a second choice remained: which cities would be destroyed? The American military group selected cities which made important contributions to the Japanese war effort. One of these was Kyoto, from a military point of view the most desirable of targets. But this choice was vetoed by the Secretary of War, on the grounds that the city was a former capital of Japan and a great center of culture and historical tradition. Though Stimson was well aware of the great loss of life involved in dropping the bomb on *any* city, he eliminated the most obvious choice. Clearly the decision on this target was not made, then, purely on military grounds or reasons of expediency. Other considerations involving moral choices served to restrain action.

What conclusions are we to draw from the decision to use the atomic bomb against Japan, the casual suggestion by Stalin, and the Allied fire raids on Germany and Japan? The first is that as the technical means of destruction in wartime have grown, so has tolerance for destructiveness. When gunpowder was first applied to military uses, many were offended. During World War I, the civilized world was appalled at the loss of life in trench warfare, killing of civilians by long-range artillery, maiming of soldiers with mustard gas, and dropping of puny bombs from airplanes. In World War II the Germans were characterized as barbarous and inhumane (the real atrocities were not yet even known) for their massive air raids on Coventry, London, Rotterdam, and Warsaw. Within a year or two those among the Allied powers who were outraged at these German military actions applauded when their own armed forces retaliated in similar, though more thorough, fashion against German and Japanese cities. Were a nuclear war to break out in our own era, policy-makers would still make the same kinds of calculations that they did in deciding to drop atomic bombs on Hiroshima and Nagasaki rather than to invade the islands. Military advisers would likely regard their problems from a professional and technical point of view, quite immune from considerations of individual suffering. It remains for civilian policy-makers to inject, if they are capable or strong enough, ethical and moral factors in the use of the instruments of violence, and to reject certain alternatives offered by their military advisers on the ground that they are ethically reprehensible or politically impracticable.

The second point about these decisions is that they were exceptional rather than typical, taken by policy-makers in circumstances of acute tension, of total war. While on hindsight other alternatives might have been possible, the alternatives that *were* considered would probably have involved even greater suffering.

A third aspect of these decisions is that some, like Stalin's suggestion, were made ultimately by individuals with supreme authority, where their perceptions of reality, prejudices, and personal ethical orientations were clearly revealed. Others, like most foreign policy decisions, were products of lengthy consultation among many governmental organizations and individual specialists. Stalin's suggestion of liquidating the German officer corps was not in all probability a serious policy alternative which had been worked out in the Soviet bureaucracy. But the decision to drop the bomb or, for instance, to make a loan offer to an underdeveloped country, is the result of complicated negotiations among various agencies in the government of the donor; it is much less likely to display so dramatically the value orientations of any single policy-maker.

Moreover, we must remember that those who make and carry out foreign policies are "role" players. They are officials, which means that they conform more or less to the legal limitations of a particular office, as well as to the expectations of numerous constituents. Role tends to mediate individual attitudes and values to such an extent that a policy-maker is not always free to use his official position to institute his personal ethics, beliefs, or prejudices. As Louis Halle points out, the position of the foreign policy official is similar to that of the corporate director who, however much he may believe in charity, cannot give away the stock-holders' assets as if they were his own.[5] Policy-makers are responsible for pursuing and protecting collective objectives, and in this capacity cannot always follow the dictates of their conscience. If they honestly disagree with a course of action, they can resign as one means of protest—though in totalitarian governments such a course of action can lead to imprisonment or even liquidation. Despite the effect of role factors on policy-making, it should not be assumed that "state" behavior is necessarily less ethical than private behavior. Given the difficult situations with which officials have to deal, their behavior is frequently no less moral than that of private citizens.[6]

Finally, statesmen who make the types of decisions examined above do not spend sleepless nights in remorse, because they make their choices in terms of collective images which conceal the plight of individuals who will suffer. Collective images, which are the basis for most foreign policy decisions, blunt moral sensitivity even among those who in their private lives uphold the strictest moral principles.[7]

## Ethical Restraints in Three Levels of Policy

Ethics and moral principles can be related to foreign policy behavior at three different levels: (1) statements of general foreign policy objectives, (2) "rules" or doctrines which governments profess to observe when they

[5] Louis J. Halle, "Morality and Contemporary Diplomacy," in *Diplomacy in a Changing World*, ed. Stephen Kertesz and M. A. Fitzsimmons (Notre Dame, Indiana: University of Notre Dame Press, 1959), p. 32.

[6] Arnold Wolfers, "Statesmanship and Moral Choice," *World Politics*, I (1949), 178–80.

[7] W. W. Kulski, *International Politics in a Revolutionary Age* (Philadelphia: J. B. Lippincott Company, 1964), pp. 416–17.

conduct relations with other states, and (3) day-to-day problem solving. Much of the confusion arising from discrepancies between a government's diplomatic rhetoric and its actual behavior in a specific set of circumstances could be avoided if these distinctions are kept clearly in mind.

First, when governments proclaim their objectives, or their vision of a "just" world order, they often emphasize the ethical and moral imperatives underlying those goals. Such long-range goals as "peace," "the rule of law," "justice," "stability," "national security," or a "world federation of socialist states" are not only ethically desirable to their proponents, but the proponents often are convinced that they are also great human objectives, endowed with ethical value to which all good men aspire. Lord Wolseley maintained once:

> I have but one great object in this world, and that is to maintain the greatness of the British Empire. But apart from my John Bull sentiment on this point, I firmly believe that in doing so I work in the cause of Christianity, of peace, of civilization, and the happiness of the human race generally.[8]

Similarly, President Wilson was convinced that in "making the world safe for democracy" and pursuing the objective of "self-determination," the objectives of the American government were in complete harmony with the aspirations of mankind.

The problem, of course, is that what may seem perfectly just and legitimate as a goal to one government may seem just the opposite to another. To the United States, a world of free, independent states, regulating their relations according to law, is eminently just and ethical. A Communist views this order as representative of American world domination, slavery under capitalism, and an international law which perpetuates inequalities between states and economic exploitation of underdeveloped countries by imperialists. Observed in this light, the goals hardly seem just and ethical. Whether or not these goals *are* ethical depends very much from which position they are being viewed.

Second, governments also pronounce their fidelity to principles of conduct in foreign policy. These are the major written and unwritten rules accepted as a legitimate basis for conducting relations within an international system. These rules, which today are contained under such slogans as "free trade," "non-interference in internal affairs," "self-determination," "observance of treaty obligations," or "pacific settlement of disputes" relate not to goals but to the methods by which governments seek to influence the behavior of other states. They establish the distinc-

---

[8] Quoted in Kenneth W. Thompson, *Political Realism and the Crisis of World Politics* (Princeton: Princeton University Press, 1960), p. 151.

tions between legitimate and illegitimate means of utilizing a state's capabilities.

Third, the role of ethical principles in actual decision-making situations may be quite different than appears in the official rhetoric regarding such generalizations as long-range goals and rules. What may be much more important to policy-makers is *how* they conduct their relations, or the style of their actions and responses. A government may be devious, petty, and self-righteous, and still observe scrupulously the major rules of international law. Another government may pursue its objectives in a patient and conciliatory manner, consulting broadly among its friends and allies, respecting the interests and rights of others, and still violate treaty obligations. Which government is behaving in a more "ethical" manner? In either case, ethical limitations will operate to preclude considerations of some policy alternatives. But the latter government will probably be judged more "ethical" because its diplomatic style is more sensitive to the interests of other states. Thus, it is in this realm of "how" states pursue their objectives that ethics might seem most immediately relevant to foreign policy. Since there may still be obvious advantages to following these rules, self-interest and ethics coincide.

Most problems which confront the policy-maker daily do not appear to him as moral problems. They are practical problems which demand practical responses and actions.[9] Some people claim, for example, that it is immoral for a democratic government to maintain an alliance with a regime which practices certain domestic policies not in accordance with democratic principles. But the policy-maker is primarily concerned with a security problem, not with the ethical characteristics of foreign political systems. The policy-maker would then argue that the alliance partner's internal affairs are irrelevant to the alliance relationship, just as he does not pass judgment on his grocer's private life before he is willing to buy food from him. The grocer's morals are largely irrelevant to the selling and purchasing relationship.[10]

Is a decision to make an alliance with a dictator really devoid of ethical content? Is this really expediency forsaking principle? It is difficult to predict the costs of *not* making the alliance, but if by not making the alliance, war is the result, who is right in arguing that alliances with dictators are immoral? And, in any case, the policy-maker could, instead of forming an alliance, order the invasion and occupation of the dictator's country, thereby creating a more effective deterrent. This would be perhaps a more practical course of action, but the policy-maker's values

[9] Halle, *Diplomacy in a Changing World*, pp. 28–29.
[10] *Ibid.*

would probably preclude even consideration of such an alternative. *Any* choice of policy alternatives involves selection among ethical standards and values. There is no such thing as a pure realist if by that term we mean one who sacrifices all values for the quickest gratification of his self-interest. In most diplomatic situations, ethical restraints are not very conspicuous in the sense that policy is deduced from moral maxims; but they can be observed in the policies that were *not* adopted, and in the general manner, whether courteous, respectful, and honest, or brusque and deceitful, in which actions were carried out with other involved countries.

In these examples we can see the extent to which both moralists and realists oversimplify. The moralists fail to observe the necessities imposed on the policy-maker by conditions abroad over which he has no control; they also neglect the possibility that strict observance of rules and commitments might lead to catastrophic consequences. And they often fail to realize that policy-makers are sometimes cast into a situation where all the alternatives are equally unpleasant. The realists, who say that policy-makers' behavior is, or should be, dictated only by "reasons of state," also fail to observe the role of ethical limitations in ruling out what may be more expedient alternatives. Moreover, in focusing on behavior in crisis situations, the realists fail to acknowledge thousands of transactions between states in which diplomatic positions conform rigidly to the principles of international law and the Charter of the United Nations. If in some situations all possible courses of action are ethically reprehensible, in many others, self-interest and ethical behavior are highly compatible.

Misunderstandings about the role of ethics in foreign relations often arise when people fail to distinguish among these three levels of policy. Because governments advocate and justify their actions in terms of long-range goals and doctrines, the average interested citizen will judge his government's daily behavior according to these pronouncements. Diplomatic rhetoric and appeals to general principles and popular sentiments make communications between governments and domestic and foreign audiences much easier. Statements of principles also evoke popular enthusiasm for policies because they are held to be inherently righteous,[11] while technical discourses on foreign policies are more likely to create apathy. When governments are groping to find an adequate course of action in a difficult set of circumstances, they often hide their uncertainty under the veil of vague principles. Thus, government leaders

[11] George Modelski, *A Theory of Foreign Policy* (New York: Frederick A. Praeger, Publisher, Inc., 1962), p. 95.

often speak in two languages to different audiences. To their own people, and often to their allies, they express themselves in terms of moral purposes, ultimate values, and the importance of observing the "rules of the game." Among themselves, however, they discuss the preservation and pursuit of various objectives, deterrents, bargaining strategies, and complex technical transactions.[12] Even here, ethical principles do not cease operating as limitations.

In situations where a state's objectives, interests, and values are threatened or frustrated, high-sounding platitudes and general principles do not often serve as realistic guides to action. No foreign policy can be conducted exclusively by deducing actions from vague moral principles.[13] Leaders like Jawaharlal Nehru and Woodrow Wilson, who stressed the importance of observing legal and ethical standards of conduct in international relationships, did not behave in practical situations very differently from other political leaders who claimed to be "realists." It is, for example, easy for a government to forswear the use and threat of force in its relations with other states. No government admits that it is anything but "peace-loving." But what if that government is subsequently threatened by a neighbor when the international organization is paralyzed because of a veto, and little diplomatic support elsewhere can be obtained? Does the general principle of non-use of power suggest any practical policy in this situation? From the point of view of the observer-moralist, is it ethically more correct to remain faithful to principle and endure certain invasion than to try to create an effective defense with which to deter the perceived enemy? Or, suppose that a government had in its policy statements solemnly declared its faith in the principles of international law, but found later that a treaty to which it was a partner imposed not only heavy, but clearly unjust, burdens, and that the other signatory was unwilling to adjust the treaty through negotiations. When justice and the principle of treaty observation conflict, which is the correct course of action? Is public declaration in support of the "rule of law" a meaningful guide by which to formulate policy in this situation?

Despite their rhetoric, policy-makers have to choose constantly among courses of action which represent conflicting values, and often feel compelled to accept not the "best" solution, but the one which requires the least sacrifice of direct interests and values. When governments are

---

[12] Kenneth W. Thompson, *American Diplomacy and Emergent Patterns* (New York: New York University Press, 1962), p. 24.

[13] A former Secretary of State, Dean Acheson, has repeatedly made this point in attempting to show that policy-makers do not approach problems solely from an ethical point of view. See, for example, his "Morality, Moralism, and Diplomacy," *Yale Review*, XLVII (1958), 481–93.

not deeply involved in a critical situation, they can afford to proclaim fidelity to ultimate purposes and commonly recognized rules, but when they are in the middle of conflict, vague principles such as those in the United Nations Charter may not help very much.

The appeasement strategy of England in the 1930's is a good example of the kinds of conflicting principles and values with which policy-makers have to struggle. In this case, British government leaders believed that peace and the principles of conduct in the Covenant of the League of Nations had to be observed. They also believed that reasonable negotiations with the Nazi regime could avert the holocausts experienced during World War I. Prime Minister Chamberlain was a man of great rectitude, and he personally abhorred organized violence. His principles and intentions were above approach. By surrendering one position after the other through diplomatic negotiations he was able to keep the peace for two years, but in the process he and his colleagues sacrificed the independence of Austria, Danzig, and Czechoslovakia. Was two years of "peace" and strict adherence to the League Covenant worth this price? The principles the British observed were commendable, but they did not help to create any effective policies for the Nazi threat.

To cite a more recent, and perhaps more typical, example, in 1964 the British economy was undergoing serious strains caused by a growing imbalance between imports and exports. Public confidence in British currency was declining, speculators were purchasing foreign currency in expectation of a devaluation of the pound, and by doing so were further decreasing the foreign currency holdings of the British government. In short, Great Britain was nearing bankruptcy; it was threatened with losing its ability to pay for the imports needed to survive. Facing this critical situation, the Labour government decided to increase tariffs by 15 per cent on a long list of import goods. This action, the government hoped, would reduce the flow of imports and stimulate a decline in the outflow of foreign exchange earnings. By putting this policy into effect, the British government violated provisions of 18 bilateral and multilateral trade treaties to which it was a signatory. The British government claims in its statements of foreign policy principles to uphold the rule of law in international relations as a general guide to behavior. But in this set of circumstances the British cabinet and its financial experts believed that continued observance of treaty obligations would have brought major disaster to Britain's economy.

The response of the British government was not unusual. Policy-makers confront difficult choices, and absolute fidelity to treaty obligations and other standards of diplomatic behavior may require sacrifices which few people would willingly condone. Fortunately, in most cases the pursuit of interests and values does not conflict so obviously with the principles which a government declares as guides to its external behavior.

### Ethical Restraints as a Function
### of the Pattern of Relations Between Nations

It is still inadequate to argue that in some cases commitment to ethical or legal principles may cause disaster or unethical consequences. We must also qualify the relationship of ethics to foreign policy by emphasizing that they combine in different ways depending upon the situation abroad, the level of involvement of a state in a conflict, and also on the general nature of relations between any two states. We do not hear much criticism about the lack of morality in Swedish-Norwegian, Costa Rican-Panamanian, or British-American relations. In these types of relationships —which comprise the vast majority of all international relations— governments and their diplomatic representatives almost always observe rigorously the accepted forms of diplomatic etiquette, frankness, honesty, good faith, and tolerance. The techniques used to influence each other are almost always within the bounds of international law and the United Nations Charter. Unfortunately, since these relationships seldom make headlines, we are seldom aware of the high standards to which they conform.

But when serious conflicts develop, the objectives of two or more states are fundamentally incompatible, and there is no tradition of responsiveness, characteristically any government will be likely to use threats and military force. Observation of treaties, diplomatic niceties, and rules against interference give way to other forms of behavior. But does one instance of the use of violent power, even for unworthy objectives, mean that that state's policy-makers are immoral in *all* of their relationships? Or does it warrant the cynicism of some observers, who claim that in any case power is always the final arbiter in international politics, and that might makes right?

The despair of the moralists and the cynicism of some observers is easy to understand, for it is precisely in these conflict situations that governments most often invoke the rhetoric of high sounding principles to justify their actions. When the British and French are enjoying good mutual relations, their governments do not need to point to the high principles they are observing in their transactions. But when, for example, the United States breaks treaty obligations or diplomatic proclamations to sponsor an invasion of Cuba or launch air strikes against North Vietnam, it appeals to such principles as "the defense of freedom." These appeals are designed primarily for public consumption, and do not necessarily indicate the actual role that the concept of "freedom" plays in the decision-making process. To the policy-makers confronting the Cuban and Vietnamese situations, the principles of treaty observation, non-interference, and avoidance of making military threats may not be relevant data in their considerations at all. Rather, they confront situations which they consider serious threats to their country's interests and values and seek pragmatically an answer to these threats. Sometimes, of course, the policy-makers decide that for various reasons they must observe the principles they have enunciated publicly, no matter what the consequences, but in most instances one principle can always be sacrificed in the name of another. Who can judge which principles should be given more weight, particularly if all of them lead to undesirable results?

We should not conclude that violations of some ethical standards in coercive and violent relationships mean that "power politics" have replaced all decency as the basis for a country's foreign policies. Even in violent relationships, as many examples illustrate, ethical norms still limit the vision of policy-makers and exclude some policy alternatives which might, in view of the circumstances, be the most expedient. In the most frigid periods of the cold war, the major antagonists have refrained from taking certain actions which might have achieved key objectives at a minimum of risk or cost. There are at least tacit agreements, for instance, that neither side would assassinate the leaders of the other, give nuclear weapons to allies, or sabotage each other's economies. These agreements, as well as others, seem to involve modes of conduct where both sides see a common correspondence of self-interest and ethical principles.

During the American-Soviet crisis of 1962 over Cuba (discussed in Chapter XII), when the Soviet government had secretly shipped missiles to the island to protect, it claimed, Castro's regime from an expected American invasion, several high officials of the American government, including President Kennedy, had to decide among several alternative courses of action in attempting to remove the missiles; two eventually remained for serious consideration. The most practical action would have been to destroy the missiles and bases by a rapid series of bombing raids. Such action would have demonstrated dramatically to the Soviet government that introduction of more missiles would only end in their destruction. Nevertheless, President Kennedy asked his intelligence advisers how many persons would be killed if the United States conducted the bombing raids. The answer was 25,000, including many civilians. The President chose the second alternative—a quarantine of the island by naval forces—partly on the ground that the United States could not be the perpetrator of a Pearl Harbor-type attack on Cuba.[14] He chose a course of action which was less certain of accomplishing the stated objective, but which would cost less lives, even in the territory of a hostile nation. Ethical considerations were operating here, as in many other cases, as criteria upon which to base policies.

### The Sanctions for Ethical Foreign Policy Behavior

The sanctions, or pressures for conformity to ethical principles, are found within the individual policy-makers, in foreign policy organizations, governments in general, and in the expectations of other states and people. In the case of President Kennedy's decision on Cuba in 1962, the sanctions were internal—in his conscience—and external—in the anticipation of unfavorable responses around the world to a Pearl Harbor-type attack. In other cases the attitudes and anticipated reaction of a political party, legislative body, pressure group, or the public at large may prompt officials to conform to certain standards of behavior.

Policy-makers may also be sensitive to the prestige, reputation, and credibility of their country as viewed by other governments and peoples. On the personal level, diplomats are more or less effective and persuasive to the extent that they are believed and believable. A diplomat is not, as one sixteenth century observer wrote, sent abroad to lie for his country, for if he did he would only hinder his chances of successfully completing his mission. A trustworthy, responsible, and frank envoy is more likely than a deceitful and irresponsible diplomat to achieve his objectives.[15] Similarly, at the national level a country's prestige and reputation abroad are no less connected to a successful foreign policy than are the personal qualities of its diplomats. A government which persistently breaks obligations, becomes unreliable towards its allies, or launches its military forces on slight pretext is not likely to elicit as much prestige as the country which, given similar capabilities, abstains from such behavior. A bad reputation is usually the result of behavior consistently at odds with accepted standards of conduct.[16]

Since reputation is a question of perceptions, governments will be constrained more by anticipated reactions of allies and friends than by states

---

[14] The President's brother, Robert Kennedy, revealed this aspect of the Cuban missile crisis in a speech in New York on October 13, 1964, reported in *The New York Times,* October 14, 1964, p. 1. Other considerations of costs, risks, and probable Soviet responses were also involved in the final choice.

[15] This point is raised by Kenneth W. Thompson, *American Diplomacy and Emergent Patterns,* p. 45.

[16] See Modelski, *A Theory of Foreign Policy,* p. 57.

with which they are not involved or by enemies. It is the diversity of cultural values in the world, and the greatly varying perspectives with which different people view reality and legal norms, that raises the problem of whether or not there are, in fact, universal standards for judging the actions of a state. Certainly most states, including the Communist countries which profess an ethical system alien to the Western tradition, claim to uphold the major rules of the international system, and do so in most actions and transactions. But to a Communist, aggression or internal interference by "imperialist" states is not at all the same thing as the Communist promotion of "wars of national liberation," though a completely neutral observer would see that they do involve similar types of action. Are there yet, then, system-wide sanctions for observing those rules and conducting relations in accordance with ethical principles? Some would argue that it is necessary to have a true sense of community and a public consensus as to what behavior is moral before governments can be expected to observe ethical principles in their foreign policies.[17] Others argue that such a rudimentary consensus already exists in the form of "world public opinion" and that this opinion, expressed through diverse channels, does force governments to act in conformity with ethical and legal norms. The previous chapter suggests, however, that "world public opinion" cannot be viewed in most cases as an effective restraint.

### Summary

No topic in the study of international politics has created more controversy than the role of ethics and morals in a country's foreign policies. The two main schools of thought on this question usually oversimplify the relationship and conclude that all foreign policies are "struggles for power," or that governments honestly attempt to fashion their behavior in accordance with moral and legal maxims. Part of the oversimplification arises from actions of government officials themselves, for their public pronouncements often refer to foreign policy in terms of ultimate ends or transaction doctrines rather than as practical problems which must be resolved. Slogans and principles are useful for mobilizing foreign and domestic opinion, but they are neither substitutes for policy nor necessarily the frames of reference in which actual decisions are made. In their day-to-day positions, policy-makers do not approach their problems from the point of view of ethics any more than most business organizations

[17] Manfred Halpern, *The Morality and Politics of Intervention* (New York: Council on Religion and International Affairs, 1963), p. 18.

resolve issues by deducing rules of action from ethical or legal principles. Nevertheless, ethics, morals, and values are constantly brought to bear on a government's behavior towards other states. Sometimes the relationship may be explicit where, for example, a policy-making body is aware of, and acts to implement, a rule of international law or a prior commitment to an ally. More often the relationship is more subtle, where ethics and values unconsciously block out consideration of policy alternatives.

For reasons of conscience, prestige, and self-interest, governments in most cases conduct their relations with each other in accordance with the commonly accepted "rules of the game." But in many instances policy-makers are confronted with situations in which they have to choose between courses of action that help to secure national values and interests (or minimize sacrifices) and those which are consistent with legal and moral obligations and ethical precepts. When the two courses of action conflict, it is not unusual for governments to choose the path which attains or defends national values and interests. More often, policy represents some sort of compromise between the demands of ethical considerations and rules and the demands of effective action.

The role of ethical and legal restraints on the use of various instruments of policy can also be related to the general type of relationship between any two countries. Good friends and allies are not likely to exploit economic dependency (except in the manner of offering rewards), interfere indiscreetly in their internal affairs, conduct hostile propaganda toward each other, or exploit ethnic, religious, or social cleavages in each other's societies. In relations between hostile states which have little responsiveness to each other's needs and values, these instruments of policy are very likely to be employed when important conflicts of interest arise—despite legal and ethical prohibitions against their use.

Finally, governments are constrained in their behavior by the expectations and expressed opinions of their friends and allies, but it is doubtful whether they are often sensitive to expressions of opinion from sources which are organized by hostile governments of professional agitators. Moreover, the varying cultural backgrounds and historical experiences of different peoples affect the way they perceive and ascribe meanings to reality. Government officials are usually aware of more obvious discrepancies of opinion, or "misunderstandings," and attempt through diplomacy and propaganda to dispel them. But if they fail, they do not often change their policies just to appease hostile sentiments.

## SELECTED BIBLIOGRAPHY

Acheson, Dean, "Morality, Moralism, and Diplomacy," *Yale Review,* XLVII (1958), 481–93.

Butterfield, Herbert, *International Conflict in the Twentieth Century: A Christian View.* New York: Harper & Row, Publishers, 1960.

————, "The Scientific versus the Moralistic Approach in International Affairs," *International Affairs,* XXVII (1951), 411–22.

Eayrs, James, *Right and Wrong in Foreign Policy.* Toronto: Toronto University Press, 1966.

Friedrich, Carl J., *Inevitable Peace.* Cambridge, Mass.: Harvard University Press, 1948.

Giovannitti, Len, and Fred Freed, *The Decision to Drop the Bomb.* New York: Coward-McCann, Inc., 1965.

Good, Robert C., "National Interest and Moral Theory: The 'Debate' among Contemporary Political Realists," in *Foreign Policy in the Sixties: The Issues and the Instrument,* ed. Roger Hilsman and Robert C. Good. Baltimore: The Johns Hopkins Press, 1965.

Halle, Louis J., "Morality and Contemporary Diplomacy," in *Diplomacy in a Changing World,* ed. Stephen Kertesz and M. A. Fitzsimmons. Notre Dame, Indiana: University of Notre Dame Press, 1959.

Halpern, Manfred, *The Morality and Politics of Intervention.* New York: Council on Religion and International Affairs, 1963.

Lefever, Ernest, *Ethics and United States Foreign Policy.* New York: Meridian Books, 1957.

Machiavelli, N., *The Prince* (1513), trans. Luigi Ricci, rev. by E. R. P. Vincent. London: Oxford University Press, 1935.

Marshall, Charles Burton, *The Exercise of Sovereignty: Papers on Foreign Policy.* Baltimore: The Johns Hopkins Press, 1965.

Morgenthau, Hans J., "The Twilight of International Morality," *Ethics,* LVIII (1948), 77–99.

Nagle, William J., ed., *Morality and Modern Warfare.* Baltimore: Helicon Press, Inc., 1960.

Niebuhr, Reinhold, *Christian Realism and Political Problems.* New York: Charles Scribner's Sons, 1953.

Thompson, Kenneth W., *Christian Ethics and the Dilemmas of Foreign Policy.* Durham, North Carolina: Duke University Press, 1959.

————, *Political Realism and the Crisis of World Politics.* Princeton: Princeton University Press, 1960.

Wolfers, Arnold, "Statemanship and Moral Choice," *World Politics,* I (1949), 175–95.

# Resolving International Conflicts

Incompatible objectives and policy actions between interacting nations form the basis of most international conflicts. Governments pursue or promote a variety of objectives, some readily identifiable, such as a demand for a piece of territory or inclusion of rebel representatives in a coalition government, and others which are less tangible, such as the values inherent in the objectives of "peace," "security," or "just international order." To achieve objectives, governments make different types of demands on their neighbors and on other nations in the system, some of which lead to conflict because their realization can be achieved only at the expense of the interests and core values of other states. In other situations, of course, a demand or request by one state can increase the advantages of both. This is the basis for cooperative and collaborative interactions.

Relationships involving conflicting forms of state behavior can be divided according to the sources from

° Portions of this chapter appeared under the title "Resolving International Conflicts: A Taxonomy of Behavior and Some Figures on Procedures," in *The Journal of Conflict Resolution,* X (1966), 272–96. They are reprinted here with the permission of the Center for Research on Conflict Resolution, University of Michigan.

# Chapter XV

which they arise and the types of actions and counter-actions in which they commonly result. Is a border incident between Chile and Argentina involving the loss of several lives to be regarded as a "conflict" in the same sense that many aspects of contemporary Soviet-Chinese relations are conflicting? In this chapter, we will make distinctions among (1) *disputes* caused by accidents and minor provocations; (2) *conflicts* arising from incompatible collective objectives; and (3) more general *tensions* between two or more states. Disputes grow out of border incidents, diplomatic embarrassments, or *unauthorized* provocations made by military forces in a neighbor's territory. Presumably, they are relatively easy to settle, because the causes are clearly identifiable and they involve specific grievances—usually to private citizens—rather than the incompatibility of collective, national objectives. To cite some examples: accidental shooting of farm animals near the frontier by border police of a neighboring state; accidental destruction of fishing boats by another nation's naval vessels; violation of an international frontier by a group of armed bandits; frontier guards or patrols from neighboring states shooting at each other; or an armed aircraft accidentally destroying lives and property in a foreign state. When such incidents occur between nations whose relations are already typified by hostile attitudes, they may lead to violent responses and even to war (the sinking of the *Maine* in Havana harbor provided the excuse for the United States to go to war against Spain), but generally they can be resolved through peaceful means, such as indemnification of those who have suffered.

Most international *conflicts* also have sources which are relatively easy to identify. The most common cause historically has been the demand by one political group for territorial rights or resources controlled by another, or the effort by one society to impose military, political, or economic controls over alien populations. These demands often cannot be satisfied except at the sacrifice of other states' core values and interests, hence conflict arises and continues until the initiator either withdraws its demands, induces the other state to compromise, or forces it to submit through threats or military action. Another source of international conflict, which has appeared with increasing frequency, is the domestic rebellion which attracts outside intervention. Unlike the simple territorial conflict, there are usually four parties involved in the internal-international conflict: the domestic government and the rebellious faction, and two outside powers intervening to support either domestic group.

The type of relationship we have called tensions arises from a juxtaposition of historical, economic, religious, or ethnic conditions, and is perpetuated by widespread and deep-seated public attitudes of hostility between two or more societies. Incompatible territorial and security objectives may be involved in tensions, but by themselves do not give rise to, or perpetuate, *all* of the forms of hostile behavior between the involved states. The cold war and Arab-Israeli tensions could not be resolved conclusively by settlement of just one of the component issues. The Korean armistice of 1953 has had little effect on hostile public attitudes in the main antagonists of the cold war; and few believe that a future settlement over Berlin would end all the fears and lack of trust that typify relations between the Soviet Union and the West. Sometimes, of course, a conflict over concrete objectives such as a piece of territory may become a symbol of a more complicated relationship, and its resolution could begin a process leading to over-all reconciliation. However, such territorial questions seldom cause by themselves the great religious, ideological, or national rivalries observed throughout history.

Since tensions have no single source, they are more difficult to resolve than those conflicts whose origins lie in expansive demands and in the incompatibility of recognizable objectives. Irrational fears, distorted perceptions, and traditional social hatreds between the French and Germans, the Austrians and Balkan Slavs, as well as important trade and colonial rivalries, the Anglo-German naval armaments race, and more specific conflicts over territory such as Alsace-Lorraine, were important conditions underlying the crisis in the summer of 1914. The European system might have been capable of allaying the immediate crisis, if not all the hostile attitudes, had it been confined to the tangible rivalries. But by July, 1914, there were few specific sources of hostility which could have become the subject of negotiation or mediation. Perhaps the frantic efforts of European diplomats to arrange negotiations while the military organizations were mobilizing as rapidly as possible failed because there were such pronounced hostile attitudes and so few definable areas of disagreement whose solution could have saved the peace.

The discussion that follows will exclude disputes and tensions, and focus primarily on conflicts which have identifiable causes, involve the threat or use of force, and whose settlement usually signifies restoration of friendly relations between states. Some of the specific cold war crises can be considered as separate conflicts, though the cold war itself, just as the religious wars of the sixteenth and seventeenth centuries, or the hostility which resulted in World War I, is not amenable to over-all settlement by resolution of specific issues. Tensions are resolved only within lengthy historical processes which lead either to eventual reconciliation or cataclysmic wars.

## Behavior Leading to the Resolution of International Conflicts

A typical conflict arising from incompatibility of readily identifiable objectives, interests, or actions may proceed as follows. One state presents demands or takes physical actions to change the *status quo*. Another party communicates to the first that these actions or demands are a violation of a treaty or some unwritten understanding, a threat to its security or "vital interests," or incompatible with its own aspirations. The first state responds by claiming that its actions or demands are fully justified according to various criteria, and that it has no intention of withdrawing them, although it is certainly willing to negotiate. The second party thereupon threatens to respond, perhaps by use of force, to protect its interests or block the fulfillment of the first state's demands. Moreover, it usually refuses to negotiate until the other party has first withdrawn its demands or physical presence from the field or area under dispute. The first government is publicly committed to its demands or course of action and refuses to withdraw, though it still offers to negotiate. At this point the second party breaks diplomatic relations or institutes other countermeasures, including the use of force, if the other state is physically occupying an area not formerly its own.[1] What alternatives are there for resolving this kind of situation?

At least six theoretical modes of behavior and outcomes are available to two or more parties when they seek to achieve or defend incompatible goals, values, interests, or positions: (1) avoidance-voluntary withdrawal, (2) violent conquest, (3) forced submission or withdrawal, (4) compromise, (5) award, and (6) "passive settlement."[2] No matter which alternative is chosen by policy-makers, it is always the result of bargaining—making commitments, offering rewards, or threatening punishments or deprivation—between two or more governments. This bargaining can be implied where, for example, two sides display their military forces, or more explicitly, exchange written messages or negotiate directly through diplomatic representatives. In fact, bargaining in any conflict

[1] A similar situation and course of events can be observed in the following conflicts since 1945: Netherlands-Indonesia, 1947–1949; Iran–Great Britain, 1951–1953; Netherlands-Indonesia, 1954–1962; India-Portugal, 1961–1962; Cuba–U.S.A., 1960–1961; Tunisia-France, 1961–1962; India-China, 1962; Algeria-Morocco, 1963–1964; Indonesia-Malaysia, 1963–1966.

[2] These are a modification and extension of the categories of conflict behavior discussed by Kenneth E. Boulding in his *Conflict and Defense: A General Theory* (New York: Harper & Row, Publishers, 1962).

usually includes both kinds of communication. If one government mobilizes its troops, institutes measures of civil defense, or increases the size of its military budget after demands or actions against it have been made, it is signalling to its adversary that it is willing to use force to protect or extend its interests and values. A government bargains simultaneously by making explicit threats or offers of rewards through written or verbal communications.

### Avoidance

When incompatibility of goals, values, or interests is perceived by both sides, and after bargaining has commenced, one possible course of action is for one or both parties to terminate the conflict by withdrawing from a physical or bargaining position, or by ceasing the acts which originally caused hostile responses. Although this may not seem a very common form of behavior, in fact it is probably the most common of all among governments that normally maintain friendly relations.[3] This occurs when, for instance, one government initiates a proposal with its neighbors to make certain frontier adjustments. When the neighbors insist that the *status quo* be maintained, the initiator may, not wishing to create bad relations, withdraw the demand and forget about it. In several instances since World War II, the major powers have voluntarily (e.g., not under threat of force) withdrawn from colonies or foreign military bases, thus avoiding friction with indigenous peoples. The issue may be more procedural, such as a proposal to hold a conference on some matter of mutual concern which, when disapproved by other states, is quietly withdrawn by the sponsoring government. Some recent examples would include the American government's implied abandonment of the plan for a multilateral NATO naval fleet, and the Soviet government's withdrawal of its demand for creating a "troika" arrangement for the Secretary-Generalship of the United Nations, where each bloc—Western, Communist, and non-aligned —would elect one person for the three positions.

### Conquest

A second method for resolving a conflict is by physically overwhelming the opponent through the use of force. But even the termination of violent conflict involves some agreement and bargaining between the antagonists. One side must be made to realize that peace, even under terms of unconditional surrender, is more desirable than continuation of

[3] *Ibid.*, p. 308.

violence.[4] This may be achieved in several ways, by making certain, for example, that the loser perceives that the possibilities of achieving even reduced objectives or successfully defending itself have disappeared. Such realization may come only after some symbolic military catastrophe, such as the defeat of the Spanish Armada, the Battle of Waterloo, the Nazi occupation of Paris, or the fall of Dien Bien Phu. The conflict may be terminated, also, if one side offers lenient peace terms, where the alternative to their acceptance would be more severe terms later on. Or the policy-makers of the losing side may be induced to believe that they can still salvage something—their military forces, an intact economy, or avoidance of foreign occupation—by suing for peace.

No government arrives at such a decision easily. Indeed, the most agonizing position for civilian and military leaders during a war comes when a decision has to be made whether or not to terminate armed resistance and capitulate to the enemy. No one can know for certain at what point the best terms of settlement can be achieved, and there are always those on the losing side who claim that further resistance can strengthen their bargaining position, just as some argue that immediate surrender will bring the most favorable terms of settlement. In 1940 the French surrendered quickly to the German forces, expecting that early capitulation would lead to softer peace terms. This strategy, though considered by many as a blot to France's honor, succeeded in part because it enabled the French to keep their navy—an important bargaining instrument against Nazi Germany in the future—and to maintain the southern portion of the country free of German occupation forces.[5]

## Submission-Withdrawal

A similar situation occurs when one party to a conflict decides to submit to the other's demands or actions even though no violence has taken place. The criterion used to distinguish the concept of submission from conquest is whether or not a threat to employ force is implemented. It could be argued that when one side submits merely to a violent threat, a peaceful settlement ensues. But it is more appropriate to consider submission resulting from military threats or *ultimata* as non-pacific modes of conflict resolution.

Conflict resolution through submission can also be analyzed as an

[4] Lewis A. Coser, "The Termination of Conflict," *Journal of Conflict Resolution,* V (1961), 349.
[5] See Paul Kecskemeti, *Strategic Surrender* (Stanford: Stanford University Press, 1958).

example of effective deterrence, where the second party, by raising a counter-threat, induces the first party to withdraw its "offensive" demands or actions. The deterrent, whether it is a threat of diplomatic, military, or economic retaliation, attempts to persuade the antagonist that the probable risks and costs of pursuing its actions or objectives outweigh the costs of retreating or withdrawing.

One problem with using the concept of deterrence is that most behavior in conflict situations involves calculations of risks, costs, and threatening responses by other parties. Even in avoidance behavior, elements of deterrence are always present in the sense that the party making the initial demands or proposals concludes that their fulfillment is not worth the cost of alienating other governments. However, we can use the concept of deterrence as a form of submission-withdrawal behavior where the target of the initial demands or actions threatens to retaliate *with the use of force.* If, in the face of a large mobilization combined with a threat of retaliation, an initiator of demands or hostile actions withdraws them, we will assume that the withdrawal was primarily a response to the deterrent. Though we have little documented proof, most observers believe that the Allied military buildup in Berlin and West Germany in 1961 induced the Soviet government to withdraw its plans to sign a separate peace treaty with East Germany, an action which would have seriously jeopardized the freedom of West Berlin.

### Compromise

A fourth possibility for settling international conflicts is through the arrangement of some sort of compromise in which *both* sides agree to a partial withdrawal of their initial objectives, positions, demands, or actions.[6] The withdrawal need not be of the same cost or magnitude (symmetrical) to both parties. Hence, some diplomatic compromises are criticized by pressure groups, editorialists, and opposition political parties as being a "sell-out" to the enemy, a submission to its demands without receiving adequate compensation. From a neutral observer's point of view, any agreement which entails some sacrifice of objectives, interests, or position by *both* sides can be considered a compromise even if one side seems to get the better bargain.

The major problem in achieving a solution to a conflict through compromise arrangements is to have both sides realize that the price of continued conflict is higher than the costs, whatever they may be, of

[6] Boulding, *Conflict and Defense,* pp. 309–10.

reducing demands or withdrawing from a diplomatic or military position. Unfortunately, many international issues are not raised to be settled short of "victory."

Armchair observers of international politics frequently demand that the parties to a conflict immediately begin negotiations. Negotiations are useful in a conflict situation if both sides maintain flexible commitments to their goals and are willing to accept some settlement short of achieving their maximum objectives. But if a government places exclusive value on total "victory," negotiations are likely to lead either to inconclusive results or capitulation by one party. European publics and statesmen were short-sighted in pleading for negotiations and compromise with Hitler over his demands upon Austria, Czechoslovakia, and Poland because he was absolutely committed to destruction of those nations' independence, either through threats or physical conquest. Hitler viewed the compromise of the Munich Conference in 1938 as only a temporary settlement, while Premier Daladier of France and Prime Minister Chamberlain of England believed that they had succeeded through oral persuasion in limiting Hitler's objectives to the Sudetenland. The only way to have resolved the German-bred conflicts short of submission by the victims would have been through the physical removal of Hitler or by a combined display of deterrent military force which might have persuaded him that the personal and national costs of continued aggression would outweigh the advantages. Compromise requires two agreements between the antagonists: both parties must initially agree that partial withdrawal of demands or positions is preferable to continued conflict, and only after this decision has been reached can they begin discussing the substantive terms of a compromise agreement. There are, however, a number of characteristics of diplomatic behavior in a crisis situation which make these two types of agreement difficult to achieve.

One is the tendency for governments to attach symbolic value to conflicts arising from rather simple sources. In our era, at least, conflicts tend to "escalate" not only militarily, but also in terms of their diplomatic and public "ideology." As the issues in a conflict—often relatively simple at the beginning—become encrusted with ideological verbiage, they become harder to resolve through compromise because government officials and publics alike tend to regard any withdrawal as a sacrifice of some great principle. International conflicts are seldom acknowledged as involving merely a piece of territory, but are usually symbolized in terms of the "defense of freedom," "defense against imperialist aggression," or "vindication of national honor." The technique of escalating simple issues into matters of principle is useful in establishing a commitment to a bargaining position, but it is a double-edged sword which can also cut off escape routes and destroy bargaining flexibility.[7] It is much more difficult for a diplomat to compromise on "freedom" than to give up a small piece of territory to the antagonist.

The outbreak of violence has often been cited as another impediment to compromise as a mode of conflict resolution.[8] Many would agree that once antagonists attempt to induce submission or withdrawal by the use of widespread violence, it becomes even more difficult ultimately to resolve the conflict through processes aimed at compromise. But there are too many historical exceptions to allow us to accept this as a totally valid assertion. One can also argue that development of a military stalemate or controlled display or use of force may actually help to induce one side to conclude that a reduction of demands, withdrawal from positions, or partial settlement is preferable to continued violence.[9] One example of this proposition occurred during the Korean War. No one was willing to discuss peace offers so long as either party was faced with submission or the possibility of victory. When United Nations' forces had occupied most of North Korea in the autumn of 1950, North Korea was no more prepared to discuss peace than it had been in the summer of 1950, when its own forces had occupied most of South Korea. But by late 1951, neither side had developed a capacity to overwhelm the other, a military stalemate ensued, and subsequently both parties were willing to discuss an armistice agreement which required each to withdraw from its original political-military objectives.[10]

During the early stages of a conflict, one party may not be entirely clear how committed its opponent is to a stated position. It may then display or use controlled force to test the opponent's reactions and commitments. If the opponent responds by mobilizing forces, both sides may then decide that a compromise or withdrawal is preferable to war. A good case of this form of behavior was in the crisis over Trieste in 1953. This city had been a center of dispute between Italy and Yugoslavia for many years. A temporary solution was imposed by the Allies in 1948 when they decided to make the port of Trieste a free city, with surrounding areas divided into two zones controlled respectively by Yugoslav and Anglo-American troops. Suddenly in 1953 the American Secretary of State, Dulles, and his

---

[7] E. James Lieberman, "Threat and Assurance in the Conduct of Conflict," in *International Conflict and Behavioral Science,* ed. Roger Fisher (New York: Basic Books, Inc., 1964), p. 105.

[8] Boulding, *Conflict and Defense,* pp. 323–24.

[9] Lewis A. Coser, *The Functions of Social Conflict* (New York: Free Press of Glencoe, Inc., 1956), p. 137.

[10] President Eisenhower's threat to use nuclear weapons in Korea may have been an important additional factor in inducing the Communists to agree to negotiate a cease fire—that is, to withdraw from their stated objectives.

British counterpart announced that the Allied troops would be with-drawn, to be replaced by an Italian occupation regime. This annoucement implied clearly that Britain and the United States were prepared to give up their zone to Italian sovereignty without even consulting Yugoslavia, which itself claimed the area in dispute. The Yugoslav government let it be known that if the Allies withdrew from their zone and permitted it to be occupied by Italian officials, Yugoslavia would send in troops, creating the likelihood of a war between Italy and Yugoslavia. To back up the threat, the Yugoslavs mobilized their military forces. Once the American, British, and Italian governments were convinced that Yugoslavia would indeed fulfill its threat to prevent Italian annexation, they became willing to negotiate a compromise. Ultimately the settlement approximated the one unilaterally declared by the Allies, but at least it was a settlement achieved through diplomatic bargaining in which Yugoslavia was repre-sented.

Decline of open communication among disputants, another frequent characteristic of diplomatic crisis behavior, may be a third impediment against bargaining that leads to a compromise settlement.[11] Though there is always implicit communication in the use or display of force, one of the first casualties of the outbreak of violence or development of international conflict into the crisis stage is the breakdown or constriction of formal communications between disputing parties. It is traditional diplomatic practice to sever formal relations even when serious disputes occur between nations, and it is not less true during international conflicts. This act may be symbolic, designed to impress the other party of the serious-ness of the quarrel, but it nevertheless decreases the possibility of exploring the actual degree of commitment the other party holds toward its position. Hence, the only way to judge that commitment in the absence of formal communication may be to take actions which should increase the likelihood of war. The importance of formal communication to compromise agreements can be seen in the frequent attempts of third parties to get hostile governments to discuss their conflict. Such efforts are usually based on the assumption that while the parties are conducting negotiations, they will avoid provocative actions.

A fourth characteristic of international crises which also impedes negotiations leading to compromise is lack of trust between antagonists. Though little systematic research on the element of trust in diplomatic bargaining has been completed, laboratory and game theoretical studies

[11] Ole R. Holsti, "The 1914 Case," *The American Political Science Review*, LIX (1965), 365–78; Paul Smoker, "Sino-Indian Relations: A Study of Trade, Communica-tion and Defense," *Journal of Peace Research*, II (1964), 65–76.

indicate that lack of trust is a factor in preventing open communication and cooperative forms of behavior.

The theme of distrust toward the Soviet Union is found recurrently in the memoirs and statements of Western diplomats who have negotiated with the Russians, as well as in the statements of leading organs of public opinion ("You can't trust the Russians"). Having found that Stalin and Molotov used verbal agreements mainly as negotiating ploys rather than genuine commitments, Western diplomats have often maintained that Soviet promises or oral agreements are worthless. A similar indication of lack of trust in Soviet-Western bargaining over political matters—and no doubt a further impediment to bargaining leading to compromises—is the view held by both sides, but emphasized more publicly in the West, that one can only negotiate successfully from a "position of strength," and that any military weakness would be exploited by the opposition.[12] Advice offered by Western statesmen such as Harry S. Truman, James Byrnes, Dean Acheson, John Foster Dulles, Adlai Stevenson, John F. Kennedy, and Winston Churchill states that the only way to achieve agreement with the Soviets is through displays of strength. Though it is undoubtedly true that Communist negotiators tend to exploit weakness in their adversaries, the assumption that settlements arranged through diplomatic bargaining are achieved more easily through threats of violence needs to be examined carefully before accepted. Certainly Communist governments have *submitted* and *withdrawn* in the face of superior strength and threats, but there is inadequate evidence to prove that they are more amenable to *compromise* as a form of conflict resolution when confronted with superior force.

If lack of trust and communication are factors inhibiting diplomatic bargaining and compromise, it would seem that where these are present, along with other variables such as the degree of responsiveness to others' needs and sensitivities, willingness to compromise during a conflict will be rather pronounced. When contentious issues arise between allies, there seems to be a strong presumption in favor of immediate diplomatic negotiations, a maximum of communication and explanation of positions, and a mutual willingness to reduce demands. A conflict or "misunderstanding" between Washington and London, for example, leads to the hurried dispatch of special emissaries to explain positions or arrange meetings between the foreign ministers or the president and prime minister. Once negotiations have commenced, the informal and understood rules of procedure and etiquette are quite different from those

[12] Coral Bell, *Negotiating from Strength* (London: Chatto and Windus, Ltd., 1962).

present in negotiations between hostile states. The element of trust in negotiations between friendly countries is maintained by scrupulous observance of certain unwritten rules, including avoidance of lies, misrepresentation, and impugning of motives, execution of all verbal or written agreements, payment of debts of gratitude, and maintenance of procedures which facilitate rather than block easy communication. Such behavior arises from trust that already exists, but it also reinforces that trust and, hence, reduces hostility and presumably makes compromise easier to achieve.[13]

Little need be said regarding the actual negotiation of compromise agreements. Some of the major bargaining tactics and techniques of inducement using economic and military threats have already been assessed in previous chapters. At some point in the proceedings, however, both sides revise their objectives, partly withdraw from their maximum demands, or remove themselves physically from a geographical position, in return for some concessions from the other party. It is almost impossible to predict at what point a compromise is possible, since it depends upon unique factors such as the skill of bargainers, capabilities they can mobilize to offer rewards or make threats, the desire to reach agreement, degrees of need, dependence, and responsiveness, and diplomatic pressures of allies and neutrals.

## Awards

A further method for resolving international conflicts—where a third party has the authority to announce the terms of settlement—is through arbitration or adjudication. The unique feature of awards is that the conflicting parties agree to give up on their own efforts and hand the power of decision to some impartial outsider, whether it is flipping a coin (chance) or an international tribunal. In such cases, the decision, or award, is usually made to accord with certain prescribed rules in specific international treaties, custom, or in general principles of international law. Most important conflicts are not, of course, resolved through this procedure because in arbitration or adjudication a state relinquishes the instruments of inducement to a third party which decides the issue on the basis of impartial law.[14] Moreover, conflict resolution through award requires at least three, and sometimes four, prior agreements among the disputants. First, they have to agree that some form of settlement—even

[13] Fred C. Iklé, *How Nations Negotiate* (New York: Harper & Row, Publishers, 1964), p. 87.
[14] Charles De Visscher, *Theory and Reality in Public International Law*, trans. Percy E. Corbett (Princeton: Princeton University Press, 1957), p. 330.

one involving loss of position—is preferable to continued conflict; second, they have to agree to resolve the conflict on the basis of legal standards rather than according to military, political, economic, or social criteria; third, they have to agree to the jurisdiction of a specific court; and, if the case is presented to an *ad hoc* arbitral tribunal, the parties also have to agree on a neutral chairman for the court. If parties to a conflict normally fail to maintain open communications with each other and lack trust in each other's motives and actions, it is little wonder that they do not accept judicial procedures for settlement, because such procedures imply considerable consensus among the disputants before the case is even heard. If one of the parties in the conflict has a weak legal position, it is not likely to accept the jurisdiction of a third party and will continue to seek to achieve its objectives by direct bargaining. On the other hand, if a stalemate develops and both sides trust the third party and expect a "fair" award, they might be induced to accept impartial determination of the case by a court.

An award settlement need not be made through judicial proceedings. As long as some external and impartial criterion for settlement is accepted by both sides, the settlement may be termed an award, even though it is administered by a non-judicial institution. A plebiscite to determine allocation of territory and population is an impartial device often used to settle both disputes and conflicts. Again, however, both parties have to agree first that the criterion of majority will should serve as a basis for settlement.

### "Passive Settlement"

Sometimes international conflicts are not formally settled through avoidance, submission, withdrawal, compromise, or award, but persist until the parties involved implicitly accept a new *status quo* as partially legitimate. When such a point has been reached, the involved nations have quietly reduced the degree of their commitment to a specific objective. Some of the post-war territorial conflicts in which the Soviet Union and the United States have had a stake have been resolved through slow acceptance of a new position rather than formal agreement. Consider, for example, the Korean problem. The division of that country at the 38th parallel after World War II was considered at first only a temporary arrangement to be succeeded by negotiations leading to unification of the country. By 1948, however, Communist and pro-Western regimes had become established in the two zones and neither would consent to unification of the country on the other's terms. In 1950 the North Koreans attempted to unify the country by force, as did the United

Nations forces before the intervention of Communist China into the war. Since the armistice, both Korean governments have maintained a symbolic commitment to unification and have actively promoted nationalist propaganda, but neither has taken realistic steps to achieve this objective. All parties to the conflict have more or less accepted the division of the country as a permanent fact, and Korea has been removed at least temporarily as one of the crisis areas of the cold war. There have been no formal negotiations, no agreements, no explicit compromises and no attempts at conquest since 1953, yet all the parties have helped to resolve the issue by passively accepting decisions that were designed in 1945 to be only temporary. Other cold war issues which have been settled in this manner would include the Soviet acceptance of West Germany as an independent government, and Western acquiescence to the Berlin Wall. Such settlements may never be very secure, of course, but since many conflicts have been temporarily resolved in this fashion, it suggests that often a conflict cannot be handled effectively when it has reached a crisis stage, and sometimes the least violent method of settlement—if it is a settlement at all—is one in which both sides learn to live with their common problem until neither is tempted to impose a solution by force.

### Procedures for the Pacific Settlement of International Disputes and Conflicts

One of the commonly recognized features of contemporary international politics is that few conflicts affect only those whose interests and values are directly involved. Even in primitive systems where violence was limited by crude technology, parties not immediately involved in tribal, feudal, or city state conflicts held some interest in seeing that issues were resolved peacefully. During the nineteenth century use of force was commonly regarded as an unlimited prerogative of the sovereign, but others saw that despite rules of neutrality which tended to limit the scope of conflicts, no war could fail to have an impact on the interests of surrounding states. Hence, delegates attending the first Hague Conference in 1899 drafted a "General Act for the Pacific Settlement of International Disputes" in which one article not only permitted, but encouraged, third parties to intervene in quarrels. Since that time it has been a recognized principle of international and regional organizations that they have a duty as representatives of a larger community to intervene in disputes and conflicts among their members, and that any threat to the peace, act of aggression, or violent conflict is a matter of concern to all states. Which particular procedures should be used in attempting to effect a settlement depends upon the nature of the conflict, including the issues in contention, scope of violence, willingness of the parties to negotiate or compromise, and legal aspects of the case. The following procedures involving third party intervention have been developed and used to settle conflicts in diverse international systems: (1) good offices, (2) mediation, (3) conciliation, (4) arbitration, and (5) adjudication. The first three procedures are usually associated with settlements accomplished through withdrawal, compromise, or "passive" behavior, while the last two are used once the involved parties have initially accepted the risks involved in handing a dispute to a third party.

Good offices is the term applied to the efforts of a third party to facilitate communication between the parties to a conflict, and to get them to agree to formal negotiations. The party that proffers its good offices does not take part in subsequent negotiations unless its proposal to act as a mediator is also accepted, but it relays peace overtures between governments which are not formally communicating with each other because of hostility, proposes sites for holding negotiations, and takes care of any arrangements for formal diplomatic meetings. Because in times of crisis or during actual hostilities communication between the disputants is usually limited to implicit bargaining through displays of force or actual violence, a third party which can facilitate formal negotiations may make an important contribution to settlement, particularly if both parties to the conflict are already disposed to substitute diplomatic bargaining for violence. In many conflict situations both disputants may be embarrassed or reluctant to propose negotiations for fear of appearing weak, but are sometimes willing to accept arrangements suggested by disinterested parties. Some successful uses of this procedure include President Theodore Roosevelt's offer of good offices to the belligerents in the Russo-Japanese war, the Swedish role that helped to end both the Russo-Finnish wars in 1940 and 1944, and the Swiss government's role in establishing communications that led to the end of hostilities between the United States and Japan in 1945.

Mediation, according to Article 4 of the Hague Convention, involves "reconciling the opposing claims and appeasing the feelings of resentment which may have arisen between the States at variance." Often the party that offers good offices also proposes that it mediate as well. A mediator may represent another government or, more frequently today, be appointed by the United Nations or some regional organization. The practices of mediators vary considerably, but usually they attempt to convince the disputants of the concern of other governments in the outcome of the conflict, and of the advantages to be gained by compromise, cease-fires, separation of forces, or mutual withdrawal. The mediator can also focus discussion on the original causes of conflict or on some obvious basis for a compromise agreement. He may propose terms of settlement, but often spends most of his time keeping discussions from breaking down. If the mediator or conciliating body is representative of the sentiments of a large number of relatively non-involved governments—as a United Nations mediator usually is—there is at least an implied obligation for the disputants to communicate with the mediator, accept *some* proposals which would alleviate tensions, and avoid hostile acts while efforts at settlement are in progress. The history of mediations by the League of Nations also indicates that when an agent of an international organization intervenes into a conflict between two small states, he can often virtually impose a settlement. A third party mediator often does not achieve a complete settlement to a conflict, but his actions can at least result in ending hostilities, institution of a "cooling off" period, and possibly direct negotiations between disputants. Finally, because of the mediator's impartiality toward the antagonists' actions and demands, he can help cut through the ideological verbiage surrounding the situation and promote discussions on the immediate sources of conflict. The following conflicts and disputes were resolved through compromises or mutual withdrawals largely as a result of mediation by third parties: the Mexican-American dispute in 1914, mediated by Argentina, Brazil, and Chile; the Indonesia-Netherlands conflict over West Irian, 1955–1962, mediated by the United States; the violent border conflict between Algeria and Morocco in 1963, mediated successfully by Haile Selassie, Emperor of Ethiopia, with the aid of some other members of the Organization of African Unity; and the Pakistan-Indian war over Kashmir in 1965, mediated by the Premier of the Soviet Union.

There is no precise distinction between mediation and conciliation, except that in the latter procedure the communication and reconciling functions are performed by a formally-constituted group of individuals representing several states or an international organization, rather than by one person or government. Conciliation also often includes systematic gathering of facts through on-the-spot investigation. These facts are subsequently employed to base recommendations on the terms of settlement, and sometimes to establish responsibility for actions which gave rise to a dispute. As in mediation, procedures for establishing commissions of inquiry and conciliation were first spelled out formally in the Hague Convention of 1899. Although many bilateral treaties of the late nineteenth and early twentieth centuries provided for creation of commissions of conciliation in the event that certain types of disputes arose, they were seldom utilized. It was under the auspices of the League of Nations that this procedure was first used frequently, especially for handling disputes that originated over "incidents" between small states. Like its predecessor, the United Nations has appointed special commissions of inquiry (Greece, 1946–1951, Hungary, 1956, Laos, 1959) and conciliation, usually with the double task of investigating the charges and countercharges of the antagonists and recommending solutions. Only in the conflict between Indonesia and the Netherlands, 1947–1949, was this procedure successful, however. The Lytton Commission (formally only a commission of inquiry) sent by the League of Nations to explore the Japanese-Chinese conflict over Manchuria in 1931 published a long report on the facts of the case and made recommendations for settlement, but these were never implemented after Japan refused to accept them and withdrew from the League. A commission of conciliation appointed by the General Assembly to arrange a settlement to the Palestine war in 1948 also failed. The experience of these efforts indicates that, as with mediation, the main ingredient for success lies in prior agreement of the antagonists that a compromise solution or withdrawal is preferable to the full achievement of their objectives. When the possibility of success through use of force, diplomatic intransigence, or other methods of inducement persists, at least one side is usually reluctant to give way to compromise. Conciliation procedures would appear to be most useful for settling minor disputes arising out of "incidents," where the facts and responsibility are not well established, and the two countries' foreign policy objectives are not otherwise incompatible.

Arbitration and adjudication differ from other procedures in several respects. First, the basis of award (arbitration) or decision (adjudication) is a legal norm rather than a compromise or withdrawal formula. Second, as distinct from mediation or conciliation where terms of settlement can only be *recommended*, once the parties have agreed to the jurisdiction of an arbitral tribunal or international court, they are bound by the decision of that body. Third, compromise is ruled out since under law there can only be a correct position and an incorrect position. When many separate legal issues are raised in a single case, however, a court need not decide all of them in favor of one party.

The distinctions between arbitration and adjudication refer primarily to procedure rather than to the basis upon which a case is decided. Under arbitration, the parties to the dispute or conflict normally name the arbitrators. Each side appoints one or more arbitrator and then both have to agree upon a neutral chairman. Adjudication takes place, on the other hand, in a permanent international tribunal, such as the International Court of Justice. Most arbitral courts are appointed to dispose of particular disputes or conflicts, and in some cases the disputants themselves may designate the body of rules or facts upon which the award must be based.

Many of the bilateral treaties which call for the institution of arbitral procedures spell out specifically which parts of a treaty being contested can be submitted to arbitration, and under what rules such procedures should take place. Once an international tribunal has achieved jurisdiction over a case, however, it is free to apply to a case whatever legal standards and procedures are provided for in its own constitution or charter.

### The Development of Institutions for Pacific Settlement

These procedures for settlement of disputes and conflicts have evolved over many centuries and can be found in diverse international systems. In some primitive tribal systems, for example, there were (and are still today, in some cases), well-established social roles for mediators, often ritual specialists and men of great prestige who could intervene into private disputes (between members of two different tribes, clans, or lineage groups) or into conflicts involving entire social collectivities, and order compensation or sanction various forms of revenge.[15]

In the Greek system of independent city states, the political units occasionally employed procedures, usually spelled out in bilateral treaties, for arbitrating conflicts arising over territorial frontiers, seizure of land for compensation of debts, partition of booty taken from third states, and religous observances. High esteem, honor, and influence were attached to the arbitrator's role, so that his offer of intervention and subsequent decisions were usually accepted by the disputants. Unlike contemporary arbitral proceedings, in the Greek city state system the arbitrator, who represented another city state or an alliance, could stand by his decisions and enforce them by the use of arms if necessary. Since the Greeks did not possess a formal body of international law, but relied more on religious principles, customs, and treaties as the basis for their claims, the arbitrator, instead of attempting to find one party guilty of a legal infraction and giving the other an award, sought to fashion a compromise and reconcile feuding city states on any basis he could discover.[16]

In the medieval and renaissance periods the third party function in conflicts and disputes between city states, kings and lords, lords and vassals, and between the emerging dynastic states, was sometimes per-

---

[15] For example, Lucy Mair, *Primitive Government* (Middlesex: Penguin Books, Ltd., 1962), pp. 48, 53; Igor Kopytoff, "Extension of Conflict as a Method of Conflict Resolution among the Suku of the Congo," *Journal of Conflict Resolution*, V (1961), 61–69.

[16] Marcus N. Tod, *International Arbitration Amongst the Greeks* (Oxford: The Clarendon Press, 1913), p. 62.

formed by the Roman church which, with its power of interdiction and excommunication, could intervene and in effect order an end to a quarrel. The evidence does not suggest that the Popes regularly conceived their role as including the duty of serving as arbiters of political quarrels. The church did not play an important part in helping to resolve international conflicts, though in several instances, such as during the great colonial rivalry between Spain and Portugal, the Pope intervened to draw the line between each dynasty's sphere of influence.

From the rise of the modern nation state until the end of the nineteenth century, there were no international institutions which provided mediatory, conciliatory, or arbitration services. This was the era of sovereign absolutism, where each ruler or dynast looked upon the use of force as a legitimate instrument of inducement, subject only to those limitations to which he had freely given his consent. There was no commonly recognized prohibition against use of force to resolve conflicts, though many of the written and unwritten rules of the period, combined with a crude military technology, helped restrict the scope of violence.

During the nineteenth century, a number of states concluded treaties which called for arbitration of disputes, and almost 300 unimportant international disputes were resolved through *ad hoc* arbitral proceedings. In the latter part of the century, due partly to the influence of the successful arbitration of a dispute verging on conflict between the United States and Great Britain (The Alabama Claims case, 1871), a number of private groups began to agitate for creation of permanent international institutions for handling conflicts and disputes. They argued that establishment of a permanent international tribunal, armed with enforcement powers and supported by limitations on armaments, would give rise to a new era of peace. These sentiments eventually influenced some governments and in 1899 and 1907 they reluctantly convened international conferences at The Hague to discuss plans for such institutions. The only important result of the first meeting was the "General Act for the Pacific Settlement of International Disputes" (amended in 1907), to which almost 50 states eventually adhered. The delegates also drafted a convention establishing the Permanent Court of Arbitration, which was neither permanent nor a court, but a list of arbitrators (nominated by members of the convention) who could be selected by disputing states to decide a particular case. The convention also delineated common rules of procedure for all arbitral cases. Though Article 38 of the General Act urged the signatories to use arbitral procedures for "questions of a legal nature, . . . especially in the interpretation or application of international conventions," the same document exempted states from submitting disputes or conflicts involving questions of "national honor." It was left to the states themselves to decide which situations involved "national honor." These arrangements thus provided only a weak basis for the Court's jurisdiction, and failed to provide it with means for enforcing those few decisions referred to it. As today, submission of cases to arbitral procedures was based on the principle of voluntarism.

In addition to the multilateral institutions and conventions created in 1899 and 1907, beginning in the latter part of the nineteenth century and continuing to the present, many governments have signed hundreds of commercial, taxation, citizenship, and territorial treaties containing clauses calling for arbitral procedures to be instituted in case of disagreement over their interpretation or violation. Other treaties have established specific classes of disputes which should be solved by arbitration or adjudication. The majority of these treaties requires the parties to appoint *ad hoc* arbitral tribunals to settle certain disputes, while a rather small minority gives automatic jurisdiction to the International Court of Justice.[17]

The most far-reaching innovation in establishing procedures for peaceful resolution of international conflicts, as well as disputes, came with the creation of the League of Nations. The major new principle of the League's Covenant was that the international community had not only a right but a duty to intervene in international conflicts and, correspondingly, that the parties to a conflict or dispute also had the obligation to submit their differences to some procedure for pacific settlement, ranging from bilateral negotiations to submission of the case to the Permanent Court of International Justice. Primary responsibility for recommending solutions to disputes and conflicts was lodged in the League Council, made up of some of the major powers plus other elected countries whose number ranged from six in 1922 to eleven in 1936. Under Article 13 of the Covenant, which provided for judicial or arbitral procedures, the members accepted the obligation not to resort to force to challenge the decisions or awards of international tribunals. To help prevent non-compliance with such decisions, Article 16 empowered the Council to order economic or military sanctions. Under Article 15, the Council was authorized to consider any matter brought before it, even if one party did not accept the "jurisdiction" of the League. Once the case came before the Council, it could attempt to effect a settlement through any means it wished. In practice the Council used a variety of procedures, including mediation (often performed by the President of the Council), commissions of inquiry, and conciliation commissions. In one case (the conflict

[17] L. Jullin, "Arbitration and Judicial Settlement: Recent Trends," *American Journal of International Law*, XLVIII (1954), 380–407.

between Poland and Lithuania in 1921 over the city of Vilna), it planned to send an international force to the scene of hostilities to separate the combatants and organize a cease-fire. In other instances the League supervised plebiscites to determine the outcome of territorial claims. If the Council could not achieve a settlement through these methods, it was authorized to submit a report recommending the terms of settlement. If the report was adopted unanimously by the Council (parties to the conflict had no vote), no member of the League could use force against the party which complied with the report, upon penalty of having economic or military sanctions imposed upon it. But if the Council could not agree unanimously on the report and its recommendations, the parties to the conflict were free to do as they wished, provided they did not go to war for a period of three months following the vote on the report.

Article 16 of the Covenant provided for automatic sanctions if any member should "resort to war in disregard of its covenants under Articles 12, 13, or 15." All members of the League were to consider the use of force in violation of these articles as an attack on themselves. While the provisions for economic and military sanctions were designed to deter aggression and assure compliance with all decisions or plans of settlement reached through the various settlement procedures, the history of the League in fulfilling these commitments was disappointing. In 1921 three Scandinavian states introduced a resolution which proposed that each member of the League, rather than the Council, should decide for itself when a breach of the Covenant had occurred; in 1923 the Canadian government sponsored another resolution which further reserved for each member the decision whether or not aggression had occurred and whether or not each should apply sanctions. Though the resolution did not pass, it had only one vote (Persia) against it, indicating clearly that the vast majority of states were not ready to relegate to the Council the authority to order sanctions—or even to determine that an act of aggression had occurred. Thus, the League Council was stripped of whatever authority it had under the Covenant to undertake action on its own authority. From 1923 to 1939, European governments displayed repeatedly that they, rather than the League Council, would make all final decisions relating to implementation of the League's efforts in the pacific settlement of disputes and collective security. The League of Nations was notable for introducing flexible procedures to help reach accommodations in disputes and conflicts involving small nations, but when action had to be taken against the aggressions of the major powers, it was powerless.

Under the Charter of the United Nations, provision is again made for use of diverse procedures for handling disputes and conflicts. Chapter VI, entitled "The Pacific Settlement of Disputes" (Articles 33 through 38) obligates the parties to a conflict or dispute "likely to endanger . . . international peace and security" to submit it to some procedure for pacific settlement, whether negotiation, enquiry, mediation, conciliation, arbitration, judicial settlement, resort to some regional agency, or any other method the parties can devise. Under Article 2, the members are prohibited from using force, even if these procedures should fail. There is no assumption in the Charter that the United Nations should, or would, become involved in most threats or breaches of the peace, although Article 37 stipulates that conflicts or disputes *not* resolved outside of the United Nations must be referred ultimately to the Security Council. Any party, whether or not a member of the United Nations, can submit an issue to the Organization; the General Assembly may notify the Security Council of any dangerous situation; and under Article 99 the Secretary General may also bring to the attention of the Security Council any matters which in his opinion threaten the maintenance of peace. On its own authority, the Security Council may, if the five permanent members agree, investigate any situation (Article 34) and may recommend at any time "appropriate procedures or methods of adjustment" (Article 36). Any action taken under Chapter VI, including dispatch of mediators or commissions of inquiry, is of a recommending nature only, however, and can be carried out only with the consent of the states directly involved in the conflict or dispute.

In Chapter VII, however, the Security Council is provided with enforcement powers if it has previously determined that there exists a threat to the peace, a breach of the peace, or an act of aggression. If it comes to such a conclusion, as in the Congo crisis of 1960, it can order the parties to a conflict and all member states to accept "provisional measures" (Article 40), such as a cease-fire or an order prohibiting intervention by outside powers. Under Article 41 the Security Council may "decide what measures not involving the use of armed force are to be employed to give effect to its decisions," and may call upon the members of the United Nations to apply such measures. These may include complete or partial interruption of economic relations, that is, boycotts and embargoes. If these measures are considered inadequate as a means of halting aggression or obtaining implementation of provisional measures taken under Article 40, the Security Council can use force. Under Article 43, which has never been implemented, the members of the United Nations are to make available to the Security Council "on its call . . . armed forces, assistance, and facilities, including the right of passage, necessary for the purpose of maintaining international peace and security."

These forces are not to be confused with the international peace groups created for the Suez, Congo, and Cyprus conflicts. The latter forces were formed primarily to effect cease-fires, separate combatants, supervise withdrawal of forces, and patrol frontiers. They are not fighting forces in the sense that their function is to halt aggression. The successful efforts of UNEF, UNOC, and UNICYP have been taken under Chapter VI of the Charter, which deals with pacific settlement of disputes. The forces, made up of contingents from many nations, have no directives to engage in hostilities, except in self-defense, and have been able to function only because the parties directly involved in the conflicts have accepted their presence. Without this consent, which is the basis of all action and decisions taken under Chapter VI, the peace forces could not have operated. It remains, however, for the United Nations to organize an international army which could be used as an instrument of collective security to repel aggression through force of arms.

The Charter gives to the General Assembly only a secondary role in handling international conflicts. While the Assembly may *discuss* any situation, it can recommend procedures or terms of settlement only if the Security Council is *not* considering the situation. Under the Uniting for Peace resolution of 1950, however, the General Assembly has given itself the authority to determine a threat to the peace, or act of aggression, and recommend appropriate action to its members in case the Security Council, on account of the veto, fails to act. It was under this resolution that the General Assembly organized the United Nations Emergency Force for the Suez crisis to supervise cessation of hostilities and secure a line dividing the combatants. The Hungarian question (1956) was also considered in the General Assembly, although its recommendations were never accepted by the Soviet Union. In 1960, the General Assembly played a key role in the Congo crisis after the agreement of the major powers in the Security Council had broken down.

While the United Nations Charter has covered some of the gaps that were found in the League Covenant, the procedures for pacific settlement are restricted by the necessary agreement among the five permanent members of the Security Council and by the principle that any actions taken under Chapter VI need the consent of the parties to a conflict. In effect, two agreements normally have to be achieved before the Security Council can deal effectively with a dangerous situation or a breach of the peace: the antagonists, with some exceptions, should agree to submit their conflict to this body, and then the five permanent members of the Council have to agree on the procedures to be used in attempting to effect reconciliation. The Security Council can discuss any situation brought to its attention, but any recommendations or actions, such as establishing commissions of inquiry, are subject to the veto.

Since 1945 the Security Council and General Assembly have used almost all of the devices and procedures for handling conflicts and disputes. They have debated and investigated dangerous situations, passed resolutions urging disputants to avoid hostile actions, established conciliation commissions, created mediators (often the Secretary-General or one of his appointees), organized international forces to separate combatants and secure cease-fires, and constructed truce supervisory teams to police cease-fire lines and armistice agreements. At other times they have deliberately avoided involvement in conflicts, pending efforts at pacific settlement outside of the United Nations structure. There is, then, no lack of institutions or procedures for peaceful resolution of international disputes and conflicts. Much could be done to improve them, such as organization of a permanent peace-keeping force, but an analysis of conflicts since 1919 suggests that the main failure in handling them lies not in the lack of institutions or procedures, but in the unwillingness of antagonistic parties to use them or to accept their recommendations for settlement. Without enforcement powers, no international institution can consistently dissuade antagonists from using violence if they are fully committed to a policy of "victory."

### Behavior and Procedures
### in International Conflicts:
### The Record Since 1919

One way to form some conclusions about the successes and failures of pacific settlement procedures is to examine the international conflicts that have occurred since 1919 and categorize each in terms of the governmental *behavior* that brought a settlement—either through peaceful forms such as avoidance, compromise, award, or "passive," or through violent conquest or effective deterrence. Second, we can also list the methods or *procedures* that were employed in attempting to resolve the conflicts. For the sake of comparison, the period 1919-1965 can be divided into two 20-year sections, the interwar period from 1919 to 1939, and the post-war period between 1945 and 1965. An almost equal number of conflicts occurred in the two periods, 38 prior to 1939, and 39 after World War II. No *disputes* are included in the figures. A conflict was identified as any situation where one or more governments threatened, mobilized, or actually used force against others to achieve or defend their objectives.

Applying first our concepts regarding the modes of behavior leading to conflict resolution, how do the two periods compare? First, it is clear that the record of peaceful settlement has improved significantly since World War II. In the interwar period, almost two out of three conflicts were ultimately settled by military conquest, forceful annexation, deterrence, or forced submission; 42 per cent of the conflicts were resolved by conquest. In contrast, in the period in which the United Nations has operated, only 15 per cent of the conflicts involved outright conquest, while 26 per cent were settled by compromise, 8 per cent by awards of various types, 8 per cent by "passive" behavior, and 18 per cent by voluntary withdrawals, or avoidance. The distinguishing feature of the interwar period, aside from the large number of conflicts resolved through force, violence, and subsequent surrender of the weaker party, was the number of conflicts resolved by awards. Eight of the 38 conflicts (21 per cent) were settled fully or partly by judicial decisions of the Permanent Court of International Justice, plebiscites, or plans drafted by the League Council which were accepted by the antagonistic parties. There is no question that outright aggression, forced annexation, or surrender under threats of invasion were important features of international conflict situations in the 1920's and 1930's, whereas today they occur relatively infrequently. Though almost all of the conflicts since 1945 have involved use of force, most have been resolved in one way or another before they broke out into full-scale war. Many of the "passive" settlements have not restored friendly relations between the countries which were quarreling, but at least they have but an end to violence.

What kinds of procedures were most often used in attempts to settle the 77 conflicts studied in the two 20-year periods? Of the *formal* attempts at settlement—excluding informal negotiations, for example, that may occur in the corridors or bars of the United Nations—a large number involved bilateral negotiations. However, contrary to the common belief that international conflicts are almost always resolved through bilateral bargaining procedures, the role of international organizations has been growing steadily. In fact, in the two 20-year periods under examination, almost as many attempts to settle the 77 conflicts were made through international organizations as in bilateral negotiations. Negotiations seem to have a relatively better chance of succeeding, however. Since 1945, of the 26 formal negotiations taking place between antagonistic nations, 14 ended successfully in some sort of compromise settlement.

Mediation and conciliation outside of the framework of international organizations seldom occurs any longer. Of the 130 formal attempts to settle the 77 conflicts under review, third-power mediation or conciliation was attempted only nine times, and succeeded or helped in bringing about a settlement in only two cases. Most mediation today is undertaken by officials of the United Nations, persons charged by the Security Council or Secretary-General with getting the conflicting parties together and discussing various peace formulas.

Multilateral conferences are employed occasionally to bring some types of conflicts, particularly those that involve more than two parties, to an end. In 1954, for instance, the major powers and the states of Indochina assembled in Geneva to terminate the Indochinese war and arrange for withdrawal of French forces after they had been defeated by the Viet Minh. Eight years later the same governments met again in Geneva to work out a peace settlement for Laos, a country which had been torn for several years by internal strife and American, Chinese, Soviet, and North Vietnamese intervention. Nine per cent (7 out of 77) of all the conflicts in the two 20-year periods were partially or entirely resolved in formal multilateral conferences.

As could be expected, the role of international organizations in resolving international conflicts has grown consistently, if not dramatically. This indicates that the idea of a community interest in conflict, no matter where it may occur, has become established. Though the League of Nations made only 18 formal attempts at settlement of conflicts on its agenda in a 20-year period, the United Nations and various regional organizations have tried actively to resolve 28 crises in a similar period of time. It is difficult to estimate the real influence of these organizations because in many instances a body such as the General Assembly passes resolutions "urging" the antagonists to settle their quarrel without recourse to violence, or "deplores" non-compliance with such resolutions, without undertaking itself any steps toward mediation. The impact of "opinion" resolutions is hard to gauge, but it is apparent that they often do not lead to desired results. Under the principle of voluntarism in Chapter VI of the Charter, any government is free to ignore resolutions passed by the General Assembly, or even the Security Council. Despite the constitutional and political weaknesses of the United Nations and the League of Nations, however, nations continue to refer their conflicts to international bodies. Of the 130 formal attempts to settle the 77 conflicts that were examined, 47 took the form of bilateral negotiations, and 46 involved various proposals, procedures, or plans of settlement worked out by international organizations or their mediators.

How successful have these international organizations been in bringing about actual settlements to conflicts? The records reveal that 16 out of the 77 conflicts in the two 20-year periods were partially or fully settled through the procedures offered by the United Nations and its predecessor. While this may not seem a particularly high figure, only six more conflicts were resolved by bilateral negotiations.

The main weaknesses of the United Nations have appeared in its attempts to settle the many conflicts involving direct confrontations between the main protagonists of the cold war. In fact, this organization has played a major role in only two cold war crises in 20 years: the Soviet evacuation of Iran in 1946, and during the Korean armistice discussions. Similarly, the League of Nations was most successful in handling conflicts between small states, and least successful in coping with the major aggressions committed by Japan, Italy, Nazi Germany, and Soviet Russia.

Another weakness of the United Nations has been its inability in promoting formal and lasting settlements, and particularly in alleviating the *causes* of international conflicts. Usually the organization has not become involved in a conflict situation until it has already developed into violence. Its main concern has been to reduce violence, not to deal with the causes of violence. The organization has thus developed means which, while not actually resolving conflicts in terms of formal settlements or removing the causes of conflict, have nevertheless helped to "freeze" them, isolate them from great power intervention, and impose controls on the amount of violence. By drafting and ordering terms for cease-fire agreements, sending truce supervisory organizations to implement and police them, and organizing international peace-keeping forces to separate combatants, the United Nations has successfully imposed limitations on the scope of violence and on the number of parties becoming directly involved in international conflicts and domestic rebellions. As Inis Claude has put it, the main contribution of the United Nations to international peace has been to stumble upon techniques of "pacific non-settlement" or "not-quite-pacific settlement" of conflicts.[18]

In the Suez, Lebanon, Congo, and Cyprus crises, the quick intervention of the United Nations forestalled initiatives by the great powers to introduce or maintain their own troops in the crisis area. By intervening in these situations—three of which started as internal rebellions—the United Nations had at least an indirect effect on the main bloc conflicts by preventing their extension into new geographic areas. And while the intervention of the United Nations has usually resulted in a stalemate between two nations or between two warring factions within a country, such an arrangement may eventually lead to "passive" settlements or formal agreements, while unilateral intervention by outside powers usually has the purpose of gaining a clear victory for one side. A stalemate, though not a solution, probably involves fewer risks to the rest of the world than does the unilateral intervention and counter-intervention of the great powers.

If we consider the example of the Cyprus conflict, the advantages of United Nations intervention and stalemate can be observed. In 1964 the

[18] Inis L. Claude, Jr., *Swords into Plowshares: The Problems and Prospects of International Organization,* 2nd ed. (New York: Random House, Inc., 1959), p. 242.

United Nations sent to that island a peace-keeping force which established and policed cease-fire lines between the Greek-speaking majority and the Turkish minority. Simultaneously, a United Nations mediator attempted to get the leaders of both sides to negotiate some form of agreement which would enable the two ethnic groups to live together peacefully on the island. While the international force operated on Cyprus, both Greece and Turkey, as "protectors" of the two ethnic groups, smuggled "volunteers" and military supplies onto the island, but generally the United Nations was able to create and enforce a stalemate between the two sides. We can only speculate on the outcome of the crisis had the United Nations failed to act, but on the basis of the direction in which the crisis was developing in late 1963 and early 1964, it is not difficult to predict that Turkey might have intervened directly, as it was authorized to do under international treaty, to protect the Turkish-speaking minority on Cyprus. Such action may have led to counter-intervention by Greece, and possible war between these two NATO allies. Since Great Britain controlled a military base on the island and considered it an important strategic area, it might have become involved as well, thus inviting some form of intervention by the Soviet Union to "protect" the Greek Cypriots against the Turkish and English "imperialists." By such preventive diplomacy in the Kashmir, Congo, Cyprus, and Middle East crises, the United Nations has made important contributions by establishing and policing cease-fires, preventing arms build-ups, and creating stalemates that may eventually lead to "passive" settlements or more formal agreements.

### Problems and Prospects
### of Settlement Through Awards

In the history of international politics since 1919, at least 77 dangerous crises have arisen; of those settled by peaceful means, the vast majority employed the procedures of bilateral negotiations, mediation and conciliation by international organizations, and negotiations in multilateral conferences. But what of judicial procedures? Certainly there is no lack of opportunities for governments to resolve their conflicts through the method of award, for almost all conflicts involve legal questions or problems that could be settled through plebiscites. And there is no lack of institutions and procedures to use. The Permanent Court of International Justice was established in 1921, and in 1946 its successor, the International Court of Justice, heard its first case. Many states also adhere to the Hague Convention for the Pacific Settlement of International Disputes, which calls upon its signatories to avail themselves of arbitral procedures where legal issues are involved.[19] Today over 50 treaties of alliance, amity, commerce, and navigation contain clauses stipulating that disputes over their interpretation should be referred to the International Court of Justice.[20] In view of the existence of both treaties and institutions which obligate states to submit certain kinds of disputes or conflicts to arbitral and adjudication procedures, what has been the record of settlement through awards?

Since 1921, international tribunals have resolved or helped to settle only 6 conflicts, and only 9 per cent of all attempts to settle international conflicts have been made through judicial institutions or other award procedures. Even if we consider the role of various international tribunals in disputes as well as conflicts, the figures are not particularly impressive. It is true that between 1920 and 1940 arbitral tribunals handed down 60 awards of some consequence,[21] but the Permanent Court of International Justice resolved only 15 major cases, while its successor made only 14 decisions up to 1964, excluding advisory opinions and those decisions in which it ruled lack of jurisdiction. Moreover, of the hundreds of arbitration and conciliation treaties, only a few have been used as the basis of settlement; the vast majority of cases handled through arbitration have involved minor issues, often complaints of private citizens which were taken up on their behalf by their governments, but certainly not the kinds of disputes which lead to serious political conflicts. Despite the willingness of the International Court of Justice to consider at least the legal aspects of dangerous conflicts, most governments have not been willing to avail themselves of this procedure.

Part of the explanation for limited use of international tribunals lies in the uncertainty surrounding their jurisdiction. Here are the methods by which they can obtain jurisdiction over a dispute or conflict:

1. The two parties to a dispute may agree through a *compromis* to submit their differences to an international tribunal.

2. Both governments can agree to implement a previous treaty which stipulates use of arbitral or judicial procedures for certain classes of disputes.

3. Both parties can honor clauses in other treaties which call upon them

---

[19] However, as of 1966, only a few governments have ratified the revised "General Act for the Pacific Settlement of International Disputes" drafted in the United Nations.

[20] Kenneth W. Thompson, *Political Realism and the Crisis of World Politics* (Princeton: Princeton University Press, 1960), p. 208.

[21] Jullin, "Arbitration and Judicial Settlement," 382.

to submit any differences of interpretation, or violation, to the International Court of Justice.

4. States can adhere to the "Optional Clause" (Article 36) of the Statute of the International Court of Justice and thereby declare that they recognize as compulsory the jurisdiction of the court on all *legal* disputes.

Though these techniques may seem to devolve upon international tribunals considerable authority, in fact they contain many conditions which make the tribunals' jurisdiction almost completely dependent upon voluntary submission of cases by the parties to a conflict or dispute. For example, both the Permanent Court of International Justice and its successor have ruled that they cannot decide cases unless *both* parties accept the court's jurisdiction. Obviously a government which knows it has a weak legal case will not readily accept such jurisdiction. Moreover, fewer than 40 governments have accepted, through the "Optional Clause," compulsory jurisdiction of the Court, and even among those which have adhered to Article 36, many have made such important reservations that for all practical purposes it is no longer the Court, but the state, which decides whether or not a case is justiciable. The United States, for example, adheres to Article 36, but through the Connally Amendment may exclude from the Court's jurisdiction any matter which is "essentially within the domestic jurisdiction of the United States." It is for the American government, not the International Court of Justice, to decide what is "essentially" a domestic matter. In short, by invoking the criterion of "domestic affairs," or arguing that the case is not primarily a legal one, any government can prevent the Court's compulsory jurisdiction from operating.

These are rather technical reasons for explaining why international tribunals have considered so few important cases. More important reasons, reflecting ideological cleavages of our era, divisions of legal philosophy, and attitudes toward sacrificing the possibility of achieving objectives through bargaining or force, are involved. International lawyers have for many years tried to draw distinctions between political and legal disputes, or between disputes and conflicts. Some have argued that only unimportant disputes are amenable to resolution through award. Others point out that a dispute is a situation in which two parties disagree over the meaning of *existing* laws or treaties, or where one party has violated its treaty obligations, while in a conflict a party seeks to *change* the other's rights, privileges, or obligations. A conflict may have important legal aspects to it (as in the Berlin, Kashmir, Vietnam, and Suez problems), but obviously one or both antagonists does not wish to characterize the situation exclusively in legal terms because its objectives and actions are incompatible with *existing* legal principles or treaties. If, for example, one government wishes to subvert a neighbor's society and proceeds to infiltrate its territory with agents and guerrilla warriors, it is seeking to achieve an objective contrary to the established order, by means which are clearly illegal. It would be almost impossible to resolve this conflict through judicial procedures because one party obviously does not accept the legitimacy of the *status quo,* whereas this is the basis upon which any international tribunal must make its award. There were legal aspects to the Nazi seizure of the Rhineland, Austria, and Czechoslovakia, but no person could have suggested seriously that the conflicts Hitler raised could have been resolved by applying pre-1933 treaties or the League of Nations Covenant. A Canadian diplomat summarized the problem of adjudicating conflicts when he stated:

> The fact is that international relations do not give rise to political problems which have a legal aspect, any more than they give rise to legal problems which have a political aspect. In my view, the basic distinction between disputes that are legal and disputes that are political is the readiness of the states concerned to regard them as legal, to consider them in terms of international law. But reluctance to think about and articulate problems in legal terms is not necessarily due to lack of interest in or respect for international law. It may arise because the realities of the issue are obscured, not clarified, by defining them in legal terms. Or the reluctance to litigate may be due to a belief that the law, as it is, is unjust or inadequate and must be changed.[22]

This last point has been increasingly apparent as one of the problems of resolving conflicts on the basis of legal criteria. Many of the new states are not enthusiastic supporters of certain parts of international law which originated in Europe and were designed to protect the investments of European and American business enterprises or provide a legal basis for colonial type relationships. One can single out, in particular, the law relating to expropriation of private property and the question of using force to obtain independence or self-determination. The condition and aspirations of these new states raise unprecedented problems for award-type conflict resolution because the history of cases before the major international tribunals reveals quite clearly that both parties which have availed themselves of the award mode of settlement have usually accepted the legitimacy of *existing* law. Moreover, many of the disputes and conflicts submitted to international tribunals have involved states which

[22] Speech by Paul Martin, Secretary of State for External Affairs, to the Toronto Branch of the International Law Association, October 14, 1964, reprinted by the Department of External Affairs, Information Division, "Statements and Speeches," No. 64/24, p. 2.

normally maintain friendly relations—for example, Belgium and the Netherlands, the United States and Switzerland, Germany and Austria, Great Britain and France, and France and Norway. An examination of these disputes and conflicts suggests that the importance of the issues to the litigants was quite small compared to their common interests.

The conclusion from this investigation is apparent. Most conflicts involve considerable bargaining between the antagonists and, in all modes of resolution except award, that bargaining can continue until some point of accommodation is reached. But in an award, bargaining ceases when both sides have agreed to resolve the issue on the basis of an impartial arbitrator, judge, or objective criterion such as majority will. At best there is only an even chance of winning the award, and if the chances are better, one side has a very weak legal case and will be naturally reluctant to agree to judicial procedures. But if there are no visible trends toward acceptance of legal procedures for conflict resolution, other figures are more heartening. Compared to the interwar period, the record of pacific settlement or "pacific non-settlement" has improved since 1945. No doubt where the vital interests of the major powers are directly incompatible, international organizations will continue to play a minor role. But if they can impose their presence in less awesome quarrels, isolate areas of confrontation, and impose cease-fire and armistice agreements, they will have made an important contribution to maintenance of international peace and security.

In all types of international systems, component political units have formulated objectives, whether derived from ideological imperatives, domestic socio-economic needs, or ambition of political leaders, whose fulfillment could only be achieved at the expense of other tribes', city states', or nations' core interests and values. Though conflict is by no means the most predominant type of relationship in all international systems, it persists, just as many domestic societies feature conflict, cooperation, and domination between individuals and institutions. The difference is that in most domestic societies, the element of force is effectively regulated by administrative authorities, while in an international system (excepting, perhaps, the hierarchical variety) each unit decides for itself when and under what circumstances it will use the ultimate means of inducement. It must not be assumed that force or threat of its use are the normal means of seeking to achieve objectives or accommodating incompatible goals. Aside from the thousands of conflicts which have been resolved through peaceful diplomatic bargaining, one only has to regard today the states which normally maintain friendly relations, despite diverging and often conflicting objectives, to see that there are many peaceful ways of reaching accommodation.

## SELECTED BIBLIOGRAPHY

Alger, Chadwick F., "Non-resolution Consequences of the United Nations and Their Effect on International Conflict," *Journal of Conflict Resolution*, V (1961), 128–45.

Aubert, Vilhelm, "Competition and Dissensus: Two Types of Conflict and of Conflict Resolution," *Journal of Conflict Resolution*, VII (1963), 26–42.

Barkun, Michael, "Conflict Resolution Through Implicit Mediation," *Journal of Conflict Resolution*, VIII (1964), 121–30.

Bloomfield, Lincoln P., ed., *International Military Forces: The Question of Peacekeeping in an Armed and Disarming World.* Boston: Little, Brown and Company, 1964.

Boulding, Kenneth E., *Conflict and Defense: A General Theory.* New York: Harper & Row, Publishers, 1962.

Brownlie, Ian, *International Law and the Use of Force by States.* London: Oxford University Press, 1963.

Burns, Arthur L., and Nina Heathcote, *Peace-Keeping by U.N. Forces: From Suez to the Congo.* New York: Frederick A. Preager, Publisher, Inc., 1963.

Burton, John W., *Peace Theory: The Preconditions of Disarmament.* New York: Alfred A. Knopf, Inc., 1962.

Claude, Inis L., Jr., *Swords into Plowshares: The Problems and Prospects of International Organization*, 2d ed. New York: Random House, Inc., 1959.

———, "The United Nations and the Use of Force," *International Conciliation*, No. 532 (1961), 325–94.

Coser, Lewis A., "The Termination of Conflict," *Journal of Conflict Resolution*, V (1961), 347–53.

Etzioni, Amitai, "On Self-encapsulating Conflicts," *Journal of Conflict Resolution*, VIII (1964), 242–55.

Fisher, Roger, ed., *International Conflict and Behavioral Science.* New York: Basic Books, Inc., 1964.

Goodrich, Leland M., and Anne P. Simons, *The United Nations and the Maintenance of International Peace and Security.* Washington, D.C.: The Brookings Institute, 1962.

Holsti, Ole R., "The Value of International Tension Measurement," *Journal of Conflict Resolution*, VII (1963), 608–17.

———, Richard Brody, and Robert C. North, "Affect and Action in International Reaction Models," *Journal of Peace Research*, Nos. 3–4 (1964), 170–90.

Honig, F., "The Diminishing Role of the World Court," *International Affairs*, XXXIV (1958), 184–94.

Jullin, L., "Arbitration and Judicial Settlement: Recent Trends," *American Journal of International Law*, XLVIII (1954), 380–407.

Kecskemeti, Paul, *Strategic Surrender*. Stanford: Stanford University Press, 1958.

Larson, Arthur, *When Nations Disagree*. Baton Rouge: Louisiana State University Press, 1961.

Levi, Werner, "On the Causes of War and the Conditions of Peace," *Journal of Conflict Resolution*, IV (1960), 411–20.

McClelland, Charles A., "Action Structures and Communication in Two International Crises: Quemoy and Berlin," *Background*, VII (1964), 201–15.

Modelski, George, "International Settlement of Internal War," in *International Aspects of Civil Strife*, ed. James N. Rosenau. Princeton: Princeton University Press, 1964.

Russell, Ruth B., *United Nations' Experience with Military Forces: Political and Legal Aspects*. Washington, D.C.: The Brookings Institute, 1964.

Schelling, Thomas C., *The Strategy of Conflict*. Cambridge, Mass.: Harvard University Press, 1960.

Stone, Julius, *Legal Controls of International Conflicts*. New York: Holt, Rinehart & Winston, Inc., 1959.

Sørenson, Max, "The International Court of Justice: Its Role in Contemporary International Relations," *International Organization*, XIV (1960), 261–76.

Wright, Quincy, "The Escalation of International Conflicts," *Journal of Conflict Resolution*, IX (1965), 434–49.

# Conflict and Collaboration in Security Communities

Our contemporary international system should not be viewed as comprising only a multitude of totally independent nation states, all using their capabilities, and sometimes force, to pursue or defend their interests, values, and objectives. There are also many loose groupings of states, sometimes formed into international or supranational organizations, where the char acteristics of conflict and collaboration may be somewhat different than customarily found in international politics. Western Europe contains overlapping networks of states representing diverse economic, political, and defense objectives and different degrees of economic or political integration: the five nations of the Nordic Council; the six nations of the European Economic Community (Common Market); the seven members of the European Free Trade Association; the seven members of the Western European Union; the 18 nations of the Organization for Economic Cooperation and Development; the three members of the Benelux

# Chapter XVI

customs union; the 15 members of NATO; and the 15 members of the Council of Europe. All of the states of non-Communist Europe belong to at least two of these organizations, some belong to six, but none belongs to all. The bilateral model of the state A–state B relationship used throughout this book therefore describes only one aspect (though the most important) of contemporary international politics, for in some of these groupings and associations the wielding of influence assumes unique forms. Moreover, on some questions—for example, the Common Market's external tariff—these associations of states act as a single unit vis-à-vis other states or groups of states. They have one common policy, reflecting their membership's common objectives.

If we are to have a wide perspective on international politics and avoid undue emphasis on violence and the ineffectiveness of legal or ethical restraints in relations among states, we must also have some understanding of the way disputes and conflicts are handled in these associations. What conditions tend to ameliorate hostility when conflicts develop in such relationships, where two members of, let us say, the Nordic Council develop misunderstandings or make demands on each other that are incompatible? Why, despite some serious conflicts over territory, foreign policy objectives, and economic interests, has there been no war between the United States and Canada? If there are such conflicts, why don't the parties make violent threats? As partial explanations, historians can cite the similar cultural and political traditions of Canada and the United States and the role of Great Britain in the nineteenth century as a deterrent against American expeditions into Canada. But peaceful conditions can also exist between countries with cultural and political differences. For example, there has been no threat of war between Mexico and the United States since 1915. Similar questions could be asked with regard to the Scandinavian states, Western Europe, and parts of Latin America. Not only has violence been avoided in relationships and transactions between countries in some of these areas, but when differences do arise, the governments involved seldom even consider using military capabilities as instruments of inducement. Conflicts are almost always settled by the modes of behavior associated with compromise, avoidance, and awards. Deterrence and forced submission are conspicuous by their very rare occurrence. Violent international conflict, while recurring in international politics, is therefore by no means the *only*, or even typical, kind of conflict. In this chapter we will investigate what social, economic, and political conditions are associated with development of these typically peaceful kinds of relationships, and how conflicts are handled when they do occur. Finally, we can draw some comparisons with the observations of the preceding chapter.

Pioneering work on political integration and peaceful relations between independent political units has been conducted by American political scientist Karl Deutsch. He has given the name "security community" to those areas where relationships between independent or integrating political units are predictably peaceful, and where conflicts are resolved by compromise, avoidance, and awards rather than by force. Deutsch has distinguished pluralistic security communities, where there is no integration of political institutions or authority (Canada and the United States, for example), from amalgamated security communities, where two or more independent political units merge to create a larger entity with a common structure of political authority. Historical examples of the processes leading to amalgamated security communities would include creation of Italy out of a conglomeration of formerly warring city states, papal holdings, and small kingdoms on the Italian peninsula; establishment of federal authority and nationhood out of 13 colonies in America; amalgamation of the former nations of Scotland, Wales, Ireland, and England into the United Kingdom by the early eighteenth century; and unification of Germany out of hundreds of principalities, semi-sovereign towns and cities, and dynastic states during the nineteenth century.

According to Deutsch, the significant fact about a security community is not whether a number of formerly independent political units officially amalgamate into one large state. The distinguishing feature of a security community, as compared to ordinary diplomatic dyads, is achievement of "integration," which Deutsch defines as a "sense" of community, and development of institutions and diplomatic-political-military practices which assure "for a long time" the expectation of only peaceful relations among the populations.[1]

[1] Karl Deutsch, *et al., Political Community and the North Atlantic Area* (Princeton: Princeton University Press, 1957), p. 5. Another political scientist, Ernst Haas, argues that true integration and community can only develop where supranational, federal, or confederal institutions exist with powers to direct the policies of the units which are amalgamating. Haas states that while avoidance of force can be achieved outside of the context of such institutions, the creation and perpetuation of a new national consciousness cannot be expected to develop unless central political authorities and institutions are established. See Ernst B. Haas, *The Uniting of Europe* (Stanford; Stanford University Press, 1957), p. 7. Amitai Etzioni, a political sociologist, defines a political community as synonymous with a unitary or federal state, with a distinct central authority which is the dominant focus of political identification for the population. Anything less, he claims, is an international system which may be more or less integrated, but which is not a political community. See his *Political Unification* (New York: Holt, Rinehart & Winston, Inc., 1965), p. 3–13. Stanley Hoffmann also makes the point that it takes more than the absence of violence between two groups to indicate the existence of a true community. See his "Discord in Community: The North Atlantic Area as a Partial International System," in *The Atlantic Community: Progress and Prospects,* ed. Francis O. Wilcox and H. Field Haviland (New York: Frederick A. Praeger, Publisher, Inc., 1963), pp. 9–10. To avoid confusion over the term "community" we shall continue to use it in the sense that Deutsch introduces it.

In Chapter VII we pointed out that avoidance of threats to use force and absence of military forces "targeted" toward the other state are essential indicators of "relations of consensus." Deutsch similarly claims that the two main indicators of the existence of a security community are revealed in situations (1) where the policy-makers of two or more political units, and their societies in general, cease to contemplate the possibility of mutual warfare, and (2) where the two or more states cease to allocate resources for building military capabilities aimed at each other.[2]

Of course it may not be easy to state at what particular point in history a security community has emerged between two or more political units. The Rush-Bagot Treaty of 1819 demilitarized the Canadian-American frontier, and there were few official government plans after 1865 indicating any expectation of war between the two countries. Yet there were several instances during the late nineteenth century when some Canadians and Americans expected or planned use of violence against each other. In terms of public attitudes, a true security community between the two countries probably dates only from the early twentieth century. Similarly, there have been no Swedish and Norwegian military forces "targeted" toward each other since the breakup of the Swedish-Norwegian union in 1905, but there were segments of the population in each country which did consider the possibility of warfare against the other until the end of World War I. Another problem of identification arises when two states continue to make routine preparations for defending their borders against each other, even though the societies and governments concerned would not have any expectation of using or threatening force against the neighbor.[3]

A third indicator of the existence of a security community could be mutual acceptance and rigorous observance of certain rules of international law and bilateral treaties when collective objectives of the units are not in harmony. These would include, as well as avoidance of military threats, meeting of treaty obligations (except in emergencies, where prior consultation would pave the way for special dispensations), avoidance of interference in the other unit's internal affairs, and observance of normal diplomatic protocol and etiquette in all transactions and negotiations. If behavior conforms to these three indicators—no "targeted" military forces, no public expectations of war, and full observance of treaties—we can say that a security community exists between two or more independent political units, or within an area where the political units are formally amalgamating.

[2] Deutsch, *Political Community*, pp. 31–33.
[3] Deutsch, *Political Community*, pp. 115–16.

One might object that in such relationships the essential collective objectives and values of the political units are so similar that serious conflicts never arise anyway. The indicators of a security community are obvious characteristics of any relationship where goals and values are compatible to begin with. The concept is thus a tautology. But this criticism fails to acknowledge that some very serious differences have arisen among states in security communities, and that some special characteristics of these relationships have prevented the quarreling governments from adopting forms of behavior typical in conflicts involving threat or use of force. For example, relations between France and the United States since World War II have often been strained by diverging collective interests and different long-range goals or concepts regarding the future organization of Europe. Throughout the 1950's the Algerian rebellion caused considerable mutual recrimination and lack of understanding between the French and American governments; in 1966 President de Gaulle asked the United States and Canada to remove their troops and facilities from French soil, and announced his plans to withdraw French commanders from NATO headquarters; ever since the organization of NATO in 1949, there have been unbridgeable differences of view on appropriate military strategies for alliance forces, control over the strategic deterrent held by the United States, and development of independent nuclear capabilities in certain NATO countries. In each case, the French and American governments have sought to change the behavior of each other to conform to their own interests through normal techniques of persuasion, by offering rewards, attempting to persuade by citing common advantages, and in some cases making non-violent threats of deprivations or punishments. But in no instance did one party conceive of, or threaten to, employ force against the other; no military capabilities were mobilized to signify total commitment to an objective, and communication between Paris and Washington did not break down. The question arises, why were characteristics associated with violent conflicts not displayed in conflicts occurring within security communities? The absence of targeted military capabilities and preparations for violence are only *indicators* of a special type of relationship; we also want to ask why these indicators appear in the relations between some political units and not among others?

## "Background Conditions" of Security Communities

Studying the integration of Switzerland, Italy, Germany, the United Kingdom, the United States, and Canada out of previously independent political units, as well as dissolution of the Austro-Hungarian empire and the Norwegian-Swedish union, Deutsch and his colleagues found that the following "background conditions," among others, were necessary for successful integration into an *amalgamated* security community:

1. Mutual compatibility of values between the units (city states, principalities, provinces, colonies) that were in the process of amalgamating.

2. Distinctive way of life. There had to be some appreciation, primarily among political and economic elites, of the differences and distinctions between the units that were amalgamating, on the one hand, and "foreigners" on the other.

3. Anticipation of increased economic gains. In almost all historical examples of amalgamation, including some not studied by Deutsch and his colleagues, a strong impetus for integration was expectation by the elites of the amalgamating units that economic benefits would result from political union. As we will see below, the economic motive for integration in Europe has been particularly prominent.

4. This study also found that it was necessary for at least several of the amalgamating units to have highly developed political and administrative capabilities. Since one source of support for union was expectation of increased benefits to the units involved, it was necessary to have the governmental capability to help realize these expectations. In the cases of amalgamation studied, the presence of one center, with established administrative capabilities, was always prominent. The role of Prussia and Piedmont in the unification of Germany and Italy are notable examples.

5. Superior economic growth rates and opportunities of some, usually the leading, units of the unification movement.

6. Prevalence of communication between the units. This condition includes not only formal communication through mass media or direct personal contact, but also development of organizations of intellectual, economic, religious, pedagogical, and scientific elites, cutting across political boundaries. In many instances this communication within transnational organizations was assisted by development of institutions for standardizing commercial laws, customs, weights and measures, and so on.

7. Broadening of the political elites of the amalgamating units. This included, for example, the entry of commercial elites and other economic groups into positions of political influence.

8. Mobility and opportunities for the politically relevant strata of the societies that were integrating. For example, popular support for integration was seldom observed where all political power was effectively concentrated in small court circles.[4]

---

[4] Etzioni found that one factor contributing to the dissolution of the West Indies Federation was concentration of support for the idea of federation among only a small political and social elite, while the masses of people were unknowledgeable and apathetic toward the project. *Political Unification*, pp. 166–70.

9. Multiplicity of types of transactions among the amalgamating units, including trade, social communication, education, and common military endeavors. Amalgamation thus seems to require a previous sense of involvement and constant communication between different political units.

10. A final characteristic which, according to Deutsch, could probably be classified as a necessary background condition for amalgamation, was mutual predictability of behavior; the units under investigation seemed to have at least some knowledge of, and ability to predict, each other's political and economic actions.[5]

Which of these conditions were necessary for the development of *pluralistic* security communities? Deutsch and his colleagues found that any of those background conditions necessary for successful amalgamation were helpful, but they concluded that only three conditions were mandatory: (1) compatibility of major social, political, and economic values; (2) responsiveness and sensitivity to each other's needs (see below); and (3) some mutual predictability of behavior.[6] Pluralistic security communities such as the Swiss confederation during the seventeenth and eighteenth centuries, the United States and Great Britain since approximately 1871, the Scandinavian states since the early twentieth century, or Britain and the low countries in the same period, have developed and flourished without the presence of many of the background conditions necessary for political amalgamation. In some of these relationships, one party was far predominant in military and economic capacity without using that capacity to crush or dominate weaker neighbors.

Deutsch's studies also demonstrated that several conditions often assumed important for the development of pluralistic or amalgamated security communities were only mildly helpful. One was the presence of a common military threat. These threats usually resulted in alliances, but the investigators found no evidence that alliances were by themselves sufficient to foster integration or the habit of pacific modes of conflict resolution. Another was strong economic ties. Though they noted that expectations of increased economic benefits were an important stimulus to integration movements, a high volume of trade or economic dependency was not essential to the development of either type of security community.[7]

How relevant are these historical background conditions to the proc-

---

[5] Deutsch, *Political Community*, pp. 46–58.
[6] Deutsch, *Political Community*, pp. 65–70.
[7] Deutsch, *Political Community*, pp. 44, 157.

esses of economic or political integration or the development of pluralistic security communities? Ernst Haas has been critical of applying conclusions from historical studies to the contemporary situation. In his own careful studies of the process of European economic integration, he has underlined the importance of some conditions which are unique to highly industrialized societies and to Western Europe. He argues, for example, that in the post-World War II era there have been no important political issues separating the six nations which formed the European Coal and Steel Community in 1951 and the Common Market and Euratom in 1957. The foreign policy goals of these nations, at least as they impinged on each other's interests, were basically compatible. Moreover, there has been a striking degree of cultural unity among the integrating states, with strong legal, economic, and political similarities as well. Finally, there has developed throughout the Western European countries since 1945 two types of political parties—the Christian Democrats and the Social Democrats—which have had strong trans-national connections, and have held within their ranks similar views on questions of economic integration, planning, and social welfare within a united Europe.[8] While some of these conditions may be unique to Europe in the last two decades, they do not necessarily refute the importance of the background conditions found to be necessary for amalgamation in historical cases.

In fact, in a later study which incorporates data from many contemporary integration movements around the world, Haas and a colleague have noted the importance of the following "background conditions" necessary for successful economic and political integration. Note how these conditions in some cases overlap with those outlined by Deutsch and his colleagues:

1. The size and power of the units or economic sectors which are integrating must be roughly similar so that no one country or economic sector can predominate over the others. In the case of the European Coal and Steel Community, it is true that in terms of *national* military and economic resources France and Germany far outweigh the Netherlands and Luxembourg; but in terms of the integration of the coal and steel sectors alone, the predominance of France and Germany is not so apparent.

2. There must be compatibility of the major social, economic, political, and cultural values among the integrating units in order to move from some forms of economic integration into political amalgamation. Haas notes that in Europe, for example, all of the members of the three Communities (Coal and Steel, Common Market, and Euratom) have

[8] Haas, *The Uniting of Europe,* pp. 290–91.

similar "pluralistic" (democratic) social and political orders, with some regional exceptions such as southern Italy, where a more traditional form of economy and society prevails.

3. There must be complementarity among national elites.

4. Finally, there must be a high rate of transactions between independent political units in the process of economic and political integration.[9]

When turning to the specific reasons and interests, rather than background conditions, which prompted various groups in the amalgamating countries to support economic integration, the importance of short-run advantages and economic rewards becomes apparent. In his thorough study of the European Coal and Steel Community, Haas points out that those political parties, trade unions, and trade associations which favored the Community did so for clear reasons of self-interest, not because of some "ideology" of Europeanism. German steel firms, for example, saw clear profit and marketing advantages in pooling Europe's coal and steel resources and abolishing trade barriers on these raw materials. Many European trade unions saw the Community as a potential instrumentality for improving working conditions in collieries and steel mills, while others opposed the plan on the grounds that foreign competition would destroy their own nation's coal and steel industries, thereby creating unemployment problems. Some governments and professional economists loaned their support to integration in the hope of creating a continental market, noting the impressive rate of growth which had occurred in the United States where there were no tariff barriers between states or regions.[10] The French government, though aware of the economic advantages (and some serious disadvantages as well) of integration, proposed the plan mainly as a means of bringing about eventual federation in Europe, thereby putting to an end the problem of German nationalism. Haas points out that the central aim of the Schuman plan (as the Coal and Steel project was known, in honor of the French foreign minister who first publicized the scheme) was to develop French and German coal and steel resources into an integrated economic unit, under the primary control of a supranational organization and responsible neither to the French nor German governments. By creating such a "community," it was hoped that war between France and Germany would be made virtually impossible.[11]

[9] Ernst B. Haas and Philippe C. Schmitter, "Economic and Differential Patterns of Political Integration: Projections About Unity in Latin America," *International Organization,* XVIII (1964), 708–17. See also Ernst B. Haas, "International Integration: The European and Universal Process," *International Organization,* XV (1961), 374.

[10] See Richard Mayne, *The Community of Europe* (New York: W. W. Norton & Company, Inc., 1963), pp. 62–63.

[11] Haas, *The Uniting of Europe,* p. 243.

The French government and many other Europeans also expected that integration of coal and steel production and trade in Europe would lead to eventual integration of transportation policies and, ultimately, to complete economic unity under a common market.

Even if all of these background conditions, as well as circumstances and interests unique to Europe, exist in a particular area, are pluralistic and amalgamated security communities a natural result? As Stanley Hoffmann has pointed out,[12] common values and high rates of economic and social transactions have not always prevented wars in the past. After all, amalgamation or a low probability of violence between political units do not necessarily result from the presence of certain of these background conditions. They must be created through policies. If political leadership can create unity, so can it destroy those background conditions which would seem to lead to development of integrated communities or pluralistic security communities. Moreover, patterns of behavior in these communities seem to be confined to specific issue-areas. It is possible, for example, to find that conflicts on issues relating to postal communication between the Soviet Union and the United States are resolved through compromise, avoidance, and awards. This does not mean that, on other issues, both sides will avoid making threats or using force against each other.

Most students of European integration would not yet predict that successful integration in economic and technical sectors will have much influence on the ways with which diplomatic and military problems are handled between the same governments. As Haas points out, integration forces have an impact on further integration, but not necessarily in integration of other types of political or economic activities[13] such as development of common foreign or defense policies. Another student of the process of amalgamation, Amitai Etzioni, has hypothesized that different types of international or supranational organizations have different potentials for "spilling over" their cooperative patterns of behavior and unique methods of resolving conflicts into other areas. He suggests, for example, that international technical organizations such as postal services or systems of police cooperation between nations have little influence in promoting cooperation between governments on major political or economic issues. International organizations concerned with labor, health, or cultural problems have had somewhat more influence on the political sectors. Etzioni, like others, also points out that the military

[12] Hoffmann, in *The Atlantic Community: Progress and Prospects,* p. 8.
[13] Haas, "International Integration," 372–74; see also Leon Lindberg, "Decision-Making and Integration in the European Community," *International Organization,* XIX (1965), 72–77.

sector is highly autonomous; even if alliances involve integration of military forces, common military planning, and exchange of defense information, the habits of cooperation and conflict resolution in these organizations do not seem to "spill over" automatically, or create any impetus, for economic or political integration.[14] It is economic integration, with its pervasive influence on all sectors and groups of society, which seems to have the highest potential for inducing political amalgamation and spilling over its patterns of decision-making and bargaining into diplomatic relations between states.[15]

Perhaps the single most important condition which dampens potential hostility in conflicts and makes contemplation or use of military violence as an instrument of inducement highly unlikely is the concept of *responsiveness*, already discussed in Chapter VII. Responsiveness is the disposition of policy-makers to greet with sympathy requests made by other governments, and to consult broadly regarding issues of common interest. According to Bruce Russett, responsiveness can also be defined as the probability that the demands and requests of another government will be met.[16] Deutsch has also indicated that *sensitivity* to the vital interests of other states is one important aspect of a security community. Conceived in these ways, responsiveness implies that the policy-makers of one government will possess considerable information regarding the other state's social, economic, and political characteristics, and its vital needs or interests. This further implies the presence of free communication between the units and lack of distortion due to crude images, rigid stereotypes, and traditional hostile attitudes. Though common institutions may help to impart knowledge of needs and promote consultation prior to initiation of new policies, such institutions are not required for unique patterns of collaboration and conflict resolution to develop. No doubt the Common Market has helped bring to the participating European governments knowledge and appreciation of each other's needs and problems, but lack of such integrating institutions has not prevented similar responsiveness from developing between, for example, the Nordic states, and the United States and its immediate neighbors. The exact relationship between the characteristic of responsiveness and avoidance of violence is not known, but without responsiveness, it is unlikely that any true security community can develop.

[14] Amitai Etzioni, "The Dialectics of Supranational Unification," *The American Political Science Review*, LVI (1962), 931–32.

[15] However, see Deutsch, *Political Community*, p. 189, for a partly dissenting view.

[16] Bruce Russett, *Trends in World Politics* (New York: The Macmillan Company, 1965), pp. 18–19.

## Policy-Making and Handling of Conflicts in Security Communities

While conflicts in pluralistic security communities are seldom danger-ous in the sense that they involve actual or potential violent behavior, their settlement still requires diplomatic bargaining typical of any two states with conflicting objectives. There is evidence, however, that bargaining and settlements related to conflicts in *integrated communities* such as the Common Market and the Coal and Steel Community display some characteristics different from ordinary diplomatic negotiation. These differences in the modes and procedures of conflict resolution and bar-gaining are partly explained by the unique institutional and policy-making arrangements in the European communities.

The main institutions of the Common Market, Euratom, and the Coal and Steel Community combine features of both ordinary intergovern-mental organizations such as NATO or the United Nations, where the members negotiate and bargain with each other until they can reach some kind of settlement or common policy, and of a type of supranational organization, where international civil servants, not responsible to any one government, possess some authority to make binding decisions over member states and their citizens. This is the most important distinction among institutions of an integrated community, diplomatic-type organiza-tions in pluralistic security communities, and intergovernmental organiza-tions. Several other distinctions are also evident. In the European com-munities, most decisions made by the member governments are reached through majority votes; policies resulting from these votes are binding on all members, including those who oppose them. In the United Nations, on the other hand, no state is compelled to accept or implement decisions reached in the organization relating to pacific settlement of disputes and conflicts. Second, the European communities possess institutions which themselves administer a common policy; to implement these policies, they are not dependent, in many cases, on national administrative structures, although these necessarily have to cooperate. This feature is seldom observed in intergovernmental organizations. Third, the European com-munities, through their executive commissions, have some direct authority over citizens and corporations within the member states, and may enforce their policies by bringing suit or levying fines against those individuals or corporations which do not conform to the policies established by the organizations. Such diversion of law-enforcing authority to a suprana-tional administration is not an ordinary feature of international organi-zations.

The institutions of the communities which possess these mixed characteristics of intergovernmental and supranational powers include:

1. The executive Commissions of the Common Market and Euratom, and the High Authority of the Coal and Steel Community, combined into one executive body in 1966. The Commission is comprised of technical experts appointed by common agreement among the member governments, and responsible only to the organization. They may initiate policy recommendations and administer those policies that have been approved by the member governments.

2. The Council of Ministers, attended by national representatives, which has the final authority to formulate and approve common policies, and to bargain with other member states.

3. The Assembly, made up of representatives chosen by national legislatures, with the authority to discuss and review the policies and actions of the Commission and Council of Ministers.

4. The Court of Justice of the communities, which reviews the legality of Commission and Council decisions and disposes of legal cases arising under the founding treaties. It considers conflicts brought by governments against each other, by governments against the Commission, and by individuals or business enterprises against the Commission. By 1965, the Court had disposed of over 1,000 cases involving individual, intergovernmental, and organizational matters.

Within these institutions, creation of common policies and resolution of conflicting points of view is unique in international relationships. Two studies (by Leon Lindberg and Ernst Haas, respectively) of the Common Market and the Coal and Steel Community illustrate the differences between the way diplomatic bargaining, threats, and violence are commonly employed to settle conflicts in traditional diplomatic relations and the procedures used in these organizations. Investigating the formulation of the Common Market's agricultural policy, Lindberg noted first that the Commission *initiated* the proposals for a common price structure and removal of tariff barriers. These proposals were submitted, after careful research, to the Council of Ministers, where a marathon of bargaining and negotiation between national ministers ensued. At the same time the ministers were attempting to advance or protect their own governments' and farmers' interests, members of the Commission were travelling through the countries of the Common Market, addressing agricultural interest groups and political parties, interviewing national administrators, and prevailing upon them to support the Commission's initiative. Such lobbying activity by the Commission was necessary in view of the impact the proposals would have on various governments and agricultural groups. The policy, as initiated by the Commission, consisted of approximately 300 regulations which were to be binding on each member state. According to Lindberg, implementation of the agricultural common market meant that a large portion of the major decisions formerly taken by national governments to regulate their own agricultural communities were now relinquished to the Commission.[17] Moreover, appeals addressed to the council to lift various regulations in favor of the immediate interests of national farmers were seldom accepted if opposed by the Commission.[18]

Such a pattern of policy-making indicates the supranational characteristics of the Common Market. All basic policy decisions are, to be sure, still made by national governments in the light of their own interests and requirements. But the High Authority of the Coal and Steel Community and the Commissions of Euratom and the Common Market have had a strong impact on the manner in which national prerogatives are reduced to a common policy, as defined by the Commissions. A clear impression from the history of these organizations is that short-run economic disadvantages to member states do not necessarily result in vetoes which prevent implementation of goals set by the organization with the aid of its members. If the pattern of policy-making in the European communities is unique, the manner of bargaining when conflicts arise is also of special significance.

To compare the behavior of governments engaged in conflicts involving violence and the procedures used in integrating communities such as the Common Market, let us first review some of the main characteristics of bargaining and conflict behavior discussed in the previous chapter. First, there is a notable decline or constriction of communication between the hostile states, and marked reluctance to negotiate directly between the adversaries. Second, willingness to compromise is related to the effectiveness of threats of violence, deterrence, or development of a stalemate. Displays of rigid commitments to bargaining positions are also typical characteristics of violent international conflicts and disputes. Third, if and when direct negotiations commence, there is often marked lack of trust between the antagonists, hence an unwillingness to accept promises not backed by guarantees or exemplary actions. Fourth, the disputants tend to use negotiations and conferences for propaganda purposes, to denounce or embarrass the other side, rather than to seek a point around which a compromise can be fashioned. Other rules, conventions, and etiquette of quiet diplomacy also suffer during bargaining in violent conflicts and disputes.

[17] Lindberg, "Decision-Making and Integration," 67.
[18] *Ibid.*, p. 69.

In his detailed examination of the Coal and Steel Community, Haas has found that the methods of reconciling conflicting interests among member states are decidedly different from those employed by states in a violent conflict or dispute. The members, for one thing, readily accept the technical advice of a third party, the High Authority. Such is seldom the case in mediation or conciliation. The High Authority's expert studies and recommendations, which reflect the interests and objectives of the organization, tend to overpower strictly national imperatives. Moreover, conflicts are not necessarily resolved on the basis of the will of the least cooperative member. In ordinary diplomatic bargaining, both sides usually trade roughly equal concessions until the point is reached where one party will concede nothing more. If this point is not sufficient for a settlement, nothing more can be achieved through negotiation. But in the European communities, there is a strong presumption among the members that no one government will deliberately veto or hold up agreement.[19] Though the ministers attending the Council meetings are, as in traditional international organizations, instructed by their governments to achieve or defend certain national viewpoints and interests, the spirit of the meetings is such that these instructions are often changed or even disregarded when the ministers are confronted with the views of other governments, and particularly with the expert advice of the Commission.[20] According to Haas, personal friendship among ministers also has important consequences on bargaining behavior. In conventional diplomatic negotiations, final settlements do not necessarily reflect the technical correctness of a position, but rather degrees of need, dependence, and threat credibility, and the bargaining skills of each side. In the negotiations among the ministers, however, compromises are often reached on the basis of technical criteria. The ministers' knowledge of each other and of the needs of other member governments (responsiveness) enables them to distinguish between arguments based on bargaining points and arguments based on real needs and interests. The result is that the discussions focus mainly around technical considerations rather than ideological, sentimental, or national positions.[21]

In this type of bargaining system, decisions and settlements are based less on the power, prestige, capabilities, or reputation of member govern-

[19] Haas, "International Integration," 367–68. President de Gaulle's actions on some aspects of the Common Market's policies are important exceptions to this generalization.

[20] For a description of this phenomenon in the Council of Ministers of the Coal and Steel Community, see Haas, *The Uniting of Europe,* pp. 490–91.

[21] Haas, *The Uniting of Europe,* p. 291.

ments, and more on the objectives of the organization and legitimate needs of its members. It does not make much difference that Luxembourg is geographically small and militarily weak compared to Germany. In the Coal and Steel Community, at least, French Ministers have often reduced their demands to accommodate the Netherlands, while on other issues the Germans or Italians have retreated from their bargaining positions in order to placate the Belgians. In other words, no government consistently gains or withdraws from its objectives because it is economically or militarily weak or strong.[22]

What conclusions are we to draw from these comparisons of bargaining behavior and conflict resolution in an integrating community and in violent conflicts and disputes? First, we must remember that problems in the European communities are concerned primarily with economic questions, involving issues where technical factors and information can be easily used to influence negotiators. In conflicts arising out of incompatible ideological values, long-range objectives, territorial claims, or more diffuse national aspirations, no such precise criteria for agreement exist. Second, the member governments and their negotiating representatives in the European communities are aware of long-run common advantages which can be used to justify short-run economic sacrifices. But when one state makes demands on another country's territory, or in some other way threatens its core interests, it is difficult to convince the victim that it will gain some advantage by acceding to those demands or threats. Third, the pattern of negotiations and conflict resolution within economically integrating communities has not yet been completely duplicated in negotiations on military and political questions between the same governments. Within NATO, for example, negotiations on military questions resemble classical bargaining behavior, where agreement is usually based on the lowest common denominator and the military capacity of each member plays an important role in determining its influence in the bargaining process.

On the other hand, within such non-integrated organizations as NATO, diplomatic bargaining, conflict resolution, and policy-making often display the characteristics of responsiveness, adherence to strict rules of negotiating etiquette, and avoidance of military threats to achieve objectives. In short, resolution of conflicts within pluralistic security communities and many international organizations falls somewhere between the patterns of behavior found in integrating communities and in conflicts involving violence.

[22] Haas, *The Uniting of Europe,* pp. 524–25.

## Resolving Conflicts
## in Security Communities—
## The Record

It is clear from a review of diplomatic relations between governments belonging to pluralistic security communities that the results of responsiveness and other characteristics creating bonds of unity have imposed restraints on national behavior that did not exist previously. Consider, for example, relations among states in Europe. In the 1920's, there were conflicts, some of which involved large-scale violence, between Sweden and Finland, France and Germany, Poland and Lithuania, Poland and Czechoslovakia, Hungary and Austria, and Bulgaria and Greece; in the 1930's the number of conflicts resolved by conquest, annexation, and forced submission grew, as did the involvement of the major powers. Since 1945, however, there have been no violent quarrels within Western Europe including Scandinavia, with the possible exception of the crisis between Yugoslavia and Italy over Trieste. The major conflicts—Berlin, Hungary, and Yugoslavia—have involved primarily non-European powers, while conflicts involving Greece and Turkey would not be classified as "Western" European. Considering the past history of violence on the continent, this is a significant development in international politics. Part of the explanation for this phenomenon of solidarity comes from the presence of a common potential enemy, Soviet Russia, but there are many other background conditions which help to account for the exceptional degree of responsiveness and non-violent behavior among these states. Peaceful relations in Eastern Europe have ensued partly from Soviet domination, and partly from an ideological homogeneity which has covered over traditional national and territorial quarrels. As in Western Europe, the Communist states surrounding the Soviet Union have reached a stage where conflicts between them are resolved through means other than the threat or use of force. On the other hand, the East European area is potentially unstable should one of the states attempt, as Yugoslavia and Hungary did, to remove itself from the Soviet bloc. But in general, the Eastern and Western European nations have within their own regions abandoned the threat or use of force, subversion, or hostile propaganda as instruments of policy and techniques of inducement. This proposition would apply also to North America, Australia and New Zealand, some parts of Latin America and Asia, and the former British colonies in the West Indies.

For the rest of the world, the record is not so favorable, for there are few other areas which, using the criterion of the possibility of armed violence between independent political units, could be classified as genuine and well-established pluralistic security communities. There are many non-European regional organizations such as the Arab League, the Organization of African Unity, and the Latin American Free Trade Association. Attempts at amalgamation between the territories of the West Indies or between Egypt and Syria have also been made, but with no success.[23] Generally, none of the non-European regional or federal organizations displays the degree of integration, ideological and cultural homogeneity, or bargaining patterns and procedures for resolving conflicts found in Europe, North America, and Australia–New Zealand. Not only are there important territorial and ethnic disputes which occur occasionally to mar the unity of these areas, but because of their political and economic instability, they make prime targets for domestic and foreign-inspired intrigues, subversion, and revolution.

In the future, most international crises will probably have as their source the civil wars, *coups d'état,* and revolutions that will occur intermittently in underdeveloped countries. These, in turn, will be exploited by the major powers for their own ends, or the domestic factions will appeal to outside powers to intervene on their behalf. Recent agendas of the United Nations indicate that the most serious diplomatic and military crises are related to the problems of building viable nations and establishing within those states regular procedures for transferring political power. The Congo, Lebanon, Laos, Yemen, Cyprus, and the Dominican crises were originally domestic quarrels in which one or more of the major powers intervened, thus turning them into international crises involving the possibility of war. It is these domestic-international conflicts which will probably be most difficult to resolve peacefully because they involve the interests and values of at least four parties (the United States and China or the Soviet Union, as well as the two major domestic factions), whereas other international conflicts are essentially bilateral confrontations. This is one legacy of the cold war.

Governments will continue, as in the past, to seek their objectives and defend their interests against the demands and actions of others by the traditional means of offering rewards, threatening or implementing punishments, diplomatic bargaining, and using force. Within pluralistic and amalgamated security communities, the probabilities are low that conflicts will be resolved through violent threats, deterrence, or conquests. In these types of relationships, the "power" model of international politics—where

---

[23] For an analysis of these failures, see Etzioni, *Political Unification,* Chaps. 4–5.

states seek to increase their "power" at the expense of others—is a particularly inappropriate tool of analysis. Conflicts arise, but legal and ethical restraints, as well as habits of "getting along," are highly effective in keeping friction to a minimum and helping to provide for settlements by bargaining, compromise, and awards.

Elsewhere, the paths to security, peace, and pacific settlement of conflicts will be dangerous and strewn with failures. With the problems most nations in the world face, including building viable states and organizing minimally satisfactory economic systems, it may be a wonder that there has not been more international conflict in recent years. Various approaches to the goals of economic well-being and international peace have been, and continue to be, advanced by different observers of international politics. To some, world federalism is the answer; others argue that legal norms must be perfected before they can be expected to restrain effectively the actions of states when their objectives are incompatible. Many believe that international relationships will not improve until the underdeveloped nations become "developed," a view that overlooks some of the horrendous social problems faced by populations in "developed" states. Still others, perpetuating a long history of simplistic thinking, assume that the only road to international stability is the one that emphasizes perfection of national capacities to threaten and inflict violent punishments. Whatever the panacea, plan, or nostrum, none will work by itself, and none can lead to the goal quickly.

Despite their failures, international organizations have made great contributions to peace in what is, historically, a wisp of time. But this has been possible only because of changing public attitudes toward war and violence. One only has to compare the bellicose views of statesmen, politicians, and publics at the turn of the century with their attitudes today. Then, war was commonly regarded as a positive good, a means of steeling national character and weeding out the poor and weak from the strong and wealthy. It was a game to vindicate honor and prestige, an opportunity to demonstrate the latest toy of destruction. After two world wars, such views seem ludicrous to most people. Today, international violence is mostly seen as a tragedy and an unpromising way of accomplishing national goals. Without such views, it is unlikely that security communities could grow, international organizations flourish, or stability develop. Underlying any improvements in the techniques and practices of resolving international conflicts peacefully is the attitudes and ethical principles of those who wield power and those in the general public who support or criticize their leaders. Without the proper values and attitudes, including willingness to experiment in international programs, concede short-run national disadvantages for common long-range advantages, and exercise great caution in the use of military power, mere institutions, laws, plans, and proposals will be inadequate to the task.

## SELECTED BIBLIOGRAPHY

Deutsch, Karl W., *Political Community at the International Level: Problems of Definition and Measurement.* Garden City, N.Y.: Doubleday & Co., Inc., 1954.

——, et al., *Political Community and the North Atlantic Area.* Princeton: Princeton University Press, 1957.

Etzioni, Amitai, "The Dialectics of Supranational Unification," *The American Political Science Review,* LVI (1962), 927–55.

——, "The Epigenesis of Communities at the International Level," *American Journal of Sociology,* LXVIII (1963), 407–21.

——, *Political Unification.* New York: Holt, Rinehart & Winston, Inc., 1965.

Haas, Ernst B., *Beyond the Nation State: Functionalism and International Organization.* Stanford: Stanford University Press, 1964.

——, *Consensus Formation in the Council of Europe.* Berkeley: University of California Press, 1960.

——, "International Integration: The European and Universal Process," *International Organization,* XV (1961), 366–92.

——, *The Uniting of Europe: Political, Social, and Economic Forces, 1950–1957.* Stanford: Stanford University Press, 1958.

——, and Philippe C. Schmitter, "Economic and Differential Patterns of Political Integration: Projections about Unity in Latin America," *International Organization* XVIII (1964), 705–37.

Jacob, Philip E., and James V. Toscano, eds., *The Integration of Political Communities.* Philadephia: J. B. Lippincott Company, 1964.

Levi, Werner, "The Concept of Integration in Research on Peace," *Background,* IX (1965), 111–26.

Lindberg, Leon, "Decision-Making and Integration in the European Community," *International Organization,* XIX (1965), 56–80.

——, *The Political Dynamics of European Economic Integration.* Stanford: Stanford University Press, 1963.

Shokking, Jan J., and Nels Anderson, "Observations on the European Integration Process," *Journal of Conflict Resolution,* IV (1960), 385–460.

Springer, Hugh, *Reflections on the Failure of the First West Indies Federation.* Cambridge, Mass.: Center for International Affairs, Harvard University, 1962.

# Index

Acheson, Dean, 452
Adjudication, 458–59
Afghanistan, 282, 291–92
Aix-la-Chapelle, Congress of, 216
Alexander the Great, 50
Alliance for Progress, 301
Alliances, 110–20
  American-Pakistan, 117
  Anglo-Austrian (1740), 117
  ANZUS Treaty, 113
  Austro-German (1879), 114
  Brussels Treaty, 113
  *casus foederis,* 112–13
  criteria for classifying, 112
  deterrence function, 116
  and domestic needs, 110–11
  Franco-Prussian (1741), 117
  German-Italian (1939), 112
  in Greek city state system, 45, 48
  impact of nuclear weapons, 119–20
  and international systems, 110
  NATO, 111, 113, 114, 115, 480, 491
  Nazi-Soviet (1939), 118
  and perception of threat, 111
  Quadruple (1815), 30, 341
  and security communities, 482
  strains in, 116–20
  territorial coverage, 115
  types, 112–16
  Warsaw Treaty, 111
  in World War II, 118

Allies, Western, 234
Anti-ballistic missiles, 374–76
Antonescu, Ion, 294
Arab unity, 272–73
Arbenz, Captain Jacobo, 331–33
Arbitration, 458–59
Armas, Carlos Castillo, 332–34
Arms control, 378–84
  Baruch plan, 383
  nuclear test-ban treaty, 382
  Washington Conference (1922), 378
  Washington Naval Convention (1922), 382
Athens, 43, 45–48 (*see also* Greece)
Atomic bomb, 425–29
Austria, 103, 231

Barghoorn, Frederick, 264, 274
Bay of Pigs, 340, 391
Belgium, 103, 109
Belief systems, 161–63
Beneš, Eduard, 327, 330
Blockade (*see* International trade)
Boulding, Kenneth E., 233
Boycott, trade, 285, 290–91
Brest-Litovsk, Treaty of, 134
Brown, J. A. C., 255
Bulgaria, 293–94
Bülow, Prince Bernhard von, 1

Bundy, McGeorge, 362
Byrnes, James F., 452

Callières, François de, 11, 205
Canada, 462, 477, 479
Capabilities:
  definition, 194
  measurement, 198–200
  mobilizing, 198
  in negotiations, 228–30
  perceptions of, 200–201
  as policy restraints, 422
  and power, 198–99
Central Intelligence Agency, 316
Chamberlain, Neville, 435
Charles V, 129
Charter of Bogotá, 342
China:
  Chou dynasty international system,
      29–42
    attached states, 32, 37
    boundaries, 30
    forms of diplomacy, 38
    forms of interaction, 37–40
    leagues of states, 35–36
    legal restraints, 40–41, 397–98
    nature of political units, 30–32
    role of neutrals, 35
    rules of the system, 40–41
    structure of the system, 32–36, 91–
        92
    subversion, 39–40
    warfare, 39
  Communist, 75
    foreign trade policies, 288–89
    guerrilla war, 336
    imperialism, 137
    and Japan, 288–89
  Han dynasty, 35
Churchill, Winston, 360, 380, 408, 425,
    452
Civil defense, 376–78
Claude, Inis L., 468
Collaboration:
  and conflict, 148
  definition, 147–49
Comintern, 316
Commitments, diplomatic, 234–35
Common Market (see European Eco-
    nomic Community)
Communication, diplomatic, 226–28
Communism:
  front organizations, 266–68
  image of world order, 140–43
  and international law, 407

Communism (Cont.)
  relation to Soviet foreign policy, 163–
      64
Concert of Europe, 401
Conciliation, 457–58, 466
Conflict:
  definition, 149–50, 443
  forms of resolution, 445–55
    avoidance, 446
    awards, 453–54, 469–73
    compromise, 448–53
    conquest, 446–47
    passive settlement, 452–53
    submission, 447–48
  institutions for resolution,   459–65,
      467–73
  procedures for resolution,   455–59,
      465–67
  in security communities, 489–92
Congo, 416–17
Congress of Aix-la-Chapelle, 216
Congress of Vienna, 216
Consulates, 220
Control of armaments (see Arms con-
    trol)
Counterforce strategy, 372–73
Craig, Gordon, 217
Cuba:
  missile crisis, 170, 242, 361–64, 437–
      38
  as non-aligned state, 105
  and United States, 201
Cyprus, 468–69
Czechoslovakia, subversion of, 324–31

Dahl, Robert, 198
Dangerfield, Royden, 297
Decision-making,  in  crisis  situations,
    183–84, 357–64
De Gaulle, Charles, 126, 143–44, 167
Delian League (see Greece)
Dependence, 150–52
Deterrence, 352–78
  and anti-ballistic missiles, 374–76
  and arms control, 378–84
  assumptions, 352
  capability requirements, 365–69
  and civil defense, 376–78
  credibility, 353–56
  in crisis situations, 357–64
  definition, 352
  sources of failure, 357
  stability of, 356
  strategies of, 364–78
  and targeting policy, 371–74

Deutsch, Karl W., 478–79, 481–82
De Visscher, Charles, 414
Diplomacy:
    in Chou international system, 37–38
    commitments, 234–35
    duplicity in, 241–42
    formal language, 217
    among Greek city states, 48
    heads of state, 215
    immunities, 217–19
    institutions, 212–15
    interference in internal affairs, 219–20
        (see also Interference)
    multilateral, 213–14
    negotiation process, 228–44
        bargaining reputation, 230
        bargaining skills, 229
        bargaining tactics, 231–36
        capabilities, 228–30
    origins, 213
    and propaganda, 227–28, 239–40, 269
    protocol, 216–17
    rank, 216–17
    recall of ambassadors, 218–19
    in Renaissance Italy, 55
    rewards, 204–5
    secret, 244
    in security communities, 487–92
    threats in, 205, 232–34
    in United Nations, 244
Diplomatic style:
    Great Britain, 237–39
    Nazi Germany, 239–41
    Soviet Union, 200, 239–43
    United States, 237–39
Diplomats:
    functions, 220–26
        advisory, 222–26
        information, 221–22
        policy making, 223–26
        protection of nationals, 220
        symbolic representation, 220–21
    Soviet, 225–26, 240–41
Disarmament, 378–84
    Baruch plan, 383
    nuclear test-ban treaty, 382
    and propaganda, 269
    Washington Conference (1922), 378
    Washington Naval Convention (1922),
        382
Disputes, diplomatic, 443
Doctrines, effects on foreign policy, 163–
    65, 187
Domination, 150–52
Dominican Republic, 323

Dulles, John Foster, 162, 220, 223, 318,
    332, 370, 381–82, 452

East Germany, 234
Economic assistance (see Foreign aid)
Economic warfare, 295–97
Eden, Anthony, 166, 228
Egypt:
    and Arab unity, 272–73
    imperialism, 137–38
    as non-aligned state, 106
    propaganda, 271–74
    subversion, 322
Eisenhower, Dwight D., 161, 381
Embargo, trade, 285, 289–90
Equality, legal, 83
Ethiopia, 102
Etzioni, Amitai, 485
Euratom, 487–92
Europe, eighteenth century international
    politics, 62–65
European Coal and Steel Community,
    482–83, 487–92
European Economic Community, 487–92

Faisal, King, 273
Falk, Richard A., 393
Ferdinand, Archduke Francis, 358
Finland:
    as non-aligned state, 104, 108–9
    and Soviet Union, 236, 287–88, 319
Fleury, Cardinal, 130
Foreign aid:
    conditions, 306–7
    Great Britain, 298
    history, 297–98
    objectives, 301–6
    Soviet Union, 298, 302, 305–6
    types, 299–301
    United States, 298–300, 302, 304–5
Foreign policy:
    ethical restraints on, 423–40
    impact of system on, 97–99, 169–72
    and international politics, 20–22
    and international relations, 20–22
    and legal restraints, 406–11
    mood, 176
    objectives:
        and bureaucracy, 181–84
        and capabilities, 175–76, 186–87
        classification, 131–32
        core interests and values, 132–35
        definition, 126
        De Gaulle's, 126, 143–44

Foreign policy ( *Cont.* )
  effect of doctrines on, 163–65, 187
  effect of ideology on, 163–65
  Hitler's, 139
  images and, 156–60
  impact of domestic needs, 173–75, 186–87
  impact of national role, 172–73, 186–87
  Lenin's, 128, 134, 138, 140–41
  long-range, 138–46
  of Louis XIV, 130
  middle-range, 135–38
  and public opinion, 176–81, 186–87
  role of beliefs in defining, 161–62, 187
  role of values in defining, 161, 186–87
  Stalin's, 142–43
  types in historical systems, 128–31
  orientations:
    alliances and coalitions, 110–20
    isolation, 99–102
    non-alignment, 103–10
Foreign trade ( *see* International trade)
France:
  and Coal and Steel Community, 484–85
  foreign aid, 298
  and international law, 392–93
  and Middle East, 201
  and NATO, 480
  role in Europe, 144
  surrender in 1940, 447
  and the United States, 480
  view of U.S. deterrent, 119–20
Frankel, Joseph, 183
Frederick the Great, 130
Fulbright, J. William, 364


General Act for Pacific Settlement of Disputes, 455–57, 460, 470
Genocide Convention, 403, 414
George V, 359
Germany:
  Nazi:
    and Bulgaria, 293–94
    and Czechoslovakia, 258
    diplomatic style, 239–41
    foreign policy, 167
    foreign trade policies, 283, 292–95
    non-aggression treaty with Soviet Union ( 1939), 118
    propaganda, 257–58, 275

Germany ( *Cont.* )
  and Romania, 294
  subversion, 324–26
Gestapo, 316
Good offices, 456
Gordon, David L., 297
Gottwald, Klement, 327, 330
Gouré, Leon, 376
Great Britain:
  and appeasement, 435
  diplomatic style, 237–39
  domestic needs and foreign policy, 174–75
  foreign aid, 298
  imperialism, 173–74
  and Middle East, 201
  rise of national government, 60–61
  and Trieste, 450–51
Greater East Asia Co-Prosperity Sphere, 175
Greece:
  city state international system, 42–50, 92
    colonies, 44
    Delian League, 45, 48
    diplomacy, 48
    forms of interaction, 46–48
    Hellenic League, 45
    nature of political units, 43–44
    Peloponnesian League, 45, 92
    rules of the system, 49
    structure, 44–46, 92
    system boundaries, 42–43
    tributary states, 44
    warfare, 47–48
  and United States, 319–20
Gromyko, Andrei, 241, 242
Grotius, Hugo, 400
Guatemala:
  subversion in, 331–34


Haas, Ernst B., 483–85, 488, 490
Hague Conferences, 213, 378, 455
Halle, Louis J., 430
Hamilton, Alexander, 423
Hammarskjöld, Dag, 244
Henlein, Konrad, 324–26
Hitler, Adolf, 139, 162–63, 167, 168
Hoffmann, Stanley, 172, 485
Holsti, Rudolf W., 396
Holy Roman Empire, 82, 129
Hull, Cordell, 238
Hundred Years' War, 52
Hussein, King, 322

Ideology:
  communism and foreign policy, 163–64
  definition, 158–59
  distortions of reality, 159–60
  effect on foreign policy, 163–65, 187
Images:
  in foreign policy decisions, 158–60
Immunities, diplomatic, 217–19
Imperialism, 137–38
India, 304
  international mediation, 106
  as non-aligned state, 105–6
  prestige, 72, 76
Indo-China, 371
Indonesia:
  imperialism, 137
  as non-aligned state, 105–6
Influence:
  and capabilities, 198–99
  definition, 194
  determining variables, 200–204
  and deterrence, 352–56, 369
  economic means of, 284–92
  exercise of, 204–5
  measurement, 203–4
  patterns of, 206–8
  and responsiveness, 202–3
Interference, diplomatic, 317–20
International Court of Justice, 469–71
International law:
  in Chou system, 397–98
  development, 399–402
  and foreign policy, 406–11
  France, 392–93
  in the Hindu system, 397
  Israel, 392
  obsolescence, 404–5
  in primitive systems, 395–96
  as propaganda, 409
  restraint on policies, 389–99, 406–11
  sanctions, 411–15
  sources, 402–3
  Soviet Union, 391–92
  United States, 391
  unwritten rules, 394
  violations, 391, 393, 409
International politics:
  approaches to the study of, 7–9
    levels of analysis, 15–17
    need for organizing devices, 13–15
  biases in study of, 22–24
  in the Chou dynasty, 29–42 (see China)
  Communist theory of, 14

International politics (Cont.)
  development of field of study, 4–6
  in eighteenth century Europe, 62–65
  and foreign policy, 20–22
  framework for analyzing, 17–20
  among Greek city states, 42–50 (see Greece)
  as an interdisciplinary study, 12–13
  and international relations, 20–22
  of nineteenth century, 65–68
  prediction, 8–9
  in Renaissance Italy, 50–59 (see Italy)
  research in, 10–11
  theories of, 7–9, 15
International relations, and international politics, 20–22
International systems:
  and alliances, 110
  boundaries of, 28
  Chou dynasty, 29–42, 92 (see also China)
  contemporary, 69–91
    decline of polarity, 89
    forms of interaction, 78–82
    maintenance of polarity, 87–89
    major rules, 82–84
    nature of units, 70–73
    sources of instability, 85–87
    stratification, 73–76
    structure, 76–78
  definition, 27
  effect of weapons on, 349–50
  eighteenth century Europe, 62–65, 92
  forms of interaction, 29
  Greek city states, 42–50, 92 (see also Greece)
  impact on foreign policy, 97–99, 169–72
  and international law, 395–402
  nineteenth century, 65–68, 92
  regulation, 29
  Renaissance Italy, 50–59, 92 (see also Italy)
  structure of, 28–29
  types, 91–94
International trade, 280–81
  Afghanistan-Pakistan, 291–92
  blockade, 295–96
  economic warfare, 295–97
  NATO-Soviet, 289–90
  Nazi German, 283, 292–95
  Soviet, 282, 283–84, 287–88
  United States, 285, 290–91
Intervention, military, 338–40, 342
Ireland, 104. 105

Isolation, 99–102
  Ethiopia, 102
  Japan, 101
  Nepal, 101
  United States, 101–2
Israel, 392
Italy:
  Renaissance international system:
    boundaries, 51–52
    diplomacy, 55
    ethics and rules, 57–58
    Most Holy League, 54–55, 58
    nature of political units, 52–53
    structure, 53–55, 92
    subversion, 56–57
    warfare, 55–56
  and Trieste, 450–51


Janos, Andrew, 336
Japan:
  alliances, 113
  attack on Pearl Harbor, 159, 365
  and Communist China, 188–89
  defeat of, 428–29
  domestic needs and foreign policy,
      174–75
  isolation, 101
Jefferson, Thomas, 423
Johnson, Lyndon B., 368
Jordan, 272, 304, 322–23, 350


Kadar, Mrs. Janos, 270
Kahn, Herman, 377
Kautilya, 5, 98, 206
Kaznacheev, Alexandr, 226, 321
Kecskemeti, Paul, 270, 274
Kellogg-Briand Pact, 378
Kennan, George, 354
Kennedy, John F., 170, 242, 355, 361,
      362–64, 437–38, 452
Khrushchev, Nikita S., 141, 264, 315,
      319, 363
Kissinger, Henry, 370
Korea, 369, 454–55 (see also War,
      Korean)


Laos, 339–40
  as neutralized state, 103–4, 109
League of Nations, 461–62
  settlement of conflicts, 466–69
  and use of force, 390
Lebanon, 339
Legal equality, 83

LeMay, General Curtis, 368
Lenin, V. I., 128, 138, 140, 240
Lichnowsky, Prince, 225
Lindberg, Leon, 488–89
Litvinov, Maxim, 380
Locarno, Treaty of (1925), 114
Lodge, Henry Cabot, 333
Lodi, Peace of (1454), 54, 58
Louis XIV, 130
Luxembourg, 103


Machiavelli, Niccolo, 5, 56, 424
McNamara, Robert, 372–74, 375
Mao Tse-tung, 336
Masaryk, Jan, 330
Massive retaliation, doctrine of, 233, 355,
      370
Mediation, 456–57, 466
Mencius, 5
Mikoyan, Anastas, 283
Molotov, Vyacheslav, 228, 231
Moltke, Count Helmuth von, 360–61
Morgenthau, Hans J., 303–4
Most Holy League (see Italy)
Munich Conference (1938), 449
Mussolini, Benito, 168


Napoleon, 168
Nasser, Gamal Abdel, 272–73
National interest, concept of, 125–26
Nationalism:
  effects on foreign policy, 65–66
  and propaganda, 267–68
Negotiation, 466 (see also Diplomacy)
Nepal, 101, 304
Neutrality, 103
Neutralization, 103–4
Nicholas II, 359
Nicolson, Arthur, 360
Nicolson, Sir Harold, 238
Non-aligned states, and bloc conflicts, 86,
      90
Non-alignment, 103–10
  distinguished from neutrality, 103
  and foreign aid, 106
  reasons for adopting, 106–8
  requirements for success, 109–10
North Atlantic Treaty Organization, 266–
      67, 289 (see also Alliances)
Norway, 109, 479
Nuclear Test-ban Treaty (1963), 382
Nuclear weapons, effects on policy-mak-
      ing, 85–86
Nuremberg war crime trials, 378, 403

Oppenheimer, Robert, 67, 428
Optional clause, 471
Organization of American States, 342–43

Pacific settlement of conflicts, 455–59, 465–69
Pakistan, 275, 282, 291–92
alliance with U.S., 117
Pathet Lao, 339
Peace of Lodi (1454), 54, 58
Peace research, 11
Peloponnesian League (*see* Greece)
Peloponnesian Wars, 45, 46, 100
Permanent Court of Arbitration, 460
Permanent Court of International Justice, 469–71
Philip of Macedonia, 43
Power:
and capabilities, 198–200
definition, 192–95
indicators, 199
Propaganda:
and attitude change, 251–55
creating impact, 256–57
definitions, 249–50
and diplomacy, 227–28, 239–40, 269
effectiveness, 274–76
Egyptian, 271–74
through front organizations, 266–68
and nationalism, 267–68
Nazi, 257–58, 275
selecting targets, 250–55
Soviet, 254, 257, 263–71, 275
techniques, 257–58
in United Nations, 227
United States, 260–63, 275
and youth, 254
Protocol, diplomatic, 216–17
Public opinion:
and foreign policy, 176–81
in General Assembly, 417–18
as restraint on policy, 415–19
Puerifoy, John, 320, 332, 333
Pufendorf, Samuel, 400
Punishment, diplomatic, 205

Quadruple Alliance (1815), 341
Qualter, Terrence, 249
Quotas, trade, 285

Responsiveness, 486
and influence, 202–3
Restraints, policy:
capabilities, 422

Restraints, policy (*Cont.*)
definition, 388
ethical, 423–40
legal, 389–99, 406–11
public opinion, 415–19, 422–23
Rewards, diplomatic, 204–5
Ritter, Gerhard, 57
Romania, 294
Roosevelt, Franklin D., 159, 167, 179, 181
Roosevelt, Theodore, 348
Rush-Bagot Treaty, 479
Russell, Richard B., 364
Russia (*see* Soviet Union)

Saud, King Ibn, 273
Saudi Arabia, 273
Schelling, Thomas, 369, 370, 384
Schuman, Maurice, 484
Seabury, Paul, 125, 127
Security communities:
background conditions, 480–86
bargaining in, 488–92
definition, 478–79
and responsiveness, 486
Simulation, 11
Smith, Ian D., 2, 4
Sorenson, Theodore, 362, 363
Sovereignty, 82
Soviet Union:
and Afghanistan, 291–92
alliances, 111, 112, 113, 118
and arms control, 379
clandestine actions, 321–22
and Communist China, 139, 305
and Cuban missile crisis, 361–64
diplomatic interference, 318–19
diplomatic style, 200, 239–43
diplomats, 225–26, 240–41
and East Germany, 234
effect of ideology on foreign policy, 163–64
and Finland, 236, 287–88, 319
foreign aid, 298, 302, 305–6
foreign trade policies, 282, 283–84, 287–88
and front organizations, 266–68
and Hungary, 339
image of world order, 140–43
imperialism, 137
and Indonesia, 306
and international law, 391–92, 409–11
long-range objectives, 139–43
non-aggression treaty with Germany, 118
propaganda, 254, 257, 263–71, 275

Soviet Union (*Cont.*)
  sources of foreign policy, 184–85
  subversion, 316, 330–31
  and Yugoslavia, 287
Spain, 296–97
Sparta, 45–48 (*see also* Greece)
Stalin, Joseph, 128, 142–43, 168, 181, 230, 264, 425
Standley, William H., 236
State Department (*see* U.S., Department of State)
Stevenson, Adlai, 242, 452
Stimson, Henry L., 426, 428
Stockholm Peace Appeal (1951), 267
Stratification, international, 29, 73–76
Subversion:
  in Africa, 313
  American, 331–34
  in the Chou international system, 39–40
  communist, 326–31
  conditions favoring, 313–15
  in contemporary international politics, 81–82
  of Czechoslovakia, 324–31
  definition, 322
  by major powers, 312
  in the Middle East, 312, 322
  Nazi German, 324–26
  in Renaissance Italy, 56–57
  Soviet, 316, 330–31
  stages of, 334
  Sudetenland, 324–26
Suez Canal, 418
Sweden, 479
  as non-aligned state, 104, 105, 108
  in World War II, 295–96
Switzerland, 104, 108

Tariffs, 285
Technical assistance, 299–300
Tensions, international, 443–44
Territoriality, 84–85
Theory of games, 11
Thirty Years' War (1618–1648), 2, 129–30
Threats, diplomatic, 205, 232–34 (*see also* Diplomacy)
Thucydides, 111
Treaty of Venice (1454), 58
Treaty of Westphalia (1648), 82
Trieste, 450–51
Trotsky, Leon, 240
Truman, Harry S., 379, 426, 452

Unconventional warfare (*see* War, guerrilla)
Underdeveloped countries:
  and international law, 472
  as non-aligned states, 104–5
  as sources of instability, 86–87, 493
United Arab Republic (*see* Egypt)
United Fruit Company, 332
United Nations:
  diplomacy in, 244
  intervention, 343
  propaganda in, 227
  and public opinion, 417–18
  settlement of conflicts, 462–69
  and use of force, 390, 403, 405, 414
  weaknesses, 467–68
United States:
  alliances, 113, 119
  alliance with Pakistan, 117
  and arms control, 379
  and atomic bomb, 425–29
  and Canada, 477, 479
  Central Intelligence Agency, 316
  clandestine actions, 321
  and Cuba, 201, 290–91, 340, 361–64
  Department of State, 183, 203, 260
  diplomatic interference, 319–20
  diplomatic style, 237–39
  effect of ideology on foreign policy, 165
  effect of role on foreign policy, 173
  foreign aid, 298–300, 302, 304–5
  foreign trade policies, 285, 290–91
  and France, 480
  and Greece, 319–20
  image of England, 416
  image of Soviet Union, 415
  imperialism, 155–56
  Information Agency (U.S.I.A.), 260–62
  and International Court of Justice, 471
  isolation, 101–2
  Korean War, 369
  and Lebanon, 339
  legal violations, 391, 409
  long-range objectives, 144–45
  propaganda, 260–63, 275
  subversion in Guatemala, 331–34
  and Trieste, 450–51
  and Venezuela, 201
Universal Postal Union, 214
U Thant, 244
Uzbekistan, 268

Values, 161

Vattel, Emerich de, 400
Venezuela, 201
Venice, 51–53
Venice, Treaty of (1454), 58
Vienna, Congress of (1815), 216
Vietnam, 166, 304–5
Voice of America, 260, 274
Vyshinski, Andrei, 242, 243


Walpole, Sir Robert, 130
War:
    arms control in, 379
    of Austrian Succession, 130
    in the Chou international system, 39
    economic, 295–97
    effect of technology on, 66–67, 348–50
    escalation, 358–61
    of French Revolution, 68
    among Greek city states, 47–48
    guerrilla, 335–38
    Hundred Years', 52
    Korean, 369, 379, 450
    limited, 370–71
    Peloponnesian, 45, 46
    in Renaissance Italy, 55–56

War (*Cont.*)
    Seven Years' (1757–63), 130–31
    Thirty Years' (1618–1648), 2, 129–30
Washington Conference (1922), 378
Washington Naval Convention (1922),
        382
Weapons:
    effects on international system, 349–50
    as instruments of policy, 348–50
    thermonuclear, 349
        proliferation, 350–51
Westphalia, Treaty of (1648), 82
Wilhelm II, 225, 359–60
Wilson, Harold, 2
Wilson, Woodrow, 162, 423–24
Wolfers, Arnold, 132
World Peace Movement, 266–68
World War I, 358–61
World War II:
    atomic bomb, use of, 425–29
    economic warfare, 295–97
Wright, Quincy, 346–47, 403


Young, Kimball, 249
Yugoslavia:
    and Soviet Union, 287
    and Trieste, 450–51